Philosophy, Religion, and Science

PHILOSOPHY RELIGION and SCIENCE

An Introduction to Philosophy

CHARLES H. MONSON,. JR.
University of Utah

CHARLES SCRIBNER'S SONS
NEW YORK

A-9.63[H]

Printed in the United States of America
Library of Congress Catalog Card Number 63-10502

TO VIVIAN

Contents

RELIGION

PREFACE

During the past dozen years I have tried many different ways to organize and teach the introductory course in philosophy. Early in my experiments I became aware that certain forms of presentation encouraged memorization, and others failed to relate the importance of philosophical ideas to a student's life, and that these pitfalls should be avoided. Gradually, however, I became convinced of three principles which form the premises for this book.[1]

First, I became convinced that students of college age are intellectually and emotionally prepared to discuss philosophical issues, although they do not recognize these problems as being uniquely philosophical. They are prepared, even eager, to argue Truth, debate Knowledge, and discuss Goodness, but in terms of whether their own religion is true, whether a university education results in knowledge, or whether a free society is good. They see philosophical problems in terms of particular issues which, strictly speaking, are not philosophical, and this difficulty led me to wonder whether a *rapport* might be easier if I did not identify the study of philosophy exclusively with the great names of the tradition.

I also came to recognize that the word "philosophy" has two distinct meanings. Originally, it meant "love of wisdom," and it is this meaning which is reflected in the thought of the earliest philosophers, Socrates, Plato, and Aristotle, for they included all knowledge, physics and metaphysics, psychology and ethics, as a part of their philosophy. In this sense philosophy was not limited to any definite procedure or group of answers; its only limitations were those inherent in the quest for wisdom. However, "philosophy," frequently given a narrower meaning today, is identified with the problems, procedures, and thoughts of those men who are part of the philosophical tradition. To study philosophy in this sense is to learn about the ideas of Descartes and Locke, Hume and Kant, Dewey and Russell. This meaning, which arose from the increasing demands of specialization, assumes that philosophy is different from psychology and physics, religion and art; it equates philosophy with a certain group of writers and problems and with certain procedures for answering those problems.

This narrower meaning has come to dominate the teaching of philosophy today, but as the title of this book indicates, I am con-

[1] The 1958 organization of the course is discussed in *The Journal of Higher Education,* XXIX (October, 1958), 386-389.

vinced that both meanings should be considered. Following the path of the philosophical tradition, the narrower meaning, is one important way to gain knowledge, but many people also have been engaged in the quest for wisdom, and thus are part of philosophy in its original meaning. Recognition of these two meanings allowed me certain important advantages. I could consider the philosophical tradition in the usual way, but I had greater latitude in stating philosophical issues. I discovered more opportunities to bring students from their present thinking to a more sophisticated level. I could compare alternative methods and answers, and so could teach traditional philosophy by comparison as well as analysis. I could consider philosophical ideas regardless of their origin.

Finally, I became convinced that philosophy in the narrower sense should act as a check on philosophy in the larger sense. Such checking requires that the competing ways for gaining wisdom must be considered sympathetically, but with the same rigor and honesty used to analyze the claims of the traditional philosophers. Definitions should be analyzed, evidence should be examined and implications should be discerned before one accepts any claim as constituting wisdom, but such a goal requires a careful philosophical analysis of all claims and of the techniques for arriving at them.

My approach to philosophy, then, tries to help students understand the problems, procedures, and answers of traditional philosophy as well as the problems, procedures, and answers of alternative ways for gaining knowledge. In this broader view of philosophy I hope students will learn of the ideas formluated by the great thinkers of the world and the importance which these ideas have on their own lives, but more importantly, I hope that they themselves will be stimulated and will have a greater competence to engage in the search for wisdom.

I wish to acknowledge my indebtedness to those who have helped me in my efforts: to the publishers who have allowed me to use copyrighted materials; to my colleagues for their advice; to my secretary, Mrs. Delpha Barry, for her accuracy and diligence; to the editorial staff of Charles Scribner's Sons for their many valuable suggestions; to my wife and family for their patience. Most of all I acknowledge the many unnamed students who have helped me understand my failures and successes.

CHARLES H. MONSON, JR.

Salt Lake City, Utah
May, 1963

A NOTE TO THE READER

The most important parts of this book are contained in Chapters Two to Four, Six to Eight, and Ten to Twelve. These chapters consist of selections from many of the world's most influential thinkers, past and present, from the East and West, philosophically sophisticated and otherwise. (The titles of all the selections have been supplied by the editor.) These selections are of moderate length so that you can read each of them carefully and thoughtfully. In each selection look for the author's conclusion/s, and for the evidence or reasons he uses to support it/them. Then, think about what you have read, evaluating his thought in the light of your own reasons and conclusions. If you will do this for each author you will learn (1) what he believes and (2) why, and (3) whether you agree with him. In more general terms, you should learn (a) what ideas there are, (b) what reasons can be given to justify them, and (c) what you yourself believe.

Following each selection you will find a bibliography divided into two lists, *Readings for Immediate Reference* and *References for Comprehensive Knowledge*. There is also a General Bibliography similarly divided at the end of each chapter but Chapter One. These are intended to help you learn more about the author and his ideas. The first list contains the whole chapter or section from which your reading selection was taken, other selections by the same author pertaining to the subject, and selections from other authors who either defend or criticize the point of view expressed in the selection. The second list contains the major works of the author not previously mentioned, the most important commentaries on his work, and books by other authors who have been concerned with the same subject. In addition, you should find the material in the glossary (page 549) of this book and in such standard encyclopedias as *Britannica, Americana* and *Collier's* helpful in understanding a man's thought. Do not hesitate to use these sources; they exist to help you clarify and expand your knowledge.

Of the remaining chapters, the first explains the basic organization of the book. Chapters Five, Nine and Thirteen are directly related to the three chapters preceding them. In Chapters Five, Nine, and Thirteen I have tried to raise certain general philosophical issues, and to show how the authors in the reading selections have dealt with these problems. These chapters are designed to serve three purposes: to provide a framework for discussing some of the more general issues of philosophy; to establish a basis for discerning similarities and differences among authors and ways of thought; and to act as an additional resource for understanding particularly difficult writers. Chapter Fourteen contains my own conclusions, ones which I shall try to convince you are correct.

A special comment should be made about Chapter Two. After reading the first chapter you will see how the selections from Socrates, Descartes, and Russell fit into the general format. However, this chapter also serves two other important functions: first, to raise, respectively, the questions of methodology, metaphysics, and ethics so you will have some idea of what issues are involved in each subject when you read the later chapters; and second, to present some of the principles of elementary logic so that a framework—and an attitude—of careful philosophical reasoning can be established at the beginning, one which should be carried on in the remaining chapters.

When you finish reading the book, certain values should have emerged. (1) You will have a wider and deeper understanding of the realm of ideas. (2) You will be able to think more clearly and carefully about issues and problems, regardless of their origin or nature. (3) You will know some of the thoughts of the great thinkers of the world. (4) You will recognize more clearly what a philosophical problem is and why it is important. (5) You will understand more fully alternative ways for answering problems. And (6) you should understand your own beliefs more fully. Other values might also emerge, but to test whether any values do result from your reading let me suggest you test yourself. As soon as you finish reading this paragraph take a few minutes and write out what you take to be your own attitude toward life. What do you really believe? What do you judge to be valuable? What is most important in your life? Write as clearly and cogently as you can, then put your paper out of sight and mind until you have finished reading and thinking about the material between this page and Chapter Fourteen. Then take out your paper and compare your present thinking with what you wrote. The difference should provide you with evidence about which of the six values you have satisfied, and how well you have satisfied them.

C. M.

Philosophy, Religion, and Science

Chapter One

INTRODUCTION

I

When one picks up a philosophy book to read he might have been motivated by any number of purposes: idle curiosity; to have something to do when the television set is broken; to fill an assignment. Or, he might have been prompted by more serious intent: to gain information, for instance. When did Plato live in comparison to Socrates and Aristotle? What did Descartes believe? Why are John Dewey's educational theories controversial? Who said he was not sure whether he was a man dreaming he was a butterfly or a butterfly dreaming he was a man?

If this is one's purpose, then he will view a philosophy book as he would any other book, wanting to learn something he did not already know, or knew only partially. The only difference would be in what he wanted to know, for instead of being shocked (or titillated) by an account of American suburban life, or being enlightened (or shocked) by a rehearsal of the turns of Russian foreign policy, he would be seeking information regarding the lives and ideas of reflective men, past and present.

Just as information from other books has its values, so knowledge from a philosophy book can be useful. It might satisfy a gnawing curiosity: "So that's what Bertrand Russell believes!" It might make travel more interesting if one knows that Josiah Royce was born in Grass Valley, California, that Karl Marx is buried in London and that Baruch Spinoza's home in The Hague still stands. It might help one to understand the world in which he lives, for to learn about the philosophical theory of Dialectical Materialism is to learn about Communism, and to know of Greek philosophy is to understand much of Christianity. Such information might even have personal value, for the Stoics tell one how to find peace of mind and Bentham tells one how to calculate pleasure. Knowledge from a philosophy book, then, can be useful as well as informative.

However, if a philosophy book provided no more than information, no matter how useful, its author would be disappointed, for he views philosophy not as a body of facts, however interesting, but as a goad to stimulate further reflective thought. In this sense he simply is continuing a tradition first started by Socrates, the first of the great philosophers.

Socrates grew to manhood during the Golden Age of Athens, a time when democratic government, high cultural achievement and great economic progress were present. However, in 431 B.C., when Socrates was thirty-nine years old, a war with Sparta, the Peloponnesian War, started. A great plague swept the city, killing Pericles, the military leader for thirty years, and many others, and continual military defeats imposed a sense of despair on the people's confidence in democratic government and, ultimately, in human reasoning itself. Socrates, who served as a foot soldier during the first decade of the war, returned to Athens to walk the streets asking people questions about subjects on which they were supposed to be knowledgeable. He asked educators about knowledge, religious leaders about piety, political leaders about justice; he even asked military leaders about courage. Plato records it this way:

Socrates: Come, then, Laches, and try to tell me what I have asked: what is courage?

Laches: Good Lord, Socrates, there's nothing hard about that. If a person voluntarily stays at his post and wards off the enemy, you'd surely call him courageous.

Socrates: Perhaps I should, Laches, but I fear you have not entirely answered my question. I wanted your view not only as to soldiers but of courage in other pursuits as well. What of those who display courage amid peril at sea, in disease and poverty, and in giving battle to unworthy temptations? Are not they too courageous?

Laches: O, decidedly.

Socrates: Well, now, if I had asked you the meaning of quickness, you would not have confined your definition to quickness of running or quickness of playing the harp; for there is a quickness in practically every action worth mentioning, whether of hands or legs or mouth or voice or mind. If anyone were to ask me: "Socrates, what do you mean by this which in all these cases you term quickness?" I would reply: the capacity of accomplishing much in little time I call quickness, whether with respect to a voice or a man or anything.

Laches: That would be quite correct.

Socrates: Try yourself, then, Laches, to give me a similar reply in the case of courage: what kind of capacity is it apart from pleasure or pain or any of the other particular circumstances in which it may be found?

Laches: You mean, you wish me to state the natural quality present in all instances of courage? Well, it strikes me as being a kind of endurance of the soul.

Socrates: Yet I doubt whether every case of endurance without exception can appeal to you as courageous. In warfare, if a man endures in a willingness to fight because he has wisely calculated that his allies can be counted on for support and that the enemy's forces are fewer and feebler than his own, and that he holds the more advantageous position —you would call a man who endured because of such wisdom and foresight courageous, would you not?

Laches: Quite the contrary. It is rather the man who endures without the benefit of such calculations that I should call courageous.

Socrates: Yet his endurance is more foolish than that of the first man.

Laches: That is true.

Socrates: Similarly, would you not say that he who endures in a cavalry fight without a knowledge of horsemanship displays more courage than an expert horseman? And that he who dives into a pool without much knowledge of how to swim is more courageous than an expert swimmer?

Laches: How could anyone deny it, Socrates?

Socrates: But such individuals in exposing themselves to danger and enduring it with fortitude behave more foolishly than those who do the same thing with proper skill?

Laches: Apparently.

Socrates: Then you have admitted the same individuals to be courageous and foolish at once.[1]

In such a conversation, and there were many, Socrates, at once, provoked the enmity of some and evoked the admiration of others in the city. At the end of the war, the former brought him to trial charging him, among other things, with teaching young people not to respect their elders, while one of the latter group, a young man in his twenties nicknamed Plato, undertook to preserve Socrates' memory by reproducing some of these discussions in written dialogue form.

Why did Socrates question and criticize the thinking of people in this way? He was not trying to demonstrate his own argumentative skills, nor was he trying to hold others up to reproach. He simply was searching for wisdom and was trying to stimulate others to participate in the quest. As he said at his trial:

And now, Athenians, I am not arguing in my own defense at all, as you might expect me to do, but rather in yours, in order that you may not

[1] Plato, *The Laches,* translated by Philip Wheelwright in *A Critical Introduction to Ethics.* 3rd ed. New York: The Odyssey Press, 1959, pp. 184-186. Reprinted by permission.

make a mistake about the gift of the god to you by condemning me. For if you put me to death, you will not easily find another who, if I may use a ludicrous comparison, clings to the state as a sort of gadfly to a horse that is large and well-bred but rather sluggish because of its size, so that it needs to be aroused. It seems to me that the god has attached me like that to the state, for I am constantly alighting upon you at every point to arouse, persuade, and reproach each of you all day long. You will not easily find anyone else, my friends, to fill my place; and if you are persuaded by me, you will spare my life. You are indignant, as drowsy persons are when they are awakened, and, of course, if you are persuaded by Anytus, you could easily kill me with a single blow, and then sleep on undisturbed for the rest of your lives, unless the god in his care for you sends another to arouse you.

* * * * *

Perhaps someone will say, "Why cannot you withdraw from Athens, Socrates, and hold your peace?" It is the most difficult thing in the world to make you understand why I cannot do that. If I say that I cannot hold my peace because that would be to disobey the god, you will think that I am not in earnest and will not believe me. And if I tell you that no greater good can happen to a man than to discuss human excellence every day and the other matters about which you have heard me arguing and examining myself and others, and that the unexamined life is not worth living, then you will believe me still less. But that is so, my friends, though it is not easy to persuade you.[1]

Socrates thought of himself as a "gadfly" whose function was to arouse individuals from their intellectual lethargy, and he did so because he believed that "the unexamined life was not worth living." This was the heart of his defense, and this has been the creed of philosophers ever since. They believe that every individual—and society—will be better if he thinks about the fundamental problems of life, about virtue and truth, knowledge and goodness, and if he does so with discriminating intelligence. Hence, philosophers view themselves, and their books, partly as gadflies, alighting on their sluggish but well-bred reader, seeking to stimulate him into a more careful, systematic and profound analysis of life, its meaning and values.

However, valuable and important as stimulation is, Socrates did not view it as an end in itself. He believed that critical thinking was important and, in the face of complacency, should be encouraged continuously, but it is only a means for achieving more important purposes. For, as Plato said:

[1] Reprinted from *Euthyphro–Apology–Crito* by Plato, copyright © 1948, 1956 by The Liberal Arts Press, Inc., by special permission of The Bobbs-Merrill Company, Inc. Pages 36-37.

There is danger lest they should taste the dear delight too early; for youngsters, as you may have observed, when they first get the taste in their mouths, argue for amusement, and are always contradicting and refuting others in imitation of those who refute them; like puppy dogs, they rejoice in pulling and tearing at all who come near them.

Yes, he said, there is nothing which they like better.

And when they have made any conquests and received defeats at the hands of many, they violently and speedily get into a way of not believing anything which they believed before, and hence, not only they, but philosophy and all that related to it is apt to have a bad name with the rest of the world.

Too true, he said.[1]

Socrates feared that critical thinking might become mere argumentation, and for that reason he viewed his task primarily as the quest for clarification. This search involves four distinct activities. First, a consideration of the alternative answers which could be used in answering a question. Second, what reasons could be given to support each alternative. Third, an understanding of the implications which would follow from each alternative. And fourth, a choice as to which would be the best.

To take a nonphilosophical example, suppose you leave the grocery store without paying for a bag of flour the clerk put directly in your car. What should you do? First, what alternatives are open to you? Return to the store and pay. Rush home. Pretend you haven't noticed the mistake, etc. Second, what reasons would you give for doing each? Someone might have seen what happened, so you should return. You are low on money, the grocer was careless, and hence he should be blamed; and besides you always wanted to get back at him for his high prices, so you should rush home. Be nonchalant because then you can pay if caught and have the free flour if not. Third, what are the implications of each alternative? If you pay because you fear other's opinions, then aren't you letting others decide what your life's activities will be and not living your own life? If you blame the grocer's carelessness, then are you willing to apply the same principle and congratulate the skillful burgler who successfully enters your home? If you delay your decision aren't you really saying that you pay your bills only when forced to do so, and hence are an egoist? And finally, which alternative would be best? Different people might make different choices, but the point is that the choice which is made will be better if it results from a

[1] Plato, *The Republic,* translated by Benjamin Jowett. New York: Oxford University Press, 1892, Book VII, 539a.

clear understanding of the nature, evidence, and implications of alternative answers.

The same principles for clarification are equally applicable to philosophical problems. What is knowledge? First, what alternative answers have been proposed? Information which comes from sense experience. From intuition. From logical deduction. From revelation, etc. Second, what reasons can be given to support each claim? Agreement among people. Ability to control natural processes. Personal experience, etc. Third, what are the implications of each view? If all knowledge comes from sense experience, then there is no knowledge when there is no such experience, so how do you know you exist when you are sleeping? If knowledge comes from revelation, then it follows that man is only the receiver, not the originator, of knowledge. And finally, which alternative should be chosen?

The purpose of philosophical stimulation, then, is to help people make intelligent choices. This can be done by elucidating and clarifying alternatives, and by examining the evidence and implications of each. Before one chooses answers, especially answers to the fundamental problems of life, he should know what answers might be given and what is to be said for and against each alternative. To provide those alternatives and reasons is a purpose of any philosophy book, for ultimately philosophy rests on the belief that a life based on reasoned and deliberate choice is best, for then one knows not only what he believes, but why he believes what he does.

Thus, any philosophy book, besides relieving boredom or fulfilling assignments, can provide information, create stimulation and help to develop an ability to make intelligent choices. It can tell one some of the ideas of influential thinkers and, in doing so, should provide stimulation for his thinking about those same problems. An observant reader will also notice how these men analyze and clarify, weigh alternatives and consider advantages, and thereby learn how to use the tools needed for clear and intelligent thinking. As one develops this ability to follow lines of reasoning in others, he usually finds that his own life becomes more meaningful, that he can face the problems presented by life with greater understanding and that he can find a sensitivity and depth of comprehension he never knew before. In the final analysis, then, a philosophy book should help one to broaden his outlook and deepen his insight into the meaning of life itself, and hence it can satisfy one of its readers' most important, even though initially unrecognized, needs.

II

This philosophy book rests on the belief that all three purposes should be satisfied. For those seeking information, the relevant facts about each writer's life are to be found at the beginning of each selection. In addition, important ideas like the Categorical Imperative and the Moral Calculus, and important questions like whether we can know of God's existence or can know anything to be certainly true are discussed in the readings.

However, the gadfly's function is never far from the philosopher's mind, and so the book also contains selections designed to challenge, perhaps disprove, some cherished beliefs. Is American society in the mid-twentieth century the best kind of civilization? Nietzsche and Fromm have some comments which might be challenging. Should there be moderation in all things? What do Aristotle and Buddha say? Hume points out why there is no basis for believing there is a Self which continues to exist over a period of time. Are Freud's theories scientifically respectable? Is religion intellectually respectable? These are the kinds of problems, and some of the answers, that are considered in the following chapters, and what these authors have had to say should provide some stimulation for a careful and critical examination of their opinions, as well as one's own.

The contents of this book, then, will provide information and stimulation; its organization is designed to provide clarification in two senses: knowing what traditional philosophy is and how philosophers have dealt with their problems; and in knowing what one's own belief might be, together with the evidence which could be used to justify them. To achieve clarification in these ways we must investigate two different kinds of problems: what issues are most fundamental in human experience; and what alternative kinds of attitude could provide answers to them.

First, to the problems. Man's experience during the past three millennia demonstrates that there are three general questions which any general attitude toward life must consider. First, methodology, the problem of method. How does one obtain information he considers to be reliable? Is human reason competent, and, if so, to what extent and under what circumstances? Is repeatable verification a necessary element? How important is the making of definitions, and how can they be made? Or are nonrational methods to be trusted, and, if so, when? These are some of the problems of methodology: how do we obtain reliable knowledge; how can we arrive at conclusions we are willing to accept as justified?

Secondly, there is the problem of morality. This is a part of the larger problem of axiology, the problem of what is valuable, the part dealing with one's relationships to other people. How should one act toward others? What does the word "good" mean? Or the word "right"? What ought I to do? What are the rights and obligations all human beings should enjoy? Or are there any universal principles? Is pleasure the highest good? Or is there a single highest good? Why should I keep my promises? These are some aspects of the problem of morality.

Finally, there is the problem of metaphysics, the problem of reality. Do my senses tell me what really exists or only what I experience to exist? Is life purposive? How can we give the same name to objects which differ in every particular respect? Is the world more like a machine or a growing organism—or neither? Does Reality change or is it permanent? What beliefs can give meaning to life? Or is life without meaning? These are the kinds of problems included in the study of metaphysics, and part of the purpose of this book is to elucidate and clarify the alternative answers which might be given to them.

These three general problems do not exhaust the issues human beings face, but they are of critical importance in any reasoned attitude toward life. Take the moral question. Many people contend this is the crucial problem facing mankind today, for while we have made great scientific progress during the past few centuries, our moral progress has been slight. Juvenile delinquency is increasing, as is alcoholism, suicide, homicide and other forms of crime; one out of every three marriages, originally made, presumably, by couples who thought they were in love, ends in divorce; wars are becoming more widespread, frequent and terrifying. Indeed, regardless of where we look it seems clear that people do not know how to live peacefully with each other.

No doubt this is due partly to man's continual struggle—and failure—to make practical his ideals. Moreover, religion's growing loss of authority has made suspect the traditional way for justifying moral standards. And many people have embraced ethical relativism, believing that since each society has its own standards, there is no standard by which a society's values themselves can be evaluated. For these and other reasons we seem to live in an age of moral skepticism and uncertainty. And yet, moral problems, ones demanding immediate answers, face us every day. How can we find answers to these problems? How can we know what we ought to do? What is right? Is there a universal good? Before we can answer these questions intelligently we must know what answers could be given, and what evidence would be offered to justify the answers, as well as what implications follow from them. What better place is there to start this inquiry than with the writings of men who have thought deeply and systematically about these problems?

Or take the area of metaphysics. Most people do not consider these problems frequently, but when they do the issues are of critical importance to their entire outlook on life. Who does not have to decide whether he believes life is purposive? Who does not wonder whether God exists, or whether immortality is only a hope? Who has not been impressed with the regularity and predictability of nature and wondered whether human life, too, is deterministic and hence predictable? Metaphysical questions are fundamental to our whole way of thinking; hence in the interests of mental peace it is fortunate we do not examine them continually. Nevertheless, because they are so basic, intelligent answers to them must be found, and this, again, requires first an understanding of what answers might be given.

However, before answers to moral and metaphysical questions can be given, we must decide how those answers can be obtained; what is a reliable method for gaining knowledge. If one were told he should love his neighbor and the reason given for doing so was that God has commanded it, this reason would not be a satisfactory justification if he doubted God's existence. If he were told Darwin's theory should be accepted because it explains the similarities among animals, this reason would not be justified if he believed all reliable knowledge came only from the Scriptures. Before any question can be answered, then, one must decide how such an answer can be obtained. Hence, to know what competing methodologies are available, and what is implied by each, is also an important part of one's beliefs.

We recognize three crucial questions any reasoned attitude toward life must answer; and experience also demonstrates there are three general approaches to life which might be adopted. The obvious attitude is the one which dominates our lives in the twentieth century, Science. Not only has science remade the technological world in which we live, it is remaking our attitudes as well. Unusual phenomena are attributed to natural, although unknown, causes rather than divine intervention. The law, that sanctuary of conservatism, now looks as much to evidence as it does to precedent. The theory and practice of education has been revolutionized by science. The medicine of a decade ago is greatly changed today. Textbooks in the physical sciences are mimeographed because they are outdated so rapidly. Since science has been so successful in understanding and controlling nature, many people consider that the attitude of the scientist is the most satisfactory attitude they might adopt toward life.

Another alternative widely accepted, although more so in earlier centuries than our own, is Religion, for it, too, gives people moral advice, helps them to decide whether life is purposive and has a way of answering the questions of men. Religion sees man's life in the context of a larger, usually supernatural, meaning, and hence it provides guidance, encouragement and, if need be, solace for the living of this life. Moreover, since these standards of wisdom transcend the frailties of human origins, many people find that religious beliefs provide a satisfying and meaningful way to view life.

The third alternative, Philosophy, is one whose adherents, relative to the other two, have been few, but whose influence has been considerable. Philosophers, too, have provided counsel and guidance for moral behavior and, to some people, metaphysics is the essence of philosophical thought. The method of precise analytical reasoning about abstract theoretical problems places emphasis on man's creative intellect for gaining knowledge, and this method has been appealing to many people. In the final analysis, many believe that philosophy provides the only satisfactory basis for a reasoned attitude toward life.[1]

The chapters which follow are based on this two-fold tripartite division. Science, Religion and Philosophy are not the only attitudes toward life one might adopt; nor are methodological, moral and metaphysical questions the only ones which might be answered. However, each of the former is widely accepted, and each of the latter is of vital importance. Hence, if one knows how those who accept each attitude toward life would answer each kind of question, he will have gained at least some of the knowledge necessary for making intelligent judgments about his own attitude toward life.

When this inquiry is completed, one should be much clearer on a number of matters. First, he should know what a philosophical attitude toward life is, for he will have read and discussed philosophers' ideas, observed how they investigate their problems, and he will have examined ideas himself. Second, he should have the same knowledge about what is involved in a religious or a scientific attitude, and for the same reasons. Third, he should have a clearer and firmer basis for comparing the three, for dealing intelligently with

[1] A short history of the origins in philosophy will be found on pages 226-227.

questions like: "Is there a conflict between science and religion?" or "Can one be both philosophical and scientific?" Fourth, he will be able to make judgments regarding the relative strengths and weaknesses of each, for if a satisfactory way of life must provide answers to all three questions, then each attitude will be adequate to the degree that it does provide those answers.

Finally, and perhaps most importantly, he should be in a better position to make intelligent choices regarding his own beliefs and values, his own attitude toward life, for he will know what problems are important, how they might be answered, and the evidence and implications of each. Or he might have read some authors who, initially, seemed so reasonable that he learned more about their thought, thereby allowing them to help guide his thinking. In either case, the information he discovers, and the stimulation which emerges, will but provide the means for intelligent decision making, and that, perhaps, is the ultimate purpose of any philosophy book.

PHILOSOPHY

Chapter Two

PHILOSOPHICAL METHOD

1. SOCRATES

Socrates was born about 470 B.C., the son of Sophroniscus, who probably was a stone mason, and Phaenarete, who might have been a midwife. Little is known of his youth, but he grew to manhood during the Golden Age of Athens and probably occupied a position of some respect in the city. He fought in several battles during the Peloponnesian War, but his fame rests on his activities after his military service. He returned to Athens to spend his time conversing with people from all walks of life on all kinds of subject. He claimed he was trying to understand the oracle's pronouncement that he was the wisest of all men, but he also thought of himself as a "gadfly" arousing others from their intellectual complacency. In appearance he was short and stout with widely separated eyes, a snub nose, broad nostrils and a wide mouth, and his contemporaries tell us he wore the same coat, winter and summer, with neither shoes nor shirt. He finally came to understand that his superior wisdom lay in the realization that he knew how much he did not know, while others were ignorant of the extent of their ignorance, and he so aroused others that in 399 he was brought to trial for "corrupting the youth" and "not believing in the divinities." Despite an eloquent defense he was judged guilty and sentenced to drink the hemlock. When the time came, he did so "in the easiest and gentlest of manners," chastizing some friends for weeping, requesting others to care for his wife, Xanthippe, and three small children, and anticipating with pleasure the opportunity to ask a few questions of those who had lived at an earlier time.

The following selection is a good example of the Socratic Method. It consists of six definitions of "piety," together with an analysis of each. In your reading be particularly attentive to the way Socrates analyzes each definition, for the techniques he employs are characteristic of the methods philosophers use to gain reliable knowledge.

What Is Piety?[1]

Euthyphro: What in the world are you doing here in the king's hall, Socrates? Why have you left your haunts in the Lyceum? You surely cannot have a suit before him, as I have.

Socrates: The Athenians, Euthyphro, call it a prosecution, not a suit.

Euthyphro: What? Do you mean that someone is prosecuting you? I cannot believe that you are prosecuting anyone yourself.

Socrates: Certainly I am not.

Euthyphro: Then is someone prosecuting you?

Socrates: Yes.

Euthyphro: Who is he?

Socrates: I scarcely know him myself, Euthyphro; I think he must be some unknown young man. His name, however, is Meletus, and his town Pitthis, if you can call to mind any Meletus of that town—a hook-nose man with long hair, and rather a scanty beard.

Euthyphro: I don't know him, Socrates. But, tell me, what is he prosecuting you for?

Socrates: What for? Not on trivial grounds, I think. It is no small thing for so young a man to have formed an opinion on such an important matter. For he, he says, knows how the young are corrupted, and who are their corrupters. He must be a wise man, who, observing my ignorance, is going to accuse me to the city, as his mother, of corrupting his friends. I think that he is the only man who begins at the right point in his political reforms; for his first care is to make the young men as perfect as possible, just as a good farmer will take care of his young plants first, and, after he has done that, of the others. And so Meletus, I suppose, is first clearing us away who, as he says, corrupt the young men as they grow up; and then, when he has done that, of course he will turn his attention to the older men, and so become a very great public benefactor. Indeed, that is only what you would expect, when he goes to work in this way.

Euthyphro: I hope it may be so, Socrates, but I have very grave doubts about it. It seems to me that in trying to injure you, he is really setting to work by striking a blow at the heart of the state. But how, tell me, does he say that you corrupt youth?

Socrates: In a way which sounds strange at first, my friend. He says that I am a maker of gods; and so he is prosecuting me, he says, for inventing new gods and for not believing in the old ones.

Euthyphro: I understand, Socrates. It is because you say that you always have a divine sign. So he is prosecuting you for introducing novelties into religion; and he is going into court knowing that such matters are easily misrepresented to the multitude, and consequently meaning to slander you

[1] Plato, *Euthyphro,* translated by F. J. Church in *The Trial and Death of Socrates.* London: Macmillan Co., 1888, pp. 1-31. [All selection titles have been supplied by the editor.]

there. Why they laugh even at me, as if I were out of my mind, when I talk about divine things in the assembly, and tell them what is going to happen: and yet I have never foretold anything which has not come true. But they are jealous of all people like us. We must not worry about them; we must meet them boldly.

Socrates: My dear Euthyphro, their ridicule is not a very serious matter. The Athenians, it seems to me, may think a man to be clever without paying him much attention, so long as they do not think that he teaches his wisdom to others. But as soon as they think that he makes other people clever, they get angry, whether it be from jealousy, as you say, or for some other reason.

Euthyphro: I am not very anxious to try their disposition toward me in this matter. . . .

Socrates: And what is this suit of yours, Euthyphro? Are you suing, or being sued?

Euthyphro: I am suing—a very old man.

Socrates: Who is he?

Euthyphro: He is my father.

Socrates: Your father, my good sir?

Euthyphro: He is indeed.

Socrates: What are you prosecuting him for? What is the charge?

Euthyphro: Murder, Socrates.

Socrates: Good heavens, Euthyphro! Surely the multitude are ignorant of what makes right. I take it that it is not everyone who could rightly do what you are doing; only a man who was already well advanced in wisdom.

Euthyphro: That is quite true, Socrates.

Socrates: Was the man whom your father killed a relative of yours? But, of course, he was. You would never have prosecuted your father for the murder of a stranger?

Euthyphro: You amuse me, Socrates. What difference does it make whether the murdered man were a relative or a stranger? The only question that you have to ask, is did the slayer slay justly or not? If justly, you must let him alone; if unjustly, you must indict him for murder, even though he share your hearth and sit at your table. The pollution is the same if you associate with such a man, knowing what he has done, without purifying yourself, and him too, by bringing him to justice. In the present case the murdered man was a poor laborer of mine, who worked for us on our farm in Naxos. While drunk he became angry with one of our slaves and killed him. My father therefore bound the man hand and foot and threw him into a ditch, while he sent to Athens to ask the seer what he should do. While the messenger was gone, he entirely neglected the man, thinking that he was a murderer, and that it would be no great matter even if he were to die. And that was exactly what happened; hunger and cold and his bonds killed him before the messenger returned. And now my father and the rest of my family are indignant with me because I am prosecuting my father for the murder of this murderer. They assert that he did not kill the man at all; and they say that, even if he had killed him over and over again, the man himself was a murderer, and that I ought not to concern myself about such a person because it is impious for a son to prosecute his father for murder. So little, Socrates, do they know the divine law of piety and impiety.

Socrates: And do you mean to say, Euthyphro, that you think that you understand divine things and piety and impiety so accurately that, in such a case as you have stated, you can bring your father to justice without fear that you yourself may be doing an impious thing?

Euthyphro: If I did not understand all these matters accurately, Socrates, I should be no use, and Euthyphro would not be any better than other men. . . .

Socrates: Tell me, then; what is piety, and what is impiety?

DEFINITION I

Euthyphro: Well, then, I say that piety means prosecuting the wrongdoer who has committed murder or sacrilege, or any other such crime, as I am doing now, whether he be your father or your mother or whoever he be; and I say that impiety means not prosecuting him. And observe, Socrates, I will give you a clear proof, which I have already given to others, that it is so, and that doing right means not suffering the sacrilegious man, whosoever he may be. Men hold Zeus to be the best and the most just of the gods; and they admit that Zeus bound his own father, Cronos, for wrongfully devouring his children; and that Cronos, in his turn, castrated his father for similar reasons. And yet these same men are angry with me because I proceed against my father for doing wrong. So, you see, they say one thing in the case of the gods and quite another in mine.

Socrates: Is not that why I am being prosecuted, Euthyphro? I mean, because I am displeased when I hear such things about the gods? I expect that I shall be called a sinner because I doubt those stories. But tell me, in the name of friendship, do you really believe that these things have actually happened?

Euthyphro: Yes, and stranger ones, too, Socrates, which the multitude do not know of.

Socrates: Then you really believe that there is war among the gods, and bitter hatreds, and battles, such as the poets tell of, and which the great painters have depicted in our temples, especially in the pictures which cover the robe that is carried up to the Acropolis at the great Panathenaic festival? Are we to say that these things are true, Euthyphro?

Euthyphro: Yes, Socrates, and more besides. As I was saying, I will relate to you many other stories about divine matters, if you like, which I am sure will astonish you when you hear them.

Socrates: I dare say. You shall relate them to me at your leisure another time. At present please try to give a more definite answer to the question which I asked you just now. What I asked you, my friend, was, what is piety? and you have not explained it to me to my satisfaction. You only tell me that what you are doing now, namely, prosecuting your father for murder, is a pious act.

Euthyphro: Well, that is true, Socrates.

Socrates: Very likely. But many other actions are pious, are they not, Euthyphro?

Euthyphro: Certainly.

Socrates: Remember, then, I did not ask you to tell me one or two of all the many pious actions that there are; I want to know what is the essential form of piety which makes all pious actions pious. You said, I think, that there is one characteristic which makes all pious actions pious, and another characteristic which makes all impious actions impious. Do you not remember?

Euthyphro: I do.

Socrates: Well, then, explain to me what is this characteristic, that I may have it to turn to, and to use as a standard whereby to judge your actions and those of other men, and be able to say that whatever action resembles it is pious, and whatever does not, is not pious.

Euthyphro: Yes, I will tell you that, if you wish it, Socrates.

Socrates: Certainly I wish it.

DEFINITION II

Euthyphro: Well, then, what is pleasing to the gods is pious, and what is not pleasing to them is impious.

Socrates: Beautiful, Euthyphro. Now you have given me the answer that I wanted. Whether what you say is true, I do not yet know. But, of course, you will go on to prove the truth of it.

Euthyphro: Certainly.

Socrates: Come, then, let us examine our words. The things and the men that are pleasing to the gods are pious, and the things and the men that are displeasing to the gods are impious. But piety and impiety are not the same; they are as opposite as possible; was not that what we said?

Euthyphro: Certainly.

Socrates: And I think it was very well said.

Euthyphro: Yes, Socrates, it certainly was.

Socrates: Have we not also said, Euthyphro, that there are factions and disagreements and hatreds among the gods?

Euthyphro: We have.

Socrates: But what kind of disagreement, my friend, causes hatred and anger? Let us look at the matter thus. If you and I were to disagree as to whether one number were more than another, would that provoke us to anger, and make us enemies? Should we not settle such dispute at once by counting?

Euthyphro: Of course.

Socrates: And if we were to disagree as to the relative size of two things, we should measure them, and put an end to the disagreement at once, should we not?

Euthyphro: Yes.

Socrates: And should we not settle a question about the relative weight of two things by weighing them?

Euthyphro: Of course.

Socrates: Then what is the question which would provoke us to anger and make us enemies, if we disagreed about it, and could not come to a settlement? Perhaps you have not an answer ready: but listen to me. Is it not the question of the right and wrong, of the honorable and the base, of the good and the bad?

Is it not questions about these matters which make you and me and everyone else quarrel, when we do quarrel, if we differ about them, and can reach no satisfactory settlement?

Euthyphro: Yes, Socrates, it is disagreements about these matters.

Socrates: Well, Euthyphro, you say that some of the gods think one thing just, the others another; and that what some of them hold to be honorable or good, others hold to be base or evil. For there would not have been factions among them if they had not disagreed on these points, would there?

Euthyphro: You are right.

Socrates: And each of them loves what he thinks honorable, and good, and right, and hates the opposite, does he not?

Euthyphro: Certainly.

Socrates: But you say that the same action is held by some of them to be right, and by others to be wrong; and that then they dispute about it, and so quarrel and fight among themselves. Is it not so?

Euthyphro: Yes.

Socrates: Then the same thing is hated by the gods and loved by them; and the same thing will be displeasing and pleasing to them.

Euthyphro: Apparently.

Socrates: Then, according to your account, the same thing will be pious and impious.

Euthyphro: So it seems.

Socrates: Then, my good friend, you have not answered my question. I did not ask you to tell me what action is both pious and impious; but it seems that whatever is pleasing to the gods is also displeasing to them. And so, Euthyphro, I should not wonder if what you are doing now in punishing your father is an action well pleasing to Zeus, but hateful to Cronos and Uranus, and acceptable to Hephaestus, but hateful to Hera; and if any of the other gods disagree about it, pleasing to some of them and displeasing to others.

DEFINITION III

Euthyphro: But on this point, Socrates, I think that there is no difference of opinion among the gods; they all hold that if one man kills another wrongfully, he must be punished.

Socrates: What, Euthyphro? Among mankind, have you never heard disputes whether a man ought to be punished for killing another man wrongfully, or for doing some other wrong deed?

Euthyphro: Indeed, they never cease from these disputes, especially in courts of justice. They do all manner of wrong things; and then there is nothing which they will not do and say to avoid punishment.

Socrates: Do they admit that they have done wrong, and at the same time deny that they ought to be punished, Euthyphro?

Euthyphro: No, indeed, that they do not.

Socrates: Then it is not every thing that they will do and say. I take it, they do not dare to assert or argue that they must not be punished if they have done something wrong. What they say is that they have not done wrong, is it not?

Euthyphro: That is true.

Socrates: Then they do not dispute the question that the wrongdoer must be punished. They disagree about the question, who is a wrongdoer, and when and what is a wrong deed, do they not?

Euthyphro: That is true.

Socrates: Well, is not exactly the same thing true of the gods if they quarrel about right and wrong, as you say they do? Do not some of them assert that the others are doing wrong, while the others deny it? No one, I suppose, my dear friend, whether god or man, ventures to say that a person who has done wrong must not be punished.

Euthyphro: No, Socrates, that is true, in the main.

Socrates: I take it, Euthyphro, that the disputants, whether men or gods, if the gods do dispute, dispute about each separate act. When they quarrel about any act, some of them say that it was done rightly, and others that it was done wrongly. Is it not so?

Euthyphro: Yes.

Socrates: Come, then, my dear Euthyphro, please enlighten me on this point. What proof have you that all the gods think that a laborer who has been imprisoned for murder by the master of the man whom he has murdered, and who dies from his imprisonment before the master has had time to learn from the seers what he should do, dies unjustly? How do you know that it is right for a son to indict his father, and to prosecute him for the murder of such a man? Come, see if you can make it clear to me that the gods necessarily agree in thinking that this action of yours is right; and if you satisfy me, I will never cease singing your praises for wisdom.

Euthyphro: I could make that clear enough to you, Socrates; but I am afraid that it would be a long business.

Socrates: I see you think that I am duller than the judges. To them, of course, you will make it clear that your father has done wrong, and that all the gods agree in hating such deeds.

Euthyphro: I will indeed, Socrates, if they will only listen to me.

Socrates: They will listen if they think that you speak well. But while you were speaking, it occurred to me to ask myself this question: suppose that Euthyphro were to prove to me as clearly as possible that all the gods think such a death unjust, how has he brought me any nearer to understanding what piety and impiety are? This particular act, perhaps, may be displeasing to the gods, but then we have just seen that piety and impiety cannot be defined in that way; for we have seen that what is displeasing to the gods is also pleasing to them. So I will let you off on this point, Euthyphro; and all the gods shall agree in thinking your father's action wrong and in hating it, if you like. But shall we correct our definition and say that whatever all the gods hate is impious, and whatever they all love is pious; while whatever some of them love, and others hate, is either both or neither? Do you wish us now to define piety and impiety in this manner?

Euthyphro: Why not, Socrates?

Socrates: There is no reason why I should not, Euthyphro. It is for you to consider whether that definition will help you to instruct me what you promised.

Euthyphro: Well, I should say that

piety is what all the gods love, and that impiety is what they all hate.

Socrates: Are we to examine this definition, Euthyphro, and see if it is a good one? Or are we to be content to accept the bare assertions of other men, or of ourselves, without asking any questions? Or must we examine the assertions?

Euthyphro: We must examine them. But for my part I think that the definition is right this time.

DEFINITION IV

Socrates: We shall know that better in a little while, my good friend. Now consider this question. Do the gods love piety because it is pious, or is it pious because they love it?

Euthyphro: I do not understand you, Socrates.

Socrates: I will try to explain myself; we speak of a thing being carried and carrying, and being led and leading, and being seen and seeing; and you understand that all such expressions mean different things, and what the difference is.

Euthyphro: Yes, I think I understand. . . .

Socrates: Well, then, Euthyphro, what do we say about piety? Is it not loved by all the gods, according to your definition?

Euthyphro: Yes.

Socrates: Because it is pious, or for some other reason?

Euthyphro: No, because it is pious.

Socrates: Then it is loved by the gods because it is pious; it is not pious because it is loved by them.

Euthyphro: It seems so.

Socrates: But then what is pleasing to the gods is pleasing to them, and is in a state of being loved by them, because they love it?

Euthyphro: Of course.

Socrates: Then piety is not what is pleasing to the gods, and what is pleasing to the gods is not pious, as you say, Euthyphro. They are different things.

Euthyphro: And why, Socrates?

Socrates: Because we are agreed that the gods love piety because it is pious, and that it is not pious because they love it. Is not this so?

Euthyphro: Yes.

Socrates: And that what is pleasing to the gods because they love it, is pleasing to them by reason of this same love, and that they do not love it because it is pleasing to them.

Euthyphro: True.

Socrates: Then, my dear Euthyphro, piety and what is pleasing to the gods are different things. If the gods had loved piety because it is pious, they would also have loved what is pleasing to them because it is pleasing to them; but if what is pleasing to them had been pleasing to them because they loved it, then piety, too, would have been piety because they loved it. But now you see that they are opposite things, and wholly different from each other. For the one is of a sort to be loved because it is loved, while the other is loved because it is of a sort to be loved. My question, Euthyphro, was, what is piety? But it turns out that you have not explained to me the essential characteristic of piety; you have been content to mention an effect which belongs to it—namely, that all the gods love it. You have not yet told me what its essential characteristic is. Do not, if you please, keep from me what piety is; begin again and tell me that. Never mind whether the gods love it, or whether it has other effects; we shall not differ on that point. Do your best to make clear to me what is piety and what is impiety.

Euthyphro: But, Socrates, I really don't know how to explain to you what is in my mind. Whatever statement we put forward always somehow moves round in a circle, and will not stay where we place it.

Socrates: I think that your statements, Euthyphro, are worthy of my ancestor Daedalus. If they had been mine and I had set them down, I dare say you would have made fun of me, and said that it was the consequence of my descent from Daedalus that the definitions which I construct run away, as his statues used to, and will not stay where they are placed. But, as it is, the definitions are yours, and the jest would have no point. You yourself see that they will not stay still.

Euthyphro: Nay, Socrates, I think that the jest is very much in point. It is not my fault that the statement moves round in a circle and will not stay still. But you are the Daedalus, I think; as far as I am concerned, my definitions would have stayed quiet enough.

Socrates: Then, my friend, I must be a more skillful artist than Daedalus; he only used to make his own works move, while I, you see, can make other people's works move, too. And the beauty of it is that I am wise against my will. I would rather that our definitions had remained firm and immovable than have all the wisdom of Daedalus and all the riches of Tantalus to boot. But enough of this. I will do my best to help you to explain to me what piety is, for I think that you are lazy. Don't give in yet. Tell me, do you not think that all piety must be just?

Euthyphro: I do.

DEFINITION V

Socrates: Well, then, is all justice pious, too? Or, while all piety is just, is a part only of justice pious, and the rest of it something else?

Euthyphro: I do not follow you, Socrates.

Socrates: Yet you have the advantage over me in your youth no less than your wisdom. But, as I say, the wealth of your wisdom makes you lazy. Exert yourself, my good friend: I am not asking you a difficult question. I mean the opposite of what the poet said, when he wrote:

> "You shall not name Zeus the creator, who made all things: for where there is fear there is also reverence."

Now I disagree with the poet. Shall I tell you why?

Euthyphro: Yes.

Socrates: I do not think it true to say that where there is fear, there also is reverence. Many people who fear sickness and poverty and other such evils seem to me to have fear, but no reverence for what they fear. Do you not think so?

Euthyphro: I do.

Socrates: But I think that where there is reverence, there also is fear. Does any man feel reverence and a sense of shame about anything, without at the same time dreading and fearing the reputation of wickedness?

Euthyphro: No, certainly not.

Socrates: Then, though there is fear wherever there is reverence, it is not correct to say that where there is fear there also is reverence. Reverence does not always accompany fear; for fear, I take it, is wider than reverence. It is a part of fear, just as the odd is a part of number, so that where you have the odd you must also have number, though where you have number you do not necessarily have the odd. Now I think you follow me?

Euthyphro: I do.

Socrates: Well, then, this is what I meant by the question which I asked you. Is there always piety where there is justice? Or, though there is always justice where there is piety, yet there is not always piety where there is justice, because piety is only a part of justice? Shall we say this, or do you differ?

Euthyphro: No, I agree. I think that you are right.

Socrates: Now observe the next point. If piety is a part of justice, we must find out, I suppose, what part of justice it is? Now, if you had asked me just now, for instance, what part of number is the odd, and what number is an odd number, I should have said that whatever number is not even is an odd number. Is it not so?

Euthyphro: Yes.

Socrates: Then see if you can explain to me what part of justice is piety, that I may tell Meletus that now that I have learned perfectly from you what actions are pious and holy, and what are not, he must give up prosecuting me unjustly for impiety.

DEFINITION VI

Euthyphro: Well, then, Socrates, I should say that holiness and piety are that part of justice which has to do with the attention which is due to the gods; and that what has to do with the attention which is due to men is the remaining part of justice.

Socrates: And I think that your answer is a good one, Euthyphro. But there is one little point about which I still want to hear more. I do not yet understand what the attention or care which you are speaking of is. I suppose you do not mean that the care which we show to the gods is like the care which we show to other things. We say, for instance, do we not, that not everyone knows how to take care of horses, but only the trainer of horses?

Euthyphro: Certainly.

Socrates: For I suppose that the art that relates to horses is the art of taking care of horses.

Euthyphro: Yes.

Socrates: And not everyone understands the care of dogs, but only the huntsman.

Euthyphro: True.

Socrates: For I suppose that the huntsman's art is the art of taking care of dogs.

Euthyphro: Yes.

Socrates: And the herdsman's art is the art of taking care of cattle.

Euthyphro: Certainly.

Socrates: And you say that piety and righteousness mean the care of the gods, Euthyphro?

Euthyphro: I do.

Socrates: Well, then, has not all care the same object? Is it not for the good and benefit of that on which it is bestowed? For instance, you see that horses are benefited and improved when they are cared for by the art which is concerned with them. Is it not so?

Euthyphro: Yes, I think so.

Socrates: And dogs are benefited and improved by the huntsman's art, and cattle by the herdsman's, are they not? And the same is always true. Or do you think care is ever meant to hurt that on which it is bestowed?

Euthyphro: No, indeed; certainly not.

Socrates: But to benefit it?

Euthyphro: Of course.

Socrates: Then is piety, which is the care which we bestow on the gods, intended to benefit the gods, or to improve them? Should you allow that you make any of the gods better, when you do a pious action?

Euthyphro: No indeed; certainly not.

Socrates: No, I am quite sure that is not your meaning, Euthyphro. It was for that reason that I asked you what you meant by the attention due to the gods. I thought that you did not mean that.

Euthyphro: You were right, Socrates. I do not mean that.

* * * * *

Socrates: Then we must begin again and inquire what piety is. I do not mean to give in until I have found out. Do not regard me as unworthy; give your whole mind to the question, and this time tell me the truth. For if anyone knows it, it is you; and you are a Proteus whom I must not let go until you have told me. It cannot be that you would ever have undertaken to prosecute your aged father for the murder of a laboring man unless you had known exactly what piety and impiety are. You would have feared to risk the anger of the gods, in case you should be doing wrong, and you would have been afraid of what men would say. But now I am sure that you think that you know exactly what is pious and what is not; so tell me, my excellent Euthyphro, and do not conceal from me what you hold it to be.

Euthyphro: Another time, then, Socrates. I am in a hurry now, and it is time for me to be off.

QUESTIONS FOR DISCUSSION

1. Did Socrates satisfactorily disprove each of Euthyphro's definitions? Look again at his discussion, particularly definitions 2, 5 and 6.
2. List the techniques of reasoning Socrates uses in his analyses and apply each of them to another example. Can you find examples of each in newspaper editorials or other textbooks?
3. Can you provide a more adequate definition of "piety" than any of Euthyphro's?

READINGS FOR IMMEDIATE REFERENCE

Plato. *The Apology, The Crito, The Phaedo.*

Thilly, Frank and Wood, Ledger. *A History of Philosophy,* 3rd ed. New York: Henry Holt, 1956, pp. 66 ff.

Wheelwright, Philip. *A Critical Introduction to Ethics,* 3rd ed. New York: The Odyssey Press, 1959, pp. 41 ff.

Windelband, Wilhelm. *A History of Philosophy.* New York: Macmillan, 1893, pp. 94 ff.

REFERENCES FOR COMPREHENSIVE KNOWLEDGE

Aristophanes. *Clouds.*

Xenophon. *Memorabilia.* Portrayals of Socrates by contemporaries less impressed by him than Plato.

Robinson, Richard. *Plato's Earlier Dialectic,* 2nd ed. Oxford: Clarendon Press, 1953. An analysis of the arguments in each of the Socratic dialogues.

Taylor, A. E. *Socrates.* Boston: Beacon Press, 1933. A brief biography which also examines the sources of our knowledge.

Also see:

Cornford, F. M. *Before and After Socrates.* Cambridge: Cambridge University Press, 1932.

Cross, R. *Socrates: The Man and His Mission.* New York: Oxford University Press, 1914.

Rogers, Arthur K. *The Socratic Problem.* New Haven: Yale University Press, 1933.

Winspear, A. D. and Silverberg, T. *Who Was Socrates?,* 2nd ed. New York: Russell and Russell, 1960.

Zeller, Edward. *Socrates and the Socratic Schools.* New York: Oxford University Press, 1885.

II. RENÉ DESCARTES

Descartes was born in 1596, the third child of a councillor in the Parliament of Brittany. He was educated at La Fléche, a famous Jesuit school, where he was recognized as a promising young scholar. However, he tired of the strict training and left the school when he was eighteen to become a gentleman soldier in the armies of Maurice of Nassau and Maximilian of Bavaria. After six years of travel in Europe, followed by a three-year residence in Italy and Paris, he finally settled in Holland where he published his philosophical works and wrote treatises on music, anatomy and mathematics (he invented the analytic geometry), besides maintaining a voluminous correspondence with all the leading intellectuals in Europe. Publication of his philosophical works attracted much attention to him, and in the fall of 1649 he was invited to go to Sweden, there to instruct Queen Christine, a vigorous young woman who could spend ten hours in the saddle without fatigue, was an excellent shot, spoke six languages and read Tacitus for relaxation. Unfortunately, the only hour she had time for instruction was 5 a.m., which must have been a great shock to Descartes who never had enjoyed good health and who was accustomed to lying in bed meditating and working until noon. He died in February, 1650.

Descartes' philosophy is both critical and constructive. As a critical philosopher, he undertakes a careful examination of all he has learned, to see if there are any ideas which are so "clear and distinct" that he could not possibly doubt their truth; as a constructive philosopher, he shows what implications follow from the one idea he knows to be true: *"Cogito, ergo sum."* In reading the selection pay careful attention to the arguments he gives to prove his points, both critical and constructive. Do you agree with his conclusions? Or is there any knowledge which is certainly and absolutely true?

The Quest for Certainty[1]

Several years have now elapsed since I first became aware that I had accepted, even from my youth, many false opinions for true, and that consequently what I afterward based on such principles was highly doubtful; and from that time I was convinced of the necessity of undertaking once in my life to rid myself of all the opinions I had adopted, and of commencing anew the work of building from the foundation, if I desired to establish a firm and abiding superstructure in the sciences. But as this enterprise appeared to me to be one of great magnitude, I waited until I had attained an age so mature as to leave me no hope that at any state of life more advanced I should be better able to execute my design. . . . Today, since I have opportunely freed my mind from all cares, and since I am in the secure possession of leisure in a peaceable retirement, I will at length apply myself earnestly and freely to the general overthrow of all my former opinions. But to this end, it will not be necessary for me to show that the whole of these are false—a point, perhaps, which I shall never reach; . . . nor will it be necessary to deal with each belief individually, which would be truly an endless labor. But, as the removal from below of the foundation necessarily involves the downfall of the whole edifice, I will at once approach the criticism of the principles on which all my former beliefs rested.

All that I have, up to this moment, accepted as possessed of the highest truth and certainty, I received either from or through the senses. I observed, however, that these sometimes misled us; and it is the part of prudence not to place absolute confidence in that by which we have even once been deceived.

But it may be said, perhaps, that although the senses occasionally mislead us respecting minute objects, and such as are so far removed from us as to be beyond the reach of close observation, there are yet many other of their presentations of the truth of which it is manifestly impossible to doubt; as for example, that I am in this place, seated by the fire, clothed in a winter dressing gown, and that I hold in my hands this piece of paper, with other intimations of the same nature. . . .

Though this be true, I must nevertheless here consider that I am a man, and that, consequently, I am in the habit of sleeping, and representing to myself in dreams those same things, or even sometimes others less probable, which the insane think are presented to

[1] From *Meditations on First Philosophy* by René Descartes, Meditations I-III, and *The Discourse on Method,* Part IV, translated by John Veitch. New York: Tudor Publishing Co., 1905. [The order of some paragraphs have been modified. C.M.]

them in their waking moments. How often have I dreamt that I was in these familiar circumstances, that I was dressed, and occupied this place by the fire, when I was lying undressed in bed? At the present moment, however, I certainly look upon this paper with eyes wide awake; the head which I now move is not asleep; I extend this hand consciously and with express purpose, and I perceive it; the occurrences in sleep are not so distinct as all this. But I cannot forget that, at other times I have been deceived in sleep by similar illusions; and, attentively considering those cases, I perceive so clearly that there exist no certain marks by which the state of waking can ever be distinguished from sleep, that I feel greatly astonished; and in amazement I almost persuade myself that I am now dreaming.

Let us suppose, then, that we are dreaming, and that all these particulars —namely, the opening of the eyes, the motion of the head, the forth-putting of the hands—are merely illusions; and even that we really possess neither an entire body nor hands such as we see. Nevertheless, it must be admitted at least that the objects which appear to us in sleep are, as it were, painted representations which could not have been formed unless in the likeness of realities; and, therefore, that those general objects, at all events, are not simply imaginary, but really existent. . . .

To this class of objects seem to belong corporeal nature in general and its extension; the figure of extended things, their quantity or magnitude, and their number, as also the place in and the time during which they exist, and other things of the same sort.

* * * * *

Let us consider, then, the objects that are commonly thought to be the most distinctly known, viz., the bodies we touch and see; not, indeed, bodies in general, for these general notions are usually somewhat more confused, but one body in particular. Take, for example, this piece of wax; it is quite fresh, having been but recently taken from the beehive; it has not yet lost the sweetness of the honey it contained; it still retains somewhat of the odor of the flowers from which it was gathered; its color, figure, size, are apparent to the sight; it is hard, cold, easily handled; and sounds when struck upon with the finger. In fine, all that contributes to make a body as distinctly known as possible is found in the one before us. But, while I am speaking, let it be placed near the fire—what remains of the taste exhales, the smell evaporates, the color changes, its figure is destroyed, its size increases, it becomes liquid, it grows hot, it can hardly be handled, and although struck upon, it emits no sound. Does the same wax still remain after this change? It must be admitted that it does remain; no one doubts it, or judges otherwise. What, then, was it I knew with so much distinctness in the piece of wax? Assuredly, it could be nothing of all that I observed by means of the senses, since all the things that fell under taste, smell, sight, touch, and hearing are changed, and yet the same wax remains. It was perhaps what I now think, viz., that this was neither the sweetness of honey, the pleasant odor of flowers, the whiteness, the figure, nor the sound, but only a body that a little before appeared to me conspicuous under these forms, and which is now perceived under others. But, to speak precisely, what is it that I imagine when I think of it in this way?

Let it be attentively considered, and retrenching all that does not belong to the wax, let us see what remains. There certainly remains nothing, except something extended, flexible, and movable. But what is meant by flexible and movable? Is it not that I imagine that the piece of wax, being round, is capable of becoming square, or of passing from a square into a triangular figure? Assuredly such is not the case, because I conceive that it admits of an infinity of similar changes; and I am, moreover, unable to compass this infinity by imagination, and consequently this concept which I have of the wax is not the product of the faculty of imagination. But what now is this extension? Is it not also unknown? For it becomes greater when the wax is melted, greater when it is boiled, and greater still when the heat increases; and I should not conceive clearly and according to truth the wax as it is, if I did not suppose that the piece we are considering admitted even of a wider variety of extension than I ever imagined. I must, therefore, admit that I cannot even comprehend by imagination what the piece of wax is.

* * * * *

I suppose, accordingly, that all the things which I see are fictitious; I believe that none of those objects which my fallacious memory represents ever existed; I suppose that I possess no senses; I believe that body, figure, extension, motion, and place are merely fictions of my mind. What is there, then, that can be esteemed true? . . .

How do I know that there is not something different altogether from the objects I have now enumerated, of which it is impossible to entertain the slightest doubt? Is there not a God, or some being, by whatever name I may designate him, who causes these thoughts to arise in my mind?

* * * * *

How do I know that He has not arranged that there should be neither earth, nor sky, nor any extended things, nor figure, nor magnitude, nor place, providing at the same time, however, for the persuasion that these do not exist otherwise than as I perceive them. But as I sometimes think that others are in error respecting matters of which they believe themselves to possess a perfect knowledge, how do I know that I am not also deceived? . . . But perhaps Deity has not been willing that I should be thus deceived, for He is said to be supremely good. If, however, it were repugnant to the goodness of Deity to have created me subject to constant deception, it would seem likewise to be contrary to his goodness to allow me to be occasionally deceived; and yet it is clear that this is permitted.

* * * * *

[Moreover], I can suppose not that Deity, who is sovereignly good and the fountain of truth, but that some malignant demon who is at once exceedingly potent and deceitful, has employed all his artifice to deceive me; I will suppose that the sky, the air, the earth, colors, figures, sounds and all external things, are nothing better than the illusions of dreams, by means of which this being has laid snares for my credulity; I will consider myself as without hands, eyes, flesh, blood, or any of the senses, and as falsely believing that I am possessed of these; I will continue resolutely fixed in this belief, and if indeed by this means it be not in my power to arrive at the knowledge of truth, I shall at least do what is in my power, viz., suspend my judgment, and guard with settled purpose against giving my assent to what is false. . . .

The Meditation of yesterday has filled my mind with so many doubts that it is no longer in my power to forget them. Nor do I see, meanwhile, any principle on which they can be resolved; and, just as if I had fallen all of a sudden into very deep water, I am so greatly disconcerted as to be unable either to plant my feet firmly on the bottom or sustain myself by swimming to the surface. . . .

[But when I reflected on these thoughts, I was persuaded] that I was at least something. Before I denied that I possessed senses or a body, . . . I existed. Before I had the persuasion that there was absolutely nothing in the world, that there was no sky and no earth, neither minds nor bodies; was I not, therefore, at the same time persuaded that *I* did not exist? Far from it; I assuredly existed, since I was persuaded.

But [suppose] there is I know not what being, who is possessed at once of the highest power and the deepest cunning, who is constantly employing all his ingenuity in deceiving me. Nevertheless, it can not be doubted that I exist, since I am deceived; and, let him deceive me as he may, he can never bring it about that I am nothing, as long as I shall be conscious that I am something. So that it must, in fine, be maintained, all things being maturely and carefully considered, that this proposition, *cogito, ergo sum,* I think, therefore I exist, is necessarily true each time it is expressed by me, or conceived by my mind.

But I do not yet know with sufficient clearness what I am, although assured that I am; and hence, in the next place, I must take care, lest perchance I inconsiderately substitute some other object in place of what is properly myself and thus wander from truth, even in that cognition which I hold to be of all others the most certain and most evident. For this reason, I will now consider anew what I formerly believed myself to be before I entered on the present train of thought; and of my previous opinions I will retrench all that can in the least be invalidated by the grounds of doubt I have adduced, in order that there may at length remain nothing but what is certain and indubitable. What then did I formerly think I was? Undoubtedly I judged that I was a man. But what is a man? Shall I say a rational animal? Assuredly not; for it would be necessary forthwith to inquire into what is meant by animal, and what by rational, and thus, from a single question, I should insensibly glide into others, and these more difficult than the first. . . .

I thought, then, that I possessed a countenance, hands, arms, and all the fabric of members that appears in a corpse, and which I call by the name of body. . . . By body I understand all that can be terminated by a certain figure; that can be comprised in a certain place, and so fill a certain space as therefrom to exclude every other body; that can be perceived either by touch, sight, hearing, taste, or smell; that can be moved in different ways, not indeed of itself, but by something foreign to it by which it is touched. . . .

But, since I suppose there exists an extremely powerful, and, if I may so speak, malignant being, whose whole endeavors are directed toward deceiving me, can I affirm that I possess any one of all those attributes of which I have lately spoken as belonging to the nature of body? After attentively considering them in my own mind, I find none of them that can properly be said to belong to myself. To recount them is idle and tedious. . . .

Let us pass, then, to the attributes of the soul. The first mentioned were the powers of nutrition and walking; but if it be true that I have no body, it is true likewise that I am capable neither of walking nor of being nourished. Perception is another attribute of the soul; but perception too is impossible without a body; besides, I have frequently, during sleep, believed that I perceived objects which I afterwards observed I did not in reality perceive. Thinking is another attribute of the soul; and here I discover what properly belongs to myself. This alone is inseparable from me. I am—I exist: this is certain; but how often? As often as I think; for perhaps it would even happen, if I should wholly cease to think, that I should at the same time altogether cease to be. I now admit nothing that is not necessarily true. I am therefore, precisely speaking, only a thinking thing, that is a mind, understanding, or reason, terms whose signification was before unknown to me. I am, however, a real thing, and really existent; but what thing? The answer was, a thinking thing!!

* * * * *

I will now close my eyes, I will stop my ears, I will turn away my senses from their objects, I will even efface from my consciousness all the images of corporeal things; or at least, because this can hardly be accomplished, I will consider them as empty and false; and thus, holding converse only with myself, and closely examining my nature, I will endeavor to obtain by degrees a more intimate and familiar knowledge of myself. I am a thinking thing, that is, a being who doubts, affirms, denies, knows a few objects, and is ignorant of many, —who loves, hates, wills, refuses, who imagines likewise and perceives for as I have remarked, although the things which I perceive or imagine are perhaps nothing at all apart from me, I am nevertheless assured that those modes of consciousness which I call perceptions and imaginations, in as far only as they are modes of consciousness, exist in me. And in the little I have said I think I have summed up all that I really know, or at least all that up to this time I was aware I knew.

* * * * *

But, among these my ideas, besides that which represents myself, respecting which there can be no difficulty, there is one that represents a God; others that represent corporeal and inanimate things; others angels; others animals; and finally, there are some that represent men like myself. But with respect to the ideas that represent other men, or animals, or angels, I can easily suppose that they were formed by the mingling and composition of the other ideas which I have of myself, of corporeal things, and of God, although they were, apart from myself, neither men, animals, nor angels.

With regard to corporeal objects, I never discovered in them anything so great or excellent which I myself did not appear capable of originating; for by considering these ideas closely and scrutinizing them individually, in the same way that I examined the idea of wax, I find that there is but little in them that is clearly and distinctly perceived. With regard to light, colors, sounds, odors, tastes, heat, cold, and the other tactile qualities, they are thought with so much obscurity and confusion, that I cannot determine whether or not the ideas I have of these qualities are in truth the ideas of real objects. . . . Thus, for example, the ideas I have of cold and heat are so far from being clear and distinct, that I am unable from them to discover whether cold is only the privation of heat, or heat the privation of cold; or whether they are or are not real qualities; and since, ideas being as it were images there can be none that does not seem to us to represent some object, the idea which represents cold as something real and positive will not improperly be called false, if it be correct to say that cold is nothing but the privation of heat; and so in other cases. To ideas of this kind, indeed, it is not necessary that I should assign any author besides myself. . . .

There only remains, therefore, the idea of God, in which I must consider whether there is anything that cannot be supposed to originate with myself. By the name God, I understand a substance infinite, eternal, immutable, independent, all-knowing, all-powerful and by which I myself, and every other thing that exists, if any such there be, were created. But these properties are so great and excellent, that the more attentively I consider them the less I feel persuaded that the idea I have of them owes its origin to myself alone. And thus it is absolutely necessary to conclude that God exists; for though the idea of substance be in my mind owing to this, that I myself am a substance, I should not, however, have the idea of an infinite substance, seeing I am a finite being, unless it were given me by some substance which in reality is infinite.

And I must not imagine that I do not apprehend the infinite by a true idea, but only by the negation of the finite, in the same way that I comprehend repose and darkness by the negation of motion and light: since, on the contrary, I clearly perceive that there is more reality in the infinite substance than in the finite, and therefore that in some way I possess the notion of the infinite before that of the finite, that is, the perception of God before that of myself, for how could I know that I doubt, desire, or that something is wanting to me, and that I am not wholly perfect, if I possessed no idea of a being more perfect than myself, by comparison of which I knew the deficiencies of my nature?

* * * * *

In the next place, and reflecting on the circumstance that I doubted, and that consequently my being was not wholly perfect (for I clearly saw that it was a greater perfection to know than to doubt), I was led to inquire whence I had learned to think of something more perfect than myself; and I clearly recognized that I must hold this notion from some Nature which in reality was more perfect. As for the thoughts of many other objects external to me, as of the sky, the earth, light, heat, and a thousand more, I was less at a loss whence these came, for since I remarked in them nothing which seemed to render them superior to myself, I could believe that, if these were true, they were dependencies on my own nature, in so far as it possessed a certain perfection; and, if they were false, that I held them from nothing, that is to say, that they were in me because of a certain imperfection in my nature. But this could not be the case with the idea of a Nature more perfect than myself; for to receive it from nothing was a thing manifestly impossible; and because it is not less repugnant that the more perfect should be an effect of and dependence on the less perfect, than that something should proceed from nothing, it was equally impossible that I could hold it from myself: accordingly, it but remained that it had been placed in me by a Nature which was in reality more perfect than mine, and which even possessed within itself all the perfections of which I could form any idea: that is to say, in a single word, which was God.

And to this I added that, since I knew some perfections which I did not possess, I was not the only being in existence, (I will here, with your permission, freely use the terms of the Schools); but on the contrary, that there was of necessity some other more perfect Being upon whom I was dependent and from whom I had received all that I possessed; for if I had existed alone, and independently of every other Being, so as to have had from myself all the perfection, however little, which I actually possessed, I should have been able for the same reason, to have had from myself the whole remainder of perfection, of the want of which I was conscious, and thus could of myself have become infinite, eternal, immutable, omniscient, all-powerful, and, in fine, have possessed all the perfections which I could recognize in God.

QUESTIONS FOR DISCUSSION

1. Why is Descartes doubtful that sense experience is a reliable source for gaining knowledge? Are you? If you do not share his opinion, how would you meet his objections? If you do, how is reliable knowledge to be obtained?
2. What is the point of his frequent references to dreams? How can you distinguish between waking and dreaming? Will pinching yourself make the distinction?
3. Why is Descartes certain he is thinking? Could the evil genius be fooling him about this matter? What is Descartes' answer to this objection? Is the answer satisfactory?
4. How does he prove God's existence? Do you find his proofs convincing?
5. How inventive are you? On the basis of what you have read, how could Descartes prove the existence of a world outside his own mind —or could he?

READINGS FOR IMMEDIATE REFERENCE

Descartes, René. *Discourse on Method,* Parts I-V; *Meditations,* I-III, V.

Augustine. *The City of God,* Book XI, Sections 26-27.

Bouwsma, O. K. "Descartes' Evil Genius," *The Philosophical Review,* LVIII (March, 1949), 141-151.

Ryle, Gilbert. *The Concept of Mind.* Hutchinson, 1949, Chapters 1, 2.

REFERENCES FOR COMPREHENSIVE KNOWLEDGE

Descartes, René. *Rules for the Direction of the Mind.*

———. *Principles of Philosophy.*

Gibson, A. B. *The Philosophy of Descartes.* New York: Oxford University Press, 1932. Considers Descartes' philosophy as it developed during his life.

Haldane, E. S. *Descartes, His Life and Times.* New York: Macmillan, 1905. A standard biography.

Smith, Norman Kemp. *Studies in the Cartesian Philosophy.* London: Allen and Unwin, 1902.

———. *New Studies in the Philosophy of Descartes.* New York: Macmillan, 1952. A half century of thought by one of Britain's most penetrating critics.

Also see:

Balz, A. G. A. *Cartesian Studies.* New York: Columbia University Press, 1951.

Fischer, Kuno. *Descartes and His School.* New York: Macmillan, 1887.

Keeling, S. V. *Descartes.* London: Allen and Unwin, 1934.

Maritain, J. *The Dream of Descartes.* New York: Philosophical Library, 1944.

III. BERTRAND RUSSELL

Born in 1872, Russell was the godson of John Stuart Mill and was descended on both sides from English aristocracy. Both of his parents died before he was three and he was educated by private tutors until he entered Cambridge at the age of eighteen. He obtained a first class with distinction in Philosophy, but following graduation he spent the next two decades working largely in the field of mathematics, publishing in 1910-1913, with Alfred North Whitehead, the influential *Principia Mathematica.* During World War I Russell was a pacifist and he not only lost his lectureship at Cambridge and his personal library because of his beliefs, but also was forcibly prevented from lecturing and writing, and finally spent six months in jail. Following the war he went to both Russia and China to teach, returning in 1922. In 1926, with his second wife, he started an experimental school for young children, all the while adding to his voluminous list of books and articles, both technical and popular. In 1938 he lectured in America, causing considerable controversy because of his views on marriage and morals. In 1944 he returned to England (where he did not oppose the war effort), there to live and write and lecture to the present time. He was awarded the Order of Merit in 1949 and the Nobel Prize for Literature in 1950. During his lifetime he has published some seventy-three books, more than half of them being important contributions to the philosophical literature, and in recent years he has published several volumes of short stories. From 1957 to 1963 he was the leader of the pacifist "ban the bomb" movement in England.

This selection should be read with two purposes in mind: first, to notice, again, the techniques of analysis a philosopher uses when discussing ideas and beliefs. Are these techniques the same as those used by Socrates and Descartes? Secondly, this article should introduce you to some of the problems of ethical theory: the meanings of ethical terms; the relationship between theory and conduct; the way ethical judgments can be made. Be sure you find out not only what these problems are, but also how Russell says they should be solved. Keep his points in mind while you read the next chapter to see if you think he might be mistaken, for shortly after this article was published, Russell said he believed his conclusions were incorrect. Can you understand why he would do so?

The Elements of Ethics[1]

The study of Ethics is perhaps most commonly conceived as being concerned with the questions "What sort of actions ought men to perform?" and "What sort of actions ought men to avoid?" It is conceived, that is to say, as dealing with human conduct, and as deciding what is virtuous and what vicious among the kinds of conduct between which, in practice, people are called upon to choose. Owing to this view of the province of ethics, it is sometimes regarded as *the* practical study, to which all others may be opposed as theoretical; the good and the true are sometimes spoken of as independent kingdoms, the former belonging to ethics, while the latter belongs to the sciences.

This view, however, is doubly defective. In the first place, it overlooks the fact that the object of ethics, by its own account, is to discover true propositions about virtuous and vicious conduct, and that these are just as much a part of truth as true propositions about oxygen or the multiplication table. The aim is not practice, but propositions about practice; and propositions about practice are not themselves practical, any more than propositions about gases are gaseous. One might as well maintain that botany is vegetable or zoology animal. Thus the study of ethics is not something outside science and co-ordinate with it: it is merely one among sciences.

In the second place, the view in question unduly limits the province of ethics. When we are told that actions of certain kinds ought to be performed or avoided, as, for example, that we ought to speak the truth, or that we ought not to steal, we may always legitimately ask for a reason, and this reason will always be concerned, not only with the actions themselves, but also with the goodness or badness of the consequences likely to follow from such actions. We shall be told that truth-speaking generates mutual confidence, cements friendships, facilitates the dispatch of business, and hence increases the wealth of the society which practices it, and so on. If we ask why we should aim at increasing mutual confidence, or cementing friendships, we may be told that obviously these things are good, or that they lead to happiness, and happiness is good. If we still ask why, the plain men will probably feel irritation, and will reply that he does not know. His irritation is due to the conflict of two feelings—the one, that whatever is true must have a reason; the other, that the reason he has already given is so obvious that it is merely contentious to demand a reason for the reason. In the second of these feelings he may be right; in the first, he is certainly wrong. In ordinary life, people only ask *why* when they are unconvinced. If a reason is given

[1] From *Philosophical Essays* by Bertrand Russell. Originally published by Longmans, 1910, Sections 1-3, 6. Reprinted by permission of the author and George Allen and Unwin, Ltd.

which they do not doubt, they are satisfied. Hence, when they do ask *why,* they usually have a logical right to expect an answer, and they come to think that a belief for which no reason can be given is an unreasonable belief. But in this they are mistaken, as they would soon discover if their habit of asking *why* were more persistent.

It is the business of the philosopher to ask for reasons as long as reasons can legitimately be demanded, and to register the propositions which give the most ultimate reasons that are attainable. Since a proposition can only be proved by means of other propositions, it is obvious that not all propositions can be proved, for proofs can only begin by assuming something. And since the consequences have no more certainty than their premises, the things that are proved are no more certain than the things that are accepted merely because they are obvious, and are then made the basis of our proofs. Thus in the case of ethics, we must ask why such and such actions ought to be performed, and continue our backward inquiry for reasons until we reach the kind of proposition of which proof is impossible, because it is so simple or so obvious that nothing more fundamental can be found from which to deduce it. . . .

The first step in ethics, therefore, is to be quite clear as to what we mean by good and bad. Only then can we return to conduct, and ask how right conduct is related to the production of goods and the avoidance of evils. . . .

Good and Bad, in the sense in which the words are here intended (which is, I believe, their usual sense), are ideas which everybody, or almost everybody, possesses. These ideas are apparently among those which form the simplest constituents of our more complex ideas, and are therefore incapable of being analyzed or built up out of other simpler ideas. When people ask "What do you mean by *Good?*" the answer must consist, not in a verbal definition such as could be given if one were asked "What do you mean by *Pentagon?*" but in such a characterization as shall call up the appropriate idea to the mind of the questioner. This characterization may, and probably will, itself contain the idea of *good,* which would be a fault in a definition, but is harmless when our purpose is merely to stimulate the imagination to the production of the idea which is intended. It is in this way that children are taught the names of colors: they are shown (say) a red book, and told that that is red; and for fear they should think *red* means *book,* they are shown also a red flower, a red ball, and so on, and told that these are all red. Thus the idea of redness is conveyed to their minds, although it is quite impossible to analyze redness or to find constituents which compose it.

In the case of *good,* the process is more difficult, both because goodness is not perceived by the senses, like redness, and because there is less agreement as to the things that are good than as to the things that are red. This is perhaps one reason that has led people to think that the notion of *good* could be analyzed into some other notion, such as *pleasure* or *object of desire.* A second reason, probably more potent, is the common confusion that makes people think they cannot understand an idea unless they can define it —forgetting that ideas are defined by other ideas, which must be already understood if the definition is to convey any meaning. When people begin to philosophize, they seem to make a point of forgetting everything familiar and ordinary; otherwise their acquaintance with redness or any other color might show them how an idea can be intelligible where definition, in the sense of analysis, is impossible. . . .

It might be thought that *good* could be defined as the quality of whatever we ought to try to produce. This would merely put *ought* in the place of *good* as our ultimate undefined notion; but as a matter of fact the good is much wider than what we ought to try to produce. There is no reason to doubt that some of the lost tragedies of Aeschylus were good, but we ought not to try to re-write them, because we should certainly fail. What we ought to do, in fact, is limited by our powers and opportunities, whereas the good is subject to no such limitation. And our knowledge of goods is confined to the things we have experienced or can imagine; but presumably there are many goods of which we human beings have absolutely no knowledge. Such goods are still goods, although human conduct can have no reference to them. Thus, the notion of good is wider and more fundamental than any notion concerned with conduct; we use the notion of good in explaining what right conduct is, but we do not use the notion of right conduct in explaining what good is.

A fairly plausible view is that *good* means the same as *desired,* so that when we say a thing is good we mean that it is desired. Thus anything is good which we either hope to acquire or fear to lose. Yet it is commonly admitted that there are bad desires; and when people speak of bad desires, they seem to mean desires for what is bad. For example, when one man desires another man's pain, it is obvious that what is desired is not good but bad. But the supporter of the view that *good* means *desired* will say that nothing is good or bad in itself, but is good for one person and perhaps bad for another. This must happen, he will say, in every case of a conflict of desires; if I desire your suffering, then your suffering is good for me, though it is bad for you. But the sense of *good* and *bad* which is needed in ethics is not in this way personal; and it is quite essential, in the study of ethics, to realize that there is an impersonal sense. In this sense, when a thing is good, it ought to exist on its own account, not on account of its consequences, nor yet of who is going to enjoy it. We cannot maintain that for me a thing ought to exist on its own account, while for you it ought not; that would merely mean that one of us is mistaken, since in fact everything either ought to exist or ought not. Thus the fact that one man's desire may be another man's aversion proves that *good,* in the sense relevant to ethics, does not mean the same as *desired,* since everything is in itself either good or not good, and cannot be at once good for me and bad for you. . . .

It is important to realize that when we say a thing is good in itself, and not merely as a means, we attribute to the thing a property which it either has or does not have, quite independently of our opinion on the subject. Most men are inclined to agree with Hamlet: "There is nothing good or bad but thinking makes it so." It is supposed that ethical preferences are a mere matter of taste, and that if X thinks A is a good thing, and Y thinks it is a bad thing, all we can say is that A is good for X and bad for Y. This view is rendered plausible by the divergence of opinion as to what is good and bad, and by the difficulty of finding arguments to persuade people who differ from us in such a question. But difficulty in discovering the truth does not prove that there is no truth to be discovered. If X says A is good, and Y says A is bad, one of them must be mistaken, though it may be impossible to discover which. If this were not the case, there would be no difference of opinion between them. If, in asserting that A is good, X meant merely to assert that A had a certain relation to himself, say of pleasing his taste in some way; and if Y, in saying that A is not good, meant merely to deny that A had a like relation to himself: then there would be no subject of debate between them. It would be absurd, if X said "I am eating a pigeon pie," for Y to answer "that is false: I am eating nothing." But this is no more absurd than a dispute as to what is good, if, when we say A is good, we mean merely to affirm a relation of A to ourselves.

* * * * *

One very important consequence of the indefinability of *good* must be emphasized, namely, the fact that knowledge as to what things exist, have existed, or will exist, can throw absolutely no light upon the question as to what things are good. . . . We cannot infer any results as to what is good or bad from a study of the things that exist. This conclusion needs chiefly, at the present time, to be applied against evolutionary ethics. The phrase "survival of the fittest" seems to have given rise to the belief that those who survive are the fittest in some ethical sense, and that the course of evolution gives evidence that the later type is better than the earlier. On this basis, a worship of force is easily set up, and the mitigation of struggle by civilization comes to be deprecated. It is thought that what fights most successfully is most admirable, and that what does not help in fighting is worthless. Such a view is wholly destitute of logical foundation. The course of nature is irrelevant in deciding as to what is good or bad. *A priori,* it would be as probable that evolution should go from bad to worse, as that it should go from good to better. What makes the view plausible is the fact that the lower animals existed earlier than the higher, and that among men the civilized races are able to defeat and often exterminate the uncivilized. But here the ethical preference of the higher to the lower animals, and of the exterminators to be exterminated, is not based upon evolution, but exists independently, and unconsciously intrudes into our judgment of the evolutionary process.

* * * * *

[If we now turn to the] judging of conduct we find at the outset two widely divergent methods, of which one is advocated by some moralists, the other by others, while both are practiced by those who have no ethical theory. One of these methods, which is that advocated by utilitarians, judges the rightness of an act by relation to the goodness or badness of its consequences. The other method, advocated by intuitionists, judges by the approval or disapproval of the moral sense or conscience. I believe that it is necessary to combine both theories in order to get a complete account of right and wrong. There is, I think, one sense in which a man does right when he does what will probably have the best consequences, and another in which he does right when he follows the dictates of his conscience, whatever the probable consequences may be. Let us begin by considering the second of these senses.

The question we have to ask ourselves is: What do we mean by the dictates of the moral sense? If these are to afford a *definition* of right conduct, we cannot say that they consist in judging that such and such acts are *right,* for that would make our definition circular. We shall have to say that the moral sense consists in a certain specific *emotion* of *approval* towards an act, and that an act is to be called right when the agent, at the moment of action, feels this emotion of approval towards the action which he decided to perform. There is certainly a sense in which a man ought to perform any act which he approves, and to abstain from any act which he disapproves; and it seems also undeniable that there are emotions which may be called approval and disapproval. Thus this theory, whether adequate or not, must be allowed to contain a part of the truth.

It is, however, fairly evident that there are other meanings of right conduct, and that, though there is an emotion of approval, there is also a judgment of approval, which may or may not be true. For we certainly hold that a man who has done an action which his conscience approved may have been mistaken, and that in some sense his conscience ought not to have approved his action. But this would be impossible if nothing were involved except an emotion. To be mistaken implies a judgment; and thus we must admit that there is such a thing as a *judgment* of approval. If this were not the case we could not reason with a man as to what is right. . . .

Thus in order to give a meaning to the judgment of approval, it is necessary to admit a sense of *right* other than approved. In this sense, when we approve an act we judge that it is right, and we may be mistaken in so judging. This new sense is *objective,* in the sense that it does not depend upon the opinions and feelings of the agent. Thus a man who obeys the dictates of his conscience is not always acting rightly in the objective sense. When a man does what his conscience approves, he does what he *believes* to be objectively right, but not necessarily what *is* objectively right. . . .

What is objectively right, then, is in some way dependent on consequences. The most natural supposition to start from would be that the objectively right act, under any circumstances, is the one which will have the best consequences. We will define this as the *most fortunate* act. The most fortunate act, then, is the one which will produce the greatest excess of good over evil, or the least excess of evil over good. But we cannot maintain that the most fortunate act is always the one which is objectively right, in the sense that it is what a wise man will hold that he ought to do. For it may happen that the act which will in fact prove the most fortunate is likely, according to all the evidence at our disposal, to be less fortunate than some other. In such a case, it will be, at least in one sense, objectively wrong to go against the evidence, in spite of the actual good result of our doing so. There have certainly been some men who have done so much harm that it would have been fortunate for the world if their nurses had killed them in infancy. But if their nurses had done so their action would not have been objectively right, because the probability was that it would not have the best effects. Hence it would seem we must take account of probability in judging of objective rightness. . . .

One further addition is required for the definition of the objectively right act, namely, that it must be *possible*. Among the acts whose consequences are to be considered we must not include such as are either physically impossible to perform or impossible for the agent to think of. This last condition introduces difficulties connected with Determinism (which are not discussed in this section). Ignoring these difficulties, we may say that the objectively right act is that one which, of all that are possible, will probably have the best consequences.

* * * * *

In order to complete our account of ethics, it would be natural to give a list of the principle goods and evils of which we have experience. I shall, however, not attempt to give such a list, since I hold that the reader is probably quite as capable as I am of judging what things are good and what bad. All that I propose to do is to examine the view that we can never know what is good and what bad, and to suggest methods to be employed and fallacies to be avoided in considering intrinsic goodness or badness.

There is a widespread ethical scepticism, which is based upon observation of men's differences in regard to ethical questions. It is said that A thinks one thing good, and B thinks another, and there is no possible way in which either can persuade the other that he is wrong. Hence, it is concluded, the whole thing is really only a matter of taste, and it is a waste of time to ask which is right when two people differ in a judgment of value.

It would be absurd to deny that, as compared with physical science, ethics does suffer from a measure of the defect which such sceptics allege. It must be admitted that ultimately the judgment "this thing is good" or "that thing is bad" must be an immediate judgment, which results merely from considering the thing appraised, and cannot be proved by any argument that would appeal to a man who had passed an opposite immediate judgment. I think it must also be admitted that, even after every possible precaution against error has been taken, people's immediate judgments of value do still differ more or less. But such immediate differences seem to me to be the exception; most of the actual differences are of a kind which argument might lessen, since usually the opinion held is either one of which the opposite is demonstrable or one which is falsely believed to be itself demonstrable. . . .

In regards to the things that are good or bad, in themselves, and not merely on account of their effects, there are two opposite errors of this sort to be avoided —the one the error of the philosopher, the other that of the moralist. The philosopher, bent on the construction of a system, is inclined to simplify the facts unduly, to give them a symmetry which is fictitious, and to twist them into a form in which they can all be deduced from one or two general principles. The moralist, on the other hand, being primarily concerned with conduct, tends to become absorbed in means, to value the actions men ought to perform more than the ends which such actions serve. This latter error—for in theorizing it is an error—is so forced upon us by the exigencies of practice that we may easily come to feel the ultimate ends of life far less important than the proximate and intermediate purposes which we consciously endeavor to realize. And hence most of what they value in this world would have to be omitted by many moralists from any imagined heaven, because there such things as self-denial and effort and courage and pity could find no place. The philosopher's error is less common than the moralist's, because the love of system and of the intellectual satisfaction of a deductive edifice is rarer than the love of virtue. But among writers on ethics the philosopher's error occurs oftener than the other, because such writers are almost always among the few men who have the love of system. Kant has the bad eminence of combining both errors in the highest possible degree, since he holds that there is nothing good except the virtuous will—a view which simplifies the good as much as any philosopher would wish, and mistakes means for ends as completely as any moralist could enjoin. . . .

Another source of apparent differences is that some things which in isolation are bad or indifferent are essential ingredients in what is good as a whole, and some things which are good or indifferent are essential ingredients in what is bad as a whole. In such cases we judge differently according as we are considering a thing in isolation or as an ingredient in some larger whole. To judge whether a thing is in itself good, we have to ask ourselves whether we should value it if it existed otherwise than as an ingredient in some whole which we value. But to judge whether a thing ought to exist, we have to consider whether it is a part of some whole which we value so much that we prefer the existence of the whole with its possibly bad part to the existence of neither. Thus, compassion is a good of which someone's misfortune is an essential part; envy is an evil of which some one's good is an essential part. Hence the position of some optimists, that all the evil in the world is necessary to constitute the best possible whole, is not logically absurd, though there is, so far as I know, no evidence in its favor. Similarly the view that all the good is an unavoidable ingredient in the worst possible whole is not logically absurd; but this view, not being agreeable, has found no advocates. . . .

* * * * *

I conclude, therefore, that although some ultimate ethical differences must be admitted between different people, by far the greater part of the commonly observed differences are due either to asking the wrong question (as, e.g., by mistaking means for ends), or to the influence of a hasty theory in falsifying immediate judgments. There is reason to hope, therefore, that a very large measure of agreement on ethical questions may be expected to result from clearer thinking; and this is probably the chief benefit to be ultimately derived from the study of ethics.

QUESTIONS FOR DISCUSSION

1. Why does Russell say "good" is an undefinable quality? Are his reasons adequate?
2. What is the difference between utilitarianism and intuitionism, and why does he say both are necessary for judging conduct?
3. What are the errors philosophers and moralists make in judging things to be good or bad? Do you agree that they are errors?
4. List the techniques of reasoning Russell has used. Is your list similar to the one you made after reading the selection from Socrates?
5. Try to think of how many ways you can use the word "good" in a sentence. Do these meanings of the word have anything in common?

READINGS FOR IMMEDIATE REFERENCE[1]

Russell, Bertrand. *Philosophical Essays.* London: Allen and Unwin, 1910, pp. 3-57.

———. *The Conquest of Happiness.* London: Allen and Unwin, 1930, Chapters 1-7.

Moore, G. E. *Principia Ethica.* Cambridge: Cambridge University Press, 1903, Chapters 1, 5.

[1] This is a bibliography for one aspect of contemporary ethical theory. For Russell's bibliography see pp. 512-513.

Prichard, H. A. "Does Moral Philosophy Rest on a Mistake?" *Moral Obligation*. Oxford: Clarendon Press, 1949, pp. 1-17.

REFERENCES FOR COMPREHENSIVE KNOWLEDGE

Russell, Bertrand. *Marriage and Morals*. London: Allen and Unwin, 1929.

———. *Human Society in Ethics and Politics*. New York: Simon and Schuster, 1954.

Ewing, A. C. *The Definition of Good*. Oxford: Clarendon Press, 1930. "Ought" is the fundamental indefinable quality.

Ross, W. D. *The Right and the Good*. Oxford: Clarendon Press, 1930. "Right" is the fundamental indefinable quality.

Also see:

Carritt, E. F. *The Theory of Morals*. New York: Oxford University Press, 1928.

Ewing, A. C. *Ethics*. New York: Macmillan, 1953.

Prichard, H. A. *Duty and Interest*. New York: Oxford University Press, 1928.

BIBLIOGRAPHY FOR CHAPTER TWO

READINGS FOR IMMEDIATE REFERENCE

Beardsley, Monroe. *Practical Logic*. New York: Prentice-Hall, 1950, Chapters 1, 6-11.

Copi, Irving M. *Introduction to Logic*, rev. ed. New York: Macmillan, 1961, Chapters 1-6, 11-13.

REFERENCES FOR COMPREHENSIVE KNOWLEDGE

Dewey, John. *How We Think*, rev. ed. New York: D. C. Heath, 1933. Philosophical thinking is intelligent problem solving.

Montague, W. P. *The Ways of Knowing*. New York: Macmillan, 1925. The six ways are Authoritarianism, Mysticism, Empiricism, Rationalism, Pragmatism, Skepticism. This standard text gives a careful analysis of each.

Murphy, Arthur E. *The Uses of Reason*. New York: Macmillan, 1943. A vigorous statement of the need for more philosophical reasoning in facing today's moral, social, and political problems.

Also see:

Nagel, Ernest. *Sovereign Reason*. Glencoe, Ill.: Free Press, 1954.

Stebbing, L. Susan. *Thinking to Some Purpose*. London: Pelican Books, 1959.

Woozley, A. D. *Theory of Knowledge*. London: Hutchinson, 1957.

Chapter Three

PHILOSOPHICAL MORALITY

1. FRIEDRICH NIETZSCHE

Nietzsche was born in 1844, the son and grandson of Protestant ministers. He attended the University of Bonn intending to prepare himself for the ministry, but under the influence of his philology professor, Ritschel, and the author, Schopenhauer, he broke completely with the family tradition and wishes. He immersed himself in scholarly studies and at graduation was so highly thought of by his professors that he was recommended for the chair of Professor of Classical Philology at the University of Basle even though he was only twenty-four. He taught at the University for many years, was a close friend of Richard Wagner and sought, with him, to purge German culture of all vestiges of romanticism and sentimentality. In 1879, however, he broke with Wagner, who was then writing *Parsifal,* resigned his university position, and spent the next decade living in seclusion in northern Italy and Switzerland writing no less than eleven books, including *Thus Spake Zarathustra, Beyond Good and Evil* and *The Genealogy of Morals.* His works were largely unknown until 1888 when a course on Nietzsche's philosophy was offered in Copenhagen. After that his fame spread rapidly, but he did not know of it, for in 1889 he suffered a complete mental breakdown from which he never recovered. He died in 1900.

In this short selection try to approach it with the same attitude and techniques you have seen philosophers using in the preceding chapter: discern the reasons Nietzsche gives for believing that the "herding-animal" morality encouraged by Christianity and democracy is inferior to the morality practiced by the Superman. Do you believe his judgments are correct?

Herding Animals and Supermen[1]

Morality in Europe at present is herding-animal morality; and therefore, as we understand the matter, only one kind of human morality, besides which, before which, and after which many other moralities, and above all *higher* moralities, are or should be possible. Against such a "possibility," against such a "should be" however, this morality defends itself with strength; it says obstinately and inexorably: "I am morality itself and nothing else is morality!" Indeed, with the help of a religion which has humored and flattered the sublimest desires of the herding-animal, things have reached such a point that we always find a more visible expression of this morality even in political and social arrangements: the democratic movement is the inheritance of the Christian movement.

* * * * *

To refrain mutually from injury, from violence, from exploitation, and put one's will on a par with that of others: this may result in a certain rough sense in good conduct among individuals. As soon, however, as one wished to take this principle more generally, and if possible even as the fundamental principle of society, it would immediately disclose what it really is—namely, a Will to the denial of life, a principle of dissolution and decay. Here one must think profoundly to the very basis and resist all sentimental weakness: life itself is *essentially* appropriation, injury, conquest of the strange and weak, suppression, severity, obtrusion of peculiar forms, incorporation, and at the least, putting it mildly, exploitation. Even the organization within which, as was previously supposed, the individuals treat each other as equals must itself, if it be a living and not a dying organization, do all that towards other bodies, which the individuals within it refrain from doing to each other; it will have to be the incarnated Will to Power, it will endeavor to grow, to gain ground, attract to itself and acquire ascendancy—not owing to any morality or immorality, but because it lives, and because life is precisely Will to Power.

On no point, however, is the ordinary consciousness of Europeans more unwilling to be corrected than on this matter; people now rave everywhere, even under the guise of science, about coming conditions of society in which "the exploiting character" is to be absent—that sounds to my ears as if they promised to invent a mode of life which should refrain from all organic func-

[1] From *Beyond Good and Evil,* by Friedrich Nietzsche, translated by Helen Zimmern. London: Allen and Unwin, Ltd., copyright 1924, Sections 202, 259, 260, 262. Reprinted by permission.

tions. "Exploitation" does not belong to a depraved, or imperfect and primitive society: it belongs to the nature of the living being as a primary organic function; it is a consequence of the intrinsic Will to Power, which is precisely the Will to Life.

Granting that as a theory this is a novelty—as a reality it is the *fundamental fact* of all history: let us be so far honest towards ourselves!

In a tour through the many finer and coarser moralities which have hitherto prevailed or still prevail on the earth, I found certain traits recurring regularly together, and connected with one another, until finally two primary types revealed themselves to me, and a radical distinction was brought to light. There is master-morality and slave-morality. The distinctions of moral values have either originated in a ruling caste, pleasantly conscious of being different from the ruled—or among the ruled class, the slaves and dependents of all sorts.

In the first case, when it is the rulers who determine the conception "good," it is the exalted, proud disposition which is regarded as the distinguishing feature, and that which determines the order of rank. The noble type of man separates from himself the beings in whom the opposite of this exalted, proud disposition displays itself: he despises them. Let it at once be noted that in this first kind of morality the antithesis "good" and "bad" means practically the same as "noble" and "despicable"; the antithesis "good" and "evil" is of a different origin. The cowardly, the timid, the insignificant, and those thinking merely of narrow utility are despised; moreover, also the distrustful, with their constrained glances, the self-abasing, the dog-like kind of men who let themselves be abused, the mendicant flatterers, and above all the liars:—it is a fundamental belief of all aristocrats that the common people are untruthful. "We truthful ones"—the nobility in ancient Greece called themselves. It is obvious that everywhere the designations of moral value were at first applied to men, and were only derivatively and at a later period applied to actions; it is a gross mistake, therefore, when historians of morals start with questions like, "Why have sympathetic actions been praised?" The noble type of man regards himself as a determiner of values; he does not require to be approved of; he passes the judgment: "What is injurious to me is injurious in itself"; he knows that it is he himself only who confers honor on things; he is *a creator of values.*

He honors whatever he recognizes in himself: such morality is self-glorification. In the foreground there is the feeling of plenitude, or power, which seeks to overflow, the happiness of high tension, the consciousness of a wealth which would fain give and bestow: the noble man also helps the unfortunate, but not—or scarcely—out of pity, but rather from an impulse generated by the superabundance of power. The noble man honors in himself the powerful one, him also who has power *over* himself, who knows how to speak and how to keep silence, who takes pleasure in subjecting himself to severity and hardness, and has reverence for all that is severe and hard.

"Wotan placed a hard heart in my breast," says an old Scandinavian Saga: it is thusly rightly expressed from the soul of a proud Viking. Such a type of man is even proud of not being made for sympathy; the hero of the Saga therefore adds warningly: "He who has not a hard heart when young, will never have one." The noble and brave who think thus are the furthest removed from the morality which sees precisely in sympathy, or in acting for the good of others, or in *dèsintéressement,* the characteristic of the moral; faith in oneself, pride in oneself, a radical enmity and irony towards "selflessness," belong as definitely to noble morality, as do a careless scorn and precaution in presence of sympathy and the "warm heart." It is the powerful who know how to honor, it is their art, their domain for invention. . . . The ability and obligation to exercise prolonged gratitude and prolonged revenge—both only within the circle of equals,—artfulness in retaliation, *raffinement* of the idea in friendship, a certain necessity to have enemies (as outlets for the emotions of envy, quarrelsomeness, arrogance—in fact, in order to be a good friend): all these are typical characteristics of the noble morality.

It is otherwise with the second type of morality—slave-morality. Supposing that the abused, the oppressed, the suffering, the unemancipated, the weary, and those uncertain of themselves, should moralize, what will be the common element in their moral estimates? Probably a pessimistic suspicion with regard to the entire situation of man will find expression, perhaps a condemnation of man, together with his situation. The slave has an unfavorable eye for the virtues of the powerful; he has a scepticism and distrust, a *refinement* of distrust of everything "good" that is there honored—he would fain persuade himself that the very happiness there is not genuine. On the other hand *those* qualities which serve to alleviate the existence of sufferers are brought into prominence and flooded with light; it is here that sympathy, the kind, helping hand, the warm heart, patience, diligence, humility, and friendliness attain to honor; for here these are the most useful qualities, and almost the only means of supporting the burden of existence.

Slave-morality is essentially the morality of utility. Here is the seat of the origin of the famous antithesis "good" and "evil"; power and dangerousness are assumed to reside in the evil, a certain dreadfulness, subtlety and strength, which do not admit of being despised. According to slave-morality, therefore, the "evil" man arouses fear; according to master-morality, it is precisely the "good" man who arouses fear and seeks to arouse it, while the bad man is regarded as the despicable being. The contrast attains its maximum when, in accordance with the logical consequences of slave-morality, a shade of depreciation at last attaches itself to the "good" man of this morality; because, according to the servile mode of thought, the good man must in any case be the *safe* man: he is good-natured, easily deceived, perhaps a little stupid, *un bonhomme.*

* * * * *

A species originates, and a type becomes established and strong in the long struggle with essentially constant unfavorable conditions. On the other hand, it is known by the experience of breeders that species which receive superabundant nourishment, and in general a surplus of protection and care, immediately tend in the most marked way to develop variations and monstrosities. Look at an aristocratic commonwealth, say an ancient Greek *polis,* or Venice, as a voluntary or involuntary contrivance for the purpose of rearing *human* beings; there are the men beside one another, thrown upon their own resources, who want to make their species prevail, chiefly because they *must* prevail, or else run the terrible danger of being exterminated. . . . The most varied experience teaches it what are the qualities to which it principally owes the fact that it still exists, in spite of all Gods and men, and has hitherto been victorious: these qualities it calls virtues, and these virtues alone it develops to maturity. It does so with severity, indeed it desires severity; every aristocratic morality is intolerant in the education of youth, in the control of women, in the marriage customs, in the relations of old and young, in the penal laws (which have an eye only for the degenerating); it counts intolerance itself among the virtues. . . . Finally, however, a happy state of things results, the enormous tension is relaxed, there are perhaps no more enemies, and the means of life, even of the enjoyment of life, are present in superabundance. With one stroke the bond and constraint of the old discipline severs: it is no longer regarded as necessary, as a condition of existence. . . . At this turning point of history, this morality which piled up the strength so enormously, which bent the bow in so threatening a manner; it is now out of date. The dangerous and disquieting point has been reached when the greater, more manifold, more comprehensive life is *lived beyond* the old morality. The individual stands out, and is obliged to have recourse to his own law-giving, his own arts and artifices for self-preservation, self-elevation and self-deliverance. Nothing but new "whys," nothing but new "hows," no common formulas any longer, misunderstanding and disregard in league with each other, decay, deterioration, and the loftiest desires frightfully entangled. . . . Danger is again present, the mother of morality, great danger; this time shifted into the individual, into the neighbor and friend, into the street, into their own child. What will the moral philosophers who appear at this time have to preach? They discover, these sharp onlookers and loafers, that the end is quickly approaching, that everything around them decays and produces decay, that nothing will endure until the day after tomorrow, except one species of man, the incurably mediocre. The mediocre alone have a prospect of continuing and propagating themselves—they will be the men of the future, the sole survivors; "be like them! become mediocre!" is now the only morality which has still a significance, which still obtains a hearing.

QUESTIONS FOR DISCUSSION

1. Why does Nietzsche believe Christianity and democracy encourage "herding-animal morality"? Do you agree? Is this bad?
2. Is twentieth century civilization different from what Nietzsche found nineteenth century society to be? Are we improving in our moral relationships or not?
3. Would you like to live in the kind of society Nietzsche advocates?

READINGS FOR IMMEDIATE REFERENCE

Nietzsche, Friedrich. *Beyond Good and Evil,* Chapters 3, 5, 7, 9.

———. *The Genealogy of Morals,* Essay I.

———. *Ecce Homo,* Chapters 1-3.

The Gospel According to Matthew, Chapters 5-7.

Riesman, David. *The Lonely Crowd.* New Haven: Yale University Press, 1950, Chapters 6, 7.

Wilson, Colin. *The Outsider.* Boston: Houghton Mifflin, 1956, Chapters 1-3, 8, 9.

REFERENCES FOR COMPREHENSIVE KNOWLEDGE

Kaufmann, Walter. *Nietzsche: Philosopher, Psychologist, Anti-Christ.* Princeton: Princeton University Press, 1950. A careful analysis of Nietzsche's thought by America's leading interpreter.

Knight, A. H. J. *Some Aspects of the Life and Work of Nietzsche.* Cambridge: Harvard University Press, 1941. Emphasizes the importance of Nietzsche's Greek studies.

Morgan, G. A. *What Nietzsche Means.* Cambridge: Harvard University Press, 1941. Presents the argument that Nietzsche is an Existentialist.

Also see:

Brinton, Crane. *Nietzsche.* Cambridge: Harvard University Press, 1941.

Copleston, Frederick. *Nietzsche, Philosopher of Culture.* London: Burns and Oates, 1952.

II. JEREMY BENTHAM

Bentham was born in 1748, the son of a well-to-do lawyer. He graduated from Oxford at fifteen and studied law in London, being admitted to practice when he was twenty-one. However, he was less interested in legal practice than in legal theory and social reform, and much of his life was devoted to writing treatises on law and government, codifying the laws, and working for the reform of the debtor laws, working hours for women and children, prison conditions, and legal practices themselves. He traveled extensively, was made an honorary citizen of France, started the *Westminister Review,* and was consulted frequently by the most important political leaders in the early nineteenth century. He was a close friend of Adam Smith whose *Wealth of Nations* (1776) is the classic statement of *laissez faire* economics, and also of James Mill, the leading associationalist psychologist, whose son, John Stuart, was to become one of the most influential philosophers in the nineteenth century. When he died in 1832 at the age of eighty-five, his body was dissected and his skeleton preserved at University College, London, where it remains today.

The form of ethical philosophy presented in this selection is known as "hedonism": the meaning of "pleasure" and "good" are intimately related, if not identical. In reading, look for three points: a description of the conditions present in a pleasurable life; an account of the best means for achieving this pleasure; and the justifying reasons Bentham would give if he were asked why pleasure is the highest good.

The Conquest of Pleasure[1]

Nature has placed mankind under the governance of two sovereign masters, pain and pleasure. It is for them alone to point out what we ought to do, as well as to determine what we shall do. On the one hand the standard of right and wrong, on the other the chain of causes and effects, are fastened to

[1] From *An Introduction to the Principles of Morals and Legislation,* rev. ed. by Jeremy Bentham. Oxford: Clarendon Press, 1823, Chapters 1, 3, 4. [The paragraph numbers have been omitted. C.M.]

their throne. They govern us in all we do, in all we say, in all we think: every effort we can make to throw off our subjection will serve but to demonstrate and confirm it. In words a man may pretend to abjure their empire: but in reality he will remain subject to it all the while. The principle of utility recognizes the subjection, and assumes it for the foundation of that system, the object of which is to rear the fabric of felicity by the hands of reason and of law. Systems which attempt to question it deal in sounds instead of sense, in caprice instead of reason, in darkness instead of light.

But enough of metaphor and declamation: it is not by such means that moral science is to be improved.

The principle of utility is the foundation of the present work: it will be proper therefore at the outset to give an explicit and determinate account of what is meant by it. By the principle of utility is meant that principle which approves or disapproves of every action whatsoever, according to the tendency which it appears to have to augment or diminish the happiness of the party whose interest is in question: or, what is the same thing in other words, to promote or to oppose that happiness. I say of every action whatsoever; and therefore not only of every action of a private individual, but of every measure of government.

By utility is meant that property in any object, whereby it tends to produce benefit, advantage, pleasure, good or happiness (all this in the present case comes to the same thing) or (what comes again to the same thing) to prevent the happening of mischief, pain, evil, or unhappiness to the party whose interest is considered: if that party be the community in general, then the happiness of the community: if a particular individual, then the happiness of that individual. . . .

It is in vain to talk of the interest of the community, without understanding what is the interest of the individual. A thing is said to promote the interest, or to be for the interest, of an individual, when it tends to add to the sum total of his pleasures: or, what comes to the same thing, to diminish the sum total of his pains.

An action then may be said to be conformable to the principle of utility, or, for shortness' sake, to utility, when the tendency it has to augment the happiness of the community is greater than any it has to diminish it. . . .

Has the rectitude of this principle ever been formally contested? It should seem that it had, by those who have not known what they have been meaning. Is it susceptible of any direct proof? It should seem not: for that which is used to prove everything else, cannot itself be proved: a chain of proofs must have their commencement somewhere. To give such proof is as impossible as it is needless.

Not that there is nor ever has been that human creature breathing, however stupid or perverse, who has not on many, perhaps on most occasions of his life, deferred to it. By the natural constitution of the human frame, on most occasions of their lives men in general embrace this principle, without thinking of it: if not for the ordering of their own actions, yet for the trying of their own actions, as well as of those of other men. There have been, at the same time, not many, perhaps, even of the most intelligent, who have been disposed to embrace it purely and without reserve. There are even few who have not taken some occasion or other to quarrel with it, either on account of their not understanding always how to apply it, or on account of some prejudice or other which they were afraid to examine into, or could not bear to part with. For such is the stuff that man is made of: in principle and in practice, in a right track and in a wrong one, the rarest of all human qualities is consistency.

When a man attempts to combat the principle of utility, it is with reasons drawn, without his being aware of it, from that very principle itself. His arguments, if they prove anything, prove not that the principle is wrong, but that, according to the applications he supposes to be made of it, it is misapplied. Is it possible for a man to move the earth? Yes; but he must first find out another earth to stand upon.

To disprove the propriety of it by arguments is impossible; but, from the causes that have been mentioned, or from some confused or partial view of it, a man may happen to be disposed not to relish it. Where this is the case, if he thinks the settling of his opinions on such a subject worth the trouble, let him take the following steps, and at length, perhaps, he may come to reconcile himself to it.

Let him settle with himself, whether he would wish to discard this principle altogether; if so, let him consider what it is that all his reasonings (in matters of politics especially) can amount to?

If he would, let him settle with himself, whether he would judge and act without any principle, or whether there is any other he would judge and act by?

If there be, let him examine and satisfy himself whether the principle he thinks he has found is really any separate intelligible principle; or whether it be not a mere principle in words, a kind of phrase, which at bottom expresses neither more nor less than the mere averment of his own unfounded sentiments; that is, what in another person he might be apt to call caprice?

If he is inclined to think that his own approbation or disapprobation, annexed to the idea of an act, without any regard to its consequences, is a sufficient foundation for him to judge and act upon, let him ask himself whether his sentiment is to be a standard of right and wrong, with respect to every other man, or whether every man's sentiment has the same privilege of being a standard to itself? And if so,

In the first case, let him ask himself whether his principle is not despotical, and hostile to all the rest of the human race?

In the second case, whether it is not anarchical, and whether at this rate there are not as many different standards of right and wrong as there are men? and whether even to the same man, the same thing, which is right today, may not (without the least change in its nature) be wrong tomorrow? and whether the same thing is not right and wrong in the same place at the same time? and in either case, whether all argument is not at an end? and whether, when two men have said, "I like this," and "I don't like it," they can (upon such a principle) have anything more to say?

* * * * *

It has been shown that the happiness of the individuals, of whom a community is composed, that is, their pleasures and their security, is the end and the sole end which the legislator ought to have in view: the sole standard, in conformity to which each individual ought, as far as depends upon the legislator, to be made to fashion his behavior. But whether it be this or anything else that is to be done, there is nothing by which a man can ultimately be made to do it, but either pain or pleasure. Having taken a general view of these two grand objects (viz. pleasure, and what comes to the same thing, immunity from pain) in the character of final causes, it will be necessary to take a view of pleasure and pain itself, in the character of efficient causes or means.

There are four distinguishable sources from which pleasure and pain are in use to flow: considered separately, they may be termed the physical, the political, the moral, and the religious: and inasmuch as the pleasures and pains belonging to each of them are capable of giving a binding force to any law or rule of conduct, they may all of them be termed sanctions.

If it be in the present life, and from the ordinary course of nature, not purposely modified by the interposition of the will of any human being, nor by any extraordinary interposition of any superior invisible being, that the pleasure or the pain takes place or is expected, it may be said to issue from or to belong to the physical sanction.

If at the hands of a particular person or set of persons in the community, who under names correspondent to that of judge, are chosen for the particular purpose of dispensing it, according to the will of the sovereign or supreme ruling power in the state, it may be said to issue from the political sanction.

If at the hands of such chance persons in the community, as the party in question may happen in the course of his life to have concerns with, according to each man's spontaneous disposition, and not according to any settled or concerted rule, it may be said to issue from the moral or popular sanction.

If from the immediate hand of a superior invisible being, either in the present life, or in a future, it may be said to issue from the religious sanction.

Pleasures or pains which may be expected to issue from the physical, political, or moral sanctions, must all of them be expected to be experienced, if ever, in the present life: those which may be expected to issue from the religious sanction, may be expected to be experienced either in the present life or in a future.

* * * * *

Pleasures then, and the avoidance of pains, are the ends which the legislator has in view: it behoves him therefore to understand their value. Pleasures and pains are the instruments he has to work with: it behoves him therefore to understand their force, which is again, in other words, their value.

To a person considered by himself, the value of a pleasure or pain considered by itself, will be greater or less, according to the four following circumstances:

1. Its intensity.
2. Its duration.
3. Its certainty or uncertainty.
4. Its propinquity or remoteness.

These are the circumstances which are to be considered in estimating a pleasure or a pain considered each of them by itself. But when the value of any pleasure or pain is considered for the purpose of estimating the tendency of any act by which it is produced, there are two other circumstances to be taken into account; these are:

Its fecundity, or the chance it has of being followed by sensations of the same kind: that is, pleasures, if it be a pleasure; pains, if it be a pain.

Its purity, or the chance it has of not being followed by sensations of the opposite kind: that is, pains, if it be a pleasure; pleasures, if it be a pain.

These two last, however, are in strictness scarcely to be deemed properties of the pleasure or the pain itself; they are not, therefore, in strictness to be taken into the account of the value of that pleasure or that pain. They are in strictness to be deemed properties only of the act, or other event, by which such pleasure or pain has been produced; and accordingly are only to be taken into the account of the tendency of such act or such event.

To a number of persons, with reference to each of whom the value of a pleasure or a pain is considered, it will be greater or less, according to seven circumstances: to wit, the six preceding ones; viz.,

1. Its intensity.
2. Its duration.
3. Its certainty or uncertainty.
4. Its propinquity or remoteness.
5. Its fecundity.
6. Its purity.

And one other; to wit:

7. Its extent; that is, the number of persons to whom it extends; or (in other words) who are affected by it.

To take an exact account then of the general tendency of any act, by which the interests of a community are affected, proceed as follows: Begin with any one person of those whose interests seem most immediately to be affected by it: and take an account,

Of the value of each distinguishable pleasure which appears to be produced by it in the first instance.

Of the value of each pain which appears to be produced by it in the first instance.

Of the value of each pleasure which appears to be produced by it after the first. This constitutes the fecundity of the first pleasure and the impurity of the first pain.

Of the value of each pain which appears to be produced by it after the first. This constitutes the fecundity of the first pain, and the impurity of the first pleasure.

Sum up all the values of all the pleasures on the one side, and those of all the pains on the other. The balance, if it be on the side of pleasure, will give the good tendency of the act upon the whole, with respect to the interests of that individual person; if on the side of pain, the bad tendency of it upon the whole.

Take an account of the number of persons whose interests appear to be concerned; and repeat the above process with respect to each. Sum up the numbers expressive of the degrees of good tendency, which the act has, with respect to each individual, in regard to whom the tendency of it is good upon the whole: do this again with respect to each individual, in regard to whom the tendency of it is good upon the whole: do this again with respect to each individual, in regard to whom the tendency of it is bad upon the whole. Take the balance; which, if on the side of pleasure, will give the general good tendency of the act, with respect to the total number or community of individuals concerned; if on the side of pain, the general evil tendency, with respect to the same community.

It is not to be expected that this process should be strictly pursued previously to every moral judgment, or to every legislative or judicial operation. It may, however, be always kept in view: and as near as the process actually pursued on these occasions approaches to it, so near will such a process approach to the character of an exact one.

The same process is alike applicable to pleasure and pain in whatever shape they appear, and by whatever denomination they are distinguished: to pleasure, whether it be called *good* or *profit,* or *convenience,* or *advantage, benefit, emolument, happiness,* and so forth: or to pain, whether it be called *evil,* or *mischief,* or *inconvenience,* or *disadvantage,* or *loss,* or *unhappiness,* and so forth.

Nor is this a novel and unwarranted, any more than it is a useless theory. In all this there is nothing but what the practice of mankind, wheresoever they have a clear view of their own interest, is perfectly conformable to.

QUESTIONS FOR DISCUSSION

1. Does Bentham believe he can prove the principle of utility? Does he try? Can you?
2. If everyone does seek pleasure, what can it mean to say that they should seek pleasure?
3. Is the attainment of pleasure at all predictable? Try the moral calculus to help you make an intelligent choice between alternative courses of action.
4. Is pleasure the motive for or the result of moral behavior—or does pleasure have anything to do with morality?

READINGS FOR IMMEDIATE REFERENCE

Bentham, Jeremy. *An Introduction to the Principles of Morals and Legislation,* rev. ed. Oxford: Clarendon Press, 1823, Chapters 1-5, 10.

Broad, C. D. *Five Types of Ethical Theory.* London: Routledge and Kegan Paul, 1930, Chapter 6.

Mill, John Stuart. *Utilitarianism.* London: 1863, Chapters 2, 3.

REFERENCES FOR COMPREHENSIVE KNOWLEDGE

Plamenatz, John. *The English Utilitarians.* Oxford: Blackwell, 1949. A brief but comprehensive survey.

Stephen, Leslie. *The English Utilitarians.* London: Duckworth, 1900. Three volumes of comprehensive reporting and thoughtful evaluating. A standard work.

Also see:

Albee, Ernest. *Utilitarianism.* New York: Macmillan, 1902.

Baumgardt, David. *Bentham and Ethics of Today.* Princeton: Princeton University Press, 1952.

Halévy, E. *The Growth of Philosophical Radicalism.* New York: Macmillan, 1928.

Sorley, W. R. *A History of English Philosophy.* Cambridge: Cambridge University Press, 1951.

III. EPICURUS

Epicurus lived during the declining period of Athenian civilization, having been born about 341 B.C. (Socrates died in 399, Plato in 347 and Aristotle in 322). As a student, he studied Plato's works and also attended Aristotle's school, but he was most attracted to an earlier philosopher, Democritus, who taught that reality was composed of unbreakable bits of matter or "atoms." He was a teacher and an author during his life, having written over 300 works, although only a few letters remain today. He established a school inside his own walled garden where, tradition says, he required his students to memorize his lectures and not to speak unless he requested them to do so. He was honored greatly during his own life, and his school continued to exert a considerable influence on society well into the age of Roman civilization.

This selection represents another, and earlier, form of hedonism. Again, look for the author's account of the nature of happiness, the best means to achieve it, and the justifying reasons to support his belief. Do his teachings differ from Bentham's on any of these points? When you finish the selection ask yourself whether you are persuaded by either—or both—of these theories. Are you a hedonist?

The Avoidance of Pain[1]

Let no one be slow to seek wisdom when he is young nor weary in the search thereof when he is grown old. For no age is too early or too late for the health of the soul. And to say that the season for studying philosophy has not yet come, or that it is past and gone, is like saying that the season for happiness is not yet or that it is now no more. Therefore, both old and young ought to seek wisdom, the former in order that, as age comes over him, he may be young in good things because of the grace of what has been, and the latter in order that, while he is young, he may at the same time be old, because he has no

[1] From "Letters to Menoeceus and Herodotus" by Epicurus in *Diogenes Laertius: Lives of Eminent Philosophers,* translated by R. D. Hicks. Cambridge: Harvard University Press, 1925, Book X, 122–135. Reprinted by permission of the publishers and the Loeb Classical Library.

fear of the things which are to come. So we must exercise ourselves in the things which bring happiness, since, if that be present, we have everything, and, if that be absent, all our actions are directed toward attaining it. . . .

Accustom thyself to believe that death is nothing to us, for good and evil imply sensation, and death is the privation of all sensation; therefore a right understanding that death is nothing to us makes the mortality of life enjoyable, not by adding to life an illimitable time, but by taking away the yearning after immortality. For life has no terrors for him who has thoroughly understood that there are no terrors for him in ceasing to live. Foolish, therefore, is the man who says that he fears death, not because it will pain when it comes, but because it pains in the prospect. Whatsoever causes no annoyance when it is present, causes only a groundless pain in the expectation. Death, therefore, the most awful of evils, is nothing to us, seeing that, when we are, death is not come, and, when death is come, we are not. It is nothing, then, either to the living or to the dead, for with the living it is not and the dead exist no longer.

But in the world, at one time men shun death as the greatest of all evils, and at another time choose it as the respite from the evils of life. The wise man does not deprecate life nor does he fear the cessation of life. The thought of life is no offense to him, nor is the cessation of life regarded as an evil. And even as men choose of food not merely and simply the larger portion, but the more pleasant, so the wise seek to enjoy the time which is most pleasant and not merely that which is longest.

And he who admonishes the young to live well and the old to make a good end speaks foolishly, not merely because of the desirableness of life, but because the same exercise at once teaches to live well and to die well. Much worse is he who says that it were good not to be born, but when once one is born to pass with all speed through the gates of Hades. For if he truly believes this, why does he not depart from life? It were easy for him to do so, if once he were firmly convinced. If he speaks only in mockery, his words are foolishness, for those who hear believe him not.

We must remember that the future is neither wholly ours nor wholly not ours, so that neither must we count upon it as quite certain to come nor despair of it as quite certain not to come.

* * * * *

There is yet one more point to seize, namely, that the greatest anxiety of the human mind arises through the belief that the heavenly bodies are blessed and indestructible, and that at the same time they have volitions and actions and causality inconsistent with this belief; and through expecting or apprehending some everlasting evil, either because of the myths, or because we are in dread of the mere insensibility of death, as if it had to do with us; and through being reduced to this state not by conviction but by a certain irrational perversity, so that, if men do not set bounds to their terror, they endure as much or even more intense anxiety than the man whose views on these matters are quite vague. But mental tranquility means being released from all these troubles and cherishing a continual remembrance of the highest and most important truths.

* * * * *

We must also reflect that of desires some are natural, others are groundless; and that of the natural some are necessary as well as natural, and some natural only. And of the necessary desires some are necessary if we are to be happy, some if the body is to be rid of uneasiness, some if we are even to live. He who has a clear and certain understanding of these things will direct every preference and aversion toward securing health of body and tranquility of mind, seeing that this is the sum and end of a blessed life. For the end of all our actions is to be free from pain and fear, and when once we have attained all this, the tempest of the soul is laid; seeing that the living creature has no need to go in search of something that is lacking, nor to look for anything else by which the good of the soul and of the body will be fulfilled. When we are pained because of the absence of pleasure, then, and then only, do we feel the need of pleasure.

Wherefore we call pleasure the alpha and omega of the blessed life. Pleasure is our first and kindred good. It is the starting point of every choice and of every aversion, and to it we come back, inasmuch as we make feeling the rule by which to judge of every good thing. And since pleasure is our first and native good, for that reason we do not choose every pleasure whatsoever, but ofttimes pass over many pleasures when a greater annoyance ensues from them. And ofttimes we consider pains superior to pleasures when submission to the pains for a long time brings us as a consequence a greater pleasure. While therefore all pleasure because it is naturally akin to us is good, not all pleasure is choiceworthy, just as all pain is an evil and yet not all pain is to be shunned. It is, however, by measuring one against another, and by looking at the conveniences and inconveniences, that all these matters must be judged.

Sometimes we treat the good as an evil, and the evil, on the contrary, as a good. Again, we regard independence of outward things as a great good, not so as in all cases to use little, but so as to be contented with little if we have not much, being honestly persuaded that they have the sweetest enjoyment of luxury who stand least in need of it, and that whatever is natural is easily procured and only the vain and worthless hard to win.

Plain food gives as much pleasure as a costly diet, when once the pain of want has been removed, while bread and water confer the highest possible pleasure when they are brought to hungry lips. To habituate one's self, therefore, to simple and inexpensive diet supplies all that is needful for health, and enables a man to meet the necessary requirements of life without shrinking, and it places us in a better condition when we approach at intervals a costly food and it also renders us fearless of the chances of fortune.

When we say, then, that pleasure is the end and aim, we do not mean the pleasures of the prodigal or the pleasures of sensuality, as we are understood to do by some through ignorance, prejudice, or wilful misrepresentation. By pleasure we mean the absence of pain in the body and of trouble in the soul. It is not an unbroken succession of drinking-bouts and of revelry, not sexual love, not the enjoyment of the fish and other delicacies of a luxurious table, which produce a pleasant life; it is sober reasoning, searching out the grounds of every choice and avoidance, and banishing those beliefs through which the greatest tumults take possession of the soul. Of all this the beginning and the greatest good is prudence.

Wherefore prudence is a more precious thing even than philosophy; from it spring all the other virtues, for it teaches that we cannot lead a life of pleasure which is not also a life of prudence, honor and justice; nor lead a life of prudence, honor and justice, which is not also a life of pleasure. For the virtues have grown into one with the pleasant life, and a pleasant life is inseparable from them.

Who, then, is superior in thy judgment to such a man? He holds a holy belief concerning the gods, and is altogether free from the fear of death. He has diligently considered the end fixed by nature, and understands how easily the limit of good things can be reached and attained, and how either the duration or the intensity of evils is but slight. Destiny, which some introduce as sovereign over all things, he laughs to scorn, affirming rather that some things happen of necessity, others by chance, others through our own agency. For he sees that necessity destroys responsibility and that chance or fortune is inconstant; whereas our own actions are free, and it is to them that praise and blame naturally attach.

It were better, indeed, to accept the legends of the gods than to bow beneath that yoke of destiny which the natural philosophers have imposed. The one holds out some faint hope that we may escape if we honor the gods, while the necessity of the naturalists is deaf to all entreaties. Nor does he hold chance to be a god, as the world in general does, for in the acts of a god there is no disorder; nor to be a cause, though an uncertain one, for he believes that no good or evil is dispensed by chance to men so as to make life blessed, though it supplies the starting point of great good and great evil. He believes that the misfortune of the wise is better than the prosperity of the fool. It is better, in short, that what is well judged in action should not owe its successful issue to the aid of chance.

Exercise thyself in these and kindred precepts day and night, both in thyself and with him who is like unto thee; then never, either in waking or in dream, wilt thou be disturbed, but wilt live as a god among men. For man loses all semblance of mortality by living in the midst of immortal blessings.

QUESTIONS FOR DISCUSSION

1. What does Epicurus recommend as the proper attitude to be taken toward death, food, and the gods? Is he correct?
2. Do you agree that, "the end of all our actions is to be free from pain and fear"? Is this the end or is it the consequence of some other end? Or is there some one final end for which all other acts are only means?
3. Have you decided whether you are a hedonist? Should you be one? On what grounds can you make such a decision?

READINGS FOR IMMEDIATE REFERENCE

Bailey, Cyril. *Epicurus, The Extant Remains.* New York: Oxford University Press, 1926.

Oates, W. J. *The Stoic and Epicurean Philosophers.* New York: Random House, 1940, pp. 3-65.

REFERENCES FOR COMPREHENSIVE KNOWLEDGE

Bailey, Cyril. *The Greek Atomists and Epicurus.* New York: Oxford University Press, 1928. A standard scholarly exposition and discussion.

Sedgwick, H. D. *The Art of Happiness.* Oxford: Clarendon Press, 1933. Written in a popular style.

Also see:

DeWitt, N. W. *Epicurus and his Philosophy.* Minneapolis: University of Minnesota Press, 1954.

Festugiere, A. M. J. *Epicurus and His Gods.* New York: Oxford University Press, 1955.

Hicks, R. D. *Stoics and Epicureans.* New York: Scribners, 1910.

Pater, Walter. *Marius the Epicurean.* New York: Macmillan, 1903.

Taylor, A. E. *Epicurus.* London: Constable, 1911.

IV. EPICTETUS

Little is known about Epictetus' life. He was born probably near the middle of the first century A.D., was a slave during his youth, tradition saying that he was a member of Nero's bodyguard. By some unknown means he obtained his freedom but was expelled from Rome, along with all other philosophers, by the Emperor Domitian in either 89 or 93 A.D. He went to Epirus in Greece where he probably founded a school at Nicopolis. He taught there until he died, around 140 A.D. One of his pupils, Flavius Arrianus, compiled eight books of Epictetus' teachings from his lectures, of which four still remain.

This selection introduces you to the ethics of Stoicism, a philosophical school tracing its origins to the fourth century B.C. While reading Epictetus' comments on God, man and the proper attitude toward life, try to discern what reasons he is giving for saying one should not be upset by what happens to him, that he should be "stoical." Is Epictetus' ethical theory different from Epicurus'? Is it similar to any religious theories you know? Does it provide a moral philosophy you could use for guiding your own life?

Imperturbability[1]

All things serve and obey the laws of the universe; the earth, the sea, the sun, the stars, and the plants and animals of the earth. Our body likewise obeys the same, in being sick and well, young and old, and passing through the other changes decreed. It is therefore reasonable that what depends on ourselves, that is, our own understanding, should not be the only rebel. For the universe is powerful and superior, and consults the best for us by governing us in conjunction with the whole. And further; opposition, besides that it is unreasonable, and produces nothing except a vain struggle, throws us into pain and sorrows. . . .

God bids the plants to blossom and

[1] From *The Discourses, The Enchiridion,* and *The Fragments,* by Epictetus, translated by George Long. London: George Bell and Sons, 1877. [The order of some paragraphs has been modified and the paragraph numbers have been omitted. C.M.]

they blossom, to bud and they bud, to bear fruit and they bear it, to ripen it and they ripen; —and when again he bids them drop their leaves and withdraw into themselves to rest and wait, they rest and wait. Whence again are there seen on the increase and decrease of the moon, and the approach and departure of the sun, so great changes and transformations in earthly things? Have then the very leaves, and our own bodies, this connection and sympathy with the whole; and have not our souls much more? But our souls are thus connected and intimately joined to God, as being indeed members and distinct portions of His essence; and must not he be sensible of every movement of them, as belonging and connatural to himself? Can even you think of the divine administration, and every other divine subject, and together with these of human affairs also; can you at once receive impressions on your senses and your understanding, from a thousand objects; at once assent to some things, deny or suspend your judgment concerning others, and preserve in your mind impressions from so many and various objects, by which aid you can revert to ideas similar to those which first impressed you? Can you retain a variety of arts and the memorials of ten thousand things? And is not God capable of surveying all things, and being present with all, and in communication with all? Is the sun capable of illuminating so great a portion of the universe, and of leaving only that small part of it unilluminated, which is covered by the shadow of the earth, —and cannot He who made and moves the sun, a small part of himself, if compared with the whole, —cannot He perceive all things?

* * * * *

We should reason in some such manner concerning ourselves. Who are you? A man. If then indeed, you consider yourself isolatedly, it is natural that you should live to old age, should be prosperous and healthy; but if you consider yourself as a man, and as a part of the whole, it will be fit, in view of that whole, that you should at one time be sick; at another, take a voyage, and be exposed to danger; sometimes be in want; and possibly die before your time. Why, then, are you displeased? Do not you know, that otherwise you are no longer a man? For what is a man? A part of a commonwealth; first and chiefly of that which includes both gods and men; and next, of that to which you immediately belong, which is a miniature of the universal city. You are a citizen of the universe, and a part of it; not a subordinate, but a principal part. . . .

As to piety towards the Gods you must know that this is the chief thing, to have right opinions about them, to think that they exist, and that they administer the All well and justly; and you must fix yourself in this principle, to obey them, and to yield to them in everything which happens, and voluntarily to follow it as being accomplished by the wisest intelligence. For if you do so, you will never either blame the Gods, nor will you accuse them of neglecting you.

Remember that such is, and was, and will be, the nature of the world, nor is it possible that things should be otherwise than they now are; and that not only men and other creatures upon earth partake of this change and transformation, but diviner things also. For indeed even the four elements are transformed and metamorphosed; and earth becomes water, and water air, and this again is transformed into other things. And the same manner of transformation happens from things above to those below. Whoever endeavors to turn his mind toward these points, and persuade himself to receive with willingness what cannot be avoided, will pass his life in moderation and harmony. . . .

Remember that you are an actor in a drama of such sort as the author chooses. If short, then in a short one; if long, then in a long one. If it be his pleasure that you should act a poor man, see that you act it well; or a cripple, or a ruler, or a private citizen. For this is your business, to act well the given part; but to choose it, belongs to another.

Of things some are in our power, and others are not. In our power are opinion, movement toward a thing, desire, aversion; and in a word, whatever are our own acts: not in our power are the body, property, reputation, offices, and in a word, whatever are not our own acts. And the things in our power are by nature free, not subject to restraint nor hindrance: but the things not in our power are weak, slavish, subject to restraint, in the power of others. Remember then that if you think the things which are by nature slavish to be free, and the things which are in the power of others to be your own, you will be hindered, you will lament, you will be disturbed, you will blame both gods and men: but if you think that only which is your own to be your own, and if you think that what is another's as it really is, belongs to another, no man will ever compel you, no man will hinder you, you will never blame any man, you will never accuse any man, you will do nothing involuntarily, no man will harm you, you will have no enemy, for you will not suffer any harm.

If then you desire such great things, remember that you must not lay hold of them with a small effort; but you must leave alone some things entirely, and postpone others for the present. But if you wish for these things also, and power, and wealth, perhaps you will not gain even these very things because you aim also at those former things: certainly you will fail in those things through which alone happiness and freedom are secured. Straightway then practice saying to every harsh appearance, "You are an appearance, and in no manner what you appear to be." Then examine it by the rules which you possess, and by this first and chiefly, whether it relates to the things which are in our power or to things which are not in our power: and if it relates to anything which is not in our power, be ready to say that it does not concern you. . . .

Seek not that the things which happen should happen as you wish; but wish the things which happen to be as they are, and you will have a tranquil flow of life. . . .

You can be invincible, if you enter into no contest in which it is not in your power to conquer. Take care then when you observe a man honored before others or possessed of great power or highly esteemed for any reason, not to suppose him happy, and be not carried away by the appearance. For if the nature of the good is in our power, neither envy nor jealousy will have a place in us. But you yourself will not wish to be a general or senator or consul, but a free man: and there is only one way to this, to despise the things which are not in our power. . . .

Remember that it is not he who reviles you or strikes you, who insults you, but it is your opinion about these matters as being insulting. When then a man irritates you, you must know that it is your opinion which has irritated you. Therefore especially try not to be carried away by the appearance. For if you once gain time, you will more easily master yourself. . . .

When any person treats you ill or speaks ill of you, remember that he does this or says this because he thinks that it is his duty. It is not possible then for him to follow that which seems right to you, but that which seems right to himself. Accordingly if he is wrong in his opinion, he is the person who is hurt, for he is the person who has been deceived; for if a man shall suppose the true conjunction to be false, it is not the conjunction which is hindered, but the man who has been deceived about it. If you proceed then from these opinions, you will be mild in temper to him who reviles you: for you say on each occasion, "It seemed so to him." . . .

If you would have your children and your wife and your friends to live forever, you are silly; for you would have the things which are not in your power to be in your power, and the things which belong to others to be yours. So if you would have your slave to be free from faults, you are a fool; for you would have badness not to be badness, but something else. But if you wish not to fail in your desires, you are able to do that. Practice then this which you are able to do. He is the master of every man who has the power over the things which another person wishes or does not wish, the power to confer them on him or to take them away. Whoever then wishes to be free, let him neither wish for anything nor avoid anything which depends on others; if he does not observe this rule, he must be a slave.

* * * * *

In everything which pleases the soul, or supplies a want, or is loved, remember to add this to the description; what is the nature of each thing, beginning from the smallest? If you love an earthen vessel, say it is an earthen vessel which you love; for when it has been broken, you will not be disturbed. If you are kissing your child or wife, say this is a human being whom you are kissing, for when the wife or child dies, you will not be disturbed. . . .

Men are disturbed not by the things which happen, but by the opinions about the things: for example, death is nothing terrible, for if it were, it would have seemed so to Socrates; for the opinion about death, that it is terrible, is the terrible thing. When then we are impeded or disturbed or grieved, let us never blame others, but ourselves, that is, our opinions. It is the act of an ill-instructed man to blame others for his own bad condition; it is the act of one who has begun to be instructed, to lay the blame on himself; and of one whose instruction is completed, neither to blame another, nor himself. . . .

When you see a person weeping in sorrow either when a child goes abroad or when he is dead, or when the man has lost his property, take care that the appearance does not hurry you away with it, as if he were suffering in external things. But straightway make a distinction in your own mind, and be in readiness to say, it is not that which has happened that afflicts this man, for it does not afflict another, but it is the opinion about this thing which afflicts the man. So far as words then, do not be unwilling to show him sympathy, and even if it needs be, to lament with him. But take care that you do not lament internally also.

In walking about as you take care not to step on a nail or to sprain your foot, so take care not to damage your own ruling faculty: and if we observe this rule in every act, we shall undertake the act with more security.

* * * * *

It is a mark of a mean capacity to spend much time on the things which concern the body, such as much exercise, much eating, much drinking, much easing of the body, much copulation. But these things should be done as subordinate things: and let all your care be directed to the improving of the mind. . . .

The condition and characteristic of an uninstructed person is this: he never expects from himself profit nor harm, but from externals. The condition and characteristic of a philosopher is this: he expects all advantage and all harm from himself. The signs of one who is making progress are these: he censures no man, he praises no man, he blames no man, he accuses no man, he says nothing about himself as if he were somebody or knew something; when he is impeded at all or hindered, he blames himself: if a man praises him, he ridicules the praiser to himself; if a man censures him, he makes no defense; he goes about like weak persons, being careful not to move any of the things which are placed, before they are firmly fixed; he removes all desire from himself, and he transfers aversion to those things only of the things within our power which are contrary to nature: he employs a moderate movement towards every thing: whether he is considered foolish or ignorant, he cares not: and in a word he watches himself as if he were an enemy and lying in ambush.

QUESTIONS FOR DISCUSSION

1. Why does Epictetus recommend that we should be imperturbable?
2. Do you agree that everyone should "watch himself as if he were an enemy and lying in ambush"? Why does Epictetus say this?
3. Is Stoicism a form of hedonism? Is it a deterrent to economic development and progress?
4. When should one be stoical? Never? Always? At certain times? If so, when?

READINGS FOR IMMEDIATE REFERENCE

Aurelius, Marcus. *Meditations.*
Epictetus. *The Discourses.*
———. *The Enchiridion.*
Overstreet, Harry A. *The Mature Mind.* New York: W. W. Norton, 1949, Chapters 1, 2, 6, 11.

REFERENCES FOR COMPREHENSIVE KNOWLEDGE

Arnold, E. V. *Roman Stoicism.* New York: Macmillan, 1911. Sees Stoicism as the bridge between ancient and modern thought.
Murray, Gilbert. *The Stoic Philosophy.* Oxford: Clarendon Press, 1927.
———. *Stoic, Christian and Humanist.* London: Allen and Unwin, 1940. Scholarly yet lively treatments by one of this century's leading classicists.
Wenley, R. M. *Stoicism and Its Influence.* Boston: Marshall Jones, 1924. Traces Stoic thought from its origins to the nineteenth century.

Also see:
Bevan, E. R. *Stoics and Skeptics.* New York: Barnes and Noble, 1957.
Reeson, Margaret. *The Political Theory of the Old and Middle Stoa.* New York: J. J. Augustin, 1951.
Sedgwick, H. D. *Marcus Aurelius.* New Haven: Yale University Press, 1922.

V. ARISTOTLE

Aristotle, one of those rare individuals who combined rich philosophical insight with extensive empirical investigation, was born in 384 B.C., the son of the physician to the court of Amyntus of Macedonia. When he was seventeen, he was sent to Plato's school where he stayed, as student and teacher, for twenty years, leaving within a year of Plato's death. He taught in Persia for some time (and married the king's adopted daughter), but returned to Macedonia to teach Alexander, Amyntus' grandson. His tutoring lasted only seven years because Alexander became king and launched his war of conquest. However, Alexander rebuilt Aristotle's native city of Stageira and had soldiers specially commissioned to obtain animal and plant specimens to be sent to Aristotle from all parts of the Middle East. Aristotle returned to Athens and established his own school, the Lyceum, where he wrote and taught. While walking—and hence earning the name of the Peripatetic Philosopher—he lectured on almost every known subject: politics, biology, rhetoric, astronomy, ethics, mathematics, history, psychology, etc. He also invented and developed a whole new subject, logic, which has exerted a strong influence in western thought ever since. In 323 B.C. Alexander died and the Athenian resentment against Macedonian domination was directed at Aristotle. Remembering the death of Socrates, Aristotle is reported to have remarked that he would not allow the Athenians to sin against philosophy twice in the same generation, so he retired to the estate of his mother, where he died within a year at the age of sixty-three.

Aristotle's theory can be considered as another form of hedonism, although more complete than the others we have previously examined. In this selection, Aristotle is concerned with two fundamental questions: is there any good which is valued for its own sake and not as a means to some other good, a *summum bonum;* and what is the best means to achieve this good.

Happiness, Moderation, and Contemplation[1]

Every art and every kind of inquiry, and likewise every act and purpose, seems to aim at some good: and so it has been well said that the good is that at which everything aims.

But a difference is observable among these aims or ends. What is aimed at is sometimes the exercise of a faculty, sometimes a certain result beyond that exercise. And where there is an end beyond the act, there the result is better than the exercise of the faculty.

Now since there are many kinds of actions and many arts and sciences, it follows that there are many ends also; e.g. health is the end of medicine, ships of shipbuilding, victory of the art of war, and wealth of economy.

But when several of these are subordinated to some one art or science,—as the making of bridles and other trappings to the art of horsemanship, and this in turn, along with all else that the soldier does, to the art of war, and so on,—then the end of the master-art is always more desired than the ends of the subordinate arts, since these are pursued for its sake. And this is equally true whether the end in view be the mere exercise of a faculty or something beyond that, as in the above instances.

If then in what we do there be some end which we wish for on its own account, choosing all the others as means to this, but not every end without exception as a means to something else (for so we should go on *ad infinitum,* and desire would be left void and objectless),—this evidently will be the good or the best of all things.

And surely from a practical point of view it much concerns us to know this good; for then, like archers shooting at a definite mark, we shall be more likely to attain what we want.

If this be so, we must try to indicate roughly what it is, and first of all to which of the arts or sciences it belongs.

It would seem to belong to the supreme art or science, that one which most of all deserves the name of master-art or master-science.

Now Politics seems to answer to this description. For it prescribes which of the sciences a state needs, and which each man shall study, and up to what point; and to it we see subordinated even the highest arts, such as economy, rhetoric, and the art of war.

Since then it makes use of the other practical sciences, and since it further ordains what men are to do and from what to refrain, its end must include the ends of the others, and must be the proper good of man.

For though this good is the same for the individual and the state, yet the good of the state seems a grander and more perfect thing both to attain and to secure; and glad as one would be to do

[1] From Aristotle's *The Nicomachean Ethics,* translated by F. H. Peters. London: Kegan Paul, Trench, Trubner and Co., Ltd., copyright 1891, Book I, Sections 1-5; Book II, Sections 5-7; Book X, Section 7. Reprinted by permission.

this service for a single individual, to do it for a people and for a number of states is nobler and more divine.

This then is the aim of the present inquiry, which is a sort of political inquiry.

We must be content if we can attain to so much precision in our statement as the subject before us admits of; for the same degree of accuracy is no more to be expected in all kinds of reasoning than in all kinds of manufacture.

Now what is noble and just (with which Politics deals) is so various and so uncertain, that some think these are merely conventional and not natural distinctions.

There is a similar uncertainty also about what is good, because good things often do people harm: men have before now been ruined by wealth, and have lost their lives through courage.

Our subject, then, and our data being of this nature, we must be content if we can indicate the truth roughly and in outline, and if, in dealing with matters that are not amenable to immutable laws, and reasoning from premises that are but probable, we can arrive at probable conclusions.

The reader, on his part, should take each of my statements in the same spirit; for it is the mark of an educated man to require in each kind of inquiry, just so much exactness as the subject admits of: it is equally absurd to accept probable reasoning from a mathematician, and to demand scientific proof from an orator. . . .

Since—to resume—all knowledge and all purpose aims at some good, what is this which we say is the aim of Politics; or, in other words, what is the highest of all realizable goods? . . .

As to its name, I suppose nearly all men are agreed; for the masses and the men of culture alike declare that it is *eudaimonia* or happiness, and hold that "to live well" or to "do well" is the same as to be "happy."

But they differ as to what this happiness is, and the masses do not give the same account of it as the philosophers.

The former take it to be something palpable and plain, as pleasure or wealth or fame; one man holds it to be this, and another that, and often the same man is of different minds at different times,—after sickness it is health, and in poverty it is wealth; while when they are impressed with the consciousness of their ignorance, they admire most those who say grand things that are above their comprehension. . . .

As to men's notions of the good or happiness, it seems (to judge, as we reasonably may, from their lives) that the masses, who are the least refined, hold it to be pleasure, and so accept the life of enjoyment as their ideal.

For the most conspicuous kinds of life are three: this life of enjoyment, the life of the statesman, and, thirdly, the contemplative life.

The mass of men show themselves utterly slavish in their preference for the life of brute beasts, but their views receive consideration because many of those in high places have the tastes of Sardanapalus.

Men of refinement with a practical turn prefer honor; for I suppose we may say that honor is the aim of the statesman's life.

But this seems too superficial to be the good we are seeking: for it appears to depend upon those who give rather than upon those who receive it; while we have a presentiment that the good is something that is peculiarly a man's own and can scarce be taken away from him.

Moreover, these men seem to pursue honor in order that they may be assured of their own excellence,—at least, they wish to be honored by men of sense, and by those who know them, and on the ground of their virtue or excellence. It is plain, then, that in their view, at any rate, virtue or excellence is better than honor; and perhaps we should take this to be the end of the statesman's life, rather than honor.

But virtue or excellence also appears too incomplete to be what we want; for it seems that a man might have virtue and yet be asleep or be inactive all his life, and, moreover, might meet with the greatest disasters and misfortunes; and no one would maintain that such a man is happy, except for argument's sake. But we will not dwell on these matters now, for they are sufficiently discussed in the popular treatises.

The third kind of life is the life of contemplation: we will treat of it further on.

* * * * *

But perhaps the reader thinks that though no one will dispute the statement that happiness is the best thing in the world, yet a still more precise definition of it is needed.

This will best be gained, I think, by asking, What is the function of man? For as the goodness and the excellence of a piper or a sculptor, or the practicer of any art, and generally of those who have any function or business to do, lies in that function, so man's good would seem to lie in his function, if he has one.

But can we suppose that, while a carpenter and a cobbler has a function and a business of his own, man has no business and no function assigned him by nature? Nay, surely as his several members, eye and hand and foot, plainly have each his own function, so we must suppose that man also has some function over and above all these.

What then is it?

Life evidently he has in common even with the plants, but we want that which is peculiar to him. We must exclude, therefore, the life of mere nutrition and growth.

Next to this comes the life of sense; but this too he plainly shares with horses and cattle and all kinds of animals.

There remains then the life whereby he acts—the life of his rational nature, with its two sides or divisions, one rational as obeying reason, the other rational as having and exercising reason.

But as this expression is ambiguous, we must be understood to mean thereby the life that consists in the exercise of the faculties; for this seems to be more properly entitled to the name.

The function of man, then, is exercise of his vital faculties on one side in obedience to reason, and on the other side with reason.

But what is called the function of a

man of any profession and the function of a man who is good in that profession are generically the same, e.g. of a harper and of a good harper; and this holds in all cases without exception, only that in the case of the latter his superior excellence at his work is added; for we say a harper's function is to harp, and a good harper's to harp well.

Man's function then being, as we say, a kind of life—that is to say, exercise of his faculties and action of various kinds with reason—the good man's function is to do this well and beautifully.

But the function of anything is done well when it is done in accordance with the proper excellence of that thing.

Putting all this together, then, we find that the good of man is exercise of his faculties in accordance with excellence or virtue, or, if there be more than one, in accordance with the best and most complete virtue.

But there must also be a full term of years for this exercise; for one swallow or one fine day does not make a spring, nor does one day or any small space of time make a blessed or happy man.

This, then, may be taken as a rough outline of the good; for this, I think, is the proper method,—first to sketch the outline, and then to fill in the details.

* * * * *

We have next to inquire what excellence or virtue is.

A quality of the soul is either (1) a passion or emotion, or (2) a power or faculty, or (3) a habit or trained faculty; and so virtue must be one of these three. By (1) a passion or emotion we mean appetite, anger, fear, confidence, envy, joy, love, hate, longing, emulation, pity, or generally that which is accompanied by pleasure or pain; (2) a power or faculty is that in respect of which we are said to be capable of being affected in any of these ways, as, for instance, that in respect of which we are able to be angered or pained or to pity; and (3) a habit or trained faculty is that in respect of which we are well or ill regulated or disposed in the matter of our affections; as, for instance, in the matter of being angered, we are ill regulated if we are too violent or too slack, but if we are moderate in our anger we are well regulated. And so with the rest.

Now, the virtues are not emotions, nor are the vices—(1) because we are not called good or bad in respect of our emotions, but are called so in respect of our virtues or vices; (2) because we are neither praised nor blamed in respect of our emotions (a man is not praised for being afraid or angry, nor blamed for being angry simply, but for being angry in a particular way), but we are praised or blamed in respect of our virtues or vices; (3) because we may be angered or frightened without deliberate choice, but the virtues are a kind of deliberate choice, or at least are impossible without it; and (4) because in respect of our emotions we are said to be moved, but in respect of our virtues and vices we are not said to be moved, but to be regulated or disposed in this way or in that.

For these same reasons also they are not powers or faculties; for we are not called either good or bad for being merely capable of emotion, nor are we either praised or blamed for this. And further, while nature gives us our powers or faculties, she does not make us either good or bad.

If, then, the virtues be neither emotions nor faculties, it only remains for them to be habits or trained faculties.

We have thus found the genus to which virtue belongs; but we want to know, not only that it is a trained faculty, but also what species of trained faculty it is.

We may safely assert that the virtue or excellence of a thing causes that thing both to be itself in good condition and to perform its function well. The excellence of the eye, for instance, makes both the eye and its work good; for it is by the excellence of the eye that we see well. So the proper excellence of the horse makes a horse what he should be, and makes him good at running, and carrying his rider, and standing a charge.

If, then, this holds good in all cases, the proper excellence or virtue of man will be a habit or trained faculty that makes a man good and makes him perform his function well.

How this is to be done we have already said, but we may exhibit the same conclusion in another way, by inquiring what the nature of this virtue is.

Now, if we have any quantity, whether continuous or discrete, it is possible to take either a larger, or a smaller, or an equal amount, and that either absolutely or relatively to our own needs.

By an equal or fair amount I understand a mean amount, or one that lies between excess and deficiency.

By the absolute mean, or mean relative to the thing itself, I understand that which is equidistant from both extremes, and this is one and the same for all.

By the mean relative to us I understand that which is neither too much nor too little for us; and this is not one and the same for all.

For instance, if ten be larger and two be smaller, if we take six we take the mean relatively to the thing itself; for it exceeds one extreme by the same amount by which it is exceeded by the other extreme: and this is the mean in arithmetical proportion.

But the mean relatively to us cannot be found in this way. If ten pounds of food is too much for a given man to eat, and two pounds too little, it does not follow that the trainer will order him six pounds: for that also may perhaps be too much for the man in question, or too little; too little for Milo,[1] too much for the beginner. The same holds true in running and wrestling.

And so we may say generally that a master in any art avoids what is too much and what is too little, and seeks for the mean and chooses it—not the absolute but the relative mean.

Every art or science, then, perfects its work in this way, looking to the mean and bringing its work up to this standard; so that people are wont to say of a good work that nothing could be taken from it or added to it, implying that excellence is destroyed by excess or deficiency, but secured by observing the mean. And good artists, as we say, do in fact keep their eyes fixed on this in all that they do.

[1] [A famous wrestler—C.M.]

Virtue therefore, since like nature it is more exact and better than any art, must also aim at the mean—virtue of course meaning moral virtue or excellence; for it has to do with passions and actions, and it is these that admit of excess and deficiency and the mean. For instance, it is possible to feel fear, confidence, desire, anger, pity, and generally to be affected pleasantly and painfully, either too much or too little, in either case wrongly; but to be thus affected at the right times, and on the right occasions, and towards the right persons, and with the right object, and in the right fashion, is the mean course and the best course, and these are characteristics of virtue. And in the same way our outward acts also admit of excess and deficiency, and the mean or due amount.

Virtue, then, has to deal with feelings or passions and with outward acts, in which excess is wrong and deficiency also is blamed, but the mean amount is praised and is right—both of which are characteristics of virtue.

Virtue, then, is a kind of moderation, inasmuch as it aims at the mean or moderate amount. . . .

And it is a moderation, firstly, inasmuch as it comes in the middle or mean between two vices, one on the side of excess, the other on the side of defect; and, secondly, inasmuch as, while these vices fall short of or exceed the due measure in feeling and in action, it finds and chooses the mean, middling, or moderate amount. . . .

But it is not enough to make these general statements: we must go on and apply them to particulars. For in reasoning about matters of conduct general statements are too vague, and do not convey so much truth as particular propositions. It is with particulars that conduct is concerned: our statements, therefore, when applied to these particulars, should be found to hold good.

These particulars then, we will take from the following table.

Moderation in the feelings of fear and confidence is courage: of those that exceed, he that exceeds in fearlessness has no name (as often happens), but he that exceeds in confidence is foolhardy, while he that exceeds in fear, but is deficient in confidence, is cowardly.

Moderation in respect of certain pleasures and also (though to a less extent) certain pains is temperance, while excess is profligacy. But defectiveness in the matter of these pleasures is hardly ever found, and so this sort of people also have as yet received no name: let us put them down as "void of sensibility."

In the matter of giving and taking money, moderation is liberality, excess and deficiency are prodigality and illiberality. But these two vices exceed and fall short in contrary ways: the prodigal exceeds in spending, but falls short in taking; while the illiberal man exceeds in taking, but falls short in spending.

But, besides these, there are other dispositions in the matter of money: there is a moderation which is called magnificence (for the magnificent is not the same as the liberal man: the former deals with large sums, the latter with small), and an excess which is called bad taste or vulgarity, and a deficiency which is called meanness; and these vices differ from those which are opposed to liberality: how they differ will be explained later.

With respect to honor and disgrace, there is a moderation which is high-mindedness, an excess which may be called vanity, and a deficiency which is little-mindedness.

But just as we said that liberality is related to magnificence, differing only in that it deals with small sums, so here there is a virtue related to high-mindedness and differing only in that it is concerned with small instead of great honors. A man may have a due desire for honor, and also more or less than a due desire: he that carries this desire to excess is called ambitious, he that has not enough of it is called unambitious, but he that has the due amount has no name.

With regard to pleasantness in amusement, he who observes the mean may be called witty, and his character wittiness; excess may be called buffoonery, and the man a buffoon; while boorish may stand for the person who is deficient, and boorishness for his character. . . .

With regard to pleasantness in the other affairs of life, he who makes himself properly pleasant may be called friendly, and his moderation friendliness; he that exceeds may be called obsequious if he has no ulterior motive, but a flatterer if he has an eye to his own advantage; he that is deficient in this respect, and always makes himself disagreeable, may be called a quarrelsome or peevish fellow.

* * * * *

Now that we have discussed the several kinds of virtue and friendship and pleasure, it remains to give a summary account of happiness, since we assume that it is the end of all that man does. And it will shorten our statement if we first recapitulate what we have said above.

We said that happiness is not a habit or trained faculty. If it were, it would be within the reach of a man who slept all his days and lived the life of a vegetable, or of a man who met with the greatest misfortunes. As we cannot accept this conclusion, we must place happiness in some exercise of faculty, as we said before. But as the exercises of faculty are sometimes necessary (i.e. desirable for the sake of something else), sometimes desirable in themselves, it is evident that happiness must be placed among those that are desirable in themselves, and not among those that are desirable for the sake of something else: for happiness lacks nothing; it is sufficient in itself.

Now, the exercise of faculty is desirable in itself when nothing is expected from it beyond itself.

Of this nature are held to be (1) the manifestations of excellence; for to do what is noble and excellent must be counted desirable for itself: and (2) those amusements which please us; for they are not chosen for the sake of anything else,—indeed, men are more apt to be injured than to be benefited by them, through neglect of their health and fortunes.

Now, most of those whom men call happy have recourse to pastimes of this sort. And on this account those who show a ready wit in such pastimes find favor with tyrants; for they make themselves pleasant in that which the tyrant wants, and what he wants is pastime. These amusements, then, are generally thought to be elements of happiness, because princes employ their leisure in them. But such persons, we may venture to say, are no criterion. For princely rank does not imply the possession of virtue or of reason, which are the sources of all excellent exercise of faculty. And if these men, never having tasted pure and refined pleasure, have recourse to the pleasures of the body, we should not on that account think these more desirable; for children also fancy that the things which they value are better than anything else. It is only natural, then, that as children differ from men in their estimate of what is valuable, so bad men should differ from good.

As we have often said, therefore, that is truly valuable and pleasant which is so to the perfect man. Now, the exercise of those trained faculties which are proper to him is what each man finds most desirable; what the perfect man finds most desirable, therefore, is the exercise of virtue.

Happiness, therefore, does not consist in amusement; and indeed it is absurd to suppose that the end is amusement, and that we toil and moil all our life long for the sake of amusing ourselves. We may say that we choose everything for the sake of something else, excepting only happiness; for it is the end. But to be serious and to labor for the sake of amusement seems silly and utterly childish; while to amuse ourselves in order that we may be serious, as Anacharsis says, seems to be right; for amusement is a sort of recreation, and we need recreation because we are unable to work continuously.

Recreation, then, cannot be the end; for it is taken as a means to the exercise of our faculties.

Again, the happy life is thought to be that which exhibits virtue; and such a life must be serious and cannot consist in amusement.

Again, it is held that things of serious importance are better than laughable and amusing things, and that the better the organ or the man, the more important is the function; but we have already said that the function or exercise of that which is better is higher and more conducive to happiness.

Again, the enjoyment of bodily pleasures is within the reach of anybody, of a slave no less than the best of men; but no one supposes that a slave can participate in happiness, seeing that he cannot participate in the proper life of man. For indeed happiness does not consist in pastimes of this sort, but in the exercise of virtue, as we have already said.

But if happiness be the exercise of virtue, it is reasonable to suppose that it will be the exercise of the highest virtue; and that will be the virtue or excellence of the best part of us.

Now, that part or faculty—call it reason or what you will—which seems naturally to rule and take the lead, and to apprehend things noble and divine—whether it be itself divine, or only the divinest part of us—is the faculty the exercise of which, in its proper excellence, will be perfect happiness.

That this consists in speculation or contemplation we have already said.

This conclusion would seem to agree both with what we have said above, and with known truths.

This exercise of faculty must be the highest possible; for the reason is the highest of our faculties, and of all knowable things those that reason deals with are the highest.

Again, it is the most continuous; for speculation can be carried on more continuously than any kind of action whatsoever.

We think too that pleasure ought to be one of the ingredients of happiness; but of all virtuous exercises it is allowed that the pleasantest is the exercise of wisdom. At least philosophy is thought to have pleasures that are admirable in purity and steadfastness; and it is reasonable to suppose that the time passes more pleasantly with those who possess, than with those who are seeking knowledge.

Again, what is called self-sufficiency will be most of all found in the speculative life. The necessaries of life, indeed, are needed by the wise man as well as by the just man and the rest; but, when these have been provided in due quantity, the just man further needs persons towards whom, and along with whom, he may act justly; and so does the temperate and the courageous man and the rest; while the wise man is able to speculate even by himself, and the wiser he is the more is he able to do this. He could speculate better, we may confess, if he had others to help him, but nevertheless he is more self-sufficient than anybody else.

Again, it would seem that this life alone is desired solely for its own sake; for it yields no result beyond the contemplation itself, while from all actions we get something more or less besides the action itself. . . .

But a life which realized this idea would be something more than human; for it would not be the expression of man's nature, but of some divine element in that nature—the exercise of which is as far superior to the exercise of the other kind of virtue, as this divine element is superior to our compound human nature.

If then reason be divine as compared with man, the life which consists in the exercise of reason will also be divine in comparison with human life. Nevertheless, instead of listening to those who advise us as men and mortals not to lift our thoughts above what is human and mortal, we ought rather, as far as possible, to put off our mortality and make every effort to live in the exercise of the highest of our faculties; for though it be but a small part of us, yet in power and value it far surpasses all the rest.

QUESTIONS FOR DISCUSSION

1. Do you agree that every act, inquiry, and object aims at some good? Is this a definition, or could evidence be offered to support it? Does Aristotle offer any evidence? Does it also follow that there is an end "natural" to each object, i.e. it is natural for a kitten to become a cat?
2. Why does Aristotle conclude that *eudaimonia* is the highest good?

3. How is Aristotle's doctrine of *eudaimonia* related to his account of the Golden Mean? Should there be moderation in all things?
4. Why does Aristotle say "the life which consists in the exercise of reason" is best? Have any other philosophers drawn the same conclusion? Are there any dangers or deficiencies to this view? What are its advantages?

READINGS FOR IMMEDIATE REFERENCE

Aristotle. *The Nicomachean Ethics.* Books 1-3, 6, 10.

Santayana, George. *Reason in Science,* Part V of *The Life of Reason.* New York: Scribners, 1905, Chapters 8-10.

Wheelwright, Philip. *A Critical Introduction to Ethics,* 3rd ed. New York: Odyssey Press, 1959, Chapter 7.

REFERENCES FOR COMPREHENSIVE KNOWLEDGE

Aristotle. *Works,* translated by W. D. Ross. New York: Oxford University Press, 1925.

Jaeger, Werner. *Aristotle.* New York: Oxford University Press, 1934. A comprehensive reconstruction of Aristotle's thought as it developed during his life.

Ross, W. D. *Aristotle.* New York: Scribners, 1924. The best single-volume treatment of Aristotle's total philosophical thought.

Taylor, A. E. *Aristotle.* New York: Dover Publications, 1955. Aristotle as seen by the foremost modern Platonist.

Also see:

Allen, D. J. *The Philosophy of Aristotle.* New York: Oxford University Press, 1952.

Barker, Ernest. *The Political Thought of Plato and Aristotle.* New York: Oxford University Press, 1906.

Cherniss, H. *Aristotle's Criticism of Plato and the Academy.* Baltimore: Johns Hopkins University Press, 1944.

Joachim, H. H. *Aristotle: The Nicomachean Ethics.* New York: Oxford University Press, 1951.

Jones, T. E. *Aristotle's Researches on Natural Science.* New York: Oxford University Press, 1912.

Mure, G. R. G. *Aristotle.* Oxford: Clarendon Press, 1932.

VI. IMMANUEL KANT

Kant, a critic of hedonism, came to the study of philosophy relatively late in life. Born in 1724, the son of a saddlemaker, he was raised in a Pietist religious atmosphere and attended the university in his native city, Konigsberg (Kaliningrad), where, after a decade of private tutoring, he was appointed a lecturer in 1755. He taught such diverse subjects as mineralogy, astronomy, anthropology, pedagogy and geography and was so well known as a lecturer that people came from all over Europe to listen to him. In 1770, at the age of forty-six, Kant was appointed Professor of Logic and Metaphysics, a post he retained until his retirement in 1798. He published numerous scientific treatises, including the nebular hypothesis account of the earth's origin, but his first major philosophical work, *The Critique of Pure Reason,* did not appear until 1781. It was followed in the next fifteen years by no less than nine major works in which Kant undertook a thorough re-examination of the whole realm of knowledge. To produce these books Kant enforced a rigid discipline on his life, arising at five a.m., giving attention to university affairs from six to ten, writing until two p.m. after which he ate the one regular meal he had each day. Then he walked for an hour and spent the remainder of the day reading, conversing, thinking, and playing the flute until nine or ten when he went to bed. Physically, he was barely five feet tall, had a deformed right shoulder, a sunken chest and a weak voice, but he had a wide acquaintance with scientific, political, and philosophical knowledge, was an engaging conversationalist and developed his thought so rigorously and comprehensively that his ideas dominated continental philosophy during most of the nineteenth century. After becoming somewhat senile during the last two years of his life, he died in 1804.

In this selection look for Kant's answers to four questions: (1) why is the good will the only intrinsic good? (2) what is the difference between acting from and acting in accordance with virtue? (3) what is the relationship between happiness and morality? and (4) what is the difference between a hypothetical and a categorical imperative?

The Categorical Imperative[1]

Nothing in the world—indeed nothing even beyond the world—can possibly be conceived which could be called good without qualification except a good will. Intelligence, wit, judgment, and the other talents of the mind, however they may be named, or courage, resoluteness and perseverance as qualities of temperament are doubtless in many respects good and desirable. But they can become extremely bad and harmful if the will, which is to make use of these gifts of nature and which in its special constitution is called character, is not good. It is the same with the gifts of fortune. Power, riches, honor, even health, general well-being, and the contentment with one's condition which is called happiness make for pride and even arrogance if there is not a good will to correct their influence on the mind and on its principles of action, so as to make it universally conformable to its end. It need hardly be mentioned that the sight of a being adorned with no feature of a pure and good will yet enjoying uninterrupted prosperity can never give pleasure to a rational impartial observer. Thus the good will seems to constitute the indispensable condition even of worthiness to be happy. . . .

The good will is not good because of what it effects or accomplishes or because of its adequacy to achieve some proposed end; it is good only because of its willing, i.e., it is good of itself. And, regarded for itself, it is to be esteemed incomparably higher than anything which could be brought about by it in favor of any inclination or even of the sum total of all inclinations. Even if it should happen that, by a particularly unfortunate fate or by the niggardly provision of a stepmotherly nature, this will should be wholly lacking in power to accomplish its purpose, and if even the greatest effort should not avail it to achieve anything of its end, and if there remained only the good will (not as a mere wish but as the summoning of all the means in our power), it would sparkle like a jewel with its own light, as something that had its full worth in itself. Usefulness or fruitlessness can neither diminish nor augment this worth. Its usefulness would be only its setting, as it were, so as to enable us to handle it more conveniently in commerce or to attract the attention of those who are not yet connoisseurs, but not to recommend it to those who are experts or to determine its worth.

But there is something so strange in this idea of the absolute worth of the will alone, in which no account is taken of any use, that, notwithstanding the agreement even of common sense, the suspicion must arise that perhaps only highflown fancy is its hidden basis, and that we may have misunderstood the purpose of nature in its appointment of

[1] Reprinted from *Foundations of the Metaphysics of Morals* by Immanuel Kant, translated by Lewis White Beck, by permission of The University of Chicago Press, copyright 1949, Sections 1 and 2.

reason as the ruler of our will. We shall therefore examine this idea from this point of view.

In the natural constitution of an organized being, i.e., one suitably adapted to life, we assume as an axiom that no organ will be found for any purpose which is not the fittest and best adapted to that purpose. Now if its preservation, welfare—in a word, its happiness—were the real end of nature in a being having reason and will, then nature would have hit upon a very poor arrangement in appointing the reason of the creature to be the executor of this purpose. For all the actions which the creature has to perform with this intention, and the entire rule of its conduct, would be dictated much more exactly by instinct, and that end would be far more certainly attained by instinct than it ever could be by reason. And if, over and above this, reason should have been granted to the favored creature, it would have served only to let it contemplate the happy constitution of its nature, to admire it, to rejoice in it, and to be grateful for it to its beneficent cause. But reason would not have been given in order that the being should subject its faculty of desire to that weak and delusive guidance and to meddle with the purpose of nature. In a word, nature would have taken care that reason did not break forth into practical use nor have the presumption, with its weak insight, to think out for itself the plan of happiness and the means of attaining it. Nature would have taken over not only the choice of ends but also that of the means and with wise foresight would have intrusted both to instinct alone.

And, in fact, we find that the more a cultivated reason deliberately devotes itself to the enjoyment of life and happiness, the more the man falls short of true contentment. From this fact there arises in many persons, if only they are candid enough to admit it, a certain degree of misology, hatred of reason. This is particularly the case with those who are most experienced in its use. After counting all the advantages which they draw from the sciences they nevertheless find that they have actually brought more trouble on their shoulders instead of gaining in happiness; they finally envy, rather than despise, the common run of men who are better guided by mere natural instinct and who do not permit their reason much influence on their conduct. . . .

Reason is not, therefore, competent to guide the will safely with regard to its objects and the satisfaction of all our needs (which it in part multiplies), and to this end an innate instinct would have led with far more certainty. But reason is given to us as a practical faculty, i.e., one which is meant to have an influence on the will. As nature has elsewhere distributed capacities suitable to the functions they are to perform, reason's proper function must be to produce a will good in itself and not one good merely as a means. . . .

We have, then, to develop the concept of a will which is to be esteemed as good of itself without regard to anything else. It dwells already in the natural sound understanding and does not need so much to be taught as only to be brought to light. In the estimation of the entire worth of our actions it always takes first place and is the condition of everything else. In order to show this, we shall take the concept of duty. . . .

I here omit all actions which are recognized as opposed to duty, even though they may be useful in one respect or another, for with these the question does not arise at all as to whether they may be done *from* duty, since they conflict with it. I also pass over the actions which are really in accordance with duty and to which one has no direct inclination, rather doing them because impelled to do so by another inclination. For it is easily decided whether an action in accord with duty is done from duty or for some selfish purpose. It is far more difficult to note this difference when the action is in accordance with duty and, in addition, the subject has a direct inclination to do it. For example, it is in fact in accordance with duty that a dealer should not overcharge an inexperienced customer, and wherever there is much business the prudent merchant does not do so, having a fixed price for everyone, so that a child may buy of him as cheaply as any other. Thus the customer is honestly served. But this is far from sufficient to justify the belief that the merchant has behaved in this way from duty and principles of honesty. His own advantage required this behavior; but it cannot be assumed that over and above that he had a direct inclination to the purchaser and that, out of love, as it were, he gave none an advantage in price over another. Therefore the action was done neither from duty nor from direct inclination but only for a selfish purpose.

On the other hand, it is a duty to preserve one's life, and moreover everyone has a direct inclination to do so. But, for that reason, the often anxious care which most men take of it has no intrinsic worth, and the maxim of doing so has no moral import. They preserve their lives *according to* duty, but not *from* duty. But if adversity and hopeless sorrow completely take away the relish for life; if an unfortunate man, strong in soul, is indignant rather than despondent or dejected over his fate and wishes for death, and yet preserves his life without loving it and from neither inclination nor fear but from duty—then his maxim has a moral import.

To be kind where one can is a duty, and there are, moreover, many persons so sympathetically constituted that without any motive of vanity or selfishness they find an inner satisfaction in spreading joy and rejoice in the contentment of others which they have made possible. But I say that, however dutiful and amiable it may be, that kind of action has no true moral worth. . . .

But assume that the mind of that friend to mankind was clouded by a sorrow of his own which extinguished all sympathy with the lot of others. And now suppose him to tear himself, unsolicited by inclination, out of this dead insensibility and to do this action only from duty and without any inclination—then for the first time his action has genuine moral worth.

* * * * *

[Thus, the first proposition of morality is that to have moral worth an action must be done from duty.] The second proposition is: An action done from duty does not have its moral worth in the purpose which is to be achieved through it but in the maxim by which it is determined. Its moral value, therefore, does not depend on the reality of the object of the action but merely on the principle of volition by which the action is done without any regard to the objects of the faculty of desire. From the preceding discussion it is clear that the purposes we may have for our actions and their effects as ends and incentives of the will cannot give the actions any unconditional and moral worth. Wherein, then, can this worth lie? It can lie nowhere else than in the principle of the will irrespective of the ends which can be realized by such action. . . .

The third principle, as a consequence of the two preceding, I would express as follows: Duty is the necessity of an action done from respect for a law or maxim. . . . But what kind of law can that be, the conception of which must determine the will without reference to the expected result? Under this condition alone the will can be called absolutely good without qualification. Since I have robbed the will of all impulses which could come to it from obedience to any law, nothing remains to serve as a principle of the will except universal conformity of its actions to law as such. That is, *I should never act in such a way that I could not will that my maxim should be a universal law.* Mere conformity to law as such (without assuming any particular law applicable to certain actions) serves as the principle of the will, and it must serve as such a principle if duty is not to be a vain delusion and chimerical concept. The common reason of mankind in its practical judgments is in perfect agreement with this and has this principle constantly in view. . . .

I do not, therefore, need any penetrating acuteness in order to discern what I have to do in order that my volition may be morally good. Inexperienced in the course of the world, incapable of being prepared for all its contingencies, I only ask myself: Can I will that my maxim become a universal law? If not, it must be rejected, not because of any disadvantage accruing to myself or even to others, but because it cannot enter as a principle into a possible universal legislation, and reason extorts from me an immediate respect for such legislation.

* * * * *

[However], if we have derived this concept of duty from the common use of our practical reason, it is by no means to be inferred that we have treated it as an empirical concept. On the contrary, if we attend to our experience of the way men act, we meet frequent and, as we ourselves confess, justified complaints that we cannot cite a single sure example of the disposition to act from pure duty. There are also justified complaints that, though much may be done that accords with what duty commands, it is nevertheless always doubtful whether it is done from duty, and thus whether it has moral worth. . . .

It is in fact absolutely impossible by experience to discern with complete certainty a single case in which the maxim of an action, however much it may conform to duty, rested solely on moral grounds and on the conception of one's duty, for we cannot by any means conclude with certainty that a secret impulse of self-love, falsely appearing as the idea of duty, was not actually the true determining cause of the will. [Moreover], one cannot better serve the wishes of those who ridicule all morality as a mere phantom of human imagination overreaching itself through self-conceit than by conceding to them that the concepts of duty must be derived only from experience. For, by this concession, a sure triumph is prepared for them. Out of love for humanity I am willing to admit that most of our actions are in accordance with duty; but, if we look closer at our thoughts and aspirations, we everywhere come upon the dear self, which is always salient, and it is this, instead of the stern command of duty (which would often require self-denial) which supports our plans. One need not be an enemy of virtue, but only a cool observer who does not mistake even the liveliest aspiration for the good with its reality, to be doubtful sometimes whether true virtue can really be found anywhere in the world. . . .

Nor could one give poorer counsel to morality than to attempt to derive it from examples. For each example of morality which is exhibited to me must itself have been previously judged according to principles of morality to see whether it is worthy to serve as an original example, i.e. as a model. By no means could it authoritatively furnish the concept of morality. . . .

From what has been said, it is clear that all moral concepts have their seat and origin entirely *a priori* in reason. It is obvious that they can be abstracted from no empirical and hence merely contingent cognitions. . . . But since moral laws should hold for every rational being as such, the principles must be derived from the universal concept of a rational being generally.

* * * * *

Everything in nature works according to laws. Only a rational being has the capacity of acting according to the conception of laws, i.e., according to universal and objective principles. The conception of an objective principle so far as it constrains the will, is a command of reason, and the formula of this command is called an *imperative*. . . .

All imperatives command either hypothetically or categorically. The former present the practical necessity of a possible action as a *means* to achieving something else which one desires. The categorical imperative would be one which presented an action as of itself objectively necessary, *without regard to any other end*. . . . The hypothetical imperative, therefore, says only that the action is good to some purpose, possible or actual. The categorical imperative, which declares the action to be of itself objectively necessary without making any reference to a purpose, i.e., without having any other end, holds as a practical principle.

All sciences have some practical part which consists of problems of some end which is possible for us and of imperatives as to how it can be reached. These can therefore generally be called imperatives of skill. Whether the end is reasonable and good is not in question at all, for the question is only of what must be done in order to attain it. The precepts to be followed by a physician in order to cure his patient and by a poisoner in order to bring about certain death are of equal value insofar as each does that which will perfectly accomplish his purpose. Since in early youth we do not know what ends may occur to us in the course of life, parents seek to let their children learn a great many things and provide for skill in the use of means to all sorts of arbitrary ends, among which they cannot determine whether any one of them may later become an actual purpose of their child.

However, there does seem to be one end which we may suppose as actual in all rational beings so far as imperatives apply to them; there is one purpose not only which they can have but which we can presuppose that they all do have by the necessity of nature. This purpose is happiness. . . .

If it were only easy to give a definite concept of happiness, the imperatives of prudence (selfishness) could be considered as categorical. But it is a misfortune that the concept of happiness is such an indefinite concept that, although each person wishes to attain it, he can never definitely and self-consistently state what it is he really wishes and wills. The reason for this is that all elements which belong to the concept of happiness are empirical, i.e., they must be taken from experience, while for the idea of happiness an absolute whole, a maximum, of well-being is needed in my present and in every future condition. Now it is impossible even for the most clear-sighted and omnipotent but finite being to form here a definite concept of that which he really wills. If he wills riches, how much anxiety, envy, and intrigues might he not thereby draw upon his shoulders! If he wills much knowledge and vision, perhaps it might become only an eye that much sharper to show him as more dreadful the evils which are now hidden from him and which are yet unavoidable or to burden his desires—which already sufficiently engage him—with even more needs! If he wills a long life, who guarantees that it will not be long misery? If he wills at least health, how often has not the discomfort of the body restrained him from excesses into which perfect health would have led him? In short, he is not capable, on any principle and with complete certainty, of ascertaining what would make him truly happy; omniscience would be needed for this. (And thus the task of determining infallibly and universally what action will promote the happiness of a rational being is completely unsolvable.) . . .

To see how the imperative of morality is possible is, then, without doubt the only question needing an answer. . . . In attacking this problem, we need to know only whether the concept of a categorical imperative does not also furnish the formula containing the proposition which alone can be a categorical imperative.

If I think of a hypothetical imperative as such, I do not know what it will contain until the condition is stated under which it is an imperative. But if I think of a categorical imperative, I know immediately what it contains. For since the imperative contains besides the law only the necessity of the maxim of acting in accordance with this law, while the law contains no condition to which it is restricted, there is nothing remaining in it except the universality of law as such to which the maxim of an action should conform; and in effect this conformity alone is represented as necessary by the imperative.

There is, as we said before, only one categorical imperative. It is: Act only according to that maxim by which you can at the same time will that it should become a universal law. . . .

But now the question is: Is it a necessary law for all rational beings that they should always judge their actions by such maxims that they themselves could will to serve as universal laws? If it is such a law, it must be connected with the concept of the will of a rational being as such. . . . Now, I say man and, in general, every rational being exists as an end in himself and not merely as a means to be arbitrarily used by this or that will. In all his actions, whether they are directed to himself or to other rational beings, he must always be regarded at the same time as an end in himself. . . .

Thus, if there is to be a supreme practical principle and a categorical imperative for the human will, it must be one that forms an objective principle of the will from the conception of that which is necessarily an end for everyone because it is an end in itself. Hence this objective principle can serve as a universal practical law. The ground of this principle is: rational nature exists as an end in itself. Man necessarily thinks of his own existence in this way; thus far it is a subjective principle of human actions. Also, every other rational being thinks of his existence by means of the same rational ground which holds also for myself; thus it is at the same time an objective principle from which, as a supreme practical ground, it must be possible to derive all laws of the will. The practical imperative, therefore, is the following: *Act so that you treat humanity, whether in your own person or in that of another, always as an end and never as a means only*. Let us now see whether this can be achieved.

Let us turn to some examples.

First, according to the concept of necessary duty to one's self, he who contemplates suicide will ask himself whether his action can be consistent with the idea of humanity as an end in itself. If, in order to escape from burdensome circumstances, he destroys himself, he uses a person merely as a means to maintain a tolerable condition up to the end of life. Man, however, is not a thing, and thus not something to be used merely as a means; he must always be regarded in all his actions as an end in himself. Therefore, I cannot dispose of man in my own person so as to mutilate, corrupt, or kill him.

And secondly, as concerns necessary or obligatory duties to others, he who intends a deceitful promise to others sees immediately that he intends to use another man merely as a means, without the latter containing the end in himself at the same time. For he whom I want to use for my own purposes by means of such a promise cannot possibly assent to my mode of acting against him and cannot contain the end of this action in himself. This conflict against the principle of other men is even clearer if we cite examples of attacks on their freedom and property. For then it is clear that he who transgresses the rights of men intends to make use of the person of others merely as a means, without considering that, as rational beings, they must always be esteemed at the same time as ends. . . .

Thus the principle of every human will as a will giving universal laws in all its maxims is very well adapted to being a categorical imperative, provided it is otherwise correct. Because of the idea of universal law-giving, it is based on no interest, and, thus of all possible imperatives, it alone can be unconditional. Or, better, converting the proposition: if there is a categorical imperative (a law for the will of every rational being), it can only command that everything be done from the maxim of its will as one which could have as its object only itself considered as giving universal laws. For only in this case are the practical principle and the imperative which the will obeys unconditional because the will can have no interest as its foundation.

QUESTIONS FOR DISCUSSION

1. Does Kant give any reasons for saying a good will is good in itself, not for what it achieves? Does he hold this view consistently?
2. Dewey says Kant's theory is merely formal, i.e. it doesn't tell you how to act in particular situations. Suppose you were walking along the sidewalk and saw a small child about to run onto the busy highway. Could you apply Kant's theory to tell you what you should do, or is Dewey correct? (Be careful that you act from, not merely in accordance with, duty.)
3. Kant has been called the greatest Protestant moralist. Can you explain why this judgment would be made?
4. What similarities, if any, are there between Kant's theory and Aristotle's? Epictetus'? Epicurus'?
5. Does Kant's theory or a hedonistic theory—or neither—seem to you to be closer to what you would consider to be a moral theory?

READINGS FOR IMMEDIATE REFERENCE

Kant, Immanuel. *Fundamental Principles of the Metaphysics of Morals.*

———. *Perpetual Peace.*

Dewey, John. *Human Nature and Conduct.* New York: Henry Holt, 1922, Part III, Section 7.

Schweitzer, Albert. *Out of My Life and Thought.* New York: Henry Holt, 1933, Chapter 9.

REFERENCES FOR COMPREHENSIVE KNOWLEDGE

Kant, Immanuel. *Critique of Pure Reason.*

———. *Critique of Practical Reason.*

Abbott, T. K. *Kant's Theory of Ethics*. New York: Longmans, Green, 1927. A standard commentary.
Lindsay, A. D. *Kant*. New York: Oxford University Press, 1927. Perhaps the best introduction to Kant's thought for the general reader.
Paton, H. J. *The Categorical Imperative*. Chicago: University of Chicago Press, 1948. Kant's work is "indispensable for all who seek the good life intelligently."

Also see:

Korner, S. *Kant*. Baltimore: Penguin Books, 1955.
Ross, W. D. *Kant's Ethical Theory*. New York: Oxford University Press, 1954.
Singer, M. G. *Generalizations in Ethics*. New York: Scribners, 1961.
Smith, Norman Kemp. *A Commentary on Kant's Critique of Pure Reason*. New York: Oxford University Press, 1927.
Teale, Alfred E. *Kantian Ethics*. New York: Oxford University Press, 1951.
Webb, C. C. J. *Kant's Philosophy of Religion*. New York: Oxford University Press, 1926.

VII. RALPH BARTON PERRY

Perry was born in Poultney, Vermont, in 1876. He studied at Princeton, intending to become a minister, but when he went to Harvard for graduate study, the influence of such teachers as Royce, Santayana, and especially William James, turned him to philosophy. He received his doctorate in 1899, and two years later joined the faculty at Harvard. He was known as a vigorous, frequently entertaining, incisive, and kind teacher, with widely diversified interests. During the 1910's he helped to formulate a metaphysical theory known as The New Realism, and for the next quarter of a century he defined, systematized, expounded, and defended a General Theory of Value. In 1935 he published his Pulitzer prize-winning biography of William James, and from then on became increasingly involved in social and political problems: in 1939 he was seriously concerned about the rise of Naziism; by 1942, the status of civil rights in America; by 1945, plans for reconstructing the world; and from 1948, the need for intelligent decision making by citizens of the world. Retirement in 1946 made little difference in his activities, only allowing him more time to write books and his famous letters to the editors, to continue his debate with Bertrand Russell over pacifism, and to propose new ways to make philosophy available to people. He was one of six Americans invited to deliver the Gifford Lectures, he was president of the American Philosophical Association, and he published more than a dozen books. Perry died in 1958.

The last three selections in this chapter are examples of contemporary philosophical thought. In this selection, Perry says values can be related to interest in four ways. Notice what these four ways are, and why he chooses the alternative he does. Pay careful attention to the way he arrives at his conclusion regarding the need to harmonize interests. Are there any skips in his analysis?

A General Theory of Value[1]

The fundamental problem of theory of value is to define the *concept* of value. The term "definition" must not be understood to imply complexity. It may appear that value in the generic sense is unanalyzable. In that case theory of value will identify it and *point it out* as the character common to all species of the genus.

Such an undertaking is to be distinguished, in the first place, from an expression of the author's *personal bias.* In so far, for example, as Nietzsche has indicated his preference for the "strong, brave, domineering and proud" type of manhood, and his contempt for the sick and slavish type which he identifies with Christianity, he is simply manifesting his own personal bias. The pages of his works abound in explosive utterances such as "I find the joy of life in its violent and cruel struggles," "I am fond of the sea, and of all that is of the sea's kin," or "Enough! I can endure it no longer." Such utterances have social importance in proportion as they arouse a like emotion in others, and thus alter the sentiment of a group or of an epoch. Or they may have poetic value in so far as they fitly and permanently embody the emotion which they express. They indicate the existence of values, and may have the power to create values. But with the theory of value they have nothing whatsoever to do. In so far, on the other hand, as Nietzsche affirms that good is a fulfillment of "life" or of the "will to power," and in so far as he affirms that the Christian cult of self-denial is therefore an absolute inversion of good and evil, he is in fact contributing a hypothesis to theory of value. . . .

It is equally important to distinguish theory of value from rational or methodical criticism. By this is meant the application to any given subject-matter of a formulated standard. It consists of judgments of *attribution,* where the attribute itself is already defined, or employed in some ready-made acceptation. Thus most of the traditional discussions of "the good" have in reality been attempts to discover that particular thing or those particular things that are good, instead of attempts to discover *what it means* for a thing to be good. The result has been to leave the fundamental question unanswered, or to adopt some traditional answer unconsciously and uncritically. Thus hedonism, for example, although purporting to examine into fundamentals, has usually sought to prove that pleasure alone is good, in the sense of being the object of desire or the end of action. But this leaves open the prior question whether being an object of desire or end of action makes a thing good. And it is precisely this question with

[1] Reprinted by permission of the publishers from Ralph Barton Perry, *General Theory of Value*. Cambridge, Mass.: Harvard University Press, Copyright, 1926, by The President and Fellows of Harvard College; 1954 by Ralph Barton Perry, Chapters 1-5, 20-22.

which theory of value is primarily concerned. . . .

In attempting to isolate and exhibit the concept of value we shall employ what may, in the broad sense, be termed the empirical or descriptive method. This does not mean that we shall not distinguish between superior and inferior values, or between valid and false values, but that we shall find these and other such distinctions to depend upon certain given and describable differences. While the best justification of such a method will be its success, there are certain difficulties whose recognition at the outset will throw light upon the nature of the problem.

In the first place, there is a difficulty regarding the delimitation of data. According to the empirical method, we are not to start with a category and then find instances of it, but must proceed in the reverse direction, first collecting instances and then analyzing out their common characteristic. In collecting instances, however, one has to employ a principle of selection; which will turn out, unless one is cautious, to be an assumption of the very concept of which one is supposed to be in search. The difficulty is aggravated by the fact that values cannot even be physically isolated without prejudging their nature. . . .

The fact is that the word "value" instead of having a clear denotation like the word "house," or the word "Asia," refers us to a region whose nominal boundaries have yet to be agreed on. It is our task to examine the topography of this region. We shall find various natural lines of cleavage which we may adopt as its frontiers. The area which we ultimately assign to the region will depend on which of these we adopt. Our method is empirical in so far as our frontiers are natural rather than artificial; and provided this is the case, it does not greatly matter where we fix them. The important thing is the accuracy of the topographical survey. This survey must be broad enough to embrace all the claims which have been made in behalf of the term "value."

* * * * *

In discussing the definition of value, we shall be dealing constantly with the motor-affective life; that is to say, with instinct, desire, feeling, will and all their family of states, acts and attitudes. It is necessary therefore to have a term which may be used to refer to what is characteristic of this strain in life and mind, which shall be sufficiently comprehensive to embrace all of its varieties, and whose meaning we may refine as we proceed. The term *interest* is the most acceptable, and will henceforth be so employed. But where the context or common usage makes it more convenient to do so, we shall for the present employ such terms as "desire," "will" or "purpose" in the same comprehensive sense.

There are four possible relations of value to interest. In the first place, value may be, in its essential nature, quite irrelevant to interest. In this case the discussion of interest would not be germane to the definition of value. Interest might as a matter of fact be taken in value, it might be the mode of awareness by which value was immediately apprehended, or it might happen to possess value, but in any case it would not be a necessary constituent of value. In the second place, value may be held to be that character of an object which qualifies it be an end; in other words, that which implies, evokes or regulates interest. In this case value would be prior to the occurrence of any actual interest, but would prescribe in advance the character which any interest must assume. It is supposed that there is some definable character of desirability or purposiveness, which is the objective complement of interest, as intelligibility is supposed to be the complement of thought; and which may be understood in its own terms, without a psychological examination of the subjective facts of interest. In the third place, value may be assigned to the objects of certain duly qualified interests, such as the final, harmonious, absolute or imperative interest. Finally, there is the simpler and more comprehensive view, that value in the generic sense attaches promiscuously to all objects of all interest. In this case the definition of value will depend upon an analysis of interest itself, not in any qualified or honorific sense, but in the general and psychological sense.

We shall be led to adopt the last of these four alternatives as a result of the successive examination of the other three. . . .

The simplest disposition of our problem is to suppose that value neither has nor needs a definition. Good, according to this view, is a quality which needs no definition to one who has perceived it, and permits of no definition to one who has not. "My point," says Professor G. E. Moore, "is that 'good' is a simple notion, just as 'yellow' is a simple notion; that, just as you cannot, by any manner of means, explain to any one who does not already know it, what yellow is, so you cannot explain what good is." . . .

There can be only one proof of the existence of a perceptual quality, and that is the perception of it. One who upholds this view of good must be prepared to point to a distinct *quale* which appears in that region which our value terms roughly indicate, and which is different from the object's shape and size, from the interrelation of its parts, from its relation to other objects, or to a subject; and from all the other factors which belong to the same context, but are designated by words other than "good." The present writer, for one, finds no such residuum. Mr. Moore's comparison of good with the quality "yellow" remains purely hypothetical: good would be like yellow *if it were* an empirical quality. But then the fact that it does not possess the self-evidence of yellow argues that it is not an empirical quality. . . .

Indeed, the most serious defect of this type of theory is its failure to provide any systematic principle whatsoever. There are as many indefinable values as there are feeling attitudes, and since these are to be regarded as objective qualities rather than as modes of feeling, there is nothing to unite them, not even the principle of feeling. If "good" is a unique quality, then so are "pleasant," "bad" and "ought." There is no way of subsuming pleasant under good, or of defining the opposition of good and bad, or of subsuming both good and ought under a more general category such as value. If, on the other hand, value is defined in terms of interest, then the variability of interest serves to account for both the unity and the diversity of values.

* * * * *

The value of an object is now conceded to lie in its relation to interest. But how shall we conceive this relation? Shall we conceive it after the analogy of the marksman and his target, and say that the interest *directs itself* toward the object? Or shall we conceive it after the analogy of the magnet and the iron-filing, and say that the object draws the interest toward itself? In the former case value would spring from interest, and be conferred on the object; in the second case value would reside in the object as its capacity to command interest. . . .

[To take the second alternative first,] our present question thus resolves itself into the following: Is there any general character of objects which compels us to judge that such objects have been produced on purpose, or are the result of being meant to be. . . .

The commonest notion of this sort arises from the tendency on the part of a purposive being to impute to another purpose that which coincides with his own, but which has not, as a matter of fact, resulted from it. We feel *grateful* for what we like, and we *resent* what we do not like, thus implying friendly or hostile intent on the part of the environment. That which proves beneficent is construed as benevolent, and that which hurts or thwarts or fails is construed as malicious. This natural human tendency is commonly known as the "pathetic fallacy."

Suppose, for example, that in spite of my most painstaking efforts to execute a powerful stroke, the golf ball rolls ingloriously from the tee. I then turn and rend my new driver or call down maledictions upon it. I am angry not with myself but with it. I feel resentment toward it precisely as though it had meant to spite me. I virtually attribute malice to it. Now this, as my less heated partner may remind me, is unreasonable, because the golf-stick really did not mean it, or do it on purpose. It is true that in effect the stick thwarted me, and occasioned my displeasure, but it is an error to impute that displeasure to it as a motive or ground of action.

Or take another example. Basking in its warmth, I praise the sun and feel gratefully disposed to it. If I knew what the sun liked, I would gladly reciprocate. This is an innocent error, a kind of poetic license, but error it is none the less. For I have responded to the sun as though the pleasure which its rays were about to give me had actuated the sun in shedding them; whereas this effect upon my sensibilities is accidental, and in no way accountable for the radiation of the sun's light and heat.

There is, however, a positive implication in this criticism. My own action in each case is purposive. My addressing the ball, or lying in the sun, is to be accounted for by reference to the stroke or the bodily comfort that is to come. My error lies not in employing such a mode of explanation, but in misapplying it. There is a human weakness, doubtless one of the major motives in religion, which prompts one to extend to all the agencies involved in any event that purposive type of determination which really holds only of one's own participation in it. In the case of one's own agency the prospective sequel does account for the act, but in the case of the other contributory agencies this explanation is out of place. Not to discriminate between them is to commit what I shall call the pathetic fallacy.

It is not to be supposed that the pathetic fallacy is peculiar to the naive. There is a form of it which is very common among philosophers. It is often held that nature could not satisfy the scientific or philosophical purpose if it did not mean to,—if there were not a sort of complicity on the part of Nature herself. This notion can usually be found in dualistic philosophies, such as those of Descartes and Kant. Where thought and its object are supposed to have independent characters of their own, their harmonious conjunction in true knowledge becomes a gratuitous piece of good fortune which we attribute to a benevolent intent. Thus, according to Descartes, knowledge implies a sort of honorable veracity on the part of God.

* * * * *

We turn now to those views which, while admitting that value is relative to interest, insist that the interest in question must be specially qualified. That which is good, or desirable, is that which is the object of a legitimate desire. . . .

Plato is primarily responsible for the prevalence in European philosophy of the view that all purposes belong to one hierarchy culminating in the love of a supreme object, or "highest good."

He who has been instructed thus far in the things of love, and who has learned to see the beautiful in due order and succession, when he comes toward the end will suddenly perceive a nature of wondrous beauty (and this, Socrates, will be the final cause of all our former toils) —a nature . . . not fair in one point of view and foul in another, . . . but beauty absolute, separate, simple, and everlasting, which . . . is imparted to the ever-growing and perishing beauties of all other things. . . .

With important differences that do not concern us here, the same hierarchical conception appears in Aristotle. Nature is an order of substances, in which each is governed by the double principle of actualizing its own distinctive form, and at the same time of supplying the material conditions for the actualization of the form next higher in the scale. Man as the highest being of terrestrial nature is animated by the purpose of realizing the rational life, which in turn culminates in that contemplative activity of the reason which is the goal of the whole, or God. . . .

It is essential to this view that the ultimate end of the process should be conceived as directing *all* of its stages. Otherwise there would be a succession of desires or purposes instead of one all-pervading desire or purpose. *All* love is love of God:

that sustaining Love,
Which through the web of being blindly wove
By man and beast and earth and air and sea,
Burns bright or dim, as each are mirrors of
The fire for which all thirst.

There is a sublimity in this cosmic spectacle which disarms criticism. But despite its appeal to the religious and speculative imagination it involves several serious psychological errors which we shall do well to bring clearly to light. In the first place, it is affirmed that the development of desires is an orderly series, in which the flower of the old desire is the seed of the new. Or, it is affirmed that desire is cumulative, in the sense that each level of satisfaction becomes in turn the base of a new aspiration which both incorporates and supplements old aspirations. . . .

That such is unfortunately not the case, is abundantly proved by the facts of human experience. In disillusionment the satisfaction of a given interest leads to its repudiation and to the search for *other* satisfactions. Furthermore, new interests most commonly arise not through the conversion of ends into means, but through the conversion of means into ends. Finding certain instrumentalities such as money useful in satisfying his biological needs, a man thenceforth devotes himself to money getting. In short, interests burgeon from root, stem and branch, and not merely from fruit or flowers.

A further error lies in the affirmation of an absolute desideratum somehow implied in all desire. The conception of perfection becomes empty and redundant as soon as it is divorced from the *particular* interests of living creatures. The Platonic or Aristotelian good has a recognizable content so long as it is related to the human organism with its specific capacities and conditions, or to human sensibilities, or to the human craving for knowledge. But when we are invited to contemplate that culminating satisfaction in which all actual desires and all possible desires are brought to port, we are left gazing at an empty canvas framed by formulas; —unless, indeed, we are gifted with a poetic imagination by which we can paint the picture for ourselves.

* * * * *

[Coming now to the last alternative,] it is characteristic of living mind to be *for* some things and *against* others. This polarity is not reducible to that between "yes" and "no" in the logical or in the purely cognitive sense, because one can say "yes" with reluctance or be glad to say "no." To be "for" or "against" is to view with favor or disfavor; it is a bias of the subject toward or away from. It implies, as we shall see more clearly in the sequel, a tendency to create or conserve, or an opposite tendency to prevent or destroy. This duality appears in many forms, such as liking and disliking, desire and aversion, will and refusal, or seeking and avoiding. It is to this all-pervasive characteristic of the motor-affective life, this *state, act, attitude or disposition of favor or disfavor,* to which we propose to give the name of *"interest."*

This, then, we take to be the original source and constant feature of all value. That which is an object of interest is *eo ipso* invested with value. Any object, whatever it be, acquires value when any interest, whatever it be, is taken in it; just as anything whatsoever becomes a target when anyone whosoever aims at it. . . . In short, interest being constitutive of value in the basic sense, theory of value will take this as its point of departure and center of reference; and will classify and systematize values in terms of the different forms which interests and their objects may be found to assume. . . .

It may appear surprising that a doctrine so familiar, if not banal, as that just stated, should have received so little authoritative support. Rarity is the last thing that would have been expected of it, either by its advocates who regard it as sound common-sense, or by its opponents who regard it as vulgar error. It is none the less a fact that this doctrine has rarely been explicitly avowed by philosophers. The reasons for this fact are extremely illuminating, and although they have been repeatedly alluded to, a brief recapitulation of them at this point will serve to sharpen the meaning of our definition.

All of these reasons are traceable to an imperfect conception of the problem itself. Theory of value in the contemporary sense has asked a new question, to which none of the traditional philosophical doctrines is precisely relevant. It may, perhaps, be fair to say that this question has been *tacitly* asked and answered; but it is evident that a tacit answer cannot be quoted. This new question, is the question, *In what consists value in the generic sense?* It is because neither philosophy nor commonsense has ordinarily been explicitly and unambiguously concerned with this question that so few explicit and unambiguous answers to it can be found. Most theories of value are intended not as answers to this question, but as answers to some one or more of the following questions: What is uniquely valuable? What is superlatively valuable? What is reflectively or consciously valuable? The history of thought abounds in opinions which identify value with interest, but in nearly all cases these opinions are formulated in terms of one of these questions, and cannot, therefore, be cited as generic definitions of value in the sense here proposed. . . .

How is the view here proposed to be proved? What is the evidence upon which it rests?

In the first place, we have reached it by a process of systematic elimination. We have first examined and eliminated those views which affirm value to be indefinable, or to be definable independently of interest. If value cannot be successfully identified or defined without reference to interest, then we must incorporate interest into our definition. We have next examined those views which relate value to interest in some qualified and exclusive sense; first, those views which have proposed to qualify and limit the object of interest; second, those views which have proposed to qualify and limit the act or state of interest itself. The result has been to exhibit a variety of values all having the common generic character of being "object-of-interest." We have thus been led to define value as the peculiar relation between any interest and its object; or that special character of an object which consists in the fact that interest is taken in it. We are now justified in framing this hypothesis as a last remaining alternative. There is a certain presumption in favor of this remaining alternative not only because of the elimination of the others, but also because these have all betrayed a common tendency. They have not only through their failure left the field clear for our definition of value, but they have *pointed* to that definition and incidentally argued in its support.

A certain positive plausibility is given to this hypothesis by the fact that in order to create values where they did not exist before it seems to be sufficient to introduce an interest. The silence of the desert is without value, until some wanderer finds it lonely and terrifying; the cataract, until some human sensibility finds it sublime, or until it is harnessed to satisfy human needs. Natural substances or the by-products of manufacture are without value until a use is found for them, whereupon their value may increase to any degree of preciousness according to the eagerness with which they are coveted. There is no entity that can be named that does not, in the very naming of it, take on a certain value through the fact that it is selected by the cognitive purpose of some interested mind. As interests grow and expand, multiplying in number and extending their radius through experience and imagination, the store of cosmic values is enriched and diversified.

* * * * *

The problem to which we now turn is one which has been often encountered. What is that condition of an object in virtue of which it may be said to be better (or worse) than another object, or the best (or worst) among several objects, and which would therefore render true a judgment of comparative or superlative value? . . . A survey of the various notions which have been employed for the critical comparison of values [leads us to conclude that all others reduce to three:] *intensity, preference* and *inclusiveness*. . . .

There is, it would appear, a sense in which the interest in a given object may be said to be more or less intense at different times, and which may be extended to cover the case in which one of two interests (differing either subjectively or objectively) is more intense than the other. In this sense intensity means degree of arousal, or the extent to which the organism as a whole is acting under the control of the interest. It is implied in this view that all fully aroused interests are of equal intensity.

What is the sense in which one of two objects is better than the other when they are objects of the same interest? Assuming that the interest is capable of being fully aroused by either of the two, does it mean anything to say that the direction of the interest to another object *would* be better than its direction to the present object? The factor of intensity is here eliminated, and the answer must be looked for in terms of our standard of *preference*. . . .

The important feature of preference is that it arranges the objects of any given interest in an order, relatively to one another, and in a manner that cannot be reduced either to the intensity or to the inclusiveness of the interest. This order of preference has its own characteristic magnitudes, which determine comparative values. . . .

[But it is impossible to make] a preferential comparison of the values which objects derive from different orders of preference. Such comparison would depend upon establishing a prior term of equality, but this in turn would require a through and through coincidence between the two orders. It follows that two orders of preference are commensurable only when two interests prefer the same objects in the same order. . . .

When, in other words, all cognitive differences have been eliminated or discounted, and two preferences still conflict, we are confronted with two undebatable facts both of which have to be accepted by both parties, the facts, namely, that whereas in the last analysis I prefer b to a, you prefer a to b. Such a conflict of preference, like conflict of interest, is a datum of value and an instance of its ultimate and irreducible relativity. . . .

Preference can be standardized only by a common order, but such community of preference already creates a situation to which the standard of inclusiveness is applicable. Interest is added to interest in the same objects, and these objects derive augmented value from the summation of the interests taken in them. . . .

The explicit acceptance of this standard by recent philosophers, is best illustrated by the following passage from William James:

> That act must be the best act, accordingly, which makes for the *best whole,* in the sense of awakening the least sum of dissatisfactions. In the casuistic scale, therefore, those ideals must be written highest which *prevail at the least cost,* or by whose realization the least possible number of other ideals are destroyed. Since victory and defeat there must be, the victory to be philosophically prayed for is that of the more inclusive side,—of the side which even in the hour of triumph will to some degree do justice to the ideals in which the vanquished party's interests lay. The course of history is nothing but the story of men's struggles from generation to generation to find the more and more inclusive order. *Invent some manner* of realizing your own ideals which will also satisfy the alien demands,—that and that only is the path of peace.

What, more exactly, does such a standard mean and imply?

There is a fundamental characteristic of the principle of inclusiveness which must be held clearly in mind. This principle is applicable only to interests or aggregates of interests that are related as *whole and part.* The *whole* is greater than its part because it contains the part, *and* something besides; thus exceeding the part, *whatever otherwise be the magnitude of either whole or part.* . . .

We have seen that the standard of preference takes precedence of the standard of intensity, meaning that in order to create values that may be said to be roundly better, in terms of both preference and intensity, it is necessary to proceed from preference to intensity rather than in the reverse direction. There is a similar order of precedence as between preference and inclusiveness. This results from the fact that the principle of inclusiveness requires that interests shall be rendered harmonious. Their prior exercise of preference tends to preclude this reconciliation, while, on the other hand, reconciliation permits the subsequent exercise of preference. The question hinges on the application of judgments of comparative value to conflicting interests, that is, to interests that are incompatible, opposed or antagonistic.

It is the conflict of interest which most commonly provokes a judgment of comparative value, and provides the most important occasions for the application of such a judgment. The gravest choices of life are not those in which good is balanced against evil, or more good against less good, or less evil against more evil, but those in which one mixture of good and evil is balanced against another. There is good and evil in both alternatives, but there is held to be a larger net gain or a smaller net loss in the one than in the other. This occurs both in personal judgments in which a lesser interest is sacrificed to a greater, and in social judgments where one man's suffering is held to be less than the happiness of the community. What judgment of better and worse is strictly applicable in situations of this type? . . .

There remains only one comparative judgment of better or worse which is free from this relativity, and which points the way to a resolution of the conflict, namely, the judgment that the satisfaction of both interests *would be* better than the defeat of either. This is a hypothetical application of the standard of inclusiveness. To employ the language of whole and part, that which contains the good relative to both interests contains the good relative to each, together with some increment from the other; and is therefore better than that which contains the good of one to the exclusion of the good of the other. . . .

The case of Jack Sprat and his wife affords an illustration which shows that preferential disagreement may yield a sum of goods, while preferential agreements often lead to conflict. Where Jack Sprats and their wives both prefer fat, or both prefer lean, situations often develop in which one interest is served only at the expense of the other. Preferential agreement is better than preferential disagreement, then, only so far as the former escapes, while the latter causes, a conflict of interest. But may not preferential disagreement be better than preferential agreement on the same ground? The answer lies in the fact that preferential disagreement is harmonious either through the happy accident of compatibility, or through a more fundamental *agreement*. The only way in which interests can be so determined as to *guarantee* their harmony, is to be governed by some comprehensive order of preference within which their disagreements may be provided for and rendered innocuous.

Since it is only in so far as all interests are brought within one harmonious system under a universal order of preference that they can be rendered all-commensurable, it follows that such all-commensurability is best only as judged by the standard of inclusiveness. This standard thus takes precedence of the others as being the only standard by which the standardization of values can itself be justified. This greatest good will be the object of an all-inclusive and harmonious system of interests.

QUESTIONS FOR DISCUSSION

1. Can you identify an ethical theory previously discussed in this chapter with each of the four value-interest relationships discussed by Perry? Are his criticisms telling?
2. Review again the argument from the principle of "inclusiveness" to that of "harmoniousness." Do interests have to be harmonized in order to be made more inclusive?
3. Do you think Perry's attempt to make all kinds of value—i.e. ethical, economic, aesthetic—subdivisions of one central concept, interest, a worthwhile way to approach value theory, or do these aspects of life have little, if anything, in common?

READINGS FOR IMMEDIATE REFERENCE

Perry, Ralph Barton. *General Theory of Value.* Cambridge: Harvard University Press, 1926, Chapters 1-5, 20-22.

———. *The Moral Economy.* New York: Scribners, 1909.

Monson, Charles H., Jr. "Perry's Two Theories of Value," *Ethics,* Vol. LIX (January, 1959), 125-133.

Zink, Sidney. "The Principles of Inclusiveness and Harmony in Perry's Theory of Value," *Philosophical Review,* LVIII (March, 1944), 184-189.

REFERENCES FOR COMPREHENSIVE KNOWLEDGE

Perry, Ralph Barton. *The Approach to Philosophy.* New York: Scribners, 1905.

———. *The Present Conflict of Ideals.* New York: Longmans, Green, 1918.

———. *Puritanism and Democracy.* New York: Vanguard Press, 1944.

———. *Realms of Value.* Cambridge: Harvard University Press, 1954.

———. *Shall Not Perish.* New York: Vanguard Press, 1940.

———. *The Thought and Character of William James.* Boston: Little, Brown, 1935.

Also see:

Parker, Dewitt. *Human Values.* New York: Harper, 1931.

VIII. JOHN DEWEY

Probably the most famous and influential of American philosophers, Dewey was born in Burlington, Vermont, in 1859. He graduated from the University of Vermont in 1879 and received his Ph.D. from Johns Hopkins in 1884, one of the first American graduate students to receive all of his training in America. Following graduation, he taught philosophy at the Universities of Minnesota and Michigan, and then went to the University of Chicago in 1894 where he established an experimental school and began working out the "experimental logic" which, in time, became the foundation for his form of pragmatic philosophy, Instrumentalism. In 1904, he went to Columbia University where his interests in learning theory and philosophy combined with the beliefs and influence of William Kilpatrick of Teacher's College to exert a profound and lasting influence on American education. However, Dewey's interests were wider than educational practice, for in addition to his voluminous writings (for example, he published seven major works during his eighth decade) he taught in China for two years, undertook an evaluation of Turkey's educational system, headed a commission investigating Stalin's charges against Trotsky, and traveled and lectured throughout the world. He retired in 1930, but continued to write and speak and live the belief that the philosopher's task is to help people find reasonable solutions to the problems they face. He died in 1952 at the age of ninety-three.

One of Dewey's fundamental beliefs concerns the role and function of philosophy itself, and in this selection he speaks of what philosophical moral theory can and cannot do in helping to solve moral problems. Notice the reasons he gives for criticizing traditional moral philosophy, and also his conception of what philosophy's proper function is, together with its advantages.

Ethical Theory as Inquiry[1]

The impact of the alteration in methods of scientific thinking upon moral ideas is, in general, obvious. Goods, ends are multiplied. Rules are softened into principles, and principles are modified into methods of understanding. Ethical theory began among the Greeks as an attempt to find a regulation for the conduct of life which should have a rational basis and purpose instead of being derived from custom. But reason as a substitute for custom was under the obligation of supplying objects and laws as fixed as those of custom had been. Ethical theory ever since has been singularly hypnotized by the notion that its business is to discover some final end or some ultimate and supreme law. This is the common element among the diversity of theories. Some have held that the end is loyalty or obedience to a higher power or authority; and they have variously found this higher principle in Divine Will, the will of the secular ruler, the maintenance of institutions in which the purpose of superiors is embodied, and the rational consciousness of duty. But they have differed from one another because there was one point in which they were agreed: a single and final source of law. Others have asserted that it is impossible to locate morality in conformity to law-giving power, and that it must be sought in ends that are good. And some have sought the good in self-realization, some in holiness, some in happiness, some in the greatest possible aggregate of pleasures. And yet these schools have agreed on the assumption that there is a single, fixed and final good. They have been able to dispute with one another only because of their common premise.

The question arises whether the way out of the confusion and conflict is not to go to the root of the matter by questioning this common element. Is not the belief in the single, final and ultimate an intellectual product of that feudal organization which is disappearing historically and of that belief in a bounded, ordered cosmos, wherein rest is higher than motion, which has disappeared from natural science? It has been repeatedly suggested that the present limit of intellectual reconstruction lies in the fact that it has not as yet been seriously applied in the moral and social disciplines. Would not this further application demand precisely that we advance to a belief in a plurality of changing, moving individualized goods and ends, and to a belief that principles, criteria, laws are intellectual instruments for analyzing individual or unique situations?

The blunt assertion that every moral situation is a unique situation having its own irreplaceable good may seem not merely blunt but preposterous. For the established tradition teaches that it

[1] From *Reconstruction in Philosophy* by John Dewey. New York: Henry Holt and Co., copyright 1920, Chapter 7. Reprinted by permission.

is precisely the irregularity of special cases which makes necessary the guidance of conduct by universals, and that the essence of the virtuous disposition is willingness to subordinate every particular case to adjudication by a fixed principle. It would then follow that submission of a generic end and law to determination by the concrete situation entails complete confusion and unrestrained licentiousness. Let us, however, follow the pragmatic rule, and in order to discover the meaning of the idea ask for its consequences. Then it surprisingly turns out that the primary significance of the unique and morally ultimate character of the concrete situation is to transfer the weight and burden of morality to intelligence. It does not destroy responsibility; it only locates it. A moral situation is one in which judgment and choice are required antecedently to overt action. The practical meaning of the situation—that is to say the action needed to satisfy it—is not self-evident. It has to be searched for. There are conflicting desires and alternative apparent goods. What is needed is to find the right course of action, the right good. Hence, inquiry is exacted: observation of the detailed makeup of the situation; analysis into its diverse factors; clarification of what is obscure; discounting of the more insistent and vivid traits; tracing the consequences of the various modes of action that suggest themselves; regarding the decision reached as hypothetical and tentative until the anticipated or supposed consequences which led to its adoption have been squared with actual consequences. This inquiry is intelligence. . . .

More definitely, the transfer of the burden of the moral life from following rules or pursuing fixed ends over to the detection of the ills that need remedy in a special case and the formation of plans and methods for dealing with them, eliminates the causes which have kept moral theory controversial, and which have also kept it remote from helpful contact with the exigencies of practice. The theory of fixed ends inevitably leads thought into the bog of disputes that cannot be settled. If there is one *summum bonum,* or supreme end, what is it? To consider this problem is to place ourselves in the midst of controversies that are as acute now as they were two thousand years ago. Suppose we take a seemingly more empirical view, and say that while there is not a single end, there also are not as many as there are specific situations that require amelioration; but there are a number of such natural goods as health, wealth, honor, or good name, friendship, esthetic appreciation, learning and such moral goods as justice, temperance, benevolence, etc. What or who is to decide the right way when these ends conflict with one another, as they are sure to do? Shall we resort to the method that once brought such disrepute upon the whole business of ethics: Casuistry? Or shall we have recourse to what Bentham well called the *ipse dixit* method: the arbitrary preference of this or that person for this or that end? Or shall we be forced to arrange them all in an order of degrees from the highest good down to the least precious? Again we find ourselves in the middle of unreconciled disputes with no indication of the way out.

Meantime, the special moral perplexities where the aid of intelligence is required go unenlightened. We cannot seek or attain health, wealth, learning, justice or kindness in general. Action is always specific, concrete, individualized, unique. And consequently judgments as to acts to be performed must be similarly specific. To say that a man seeks health or justice is only to say that he seeks to live healthily or justly. These things, like truth, are adverbial. They are modifiers of action in special cases. How to live healthily or justly is a matter which differs with every person. It varies with his past experience, his opportunities, his temperamental and acquired weaknesses and abilities. Not man in general but a particular man suffering from some particular disability aims to live healthily, and consequently health cannot mean for him exactly what it means for any other mortal. Healthy living is not something to be attained by itself apart from other ways of living. A man needs to be healthy *in* his life, not apart from it, and what does life mean except the aggregate of his pursuits and activities? A man who aims at health as a distinct end becomes a valetudinarian, or a fanatic, or a mechanical performer of exercises, or an athlete so one-sided that his pursuit of bodily development injures his heart. When the endeavor to realize a so-called end does not temper and color all other activities, life is portioned out into strips and fractions. Certain acts and times are devoted to getting health, others to cultivating religion, others to seeking learning, to being a good citizen, a devotee of fine art and so on. This is the only logical alternative to subordinating all aims to the accomplishment of one alone—fanaticism.

This is out of fashion at present, but who can say how much of distraction and dissipation in life, and how much of its hard and narrow rigidity is the outcome of men's failure to realize that each situation has its own unique end and that the whole personality should be concerned with it? Surely, once more, what a man needs is to live healthily, and this result so affects all the activities of his life that it cannot be set up as a separate and independent good.

* * * * *

Moral goods and ends exist only when something has to be done. The fact that something has to be done proves that there are deficiencies, evils in the existent situation. This ill is just the specific ill that it is. It never is an exact duplicate of anything else. Consequently the good of the situation has to be discovered, projected and attained on the basis of the exact defect and trouble to be rectified. It cannot intelligently be injected into the situation from without. Yet it is the part of wisdom to compare different cases, to gather together the ills from which humanity suffers, and to generalize the corresponding goods into classes. Health, wealth, industry, temperance, amiability, courtesy, learning, esthetic capacity, initiative, courage, patience, enterprise, thoroughness and a multitude of other generalized ends are acknowledged as goods. But the value of this systematization is intellectual or analytic. Classifications *suggest* possible traits to be on the lookout for in studying a particular case; they suggest methods of action to be tried in removing the inferred causes of ill. They are tools of insight; their value is in promoting an individualized response in the individual situation.

Morals is not a catalogue of acts nor a set of rules to be applied like drugstore prescriptions or cook-book recipes. The need in morals is for specific methods of inquiry and of contrivance: Methods of inquiry to locate difficulties and evils; methods of contrivance to form plans to be used as working hypotheses in dealing with them. And the pragmatic import of the logic of individualized situations, each having its own irreplaceable good and principle, is to transfer the attention of theory from preoccupation with general conceptions to the problem of developing effective methods of inquiry.

Two ethical consequences of great moment should be remarked. The belief in fixed values has bred a division of ends into intrinsic and instrumental, of those that are really worthwhile in themselves and those that are of importance only as means to intrinsic goods. Indeed, it is often thought to be the very beginning of wisdom, of moral discrimination, to make this distinction. Dialectically, the distinction is interesting and seems harmless. But carried into practice it has an import that is tragic. Historically, it has been the source and justification of a hard and fast difference between ideal goods on one side and material goods on the other. So-called intrinsic goods are divorced from those interests of daily life which because of their constancy and urgency form the preoccupation of the great mass. . . .

No one can possibly estimate how much of the obnoxious materialism and brutality of our economic life is due to the fact that economic ends have been regarded as *merely* instrumental. When they are recognized to be as intrinsic and final in their place as any others, then it will be seen that they are capable of idealization, and that if life is to be worthwhile, they must acquire ideal and intrinsic value. Esthetic, religious and other "ideal" ends are now thin and meagre or else idle and luxurious because of the separation from "instrumental" or economic ends. Only in connection with the latter can they be woven into the texture of daily life and made substantial and pervasive. . . .

The other generic change lies in doing away once and for all with the traditional distinction between moral goods, like the virtues, and natural goods like health, economic security, art, science and the like. The point of view under discussion is not the only one which has deplored this rigid distinction and endeavored to abolish it. Some schools have even gone so far as to regard moral excellencies, qualities of character, as of value only because they promote natural goods. But the experimental logic when carried into morals makes every quality that is judged to be good according as it contributes to amelioration of existing ills. And in so doing, it enforces the moral meaning of natural science. When all is said and done in criticism of present social deficiencies, one may well wonder whether the root difficulty does not lie in the separation of natural and moral science. When physics, chemistry, biology, medicine, contribute to the detection of concrete human woes and to the development of plans for remedying them and relieving the human estate, they become moral; they become part of the apparatus of moral inquiry or science. The latter then loses its peculiar flavor of the didactic and pedantic; its ultra-moralistic and hortatory tone. It loses its thinness and shrillness as well as its vagueness. It gains agencies that are efficacious. But the gain is not confined to the side of moral science. Natural science loses its divorce from humanity; it becomes itself humanistic in quality. It is something to be pursued not in a technical and specialized way for what is called truth for its own sake, but with the sense of its social bearing, its intellectual indispensableness. It is technical only in the sense that it provides the technique of social and moral engineering. . . .

As long as ends are not thought of as individualized according to specific needs and opportunities, the mind will be content with abstractions, and the adequate stimulus to the moral or social use of natural science and historical data will be lacking. But when attention is concentrated upon the diversified concretes, recourse to all intellectual materials needed to clear up the special cases will be imperative. At the same time that morals are made to focus in intelligence, things intellectual are moralized. The vexatious and wasteful conflict between naturalism and humanism is terminated.

These general considerations may be amplified. First: Inquiry, discovery takes the same place in morals that they have come to occupy in sciences of nature. Validation, demonstration becomes experimental, a matter of consequences. Reason, always an honorific term in ethics, becomes actualized in the methods by which the needs and conditions, the obstacles and resources, of situations are scrutinized in detail, and intelligent plans of improvement are worked out. Remote and abstract generalities promote jumping at conclusions, "anticipations of nature." Bad consequences are then deplored as due to natural perversity and untoward fate. But shifting the issue to analysis of a specific situation makes inquiry obligatory and alert observation of consequences imperative. No past decision nor old principle can ever be wholly relied upon to justify a course of action. No amount of pains taken in forming a purpose in a definite case is final; the consequences of its adoption must be carefully noted, and a purpose held only as a working hypothesis until results confirm its rightness. Mistakes are no longer either mere unavoidable accidents to be mourned or moral sins to be expiated and forgiven. They are lessons in wrong methods of using intelligence and instructions as to a better course in the future. They are indications of the need of revision, development, readjustment. Ends grow, standards of judgment are improved. Man is under just as much obligation to develop his most advanced standards and ideals as to use conscientiously those which he already possesses. Moral life is protected from falling into formalism and rigid repetition. It is rendered flexible, vital, growing.

In the second place, every case where moral action is required becomes of equal moral importance and urgency with every other. If the need and deficiencies of a specific situation indicate improvement of health as the end and good, then for that situation health is the ultimate and supreme good. It is no means to something else. It is a final and intrinsic value. The same thing is true of improvement of economic status, of making a living, of attending to business and family demands—all of the things which under the sanction of fixed ends have been rendered of secondary and merely instrumental value, and so relatively base and unimportant. Anything that in a given situation is an end and good at all is of equal worth, rank and dignity with every other good of any other situation, and deserves the same intelligent attention.

We note thirdly the effect in destroying the roots of Phariseeism. The conception which looks for the end of action within the circumstances of the actual situation will not have the same measure of judgment for all cases. When one factor of the situation is a person of trained mind and large resources, more will be expected than a person of backward mind and uncultured experience. The absurdity of applying the same standard of moral judgment to savage peoples that is used with civilized will be apparent. No individual or group will be judged by whether they come up to or fall short of some fixed result, but by the direction in which they are moving. The bad man is the man who no matter how good he *has* been is beginning to deteriorate, to grow less good. The good man is the man who no matter how morally unworthy he has been is moving to become better. Such a conception makes one severe in judging himself and humane in judging others. It excludes that arrogance which always accompanies judgment based on degree of approximation to fixed ends.

In the fourth place, the process of growth, of improvement and progress, rather than the static outcome and result, becomes the significant thing. Not health as an end fixed once and for all, but the needed improvement in health—a continual process—is the end and good. The end is no longer a terminus or limit to be reached. It is the active process of transforming the existent situation. Not perfection as a final goal, but the ever-enduring process of perfecting, maturing, refining is the aim of living. Honesty, industry, temperance, justice, like health, wealth and learning are not goods to be possessed as they would be if they expressed fixed ends to be attained. They are directions of change in the quality of experience. Growth itself is the only moral "end."

* * * * *

If a few words are added upon the topic of education, it is only for the sake of suggesting that the educative process is all one with the moral process, since the latter is a continuous passage of experience from worse to better. Education has been traditionally thought of as preparation: as learning, acquiring certain things because they will later be useful. The end is remote, and education is getting ready, is a preliminary to something more important to happen later on. Childhood is only a preparation for adult life, and adult life for another life. Always the future, not the present, has been the significant thing in education. Education is thought of also as something needed by some human beings merely because of their dependence upon others. We are born ignorant, unversed, unskilled, immature, and consequently in a state of social dependence. Instruction, training, moral discipline are processes by which the mature, the adult, gradually raise the helpless to the point where they can look out for themselves. The business of childhood is to grow into the independence of adulthood by means of the guidance of those who have already attained it. Thus, the process of education as the main business of life ends when the young have arrived at emancipation from social dependence.

These two ideas, generally assumed but rarely explicitly reasoned out, contravene the conception that growing, or the continuous reconstruction of experience, is the only end. If at whatever period we choose to take a person, he is still in process of growth, then education is not, save as a by-product, a preparation for something coming later. Getting from the present the degree and kind of growth there is in it is education. This is a constant function, independent of age. The best thing that can be said about any special process of education, like that of the formal school period, is that it renders its subject capable of further education: more sensitive to conditions of growth and more able to take advantage of them. Acquisition of skill, possession of knowledge, attainment of culture are not ends: they are marks of growth and means to its continuing. The idea of education as preparation, and of adulthood as a fixed limit of growth, are two sides of the same obnoxious untruth. . . .

When the identity of the moral process with the processes of specific growth is realized, the more conscious and formal education of childhood will be seen to be the most economical and efficient means of social advance and reorganization, and it will also be evident that the test of all the institutions of adult life is their effect in furthering continued education. Government, business, art, religion, all social institutions have a meaning, a purpose. That purpose is to set free and to develop the capacities of human individuals without respect to race, sex, class or economic status. And this is all one with saying that the test of their value is the extent to which they educate every individual into the full stature of his possibility. Democracy has many meanings, but if it has a moral meaning, it is found in resolving that the supreme test of all political institutions and industrial arrangements shall be the contribution they make to the all around growth of every member of society.

QUESTIONS FOR DISCUSSION

1. Is Dewey correct in saying that preceding ethical theorists have been concerned with finding a *summum bonum*? Are his criticisms of this attempt justified?
2. What alternative does he propose? Do you think it is better than what he rejects? How can you decide?
3. On the basis of your reading what kind of curriculum and what methods of teaching would characterize Deweyan educational practice?

READINGS FOR IMMEDIATE REFERENCE

Dewey, John. *Human Nature and Conduct*. New York: Henry Holt, 1922, Introduction and Parts III and IV.

———. *Logic: The Theory of Inquiry*. New York: Henry Holt, 1938, Chapters 1-7, 24.

———. *Reconstruction in Philosophy*. New York: Henry Holt, 1920, Chapters 1, 5, 7, 8.

Mead, George Herbert. *Mind, Self and Society*. Chicago: University of Chicago Press, 1934, Chapters 28, 29.

REFERENCES FOR COMPREHENSIVE KNOWLEDGE

Dewey, John. *A Common Faith*. New Haven: Yale University Press, 1934.

———. *Democracy and Education*. New York: Macmillan, 1917.

———. *Ethics*, rev. ed. New York: Henry Holt, 1932.

———. *Experience and Nature*. New York: W. W. Norton, 1929.

———. *How We Think*, rev. ed. Boston: D. C. Heath, 1933.

———. *The Quest for Certainty*. New York: G. P. Putnam, 1929.

Feldman, W. T. *The Philosophy of John Dewey*. New York: Henry Holt, 1956. A vigorously critical treatment.

Geiger, George. *John Dewey in Perspective*. New York: Oxford University Press, 1958. A sympathetic restatement and defense of Dewey's main theses.

Schilpp, Paul A. *The Philosophy of John Dewey*. New York: Tudor Publishing Co., 1939. A collection of analyses by other philosophers together with Dewey's replies.

Also see:

Childs, John. *American Pragmatism and Education*. New York: Henry Holt, 1956.

Hook, Sidney. *John Dewey: An Intellectual Portrait*. New York: John Day, 1939.

Thayer, H. S. *The Logic of Pragmatism*. New York: Humanities Press, 1952.

White, Morton. *The Origins of Dewey's Instrumentalism*. New York: Columbia University Press, 1943.

IX. ALFRED J. AYER

Ayer was born in England in 1910 and was educated at Eton College. He became a student at Christ Church, Oxford in 1929 where, after receiving his degree in 1932, he stayed on as a lecturer. He also held the post of Research Student until 1944 when he was elected a Fellow and subsequently Dean of Wadham College, Oxford. In 1936, he published *Language, Truth and Logic,* a book once described as "a young man's book, lively, uncompromising, belligerent—indeed, the most readily accessible defense of classical, phenomenalistic, logical positivism." During World War II he was a Captain in the Welsh Guards and an attaché to the British Embassy in Paris in 1945. In 1946 he was appointed Grote Professor of Mind and Logic at the University of London, and in 1959 he returned to Oxford. His later philosophical work has been devoted chiefly to problems in the theory of knowledge.

Now that you have read a number of ethical theories you should be in a position to evaluate the criticism of these theories made by a leading philosopher from the Logical Positivist school of thought. Notice the four activities Ayer says have characterized traditional philosophical thought, and why he believes philosophers have little that is unique to add to them. According to Ayer, what are philosophers doing when they make ethical theories? Is he correct?

A Positivistic View of Ethical Theory[1]

The ordinary system of ethics, as elaborated in the works of ethical philosophers, is very far from being a homogeneous whole. Not only is it apt to contain pieces of metaphysics, and analyses of non-ethical concepts: its actual ethical contents are themselves of very different kinds. We may divide them, indeed, into four main classes. There are, first of all, propositions which express definitions of ethical terms, or judgments about the legitimacy or possibility of certain definitions. Secondly, there are propositions describing the phenomena of moral experience, and their causes. Thirdly, there are exhorta-

[1] From *Language, Truth and Logic* by Alfred J. Ayer. London: Victor Gollancz Co., Ltd., 1936. Published by Dover Publications, Inc., New York 14, N. Y. and reprinted through permission of the publisher.

tions to moral virtue. And, lastly, there are actual ethical judgments. It is unfortunately the case that the distinction between these four classes, plain as it is, is commonly ignored by ethical philosophers; with the result that it is often very difficult to tell from their works what it is that they are seeking to discover or prove.

In fact, it is easy to see that only the first of our four classes, namely that which comprises the propositions relating to the definitions of ethical terms, can be said to constitute ethical philosophy. The propositions which describe the phenomena of moral experience, and their causes, must be assigned to the science of psychology, or sociology. The exhortations to moral virtue are not propositions at all, but ejaculations or commands which are designed to provoke the reader to action of a certain sort. Accordingly, they do not belong to any branch of philosophy or science. As for the expressions of ethical judgments, we have not yet determined how they should be classified. But inasmuch as they are certainly neither definitions nor comments upon definitions, nor quotations, we may say decisively that they do not belong to ethical philosophy. A strictly philosophical treatise on ethics should therefore make no ethical pronouncements. But it should, by giving an analysis of ethical terms, show what is the category to which all such pronouncements belong. And this is what we are now about to do.

A question which is often discussed by ethical philosophers is whether it is possible to find definitions which would reduce all ethical terms to one or two fundamental terms. But this question, though it undeniably belongs to ethical philosophy, is not relevant to our present enquiry. We are not now concerned to discover which term, within the sphere of ethical terms, is to be taken as fundamental; whether, for example, "good" can be defined in terms of "right" or "right" in terms of "good," or both in terms of "value." What we are interested in is the possibility of reducing the whole sphere of ethical terms to non-ethical terms. We are enquiring whether statements of ethical value can be translated into statements of empirical fact.

That they can be so translated is the contention of those ethical philosophers who are commonly called subjectivists, and of those who are known as utilitarians. For the utilitarian defines the rightness of actions, and the goodness of ends, in terms of the pleasure, or happiness, or satisfaction, to which they give rise; the subjectivist, in terms of the feelings of approval which a certain person, or group of people, has towards them. Each of these types of definition makes moral judgments into a sub-class of psychological or sociological judgments; and for this reason they are very attractive to us. For, if either was correct, it would follow that ethical assertions were not generically different from the factual assertions which are ordinarily contrasted with them; and the account which we have already given of empirical hypotheses would apply to them also.

Nevertheless we shall not adopt either a subjectivist or a utilitarian analysis of ethical terms. We reject the subjectivist view that to call an action right, or a thing good, is to say that it is generally approved of, because it is not self-contradictory to assert that some actions which are generally approved of are not right, or that some things which are generally approved of are not good. And we reject the alternative subjectivist view that a man who asserts that a certain action is right, or that a certain thing is good, is saying that he himself approves of it, on the ground that a man who confessed that he sometimes approved of what was bad or wrong would not be contradicting himself. And a similar argument is fatal to utilitarianism. We cannot agree that to call an action right is to say that of all the actions possible in the circumstances it would cause, or be likely to cause, the greatest happiness, or the greatest balance of pleasure over pain, or the greatest balance of satisfied over unsatisfied desire, because we find that it is not self-contradictory to say that it is sometimes wrong to perform the action which would actually or probably cause the greatest happiness, or the greatest balance of pleasure over pain, or of satisfied over unsatisfied desire. And since it is not self-contradictory to say that some pleasant things are not good, or that some bad things are desired, it cannot be the case that the sentence "x is good" is equivalent to "x is pleasant," or to "x is desired." And to every other variant of utilitarianism with which I am acquainted the same objection can be made. And therefore we should, I think, conclude that the validity of ethical judgments is not determined by the felicific tendencies of actions, any more than by the nature of people's feelings; but that it must be regarded as "absolute" or "intrinsic," and not empirically calculable.

If we say this, we are not, of course, denying that it is possible to invent a language in which all ethical symbols are definable in non-ethical terms, or even that it is desirable to invent such a language and adopt it in place of our own; what we are denying is that the suggested reduction of ethical to non-ethical statements is consistent with the conventions of our actual language. That is, we reject utilitarianism and subjectivism, not as proposals to replace our existing ethical notions by new ones, but as analyses of our existing ethical notions. Our contention is simply that, in our language, sentences which contain normative ethical symbols are not equivalent to sentences which express psychological propositions, or indeed empirical propositions of any kind. . . .

In admitting that normative ethical concepts are irreducible to empirical concepts, we seem to be leaving the way clear for the "absolutist" view of ethics —that is, the view that statements of value are not controlled by observation, as ordinary empirical propositions are, but only by a mysterious "intellectual intuition." A feature of this theory, which is seldom recognized by its advocates, is that it makes statements of value unverifiable. For it is notorious that what seems intuitively certain to one person may seem doubtful, or even false, to another. So that unless it is possible to provide some criterion by which one may decide between conflicting intuitions, a mere appeal to intuition is worthless as a test of a proposition's validity. But in the case of moral judgments, no such criterion can be given. Some moralists claim to settle the matter by saying that they "know" that their own moral judgments are correct. But such an assertion is of purely psychological interest, and has not the slightest tendency to prove the validity of any moral judgment. For dissentient moralists may equally well "know" that their ethical views are correct. And, as far as subjective certainty goes, there will be nothing to choose between them. When such differences of opinion arise in connection with an ordinary empirical proposition, one may attempt to resolve them by referring to, or actually carrying out, some relevant empirical test. But with regard to ethical statements, there is, on the "absolutist" or "intuitionist" theory, no relevant empirical test. We are therefore justified in saying that on this theory ethical statements are held to be unverifiable. They are, of course, also held to be genuine synthetic propositions.

Considering the use which we have made of the principle that a synthetic proposition is significant only if it is empirically verifiable, it is clear that the acceptance of an "absolutist" theory of ethics would undermine the whole of our main argument. And as we have already rejected the "naturalistic" theories which are commonly supposed to provide the only alternative to "absolutism" in ethics, we seem to have reached a difficult position. We shall meet the difficulty by showing that the correct treatment of ethical statements is afforded by a third theory, which is wholly compatible with our radical empiricism.

We begin by admitting that the fundamental ethical concepts are unanalyzable, inasmuch as there is no criterion by which one can test the validity of the judgments in which they occur. So far we are in agreement with the absolutists. But, unlike the absolutists, we are able to give an explanation of this fact about ethical concepts. We say that the reason why they are unanalyzable is that they are mere pseudo-concepts. The presence of an ethical symbol in a proposition adds nothing to its factual content. Thus if I say to someone, "You acted wrongly in stealing that money," I am not stating anything more than if I had simply said, "You stole that money." In adding that this action is wrong I am not making any further statement about it. I am simply evincing my moral disapproval of it. It is as if I had said, "You stole that money," in a peculiar tone of horror, or written it with the addition of some special exclamation marks. The tone, or the exclamation marks, adds nothing to the literal meaning of the sentence. It merely serves to show that the expression of it is attended by certain feelings in the speaker.

If now I generalize my previous statement and say, "Stealing money is wrong," I produce a sentence which has no factual meaning—that is, expresses no proposition which can be either true or false. It is as if I had written "Stealing money!!"—where the shape and thickness of the exclamation marks show, by a suitable convention, that a special sort of moral disapproval is the feeling which is being expressed. It is clear that there is nothing said here which can be true or false. Another man may disagree with me about the wrongness of stealing, in the sense that he may not have the same feelings about stealing as I have, and he may quarrel with me on account of my moral sentiments. But he cannot, strictly speaking, contradict me. For in saying that a certain type of action is right or wrong, I am not making any factual statement, not even a statement about my own state of mind. I am merely expressing certain moral sentiments. And the man who is ostensibly contradicting me is merely expressing his moral sentiments. So that there is plainly no sense in asking which of us is in the right. For neither of us is asserting a genuine proposition.

What we have just been saying about the symbol "wrong" applies to all normative ethical symbols. Sometimes they occur in sentences which record ordinary empirical facts besides expressing ethical feeling about those facts: sometimes they occur in sentences which simply express ethical feeling about a certain type of action, or situation, without making any statement of fact. But in every case in which one would commonly be said to be making an ethical judgment, the function of the relevant ethical word is purely "emotive." It is used to express feeling about certain objects, but not to make any assertion about them.

It is worth mentioning that ethical terms do not serve only to express feeling. They are calculated also to arouse feeling, and so to stimulate action. Indeed some of them are used in such a way as to give the sentences in which they occur the effect of commands. Thus the sentence "It is your duty to tell the truth" may be regarded both as the expression of a certain sort of ethical feeling about truthfulness and as the expression of the command "Tell the truth." The sentence "You ought to tell the truth" also involves the command "Tell the truth," but here the tone of the command is less emphatic. In the sentence "It is good to tell the truth" the command has become little more than a suggestion. And thus the "meaning" of the word "good," in its ethical usage, is differentiated from that of the word "duty" or the word "ought." In fact we may define the meaning of the various ethical words in terms both of the different feelings they are ordinarily taken to express, and also the different responses which they are calculated to provoke.

We can now see why it is impossible to find a criterion for determining the validity of ethical judgments. It is not because they have an "absolute" validity which is mysteriously independent of ordinary sense-experience, but because they have no objective validity whatsoever. If a sentence makes no statement at all, there is obviously no sense in asking whether what it says is true or false. And we have seen that sentences which simply express moral judgments do not say anything. They are pure expressions of feeling and as such do not come under the category of truth and falsehood. They are unverifiable for the same reason as a cry of pain or a word of command is unverifiable—because they do not express genuine propositions. . . .

It is plain that the conclusion that it is impossible to dispute about questions of value follows from our theory also. For as we hold that such sentences as "Thrift is a virtue" and "Thrift is a vice" do not express propositions at all, we clearly cannot hold that they express incompatible propositions. We must therefore admit that if Moore's argument really refutes the ordinary subjectivist theory, it also refutes ours. But, in fact, we deny that it does refute even the ordinary subjectivist theory. For we hold that one really never does dispute about questions of value.

This may seem, at first sight, to be a very paradoxical assertion. For we certainly do engage in disputes which are ordinarily regarded as disputes about questions of value. But, in all such cases, we find, if we consider the matter closely, that the dispute is not really about a question of value, but about a question of fact. When someone disagrees with us about the moral value of a certain action or type of action, we do admittedly resort to argument in order to win him over to our way of thinking. But we do not attempt to show by our arguments that he has the "wrong" ethical feeling towards a situation whose nature he has correctly apprehended. What we attempt to show is that he is mistaken about the facts of the case. We argue that he has misconceived the agent's motive: or that he has misjudged the effects of the action, or its probable effects in view of the agent's knowledge; or that he has failed to take into account the special circumstances in which the agent was placed. Or else we employ more general arguments about the effects which actions of a certain type tend to produce, or the qualities which are usually manifested in their performance. We do this in the hope that we have only to get our opponent to agree with us about the nature of the empirical facts for him to adopt the same moral attitude towards them as we do. And as the people with whom we argue have generally received the same moral education as ourselves, and live in the same social order, our expectation is usually justified. But if our opponent happens to have undergone a different process of moral "conditioning" from ourselves, so that, even when he acknowledges all the facts, he still disagrees with us about the moral value of the actions under discussion, then we abandon the attempt to convince him by argument. We say that it is impossible to argue with him because he has a distorted or undeveloped moral sense; which signifies merely that he employs a different set of values from our own. We feel that our own system of values is superior, and therefore speak in such derogatory terms of his. But we cannot bring forward any arguments to show that our system is superior. For our judgment that it is so is itself a judgment of value, and accordingly outside the scope of argument. It is because argument fails us when we come to deal with pure questions of value, as distinct from questions of fact, that we finally resort to mere abuse.

In short, we find that argument is possible on moral questions only if some system of values is presupposed. If our opponent concurs with us in expressing moral disapproval of all actions of a given type t, then we may get him to condemn a particular action A, by bringing forward arguments to show that A is of type t. For the question whether A does or does not belong to that type is a plain question of fact. Given that a man has certain moral principles, we argue that he must, in order to be consistent, react morally to certain things in a certain way. What we do not and cannot argue about is the validity of these moral principles. We merely praise or condemn them in the light of our own feelings.

If anyone doubts the accuracy of this account of moral disputes, let him try to construct even an imaginary argument on a question of value which does not reduce itself to an argument about a question of logic or about an empirical matter of fact. I am confident that he will not succeed in producing a single example. And if that is the case, he must allow that its involving the impossibility of purely ethical arguments is not, as Moore thought, a ground of objection to our theory, but rather a point in favor of it.

Having upheld our theory against the only criticism which appeared to threaten it, we may now use it to define the nature of all ethical enquiries. We find that ethical philosophy consists simply in saying that ethical concepts are pseudo-concepts and therefore unanalyzable. The further task of describing the different feelings that the different ethical terms are used to express, and the different reactions that they customarily provoke, is a task for the psychologist. There cannot be such a thing as ethical science, if by ethical science one means the elaboration of a "true" system of morals. For we have seen that, as ethical judgments are mere expressions of feeling, there can be no way of determining the validity of any ethical system, and, indeed, no sense in asking whether any such system is true. All that one may legitimately enquire in this connection is, what are the moral habits of a given person or group of people, and what causes them to have precisely those habits and feelings? And this enquiry falls wholly within the scope of the existing social sciences.

It appears, then, that ethics, as a branch of knowledge, is nothing more than a department of psychology and sociology. And in case anyone thinks that we are overlooking the existence of casuistry, we may remark that casuistry is not a science, but is a purely analytical investigation of the structure of a given moral system. In other words, it is an exercise in formal logic.

When one comes to pursue the psychological enquiries which constitute ethical science, one is immediately enabled to account for the Kantian and hedonistic theories of morals. For one finds that one of the chief causes of moral behavior is fear, both conscious and unconscious, of a god's displeasure, and fear of the enmity of society. And this, indeed, is the reason why moral precepts present themselves to some people as "categorical" commands. And one finds, also, that the moral code of a society is partly determined by the beliefs of that society concerning the conditions of its own happiness—or, in other words, that a society tends to encourage or discourage a given type of conduct by the use of moral sanctions according as it appears to promote or detract from the contentment of the society as a whole. And this is the reason why altruism is recommended in most moral codes and egotism condemned. It is from the observation of this connection between morality and happiness that hedonistic or eudæmonistic theories of morals ultimately spring, just as the moral theory of Kant is based on the fact, previously explained, that moral precepts have for some people the force of inexorable commands. As each of these theories ignores the fact which lies at the root of the other, both may be criticized as being onesided; but this is not the main objection to either of them. Their essential defect is that they treat propositions which refer to the causes and attributes of our ethical feelings as if they were definitions of ethical concepts. And thus they fail to recognize that ethical concepts are pseudo-concepts and consequently indefinable.

QUESTIONS FOR DISCUSSION

1. Apply Ayer's analysis of the fourfold activity of ethical theorists to the thought of Kant, Bentham or Aristotle and determine whether these theories are subject to his criticisms.
2. Why does Ayer reject "subjectivist" and "absolutist" definitions of ethical terms? Are his reasons good ones, in your judgment?
3. Do ethical terms express feelings? Do they do any more?
4. What does Ayer mean when he says: "One really never does dispute about questions of value." Do you agree?

READINGS FOR IMMEDIATE REFERENCE

Ayer, Alfred J. *Language, Truth and Logic.* New York: Dover Publications, 1936, Chapter 5, Preface to the second edition.

Baier, Kurt. *The Moral Point of View.* Ithaca: Cornell University Press, 1958, Parts 1, 8, 9.

Stevenson, Charles L. "The Emotive Meaning of Ethical Terms," *Mind,* XLVI (January, 1937), 14-31.

REFERENCES FOR COMPREHENSIVE KNOWLEDGE

Ayer, Alfred J. *Foundations of Empirical Knowledge.* New York: Macmillan, 1940.

———. *Philosophical Essays.* New York: Macmillan, 1954.

———. *The Problem of Knowledge.* London: Penguin Books, 1956.

———. *Thinking and Meaning.* London: H. K. Lewis, 1947.

Stevenson, Charles L. *Ethics and Language.* New Haven: Yale University Press, 1944. The emotive theory of ethics as stated by a leading American exponent.

Also see:

Ewing, A. C. *The Definition of Good.* New York: Macmillan, 1947.

Hare, R. M. *The Language of Morals.* New York: Oxford University Press, 1952.

Nowell-Smith, Patrick. *Ethics.* London: Penguin Books, 1954.

Schlick, Moritz. *Problems of Ethics.* New York: Prentice-Hall, 1939.

BIBLIOGRAPHY FOR CHAPTER THREE

READINGS FOR IMMEDIATE REFERENCE

Hospers, John. *Human Conduct.* New York: Harcourt, Brace and World, 1961, Chapters 1-7.

Sedgwick, Henry. *History of Ethics,* 6th ed. New York: Macmillan, 1931.

Wheelwright, Philip. *A Critical Introduction to Ethics,* 3rd ed. New York: Odyssey Press, 1959, Parts I, II.

REFERENCES FOR COMPREHENSIVE KNOWLEDGE

Broad, C. D. *Five Types of Ethical Theory.* London: Routledge and Kegan Paul, 1930. Spinoza, Butler, Hume, Kant, Hedonism. A standard text.

Toulmin, Stephen. *The Place of Reason in Ethics.* Cambridge: Cambridge University Press, 1950. A provocative analysis of the nature and limits of reasoning about ethical theory.

Tsanoff, Radaslov A. *The Moral Ideals of our Civilization.* New York: Dutton, 1942. A survey of the history of ethical theory for the general reader.

Also see:

Bayliss, Charles A. *Ethics.* New York: Henry Holt, 1958.

Brandt, Richard. *Ethical Theory.* New York: Prentice-Hall, 1959.

Hill, Thomas E. *Ethics in Theory and Practice.* New York: Crowell, 1956.

Leys, Wayne A. R. *Ethics for Policy Decisions.* New York: Prentice-Hall, 1952.

Chapter Four

PHILOSOPHICAL METAPHYSICS

1. DAVID HUME

Born in 1711, Hume came from a landed, middle-class family who wanted him to become a lawyer. However, his interests in literature and philosophy led him to France (to Le Flèche, Descartes' school) where, after three years of frugality, he published *A Treatise of Human Nature,* a work which he thought would revolutionize philosophical thought but which, in his own words, "fell dead born from the presses." At twenty-eight, he returned to Scotland to continue writing. He applied unsuccessfully for academic appointments, but he did gain a well-known reputation for skepticism and atheism. He revised the *Treatise* and published it under the title *An Inquiry Concerning Human Understanding,* and this time his expectations were fulfilled. The controversy it generated was vigorous and sustained, and still is. In 1752, Hume became a librarian and turned his writing interests to historical and political as well as moral and philosophical topics. He was appointed Secretary of the British embassy in Paris in 1763, and was received with acclaim by Voltaire, Rousseau, and others in French intellectual society. Four years later he was made Under-Secretary of State for Scotland. In 1769 he returned to his ancestral home at Ninewells where he died several years later after a lengthy illness. He spoke of himself as "a man of mild disposition, in command of temper, of an open, social and cheerful mind, capable of attachment, but little susceptible to enmity," and the judgments of his friends support this estimate.

Descartes said we have knowledge of the existence of three things: the Self, the external world, and God. Here we examine what Hume has to say about the extent of our empirical knowledge of the first two. Read his analyses and arguments carefully, looking for the reasons he gives to support his conclusions. Is skepticism the logical result of empiricism?

Empiricism and Skepticism[1]

All the perceptions of the human mind resolve themselves into two distinct kinds, which I shall call Impressions and Ideas. The difference betwixt these consists in the degrees of force and liveliness with which they strike upon the mind, and make their way into our thought or consciousness. Those perceptions, which enter with most force and violence, we may name *impressions;* and under this name I comprehend all our sensations, passions and emotions, as they make their first appearance in the soul. By *ideas* I mean the faint images of these in thinking and reasoning; such as, for instance, are all the perceptions excited by the present discourse, excepting only, those which arise from the sight and touch, and excepting the immediate pleasure or uneasiness it may occasion.

I believe it will not be very necessary to employ many words in explaining this distinction. Every one of himself will readily perceive the difference betwixt feeling and thinking. The common degrees of these are easily distinguished; though it is not impossible but in particular instances they may very nearly approach to each other. Thus in sleep, in a fever, in madness, or in any very violent emotions of soul, our ideas may approach to our impressions: As on the other hand it sometimes happens, that our impressions are so faint and low that we cannot distinguish them from our ideas. But notwithstanding this near resemblance in a few instances, they are in general so very different, that no one can make a scruple to rank them under distinct heads, and assign to each a peculiar name to mark the difference.

There is another division of our perceptions, which it will be convenient to observe, and which extends itself both to our impressions and ideas. This division is into Simple and Complex. Simple perceptions or impressions and ideas are such as admit of no distinction nor separation. The complex are the contrary to these, and may be distinguished into parts. Though a particular color, taste, and smell are qualities all united together in this apple, 'tis easy to perceive they are not the same, but are at least distinguishable from each other.

Having by these divisions given an order and arrangement to our objects, we may now apply ourselves to consider with the more accuracy their qualities and relations. The first circumstance that strikes my eyes, is the great resemblance betwixt our impressions and ideas in every other particular, except their degree of force and vivacity. . . . When I shut my eyes and think of my chamber, the ideas I form are exact representations of the impressions I felt; nor is

[1] From *A Treatise of Human Nature* by David Hume. London: Clarendon Press, 1896, Part I, Section I; Part II, Sections I, II; Part III, Sections I, III, VI, VII; Part IV, Section V.

there any circumstance of the one, which is not to be found in the other. In running over my other perceptions, I find still the same resemblance and representation. Ideas and impressions appear always to correspond to each other. This circumstance seems to me remarkable, and engages my attention.

Upon a more accurate survey I find I have been carried away too far by the first appearance, and that I must make use of the distinction of perceptions into simple and complex, to limit this general decision, that all our ideas and impressions are resembling. I observe that many of our complex ideas never had impressions that corresponded to them, and that many of our complex impressions never are exactly copied in ideas. I can imagine to myself such a city as the New Jerusalem, whose pavement is gold and walls are rubies, tho' I never saw any such. I have seen Paris, but shall I affirm I can form such an idea of that city, as will perfectly represent all its streets and houses in their real and just proportions?

I perceive, therefore, that tho' there is in general a great resemblance betwixt our complex impressions and ideas, yet the rule is not universally true, that they are exact copies of each other. We may next consider how the case stands with our simple perceptions. After the most accurate examination, of which I am capable, I venture to affirm, that the rule here holds without any exception, and that every simple idea has a simple impression, which resembles it; and every simple impression a correspondent idea. That idea of red, which we form in the dark, and that impression, which strikes our eyes in sunshine, differ only in degree, not in nature. That the case is the same with all our simple impressions and ideas, 'tis impossible to prove by a particular enumeration of them. Everyone may satisfy himself in this point by running over as many as he pleases. But if any one should deny this universal resemblance, I know of no way of convincing him, but by desiring him to show a simple impression, that has not a correspondent idea, or a simple idea, that has not a correspondent impression. If he does not answer this challenge, as 'tis certain he cannot, we may from his silence and our own observation establish our conclusion.

In seeking for phenomena to prove this proposition, I find only those of two kinds; but in each kind the phenomena are obvious, numerous and conclusive. I first make myself certain, by a new review, of what I have already asserted, that every simple impression is attended with a correspondent idea, and every simple idea with a correspondent impression. From this constant conjunction of resembling perceptions I immediately conclude that there is a great connection betwixt our correspondent impressions and ideas, and that the existence of the one has a considerable influence upon that of the other. Such a constant conjunction, in such an infinite number of instances, can never arise from chance; but clearly proves a dependence of the impressions on the ideas, or of the ideas on the impressions. . . .

To confirm this I consider another plain and convincing phenomenon; which is, that wherever by any accident the faculties, which give rise to any impressions, are obstructed in their operations, as when one is born blind or deaf; not only the impressions are lost, but also their correspondent ideas; so that there never appear in the mind the least traces of either of them. . . . We cannot form to ourselves a just idea of the taste of a pineapple, without having actually tasted it.

[Thus we find] *that all our simple ideas in their first appearance are deriv'd from simple impressions, which are correspondent to them, and which they exactly represent*. . . . Let us apply this principle, in order to discover farther the nature of our ideas of space and time.

* * * * *

Upon opening my eyes, and turning them to the surrounding objects, I perceive many visible bodies; and upon shutting them again, and considering the distance betwixt these bodies, I acquire the idea of extension. As every idea is deriv'd from some impression, which is exactly similar to it, the impressions similar to this idea of extension, must either be some sensations deriv'd from the sight, or some internal impressions arising from these sensations.

Our internal impressions are our passions, emotions, desires and aversions; none of which, I believe, will ever be asserted to be the model, from which the idea of space is deriv'd. There remains therefore nothing but the senses which can convey to us this original impression. Now what impression do our senses here convey to us?

The table before me is alone sufficient by its view to give me the idea of extension. This idea, then, is borrow'd from, and represents some impression, which this moment appears to the senses. But my senses convey to me only the impressions of color'd points, dispos'd in a certain manner. If the eye is sensible of any thing farther, I desire it may be pointed out to me. But if it be impossible to show any thing farther, we may conclude with certainty, that the idea of extension is nothing but a copy of these color'd points, and of the manner of their appearance.

Suppose that in the extended object, or composition of color'd points, from which we first receiv'd the idea of extension, the points were of a purple color; it follows, that in every repetition of that idea we wou'd not only place the points in the same order with respect to each other, but also bestow on them that precise color, with which alone we are acquainted. But afterwards, having experience of the other colors of violet, green, red, white, black, and of all the different compositions of these, and finding a resemblance in the disposition of color'd points, of which they are compos'd, we omit the peculiarities of color, as far as possible, and found an abstract idea merely on that disposition of points, or manner of appearance, in which they agree. Nay, even when the resemblance is carried beyond the objects of one sense, and the impressions of touch are found to be similar to those of sight in the disposition of their parts; this does not hinder the abstract idea from representing both, upon account of their resemblance. All abstract ideas are really nothing but particular ones, consider'd in a certain light; but being annexed to general terms, they are able to represent a vast variety, and to comprehend objects, which, as they are alike in some particulars, are in others vastly wide of each other. . . .

As 'tis from the disposition of visible and tangible objects we receive the idea of space, so from the succession of ideas and impressions we form the idea of time, nor is it possible for time alone ever to make its appearance, or be taken notice of by the mind. A man in a sound sleep, or strongly occupy'd with one thought, is insensible of time; and according as his perceptions succeed each other with greater or less rapidity, the same duration appears longer or shorter to his imagination. . . . Wherever we have no successive perceptions, we have no notion of time, even tho' there be a real succession in the objects. Thus we conclude that time cannot make its appearance in the mind, either alone, or attended with a steady unchangeable object, but is always discover'd by some *perceivable* succession of changeable objects.

* * * * *

It may not be amiss, before we leave this subject, to explain the ideas of existence and of external existence; which have their difficulties, as well as the ideas of space and time. . . .

There is no impression nor idea of any kind, of which we have any consciousness or memory, that is not conceiv'd as existent; and 'tis evident, that from this consciousness the most perfect idea and assurance of *being* is deriv'd. From hence we may form a dilemma, the most clear and conclusive that can be imagin'd viz., that since we never remember any idea or impression without attributing existence to it, the idea of existence must either be deriv'd from a distinct impression, conjoin'd with every perception or object of our thought, or must be the very same with the idea of the perception or object.

As this dilemma is an evident consequence of the principle that every idea arises from a similar impression, so our decision betwixt the propositions of the dilemma is no more doubtful. So far from there being any distinct impression, attending every impression and every idea, that I do not think there are any two distinct impressions, which are inseparably conjoin'd. Tho' certain sensations may at one time be united, we quickly find they admit of a separation, and may be presented apart. And thus, tho' every impression and idea we remember be considered as existent, the idea of existence is not derived from any particular impression. . . .

Now since nothing is ever present to the mind but perceptions, and since all ideas are deriv'd from something antecedently present to the mind; it follows, that 'tis impossible for us so much as to conceive or form an idea of any thing specifically different from ideas and impressions. Let us fix our attention out of ourselves as much as possible: Let us chase our imagination to the heavens, or to the utmost limits of the universe; we never really advance a step beyond ourselves, nor can conceive any kind of existence, but those perceptions, which have appear'd in that narrow compass.

* * * * *

[Let us now examine the idea of cause and effect.] Let us cast our eye on any two objects, which we call cause and effect, and turn them on all sides, in order to find that impression which produces an idea of such prodigious consequence. At first sight I perceive that I must not search for it in any of the particular *qualities* of the objects; since, whichever of these qualities I pitch on, I find some object that is not possessed of it and yet falls under the denomination of cause and effect. . . .

The idea, then, of causation must be deriv'd from some *relation* among objects; and that relation we must now endeavor to discover. I find in the first place, that whatever objects are consider'd as causes or effects, are *contiguous;* and that nothing can operate in a time or place which is ever so little remov'd from those of its existence. We may therefore consider the relation of Contiguity as essential to that of causation. . . .

The second relation I observe as essential to causes and effects, is not so universally acknowledg'd, but is liable to some controversy. 'Tis that of Priority of time in the cause before the effect. Some pretend that 'tis not absolutely necessary a cause shou'd precede its effect; but that any object or action, in the very first moment of its existence, may exert its productive quality, and give rise to another object or action, perfectly co-temporary with itself. But experience in most instances seems to contradict this opinion. . . .

Having thus discover'd or suppos'd the two relations of *Contiguity* and *Succession* to be essential to causes and effects, I find I am stopped short, and can proceed no farther in considering any single instance of cause and effect. . . . Shall we then rest contented with these two relations as affording a complete idea of causation? By no means. An object may be contiguous and prior to another without being consider'd as its cause. There is a *Necessary Connection* to be taken into consideration; and that relation is of much greater importance than the other two above mention'd.

Here again I turn the object on all sides, in order to discover the nature of this necessary connection, and find the impression, or impressions, from which its idea may be deriv'd. When I cast my eye on the known *qualities* of the object, I immediately discover that the relation of cause and effect depends not in the least on them. When I consider their *relations,* I can find none but those of contiguity and succession. Shall the despair of success make me assert that I am here possessed of an idea which is not preceded by any similar impression? No, for this wou'd be too strong a proof of levity since the contrary principle has been established so firmly. How does experience, then, give rise to such a principle?

* * * * *

'Tis easy to observe that in tracing this relation of necessary connection, the inference we draw from cause to effect is not deriv'd merely from a survey of these particular objects, and from such a penetration into their essences as may discover the dependence of the one upon the other. There is no object which implies the existence of any other if we consider these objects in themselves, and never look beyond the ideas which we form of them. . . .

'Tis therefore by *Experience* only that we can infer the existence of one object from that of another. The nature of the experience is this. We remember to have had frequent instances of the existence of one species of object; and also remember that the individuals of another species of object have always attended them, and have existed in a regular order of contiguity and succession with regard to them. Thus we remember to have seen that species of object we call *flame,* and to have felt that species of sensation we call *heat.* We likewise call to mind their constant conjunction in all past instances. Without any further ceremony, we call the one *cause* and the other *effect,* and infer the existence of the one from that of the other. . . . But *there is nothing in the object, consider'd in itself, which can afford us a reason for drawing a conclusion beyond it.* . . . 'Tis a custom of the mind which makes us do so.

* * * * *

Upon the whole, then, necessity is something that exists in the mind, not in objects; nor is it possible for us ever to form the most distant idea of it, consider'd as a quality in bodies. Either we have no idea of necessity, or necessity is nothing but that determination of the thought to pass from causes to effects and from effects to causes, according to their experienc'd union.

* * * * *

There are some philosophers, who imagine we are every moment intimately conscious of what we call our *Self;* that we feel its existence and its continuance in existence; and are certain, beyond the evidence of a demonstration, both of its perfect identity and simplicity. The strongest sensation, the most violent passion, say they, instead of distracting us from this view, only fix it the more intensely, and make us consider their influence on self either by their pain or pleasure. To attempt a farther proof of this were to weaken its evidence; since no proof can be deriv'd from any fact, of which we are so intimately conscious; nor is there any thing, of which we can be certain, if we doubt of this.

Unluckily all these positive assertions are contrary to that very experience, which is pleaded for them, nor have we any idea of self, after the manner it is here explain'd. For from what impression could this idea be deriv'd? This question 'tis impossible to answer without a manifest contradiction and absurdity; and yet 'tis a question, which must necessarily be answer'd, if we wou'd have the idea of self pass for clear and intelligible. It must be some one impression, that gives rise to every real idea. But self or person is not any one impression, but that to which our several impressions and ideas are suppos'd to have a reference. If any impression gives rise to the idea of self, that impression must continue invariably the same, thro' the whole course of our lives; since self is suppos'd to exist after that manner. But there is no impression constant and invariable. Pain and pleasure, grief and joy, passions and sensations succeed each other, and never all exist at the same time. It cannot, therefore, be from any of these impressions, or from any other, that the idea of self is deriv'd; and consequently there is no such idea.

But farther, what must become of all our particular perceptions upon this hypothesis? All these are different, and distinguishable, and separable from each other, and may be separately consider'd, and may exist separately, and have no need of any thing to support their existence. After what manner, therefore, do they belong to self; and how are they connected with it? For my part, when I enter most intimately into what I call myself, I always stumble on some particular perception or other, of heat or cold, light or shade, love or hatred, pain or pleasure. I never can catch myself at any time without a perception, and never can observe any thing but the perception. When my perceptions are remov'd for any time, as by sound sleep; so long am I insensible of myself, and may truly be said not to exist. And were all my perceptions remov'd by death, and cou'd I neither think, nor feel, nor see, nor love, nor hate after the dissolution of my body, I shou'd be entirely annihilated, nor do I conceive what is farther requisite to make me a perfect non-entity. If any one upon serious and unprejudic'd reflection, thinks he has a different notion of himself, I must confess I can reason no longer with him. All I can allow him is, that he may be in the right as well as I, and that we are essentially different in this particular. He may, perhaps, perceive something simple and continu'd, which he calls himself; tho' I am certain there is no such principle in me.

But setting aside some metaphysicians of this kind, I may venture to affirm of the rest of mankind, that they are nothing but a bundle or collection of different perceptions, which succeed each other with an inconceivable rapidity, and are in a perpetual flux and movement. Our eyes cannot turn in their sockets without varying our perceptions. Our thought is still more variable than our sight; and all our other senses and faculties contribute to this change; nor is there any single power of the soul which remains unalterably the same, perhaps for one moment. There is properly no *simplicity* in it at one time, nor *identity* in different times; regardless of whatever natural propension we may have to imagine them. . . .

What then gives us so great a propension to ascribe an identity to these successive perceptions, and to suppose ourselves possessed of an invariable and uninterrupted existence thro' the whole course of our lives? . . .

We have a distinct idea of an object, that remains invariable and uninterrupted thro' a suppos'd variation of time; and this idea we call that of *identity* or *sameness*. We also have a distinct idea of several different objects existing in succession, and connected together by a close relation; and this to an accurate view afford as perfect a notion of *di-*

versity, as if there was no manner of relation among the objects. But tho' these two ideas of identity, and a sucession of related objects be in themselves perfectly distinct, and even contrary, yet 'tis certain, that in our common way of thinking they are generally confounded with each other. That action of the imagination, by which we consider the uninterrupted and invariable object, and that by which we reflect on the succession of related objects, are almost the same to the feeling, nor is there much more effort of thought requir'd in the latter case than in the former. The relation facilitates the transition of the mind from one object to another, and renders its passage as smooth as if it contemplated one continu'd object. This resemblance is the cause of the confusion and mistake, and makes us substitute the notion of identity, instead of that of related objects. However, at one instant we may consider the related succession as variable or interrupted, we are sure the next to ascribe to it a perfect identity, and regard it as invariable and uninterrupted. Our propensity to this mistake is so great from the resemblance above mention'd, that we fall into it before we are aware; and tho' we incessantly correct ourselves by reflection, and return to a more accurate method of thinking, yet we cannot long sustain our philosophy, or take off this bias from the imagination. Our last resource is to yield to it, and boldly assert that these different related objects are in effect the same, however interrupted and variable. In order to justify to ourselves this absurdity, we often feign some new and unintelligible principle that connects the objects together, and prevents their interruption or variation. Thus we feign the notion of a *soul,* and *self* and *substance* to disguise the variation.

QUESTIONS FOR DISCUSSION

1. What is Hume's doctrine concerning impressions and ideas? Do you find anything in this doctrine you disagree with?
2. Upon your own "serious and unprejudiced reflection" can you find any other source for your knowledge of such things as time and space, cause and effect, and your own Self other than that which Hume has described?
3. Is the "mind" more like a sheet of paper on which experience is recorded or is it more like a sorting machine arranging and ordering the data of experience? Or is neither metaphor applicable? What difference would it make for any of Hume's arguments if the mind were more like a machine than a sheet of paper?
4. Is Hume's philosophy skeptical?

READINGS FOR IMMEDIATE REFERENCE

Hume, David. *A Treatise of Human Nature.* Book I, Parts I, III, IV.
———. *An Inquiry Concerning Human Understanding.* Sections 4-8.
———. *Dialogues Concerning Natural Religion.* Chapters 2, 5-9.

Kant, Immanuel. *Critique of Pure Reason*. Preface to the second edition, Introduction, Parts I-III.

Laertius, Diogenes. *Pyrrho*. Loeb Classical Library. Cambridge: Harvard University Press, 1905.

REFERENCES FOR COMPREHENSIVE KNOWLEDGE

Hume, David. *An Inquiry Concerning the Principles of Morals*.

———. *Natural History of Religion*.

Laird, John. *Hume's Philosophy of Human Nature*. London: Methuen, 1932. A penetrating and comprehensive study.

Price, H. H. *Hume's Theory of the External World*. New York: Oxford University Press, 1940. A careful analysis of one of the most important aspects of Hume's thought.

Smith, Norman Kemp. *The Philosophy of David Hume*. New York: Macmillan, 1941. A thorough analysis which maintains that Hume's philosophy "originated in his preoccupation with moral questions."

Also see:

Hendel, Charles W. *Studies in the Philosophy of David Hume*. Princeton: Princeton University Press, 1925.

MacNabb, D. G. C. *David Hume, His Theory of Knowledge and Morality*. London: Hutchinson University Library, 1951.

Mossner, Ernest C. *The Life of David Hume*. Austin, Texas: University of Texas Press, 1954.

Passmore, G. A. *Hume's Intentions*. Cambridge: Cambridge University Press, 1952.

II. JOSIAH ROYCE

Born in the mining town of Grass Valley in 1855 during the height of the California gold rush, Royce grew to manhood on the American frontier. He was one of the first graduates from the University of California, having entered as an engineering student. He was financed for two years of study in Germany by prosperous friends, although he finally took his doctorate at Johns Hopkins University (ten years before Dewey) where he studied under Charles Peirce. He taught literature at Berkeley for four years, but with the help and encouragement of his friend—and chief philosophical antagonist—William James, he went to Harvard in 1884 to write, teach, and defend his philosophical beliefs until his death in 1916. Perhaps the flavor of his philosophy and personality was best captured by Ralph Barton Perry, then a junior member of the department, who compared James and Royce in this way: "James was a man of the world, by accident a teacher, whose lectures were always conversations; Royce was a teacher, by accident occasionally astray in the world, whose conversations were always lectures. . . . Royce was the battleship, heavily armored, both for defense and offense. It was natural to suppose he was impregnable and irresistible. James, however, combined the attributes of the light cruiser, the submarine and the bombing airplane. He provided the rallying point for those Athenian youths in whom the spirit of revolt was stronger than tradition and prestige."

Royce represents the school of philosophy which dominated philosophical thought during the nineteenth century: *idealism* or, more accurately, *ideaism*. This type of thought, Royce says, has two aspects. Notice what they are, for the whole selection consists of his arguments to prove each correct. Do you find any errors in his analysis?

The Two Aspects of Idealism[1]

Idealism has two aspects. It is, for the first, a kind of analysis of the world, an analysis which so far has no absolute character about it, but which undertakes, in a fashion that might be acceptable to any skeptic, to examine what you mean by all the things, whatever they are, that you believe in or experience. This idealistic analysis consists merely in a pointing out, by various devices, that the world of your knowledge, whatever it contains, is through and through such stuff as ideas are made of, that you never in your life believed in anything definable *but* ideas, that, as Berkeley put it, "this whole choir of heaven and furniture of earth" is nothing for any of us but a system of ideas which govern our belief and conduct.

Such idealism has numerous statements, interpretations, embodiments: forms part of the most various systems and experiences, is consistent with Berkeley's theism, with Fichte's ethical absolutism, with Professor Huxley's agnostic empiricism, with Clifford's mind-stuff theory, with countless other theories that have used such idealism as a part of their scheme. In this aspect idealism is already a little puzzling to our natural consciousness, but it becomes quickly familiar, in fact almost commonplace, and seems after all to alter our practical faith or to solve our deeper problems very little.

The other aspect of idealism is the one which gives us our notion of the absolute Self. To it the first is only preparatory. This second aspect is the one which from Kant, until the present time, has formed the deeper problem of thought. Whenever the world has become more conscious of its significance, the work of human philosophy will be, not nearly ended (heaven forbid an end!), but for the first time fairly begun. For then, in critically estimating our passions, we shall have some truer sense of whose passions they are.

I begin with the first and the less significant aspect of idealism. Our world, I say, whatever it may contain, is such stuff as ideas are made of. This preparatory sort of idealism is the one that, as I just suggested, Berkeley made prominent, and after a fashion familiar. I must state it in my own way, although one in vain seeks to attain novelty in illustrating so frequently described a view.

Here, then, is our so real world of the sense, full of light and warmth and sound. If anything could be solid and external, surely one at first will say, it is this world. Hard facts, not mere ideas, meet us on every hand. Ideas any one can mould as he wishes. Not so facts. In idea socialists can dream out Utopias, disappointed lovers can imagine themselves successful, beggars can ride horses, wanderers can enjoy the fireside at home. In the realm of facts, society organizes itself as it must, rejected

[1] From *The Spirit of Modern Philosophy* by Josiah Royce. Boston: Houghton Mifflin Co., 1892, Lecture XI.

lovers stand for the time defeated, beggars are alone with their wishes, oceans roll drearily between home and the wanderer. Yet this world of fact is, after all, not entirely stubborn, nor merely hard. The strenuous will can mould facts. We can form our world, in part, according to our ideas. Statesmen influence the social order, lovers woo afresh, wanderers find the way home. This, then, is the presupposition of life, that we work in a real world, where house-walls do not melt away as in dreams, but stand firm against the winds of many winters and can be felt as real. . . .

The reality of the world, however, when thus defined in terms of its stubbornness, its firmness as against the will that has not conformed to its laws, its kindly rigidity in preserving for us the fruits of our labors,—such reality, I say, is still something wholly unanalyzed. In what does this stubbornness consist? Surely, many different sorts of reality, as it would seem, may be stubborn. Matter is stubborn when it stands in hard walls against us, or rises in vast mountain ranges before the path-finding explorer. But minds can be stubborn also. The lonely wanderer, who watches by the seashore the waves that roll between him and his home, talks of cruel facts, material barriers that, just because they are material, and not ideal, shall be the irresistible foes of his longing heart. "In wish," he says, "I am with my dear ones, but alas, wishes cannot cross oceans! Oceans are material facts, in the cold outer world. Would that the world of the heart were all!" But alas! to the rejected lover the world of the heart is all, and that is just his woe. Were the barrier between him and his beloved only made of those stubborn material facts, only of walls or of oceans, how lightly might his will erelong transcend them all! Matter stubborn! Outer nature cruelly the foe of ideas! Nay, it is just an idea that now opposes him,—just an idea, and that, too, in the mind of the maiden he loves. But in vain does he call this stubborn bit of disdain a merely ideal fact.

Place me for a moment, then, in an external world that shall consist wholly of ideas,—the ideas, namely, of other people about me, a world of maidens who shall scorn me, of old friends who shall have learned to hate me, of angels who shall condemn me, of God who shall judge me. In what piercing north winds, amidst what fields of ice, in the labyrinths of what tangled forests, in the depths of what thick-walled dungeons, on the edges of what tremendous precipices, should I be more genuinely in the presence of stubborn and unyielding facts than in that conceived world of ideas! So, as one sees, I by no means deprive my world of stubborn reality, if I merely call it a world of ideas. On the contrary, as every teacher knows, the ideas of the people are often the most difficult of facts to influence. We were wrong, then, when we said that whilst matter was stubborn, ideas could be moulded at pleasure. Ideas are often the most implacable of facts. Even my own ideas, the facts of my own inner life, may cruelly decline to be plastic to my wish. . . .

No, here are barriers worse than any material chains. The world of ideas has its own horrible dungeons and chasms.

Let those who have refuted Bishop Berkeley's idealism by the wonder why he did not walk over every precipice or into every fire if these things existed only in his idea, let such, I say, first try some of the fires and the precipices of the inner life, ere they decide that dangers cease to be dangers as soon as they are called ideal, or even subjectively ideal in me.

Many sorts of reality, then, may be existent at the heart of any world of facts. But this bright and beautiful sense-world of ours,—what, amongst these many possible sorts of reality, does that embody? Are the stars and the oceans, the walls and the pictures, real as the maiden's heart is real,—embodying the ideas of somebody, but none the less stubbornly real for that? Or can we make something else of their reality? For, of course, that the stars and the oceans, the walls and the pictures have some sort of stubborn reality, just as the minds of our fellows have, our analysis so far does not for an instant think of denying. Our present question is, what sort of reality?

Consider, then, in detail, certain aspects of the reality that seems to be exemplified in our sense-world. The sublimity of the sky, the life and majesty of the ocean, the interest of a picture, —to what sort of real facts do these belong? Evidently here we shall have no question. So far as the sense-world is beautiful, is majestic, is sublime, this beauty and dignity exist only for the appreciative observer. If they exist beyond him, they exist only for some other mind, or as the thought and embodied purpose of some universal soul of nature. A man who sees the same world, but who has no eye for the fairness of it, will find all the visible facts, but will catch nothing of their value. At once, then, the sublimity and beauty of the world are thus truths that one who pretends to insight ought to see, and they are truths which have no meaning except for such a beholder's mind.

But let us look a little deeper. Surely, if the objects yonder are unideal and outer, odors and tastes and temperatures do not exist in these objects in just the way in which they exist in us. Part of the being of these properties, at least, if not all of it, is ideal and exists for us, or at best is once more the embodiment of the thought or purpose of some world-mind. About tastes you cannot dispute, because they are not only ideal but personal. For the benumbed tongue and palate of diseased bodily conditions, all things are tasteless. As for temperatures, a well-known experiment will show how the same water may seem cold to one hand and warm to the other. But even so colors and sounds are at least in part ideal. Their causes may have some other sort of reality; but colors themselves are not in the things, since they change with the light that falls on the things, vanish in the dark (whilst the things remained unchanged), and differ for different eyes. And as for sounds, both the pitch and the quality of tones depend for us upon certain interesting peculiarities of our hearing organs, and exist in nature only as voiceless sound-waves trembling through the air. All such sense qualities, then, are ideal. The world yonder may—yes, must—have attributes that give reasons why these qualities are thus felt by us; for so we assume. The world yonder may even be a mind that thus expresses its will to us. But these qualities need not, nay, cannot resemble the ideas that are produced in us, unless, indeed, that is because these qualities have a place as ideas in some world-mind. . . .

Unless, then, the real physical world yonder is itself the embodiment of some world-spirit's ideas, which he conveys to us, unless it is real only as the maiden's heart is real, namely, as itself a conscious thought, then we have so far but one result: that real world (to repeat one of the commonplaces of modern popular science) is in itself, apart from somebody's eyes and tongue and ears and touch, neither colored nor tasteful, neither cool nor warm, neither light nor dark, neither musical nor silent. . . .

But now, at this point, the Berkeleyan idealist goes one step further. The real outside world that is still left unexplained and unanalyzed after its beauty, its warmth, its odors, its tastes, its colors, and its tones, have been relegated to the realm of ideal truths, what do you now *mean* by calling it real? No doubt it is known as somehow real, but *what* is this reality *known as* being? If you know that this world is still there and outer, as by hypothesis you know, you are bound to say *what* this outer character implies for your thought. And here you have trouble. Is the outer world, as it exists outside of your ideas, or of anybody's ideas, something having shape, filling space, possessing solidity, full of moving things? That would in the first place seem evident. The sound isn't outside of me, but the sound-waves, you say, are. The colors are ideal facts; but the ether-waves don't need a mind to know them. Warmth is ideal, but the physical fact called heat, this playing to and fro of molecules, is real, and is there apart from any mind. But once more, is this so evident? What do *I mean* by the shape of anything, or by the size of anything? Don't I mean just the idea of shape or of size that I am obliged to get under certain circumstances? What is the meaning of any property that I give to the real outer world? How can I express that property except in case I think it in terms of my ideas? As for the sound-waves and the ether-waves, what are they but things ideally conceived to explain the facts of nature?

The conceptions have doubtless their truth, but it is an ideal truth. What I mean by saying that the things yonder have shape and size and trembling molecules, and that there is air with sound-waves, and ether with light-waves in it,—what I mean by all this is that experience forces upon me, directly or indirectly, a vast system of ideas, which may indeed be founded in truth beyond me, which in fact must be founded in such truth if my experience has any sense, but which, like my ideas of color and of warmth, are simply expressions of how the world's order must appear to me, and to anybody constituted like me. Above all, is this plain about space. The real things, I say, outside of me, fill space, and move about in it. But what do I mean by space? Only a vast system of ideas which experience and my own mind force upon me. Doubtless these ideas have a validity. They have *this* validity, that I, at all events, when I look upon the world, am bound to see it in space, as much bound as the king in Hamlet was, when he looked within, to see himself as guilty and unrepentant. But just as his guilt was an idea,—a crushing, an irresistible, and overwhelming idea,—but just an idea still, so, too, the space in which I place my world is one great formal idea of mine. That is just why I can describe it to other people. "It has three dimensions," I say, "length, breadth, depth." I describe each. I form, I convey, I construct, an idea of it through them. I know space, as an idea, very well. I can compute all sorts of unseen truths about the relations of its parts. I am sure that you, too, share this idea. But, then, for all of us alike it is just an idea; and when we put our world into space, and call it real there, we simply think one idea into another idea, not voluntarily, to be sure, but inevitably, and yet without leaving the realm of ideas.

Thus, all the reality that *we* attribute to our world, in so far as *we* know and can tell what we mean thereby, becomes ideal. There is, in fact, a certain system of ideas, forced upon us by experience, which we have to use as the guide of our conduct. This system of ideas we can't change by our wish; it is for us too overwhelming a fact as guilt, or as the bearing of our fellows towards us, but we know it only *as* such a system of ideas. And we call it matter.

John Stuart Mill very well expressed the puzzle of the whole thing, as we have now reached the statement of this puzzle, when he called matter a mass of "permanent possibilities of experience" for each of us. Mill's definition has its faults, but is a very fair beginning. You know matter as something that either now gives you this idea or experience, or that would give you some other idea or experience under other circumstances. A fire, while it burns, is for you a permanent possibility of either getting the idea of an agreeable warmth, or of getting the idea of a bad burn, and you treat it accordingly. A precipice amongst mountains is a permanent possibility of your experiencing a fall, or of getting a feeling of the exciting or of the sublime in mountain scenery. When you call the sun 92,000,000 miles away, you mean that between you and the sun (that is, between your present experience and the possible experience of the sun's surface) there would inevitably lie the actually inaccessible, but still numerically conceivable series of experiences of distance expressed by the number of miles in question. In short, your whole attitude towards the real world may be summed up by saying: "I have experiences now which I seem bound to have, experiences of color, sound, and all the rest of my present ideas; and I am also bound by experience to believe that in case I did certain things (for instance, touched the wall, traveled to the tropics, visited Europe, studied physics), I then should get, in a determinate order, dependent wholly upon *what* I have done, certain other experiences (for instance, experiences of the wall's solidity, or of a tropical climate, or of the scenes of an European tour, or of the facts of physics)." And this acceptance of actual experience, this belief in possible experience constitutes all that you mean by your faith in the outer world.

But, you say, Is not, then, all this faith of ours after all well founded? Isn't there really something yonder that corresponds in fact to this series of experiences in us? Yes, indeed, there no doubt is. But what if this, which so shall correspond without us to the ideas within us, what if this hard and fast reality should itself be a system of ideas, outside of our minds but not outside of every mind? As the maiden's disdain is outside the rejected lover's mind, unchangeable so far for him, but not on that account the less ideal, not the less a fact in a mind, as, to take afresh a former fashion of illustration, the price of a security or the objective existence of this lecture is an ideal fact, but real and external for the individual person, —even so why might not this world beyond us, this "permanent possibility of experience" be in essence itself a system of ideal experiences of some standard thought of which ours is only the copy? Nay, must it not be such a system in case it has any reality at all? For, after all, isn't this precisely what our analysis brings us to? Nothing whatever can I say about my world yonder that I do not express in terms of mind. Isn't it plain, then, that *if* my world yonder is anything knowable at all, it must be in and for itself essentially a mental world? Are my ideas to *resemble* in any way the world? Is the truth of my thought to consist in its *agreement* with reality? And am I thus capable, as common sense supposes, of conforming my ideas to things? Then reflect. What can, after all, so well agree with an idea as another idea? To what can things that go on in my mind conform unless it be to another mind? If the more my mind grows in mental clearness, the nearer it gets to the nature of reality, then surely the reality that my mind thus resembles must be in itself mental.

After all, then, would it deprive the world here about me of reality, nay, would it not rather save and assure the reality and the knowableness of my world of experience, if I said that this world, as it exists outside of my mind, and of any other human mind, exists in and for a standard, an universal mind, whose system of ideas simply constitutes the world? To say this, as you see, in no wise deprives our world of its due share of reality. If the standard mind knows now that its ideal fire has the quality of burning those who touch it, and if I in my finitude am bound to conform in my experiences to the thoughts of this standard mind, then in case I touch that fire I shall surely get the idea of a burn. The standard mind will be at least as hard and fast and real in its ideal consistency as is the maiden in her disdain for the rejected lover; and I, in presence of the ideal stars and the oceans, will see the genuine realities of fate as certainly as the lover hears his fate in the voice that expresses her will. . . .

If the external world is in itself mental, then, be this reality a standard and universal thought, or a mass of little atomic minds constituting the various particles of matter, in any case one can comprehend what it is, and will have to submit to its stubborn authority as the lover accepts the reality of the maiden's moods. If the world isn't such an ideal thing, then indeed all our science, which is through and through concerned with our mental interpretations of things, can neither have objective validity, nor make satisfactory progress toward truth. For as science is concerned with ideas, the world beyond all ideas is a bare "x."

But with this bare "x," you will say, this analytical idealism after all, doesn't tell us what the true world is, but only that so much of the true world as we ever get into our comprehension has to be conceived in ideal terms. Perhaps, after all, there does exist yonder an extra-mental world which has nothing to do, except by accident, with any mind, and which is the basis of experience, the source of ideas. Perhaps it is there. Yes, you will say, but *must* it be there?

* * * * *

Note the point we have reached. Either, as you see, your real world yonder is through and through a world of ideas, an outer mind that you are more or less comprehending through your experience, or else, insofar as it is real and outer it is unknowable, an inscrutable "x," an absolute mystery. Either a mind yonder, or else the unknowable; that is your choice. . . . For if that so-called unknowable, that unknown outer world there, ever could by any device, come within our ken, then it is already an ideal world. For just that is what our whole idealistic analysis has been proving. Only ideas are knowable. And nothing absolutely unknowable can exist. For the absolutely unknowable, the "x" pure and simple, the Kantian thing in itself, simply cannot be admitted. The notion of it is nonsense.

* * * * *

The world, then, is such stuff as ideas are made of. Thought possesses all things. But the world isn't unreal. It extends infinitely beyond our private consciousness, because it is the world of an universal mind. What facts it is to contain only experience can inform us. There is no magic that can anticipate the work of science. Absolutely the only thing sure from the first about this world, however, is that it is intelligent, rational, orderly, essentially comprehensive, so that all its problems are somewhere solved, all its darkest mysteries are known to the Supreme Self. . . . Beyond the seeming wreck and chaos of our finite problems, its eternal insight dwells, therefore, in absolute and supreme majesty. Yet it is not far from every one of us. There is no least or most transient thought that flits through a child's mind, or that troubles with the faintest line of care a maiden's face, and that still does not contain and embody something of this divine Logos.

QUESTIONS FOR DISCUSSION

1. Would this line from *Hamlet* accurately express all Royce claims in the first aspect of idealism: "There is nothing either good or bad, but thinking makes it so"?

2. Why does Royce say of the second aspect: "Either a mind yonder, or else the unknowable; that is your choice"? Are there other alternatives?
3. If all we know are ideas does it follow that ideas are all that exist? Does Royce argue for this conclusion?

READINGS FOR IMMEDIATE REFERENCE

Royce, Josiah. *Lectures on Modern Idealism.* New Haven: Yale University Press, 1919, Chapter 10.

———. *The Spirit of Modern Philosophy.* Boston: Houghton Mifflin, 1892, Lecture 11.

———. *The World and the Individual.* London: Macmillan, 1904, Chapters 1, 6, 7, 10.

Berkeley, George. *A Treatise Concerning the Principles of Human Knowledge,* Part I.

Moore, G. E. "The Refutation of Idealism," *Philosophical Studies.* London: Routledge and Kegan Paul, 1922, 1-30.

REFERENCES FOR COMPREHENSIVE KNOWLEDGE

Royce, Josiah. *The Philosophy of Loyalty.* New York: Macmillan, 1908.

———. *The Problems of Christianity.* New York: Macmillan, 1913.

———. *The Religious Aspects of Philosophy.* New York: Houghton Mifflin, 1885.

Berkeley, George. *Dialogues between Hylas and Philonous.* An eighteenth-century version of the idealist position.

Perry, Ralph Barton. *The Thought and Character of William James.* Boston: Little, Brown, 1935. Appendices V and VI contain the famous discussion between James and Royce on the Absolute.

Also see:

Adams, G. P. *Idealism and the Modern Age.* New Haven: Yale University Press, 1919.

Cunningham, G. W. *The Idealist Argument in Recent British and American Philosophy.* New York: Century, 1933.

Ewing, A. C. *Idealism.* London: Methuen, 1934.

Smith, J. E. *Royce's Social Infinite: The Community of Interpretation.* New York: Liberal Arts Press, 1950.

III. HENRI BERGSON

The year 1859 was particularly memorable in the history of thought, for it marked not only the publication of Darwin's *Origin of Species,* Spencer's *First Principles,* and Mill's *On Liberty,* but the birth of John Dewey, Edmund Husserl, Samuel Alexander, and Henri Bergson as well. Born of French Jewish parentage, Bergson's early education was largely in mathematics and physics, subjects in which his instructors thought he had great competence. However, in his early twenties his interests turned more to philosophy, especially to the implications of Darwin's theory for philosophical issues. He was elected Professor of Philosophy at the Collège de France in 1900, published his most influential book, *Creative Evolution,* in 1907, was elected to the French Academy in 1914, and was awarded the Nobel Prize for Literature in 1927. In addition to his teaching and writing Bergson devoted much of his time and energy to political and international affairs. He was president of the Committee for Intellectual Cooperation following World War I and held other positions of equal importance. He died in seclusion in 1941, shortly after refusing exemption from the Vichy laws governing Jews during World War II.

Bergson's philosophy, which is usually classified as *vitalist* and *intuitionist,* has both a critical and a constructive side, almost inextricably mixed. He is critical of much traditional philosophy and contemporary science because it rests on "analysis," a method which interposes symbols between the knower and reality. On the contrary, he contends, only an "intellectual sympathy" can tell us of reality as it is.

Analysis and Intuition[1]

A comparison of the definitions of metaphysics and the various conceptions of the absolute leads to the discovery that philosophers, in spite of their apparent divergencies, agree in distinguishing two profoundly different ways of knowing a thing. The first implies that we move around the object; the second that we enter into it. The first depends on the point of view at which we are placed and on the symbols by which we express ourselves. The second neither depends on a point of view nor relies on any symbol. The first kind of knowledge may be said to stop at the relative; the second, in those cases where it is possible, to attain the absolute.

Consider, for example, the movement of an object in space. My perception of the motion will vary with the point of view, moving or stationary, from which I observe it. My expression of it will vary with the systems of axes, or the points of reference, to which I relate it; that is, with the symbols by which I translate it. For this double reason I call such motion relative: in the one case as in the other, I am placed outside the object itself. But when I speak of an absolute movement, I am attributing to the moving object an interior and, so to speak, state of mind; I also imply that I am in sympathy with those states, and that I insert myself in them by an effort of the imagination. Then, according as the object is moving or stationary, according as it adopts one movement or another, what I experience will vary. And what I experience will depend neither on the point of view I may take up in regard to the object, since I am inside the object itself, nor on the symbols by which I may translate the motion, since I have rejected all translations in order to possess the original. In short, I shall no longer grasp the movement from without, remaining where I am, but from where it is, from within, as it is in itself. I shall possess an absolute.

Consider, again, a character whose adventures are related to me in a novel. The author may multiply the traits of his character, may make him speak and act as much as he pleases, but all this can never be equivalent to the simple and indivisible feeling which I should experience if I were able for an instant to identify myself with the person of the hero himself. Out of that indivisible feeling, as from a spring, all the words, gestures and actions of a man would appear to me to flow naturally. There would no longer be accidents which, added to the idea I had already formed of the character, continually enriched that idea, without ever completing it. The character would be given to me all at once, in its entirety, and the thousand incidents which manifest it, instead of adding themselves to the idea and so

[1] From Henri Bergson's *An Introduction to Metaphysics,* translated by T. E. Hulme, copyright, 1949, 1955 by The Liberal Arts Press, Inc., reprinted by special permission of the Liberal Arts Press Division of the Bobbs-Merrill Company, Inc.

enriching it, would seem to me, on the contrary to detach themselves from it, without, however, exhausting it or impoverishing its essence. . . .

It is in this sense, and in this sense only, that absolute is synonymous with perfection. Were all the photographs of a town, taken from all possible points of view, to go on indefinitely completing one another, they would never be equivalent to the solid town in which we walk about. Were all the translations of a poem into all possible languages to add together their various shades of meaning and, correcting each other by a kind of mutual retouching, to give a more and more faithful image of the poem they translate, they would yet never succeed in rendering the inner meaning of the original. A representation taken from a certain point of view, a translation made with certain symbols will always remain imperfect in comparison with the object of which a view has been taken. But the absolute, which is the object and not its representation, the original and not its translation, is perfect, by being perfectly what it is. . . .

It follows from this that an absolute could only be given in an intuition, whilst everything else falls within the province of analysis. By intuition is meant the kind of intellectual sympathy by which one places oneself within an object in order to coincide with what is unique in it and consequently inexpressible. Analysis, on the contrary, is the operation which reduces the object to elements already known, that is, to elements common both to it and other objects. To analyze, therefore, is to express a thing as a function of something other than itself. All analysis is thus a translation, a development into symbols, a representation taken from successive points of view from which we note as many resemblances as possible between the new object which we are studying and others which we believe we know already. In its eternally unsatisfied desire to embrace the object around which it is compelled to turn, analysis multiplies without end the number of its points of view in order to complete its always incomplete representation, and ceaselessly varies its symbols that it may perfect the always imperfect translation. It goes on, therefore, to infinity. But intuition, if intuition is possible, is a simple act.

Now it is easy to see that the ordinary function of positive science is analysis. Positive science works above all, with symbols. Even the most concrete of the natural sciences, those concerned with life, confine themselves to the visible form of living beings, their organs and anatomical elements. They make comparisons between these forms, they reduce the more complex to the more simple; in short, they study the workings of life in what is, so to speak, only its visual symbol. If there exists any means of possessing a reality absolutely instead of knowing it relatively, of placing oneself within it instead of looking at it from outside points of view, of having the intuition instead of making the analysis: in short, of seizing it without any expression, translation, or symbolic representation—metaphysics is that means. Metaphysics, then, is the science which claims to dispense with symbols.

There is one reality, at least, which

we all seize from within, by intuition and not by simple analysis. It is our own personality in its flowing through time —our self which endures. We may sympathize intellectually with nothing else, but we certainly sympathize with our own selves.

When I direct my attention inward to contemplate my own self (supposed for the moment to be inactive), I perceive at first, as a crust solidified on the surface, all the perceptions which come to it from the external world. These perceptions are clear, distinct, juxtaposed or juxtaposable one with another; they tend to group themselves into objects. Next, I notice the memories which more or less adhere to these perceptions and which serve to interpret them. These memories have been detached, as it were, from the depth of my personality, drawn to the surface by the perceptions which resemble them; they rest on the surface of my mind without being absolutely myself. Lastly, I feel the stir of tendencies and motor habits—a crown of virtual actions, more or less firmly bound to these perceptions and memories. All these clearly defined elements appear more distinct from me, the more distinct they are from each other. Radiating, as they do, from within outwards, they form, collectively, the surface of a sphere which tends to grow larger and lose itself in the exterior world. But if I draw myself in from the periphery towards the center, if I search in the depth of my being that which is most uniformly, most constantly, and most enduringly myself, I find an altogether different thing.

There is, beneath these sharply cut crystals and this frozen surface, a continuous flux which is not comparable to any flux I have ever seen. There is a succession of states, each of which announces that which follows and contains that which precedes it. They can, properly speaking, only be said to form multiple states when I have already passed them and turn back to observe their track. Whilst I was experiencing them they were so solidly organized, so profoundly animated with a common life, that I could not have said where any one of them finished or where another commenced. In reality, no one of them begins or ends, but all extend into each other.

This inner life may be compared to the unrolling of a coil, for there is no living being who does not feel himself coming gradually to the end of his role; and to live is to grow old. But it may just as well be compared to the continual rolling up, like that of a thread on a ball, for our past follows us, it swells incessantly with the present that it picks up on its way; and consciousness means memory.

But actually it is neither an unrolling nor a rolling up, for these two similes evoke the idea of lines and surfaces whose parts are homogeneous and superposable on one another. . . . It would be better to use as a comparison the myriad-tinted spectrum, with its insensible gradations leading from one shade to another. A current of feeling which passed along the spectrum, assuming in turn the tint of each of its shades, would experience a series of gradual changes, each of which would announce the one to follow and would sum up those which preceded it. Yet even here the successive shades of the spectrum always remain external one to another. They are juxtaposed; they occupy space. But pure duration, on the contrary, excludes all idea of juxtaposition, reciprocal externality, and extension. . . . So, even this image is incomplete. The inner life is all this at once: variety of qualities, continuity of progress, and unity of direction. It cannot be represented by images.

But it is even less possible to represent it by *concepts,* that is by abstract, general or simple ideas. . . . Concepts, especially if they are simple, have the disadvantage of being in reality symbols substituted for the object they symbolize, and demand no effort on our part. Examined closely, each of them, it would seem, retains only that part of the object which is common to it and to others, and expresses, still more than the image does, a comparison between the object and others which resemble it. . . . For on the one hand, these concepts, laid side by side, never actually give us more than an artificial reconstruction of the object, of which they can only symbolize certain general, and, in a way, impersonal aspects; it is therefore useless to believe that with them we can seize a reality of which they present to us the shadow alone. And, on the other hand, besides the illusion there is also a very serious danger. For the concept generalizes at the same time as it abstracts. The concept can only symbolize a particular property by making it common to an infinity of things. It therefore always more or less deforms the property by the extension it gives to it. . . . Thus, our duration can be presented to us directly only in an intuition, and can be suggested by images, but it can never be enclosed in a conceptual representation. . . .

It is this confusion between the function of analysis and that of intuition which gives birth to the discussions between the schools and the conflicts between systems. Psychology, in fact, proceeds like all the other sciences by analysis. It resolves the self, which has been given to it at first in a simple intuition, into sensations, feelings, ideas, etc., which it studies separately. It substitutes, then, for the self a series of elements which form the facts of psychology. But are these *elements* really *parts?* That is the whole question, and it is because it has been evaded that the problem of human personality has so often been stated in insoluble terms.

It is incontestable that every psychical state, simply because it belongs to a person, reflects the whole of a personality. Every feeling, however simple it may be, contains virtually within it the whole past and present of the being experiencing it, and, consequently, can only be separated and constituted into a "state" by an effort of abstraction, an analysis. But it is no less incontestable that without this effort of abstraction or analysis there would be no possible development of the science of psychology. What, then, is the operation by which a psychologist detaches a mental state in order to erect it into a more or less independent entity? He begins by neglecting that special coloring or the personality which cannot be expressed in known and common terms. Then he endeavors to isolate, in the person thus simplified, some aspect which lends itself to an interesting inquiry. . . . But in so doing he mistakes partial notations for real parts, and simple concepts for the rich diversity of psychical states, thus confusing the point of view of analysis and intuition, of science and metaphysics.

Philosophical empiricism is born here, of a confusion between the point of view of intuition and that of analysis. Seeking for the original in the translation, where naturally it cannot be, it denies the existence of the original on the ground that it is not found in the translation. It leads of necessity to negations; but on examining the matter closely, we perceive that these negations simply mean that analysis is not intuition, which is self-evident. From the original, and, one must add, very indistinct intuition which gives positive science its material, science passes immediately to analysis, which multiplies to infinity its observations of this material from outside points of view. It soon comes to believe that by putting together all these diagrams it can reconstitute the object itself.

But rationalism is the dupe of the same illusions. It starts out from the same confusion as empiricism, and remains equally powerless to reach the inner self. Like empiricism, it considers psychical states as so many fragments detached from an ego that binds them together. Like empiricism, it tries to join these fragments together in order to re-create the unity of the self. Like empiricism, finally, it sees this unity of the self, in the continually renewed effort it makes to clasp it, steal away indefinitely like a phantom. But whilst empiricism, weary of the struggle, ends by declaring that there is nothing else but the multiplicity of psychical states, rationalism persists in affirming the unity of the person. . . . To these detached psychical states, rationalism, in order to reconstitute personality, adds something still more unreal, the void in which these shadows move. . . .

I see in this matter only one difference between empiricism and rationalism. The former, seeking the unity of the ego in the gaps, as it were, between the psychical states, is led to fill the gaps with other states, and so on indefinitely, so that the ego, compressed in a constantly narrowing interval, tends towards zero, as analysis is pushed farther and farther; whilst rationalism, making the ego the place where mental states are lodged, is confronted with an empty space which we have no reason to limit here rather than there, which goes beyond each of the successive boundaries that we try to assign to it, which constantly grows larger, and which tends to lose itself no longer in zero, but in the infinite.

* * * * *

But if metaphysics is to proceed by intuition, if intuition has the mobility of duration as its objects, and if duration is of a psychical nature, shall we not be confining the philosopher to the exclusive contemplation of himself? Will not philosophy come to consist in watching oneself merely live, "as a sleepy shepherd watches the water flow"? To talk in this way would be to return to the error which, since the beginning of this study, we have not ceased to point out. It would be to misconceive the singular nature of duration, and at the same time the essentially active, I might almost say violent, character of metaphysical intuition. It would be failing to see that the method we speak of alone permits us to go beyond idealism, as well as realism, to affirm the existence of objects inferior and superior to us, to make them co-exist together without difficulty, and to dissipate gradually the obscurities that analysis accumulates round these great problems. Without entering here upon the study of these different points, let us confine ourselves to showing how the intuition we speak of is not a single act, but an indefinite series of acts, and how this diversity of acts corresponds to all the degrees of being.

If I seek to *analyze* duration—that is, to resolve it into ready-made concepts—I am compelled, by the very nature of the concepts and of analysis, to take two opposing views of duration in general, with which I then attempt to reconstruct it. I shall have to say, that there is on the one hand a multiplicity of successive states of consciousness, and on the other a unity which binds them together. Duration will be the "synthesis" of this unity and this multiplicity, a mysterious operation which takes place in darkness, and in regard to which, I repeat, one does not see how it would admit of shades or of degrees. . . .

If I consider duration as a multiplicity of moments bound to each other by a unity which goes through them like a thread, then, however short the chosen duration may be, these moments are unlimited in number. Looked at from the point of view of multiplicity, then, duration disintegrates into a powder of moments, none of which endures, each being an instantaneity. If, on the other hand, I consider the unity which binds the moments together, this cannot endure either, since by hypothesis everything that is changing, and everything that is really durable in duration, has been put to the account of the multiplicity of moments. . . .

It is quite otherwise if we place ourselves from the first, by an effort of intuition, in the concrete flow of duration. Certainly, we shall then find no logical reason for positing multiple and diverse durations. The intuition of our duration, far from leaving us suspended in the void as pure analysis would do, brings us into contact with a whole continuity of durations which we must try to follow, whether downwards or upwards; in both cases we can extend ourselves indefinitely by an increasingly violent effort, in both cases we transcend ourselves. In the first we advance towards a more and more attenuated duration, the pulsations of which, being rapider than ours, and dividing our simple sensations, dilute its quality into quantity; at the limit would be pure homogeneity, that pure *repetition* by which we define materiality. Advancing in the other direction, we approach a duration which strains, contracts, and intensifies itself more and more; at the limit would be eternity. No longer conceptual eternity, which is an eternity of death, but an eternity of life. A living, and therefore still moving eternity in which our own particular duration would be included as the vibrations are in light; an eternity which would be the concentration of all duration, as materiality is its dispersion. Between these two extreme limits intuition moves, and this movement is the very essence of metaphysics.

* * * * *

The inherent difficulties of metaphysics, the division into antagonistic schools, and the irreducible opposition between systems are largely the result of our applying processes which we generally employ for practical ends. They arise from the fact that we place ourselves in the immobile in order to lie in wait for the moving thing as it passes, instead of replacing ourselves in the moving thing itself, in order to traverse with it the immobile positions. They arise from our professing to reconstruct reality with concepts and percepts whose function is to make it stationary. In other words, it is clear that fixed concepts may be extracted by our thought from mobile reality; but there are no means of reconstructing the mobility of the real with fixed concepts. . . .

But the truth is that our intelligence can follow the opposite method. It can place itself within the mobile reality, and adopt its ceaselessly changing direction; in short, can grasp it by means of that intellectual sympathy which we call intuition. This is extremely difficult. The mind has to do violence to itself, has to reverse the direction of the operation by which it habitually thinks, has perpetually to revise, or rather to recast, all its categories. But in this way it will attain to fluid concepts, capable of following reality in all its sinuosities and of adopting the very movement of the inward life of things. Only thus will a progressive philosophy be built up, freed from the disputes which arise between the various schools, and able to solve its problems naturally, because it will be released from the artificial expression in terms of which such problems are posited.

QUESTIONS FOR DISCUSSION

1. Do you agree with Bergson that "analysis" gives only partial understanding? Is this an insufficient basis for one's claiming to have knowledge?
2. How does Bergson react to (a) Hume's and (b) Royce's philosophical theories? How would they react to his? In your opinion, which of the three has the most fundamental analysis? Can you give reasons to support your view?
3. How does Bergson's thought reflect and embody the theory of evolution?

READINGS FOR IMMEDIATE REFERENCE

Bergson, Henri. *Creative Evolution,* translated by Arthur Mitchell. New York: Henry Holt, 1911, Chapter 4.

Lewis, C. I. "Some Logical Considerations Concerning the Mental," *The Journal of Philosophy,* XXXVIII (April, 1941), 225-233.

Whitehead, A. N. *Science and the Modern World*. New York: Macmillan, 1925, Chapters 10, 12.

REFERENCES FOR COMPREHENSIVE KNOWLEDGE

Bergson, Henri. *Matter and Memory*. New York: Macmillan, 1912.
——. *Time and Free Will*. New York: Macmillan, 1913.
——. *The Two Sources of Morality and Religion*. New York: Henry Holt, 1935.
LeRoy, E. *The New Philosophy of Henri Bergson*. New York: Henry Holt, 1913. Has become the standard commentary.

Also see:
du Nouy, Lecomte. *Human Destiny*. New York: Longmans, Green, 1947.
Gunn, J. A. *Bergson and His Philosophy*. New York: Henry Holt, 1922.
Stallknecht, N. P. *Studies in the Philosophy of Creation*. Princeton: Princeton University Press, 1934.

IV. CHARLES S. PEIRCE

Peirce was born in 1839, the son of the distinguished Harvard mathematician, Benjamin Peirce. He graduated from Harvard in 1859 and the Lawrence Scientific School in 1862, then joined the U.S. Coast Survey where he was employed until his retirement in 1887. He tried continually to obtain a University lectureship, succeeding only to the extent of teaching at Johns Hopkins University in 1880-1881, and (with the help of William James) for one semester at Harvard in 1903. He was equally unsuccessful as an author, for although his published works today occupy eight volumes and his influence on contemporary philosophical thought continues to grow, he published only a small book on logic, the reports of some of his photometric research, and a few articles during his lifetime. However, he had an original and creative mind and a breadth of interests which enabled him to make significant contributions to such diverse fields as philology, mathematical logic, meteorology, psychophysics, metaphysics, and education. He invented the word "pragmatism" to characterize one aspect of his thought, but when others coined the word to typify their ideas he decided to call his philosophy "pragmaticism, a word so ugly no one will want to steal it." As a person he was retiring and reserved with little interest in people or social amenities. He died in pain, poverty, and seclusion in 1914.

In this article, one of the first he published, Peirce examines how thought originates, and the four ways in which doubt might be resolved. Near the end of the selection he examines the question of what we can know about reality. Does the *pragmatic* attitude toward metaphysics have more or less to recommend it than the empiricist, idealist or intuitionist?

From Doubt to Belief[1]

Few persons care to study logic, because everybody conceives himself to be proficient enough in the art of reasoning already. But I observe that this satisfaction is limited to one's own ratiocination, and does not extend to that of other men.

We come to the full possession of our power of drawing inferences, the last of all our faculties; for it is not so much a natural gift as a long and difficult art.

* * * * *

We are, doubtless, in the main, logical animals, but we are not perfectly so. Most of us, for example, are naturally more sanguine and hopeful than logic would justify. We seem to be so constituted that in the absence of any facts to go upon we are happy and self-satisfied; so that the effect of experience is continually to contract our hopes and aspirations. Yet a lifetime of the application of this corrective does not usually eradicate our sanguine disposition. Where hope is unchecked by any experience, it is likely that our optimism is extravagant. Logicality in regard to practical matters (if this be understood, not in the old sense, but as consisting in a wise union of security with fruitfulness of reasoning) is the most useful quality an animal can possess, and might, therefore, result from the action of natural selection; but outside of these it is probably of more advantage to the animal to have his mind filled with pleasing and encouraging visions, independently of their truth; and thus, upon unpractical subjects, natural selection might occasion a fallacious tendency of thought.

* * * * *

We generally know when we wish to ask a question and when we wish to pronounce a judgment, for there is a dissimilarity between the sensation of doubting and that of believing.

But this is not all which distinguishes doubt from belief. There is a practical difference. Our beliefs guide our desires and shape our actions. The Assassins, or followers of the Old Man of the Mountain, used to rush into death at his least command, because they believed that obedience to him would insure everlasting felicity. Had they doubted this, they would not have acted as they did. So it is with every belief, according to its degree. The feeling of believing is a more or less sure indication of there being established in our nature some habit which will determine our actions. Doubt never has such an effect.

Nor must we overlook a third point of difference. Doubt is an uneasy and dissatisfied state from which we struggle to free ourselves and pass into the state of belief; while the latter is a calm and

[1] Reprinted by permission of the publishers from *Collected Papers of Charles Sanders Peirce,* edited by Charles Hartshorne and Paul Weiss. Cambridge, Mass.: Harvard University Press, Copyright, 1935, by The President and Fellows of Harvard College, Vol. V, pp. 223-270.

satisfactory state which we do not wish to avoid, or to change to a belief in anything else. On the contrary, we cling tenaciously, not merely to believing, but to believing just what we do believe.

Thus, both doubt and belief have positive effects upon us, though very different ones. Belief does not make us act at once, but puts us into such a condition that we shall behave in some certain way, when the occasion arises. Doubt has not the least such active effect, but stimulates us to inquiry until it is destroyed. This reminds us of the irritation of a nerve and the reflex action produced thereby; while for the analogue of belief, in the nervous system, we must look to what are called nervous associations—for example, to that habit of the nerves in consequence of which the smell of a peach will make the mouth water.

The irritation of doubt causes a struggle to attain a state of belief. I shall term this struggle *Inquiry,* though it must be admitted that this is sometimes not a very apt designation.

The irritation of doubt is the only immediate motive for the struggle to attain belief. It is certainly best for us that our beliefs should be such as may truly guide our actions so as to satisfy our desires; and this reflection will make us reject every belief which does not seem to have been so formed as to insure this result. But it will only do so by creating a doubt in the place of that belief. With the doubt, therefore, the struggle begins, and with the cessation of doubt it ends. Hence, the sole object of inquiry is the settlement of opinion.

That the settlement of opinion is the sole end of inquiry is a very important proposition. It sweeps away, at once, various vague and erroneous conceptions of proof. A few of these may be noticed here.

1. Some philosophers have imagined that to start an inquiry it was only necessary to utter a question whether orally or by setting it down upon paper, and have even recommended us to begin our studies with questioning everything! But the mere putting of a proposition into the interrogative form does not stimulate the mind to any struggle after belief. There must be a real and living doubt, and without this all discussion is idle.

2. It is a very common idea that a demonstration must rest on some ultimate and absolutely indubitable propositions. These, according to one school, are first principles of a general nature; according to another, are first sensations. But, in point of fact, an inquiry, to have that completely satisfactory result called demonstration, has only to start with propositions perfectly free from all actual doubt. If the premises are not in fact doubted at all, they cannot be more satisfactory than they are.

3. Some people seem to love to argue a point after all the world is fully convinced of it. But no further advance can be made. When doubt ceases, mental action on the subject comes to an end; and, if it did go on, it would be without a purpose.

If the settlement of opinion is the sole object of inquiry, and if belief is of the nature of a habit, why should we not attain the desired end, by taking as answer to a question any we may fancy, and constantly reiterating it to ourselves, dwelling on all which may conduce to that belief, and learning to turn with contempt and hatred from anything that might disturb it? . . .

I have often known this system to be deliberately adopted. Still oftener, the instinctive dislike of an undecided state of mind, exaggerated into a vague dread of doubt, makes men cling spasmodically to the views they already take. The man feels that, if he only holds to his belief without wavering, it will be entirely satisfactory. Nor can it be denied that a steady and immovable faith yields great peace of mind. It may, indeed, give rise to inconveniences, as if a man should resolutely continue to believe that fire would not burn him, or that he would be eternally damned if he received his *ingesta* otherwise than through a stomach-pump. But then the man who adopts this method will not allow that its inconveniences are greater than its advantages. He will say, "I hold steadfastly to the truth, and the truth is always wholesome." And in many cases it may very well be that the pleasure he derives from his calm faith overbalances any inconveniences resulting from its deceptive character. Thus, if it be true that death is annihilation, then the man who believes that he will certainly go straight to heaven when he dies, provided he has fulfilled certain simple observances in this life, has a cheap pleasure which will not be followed by the least disappointment. A similar consideration seems to have weight with many persons in religious topics, for we frequently hear it said, "Oh, I could not believe so-and-so, because I should be wretched if I did." When an ostrich buries its head in the sand as danger approaches, it very likely takes the happiest course. It hides from the danger, and then calmly says there is no danger; and, if it feels perfectly sure there is none, why should it raise its head to see? A man may go through life, systematically keeping out of view all that might cause a change in his opinions, and if he only succeeds—basing his method, as he does, on two fundamental psychological laws—I do not see what can be said against his doing so. . . .

But this method of fixing belief, which may be called the method of tenacity, will be unable to hold its ground in practice. The social impulse is against it. The man who adopts it will find that other men think differently from him, and it will be apt to occur to him, in some saner moment, that their opinions are quite as good as his own, and this will shake his confidence in his belief. This conception, that another man's thought or sentiment may be equivalent to one's own, is a distinctly new step, and a highly important one. It arises from an impulse too strong in man to be suppressed, without danger of destroying the human species. Unless we make ourselves hermits, we shall necessarily influence each other's opinions; so that the problem becomes how to fix belief, not in the individual merely, but in the community.

Let the will of the state act, then, instead of that of the individual. Let an institution be created which shall have for its object to keep correct doctrines before the attention of the people, to reiterate them perpetually, and to teach them to the young; having at the same time power to prevent contrary doctrines from being taught, advocated, or expressed. Let all possible causes of a change of mind be removed from men's apprehensions. Let them be kept ignorant, lest they should learn of some reason to think otherwise than they do. Let their passions be enlisted, so that they may regard private and unusual opinions with hatred and horror. Then, let all men who reject the established belief be terrified into silence. Let the people turn out and tar-and-feather such men, or let inquisitions be made into the manner of thinking of suspected persons, and when they are found guilty of forbidden beliefs, let them be subjected to some signal punishment. When complete agreement could not otherwise be reached, a general massacre of all who have not thought in a certain way has proved a very effective means of settling opinion in a country. If the power to do this be wanting, let a list of opinions be drawn up, to which no man of the least independence of thought can assent, and let the faithful be required to accept all these propositions, in order to segregate them as radically as possible from the influence of the rest of the world. . . .

In judging this method of fixing belief, which may be called the method of authority, we must, in the first place, allow its immeasurable mental and moral superiority to the method of tenacity. Its success is proportionately greater; and, in fact, it has over and over again had the most majestic results. . . . But no institution can undertake to regulate opinions upon every subject. Only the most important ones can be attended to, and on the rest men's minds must be left to the action of natural causes. This imperfection will be no source of weakness so long as men are in such a state of culture that one opinion does not influence another—that is, so long as they cannot put two and two together. But in the most priest-ridden states some individuals will be found who are raised above that condition. These men possess a wider sort of social feeling; they see that men in other countries and in other ages have held to very different doctrines from those which they themselves have been brought up to believe; and they cannot help seeing that it is the mere accident of their having been taught as they have, and of their having been surrounded with the manners and associations they have, that has caused them to believe as they do and not far differently. Nor can their candor resist the reflection that there is no reason to rate their own views at a higher value than those of other nations and other centuries; thus giving rise to doubts in their minds. . . .

A different new method of settling opinions must be adopted, that shall not only produce an impulse to believe, but shall also decide what proposition it is which is to be believed. Let the action of natural preferences be unimpeded, then, and under their influence let men, conversing together and regarding matters in different lights, gradually develop beliefs in harmony with natural causes. This method resembles that by which conceptions of art have been brought to maturity. The most perfect example of it is to be found in the history of metaphysical philosophy. Systems of this sort have not usually rested upon any observed facts, at least not in any great degree. They have been chiefly adopted because their fundamental propositions seemed "agreeable to reason." This is an apt expression; it does not mean that which agrees with experience, but that which we find ourselves inclined to believe. Plato, for example, finds it agreeable to reason that the distances of the celestial spheres from one another should be proportional to the different lengths of strings which produce harmonious chords. Many philosophers have been led to their main conclusions by considerations like this; but this is the lowest and least developed form which the method takes, for it is clear that another man might find Kepler's theory, that the celestial spheres are proportional to the inscribed and circumscribed spheres of the different regular solids, more agreeable to *his* reason. But the shock of opinions will soon lead men to rest on preferences of a far more universal nature. Take, for example, the doctrine that man only acts selfishly—that is, from the consideration that acting in one way will afford him more pleasure than acting in another. This rests on no fact in the world, but it has had a wide acceptance as being the only reasonable theory.

This method is far more intellectual and respectable from the point of view of reason than either of the others which we have noticed. Indeed, as long as no better method can be applied, it ought to be followed, since it is then the expression of instinct which must be the ultimate cause of belief in all cases. But its failure has been the most manifest. It makes of inquiry something similar to the development of taste; but taste, unfortunately, is always more or less a matter of fashion, and accordingly metaphysicians have never come to any fixed agreement, but the pendulum has swung backward and forward between a more material and a more spiritual philosophy, from the earliest times to the latest. And so from this, which has been called the *a priori* method, we are driven, in Lord Bacon's phrase, to a true induction. . . .

To satisfy our doubts, therefore, it is necessary that a method should be found by which our beliefs may be determined by nothing human, but by some external permanency—by something upon which our thinking has no effect. Such is the method of science. Its fundamental hypothesis, restated in more familiar language, is this: There are Real things, whose characters are entirely independent of our opinions about them; those Reals affect our senses according to regular laws, and, though our sensations are as different as are our relations to the objects, yet, by taking advantage of the laws of perception, we can ascertain by reasoning how things really and truly are; and any man, if he have sufficient experience and he reason enough about it, will be led to the one True conclusion. The new conception here involved is that of Reality. It may be asked how I know that there are any Reals. If this hypothesis is the sole support of my method of inquiry, my method of inquiry must not be used to support my hypothesis. The reply is this: 1. If investigation cannot be regarded as proving that there are Real things, it at least does not lead to a contrary conclusion; but the method and the conception on which it is based remain ever in harmony. No doubts of the method, therefore, necessarily arise from its practice, as is the case with all the others. 2. The feeling which gives rise to any method of fixing belief is a dissatisfaction at two repugnant propositions. But here already is a vague concession that there is some *one* thing which a proposition should represent. Nobody, therefore, can really doubt that there are Reals, for, if he did, doubt would not be a source of dissatisfaction. The hypothesis, therefore, is one which every mind admits. So that the social impulse does not cause men to doubt it. 3. Everybody uses the scientific method about a great many things, and only ceases to use it when he does not know how to apply it. 4. Experience of the method has not led us to doubt it, but, on the contrary, scientific investigation has had the most wonderful triumphs in the way of settling opinion. These afford the explanation of my not doubting the method or the hypothesis which it supposes; and not having any doubt, nor believing that anybody else whom I could influence has, it would be the merest babble for me to say more about it. If there be anybody with a living doubt upon the subject, let him consider it.

* * * * *

The principles set forth in the first part of this essay lead, at once, to a method of reaching a clearness of thought of higher grade than the "distinctness" of the logicians. We have found that the action of thought is excited by the irritation of doubt, and ceases when belief is attained; so that the production of belief is the sole function of thought. . . . Most frequently doubts arise from some indecision, however momentary, in our action. Sometimes it is not so. I have, for example, to wait in a railway-station, and to pass the time I read the advertisements on the walls. I compare the advantages of different trains and different routes which I never expect to take, merely fancying myself to be in a state of hesitancy, because I am bored with having nothing to trouble me. [But] feigned hesitancy, whether feigned for mere amusement or with a lofty purpose, plays a great part in the production of scientific inquiry. However the doubt may originate, it stimulates the mind to an activity which may be slight or energetic, calm or turbulent. Images pass rapidly through consciousness, one incessantly melting into another, until at last, when all is over—it may be in a fraction of a second, in an hour, or after long years—we find ourselves decided as to how we should act under such circumstances as those which occasioned our hesitation. In other words, we have attained belief. . . .

And what, then, is belief? It is the demi-cadence which closes a musical phrase in the symphony of our intellectual life. It has three properties: First, it is something that we are aware of; second, it appeases the irritation of doubt; and, third, it involves the establishment in our nature of a rule of action, or, say for short, a *habit*. As it appeases the irritation of doubt, which is the motive for thinking, thought relaxes, and comes to rest for a moment when belief is reached. But, since belief is a rule for action, the application of which involves further doubt and further thought, at the same time that it is a stopping place, it is also a new starting place for thought.

The essence of belief is the establishment of habit; and different beliefs are distinguished by the different modes of actions to which they give rise. If beliefs do not differ in this respect, if they appease the same doubt by producing the same rules of action, then no mere differences in the manner of consciousness of them can make them different beliefs, any more than playing a tune in different keys is playing different tunes. . . .

The whole function of thought is to produce habits of action. Whatever there is connected with thought, but irrelevant to its purpose is an accretion to it, but no part of it. If there be a unity among our sensations which has no reference to how we shall act on a given occasion, as when we listen to a piece of music, why do we not call that thinking? To develop its meaning, we have, therefore, simply to determine what habits it produces, for what a thing means is simply what habits it involves.

* * * * *

Let us now approach the subject of logic, and consider a conception which particularly concerns it, that of *reality*. Taking clearness in the sense of familiarity, no idea could be clearer than this. Every child uses it with perfect confidence, never dreaming that he does not understand it. As for clearness in its second grade, however, it would probably puzzle most men, even among those of a reflective turn of mind, to give an abstract definition of the real. Yet such a definition may perhaps be reached by considering the points of difference between reality and its opposite, fiction. A figment is a product of somebody's imagination; it has such characters as his thought impresses upon it. That those characters are independent of how you or I think is an external reality. There are, however, phenomena within our own minds, dependent upon our thought, which are at the same time real in the sense that we really think them. But though their characters depend on how we think, they do not depend on what we think those characters to be. Thus, a dream has a real existence as a mental phenomenon, if somebody has really dreamt it; that he dreamt so and so, does not depend on what anybody thinks was dreamt but is completely independent of all opinion on the subject. On the other hand, considering, not the fact of dreaming, but the thing dreamt, it retains its peculiarities by virtue of no other fact than that it was dreamt to possess them. Thus we may define the real as that whose characters are independent of what anybody may think them to be.

But however satisfactory such a definition may be found, it would be a great mistake to suppose that it makes the idea of reality perfectly clear. Here, then, let us apply our rules. According to them, reality, like every other quality, consists in the peculiar sensible effects which things partaking of it produce. The only effect which real things have is to cause belief, for all the sensations which they excite emerge into consciousness in the forms of belief. The question therefore is, how is true belief (or belief in the real) distinguished from false belief (of belief in fiction). But, as we have seen, the ideas of truth and falsehood, in their full development appertain exclusively to the experiential method of settling opinion. A person who arbitrarily chooses the propositions which he will adopt can use the word truth only to emphasize the expression of his determination to hold on to his choice. Of course, the method of tenacity never prevailed exclusively; reason is too natural to men for that. But in the literature of the dark ages we find some fine examples of it. . . .

When philosophy began to awake from its long slumber, and before theology completely dominated it, the practice seems to have been for each professor to seize upon any philosophical position he found unoccupied and which seemed a strong one, to intrench himself in it, and to sally forth from time to time to give battle to the others. For him, the truth is simply his particular stronghold. . . .

When the method of authority prevailed, the truth meant little more than the Catholic faith. All the efforts of the scholastic doctors are directed toward harmonizing their faith in Aristotle and their faith in the Church, and one may search their ponderous folios through without finding an argument which goes any further. . . . Since the time of Descartes, the defect in the conception of truth has been less apparent. Still, it will sometimes strike a scientific man that the philosophers have been less intent on finding out what the facts are, than on inquiring what belief is most in harmony with their system. It is hard to convince a follower of the *a priori* method by adducing facts; but show him that an opinion he is defending is inconsistent with what he has laid down elsewhere, and he will be very apt to retract it. These minds do not seem to believe that disputation is ever to cease; they seem to think that the opinion which is natural for one man is not so for another, and that belief will, consequently, never be settled. In contenting themselves with fixing their own opinions by a method which would lead another man to a different result, they betray their feeble hold of the conception of what truth is.

On the other hand, all the followers of science are animated by a cheerful hope that the processes of investigation, if only pushed far enough, will give one certain solution to each question to which they apply it. . . . Different minds may set out with the most antagonistic views, but the progress of investigation carries them by a force outside of themselves to one and the same conclusion. This activity of thought by which we are carried, not where we wish, but to a fore-ordained goal, is like the operation of destiny. No modification of the point of view taken, no selection of other facts for study, no natural bent of mind even, can enable a man to escape the predestinate opinion. This great hope is embodied in the conception of truth and reality. The opinion which is fated to be ultimately agreed to by all who investigate, is what we mean by truth, and the object represented in this opinion is the real. That is the way I would explain reality. . . .

It seems to me, then, that we have, by the application of our rule, reached so clear an apprehension of what we mean by reality, and of the fact which the idea rests on, that we should not perhaps be making a pretension so presumptuous as it would be singular, if we were to offer a metaphysical theory of existence for universal acceptance among those who employ the scientific method of fixing belief. However, as metaphysics is a subject much more curious than useful, the knowledge of which, like that of a sunken reef, serves chiefly to enable us to keep clear of it, I will not trouble the reader with any more Ontology at this moment.

QUESTIONS FOR DISCUSSION

1. What are the advantages and disadvantages of each of the methods Peirce discusses for establishing belief? Are there any other ways he did not discuss?
2. When you make a decision, which method (s) do you use? Can you give examples from your own experience when you used each of Peirce's four methods?
3. Do you agree that reality is what competent scientific observers agree is real? Would Royce agree? What would Hume say? What would be Bergson's reaction?

READINGS FOR IMMEDIATE REFERENCE

Peirce, Charles S. *Collected Papers.* Cambridge: Harvard University Press, 1935, Vol. V.

Dewey, John. *How We Think,* rev. ed. Boston: D. C. Heath and Co., 1933, Chapter 1.

James, William. *The Will to Believe.* New York: Longmans, Green and Co., 1897, Chapter 1.

REFERENCES FOR COMPREHENSIVE KNOWLEDGE

Peirce, Charles S. *Chance, Love and Logic,* M. R. Cohen, ed. New York: Harcourt, Brace, 1923.

———. *Essays in the Philosophy of Science,* Vincent Tomas, ed. New York: Liberal Arts Press, 1951.

———. *Values in a Universe of Chance,* P. Wiener, ed. New York: Doubleday Anchor Books, 1958.

Buchler, Justus. *Charles Peirce's Empiricism.* New York: Harcourt, Brace, 1939. Approaches Peirce from the point of view of his scientific interests.

Goudge, T. A. *The Thought of C. S. Peirce.* Toronto: University of Toronto Press, 1950. Systematic and comprehensive.

Thompson, Manley H. *The Pragmatic Philosophy of C. S. Peirce.* Chicago: University of Chicago Press, 1953. Understands Peirce's basic interest to be his pragmatism.

Also see:

Feibleman, James. *An Introduction to Peirce's Philosophy.* New York: Harper, 1946.

Gallie, W. B. *Peirce and Pragmatism.* Baltimore: Penguin Books, 1952.

Murphey, Murray G. *The Development of Peirce's Philosophy.* Cambridge: Harvard University Press, 1961.

V. PLATO

Born in 428 B.C., Aristocles or "Plato," a nickname given him because of his broad shoulders, came from a distinguished Athenian family. His father was descended from the kings of Athens and his mother was independently wealthy, besides being related to many political leaders. Presumably he was raised in aristocratic surroundings, although the Peloponnesian War, in which Plato fought, made the Athenian cultural achievements less brilliant than they had been during Socrates' youth. When Plato was twenty, he began his studies with Socrates, then sixty-two, and was deeply affected by his teacher's death eight years later. He travelled some, perhaps as far as Egypt, certainly to Italy and Sicily, and even tried his hand in political life, but by 388 B.C. he returned to Athens to establish his school, The Academy. Young people, including Aristotle, came from all over the Mediterranean to study music, mathematics, astronomy, literature, and philosophy at his school, and Plato considered his teaching the most important part of his life's work. However, we know him today for the two dozen highly polished dialogues he wrote, most of them having Socrates as the main spokesman. He taught and wrote until his death at the age of eighty, and his school continued to educate the leaders of Greek and, later, of Roman society until the fall of the Roman Empire. Nor can Plato's influence on the contemporary western world be overestimated.

This selection from *The Republic,* Plato's most important single work, portrays his metaphysical theory in terms of a divided line and an allegory. Pay careful attention to the various parts of the divided line and notice how they are exemplified in the allegory. Plato believes reality consists of two aspects, that which is visible and that which is intelligible, and that the latter is the more important. Why does he believe this?

The Divided Line and the Allegory of the Cave[1]

Now take a line which has been cut into two unequal parts, and divide each of them again in the same proportion, and suppose the two main divisions to answer, one to the visible and the other to the intelligible, and then compare the subdivisions in respect of their clearness and want of clearness, and you will find that the first section in the sphere of the visible consists of images. And by images I mean, in the first place, shadows, and in the second place, reflections in water and in solid, smooth and polished bodies and the like: Do you understand?

Yes, I understand.

Imagine, now, the other section, of which this is only the resemblance, to include the animals which we see, and everything that grows or is made.

Very good.

Would you not admit that both the sections of this division have different degrees of truth, and that the copy is to the original as the sphere of opinion is to the sphere of knowledge?

Most undoubtedly.

Next proceed to consider the manner in which the sphere of the intellectual is to be divided.

In what manner?

Thus:—There are two subdivisions, in the lower of which the soul uses the figures given by the former division as images; the inquiry can only be hypothetical, and instead of going upwards to a principle descends to the other end; in the higher of the two, the soul passes out of hypotheses, and goes up to a principle which is above hypotheses, making no use of images as in the former case, but proceeding only in and through the ideas themselves.

I do not quite understand your meaning, he said.

Then I will try again; you will understand me better when I have made some preliminary remarks. You are aware that students of geometry, arithmetic, and the kindred sciences assume the odd and the even and the figures and three kinds of angles and the like in their several branches of science; these are their hypotheses, which they and everybody are supposed to know, and therefore they do not deign to give any account of them either to themselves or others; but they begin with them, and go on until they arrive at last, and in a consistent manner, at their conclusion?

Yes, he said, I know.

And do you not know also that although they make use of the visible forms and reason about them, they are thinking not of these, but of the ideal forms which they resemble; not of the figures which they draw, but of the absolute square and the absolute diameter, and so on—the forms which they draw or make, and which have shadows and reflections in water of their own, are converted by them into

[1] From Plato's *The Republic,* 2nd ed., translated by Benjamin Jowett. New York: Oxford University Press, 1891, Books VI and VII, 510-519.

images, but they are really seeking to behold the things themselves, which can only be seen with the eye of the mind?

That is true.

And of this kind I spoke as the intelligible, although in the search after it the soul is compelled to use hypotheses; not ascending to a first principle, because she is unable to rise above the region of hypothesis, but employing the objects of which the shadows below are resemblances in their turn as images, they having in relation to the shadows and reflections of them a greater distinctness, and therefore a higher value.

I understand, he said, that you are speaking of the province of geometry and the sister arts.

And when I speak of the other division of the intelligible, you will understand me to speak of that other sort of knowledge which reason herself attains by the power of dialectic, using the hypotheses not as first principles, but only as hypotheses—that is to say, as steps and points of departure into a world which is above hypotheses, in order that she may soar beyond them to the first principle of the whole; and clinging to this and then to that which depends on this, by successive steps she descends again without the aid of any sensible object, from ideas, through ideas, and in ideas she ends.

I understand you, he replied; not perfectly, for you seem to me to be describing a task which is really tremendous; but, at any rate, I understand you to say that knowledge and being, which the science of dialectic contemplates, are clearer than the notions of the arts, as they are termed, which proceed from hypotheses only: these are also contemplated by the understanding, and not by the senses: yet, because they start from hypotheses and do not ascend to a principle, those who contemplate them appear to you not to exercise the higher reason upon them, although when a first principle is added to them they are cognizable by the higher reason. And the habit which is concerned with geometry and the cognate sciences I suppose that you would term understanding and not reason, as being intermediate between opinion and reason.

You have quite conceived my meaning, I said; and now, corresponding to these four divisions, let there be four faculties in the soul—reason answering to the highest, understanding to the second, faith (or conviction) to the third; and perception of shadows to the last—and let there be a scale of them, and let us suppose that the several faculties have clearness in the same degree that their objects have truth.

I understand, he replied, and give my assent, and accept your arrangement.

And now, I said, let me show in a figure how far our nature is enlightened or unenlightened:—Behold! human beings living in an underground den, which has a mouth open towards the light and reaching all along the den; here they have been from their childhood, and have their legs and necks chained so that they cannot move, and can only see before them, being prevented by the chains from turning round their heads. Above and behind them a fire is blazing at a distance, and between the fire and the prisoners there is a raised way; and you will see, if you look, a low wall built along the way, like the screen which marionette players have in front of them, over which they show the puppets.

I see.

And do you see, I said, men passing along the wall carrying all sorts of vessels, and statues and figures of animals made of wood and stone and various materials, which appear over the wall? Some of them are talking, others silent.

You have shown me a strange image, and they are strange prisoners.

Like ourselves, I replied; and they see only their own shadows, or the shadows of one another, which the fire throws on the opposite wall of the cave.

True, he said; how could they see anything but the shadows if they were never allowed to move their heads?

And of the objects which are being carried in like manner they would only see the shadows?

Yes, he said.

And if they were able to converse with one another, would they not suppose that they were naming what was actually before them?

Very true.

And suppose further that the prison had an echo which came from the other side, would they not be sure to fancy when one of the passers-by spoke that the voice which they heard came from the passing shadow?

No question, he replied.

To them, I said, the truth would be literally nothing but the shadows of the images.

That is certain.

And now look again, and see what will naturally follow if the prisoners are released and disabused of their error. At first, when any of them is liberated and compelled suddenly to stand up and turn his neck round and walk and look towards the light, he will suffer sharp pains; the glare will distress him, and he will be unable to see the realities of which in his former state he had seen the shadows; and then conceive some one saying to him, that what he saw before was an illusion, but that now, when he is approaching nearer to being and his eye is turned towards more real existence, he has a clearer vision,—what will be his reply? And you may further imagine that his instructor is pointing to the objects as they pass and requiring him to name them, —will he not be perplexed? Will he not fancy that the shadows which he formerly saw are truer than the objects which are now shown to him?

Far truer.

And if he is compelled to look straight at the light, will he not have a pain in his eyes which will make him turn away to take refuge in the objects of vision which he can see, and which he will conceive to be in reality clearer than the things which are now being shown to him?

True, he said.

And suppose once more, that he is reluctantly dragged up a steep and rugged ascent, and held fast until he is forced into the presence of the sun himself, is he not likely to be pained and irritated? When he approaches the light his eyes will be dazzled, and he will not be able to see anything at all of what are now called realities.

Not all in a moment, he said.

He will require to grow accustomed to the sight of the upper world. And first he will see the shadows best, next the reflections of men and other objects in the water, and then the objects themselves; then he will gaze upon the light of the moon and the stars and the spangled heaven; and he will see the sky and the stars by night better than the sun or the light of the sun by day?

Certainly.

Last of all he will be able to see the sun, and not mere reflections of him in the water, but he will see him in his own proper place, and not in another; and he will contemplate him as he is.

Certainly.

He will then proceed to argue that this is he who gives the season and the years, and is the guardian of all that is in the visible world, and in a certain way the cause of all things which he and his fellows have been accustomed to behold?

Clearly, he said, he would first see the sun and then reason about him.

And when he remembered his old habitation, and the wisdom of the den and his fellow-prisoners, do you not suppose that he would felicitate himself on the change, and pity them?

Certainly, he would.

And if they were in the habit of conferring honors among themselves on those who were quickest to observe the passing shadows and to remark which of them went before, and which followed after, and which were together; and who were therefore best able to draw conclusions as to the future, do you think that he would care for such honors and glories, or envy the possessors of them? Would he not say with Homer, "Better to be the poor servant of a poor master," and to endure anything, rather than think as they do and live after their manner?

Yes, he said, I think that he would rather suffer anything than entertain these false notions and live in this miserable manner.

Imagine once more, I said, such an one coming suddenly out of the sun to be replaced in his old situation; would he not be certain to have his eyes full of darkness?

To be sure, he said.

And if there were a contest, and he had to compete in measuring the shadows with the prisoners who had never moved out of the den, while his sight was still weak, and before his eyes had become steady (and the time which would be needed to acquire this new habit of sight might be very considerable) would he not be ridiculous? Men would say of him that up he went and down he came without his eyes; and that it was better not even to think of ascending; and if any one tried to loose another and lead him up to the light, let them only catch the offender, and they would put him to death.

No question, he said.

This entire allegory, I said, you may now append, dear Glaucon, to the previous argument; the prisonhouse is the world of sight, the light of the fire is the sun, and you will not misapprehend me if you interpret the journey upwards to be the ascent of the soul into the intellectual world according to my poor belief, which, at your desire, I have expressed—whether rightly or wrongly God knows. But, whether true or false, my opinion is that in the world of knowledge the idea of Good appears last of all, and is seen only with an effort; and, when seen, is also inferred to be the universal author of all things beautiful and right, parent of light and of the lord of light in this visible world, and the immediate source of reason and truth in the intellectual; and that this is the power upon which he who would act rationally either in public or private life must have his eye fixed.

I agree, he said, as far as I am able to understand you.

Moreover, I said, you must not wonder that those who attain to this beatific vision are unwilling to descend to human affairs; for their souls are ever hastening into the upper world where they desire to dwell; which desire of theirs is very natural, if our allegory may be trusted.

Yes, very natural.

And is there anything surprising in one who passes from divine contemplations to the evil state of man, misbehaving himself in a ridiculous manner; if, while his eyes are blinking and before he has become accustomed to the surrounding darkness, he is compelled to fight in courts of law, or in other places, about the images or the shadows of images of justice, and is endeavoring to meet the conceptions of those who have never yet seen absolute justice?

Anything but surprising, he replied.

Any one who has common sense will remember that the bewilderments of the eyes are of two kinds, and arise from two causes, either from coming out of the light or from going into the light, which is true of the mind's eye, quite as much as of the bodily eye; and he who remembers this when he sees any one whose vision is perplexed and weak, will not be too ready to laugh; he will first ask whether that soul of man has come out of the brighter life, and is unable to see because unaccustomed to the dark, or having turned from darkness to the day is dazzled by excess light. And he will count the one happy in his condition and state of being, and he will pity the other; or, if he have a mind to laugh at the soul which comes from below into the light, there will be more reason in this than in the laugh which greets him who returns from above out of the light into the den.

That, he said, is a very just distinction.

But then, if I am right, certain professors of education must be wrong when they say that they can put a knowledge into the soul which was not there before, like sight into blind eyes.

They undoubtedly say this, he replied.

Whereas, our argument shows that the power and capacity of learning exists in the soul already; and that just as the eye was unable to turn from darkness to light without the whole body, so too the instrument of knowledge can only by the movement of the whole soul be turned from the world of becoming into that of being, and learn by degrees to endure the sight of being, and of the brightest and best of being, or in other words, of the good.

Very true.

And must there not be some art which will effect conversion in the easiest and quickest manner; not implanting the faculty of sight, for that exists already, but has been turned in the wrong direction, and is looking away from the truth?

Yes, he said, such an art may be presumed.

And whereas the other so-called virtues of the soul seem to be akin to bodily qualities, for even when they are not originally innate they can be implanted later by habit and exercise, the virtue of wisdom more than anything else contains a divine element which always remains, and by this conversion is rendered useful and profitable; or, on the other hand, hurtful and useless. Did you never observe the narrow intelligence flashing from the keen eye of a clever rogue—how eager he is, how clearly his paltry soul sees the way to his end; he is the reverse of blind, but his keen eyesight is forced into the service of evil, and he is mischievous in proportion to his cleverness?

Very true, he said.

But what if there had been a circumcision of such natures in the days of their youth; and they had been severed from those sensual pleasures, such as eating and drinking, which, like leaden weights, were attached to them at their birth, and which drag them down and turn the vision of their souls upon the things that are below—if, I say, they had been released from these impediments and turned in the opposite direction, the very same faculty in them would have seen the truth as keenly as they see what their eyes are turned to now.

Very likely.

QUESTIONS FOR DISCUSSION

1. What conclusions do the doctrines of the divided line and allegory of the cave point to? Does Plato offer any reasons or evidence to support his beliefs? Could he? Could you?
2. In your own thinking, are "knowledge," "opinion," "faith," and "perception" different from each other, as Plato says? How are these differences significant for the problem of deciding what is real?
3. Should the search for knowledge of unchanging truths be the basis of educational practice? How would this differ from Dewey's approach?

READINGS FOR IMMEDIATE REFERENCE

Plato. *The Republic,* Books II-VII.
———. *The Symposium.*
———. *Parmenides,* 128-135.
Aristotle. *Politics,* Book VIII.

REFERENCES FOR COMPREHENSIVE KNOWLEDGE

Plato. *Dialogues of Plato,* translated by Benjamin Jowett. New York: Oxford University Press, 1893.

Fite, Warner. *The Platonic Legend.* New York: Henry Holt, 1935. A vigorous criticism of Plato's admirers.

Grube, G. M. A. *Plato's Thought.* New York: Oxford University Press, 1935. An introductory commentary based on topics rather than dialogues.

Ritter, Constantine. *The Essence of Plato's Philosophy.* New York: Dial Press, 1933. An influential commentary. For the advanced student.

Taylor, A. E. *Plato, The Man and His Work.* London: Methuen, 1926. Detailed analyses of all the dialogues by this century's leading Platonist.

Also see:

Cornford, F. M. *Plato's Theory of Knowledge.* New York: Harcourt, Brace, 1935.

Jaeger, Werner. *Paideia.* Oxford: Basil Blackwell, 1947.

Nettleship, R. L. *Lectures on the Republic of Plato.* New York: Oxford University Press, 1939.

Popper, Karl. *The Open Society and Its Enemies.* Princeton: Princeton University Press, 1950.

Shorey, Paul. *Platonism Ancient and Modern.* Berkeley: University of California Press, 1938.

Wild, John. *Plato's Theory of Man.* Cambridge: Harvard University Press, 1946.

VI. LUCRETIUS

In addition to the thought of Plato, Aristotle, and the Stoics, Greek philosophy also produced a type of philosophy known as *atomism.* Its earliest spokesmen, Leucippus, and his younger contemporary, Democritus, lived in the fifth and fourth centuries B.C., and some of the ethical implications of their teachings were given expression in the writings of Epicurus. However, it is in the thought of Lucretius that Atomism is developed to its fullest extent. Unfortunately, little is known of his life beyond the fact that he was born about 98 B.C., lived a life of retirement and obscurity, might have been insane for portions of his later life, and probably committed suicide before he was forty years old. It is to Cicero that we owe a debt for preserving Lucretius' *The Nature of the Universe,* for he edited and published the work in 54 B.C. By the next century the work was highly regarded and was imitated by Virgil and studied by Horace and Ovid. The work was originally written in verse form.

This kind of metaphysical theory probably will sound remarkably modern to you. But do not let its modernity prevent you from considering whether the arguments Lucretius gives to support his points are justified or not. Do they seem to you to be persuasive? Or is Plato's theory a more satisfactory account of reality?

Atomism[1]

This dread and darkness of the mind cannot be dispelled by the sunbeams, the shining shafts of day, but only by an understanding of the outward form and inner workings of nature. In tackling this theme, our starting-point will be this principle: *Nothing can ever be created by divine power out of nothing.* The reason why all mortals are so gripped by fear is that they see all sorts of things happening on the earth and in the sky with no discernible cause, and these they attribute to the will of a god. Accordingly, when we have seen that nothing can be created out of nothing, we shall then have a clearer picture of the path ahead, the problem of how things are created and occasioned without the aid of the gods.

First then, if things were made out

[1] From *The Nature of the Universe* by Lucretius, translated by R. E. Latham. Penguin Books, 1951, Books I-III. Reprinted by permission.

of nothing, any species could spring from any source and nothing would require seed. Men could arise from the sea and scaly fish from the earth, and birds could be hatched out of the sky. Cattle and other domestic animals and every kind of wild beast, multiplying indiscriminately, would occupy cultivated and waste lands alike. The same fruits would not grow constantly on the same trees, but they would keep changing: any tree might bear any fruit. If each species were not composed of its own generative bodies, why should each be born always of the same kind of mother? Actually, since each is formed out of specific seeds, it is born and emerges into the sunlit world only from a place where there exists the right material, the right kind of atoms. This is why everything cannot be born of everything, but a specific power of generation inheres in specific objects. . . .

Or again, why has not nature been able to produce men on such a scale that they could ford the ocean on foot or demolish high mountains with their hands or prolong their lives over many generations? Surely because each thing requires for its birth a particular material which determines what can be produced. It must therefore be admitted that nothing can be made out of nothing, because everything must be generated from a seed before it can emerge into the unresisting air.

Lastly, we see that tilled plots are superior to untilled, and their fruits are improved by cultivation. This is because the earth contains certain atoms which we arouse to productivity by turning the fruitful clods with the ploughshare and stirring up the soil. But for these, you would see great improvements arising spontaneously without any aid from our labors.

The second great principle is this: *nature resolves everything into its component atoms and never reduces anything to nothing.* If anything were perishable in all its parts, anything might perish all of a sudden and vanish from sight. There would be no need of any force to separate its parts and loosen their links. In actual fact, since everything is composed of indestructible seeds, nature obviously does not allow anything to perish till it has encountered a force that shatters it with a blow or creeps into chinks and unknits it.

If the things that are banished from the scene by age are annihilated through the exhaustion of their material, from what source does Venus bring back the several races of animals into the light of life? And, when they are brought back, where does the inventive earth find for each the special food required for its sustenance and growth? From what fount is the sea replenished by its native springs and the streams that flow into it from afar? Whence does the ether draw nutriment for the stars? For everything consisting of a mortal body must have been exhausted by the long day of time, the illimitable past. If throughout this bygone eternity there have persisted bodies from which the universe has been perpetually renewed, they must certainly be possessed of immortality. Therefore things cannot be reduced to nothing.

Again, all objects would regularly be destroyed by the same force and the same cause, were it not that they are sustained by imperishable matter more or less tightly fastened together. Why, a mere touch would be enough to bring about destruction supposing there were no imperishable bodies whose union could be dissolved only by the appropriate force. Actually, because the fastenings of the atoms are of various kinds while their matter is imperishable, compound objects remain intact until one of them encounters a force that proves strong enough to break up its particular constitution. Therefore nothing returns to nothing, but everything is resolved into its constituent bodies.

* * * * *

Well, Memmius, I have taught you that things cannot be created out of nothing nor, once born, be summoned back to nothing. Perhaps, however, you are becoming mistrustful of my words, because these atoms of mine are not visible to the eye. Consider, therefore, this further evidence of *bodies whose existence you must acknowledge though they cannot be seen.* First, wind, when its force is roused, whips up waves, founders tall ships and scatters cloud rack. Sometimes scouring plains with hurricane force it strews them with huge trees and batters mountain peaks with blasts that hew down forests. Such is wind in its fury, when it whoops aloud with a mad menace in its shouting. Without question, therefore, there must be invisible particles of wind which sweep sea and land and the clouds in the sky, swooping upon them and whirling them along in a headlong hurricane. . . .

Then again, we smell the various scents of things though we never see them approaching our nostrils. Similarly, heat and cold cannot be detected by our eyes, and we do not see sounds. Yet all these must be composed of bodies, since they are able to impinge upon our senses. For nothing can touch or be touched except body. . . .

Again, in the course of many annual revolutions of the sun a ring is worn thin next to the finger with continual rubbing. Dripping water hollows a stone. A curved ploughshare, iron though it is, dwindles imperceptibly in the furrow. We see the cobble-stones of the highway worn by the feet of many wayfarers. The bronze statues by the city gates show their right hands worn thin by the touch of travellers who have greeted them in passing. We see that all these are being diminished, since they are worn away. But to perceive what particles drop off at any particular time is a power grudged to us by our ungenerous sense of sight. . . .

On the other hand, things are not hemmed in by the pressure of solid bodies in a tight mass. This is because *there is vacuity in things.* A grasp of this fact will be helpful to you in many respects and will save you from much bewildered doubting and questioning about the universe and from mistrust of my teaching. Well then, by vacuity I mean intangible and empty space. If it did not exist, things could not move at all. For the distinctive action of matter, which is counteraction and obstruction, would be in force always and everywhere. Nothing could proceed, because nothing would give it a starting-point by receding. As it is, we see with our own eyes at sea and on land and high up in the sky that all sorts of things in all sorts of ways are on the move. If there were no empty space, these things would be denied the power of restless movement—or rather, they could not possibly have come into existence, embedded as they would have been in motionless matter.

Besides, there are clear indications that things that pass for solid are in fact porous. Even in rocks a trickle of water seeps through into caves, and copious drops ooze from every surface. Food percolates to every part of an animal's body. Trees grow and bring forth their fruit in season, because their food is distributed throughout their length from the tips of the roots through the trunk and along every branch. Noises pass through walls and fly into closed buildings. Freezing cold penetrates to the bones. If there were no vacancies through which the various bodies could make their way, none of these phenomena would be possible.

* * * * *

It remains to show that *nothing exists that is distinct both from body and from vacuity* and could be ranked with the others as a third substance. For whatever *is* must also be something. If it offers resistance to touch, however light and slight, it will increase the mass of body by such amount, great or small, as it may amount to, and will rank with it. If, on the other hand, it is intangible, so that it offers no resistance whatever to anything passing through it, then it will be that empty space which we call vacuity. Besides, whatever it may be in itself, either it will act in some way, or react to other things acting upon it, or else it will be such that things can be and happen in it. But without body nothing can act or react; and nothing can afford a place except emptiness and vacancy. Therefore, besides matter and vacuity, we cannot include in the number of things any third substance that can either affect our senses at any time or be grasped by the reasoning of our minds. . . .

Material objects are of two kinds, atoms and compounds of atoms. The atoms themselves cannot be swamped by any force, for they are preserved indefinitely by their absolute solidity. Admittedly, it is hard to believe that anything can exist that is absolutely solid. The lightning stroke from the sky penetrates closed buildings, as do shouts and other noises. Iron glows molten in the fire, and hot rocks are cracked by untempered scorching. Hard gold is softened and melted by heat; and bronze, ice-like, is liquefied by flame. Both heat and piercing cold seep through silver, since we feel both alike when a cooling shower of water is poured into a goblet that we hold ceremonially in our hands. All these facts point to the conclusion that nothing is really solid. But sound reasoning and nature itself drive us to the opposite conclusion. Pay attention, therefore, while I demonstrate in a few lines that there exist certain bodies that are absolutely solid and indestructible, namely those atoms which according to our teaching are the seeds or prime units of things from which the whole universe is built up. . . .

If there were no empty space, everything would be one solid mass; if there were no material objects with the property of filling the space they occupy, all existing space would be utterly void. It is clear, then, that there is an alternation of matter and vacuity, mutually distinct, since the whole is neither completely full nor completely empty. There are therefore solid bodies, causing the distinction between empty space and full. And these, as I have just shown, can be neither decomposed by blows from without nor invaded and unknit from within nor destroyed by any other form of assault. For it seems that a thing without vacuum can be neither knocked to bits nor snapped nor chopped in two by cutting; nor can it let in moisture or seeping cold or piercing fire, the universal agents of destruction. The more vacuum a thing contains within it, the more readily it yields to these assailants. Hence, if the units of matter are solid and without vacuity, as I have shown, they must be everlasting.

Yet again, if the matter in things had not been everlasting, everything by now would have gone back to nothing, and the things we see would be the product of rebirth out of nothing. But, since I have already shown that nothing can be created out of nothing nor any existing thing be summoned back to nothing, the atoms must be made of imperishable stuff into which everything can be resolved in the end, so that there may be a stock of matter for building the world anew. The atoms, therefore, are absolutely solid and unalloyed. . . . To these nature allows no loss or diminution, but guards them as seeds for things.

* * * * *

Well then, since I have shown that there are completely solid indestructible particles of matter flying about through all eternity, let us elucidate whether or not there is any limit to their number. Similarly, as we have found that there is a vacuum, the place or space in which things happen, let us see whether its whole extent is limited or whether it stretches far and wide into immeasurable depths.

Learn, therefore, that *the universe is not bounded in any direction.* If it were, it would necessarily have a limit somewhere. But clearly a thing cannot have a limit unless there is something outside to limit it, so that the eye can follow it up to a certain point but not beyond. Since you must admit that there is nothing outside the universe, it can have no limit and is accordingly without end or measure. It makes no odds in which part of it you may take your stand: whatever spot anyone may occupy, the universe stretches away from him just the same in all directions without limit. Suppose for a moment that the whole of space were bounded and that someone made his way to its uttermost boundary and threw a flying dart. Do you choose to suppose that the missile, hurled with might and main, would speed along the course on which it was aimed? Or do you think something would block the way and stop it? You must assume one alternative or the other. But neither of them leaves you a loophole. Both force you to admit that the universe continues without end. . . .

Further, if all the space in the universe were shut in and confined on every side by definite boundaries, the supply of matter would already have accumulated by its own weight at the bottom, and nothing could happen under the dome of the sky—indeed, there would be no sky and no sunlight, since all the available matter would have settled down and would be lying in a heap throughout eternity. As it is, no rest is given to the atoms, because there is no bottom where they can accumulate and take up their abode.

* * * * *

And now I will explain *the motion by which the generative bodies of matter give birth to various things,* and, after they are born, dissolve them once more; the force that compels them to do this; and the power of movement through the boundless void with which they are endowed. It is for you to devote yourself attentively to my words.

Be sure that matter does not stick together in a solid mass. For we see that everything grows less and seems to melt away with the lapse of time and withdraw its old age from our eyes. And yet we see no diminution in the sum of things. This is because the bodies that are shed by one thing lessen it by their departure but enlarge another by their coming; here they bring decay, there full bloom, but they do not linger there. So the sum of things is perpetually renewed. Mortals live by mutual interchange. One race increases by another's decrease. The generations of living things pass in swift succession and like runners hand on the torch of life.

If you think that the atoms can stop and by their stopping generate new motions in things, you are wandering far from the path of truth. Since the atoms are moving freely through the void, they must all be kept in motion either by their own weight or on occasion by the impact of another atom. For it must often happen that two of them in their course knock together and immediately bounce apart in opposite directions, a natural consequence of their hardness and solidity and the absence of anything behind to stop them. . . .

It clearly follows that no rest is given to the atoms in their course through the depths of space. Driven along in an incessant but variable movement, some of them bounce far apart after a collision while others recoil only a short distance from the impact. From those that do not recoil far, being driven into a closer union and held there by the entanglement of their own interlocking shapes, are composed firmly rooted rock, the stubborn strength of steel and the like. Those others that move freely through larger tracts of space, springing far apart and carried far by the rebound—these provide for us thin air and blazing sunlight. Besides these, there are many other atoms at large in empty space which have been thrown out of compound bodies and have nowhere even been granted admittance so as to bring their motions into harmony.

This process, as I might point out, is illustrated by an image of it that is continually taking place before our very eyes. Observe what happens when sunbeams are admitted into a building and shed light on its shadowy places. You will see a multitude of tiny particles mingling in a multitude of ways in the empty space within the light of the beam, as though contending in everlasting conflict, rushing into battle rank upon rank with never a moment's pause in a rapid sequence of unions and disunions. From this you may picture what it is for the atoms to be perpetually tossed about in the illimitable void.

* * * * *

And now let us turn to a new theme —*the characteristics of the atoms of all substances, the extent to which they differ in shape and the rich multiplicity of their forms.* Note that there are not many of the same shape, but they are by no means all identical with one another. And no wonder. When the multitude of them, as I have shown, is such that it is without limit or count, it is not to be expected that they should all be identical in build and configuration.

Consider the race of men, the scaly fish that swim in silence, the lusty herds, the creatures of the wild and the various feathered breeds, those that throng the vivifying watery places, by river banks and springs and lakes, and those that flock and flutter through pathless woodlands. Take a representative of any of these diverse species and you will still find that it differs in form from others of its kind. Otherwise the young could not recognize their mother, nor the mother her young. But we see that this can happen, and that individuals of these species are mutually recognizable no less than human beings. . . .

On this principle it is quite easy to explain why the fire of lightning is far more penetrative than our fire which springs from earthly torches. You can say that the heavenly fire of the lightning is of finer texture, being composed of smaller atoms, and can therefore pass through apertures impervious to this fire of ours, which springs from wood and is generated by a torch. Again, light passes through horn, but rain is dashed back. Why, if not because the particles of light are smaller than those that form the life-giving drops of water? We see that wine flows through a strainer as fast as it is poured in; but sluggish oil loiters. This, no doubt, is either because oil consists of larger atoms, or because these are more hooked and intertangled and, therefore, cannot separate as rapidly, so as to trickle through the holes one by one.

* * * * *

The next step now is evidently to elucidate in my verses the nature of mind and of life. . . .

First, I maintain that *the mind,* which we often call the intellect, the seat of the guidance and control of life, *is part of a man,* no less than hand or foot or eyes are parts of a whole living creature for often the visible body is obviously ill, while in some other unseen part we are enjoying ourselves. No less often the reverse happens: one who is sick at heart enjoys bodily well-being.

This is no different from the experience of an invalid whose foot is hurting while his head is in no pain.

Or consider what happens when we have surrendered our limbs to soothing slumber and our body, replete and relaxed, lies insensible. At that very time there is something else in us that is awake to all sorts of stimuli—something that gives free admittance to all the motions of joy and to heart-burnings void of substance.

Next, you must understand that *there is also a vital spirit in our limbs* and the body does not derive its sentience from harmony. In the first place, life often lingers in our limbs after a large part of the body has been cut off. On the other hand, when a few particles of heat have dispersed and some air has been let out through the mouth, life forsakes the veins forthwith and abandons the bones. Hence you may infer that all the elements do not hold equal portions of vitality or sustain it equally, but it is chiefly thanks to the atoms of wind and heat that life lingers in the limbs. There is therefore in the body itself a vital breath and heat which forsakes our limbs at death. . . .

[Next I maintain] *mind and spirit are both composed of matter.* We see them propelling the limbs, rousing the body from sleep, changing the expression of the face and guiding and steering the whole man—activities that all clearly involve touch, as touch in turn involves matter. How then can we deny their material nature? You see the mind sharing in the body's experiences and sympathizing with it. When the nerve-racking impact of a spear gashes bones and sinews, even if it does not penetrate to the seat of life, there ensues faintness and a tempting inclination earthwards and on the ground a turmoil in the mind and an intermittent faltering impulse to stand up again. The substance of the mind must therefore be material, since it is affected by the impact of material weapons.

My next task will be to demonstrate to you what sort of matter it is of which this mind is composed and how it was formed. First, I affirm that *it is of very fine texture and composed of exceptionally minute particles.* If you will mark my words, you will be able to infer this from the following facts. It is evident that nothing happens as quickly as the mind represents and sketches the happening to itself. Therefore the mind sets itself in motion more swiftly than any of those things whose substance is visible to our eyes. But what is so mobile must consist of exceptionally minute and spherical atoms, so that it can be set going by a slight push. The reason why water is set going and flowing by such a slight push is of course the smallness of its atoms and their readiness to roll. The stickier consistency of honey—its relatively sluggish flow and dilatory progress—is due to the closer coherence of the component matter, consisting, as it obviously does, of particles not so smooth or so fine or so round. A high pile of poppy seed can be disturbed by a light puff of breeze, so that it trickles down from the top, whereas a heap of stones or corn ears remains immovable. In proportion as objects are smaller and smoother, so much the more do they enjoy mobility;

the greater their weight and roughness, the more firmly are they anchored. Since, therefore, the substance of the mind has been found to be extraordinarily mobile, it must consist of particles exceptionally small and smooth and round. This discovery, my dear fellow, will prove a timely aid to you in many problems.

Here is a further indication how flimsy is the texture of the vital spirit and in how small a space it could be contained if it could be massed together. At the instant when a man is mastered by the care-free calm of death and forsaken by mind and spirit, you cannot tell either by sight or by weight that any part of the whole has been filched away from his body. Death leaves everything there, except vital sentience and warmth. Therefore the vital spirit as a whole must consist of very tiny atoms, linked together throughout veins, flesh and sinews—atoms so small that, when all the spirit has escaped from the whole body, the outermost contour of the limbs appears intact and there is no loss of weight.

QUESTIONS FOR DISCUSSION

1. Describe the nature of reality as Lucretius sees it. How many and which of his views are held by contemporary scientific thought?
2. Look again at Lucretius' arguments. Can you explain such phenomena as erosion, wind, the experience of pain, the growth of vegetation, etc. in terms of any other theory than the one Lucretius adopts?
3. Does Atomism imply determinism?
4. Why do you think Plato's metaphysical theory would prevail for two millennia while Lucretius' has become prominent only during the last century? Does your answer point to any general conclusions regarding why metaphysical theories are accepted or rejected?

READINGS FOR IMMEDIATE REFERENCE

Lucretius. *The Nature of the Universe,* translated by R. E. Latham. Baltimore: Penguin Books, 1951, Books I-IV.

Democritus. *Fragments.*

Aristotle. *On Generation and Corruption.* 325 a23, 324 b35.

———. *De Anima.* 403 b30, 405 a8.

REFERENCES FOR COMPREHENSIVE KNOWLEDGE

Bailey, Cyril. *The Greek Atomists and Epicurus.* New York: Oxford University Press, 1928. Relates Epicurus and Lucretius to the larger context of Atomism.

Santayana, George. *Three Philosophical Poets.* Cambridge: Harvard University Press, 1927. Discusses both the poetic and philosophical significance of Lucretius.

Also see:

Gompers, Theodor. *Greek Thinkers,* Vol. 1. New York: Humanities Press, 1955.

Masson, J. *Lucretius, Epicurean and Poet.* New York: Oxford University Press, 1909.

Also consult the bibliography on p. 64.

VII. BARUCH SPINOZA

Spinoza was born in 1632, a Jew whose grandparents had escaped the Spanish Inquisition by settling in Holland. His mother died when he was six years old and his father, a well-to-do merchant and leader in the community, saw that he was educated in a Rabbinical school, learning the Torah and Talmud, along with Latin, Dutch and Spanish, mathematics and science, and the profession of lens grinding. Before he was twenty he began investigating the authorship of the Old Testament and concluded, among other things, that Moses did not write the Pentateuch. His friends and teachers tried to dissuade him from these investigations but no entreaty or reward moved him, so he was judged guilty of heresy and was excommunicated from the community. He was disinherited and all written records of his life were obliterated—at the age of twenty-four. He Latinized his name to Benedict and lived the remaining twenty years of his life earning his living by grinding lenses and teaching, while he wrote philosophy books during the evenings. The only challenge to this quiet occurred in 1670 when he anonymously published the results of his study of the Old Testament. Many people, Christians and Jews, were affronted and, despite his anonymity, Spinoza feared for his life. He died in 1677, probably from tuberculosis.

In the following selection, Spinoza briefly examines the condition necessary for lasting happiness: the "intellectual love of God." Notice his proofs for God's existence, his account of the proper conception of God's nature, and his conclusions regarding man's freedom.

The Intellectual Love of God[1]

After experience had taught me that all the usual surroundings of social life are vain and futile; seeing that none of the objects of my fears contained in themselves anything either good or bad, except insofar as the mind is affected by them, I finally resolved to inquire whether there might be some real good

[1] From *The Improvement of the Understanding* and *The Ethics,* Books I and II, translated by R. H. M. Elwes, from *The Chief Works,* 1951, by Spinoza. Reprinted through permission by Dover Publications, Inc., New York 14, New York. [I have omitted the geometrical form of presentation and rearranged some of the propositions. C.M.]

having power to communicate itself, which would affect the mind singly, to the exclusion of all else: whether, in fact, there might be anything of which the discovery and attainment would enable me to enjoy continuous, supreme, and unending happiness. . . .

I therefore debated whether it would not be possible to arrive at a new principle, or at any rate at a certainty concerning its existence, without changing the conduct and usual plan of my life; with this end in view I made many efforts, but in vain. For the ordinary surroundings of life which are esteemed by men (as their actions testify) to be the highest good, may be classed under the three heads—Riches, Fame, and the Pleasures of Sense: with these three the mind is so absorbed that it has little power to reflect on any different good. By sensual pleasure the mind is enthralled to the extent of quiescence, as if the supreme good were actually attained, so that it is quite incapable of thinking of any other object; when such pleasure has been gratified it is followed by extreme melancholy, whereby the mind, though not enthralled, is disturbed and dulled.

The pursuit of honors and riches is likewise very absorbing, especially if such objects be sought simply for their own sake, inasmuch as they are then supposed to constitute the highest good. In the case of fame the mind is still more absorbed, for fame is conceived as always good for its own sake, and as the ultimate end to which all actions are directed. Further, the attainment of riches and fame is not followed as in the case of sensual pleasures by repentance, but, the more we acquire, the greater is our delight, and consequently, the more are we incited to increase both the one and the other; on the other hand, if our hopes happen to be frustrated we are plunged into the deepest sadness. Fame has the further drawback that it compels its votaries to order their lives according to the opinions of their fellow-men, shunning what they usually shun, and seeking what they usually seek. . . .

All the objects pursued by the multitude not only bring no remedy that tends to preserve our being, but even act as hindrances, causing the death not seldom of those who possess them, and always of those who are possessed by them. There are many examples of men who have suffered persecution even to death for the sake of their riches, and of men who in pursuit of wealth have exposed themselves to so many dangers, that they have paid away their life as a penalty for their folly. Examples are no less numerous of men, who have endured the utmost wretchedness for the sake of gaining or preserving their reputation. Lastly, there are innumerable cases of men, who have hastened their death through over-indulgence in sensual pleasure. All these evils seem to have arisen from the fact that happiness or unhappiness is made to depend wholly on the quality of the object which we love. When a thing is not loved, no quarrels will arise concerning it, no fear, no hatred, in short no disturbances of the mind. All these arise from the love of what is perishable, such as the objects already mentioned. But love towards a thing eternal and infinite feeds the mind wholly with joy, and is itself unmingled with any sadness, wherefore it is greatly to be desired and sought for with all our strength. . . .

Thus it is apparent to everyone that I wish to direct all sciences to one end and aim, so that we may attain to the supreme human perfection. To sum up the matter in a word, all our actions and thoughts must be directed to this one end. [But what could this end be which is desired for itself alone, knowledge of which gives eternal and permanent happiness? The name commonly given to this conception is God or Substance, that which is in and by itself, unlimited by anything else. But let us proceed more carefully and begin with definitions.]

* * * * *

By *substance,* I mean that which is in itself, and is conceived through itself; in other words, that of which a conception can be formed independently of any other conception. By *attribute,* I mean that which the intellect perceives as constituting the essence of substance. By *mode,* I mean the manifestations of substance, or that which exists in, and is conceived through, something other than itself. By *god,* I mean a being absolutely infinite—that is, a substance consisting in infinite attributes, of which each expresses eternal and infinite essentiality. Note that I say absolutely infinite, not infinite after its kind, for of a thing infinite only after its kind, infinite attributes may be denied; but that which is absolutely infinite, contains in its essence whatever expresses reality, and involves no negation. That thing is called *free,* which exists solely by the necessity of its own nature, and of which the action is determined by itself alone. On the other hand, that thing is necessary, or rather constrained which is determined by something external to itself to a fixed and definite method of existence or action. . . .

[Now, it is clear that] God, or substance, consisting of infinite attributes, of which each expresses eternal and infinite essentiality, necessarily exists. This is so because of everything whatsoever a cause or reason must be assigned, either for its existence, or for its non-existence—e.g. if a triangle exists, a reason or cause must be granted for its existence; if, on the contrary, it does not exist, a cause must also be granted, which prevents it from existing, or annuls its existence. This reason or cause must either be contained in the nature of the thing in question, or be external to it. For instance, the reason for the non-existence of a square circle is indicated in its nature, namely, because it would involve a contradiction. But the reason for the existence of a triangle or a circle follows from the order of universal nature in extension. From the latter it must follow, either that a triangle necessarily exists, or that it is impossible that it should exist. So much is self-evident. It follows therefrom that a thing necessarily exists, if no cause or reason can be granted which prevents its existence.

If, then, no cause or reason can be given which prevents the existence of God, or which destroys his existence, we must certainly conclude that he necessarily does exist. If such a reason or cause should be given, it must either be drawn from the very nature of God, or be external to Him—that is, drawn from another substance of another nature. If it were of the same nature, God, by that very fact, would be admitted to exist. But, if it were of a different nature, another substance, it could have nothing in common with God, since each must exist in itself and be conceived through itself. In other words, the conception of the one does not imply the conception of the other and therefore it would be unable either to cause or to destroy his existence.

As, then, a reason or cause which would annul the divine existence cannot be drawn from anything external to the divine nature, such cause must, perforce, if God does not exist, be drawn from God's own nature, which would involve a contradiction. To make such an affirmation about a being absolutely infinite and supremely perfect is absurd; therefore, neither in the nature of God, nor externally to His nature, can a cause or reason be assigned which would annul his existence. Therefore, God necessarily exists.

[If another proof is desired, consider that] the potentiality of non-existence requires a negation of power, and contrariwise the potentiality of existence requires the presence of power. This is obvious. If, then, that which necessarily exists is nothing but finite beings, that is, beings limited in time and space, such finite beings are more powerful than a being absolutely infinite, which is obviously absurd; therefore, either nothing exists, or else a being absolutely infinite necessarily exists also. Now we exist either in ourselves, or in something else which necessarily exists, therefore, a being absolutely infinite—in other words, God, —necessarily exists. . . .

Besides God, no substance can be granted or conceived, for if any substance besides God were granted, it would have to be explained by some attribute of God, and thus two substances with the same attribute would exist, which is absurd. [Moreover,] if another substance could be conceived, it would necessarily have to be conceived as existent, but this, too, is absurd. Clearly, therefore: 1. God is one, that is, only one substance can be granted in the universe, and that substance is absolutely infinite, and 2. *extension* and *thought* are either attributes of God or manifestations of the attributes of God.

* * * * *

Thought is an attribute of God, or God is a thinking thing. This conclusion is evident from the fact that we are able to conceive of an infinite thinking being, and in proportion as a thinking being is conceived as thinking more thoughts, so it is conceived as containing more reality or perfection. Therefore a being which can think an infinite number of thoughts in an infinite number of ways, is, necessarily, in respect of thinking, infinite. As, therefore, from the consideration of thought alone we conceive an infinite being, thought is necessarily one of the infinite attributes of God. God, then, is a thinking being.

Extension, also, is an attribute of God, or God is an extended thing, as can be seen by the same reasoning. . . .

Before going any further, I wish to

recall to mind what has been pointed out before—namely, that whatsoever can be perceived by the infinite intellect as constituting the essence of substance, belongs altogether only to one substance: consequently, substance thinking and substance extended are one and the same substance, comprehended now through one attribute, now through the other. So, also, a mode of extension and the idea of that mode are one and the same thing, though expressed in two ways. Thus, whether we conceive nature under the attribute of extension, or under the attribute of thought, we shall find the same order, or one and the same chain of causes.

* * * * *

Some assert that God, like a man, consists of body and mind, and is susceptible of passions. How far such persons have strayed from the truth is sufficiently evident from what has been said. All who have in anywise reflected on the divine nature deny that God has a body. Of this they find excellent proof in the fact that we understand by body a definite quantity, so long, so broad, so deep, bounded by a certain shape, and it is the height of absurdity to predicate such a thing of God, who is a being absolutely infinite. . . . [Moreover,] if intellect and will pertain to the eternal essence of God, we must take these words in some significations quite different from those they usually bear. This I will prove as follows.

If intellect belongs to the divine nature, it cannot be in nature, as ours is generally thought to be, posterior to, or simultaneous with the things understood, inasmuch as we have shown that God is prior to all things. Wherefore the intellect of God, insofar as it is conceived to constitute God's essence, is, in reality, the cause of things, both of their essence and of their existence. As, therefore, God's intellect is the sole cause of things, it must necessarily differ from them. For a cause differs from a thing it causes, precisely in the quality which the latter gains from the former.

For example, a man is the cause of another man's existence, but not of his essence, and therefore, the two men may be entirely similar in essence, that is, they are both men; but must be different in existence, that is, they are different men. Hence, if the existence of one of them cease, the existence of the other will not necessarily cease also; but if the essence of one would be destroyed the essence of the other would be destroyed also. Wherefore, a thing which is the cause both of the essence and of the existence of a given effect, must differ from such effect both in respect to its essence, and also in respect to its existence. Now, as we have shown, the intellect of God is the cause of both the essence and the existence of our intellect; therefore the intellect of God insofar as it is conceived to constitute the divine essence, differs from our intellect both in respect to essence and existence, nor can it in anywise agree save in name. The reasoning would be identical in the case of will, as anyone can easily see. . . .

God acts solely by the laws of his own nature, and is not constrained by any one. [This follows] solely from the necessity of the divine nature, or, what is the same thing, solely from the laws of nature. All things are in God, wherefore nothing can exist outside himself, whereby he can be conditioned or constrained to act. From this it follows that: 1. there can be no cause which, either extrinsically or intrinsically, moves God to act; and 2. God is the sole free cause. For God alone exists by the sole necessity of his nature, and acts by the sole necessity of his nature. Wherefore, God is, by necessity, the only free cause. . . .

[Therefore,] a thing which has been determined to act in a particular way has necessarily been determined by God. [Moreover,] things could not have been brought into being by God in any manner or any order different from that which has in fact obtained, for if things could have been of a different nature, or could have been determined to act in a different way, God's nature would also have been able to be different from what it now is; and therefore that different nature also would have existed, and consequently there would have been able to be two or more Gods. This, of course, has been shown to be impossible. Therefore, things could not have been brought into being by God in any other manner than the way they have.

* * * * *

In the mind, there is no free will, for the mind is determined to wish this or that by a cause, which has also been determined by another cause, and this last by another cause, and so on to infinity. [This is] because the mind, as a part of nature, is a fixed and definite mode of thought; therefore it cannot be a free cause of its own actions. In other words, it cannot have an absolute faculty of positive or negative volition, but it must be determined by a cause, which has also been determined by another cause, and this last by another, etc. . . .

There might remain misconceptions which may prove a hindrance to understanding this conclusion, for experience seems to teach us especially clearly, that we are able to suspend our judgment before assenting to things which we perceive. If, therefore, we can assent to or deny a judgment, we must be free to do so.

However, all men are born ignorant of the causes of things, all have the desire to seek for what is useful to them, and they are conscious of that desire. Herefrom it follows that men think themselves free, inasmuch as they are conscious of their volitions and desires, and never even dream, in their ignorance, of the causes which have disposed them to wish and desire as they do. Secondly, men find in themselves and outside themselves many means which assist them in their search for what is useful; for instance, eyes for seeing, teeth for chewing, herbs and animals for yielding food, the sun for giving light, the sea for breeding fish, etc. Now as they are aware that they found these conveniences and did not make them, they think they have cause for believing, that some other being has made them for their use. As they look upon things as means, they cannot believe them to be self-created; but judging from the means which they are accustomed to prepare for themselves, they are bound to believe in some ruler or rulers of the universe endowed with human freedom, who have arranged and adapted everything for human use. They are bound to estimate the nature of such rulers (having no information on the subject) in accordance with their own nature, and therefore they assert that the gods ordained everything for the use of man, in order to bind man to themselves and obtain from him the highest honor. Hence, it also follows, that everyone thought out for himself, according to his abilities, a different way of worshipping God, so that God might love him more than his fellows, and direct the whole course of nature for the satisfaction of his blind cupidity and insatiable avarice. Thus the prejudice developed into superstition, and took deep root in the human mind. . . .

Therefore, all things depend on the power of God. In order that things should be different from what they are, God's will would necessarily have to be different. But God's will cannot be different, as we have just most clearly demonstrated, from God's perfection. Therefore, neither can things be different from what they are, [all which shows] that men judge of things according to their own mental disposition, and imagine that the world, nature and God are just as they understand them to be. But these explanations are mere modes of imagining, and do not indicate the true nature of anything, but only the constitution of the imagination making them.

* * * * *

It remains to point out the advantages of a knowledge of this doctrine as bearing on conduct, and this may be easily gathered.

1. Inasmuch as it teaches us to act solely according to the decree of God, and to be partakers in the Divine nature, and so much the more, as we perform more perfect actions and more and more understand God. Such a doctrine not only completely tranquillizes our spirit, but also shows us where our highest happiness and blessedness is, namely, solely in the knowledge or *intellectual love of God,* whereby we are led to act only as love and piety shall bid us. We may thus clearly understand, how far astray from the true estimate of virtue are those who expect to be decorated by God with high rewards for their virtue, and their best actions, as for having endured the direst slavery; as if virtue and the service of God were not in itself happiness and perfect freedom.

2. Inasmuch as it teaches us how we ought to conduct ourselves with respect to the gifts of fortune, or matters which are not in our own power, and do not follow from our nature. For it shows us that we should await and endure fortune's smiles or frowns with an equal mind, seeing that all things follow from the eternal decree of God by the same necessity as it follows from the essence of a triangle that the three angles are equal to two right angles.

3. This doctrine raises social life, inasmuch as it teaches us to hate no man, neither to despise, or deride, to envy or to be angry with any. Further, as it tells us that each should be content with his own, and helpful to his neighbor, not from any womanish wit, favor,

or superstition, but solely by the guidance of reason.

4. Lastly, this doctrine confers no small advantage on the commonwealth; for it teaches how citizens should be governed and led, not so as to become slaves, but so that they may do whatsoever things are best.

QUESTIONS FOR DISCUSSION

1. Do Spinoza's two proofs for God's existence seem satisfactory? Must they presuppose his definition of Substance? Is that definition satisfactory?
2. Is Spinoza's definition of "free" satisfactory? If so, can you escape his conclusions concerning man's (even God's) determinism? Does accepting this conclusion bother you?
3. How does the "intellectual love of God" lead to happiness?
4. Would you say that Spinoza's metaphysical theory is a restatement or a criticism of western religious tradition? Is it irrelevant to this tradition? To modern scientific thought?

READINGS FOR IMMEDIATE REFERENCE

Spinoza, Baruch. *The Ethics,* Parts I, IV.

———. *On the Improvement of the Understanding.*

Lippmann, Walter. *A Preface to Morals.* New York: Macmillan, 1934, Part II.

Maugham, W. Somerset. *Of Human Bondage.* New York: Doubleday, Doran, 1915. (novel)

REFERENCES FOR COMPREHENSIVE KNOWLEDGE

Spinoza, Baruch. *Tractatus Theologico-Politicus.*

———. *Tractatus Politicus.*

McKeon, Richard. *The Philosophy of Spinoza.* New York: Longmans, Green, 1928. A standard commentary.

Wolfson, Harry A. *The Philosophy of Spinoza.* Cambridge: Harvard University Press, 1934. Relates Spinoza to his background, particularly medieval thought.

Also see:

Hampshire, Stuart. *Spinoza.* Baltimore: Penguin Books, 1958.

Joachim, H. H. *A Study in the Ethics of Spinoza.* New York: Oxford University Press, 1901.

———. *Spinoza's Tractatus de Intellectus Emendationa.* New York: Oxford University Press, 1940.

Parkinson, G. H. R. *Spinoza's Theory of Knowledge.* Oxford: Clarendon Press, 1954.

Pollock, Frederick. *Spinoza: His Life and Philosophy.* New York: Oxford University Press, 1899.

VIII. MORITZ SCHLICK

Born in 1882, Schlick received his doctorate in physics from the University of Berlin where he studied under Max Planck. He taught at Kiel for some years, then in 1922 he was appointed a professor of philosophy at the University of Vienna. There he was mainly responsible for organizing a group of philosophers and scientists who met weekly to discuss problems of mutual interest. This group, known as the Vienna Circle, later joined forces with Russell, Ayer, and Wittgenstein in England and Reichenbach in Berlin to formulate the philosophy now known as *logical positivism* or *logical empiricism,* probably the single most important school of thought on the scene today. Schlick taught at Stanford in 1929 and at the University of California in 1931-32. While on his way to class in Vienna in 1936 he was shot by a student and died at the age of fifty-four.

As you read, ask yourself whether Schlick's assessment of the situation among metaphysical theories is accurate, and whether his solution is advisable. What does he take to be the purpose of philosophy?

The Turning Point in Philosophy[1]

From time to time prizes have been established for essays on the question what progress philosophy has made in a given period. The period tends to be limited on the one side by the name of some great thinker, on the other by "the present." It was thus assumed that there is some degree of clarity regarding the philosophic progress of mankind up to the time of that thinker, but that it is dubious what further contributions have been made in recent times.

Such questions clearly express a certain mistrust concerning the philosophy of the period which had recently elapsed. One has the impression of being presented only with an embarrassed formulation of the question: Has philosophy in that period made any progress whatever? For if one were sure that contributions had been made one would also know in what they consisted.

If the more remote past is regarded with less scepticism and one is rather

[1] From "The Turning Point in Philosophy," by Moritz Schlick, *Erkenntnis,* Vol. 1, No. 1, 1931, pp. 1-14. Reprinted by permission of Mrs. Schlick and Rudolph Carnap, co-editor of *Erkenntnis.*

inclined to see in its philosophy a continuous development, the explanation may be that one's attitude towards everything whose place is established in history is tinged with greater respect. A further point is that the older philosophers have at least demonstrated their historical influence. Hence in considering them one can take as one's base their historical rather than their substantive importance, especially since one often does not venture to distinguish between the two.

But it is just the ablest thinkers who most rarely have believed that the results of earlier philosophizing, including that of the classical models, remain unshakable. This is shown by the fact that basically every new system starts again from the beginning, that every thinker seeks his own foundation and does not wish to stand on the shoulders of his predecessors. Descartes (not without reason) felt himself to be making a wholly new beginning; Spinoza believed that in introducing the (to be sure quite adventitious) mathematical form he had found the ultimate philosophical method; and Kant was convinced that on the basis of the way taken by him philosophy would at last adopt the sure path of a science. Further examples are superfluous, for practically all great thinkers have sought for a radical reform of philosophy and considered it essential.

This peculiar fate of philosophy has been so often described and bemoaned that it is indeed pointless to discuss it at all. Silent scepticism and resignation seem to be the only appropriate attitudes. Two thousand years of experience seem to teach that efforts to put an end to the chaos of systems and to change the fate of philosophy can no longer be taken seriously. To point out that man has finally succeeded in solving the most stubborn problems, for example that of Daedalus, gives an informed person no comfort; for what he fears is just that philosophy will never arrive at a genuine "problem."

I refer to this anarchy of philosophical opinions which has so often been described, in order to leave no doubt that I am fully conscious of the scope and weighty significance of the conviction that I should now like to express. For I am convinced that we now find ourselves at an altogether decisive turning point in philosophy, and that we are objectively justified in considering that an end has come to the fruitless conflict of systems. We are already at the present time, in my opinion, in possession of methods which make every such conflict in principle unnecessary. What is now required is their resolute application.

These methods have been quietly developed, unnoticed by the majority of those who teach or write philosophy; and thus a situation has been created which is not comparable to any earlier one. That the situation is unique and that the turning embarked upon is really decisive can be understood only by becoming acquainted with the new paths and by looking back, from the standpoint to which they lead, upon all those efforts that have ever passed as "philosophical."

The paths have their origin in logic. Leibniz dimly saw their beginning. Bertrand Russell and Gottlob Frege have opened up important stretches in the last decades, but Ludwig Wittgenstein (in his *Tractatus Logico-Philosophicus*, 1922) is the first to have pushed forward to the decisive turning point.

It is well known that in recent decades mathematicians have developed new logical methods, at first primarily for the solution of their own problems which could not be overcome by the traditional methods of logic. But the logic thus developed has also long since shown its superiority in other ways over the old forms, and doubtless will very soon supplant them. Was I referring to this logic as the powerful means which is in principle capable of raising us above all philosophical conflicts? Does it give us general rules with whose help all the traditional problems of philosophy can at least in principle be resolved?

If this were so I should hardly have had the right to say that a wholly new situation had been created. For then there would have been only a gradual, as it were, technical progress, as for example, when the invention of the internal combustion engine finally made possible the solution of the problem of flight. However highly the value of the new methods is to be esteemed, it is plain that nothing so fundamental can be brought about by the mere development of a method. The great turning point is therefore not to be attributed to logic itself but to something quite different which was indeed stimulated and made possible by it, but which proceeds on a much deeper level: the insight into the nature of logic itself.

That the logical is in some sense the purely *formal* has been expressed early and often; however, one was not really clear concerning the nature of pure forms. The clue to their nature is to be found in the fact that every cognition is an expression or representation. That is, it expresses a fact which is cognized in it. This can happen in any number of ways, in any language, by means of any arbitrary system of signs. All these possible modes of representation—if they otherwise actually express the same knowledge—must have something in common; and what is common to them is their logical form.

So all knowledge is such only by virtue of its form. It is through its form that it represents the fact known. But the form cannot itself in turn be represented. It alone is concerned in cognition. Everything else in the expression is inessential and accidental material, not different, say, from the ink by means of which we write down a statement.

This simple insight has consequences of the very greatest importance. Above all, it enables us to dispose of the traditional problems of "the theory of knowledge." Investigations concerning the human "capacity for knowledge," in so far as they do not become part of psychology, are replaced by considerations, regarding the nature of expression, of representation, i.e. concerning every possible "language" in the most general sense of the term. Questions regarding the "validity and limits of knowledge" disappear. Everything is knowable which can be expressed, and this is the total subject matter concerning which meaningful questions can be raised. There are consequently no questions which are in principle unanswerable, no problems which are in principle insoluble. What have been considered such up to now are not genuine questions, but meaningless sequences of words. To be sure, they look like questions from the outside, since they seem to satisfy the customary rules of grammar, but in truth they consist of empty sounds, because they transgress the profound inner rules of logical syntax discovered by the new analysis.

Wherever there is a meaningful problem one can in theory always give the path that leads to its solution. For it becomes evident that giving this path coincides with the indication of its meaning. The practical following out of this path may of course be hindered by factual circumstances—by deficient human capacities, for example. The act of verification in which the path to the solution finally ends is always of the same sort: it is the occurrence of a definite fact that is confirmed by observation, by means of immediate experience. In this manner the truth (or falsity) of every statement, of daily life or science, is determined. There is thus no other testing and corroboration of truths except through observation and empirical science. Every science, (in so far as we take this word to refer to the content and not to the human arrangements for arriving at it) is a system of cognitions, that is, of true experiential statements. And the totality of sciences, including the statements of daily life, is the system of cognitions. There is, in addition to it, no domain of "philosophical" truths. Philosophy is not a system of statements; it is not a science.

But what is it then? Well, certainly not a science, but nevertheless something so significant and important that it may henceforth, as before, be honored as the Queen of the Sciences. For it is nowhere written that the Queen of the Sciences must itself be a science. The great contemporary turning point is characterized by the fact that we see in philosophy not a system of cognitions, but a system of *acts;* philosophy is that activity through which the meaning of statements is revealed or determined. By means of philosophy statements are explained, by means of science they are verified. The latter is concerned with the truth of statements, the former with what they actually mean. The content, soul and spirit of science is lodged naturally in what in the last analysis its statements actually mean; the philosophical activity of giving meaning is therefore the Alpha and Omega of all scientific knowledge. This was indeed correctly surmised when it was said that philosophy supplied both the foundation and the apex of the edifice of science. It was a mistake, however, to suppose that the foundation was made up of "philosophical" statements (the statements of theory of knowledge), and crowned by a dome of philosophical statements (called metaphysics).

It is easy to see that the task of philosophy does not consist in asserting statements—that bestowing meaning upon statements cannot be done in turn by statements. For if, say, I give the meaning of my words through explanatory statements and definitions, that is by help of other words, one must ask further for the meaning of these words, and so on. This process cannot proceed endlessly. It always comes to an end in actual pointings, in exhibiting what is meant, thus in real acts; only these acts are no longer capable of, or in need of, further explanation. The final giving of meaning always takes place therefore, through *deeds*. It is these deeds or acts which constitute philosophical activity.

It was one of the most serious errors of former times to have believed that the actual meaning and ultimate content was in turn to be formulated in statements, and so was representable in cognitions. This was the error of "metaphysics." The efforts of metaphysicians were always directed upon the absurd end of expressing the content of pure quality (the "essence" of things) by means of cognitions, hence of uttering the unutterable. Qualities cannot be "said." They can only be shown in experience. But with this showing, cognition has nothing to do.

Thus metaphysics collapses not because the solving of its tasks is an enterprise to which the human reason is unequal (as for example Kant thought) but because there is no such task. With the disclosure of the mistaken formulation of the problem the history of metaphysical conflict is likewise explained.

If our conception is in general correct we must be able to establish it historically. It would have to be capable of giving some account of the change in meaning of the word "philosophy."

Now this is actually the case. If in ancient times, and actually until recently, philosophy was simply identical with every purely theoretical scientific investigation, this points to the fact that science found itself in a state in which it saw its main task still in the clarification of its fundamental concepts. The emancipation of the special sciences from their common mother, philosophy, indicates that the meaning of certain fundamental concepts became clear enough to make successful further work with them possible. If, today, ethics and aesthetics, and frequently also psychology, are considered branches of philosophy, this is a sign that these studies do not yet possess sufficiently clear basic concepts, that their efforts are still chiefly directed upon the *meaning* of their statements. Finally, if within a well-established science the necessity suddenly arises at some point of reflecting anew on the true meaning of the fundamental concepts, and thereby a more profound clarification of their meaning is achieved, this will be felt at once as an eminent philosophical achievement. All are agreed that, for instance, Einstein's work, proceeding from an analysis of the meaning of statements about time and space, was actually a philosophical achievement. Here we should add that the decisive epoch-making forward steps of science are always of this character; they signify a clarification of the meaning of the fundamental statements and only those succeed in them who are endowed for philosophical activity. The great investigator is also always a philosopher.

Frequently also the name of philosophy is bestowed on mental activities which have as their concern not pure knowledge but the conduct of life. This is readily understandable. For the wise man rises above the uncomprehending mass just by virtue of the fact that he can point out more clearly than they the meaning of statements and questions concerning life relationships, facts and desires.

The great turning point of philosophy signifies also a decisive turning away from certain erroneous paths which have been embarked upon since the second half of the 19th century and which must lead to quite a wrong assessment and evaluation of philosophy. I mean the attempts to claim for it an inductive character and accordingly to believe that it consists solely of statements of hypothetical validity. The idea of claiming only probability for its statements was remote from earlier thinkers. They would have rejected it as incompatible with the dignity of philosophy. In this was expressed a healthy instinct for the fact that philosophy must supply the ultimate support of knowledge. The reverse side of the medal is the dogma that philosophy supplies unconditionally true *a priori* axioms, which we must regard as an extremely unfortunate expression of this instinct, particularly since philosophy does not consist of statements at all. But we too believe in the dignity of philosophy and deem incompatible with it the character of being uncertain and only probable; and we are happy that the decisive turning point makes it impossible to attribute any such character to it. For the concept of probability or uncertainty is simply not applicable to the acts of giving meaning which constitute philosophy. It is a matter of positing the meaning of statements as something simply final. Either we *have* this meaning, and then we know what is meant by the statement, or we do not possess it, in which case mere empty words confront us, and as yet no statement at all. There is nothing in between and there can be no talk of the probability that the meaning is the right one. Thus after the great turning point philosophy shows its decisive character even more clearly than before.

It is only, indeed, because of this character that the conflict of systems can be ended. I repeat: in consequence of the insights which I have sketched we may today consider it as in principle already ended. I hope that this may become increasingly clear in the pages of this journal in the new period of its existence.

Certainly there will still be many a rear-guard action. Certainly many will for centuries continue to wander further along the traditional paths. Philosophical writers will long continue to discuss the old pseudo-questions. But in the end they will no longer be listened to; they will come to resemble actors who continue to play for some time before noticing that the audience has slowly departed. Then it will no longer be necessary to speak of "philosophical problems" for one will speak philosophically concerning all problems, that is: clearly and meaningfully.

QUESTIONS FOR DISCUSSION

1. What is the "simple insight" that marks the turning point in philosophy? What are its implications for traditional metaphysical problems?
2. Do you agree that "wherever there is a meaningful problem one can in theory always give the path that leads to its solution"? Why does Schlick say this? Can you think of a meaningful problem you do not know how to solve?
3. According to Schlick, what is the purpose of philosophy? Is this different from what other philosophers take to be its purpose?
4. Do you agree with Schlick that most metaphysical problems are pseudo-problems?

READINGS FOR IMMEDIATE REFERENCE

Schlick, Moritz. "The Future of Philosophy," *Basic Problems of Philosophy,* rev. ed., ed., D. Bronstein, et al. New York: Prentice-Hall, 1956, 572-583.

Ayer, A. J. *Language, Truth and Logic.* New York: Dover Publications Co., 1936, Chapter 1.

Carnap, Rudolf. "The Elimination of Metaphysics through Logical Analysis of Language," *Logical Positivism,* ed., A. J. Ayer. Glencoe, Ill.: The Free Press, 1959.

Heidegger, Martin. *Existence and Being.* Chicago: Regnery, 1949. Introduction.

REFERENCES FOR COMPREHENSIVE KNOWLEDGE

Schlick, Moritz. "Meaning and Verification," *Philosophical Review,* Vol. XLV (July, 1936), 339-369.

———. *Philosophy of Nature.* New York: Philosophical Library, 1949.

———. *Problems of Ethics.* New York: Prentice-Hall, 1939.

———. *Space and Time in Contemporary Physics.* New York: Oxford University Press, 1917.

von Mises, Richard. *Positivism: A Study in Human Understanding.* Cambridge: Harvard University Press, 1951. A thoughtful study of the leading ideas.

Wittgenstein, Ludwig. *Tractatus Logico-Philosophicus.* New York: Harcourt, Brace, 1922. Is becoming the authoritative modern work which identifies philosophy with the analysis of meanings.

Also see:

Feigl, Herbert. *Readings in Philosophical Analysis.* New York: Appleton-Century, 1949.

Jorgensen, J. *The Development of Logical Empiricism.* Chicago: University of Chicago Press, 1951.

Russell, Bertrand. "Philosophy of Logical Atomism," *Logical Positivism,* ed., A. J. Ayer. Glencoe, Ill.: The Free Press, 1951.

IX. GEORGE SANTAYANA

Born in Madrid in 1863, Santayana was brought by his parents to Boston when he was eight years old. He graduated from Harvard in 1886, then went abroad to study at Cambridge and Berlin. He returned to Harvard in 1889 to teach, alongside his old masters, Royce and James, and with young new philosophers such as Perry, W. P. Montague, and C. I. Lewis. He resigned his position in 1912 to take up a permanent residence in England from which he traveled extensively throughout the world and published nearly two dozen books on literary criticism, philosophical analysis, poetry, and novels during the next thirty years. The last few years of his life were spent in seclusion, first in Spain and then later in a convent near Rome, where he died in 1952.

This selection is the Preface to Santayana's five-volume work, *Realms of Being,* which is his most ambitious and one of his most influential works. Notice how he describes each of the four realms, and what reasons he gives for accepting them as being part of reality. Does Santayana believe that formulating metaphysical theories is a worthwhile enterprise? How would you characterize his theory?

Realms of Being[1]

The world is old, and can have changed but little since man arose in it, else man himself would have perished. Why, then, should he still live without a sure and sufficient philosophy? The equivalent of such a philosophy is probably hereditary in sundry animals not much older than man. They have had time to take the measure of life, and have settled down to a routine of preferences and habits which keeps their heads, as a race, above water; and they are presumably visited at appropriate seasons by magic images, which are symbols to them for the world or for the cycles of their destiny. Among groups of men an equilibrium of this moral sort has been sometimes ap-

[1] Reprinted with the permission of Charles Scribner's Sons from the Introduction to the one-volume edition of *Realms of Being* by George Santayana. Copyright 1942 Charles Scribner's Sons. Canadian permission by Constable and Co., Ltd.

proached—in India, in China, under the Moslem or the Catholic regimens; and if socialist or other panaceas now exercise such a strange influence over men's hearts, it is perhaps because they are impatient of being so long the sport of divers ignorant dogmas and chance adventures, and aspire to live in a stable harmony with nature.

In fact, beneath these various complete systems which have professed but failed to be universal, there is actually a dumb human philosophy, incomplete but solid, prevalent among all civilized peoples. They all practice agriculture, commerce, and mechanical arts, with artificial instruments lately very much complicated; and they necessarily possess, with these arts, a modicum of sanity, morality, and science requisite for carrying them on, and tested by success in doing so. Is not this human competence philosophy enough? Is it not at least the nucleus of all sound philosophy? In spite of the superficial confusion reigning in the world, is not the universal wisdom of the future actually gathering about this human competence in engineering, in chemistry, in medicine, in war?

It might seem so, since the sort of knowledge involved in the arts, though it may not go very far, is compulsory so far as it goes, and being sanctioned by success, it ought to be permanent and progressive. There is indeed a circle of material events called nature, to which all minds belonging to the same society are responsive in common. Not to be responsive to these facts is simply to be stupid and backward in the arts; those who explore and master their environment cannot help learning what it is. In this direction competence involves enlightenment. Among minds forming a moral society, and able to compare their several opinions, this enlightenment in the expert is coercive over the layman also, because the same facts confront them both. Did not the same facts confront them, communication would be impossible between them, or if communication was reputed to exist by magic there would be no possible conflict or progress among their opinions, because they would not refer to the same events. Even if each declared himself competent and prosperous in his own world, he would know nothing of the world of his neighbors. Their several minds would simply be variously or similarly brilliant, like jewels signifying nothing to one another.

If any mind hopes to address another (or even itself) persuasively, as I now wish to address the reader and my own thoughts, it must assume a single system of events to which both minds are responsive, and which includes their respective bodies and actions. Assuming such a common world, it is easy to see how animals may acquire knowledge of it and may communicate it. Material events will arouse in them intuitions conformable to their several stations, faculties, and passions; and their active nature (since they are animals, not plants) will compel them to regard many of the essences so given in intuition as signs for the environment in which they move, modifying this environment and affected by it. This assumption justifies itself at every turn in practice, and establishes in the habits of all men, in proportion to their competence, an appropriate adjustment to the *Realm of Matter,* and in their imagination a suitable picture of the same.

Nevertheless, since the stations, faculties, and passions of all men are not identical, these pictures will not be similar. Different observers may be addressed to different regions of nature, or sensitive to different elements in the same region; thus dwellers in distinct planets must evidently have distinct geographies, and the same battle in the clouds will be known to the deaf only as lightning and to the blind only as thunder, each responding to a different constituent of the total event, and not simultaneously. So an eclipse—itself but one aspect of a constellation of events in the heavens—may be known in various entirely different terms; by calculation before it occurs, by sense when it is occurring, by memory immediately afterward, and by reports to posterity. All these indications are entirely inadequate to the facts they reveal in the realm of matter, and qualitatively unlike those facts; they are a set of variegated symbols by which sensitive animals can designate them. Of course, the existence and use of such languages is an added fact in nature—a fact so important and close to the egotism of the animals themselves as perhaps to obscure all else in their eyes. Their instinct, indeed, keeps their attention stretched upon the material world that actually surrounds them; but sometimes sensation and language, instead of being passed over like the ticking of the telegraph, may become objects in themselves, in all their absolute musical insignificance; and then animals become idealists. The terms in which they describe things, unlike the things they meant to describe, are purely specious, arbitrary, and ideal; whether visual, tactile, auditory, or conceptual, these terms are essentially *words.* They possess intrinsically, in their own ontological plane, only logical or aesthetic being; and this contains no indication whatever of the material act of speaking, touching, or looking which causes them to appear. All possible terms in mental discourse are essences existing nowhere; visionary equally, whether the faculty that discovers them be sense or thought or the most fantastic fancy.

Such diversity in animal experience taken in itself exhibits sundry qualities or forms of being, a part of the infinite multitude of distinguishable ideal terms which (whether ever revealed to anybody or not) I call the *Realm of Essence.* Pure intuition, in its poetic ecstasy, would simply drink in such of these essences as happened to present themselves; but for a wakeful animal they are signals. They report to his spirit, in very summary and uncertain images, the material events which surround him and which concern his welfare. They may accordingly become terms in knowledge if interpreted judiciously, and if interpreted injudiciously they may become illusions.

The dumb philosophy of the human animal, by which he rears his family and practices the arts and finds his way home, might take definite shape and establish a healthy routine in all his dealings with matter (which includes society), and yet his imaginative experience might retain all its specious originality. The control which the environment exercises over the structure and conduct of animals is decidedly loose. They can live dragging a long chain of idle tricks, diseases, and obsolete organs; and even this loose control fails almost entirely in the case of alternative senses or languages, one of which may serve as well as another. Many species survive together, many rival endowments and customs and religions. And the same control fails altogether in regard to the immaterial essences which those senses or languages call up before the mind's eyes. Adaptation is physical, and it is only the material operation in sensation or speech that can possibly be implicated in the clockwork of nature. The choice of those visionary essences which meantime visit the mind, though regular, is free; they are the transcript of life into discourse, the rhetorical and emotional rendering of existence, which when deepened and purified becomes poetry or music. . . . Poetic, creative, original fancy thus is not a secondary form of sensibility, but its first and only form. The same manual restlessness and knack which makes man a manufacturer of toys makes him, when by chance his toys prove useful, a manufacturer of implements. Fine art is thus older than servile labor, and the poetic quality of experience is more fundamental than its scientific value. Existence may revert at any moment to play, or may run down in idleness; but it is impossible that any work or discovery should ever come about without the accompaniment of pure contemplation, if there is consciousness at all; so that the inherent freedom of the spirit can never be stamped out, so long as spirit endures.

Nor is it safe to imagine that inspired people, because they dream awake in their philosophy, must come to grief in the real world. The great religious and political systems which I mentioned above have had brilliant careers. Their adepts have been far from making worse soldiers than sceptics make, or worse workmen than materialists; nor have they committed suicide or been locked up in the madhouse more often than exact philosophers. Nature drives with a loose rein, and vitality of any sort, even if expressed in fancy, can blunder through many a predicament in which reason would despair. And if the mythical systems decline at last, it is not so much by virtue of the maladjustments underlying their speculative errors—for their myths as a whole are wisely contrived—as because imagination in its freedom abandons these errors for others simply because the prevalent mood of mankind has changed, and it begins dreaming in a different key. Spirit bloweth where it listeth, and continually undoes its own work. This world of free expression, this drift of sensations, passions, and ideas, perpetually kindled and fading in the light of consciousness, I call the *Realm of Spirit.* It is only for the sake of this free life that material competence and knowledge of fact are worth attaining. Facts for a living creature are only instruments; his play-life is his true life. On his working days, when he is attentive to matter, he is only his own servant, preparing the feast. He becomes his own master in his holidays and in his sportive passions. Among these must be counted literature and philosophy, and so much of love, religion, and patriotism as is not an effort to survive materially. In such enthusiasms there is much asseveration; but what they attest is really not the character of the external facts concerned, but only the spiritual uses to which the spirit turns them.

A philosopher cannot wish to be deceived. His philosophy is a declaration of policy in the presence of the facts; and therefore his first care must be to ascertain and heartily to acknowledge all such facts as are relevant to his action or sentiment—not less, and not necessarily more. The pursuit of truth is a form of courage, and a philosopher may well love truth for its own sake, in that he is disposed to confront destiny, whatever it may be, with zest when possible, with resignation when necessary, and not seldom with amusement. The facts to which it is prudent and noble in him to bare his bosom are the morally relevant facts, such as touch his fortunes or his heart, or such as he can alter by his efforts; nor can he really discover other facts. Intuition, or absolute apprehension without media or doubt, is proper to spirit perusing essences; it is impossible to animals confronting facts. . . . What renders knowledge true is fidelity to the object; but in the conduct and fancy of an animal this fidelity can be only rough, summary, dramatic; too much refinement renders it subjective, as does too much haste. This is true of mathematical refinements no less than of verbal pedantries. The realm of matter can never be disclosed either to hypothesis or to sensation in its presumable inmost structure and ultimate extent: the garment of appearance must always fit it loosely and drape it in alien folds, because appearance is essentially an adaptation of facts to the scale and faculty of the observer. . . .

It follows from all this that knowledge of facts merely because they are facts cannot be the ultimate object of a philosopher, although he must wish to know the whole unvarnished truth about relevant matters. A liberal mind must live on its own terms, and think in them; it is not inferior to what surrounds it; fact-worship on its part would accordingly be a fault in taste and in morals. What is the function of philosophy? To disclose the absolute truth? But is it credible that the absolute truth should descend into the thoughts of a mortal creature, equipped with a few special senses and with a biased intellect, a man lost amidst millions of his fellows and a prey to the epidemic delusions of the race? Possession of the absolute truth is not merely by accident beyond the range of particular minds; it is incompatible with being alive, because it excludes any particular station, organ, interest, or date of survey: the absolute truth is undiscoverable just because it is not a perspective. Perspectives are essential to animal apprehension; an observer, himself a part of the world he observes, must have a particular station in it; he cannot be equally near to everything, nor internal to anything but himself; of the rest he can only take views, abstracted according to his sensibility and foreshortened according to his interests. . . . Mind was not created for the sake of discovering the absolute truth. The absolute truth has its own intangible reality, and scorns to be known. The function of mind is rather to increase the wealth of the universe in the spiritual dimension, by adding appearance to substance and passion to necessity, and by creating all those private perspectives, and those emotions of wonder, adventure, curiosity, and laughter which omniscience would exclude. . . .

Thus if there is a sense in which all special and separable existence is illusion, there is another sense in which illusion is itself a special and separable existence; and if this be condemned for not being absolute substance and for excluding knowledge of the absolute truth, it may also be prized for these very reasons. Sensation is true enough. All experience yields some acquaintance with the realm of essence, and some perspective of the material world; and this would always be a true perspective (since things seen at that angle and with that organ really look like that) if the appearance were not stretched to cover more than it covers in reality. Of such true perspectives the simplest and most violently foreshortened may be as good as the most complicated, the most poetical or pictorial as good as the most scientific, not only aesthetically but even cognitively; because it may report the things concerned on that human scale on which we need to measure them, and in this relation may report them correctly. Nor is the error which such very partial knowledge may breed, when inflated by precipitate judgments and vanity, altogether unavoidable. The variety of senses in man, the precarious rule of his instincts, and the range of his memory and fancy, give rise in him eventually to some sense of error and even of humor. He is almost able to pierce the illusions of his animal dogmatism, to surrender the claim to inspiration, and in one sense to transcend the relativity of his knowledge and the flightiness of his passions by acknowledging them with a good grace.

This relativity does not imply that there is no absolute truth. On the contrary, if there were no absolute truth, all-inclusive and eternal, the desultory views taken from time to time by individuals would themselves be absolute. They would be irrelevant to one another, and incomparable in point of truth, each being without any object but the essence which appeared in it. If views can be more or less correct, and perhaps complementary to one another, it is because they refer to the same system of nature, the complete description of which, covering the whole past and the whole future, would be the absolute truth. This absolute truth is no living view, no actual judgment, but merely that segment of the realm of essence which happens to be illustrated in existence. The question whether a given essence belongs to this segment or not—that is, whether a suggested idea is or is not true—has a tragic importance for an animal intent on discovering and describing what exists, or has existed, or is destined to exist in his world. He seldom has leisure to dwell on essences apart from their presumable truth; even their beauty and dialectical pattern seem to him rather trivial, unless they are significant of facts in the realm of matter, controlling human destiny. I therefore give a special name to this tragic segment of the realm of essence and call it the *Realm of Truth*.

The knowledge of relevant truth, while it has this fundamental moral importance, is far from being our only concern in the life of reason. It comes in only incidentally, in so far as a staunch and comprehensive knowledge of things makes a man master of things, and independent of them in a great measure. The business of a philosopher is rather to be a good shepherd of his thoughts. The share of attention and weight which he gives to physical speculation or to history or to psychology will express his race and disposition, or the spirit of his times; everyone is free to decide how far material arts and sciences are worth pursuing, and with what free creations they shall be surrounded. Young and ardent minds, and races without accumulated possessions, tend to poetry and metaphysics; they neglect or falsify the truth in the heat of their imaginative passion. Old men, and old nations, incline to mix their wine with larger dilutions of reality; and they prefer history, biography, politics, and humorous fictions; because in all these, while the facts are neither conceived nor tested scientifically, the savor of earth and of experience remains dominant.

By the philosopher, however, both the homeliest brew and the most meticulous science are only relished as food for the spirit. Even if defeated in the pursuit of truth, the spirit may be victorious in self-expression and self-knowledge; and if a philosopher could be nothing else, he might still be a moralist and a poet. He will do well to endow his vision of things with all the force, color, and scope of which his soul is capable. Then if he misses the truth of nature, as in many things is probable, he will at least have achieved a work of imagination. In such a case the universe, without being mapped as a whole in the fancy, will be enriched at one point, by the happy life enacted there, in one human focus of art and vision. The purer and more distinct the spirit which a philosopher can bring to light in his thoughts, the greater the intellectual achievement; and the greater the moral achievement also, if the policy so set forth is actually carried out in his whole life and conversation.

As for me, in stretching my canvas and taking up my palette and brush, I am not vexed that masters should have painted before me in styles which I have no power and no occasion to imitate; nor do I expect future generations to be satisfied with always repainting my pictures. Agreement is sweet, being a form of friendship; it is also a stimulus to insight, and helpful, as contradiction is not; and I certainly hope to find agreement in some quarters. Yet I am not much concerned about the number of those who may be my friends in the spirit, nor do I care about their chronological distribution, being as much pleased to discover one intellectual kinsman in the past as to imagine two in the future. That in the world at large alien natures should prevail, innumerable and perhaps infinitely various, does not disturb me. On the contrary, I hope fate may manifest to them such objects as they need and can love; and although my sympathy with them cannot be so vivid as with men of my own mind, and in some cases may pass into antipathy, I do not conceive that they are wrong or inferior for being different from me, or from one another. If God and nature can put up with them, why should I raise an objection? But let them take care; for if they have sinned against the facts (as I suspect is often the case) and are kicking against the pricks of matter, they must expect to be brought to confusion on the day of doom, or earlier. Not only will their career be brief and troubled, which is the lot of all flesh, but their faith will be stultified by events, which is a needless and eternal ignominy for the spirit. But if somehow, in their chosen terms, they have balanced their accounts with nature, they are to be heartily congratulated on their moral diversity. It is pleasant to think that the fertility of spirit is inexhaustible, if matter only gives it a chance, and that the worst and most successful fanaticism cannot turn the moral world permanently into a desert.

The pity of it is only that contrary souls should often fight for the same bodies, natural or political, as if space and matter in the universe were inadequate (as on earth indeed they are) for every essence in its own time to see the sun. But existence is precipitate and blind; it cannot bide its time; and the seeds of form are often so wantonly and thickly scattered that they strangle one another, call one another weeds and tares, and can live only in the distracted effort to keep others from living. Seldom does any soul live through a single and lively summer in its native garden, suffered and content to bloom. Philosophers and nations cannot be happy unless separate; then they may be single-minded at home and tolerant abroad. If they have a spirit in them which is worth cultivating (which is not always the case) they need to entrench it in some consecrated citadel, where it may come to perfect expression. Human beings allowed to run loose are vowed to perdition, since they are too individual to agree and too gregarious to stand alone. Hence the rareness of any polity founded on wisdom, like that of which ancient Greece affords some glimpses, and the equal rareness of a pure and complete philosophy, such as that of Dante or of Spinoza, conceived in some moment of wonderful unanimity or of fortunate isolation. . . .

In confessing that I have merely touched the hem of nature's garment, I feel that virtue from her has passed into me, and made me whole. There is no more bewitching moment in childhood than when the boy, to whom someone is slyly propounding some absurdity, suddenly looks up and smiles. The brat has understood. A thin deception was being practiced on him, in the hope that he might not be deceived, but by deriding it might prove he had attained to a man's stature and a man's wit. It was but banter prompted by love. So with this thin deception practiced upon me by nature. The great Sphinx in posing her riddle and looking so threatening and mysterious is secretly hoping that I may laugh. She is not a riddle but a fact; the words she whispers are not oracles but prattle. Why take her residual silence, which is inevitable, for a challenge or a menace? She does not know how to speak more plainly. Her secret is as great a secret to herself as to me. If I perceive it, and laugh, instantly she draws in her claws. A tremor runs through her enigmatical body; and if she were not of stone she would embrace her boyish discoverer, and yield herself to him altogether. It is so simple to exist, to be what one is for no reason, to engulf all questions and answers in the rush of being that sustains them. Henceforth nature and spirit can play together like mother and child, each marvellously pleasant to the other, yet deeply unintelligible; for as she created him she knew not how, merely by smiling in her dreams, so in awakening and smiling back he somehow understands her; at least he is all the understanding she has of herself.

QUESTIONS FOR DISCUSSION

1. Describe each of the four realms of Being, together with the reasons, if any, Santayana gives for accepting each. How are they related to each other?
2. Santayana's philosophy has been described as a form of naturalistic mysticism. Does that seem to you to be an accurate description?
3. What is the point Santayana makes in the last paragraph? Is it consistent with the rest of his teaching?
4. Reflect on your readings in this chapter to determine which of these authors has presented what, to you, is the most persuasive metaphysical theory. Hume? Plato? Spinoza? Schlick? etc. Is metaphysical inquiry worthwhile?

READINGS FOR IMMEDIATE REFERENCE

Santayana, George. *Reason in Religion.* New York: Scribners, 1905, Chapters 1, 10-12, 15.

———. *Skepticism and Animal Faith.* New York: Scribners, 1923, Preface.

Thilly, Frank and Wood, Ledger. *A History of Philosophy,* 3rd ed. New York: Henry Holt, 1957, pp. 618-623.

REFERENCES FOR COMPREHENSIVE KNOWLEDGE

Santayana, George. *The Life of Reason,* 5 vols. New York: Scribners, 1905.

———. *Platonism and the Spiritual Life.* New York: Scribners, 1927.

———. *Realms of Being,* 6 vols. New York: Scribners, 1927-1940.

———. *The Sense of Beauty.* New York: Scribners, 1896.

———. *Three Philosophical Poets: Lucretius, Dante, Goethe.* Cambridge: Harvard University Press, 1910.

———. *Winds of Doctrine.* New York: Scribners, 1913.

Schilpp, P. A. *The Philosophy of George Santayana.* New York: Tudor, 1940. Essays on different facets of Santayana's thought together with his replies.

Also see:

Arnett, W. E. *Santayana and the Sense of Beauty*. Boston: Houghton Mifflin, 1956.

Butler, R. *The Mind of Santayana*. New York: Philosophical Library, 1955.

Howgate, G. W. *George Santayana*. New York: Henry Holt, 1938.

BIBLIOGRAPHY FOR CHAPTER FOUR

READINGS FOR IMMEDIATE REFERENCE

Pepper, Stephen C. "The Root Metaphor Theory of Metaphysics," *The Journal of Philosophy*, Vol. XXXII (July, 1935), 365-374.

Russell, Bertrand. *An Inquiry into Meaning and Truth*. London: Allen and Unwin, 1940, Chapter 25.

Sartre, Jean-Paul. *Existentialism and Human Emotions*. New York: Philosophical Library, 1957, pp. 12-51.

REFERENCES FOR COMPREHENSIVE KNOWLEDGE

Emmet, Dorothy. *The Nature of Metaphysical Thinking*. London: Macmillan, 1957. Metaphysical thinking is based on the use of analogies.

Pepper, Stephen C. *World Hypotheses*. Berkeley: University of California Press, 1948. Compares six basic kinds of theory according to their ability to explain all the facts of experience in detail. A standard work.

Also see:

Montague, W. P. *The Ways of Knowing*. New York: Macmillan, 1925.

Northrup, F. C. S. *The Meeting of East and West*. New York: Macmillan, 1946.

Urban, W. M. *Beyond Realism and Idealism*. London: Allen and Unwin, 1949.

Chapter Five

THE PHILOSOPHICAL WAY

Voltaire once said that philosophy is "a persistent set of questions and a bewildering array of answers"; perhaps reading the preceding selections has provided ample proof to support that description. The questions do seem persistent. Are we any more successful in defining "piety" today than Euthyphro and Socrates were in the fifth century B.C.? How many times do inquiring young minds today ask the same question Descartes asked in the sixteenth century: "What can I really believe?" When Russell, a contemporary philosopher, asks what the word "good" means, his query seems timeless. What is Good? Or True? Or Just? These are problems we discuss now, as has every age and society.

Are the answers bewildering? Bentham tells us that the pleasurable is the moral; Kant denies that the search for pleasure is relevant to moral activity. Dewey contends that there are no final "goods" such as Aristotle advocates. Nietzsche says we should assert our Will, but Epictetus advises us to accept misfortune. Bergson says that sense experience is unreliable; Peirce says it can be accepted. Who should be believed? What are the correct answers? What is meant by "correct"? So we come back to the persistent questions.

The questions are persistent because they are fundamental to human experience, and different answers might not be incompatible since closer inspection reveals that they are answers to different questions. Is this the case with the preceding authors? Only a more careful inspection of the problems they are discussing can answer that question.

I. PHILOSOPHICAL METHOD

Philosophical writings are characterized by questions like: "What is meant by . . . ?" or "What evidence is there for saying that . . . ?" or "This conclusion implies that. . . ." Philosophers think in these terms because they believe that the techniques of logical analysis provide the most reliable method for gaining knowledge. What are these techniques? Consider some of them as they have appeared in these readings.

Notice, first, that words like "because" ("since," "for," "as shown by," etc.) and "therefore" ("thus," "hence," "so," etc.) perform a unique function in many sentences, for they indicate the difference between a reason and a conclusion, the former being given as evidence to justify the latter. Thus, in Definition II, Socrates says an adequate definition of "piety" cannot be "what is pleasing to the gods" because the gods do not agree on what is pleasing, and Russell says that ethical theory is concerned with propositions, and therefore not with actions.

Notice, also, that each word indicates the relative positions of the reason and the conclusion. Thus, in the example from Socrates, the word "because" indicates that the conclusion comes first, with the reason following; while in Russell's case, the "therefore" indicates that the reason comes first and the conclusion follows. Consider this example from Descartes:

> God's properties are so great and excellent, that the more attentively I consider them the less I feel persuaded that the idea I have of them owes its origin to myself alone. And thus it is absolutely necessary to conclude that God exists.

What reason does he give to prove what conclusion?

Therefore (here is a conclusion), the first point to remember when approaching sentences philosophically is to be clear about which are reasons and which are conclusions, looking for words like "because" and "therefore" to indicate the difference. Sometimes one reason is used to justify several conclusions; at other times there is one reason and one conclusion, but more frequently several reasons are given to support one conclusion. Moreover, the conclusion from one sentence might be the reason given to justify a different conclusion, and this process is not restricted to sentences only. Groups of sentences, paragraphs, even chapters or whole books are given as reasons to justify conclusions. The reasoning process, then, can be very complicated, but regardless of the complexity, any series of reasons and conclusions can be reduced to one of these three forms:

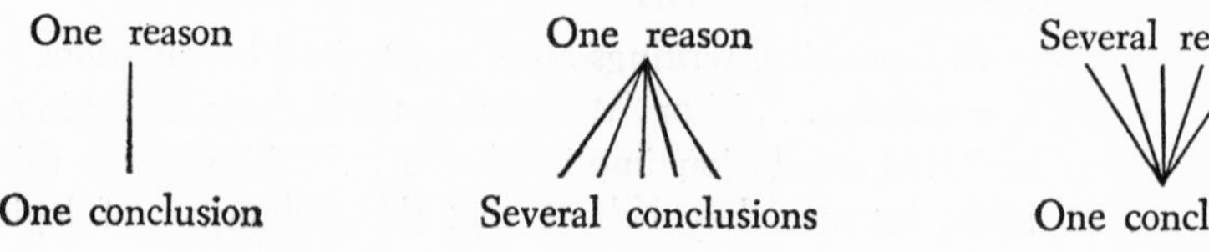

Next, consider the word "justify" in this sentence: "A reason is used to justify a conclusion." Here the rules for careful reasoning are not so easy to state, not only because of their complexity but also because a justifying reason for one person might not justify a conclusion for another. Nevertheless, there are certain principles which should always be kept in mind.

Most obviously, the reason must be relevant to the conclusion. If one said, "I'm going to the store today because Lao-tse was born in 604 B.C.," the reason he gives seems less relevant that Descartes' argument: "I am thinking because if I doubt whether I am thinking, my doubting is itself a form of thinking." In the first case, Lao-tse's birth might have some relevance to daily activities, but the connection is not immediately clear; however, before one could know whether the reason was relevant, the intermediate steps would have to be supplied. In Descartes' case, the relevance is established by using the same word, "thinking," in both the reason and the conclusion. If the reason and the conclusion are concerned with the same subject, then, the former can be a justification for the latter.

To do this is not always so easy as it sounds. What does the word "same" mean? Identical spelling? Yes, but even that is not always sufficient. For instance, suppose one said: "It is a crime the way Jones treats his wife; therefore, as one who commits a crime, he should be sent to jail." The word "crime" is the same in both reason and conclusion, yet in the former case it means "morally reprehensible" and in the latter, "a violation of a statute." To use the same word with different meanings in the reason and conclusion is to commit the fallacy of equivocation, so in looking for relevance make certain the key definitions have been kept constant.

Equivocation is only part of a still more fundamental problem in language: ambiguity. Words are ambiguous when they can be understood in different senses. As Socrates points out in Definition III, the word "wrongfully" has a different meaning for each god, and Russell says that the word "judge" can refer to quite different activities. Ambiguity also has certain values, for multiple meanings enable one to convey a variety of messages at the same time; multiple values, for example, play an important part in poetry. Consider these stanzas from Robert Herrick's "Delight in Disorder."

A sweet disorder in the dress
Kindles in clothes a wantonness.
A lawn about the shoulders thrown
Into a fine distraction;
An erring lace, which here and there

Enthralls the crimson stomacher,
A cuff neglectful, and thereby
Ribbands to flow confusedly;
A winning wave (deserving note)
In the tempestuous petticoat;
A careless shoe-string, in whose tie
I see a wild civility;—
Do more bewitch me, than when art
Is too precise in every part.

The word "art" can here be used to mean (1) style of dress, (2) the techniques of flirtatious women, or (3) a method for political rule, and the poem has successively deeper significance as each meaning is kept in mind.

Ambiguity is important in poetry, and also is the basis for punning, but one of the principles of careful reasoning is that ambiguity should be eliminated. How can this be done? This question brings us to one of the large areas of philosophical method, *semantics*, particularly to the question of how to make precise and uniform definitions. Our authors have given examples of several procedures which might be used.

1. In Definition V, Socrates defines "piety" by comparing its meaning to that of "justice." He asks whether "all justice is pious or, while all piety is just, is a part only of justice pious." Euthyphro, for once, confesses he does not know, but Socrates was only asking him which of the following alternatives represents the proper relationship between the meanings of the two words:

1.  (PJ) Piety and justice are identical in meaning; they are perfect synonyms.

2. 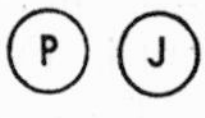 (P) (J) Piety and justice have nothing in common.

3. 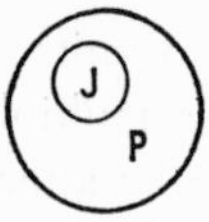 (J inside P) Justice is part of piety: every just action is pious; but not every pious action is just.

4. 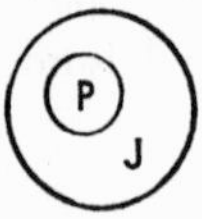 (P inside J) Piety is part of justice: every pious action is just, but not every just action is pious.

5.  (P overlapping J) Piety and justice overlap: some actions are pious and not just; others are just and not pious; still others are both pious and just.

By a series of reasons and conclusions (which can be reconsidered profitably), Socrates concludes that "though there is always justice when there is piety, yet there is not always piety where there is justice." Euthyphro agrees, although hesitantly, for he is not certain he knows which alternative Socrates has chosen. Do you?

Regardless of the conclusion, this procedure provides an example of what Aristotle called *defining by genus and differentia.* To define in this way, one looks for the characteristics that a word has in common with other words, if any, and what differences remain, if any. Thus, Aristotle defines man as a "rational animal," the word "animal" referring to the genus, or to those characteristics man shares with tigers and elephants; while the word "rational" refers to the differentia, the attributes unique to man. So, when Socrates goes on to say that piety and justice have something in common, namely, "careful attention" (eliminating alternative number 2), that every case of piety is also an instance of justice (eliminating numbers 3 and 5) and that there are some actions which are just but not pious (eliminating number 1), he has shown both what piety has in common with justice and has left the way open to explore further the differences in Definition VI.

2. Another way to make clear and precise definitions is to define *stipulatively.* This is the method Descartes employs when he says: "By God I understand a substance infinite, eternal, immutable. . . ." Russell uses it when he says that a thing is "desired" when "we either hope to acquire it or fear to lose it." Frequently you will find this kind of definition in introductory text books: "By 'pre-cambrian' is meant . . ."; "An introvert is one who . . ."; "The phrase 'kinetic energy' means. . . ."

Like the preceding method, this technique analyzes the ideas conveyed by the word, but does so arbitrarily, as the person who makes the definition defines the word so that it covers only those characteristics that he wishes it to include. In this way a word can be defined precisely, as is done with many scientific words, and without the extensive vocabulary required by the preceding method. Its chief disadvantage is its arbitrariness, for if others are not willing to grant the definition, communication ceases. For example, if one did not agree with Descartes that God is a "substance," the argument to prove His existence could not go beyond the level of one affirming and the other denying the definition. Moreover, stipulative definitions can contain ambiguities, as Socrates pointed out in Definition III.

3. Another way in which a word's meaning can be communicated, although, strictly speaking, the result is not a definition, is that of

definition by denotation. This was the method Euthyphro used in Definition I when he said: "Piety means prosecuting the wrong doer . . . as I am now doing." This method frequently is used on the common-sense level as, for instance, when parents point to an object and say to their child, "That is a cow," or "This is a chair"; for one way to define by denotation is to point to the object so named. This method can convey a word's meaning, but does not define it, for there might be a question as to precisely what is being pointed out. What characteristics make a chair deserve the name "chair"? Its color? Its height? Its four-leggedness? What must it have to be a chair? Or perhaps you shared Descartes' perplexity in trying to decide what qualities wax must have which make it distinctively "wax." This method, then, is not too satisfactory for avoiding ambiguities and, moreover, is difficult to apply to words such as "freedom" or "truth," for which there seem to be no physical referents. But many meanings can be conveyed with a minimum of effort, hence this method is used frequently.

4. In Definition VI, Socrates defines the word "care" by examining its meaning in sentences like "A huntsman's art is the art of taking care of dogs," and "A herdsman's art is the art of taking care of cattle." He says that in such sentences the word "care" means "for the good and benefit of that on which it is bestowed." This technique is known as making a *definition in use* and, like the preceding method, will convey a word's meaning without giving it a strict definition. But unlike definition by denotation, a definition in use discovers a word's meaning in its linguistic context, for a word whose meaning is unknown when it appears alone frequently has meaning when it appears in a sentence. Thus, one might find it difficult to define "erudite" as such, but put in the sentence, "If you have understood everything you have read so far, you are erudite," the word takes on a definite meaning. This method is widely used, but a word of caution is in order: a word's meaning might be applicable only to that particular context. For example, one would be well advised not to use Socrates' meaning of "care" in a sentence like: "I care for my wife."

Before leaving the subject of definition, there are two additional principles, previously mentioned, which should be made explicit. The first is that one should avoid circular definitions, for, as Russell points out, a good definition will not use one of its synonyms. To define "piety" as "not doing wrong" requires still that "wrong" be defined, just as to discover that a dictionary says that "freedom" means "liberty" and that "liberty" means "lack of restraint" and that "restraint" means "not being free" brings the definition full circle and results in an interesting, but uninformative, exercise in page turning.

The second point was raised in connection with defining a "chair," but its importance extends far beyond matters of a particular definition, even beyond the confines of semantics to the foundations of knowledge itself. When defining a word—or justifying a conclusion, or discerning the cause of a phenomenon—make certain what characteristics the word must have, as distinct from those it might have. What qualities must a chair have to be a chair? What makes piety pious? The fact that the gods love it? No, for as Socrates points out in Definition IV, this is only an accidental quality of piety, not an essential quality. Or, as Descartes reminds us, having sensory experience of an external world is not sufficient to assure its existence, for we might be dreaming of having the experience. Never confuse the essential with the accidental, whether in definitions, conclusions or causes.

Thus, ambiguity can be minimized if one knows how to make definitions properly. Each of the methods singled out for comment here has its own advantages and disadvantages, and hence should be used when its unique purposes can be achieved best. The last two will convey the meanings of many words, but only roughly. The first and fourth presuppose some knowledge of language forms. The first two give precise definitions. The third relies on experience. And so on. If one knows when a given technique is appropriate, he will have taken an important step in avoiding ambiguities and hence making his reasons relevant to his conclusions.

To see whether you can tell which method is being used, and whether it is being used well, consider the *eryximax*. What is an

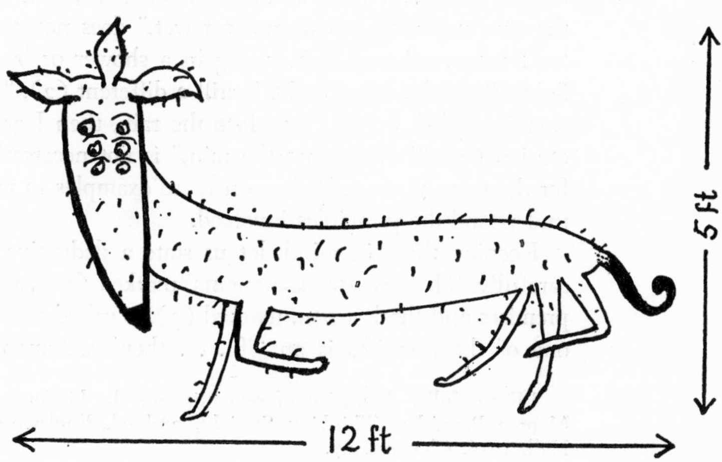

eryximax? It is: (1) stipulative—"a five-legged, three-eared, one-tailed, dehorned, brown animal that has six purple eyes, a large curving nose, and is five feet high and twelve feet long"; (2) to be understood as definition in use in a statement like: "An eryximax and an aardvark both eat ants"; (3) to be compared by stating that all eryximaxes (eryximaxi?) are aardvarks, but not all aardvarks are eryximaxes; (4) to be denoted by saying this is one!

In addition to semantics,[1] philosophical method also makes use of the principles of *deductive logic.* In general, deduction is concerned with the implications which follow from statements and is to be distinguished from semantics, which is concerned with the words' meanings, and from induction, which is concerned with the evidence used to justify statements. Thus, if the sentence "Every one ought to be happy" were to be examined semantically, we would concentrate on defining "happy" and "ought"; if inductively, we would ask for the evidence which supports the conclusion; and if deductively, we might point out that every sadistic act could be justified because it made someone happy.

But to reason deductively one must think carefully and rigorously. Deduction involves combining two sentences so that they imply a conclusion. To take an example, A, when I say, (1) "If I go into the rain, then I get wet" and (2) "I go into the rain," then the conclusion, (3) "I get wet" is implied. Likewise, example B, if I repeat (1) "If I go into the rain, then I get wet," but add a new (2), "I do not get wet," a new conclusion, (3) "I do not go into the rain," is implied.

Notice, also that the order in which the words appear is important. If, in example C, I again repeat (1) "If I go into the rain, then I get wet." but add still another (2), "I do not go into the rain," the conclusion, (3) "I do not get wet," does not necessarily follow, for I might get wet by standing in a shower or by having a water fight. Similarly, example D, if still a different (2), "I do get wet," is combined with (1) "If I go into the rain, then I get wet," the conclusion (3), "I do go into the rain," is not necessarily implied, and for the same reasons. Reflect on these examples to make certain you understand the principles involved.

Keeping these in mind, let us state a deductive argument more carefully. The first two statements, marked (1) and (2), are called premises and the last one, marked (3), is called a conclusion. When one of the premises is an "if . . . then" statement, it is called a

[1] For a fuller discussion of semantics see the bibliography on p. 45 and Monroe Beardsley, *Thinking Straight,* 2nd ed. Englewood Cliffs: Prentice Hall, 1956, Chapters 4-7.

hypothetical statement, and when this premise is combined with another premise in such a way that the conclusion *necessarily* follows, as in examples A and B, the combination is called a valid hypothetical argument. On the other hand, other combinations of premises do not necessarily imply the stated conclusion, as in examples C and D, and where the conclusion does not necessarily follow from the premises, the argument is invalid. Thus, to take our four alternatives:

A. If I go into the rain, then I get wet.
I go into the rain.
Therefore, I get wet.
Valid

B. If I go into the rain, then I get wet.
I do not get wet.
Therefore, I do not go into the rain.
Valid

C. If I go into the rain, then I get wet.
I do not go into the rain.
Therefore, I do not get wet.
Invalid

D. If I go into the rain, then I get wet.
I do get wet.
Therefore, I do go into the rain.
Invalid

Notice, again, that the first premise says, "If I go into the rain, then I get wet"; it does not say, "If I get wet, then I have gone into the rain." If you understand the difference between these two statements then you will understand why examples C and D are invalid arguments, for given the first premise, the hypothetical statement, a second premise such as "I do not go into the rain," does not necessarily imply the conclusion, "I do not get wet"; nor does adding a different second premise, "I do get wet," necessarily imply the conclusion, "I go into the rain."

Validity, then, is a matter of how premises are related to each other, but notice how cumbersome it is to write out the whole sentence each time. Why not reduce each element in the sentence to a symbol so that their relationships will be preserved, but simplified? Thus, if "gr" can stand for "go into the rain," and "gw" for "get wet," the four previous alternatives can be restated in this way:

A. If gr then gw
gr
Therefore gw

B. If gr then gw
Not gw
Therefore not gr

C. If gr then gw
Not gr
Therefore not gw

D. If gr then gw
gw
Therefore gr

However, even these can be simplified. Suppose we let "P" stand for the words after the "if" and before the "then" (the antecedent) and "Q" stand for those after the "then" (the consequent); let "$\supset$" stand for the "if . . . then" relationship; "—" for the "not"; and "$\therefore$" for the "therefore." Now the arguments look like this:

A. $P \supset Q$	B. $P \supset Q$	C. $P \supset Q$	D. $P \supset Q$
P	$-Q$	$-P$	Q
$\therefore Q$	$\therefore -P$	$\therefore -Q$	$\therefore P$
Valid	Valid	Invalid	Invalid

Compare these versions with the original statements on p. 211 and you will see that the original relationships have been maintained, both within and among the sentences. In a deductive argument, then, the meanings of the words in the premises are not as important as their relationships. Thus, the argument, "If there is an eryximax, then there is an emos, and since there is an eryximax, it follows that there is an emos," is perfectly valid, although one might wonder what it means, while the argument, "If he is a Communist, then he will dislike what I am saying, and since he dislikes what I am saying, it follows that he is a Communist" is invalid, even though some people find it persuasive.

This particular form of deduction is known as a hypothetical argument, and there were several examples in Chapter Two. In Definition II, Socrates says that if all the gods disagree, then they will disagree on the definitions of right and wrong, and since they do disagree, they disagree on these definitions. Descartes' "I think, therefore I am" is an example, although the missing hypothetical first premise must be supplied. Russell's argument against ethical relativism is another example: 'If actions are objectively good, then when people disagree, they do not understand "good" to have the same meaning, and since actions are objectively good, people do not understand "good" to have the same meaning. To remember whether a hypothetical argument is valid, only two rules must be remembered: if the second premise either (a) affirms the antecedent or (b) denies the consequent, the argument is valid. Or, if you want to be erudite, the first is called *modus ponens;* the second, *modus tollens.*[1]

Deductive logic also takes other forms. Disjunctive arguments, for instance, are characterized by an "either . . . or" rather than an

[1] Validity can be demonstrated more rigorously by the use of truth tables. See Lionel Ruby, *Logic, An Introduction.* Philadelphia: Lippincott Co., 1960, Chapter 13.

"if . . . then" statement, as when Russell says: "Since everything is in itself either good or not good, it cannot be at once good for me and bad for you." Russell makes the alternatives mutually exclusive, that is, both cannot be true. Accordingly, if he can show that one alternative is true, it necessarily follows that the other is false. However, suppose he had said: "A thing cannot be both good and profitable," and then argued that since he had shown that it was good, it could not also be profitable. Would this be a valid argument? This is not completely answerable without definitions of "good" and "profitable," but on the surface the conclusion would not necessarily follow. A thing could not be both good and not good, but it could be both good and profitable, for the alternatives do not exclude each other. Thus, the argument, "Ethelbert is either a Catholic or a Democrat, and since he is a Catholic, he is not a Democrat" is invalid, for it commits what is called the fallacy of false disjunction, that of offering alternatives which are not mutually exclusive and then concluding that because one is true the other is false.

Another principle of deductive logic is the use of contraries. When Euthyphro defines piety as that which is "loved by the gods," he also says that the gods have different opinions regarding what they love, so Socrates concludes that "the same action will be held by some of them to be just, and by others to be unjust, and hence the same thing will be both pious and impious." This is an example of a contrary, and it is an important concept in thinking because it demonstrates confused thinking so clearly. If the same action is said to be both pious and not pious, there is something wrong with the definition, just as there is difficulty understanding what a man means when he says that he is more than six feet tall and less than six feet tall.

In ordinary language such a statement would be called a contradiction, but in logical terminology that term is reserved for a more rigorous form of incompatibility. A contrary demonstrates confused thinking, but it is not always so easy to discern. Suppose someone said he was both rich and poor. Or that today is Tuesday and Wednesday. Are these contraries? Not clearly so, for he might have meant that he was rich in spirit but poor in money, or that today is Tuesday in America but Wednesday in Japan. For two propositions to be contraries, three requirements must be met: there must be different statements about (1) the same subject, one (2) affirming and the other (3) denying it. Thus, "This act is and is not pious."

One other fallacy should suffice as an introduction to the principles of deductive logic. If someone said that Shakespeare is a better writer than Spillane because people with good taste always prefer Shakespeare, and if he asked how to recognize those who have good taste he probably would feel dissatisfied if he were told they are easily identified because they are the ones who prefer Shakespeare to Spillane. In the same way Russell objects to an evolutionary ethical theory which says that the "more developed" is the "better" because by "better" we mean that which is more evolved, for while this is not a circular definition, it is the next thing to it: begging the question. This fallacy occurs when the premise contains the conclusion; so instead of there being a reason supporting a conclusion, there is only a repetition of the reason after the "therefore," although different terminology might be used. Remember that a deductive argument is supposed to lead from a set of premises to a new conclusion, a bridge, albeit a small one, from old information to new, but when the question is begged, there is no need for a bridge, for there is nothing to cross.[1]

The third general area of philosophical reasoning is *inductive logic*. As mentioned earlier, this form of thought seeks to determine relevance by determining what evidence supports the conclusion. This is one of the central elements in scientific experimentation, and so its principles will be considered more fully in Chapters Ten and Thirteen. However, there are certain fallacies in inductive reasoning which we can consider at this point.

When inductive logic is used, the reason given to support the conclusion involves an appeal to previous experience. From the experience of being short-changed by a grocery clerk one might conclude that all clerks are dishonest. In the same way, Euthyphro, in Definitions I and III, says that the meaning of piety involves "prosecuting the unjust individual as I am now doing." To thus go from a particular instance to a general conclusion is the inductive principle of generalization. Now the problem becomes: "When is a generalization justified?"

Socrates says he did not want Euthyphro "to tell me of one or two of all the many pious actions there are; I want to know what is the essential part of piety which makes all pious actions pious." Descartes says that even though he now considers himself to be at his desk, still "at other times I have been deceived in sleep by similar illusions." The point made in both cases is that one or two examples are not

[1] For a fuller discussion of deduction see the bibliographies on p. 45, and Philip Wheelwright, *Valid Thinking*. New York: The Odyssey Press, 1962, Chapters 1-7.

sufficient to justify a general conclusion; hence these are examples of what is called the fallacy of hasty generalization. The corollary also is true, for the more instances there are the more reliable the conclusion will be. So, if Descartes dreamed continually about his desk and fireplace, Euthyphro continued to bring his father to trial, and one experienced nothing but dishonest grocery clerks, the conclusions would be more reliable.

Another principle mentioned earlier, confusing the essential with the accidental, is the foundation for three other inductive fallacies: *post hoc*; forced hypothesis; and faulty analogy. The first has been given the name, *post hoc, ergo propter hoc:* "after this, therefore because of it." This fallacy identifies an accidental historical sequence with the essential cause, for it says that because one phenomenon appeared before the other, the first was the cause of the second. Thus, "Shortly after Billingsley came to the base, our efficiency rating went up, therefore Billingsley must be given the credit." It might be that Billingsley did increase the efficiency of the base, but more evidence would have to be given and alternative hypotheses considered before the conclusion would be justified.

A second fallacy is closely related: forced hypothesis. Descartes' proof for God's existence is a case in point. He says it is "absolutely necessary to conclude that God exists, for . . . I should not have the idea of an infinite substance unless it were given me by some substance which in reality is infinite." Setting aside the problem as to whether one can have an idea of an infinite substance, the question here is whether God is the only possible cause for this idea. Could it have come from any other source? Or again, a remark heard at the office: "Roger has been fighting with his wife again: look at the streaks on his face where she scratched him." Or one heard in the classroom: "Paul has been getting an *A* ever since he talked to the professor. It pays to let your teachers know who you are." Are surly wives and professors who know students the only possible causes for streaked faces and improved grades? This fallacy reminds us that one should not be forced too readily into accepting one explanation and ignoring others.

A final fallacy to be mentioned is that of faulty analogy. An argument by analogy occurs when someone says that one thing is similar to another thing and that as the first has certain characteristics, the second has those same characteristics. This is a form of argument used frequently in Plato's dialogues. In Definitions II and III, Socrates says men are similar to gods and that as men disagree on what is good, the gods do also. Definition V contains a series of analogies comparing the relationship between piety and justice to that of reverence and fear and that, in turn, to odd and number. And Russell says that if the study of ethics is concerned with its practice, it is possible to say similarly that botany is vegetable and zoology is animal.

Analogies, however, when properly used are useful tools in reasoning, for, as Socrates' discussions show, difficult points can be reduced to simple illustrations. They also are very difficult to use correctly, for the two things which are said to be similar might not be similar in their essential characteristics. Men and gods might be similar in many ways without being similar in the one way essential to the argument, so when analyzing an argument using analogies, look carefully at the two things which are said to be similar to determine whether their similarities concerns essential points, for analogies can be enlightening, entertaining, even persuasive—and all the while be faulty.[1]

The philosopher's method for ascertaining reliable knowledge, then, is the method of controlled and analytical human reasoning. His aim is to determine when a set of reasons justify a conclusion, and he does so by the use of (1) semantics, which analyzes the meaning of key words, using different techniques, depending on his purposes; (2) deductive logic, which examines the implications of sentences, distinguishing valid from invalid forms of argument; and (3) inductive logic, which determines whether the evidence is of sufficient quantity and relevance to justify the conclusion. All philosophical thinking seeks this end and makes use of these techniques; however, philosophers differ among themselves as to which of these three areas is most important.

Some, like Descartes and Spinoza, view the philosophic enterprise as essentially deductive. They believe that if one can find a basic premise which is indubitable, then all other knowledge can be derived from a logical analysis of the premise's implications. Thus, Descartes says that the fact that he is thinking can not be doubted, for to doubt whether he is thinking is to think, and from this premise he deduces other knowledge concerning God's nature and attributes and the existence and qualities of the external world. Spinoza, too, begins with a fundamental definition, "Substance is

[1] For a fuller discussion of induction see the bibliographies on p. 45, and Max Black, *Critical Thinking*. New York: Prentice-Hall, 1946, Chapters 13-19.

that which is in itself," then demonstrates, among others, the implications that substance exists, that it is one, and that man's freedom is an illusion. By a deductive procedure these philosophers are giving expression to an important motive for much of our thinking, for if there is a fundamental principle from which all other knowledge is derived, it can be applied in many different situations, bypassing the relativities of time and place, and can give a sense of security and well being to one's intellectual life. It is this outlook which gives rise to such diverse enterprises as philosophical rationalism, mathematics and much of religion.

Other philosophers, like Hume, Bentham and Peirce, use a primarily inductive approach to philosophy. They believe that there is no substitute for sense experience, regardless of the conclusions derived from logic. Hume says that all knowledge begins with sense impressions, and argues that if there is no initial impression for such ideas as a self, the necessary connection between cause and effect, and God, there is no knowledge of them. Bentham insists that experience proves all human motivation proceeds from the desire to achieve pleasure or avoid pain, and that the moral calculus is the best means to achieve this end. The procedures evidenced by these philosophers, too, is important in all thinking, for there seems to be nothing more obvious than our experiences, and to ignore that evidence, or worse, to go contrary to it, seems to deny one of our most fundamental beliefs. This is why philosophical empiricism and science, which are dominantly inductive, always have many advocates.

Other philosophers take seriously John Locke's advice: "First define your words then we can discuss the issue." Russell, for instance, argues that ethical theory deals only with the meanings of words like "good" and "right," and Schlick contends that the whole subject of speculative metaphysics can be eliminated when we clarify our linguistic forms of expression. These philosophers, also, are giving expression to a commonly held idea, that both arguments and evidence can be understood only in terms of a linguistic form; hence semantics takes precedence over induction and deduction in the search for wisdom. It is this belief which has fostered the important contemporary school of thought known as *analytical philosophy,* and has made people in all periods of history ask "What do you mean?" before they ask "What is the evidence?" or "What are the implications?"

Of course, these three are not incompatible, and some philosophers, notably Plato, Aristotle and Kant have combined them in remarkably coherent ways. Nevertheless, much of the history of man's thought is a record of his disagreement about which is the most fundamental way to gain knowledge. Which is the most important? In the final analysis, the philosopher says, only careful human reasoning can reach that decision. However, one might say, the history of reasoning simply demonstrates that reasons can be given to support each view, so how can we ever know which is right? To this objection the philosopher would simply reply: "That is still another reason for thinking of philosophy as a persistent set of questions."

II. PHILOSOPHICAL MORALITY

At first blush, the situation among those who have dealt with moral questions using the techniques of careful logical reasoning seems one of total chaos, for regardless of what someone has written, someone else has contradicted him. Aristotle says that one should be moderate in all things; Nietzsche says that one should be extreme. Epicurus says that to be happy is to be moral; Kant denies that happiness and morality are identical. Epictetus advises one to seek peace of mind; Dewey insists that there are no ultimate ends. Add to these disagreements the thought of Ayer, who contends that philosophers have nothing beyond exhortation to add to moral considerations, and, initially, it seems unlikely that philosophers can provide satisfactory answers to man's moral problems.

However, the philosophic enterprise asks that we look at the situation more closely, employing the techniques of careful analysis to determine whether these statements really are contradictions or whether these men simply are discussing different problems. Does this situation suggest inconsistencies among philosophers or does it signify the complexity of the subject? The hypothesis proposed by this section is the second, that philosophers have been concerned with many different questions, and that once several distinctions have been made, the apparent inconsistencies will be mitigated, if not entirely eliminated.

First, consider the difference between a descriptive and a prescriptive statement, the difference between describing what values people do have, and prescribing what values they should have. Descriptively, for instance, Nietzsche contends that "morality in Europe at present is herding-animal morality." Bentham contends that

"Nature has placed mankind under the governance of two sovereign masters, pleasure and pain." Aristotle believes that "there is a general agreement among the general run of men and people of superior refinement that *eudaimonia,* or happiness, is the purpose of life." Which, if any, of these men is correct?

To answer this question would require an inductive investigation. People's actions would be observed to determine whether, in fact, they do seek pleasure, behave like herding animals, or believe that *eudaimonia* is the highest good. The evidence obtained could be reduced to statistical form, and the generalization could be judged to be accurate or not. Nevertheless, the evidence would only describe the manner in which some people behave.

However, prescriptively, Nietzsche believes that the noble man ought to prevail. Bentham says that people should seek pleasure. Aristotle contends that everyone ought to seek the *summum bonum,* contemplation. Which, if any, of these statements is correct?

If inductive procedures were appropriate to answering this question, then people would be asked: "Should the noble man prevail?" "Should people seek pleasure?" "Should men be contemplative?" Notice, however, that the evidence obtained would not say whether men should be either contemplative or noble, only that a certain percentage of those interviewed thought that men should. This evidence still would be descriptive, although it would describe what people think they ought to do rather than how they actually do act. But the question is not what they believe; it is, rather, what they *ought* to believe, and in answering this question, an inductive procedure does not seem to be appropriate.

Nor is this the method used by these authors. Nietzsche says that men should be Supermen because "life itself is essentially exploitation." Bentham contends nature has made man so he has no alternative but to seek pleasure. Aristotle says that man's happiness comes from developing his unique characteristic, his reason. To justify their conclusions, these authors have given as reasons considerations much more general than the conclusions themselves. Nietzsche appeals to the struggle for life which permeates all nature and concludes that we should follow nature in this respect. Bentham, too, appeals to nature, but he says that it makes man seek pleasure. Aristotle justifies his conclusion by claiming contemplation as the unique characteristic of man. In other words, these philosophers have answered moral questions by giving answers to even more inclusive questions such as: "What is nature?" or "What is man?"

These men, then, are not content to describe the values people do have; they want to prescribe the values people should have. To give reasons to support these claims they rely not on inductive evidence but rather on deductive inference, deriving their prescriptions from the answers to more inclusive questions. Thus, the subject matter for prescriptive moral theory usually comes from metaphysics, religion, and semantics rather than from empirical data.

Staying now within the framework of prescriptive morality, we should next note that some philosophers have believed that the most important element in judging moral worth is the intent of the person committing the act. Thus, Kant begins his treatise with the pronouncement: "Nothing in the world—indeed nothing even beyond the world—can possibly be conceived which could be called good without qualification except a good will." Health and wealth could be used for either good or bad purposes, as could fame or power, courage or intellect; thus the crucial moral problem, as he sees it, is to find a maxim or law which ought to be used in guiding men's motives. Kant finds this in the concept of rationality itself, and he states it as the *"categorical imperative"*: "Act according to the maxim by which you can at the same time will that it should become a universal law." Or, what he believes is the same thing: "Act so that you treat humanity, whether in your own person or in another, always as an end and never as a means only."

Epictetus, too, locates morality in a person's attitude. He sees man living in a world governed by unchanging laws and concludes that if man is to find peace of mind he should learn to accept the world as it is. "Remember that it is not he who reviles you or strikes you who insults you, but it is your opinion about these matters that is insulting." Before you do anything, then, develop an attitude which will allow you to be content under any circumstances. If you fail a class, recognize that what will be, will be. And should you pass, be grateful that the forces in nature, your handwriting, your teacher's eyesight and reasoning operated as they did.

Other philosophers, unlike Epictetus and Kant, have insisted that the most important aspect of a moral act is the consequence. Rather than saying an act is good if the actor intended it to be good ("But I didn't mean to ruin the car, Dad."), these writers say moral worth is to be found in the results of the act. ("But Dad, ruining the car was better than having me killed, wasn't it?") Bentham, for instance, says an act is good if it results in the greatest amount of pleasure for the greatest number of people and, we might add, for the longest period of time. He believes that is the standard for judging moral behavior because the acts which are good are those which give pleasure; so the maximum of pleasure would result in the maximum good.

Perry likewise looks to the consequences for judging the moral worth of an action. He believes that moral considerations must begin with the satisfaction of interests, the broadest possible base. Since, initially, interests do not differ qualitatively (no one interest is better than another), it follows that the meaning for "better" must be found in a quantitative calculation. If the satisfaction of one interest is good, the satisfaction of more interests is better, and the satisfaction of most interests is best. However, satisfied interests can be maximized only if they are harmonized, so that "the greatest good will be the satisfaction of an all-inclusive and harmonious system of interests."

Dewey, too, places emphasis on the consequences of the action. He believes it is difficult, if not dangerous, to judge the moral worth of an actor's motives, and he contends that every moral situation is characterized by "conflicting desires and alternative apparent goods." What is needed, then, "is to find the right source of action, the right good," and this can be done best when intelligent inquiry is brought to bear in finding a solution to the unique problem one faces. Hence, if the action does have good consequences, it is morally good.

Another distinction which can be helpful in understanding philosophers' contributions to moral theory is the difference between extrinsic and intrinsic goods. This distinction is made, for example, in the selection from Aristotle in which he asks whether "there is some end of the things we do which we desire for their own sake (everything else being desired for the sake of this)," this highest good being an intrinsic good, the others being extrinsic goods in that they are not desired for themselves. Aristotle believes there is such a *summum bonum, eudaimonia,* as can be demonstrated by asking people what they value most; while some desire wealth, others fame, and still others fortune, they desire these goods only for the happiness they will bring.

Epicurus, too, makes the same distinction, believing that the "first and kindred good" is the avoidance of pain, and that to achieve this good men cultivate their minds to believe that death should not be feared, that the gods live in a world apart enjoying their own pleasures and having no interest in the affairs of men, and that involvement in social or political affairs should be avoided. If we can achieve the calm mind which these attitudes will produce, then the highest good, the avoidance of pain, will also be achieved.

Another distinction closely related to the difference between extrinsic and intrinsic goods is that of means and ends. If what Aristotle and Epicurus referred to as extrinsic goods were not judged to be goods but merely means for achieving another end, then this distinction can be recognized. Both Bentham and Aristotle, along with almost every other philosopher writing in the field of ethics, have had much to say on this point. In Bentham's case, a moral act is one which results in a maximum of pleasure, and he believes that pleasure can be measured by use of the moral calculus. Pleasure has certain ingredients—its duration, intensity, fecundity, purity. If the ingredients of pleasure involved in alternative courses of action can be calculated and compared, the best action can be determined. Thus, let us take one of Bentham's own examples: should the debtor laws be retained or not? Consider each of the elements on a scale of 1-10 according to the amount of pleasure each alternative would give for that ingredient, then perform the act

Ingredients of Pleasure	Retain laws	Abolish laws
1. Duration (How long the pleasure lasts)		
2. Intensity (How much it occupies your whole attention)		
3. Certainty (How certain you are the act will result in pleasure)		
4. Propinquity (How soon it will occur, the sooner the better)		
5. Fecundity (How much it will give rise to other pleasures)		
6. Purity (How much the act is unmixed with pain)		
7. Social Extent (How much having this pleasure gives pleasure to others)		
Totals		

having the highest total. The moral calculus is the means to achieve the desired end, pleasure.

To return to Aristotle, we can know best how to achieve *eudaimonia* if we analyze the nature of man himself, for it is man's happiness in which we are interested. To be sure, man has certain vegetative functions such as reproduction and digestion, and certain functions he shares in common with animals, such as sensory experience. But man is uniquely rational, so if he is to achieve his unique kind of happiness, the development of his reason is the means for achieving the end of happiness. But reason, also, can be used as a means to an end, as in solving problems; thus there is both an extrinsic and an intrinsic value to reason. Extrinsically, the development of reason is identified with the Golden Mean and is used as a means to achieve what is intrinsically good, being contemplative. So, observing moderation is the best method of achieving contemplation which, in turn, is the best method of acquiring happiness, which is the end of all activity since it is valued for its own sake.

These two distinctions, extrinsic-intrinsic, means-ends relationships, are important because they call attention to the need for ranking goods in their order of importance. It may be, as Dewey says, that the ends in one situation become the means in another, and that a rigid distinction between the two elements in each pair is not justified. Nevertheless, the distinctions are important in helping to judge goods in their relationship to other goods and thus in understanding the complexities and problems which characterize the moral life.

Two more distinctions will enable us to assess the philosophers' contributions to moral theory and practice. The first is the difference between making a moral judgment and knowing how to make such a judgment, between decision and method for making a decision. This distinction has been implicit in some of the previous discussion, for most philosophers are more concerned with the methodological aspects of morality; that is, they recommend the manner in which people should make decisions instead of telling them what particular decisions should be. The golden mean, the categorical imperative, the moral calculus are all examples of this concern, as is Epictetus' "Master thyself" and Epicurus' "Avoid pain."

Dewey, however, makes this problem of central concern in his ethical theory, for he is critical of traditional philosophical ethics, believing that the quest for a *summum bonum* is futile and that the uniqueness of each situation makes the search for universal moral rules, rules which work like "drugstore prescriptions or cook book recipes," unrealistic. Rather, he suggests that people should use their intelligence to solve moral problems, as intelligence is an ability "to observe the detailed makeup of the situation; analyze it into its diverse factors; clarify what is obscure; trace the consequences of the various modes of action which suggest themselves; and regard the decision reached as hypothetical and tentative." Every situation requires this same intelligent inquiry: learning how to do it well is the never-ending task of education.

Our final distinction brings us back to philosophical method. This is the difference between conclusions and reasons or, in terms more appropriate to ethical theory, the difference between the theory and its justification. Why should one be a Superman, as Nietzsche recommends? Or seek happiness? Or be imperturbable? What reasons can be given to support these conclusions?

As suggested at the beginning of this section, this kind of inquiry invariably leads our authors outside the field of ethics proper. It led Nietzsche to discussing the nature of life, emphasizing its competitiveness. It led Bentham to a discussion of human motivation, as it did Epicurus, and to the contention that the search for pleasure is the basic desire motivating all activity. Epictetus based his ethical theory on the belief that the world's processes are deterministic, while Aristotle based his on what he considered to be unique about man. Kant emphasized the differences in meaning between prudence and morality, and Dewey and Perry believe that moral inquiry should be based, finally, on human needs. So, even among these few writers, the justifying reasons they give run the gamut from psychology to metaphysics, from semantics to science, from biological striving to mechanical determinism.

For many, this aspect of moral theory is, at once, the most important and the least satisfying of the philosophers' contributions to an understanding of the moral life. It is important because the giving of reasons to support conclusions is at the very heart of the philosophic enterprise. Its unsatisfactoriness arises not only from the diversity, perhaps incompatibility, of the reasons given, but from the fact that the reasons are not themselves derived from ethical sources but are, rather, appeals to the ingredients of psychology, history, biology or metaphysics. It was this situation which prompted the British philosopher G. E. Moore to contend that many philosophers have committed the "naturalistic fallacy" of reducing the meaning of ethical terms to non-ethical concepts. To escape this fallacy he held that moral words cannot be further reduced but are undefinable qualities, knowable but incapable of different expression. This point of view was expressed in the selection from Russell, and has been the source for many discussions among contemporary philosophical writers, as can be seen by examining the bibliography on pp. 44-45.

Whether non-ethical reasons justifiably can be given to support ethical theories, whether ethical concepts are undefinable, whether the naturalistic fallacy is a fallacy: these are some of the problems occupying the attention of philosophers today. It is not our business here to try to discuss these issues farther, for they are technical and difficult, but they should not blind us to the fact that traditional philosophers have added considerably to our knowledge of the moral life. They have proposed a number of different theories, each with its own rationale, ones which can be—and are—used by people in framing the conduct and making the decisions which guide their lives. Secondly, as this section has suggested, philosophical thought has enabled us to make a number of distinctions which help to clarify the elements relevant to a moral theory. Finally, if nothing else, a study of philosophical writings on ethical theory should make one acutely aware of the complexity of the moral life and of the need to distinguish between descriptions and prescriptions, motives and consequences, means and ends, intrinsic and extrinsic goods, in judging the moral worth of an action. Moral problems are not simple nor are they likely to be solved by clichés.

If these conclusions are correct, then the inadequacy of Ayer's attack on philosophical ethical theory should be apparent. Not only have philosophers tried to do more than define ethical words, describe values, exhort others and make judgments, but there are ethical theorists who are neither subjectivists, relying on private feelings to define their words, nor objectivists, relying on "intellectual intuitions." Ethical theorists have not been merely trying to convince others of the correctness of their theory; they have been clarifying the ingredients of the moral life and presenting alternative ways to deal with these complexities. A study of philosophical morality, then, should not result in the conclusion that all is confusion and inconsistency; it should demonstrate, rather, an increasing clarification of an exceedingly complex subject.

III. PHILOSOPHICAL METAPHYSICS

On the surface, the same situation seems to prevail among the philosophical metaphysicians as among the philosophical moralists: confusion and contradiction. Empiricists like Hume, Mill and Russell believe that sense experience is the only method of gaining knowledge; others, like Hegel, Bradley and Royce, are idealists, contending that reality is known as, and composed of, ideas. Still others, like Bergson, Aristotle and Schopenhauer are vitalists, for they see reality as dynamic rather than static, as do mechanists like Lucretius and Hobbes. Moreover, the differences between those who believe reality is composed of one substance, monists, like Leibnitz or Democritus, and those who see it composed of two, dualists, like Plato or Aristotle, are as old as philosophy itself. Add to these differences those theories which defy classification, like Spinoza's, those philosophers, like Peirce, who view the whole enterprise with misgivings, and contemporary thinkers like Schlick who believe that philosophy has finally passed beyond its unexamined origins, and there seems little hope that philosophy can provide satisfactory answers to metaphysical problems.

However, if nothing else, our study of philosophy thus far should make us aware of the fallacy of hasty generalization. Perhaps the principle employed in the preceding section is equally applicable here, and we might conclude that given the proper distinctions, our authors are talking about different problems rather than contradictorily about the same one. Can a philosopher be both a mechanist and a monist? An empiricist and a vitalist? To test the hypothesis let us consider two important metaphysical problems: The One and the Many, and the adequacy of sense experience.

Historically, philosophy began when certain men living in Miletus, a city in Asia Minor, in the seventh century B.C., noticed that one kind of phenomenon seems to become another. When there is rain, they reasoned, the air turns into water, and where there is a spring, the earth becomes water. At a river's mouth, the water turns into earth, and on a sunny day the water in a jar disappears so that water becomes air once again. These men observed such phenomena and were led to ask a provocative question: "Is there any one element, a substance, which underlies all other phenomena and from which all other things are made?"

Thales, the first recorded philosopher, is known otherwise by the obscure statement Aristotle attributes to him: "Everything is water." Presumably such phenomena as rainstorms and springs led him to this conclusion, for if such universally present things as air and earth turn into water, less prevalent things must also.

But other writers were not so confident. Anaximander doubted that all the variety of physical phenomena could be just one kind of physical phenomena, for then things would not be different from each other, as they obviously are. If there is a basic substance, he reasoned, it could not be physical, and therefore would have no limits. He called this substance "the boundless." Moreover, he believed that "the beginning of that which is, is the boundless and when that which is arises, thither must it return again of necessity." Thus, all physical things are composed of, originate from and return to the non-physical boundless.

Anaximenes, a pupil (or companion) of Anaximander, found the notion of a boundless too subtle to identify. He asked how could things with length, weight and solidity be composed of a substance which is neither long, heavy nor solid. No, substance had to be physical, but it could not be water, for lakes dried up and burning wood turned into air, not water. Moreover, he noticed that when earth wears away and vegetables wither, there is nothing left; they, too, must turn into air. And air is sufficiently pliable that it can take many forms. Therefore, the one substance underlying the multiplicity of physical experience is air.

Empedocles, living a little later, considered previous thinkers mistaken in reducing all phenomena to one Substance, whether physical or non-physical. He contended that reality was composed of four basic elements, earth, air, fire and water and, moreover, that the objects we experience come together or fly apart according to certain principles which are part of the universe. "These elements never cease changing place continually, now being all united by Love into one, now being borne apart by the hatred engendered of Strife, until they are brought together in the unity of all, and become subject to it."

Still another early philosopher, Anaxagoras, believed that some things such as hair, rock and wood could not be reduced to air or water, or even to Empedocles' four elements. He said there are as many elements as there seem to be, objects differing only because each has a preponderance of one kind of element. Moreover, love and strife are part of a more fundamental reality: mind. "In all things there is a portion of everything except Mind. Mind is infinite and all-powerful and mixed with nothing, but it exists alone itself by itself."

These, then, were the beginnings of philosophy. Men, perhaps reacting to the arbitrariness of the polytheistic beliefs of their time, perhaps carefully observing natural phenomena, began to ask questions. Notice, also, that the problems became increasingly complex. Compare Thales' simple assertion about water with Anaxagoras' explanation involving the multiplicity of substances and the operations of mind through love and strife. Not only were they concerned with the basic ingredients of reality, but with the causes of them, and with the processes by which change took place. Gradually, then, the problems were expanded and deepened until later philosophers saw that they were dealing with different kinds of problems, but all of them interrelated. Experience demonstrates both a vast diversity and an extensive similarity among things. But how can there be both diversity and unity, multiplicity and uniformity? How can we give the same name to objects which are fundamentally different from each other. Or, to put the problem in the traditional form: how can there be one substance yet many objects?

One way to deal with this problem is to deny that the many objects are different in any essential respects. To be sure, chairs and cabbages are different from trees and fish, but they are all composed of the same essential elements. This is the alternative taken by Lucretius and the early Greek atomists, for they believed that every object is composed of the same kind of substance, unbreakable bits of matter they called "atoms." These particles differ quantitatively but not qualitatively (although soul atoms are more "pure and refined" than body atoms), objects differing from each other because of the number of atoms coalescing at a given time and place. Lucretius explained the creation and dissolution of objects in terms of the attraction and repulsion of atoms and thus was able to give an account of mind and the knowing process in purely atomistic terms. Thus, if the underlying substance is atomic, the problem of the one and the many can be answered.

But, can this explanation account for all phenomena? Take color, for instance. Obviously we experience different colors, but does this mean there are different colored atoms? If so, then they differ qualitatively and hence there must be a still more basic substance than atoms. But if they do not, where is color to be found? Outside atoms altogether? In the collection of atoms but not in each individual atom? In the "mind" of the person perceiving the color? Each solution was proposed by an atomist, but there are difficulties with each view. The same point can be made in regard to sound, taste and smell. And what about attention or will? What about ideas and thoughts? What about life itself? Can each of these be explained in atomic terms? These have proven to be the most difficult areas an atomic metaphysics has had to explain; nevertheless, this alternative for dealing with the problem of the one and the many has proven to have enduring qualities.

A similar kind of explanation has been given by a quite different school of thought: idealism. Royce says that "the world of your knowledge, whatever it contains, is through and through such stuff as ideas are made of." Objects differ, then, but basically are composed of the same substance: ideas. Royce reaches this conclusion by an analysis of the knowing process. He points out that our own ideas are all that we know. We know nothing about an object's length or weight, temperature or color, except our idea of it, nor do we know of its motion or beauty apart from our understanding. Therefore, so far as we know, everything is composed of ideas. Yet there does seem to be a continuity and persistence of objects independent of my ideas. How can this be explained? Very simply. All things exist as ideas, and to have an idea requires the presence of a mind. For ideas to exist continuously, then, there must be a mind existing continuously. Either accept this, Royce says, or embrace skepticism, believing things come into and go out of existence as you have or do not have an idea of them.

This doctrine has sounded strange to many people. Alexander Knox objected to the argument this way:

> There once was a man who said, "God
> Must think it exceedingly odd
> If he finds that this tree
> Continues to be
> When there's no one about in the Quad."

But the idealist recognizes this objection as the skeptical alternative to idealism. As that famous limerist, Anonymous, answered:

> Dear Sir: Your astonishment's odd,
> I am always about in the Quad.
> And that's why the tree
> Will continue to be,
> Since observed by Yours faithfully, God.

What problems does this explanation have to face? First, there seems to be a jump in the deductive part of the analysis. Inductively Royce points out that all we know we know as ideas, but he then concludes that all that exists are ideas. Do things exist without our knowledge? Of course we can't know, in one sense, until we know of their existence, but if idealism says no more than that we know of the existence of things only when we know of their existence, it has not said much. The difficulty here is in passing from an account of what we know about reality to a description of what reality is, technically speaking, moving from an epistemology to a metaphysics, and making this step always has presented a difficulty for the idealists.

A second problem should also be mentioned. Deductively, the need for an absolute mind has been shown, but inductively, among the ideas we have, do we have an idea of an absolute mind? If we do, we should be able to describe it; if we do not, we have no such knowledge. Berkeley faced this problem by saying that while we do not have an "idea" of the absolute, we do have a "notion" of it, and if you read Royce carefully on this point, you will discover that he does not give an answer. So, just as a person who adopts an atomistic metaphysics faces certain crucial problems, so does one who accepts an idealistic theory.

Another answer given to the problem of the one and the many is known as the theory of forms. This answer, first stated by Plato and later revised by Aristotle, says that every object is composed not of one but two kinds of matter. There is the material stuff which makes this object the unique object it is, but there is, in addition, a non-material form which makes the object a member of a class of objects, all given the same name. Particular bits of reality consist of both many kinds of matter and one form, and of the two the form is more important. This is so because it is unchanging, whereas the material objects, the things we know by sense experience, are coming into and going out of existence continually. Just as shadows are more fleeting than objects, so objects are less permanent than the forms in which they participate. Reliable knowledge, then, is obtained when one has knowledge of the eternal forms.

What problems does this kind of answer find to be crucially significant? If reality is composed of the changeable many of the material world and the unchangeable one of the realm of forms, then, as Plato himself points out, the most important problem is the way in which the two realms are related. In the dialogue, *The Parmenides,* Plato asks whether there are forms for "hair, mud, dirt or anything else particularly vile or worthless," whether each object "participates in the whole form or only a part of it," whether there is a hierarchy of forms such that lower forms partake of higher forms and whether "these ideas exist in nature as patterns or as separate independent entities." In addition, he asks for a more careful explanation of the "participation," "partaking" or "reflection" of objects in forms. In short, if there are two kinds of reality, how are they related to each other.

A final author whose thought can be considered in the light of this problem is Spinoza. Like Plato, Spinoza says that whether reality is one or many depends on where one looks. If he is impressed with the orderliness and coherence of the whole universe and sees it as one, he calls it substance or God. If he is interested in man's knowledge of the universe, he sees it as dual, for man knows of things only in terms of thought and extension, these being attributes of substance. And if he is most aware of the multiplicity of particular things, he sees reality as many, these being modes or manifestations of substance. Each way of viewing reality has its own uniquely appropriate method: the intuitive or mystical experience applying to the first; the study of philosophical reasoning to the second; and the techniques of science to the last. Moreover, each method has certain advantages and disadvantages, science dealing with sense experience but with an infinite number of objects to investigate; philosophy being less complicated but more abstract; intuition being indivisible but beyond all forms of rational comprehension.

The chief challenge that Spinoza's view has faced is that it is purely formal, depending entirely on stipulative definitions for its content; deny the definitions and the philosophy can be dismissed. However, there are other objections which can be raised also. It could be argued that Spinoza, too, confused epistemology with metaphysics, for we know of both God and modes only by means of attributes, hence we can say nothing about what is, only what we experience things to be. Spinoza has been criticized for his unmitigated determinism and denial of man's freedom, for the act of choosing seems to be among the most obvious of man's experiences, and he also has had to face the charge that his use of the word "God" is misleading since for the western tradition, "God" is thought to be separate from His creation, while Spinoza insists that He is all there is, with nothing existing independent of Him.

This, then, is the problem, and these are some of the possible answers, each having its own rationale and distinctive problems to answer. These are some of the answers given by philosophers; how would you deal with the same problem? How can you give the same name to objects which are totally different from each other? Or is this a problem?

A second important metaphysical problem involves the reliability of sense experience, and again the problem can be made clearest by referring to the origins of philosophy. In the sixth and fifth centuries B.C., there lived two philosophers, Heraclitus and Parmenides, whose comments and disagreements on this point suggest the reasons some people believe sense experience is the only source for reliable knowledge while others maintain it is either unreliable or insufficient—or both.

Nothing seems more obvious than the fact that much, if not all, of our knowledge originates from our senses. Blind men cannot know differences among colors, nor can deaf people appreciate the tonal nuances of sound. But notice, also, that this kind of knowledge changes continually, the senses giving us different pictures of the universe with every perception. Heraclitus was particularly impressed with this phenomena, insisting that "everything flows and nothing abides. You cannot step into the same river twice," for the second time you are not the same person, nor is the river the same as before.[1] Since everything continually is in flux, it follows that there is no "present," only the past and the future. Indeed, words like "same" or "identical" should never be used, for nothing is ever the same thing it once was. Even as you are reading this sentence, "you" are changing.

Parmenides, on the other hand, insisted that sense experience is not reliable because change is logically impossible. Consider his argument:

> There is left but this single path to tell thee of: namely that Being is. And on this path there are many proofs that Being is without beginning and indestructible; it is universal, existing alone, immovable and without end; nor was it nor will it be, since it now *is,* all together, one and continuous. From what generating of it wilt thou seek out? From what did it grow, and how? It could not come from Not-Being; for it is impossible to think or to say what Not-Being is. What thing would then have stirred it into activity that it should arise from Not-Being later rather than earlier? So it is necessary that Being either is absolutely or is not. Nor will the force of the argument permit that anything spring from Being except Being itself. Therefore, Being is continuous to Being. . . . Nor is it subject to divisions, for it is all alike; nor is anything more in it, so as to prevent cohesion, nor anything less, but all is full of Being; therefore all is continuous for Being is continuous with Being.[2]

Motion involves change, and for an object to change it must move from the place where it now is to a place where there is nothing. But Being is continuous; hence there can be no Not-Being, no place where there is nothing. (If you try to even think of nothing, you will find you can only think of the absence of something.) Since there can be no place which is empty, there is no place into which an object could move. Therefore, change is im-

[1] One of Heraclitus' followers whose name, perhaps fortunately, has been lost insisted that you cannot step into the same river even once, for while you are stepping in, both you and the river are changing.

[2] *On Nature,* translated by Thomas Davidson. *Journal of Speculative Philosophy.* XXXII (January, 1894), 34.

possible, and if the senses attest to motion, this simply proves their unreliability.

Zeno, a pupil of Parmenides, was fond of putting his teacher's beliefs in the form of paradoxes. Suppose you shoot an arrow at the target. How long will it take to arrive? If you rely on your senses you would use a stop watch, but first consider the reasoning involved. Before the arrow can arrive, it must cover half the distance between its present position and the target. But after it moves that far it still must cover half the remaining distance, and half of the distance still remaining, and half of that and half of that, and half of that. Since the remaining distance can be divided in half an infinite number of times, it follows that the arrow will always have half the remaining distance to cover and hence never can reach the target.

Indeed, when you think about it, the arrow never can get started, for before it can go half way it must cover half of that distance, and half of that, and half of that, *ad infinitum*. Or take another of Zeno's paradoxes. If Achilles races the tortoise and sleeps during the race he never can win for before he can catch his rival he must get to where the tortoise used to be, but while he is getting that far, the tortoise has moved to where he now is. Achilles must now cover that distance, but, in the meantime, the tortoise has moved to a new position which Achilles must now reach, but while he does so, the tortoise has moved again, *ad infinitum*. So, while Achilles might continually get closer, he cannot overtake the tortoise who will always be ahead by the difference between where he was and where he now is.

These paradoxes have provoked considerable discussion in the history of philosophy. Aristotle, for instance, insisted that time is as infinitely divisible as space. But in the larger view, the conflict between Heraclitus and Parmenides, between those who trust their senses and accept reality as being continually in flux and those who doubt whether their senses give reliable knowledge and are looking for an unchanging reality, is one of the great issues in philosophical metaphysics. Actually, the problem has two aspects: those who doubt whether sensory knowledge gives an accurate account of reality at all; and those who believe that even if it does, it does not give a complete understanding.

Charles Peirce's view probably represents the average initially unreflective view toward reality and sense experience. There is a world which exists independently of our knowledge about it, and which is known through our senses. This knowledge differs from imagination or dreams in that it gives rise to beliefs which can be experienced by others and thus we come to agreements on what we experience, on what is real. Accordingly, there is not as much need to speculate about this reality as there is to examine the processes by which beliefs are established, Peirce says, so he discusses the advantages and disadvantages of the methods of tenacity, authority, *a priori* reasoning and scientific method, concluding that the study of metaphysics is more curious than useful, "the knowledge of which, like that of a sunken reef, serves chiefly to enable us to keep clear of it."

Bergson, however, is not so confident about the reliability of sense experience, for a number of reasons. First, our knowledge of an object will change with every perception, and we can never say what it really is. Secondly, our senses give us only a limited view of an object, an infinite number of observation points being necessary for complete understanding. Third, two people can never have the same knowledge since they will always see objects from their own point of view and unique background. Fourth, even the same person cannot have the same knowledge at different times or places. Fifth, sense experience makes use of symbols, so one does not know things directly, but only in terms of its representation or idea, and one can never get outside those ideas to know whether the symbol is the same as the object it symbolizes. Most important, sense experience or analysis never arrives at the dynamic living qualities of things; it is able to observe only their outward manifestations. Hence, Bergson says, sense experience gives knowledge which is incomplete, relative, changeable, biased and superficial. It cannot tell us about reality; only an "intellectual sympathy" can do that.

Plato, too, was suspicious of sensory knowledge, for the same reasons; therefore he recommended that reliable knowledge could be obtained only when one left the changeable world of shadows and ascended into the intelligible world where permanence and knowledge, eternity and reason, are inextricably wed. Since Royce also employs many of the same arguments it is fair to say that philosophers from quite different traditions have been doubtful of the adequacy of sense experience to give reliable knowledge.

Indeed, even among the empiricists the point is made. Hume is an empiricist and for that reason his comments are perhaps even more damaging to the claims of sense experience. He contends that all ideas in the mind had their origin from some initial impression. These experiences which are more lively and vivid are called "impressions," to distinguish them from those less so, "ideas," but the important point is that without an original impression there is no knowledge. Do I know I exist over a period of time? When I say I do, Hume contends, I am imagining that the experience I now have of myself is identical to my past experience of myself. But do I have an impression of a self from my past which is identical to my impression of a self in the present? Hume says he can find none in his own knowledge, challenging others to find a continuing impression of their unique self in their experience. Consequently, "when my perceptions are removed by any time, as by sound sleep, so long am I insensible of myself, and may truly be said not to exist."

When we apply the same principle to another area, as when we claim something causes something else to be what it is, a careful empiricist will analyze the impressions involved. All we can observe in such a case, one billiard ball hitting another, for instance, is that the two are together in space and the cause existed prior to the effect, but we have no impression of the "necessary connection" between the two. "There is nothing in the object, considered in itself, which can afford us a reason for drawing a conclusion beyond it; 'tis a custom of the mind which makes us do so." Thus, to the partiality, incompleteness and superficiality of sense experience can be added the conclusion that it gives us no basis for believing in the continuity either of a self or a world.

For these reasons Santayana recommends that the realm of matter is not all there is to reality. Perhaps the limitations Bergson calls to our attention can be mitigated by scientific experimentation. Perhaps Hume's skepticism can be cushioned if we consider knowledge to be that which is probably true rather than that which is certainly true. Still, beyond this knowledge there is the realm of essence, the underlying principles which make for similarity in experience, one which can be apprehended "by intuition as these essences happen to present themselves." And beyond this there is the realm of spirit, the world of free expression, in which the material from sense experience provides the instruments for man's play life, "his only true life." In this realm, man is his own master as he develops his appreciation for "literature and philosophy, and so much of love, religion and patriotism as is not an effort to survive materially."

This brief examination of two important metaphysical problems should be sufficient to demonstrate how difficult it is to reconcile the diverse views of philosophers. Lucretius' view of a reality composed only of atoms and the void leaves no room for Royce's ideas or Plato's forms. Hume's contention that impressions are the only source for knowledge rules out Santayana's realms of essence and spirit.

Bergson's rejection of sensory knowledge is incompatible with Peirce's acceptance of it.

Shall we conclude with Schlick and other positivists that metaphysical inquiry is based on an improper kind of question, that of asking what kind of meaning can be given to terms whose attributes cannot be known by experience? If so, then "metaphysics is directed upon the absurd end of expressing the content of pure quality by means of cognitions, hence of uttering the unutterable." Thus, Schlick concludes, we should recognize that words have meaning only as they can be expressed and since this is the total subject of all knowledge, we can forget the problems metaphysicians have been inventing and turn our attention to problems which do lend themselves to expression, and hence solution.

Or should we conclude with Santayana that the chief difficulty with metaphysical inquiry is the presupposition that it must eventuate in agreements? Some fault can be found with any theory (some of which have been mentioned in the preceding pages) but this act of analyzing and criticizing simply provides the stimulus for renewed investigation in the realm of spirit. Metaphysics, Santayana says, grows from the "fertility of the spirit" as man experiences, criticizes and invents, trying to unravel the riddle of the great Sphinx, knowing that "nature and spirit can play together like mother and child, each marvelously pleasant to the other, yet deeply unintelligible."

Or should we conclude with the judgment expressed by Stephen Pepper in his *World Hypotheses* that different metaphysical theories simply reflect different ways for viewing reality, each with its own reasons to support it and its own persuasiveness? In this sense, philosophy both reflects the experience of men, although in a more refined and carefully stated way, and it also keeps rival world views alive and meaningful. Perhaps philosophers never will find complete agreement among themselves, since each has a fundamentally different way of viewing the world, but continual examination and discussion is necessary to clarify the alternatives and discern the weaknesses and strengths of each kind of theory. Metaphysical inquiry, then, cannot be ignored, for it arises out of the experience of human life itself.

IV. PHILOSOPHY AS A WAY OF LIFE

If one were to be basically philosophical in his attitudes, how would he approach life? What would he believe? How would he deal with the problems he experienced?

First, a philosophical attitude would be one which searched for answers and was concerned with the most profound questions of life. What is Truth? or Justice? or Knowledge? If one would be philosophical, he must take these questions seriously. Secondly, he must attempt to bring the best of human reasoning in the search for answers to these problems, making use of careful definitions, examining evidence and formulating implications; in short, stating conclusions and considering the reasons given to support them. Finally, a philosophical attitude emphasizes tentativeness, the absence of dogmatism and the continual search for knowledge, for one who accepts this way believes that truth can be found in many places and by many methods. When one can develop these characteristics to guide his life and thought he will have caught the profound insight which motivates the philosophical enterprise, one which was clearly stated by that first great philosopher, Socrates, when he said:

> No greater good can happen to a man than to discuss human excellence every day, as you have heard me examining myself and others, for, my friends, the unexamined life is not worth living.

QUESTIONS FOR DISCUSSION

1. Using the techniques of analysis provided by semantics, deductive logic, and inductive logic analyze the following argument as it might be proposed by some people: "The Democrats want to provide everyone with a satisfactory standard of living, so they like a steep progressive income tax which will yield considerable revenue which can then be used to provide more jobs, more income, more demand and more supply, the goal being that of universal opulence. Republicans, on the other hand, believe that more material goods can be produced by unfettered competition, the public benefiting from the ingenuity of some and mistakes of others. But these are simply different means to achieve the same end."
2. Apply the distinctions suggested in section II to any one of the ethical theories presented in Chapter Three to determine which kind (s) of question the author was answering.
3. Are metaphysical questions important? Are they answerable?

READINGS FOR IMMEDIATE REFERENCE

James, William. "Philosophy and Its Critics," *Some Problems of Philosophy*. New York: Longmans, Green, 1911, Chapter 1.

Montague, William P. *Great Visions of Philosophy*. LaSalle, Ill.: Open Court Publishing Co., 1950, Prologue.

Russell, Bertrand. *Problems of Philosophy*. New York: Oxford University Press, 1912, Chapter 14.

REFERENCES FOR COMPREHENSIVE KNOWLEDGE

Durant, Will. *The Story of Philosophy*. New York: Simon and Schuster, 1926. The most popular history of philosophy book. Although the definition of philosophy is broad, the reports on particular men are not always accurate, and the relative importance of different men can be disputed, the book is readable and informative.

Jones, W. T. *A History of Western Philosophy*. New York: Harcourt, Brace, 1952. Comprehensive, accurate, and incisive; complete with commentary, extended quotations, and evaluations.

Also see:

Edman, Irwin. *Four Ways of Philosophy*. New York: Henry Holt, 1937.

Fuller, B. A. G. and McMurrin, Sterling. *A History of Philosophy*, rev. ed. New York: Henry Holt, 1955.

Thilly, Frank and Wood, Ledger. *A History of Philosophy*, 3rd ed. New York: Henry Holt, 1957.

Whitehead, Alfred North. *Adventures in Ideas*. New York: Macmillan, 1933.

RELIGION

Chapter Six

RELIGIOUS MORALITY

1. THE OLD TESTAMENT

The Old Testament is a record of the Israelites from their origins to the second century B.C. It consists mainly of their history and the sayings of their prophets, but it also includes poetry, accounts of their religious practices, some metaphysical thoughts and ethical codes, precepts, and practices. This particular selection is taken from The Pentateuch, traditionally ascribed to Moses but now thought to have been compiled no earlier than the fifth century B.C. from other documents. It deals with that period of history during which Abraham, Isaac, and Jacob occupied the land promised them by Yahweh, their departure necessitated by drought, their refuge in Egypt, and their return, under Moses, to their own land. The ethical aspects of this story are those which will occupy our attention.

The reading selection consists of two parts: the first, from Genesis, is an account of the lives of Abraham, Isaac, and Jacob; the second, from Exodus, is one of the statements of the Ten Commandments, with the chapter immediately following. As you read, see if the distinctions made in the preceding chapters are helpful in understanding these moral theories, and also ask yourself whether either —or both—would make an adequate moral theory which you believe all people ought to follow.

From Abraham to Moses[1]

I

And the Lord visited Sarah as he had said, and the Lord did unto Sarah as he had spoken. For Sarah conceived, and bare Abraham a son in his old age, at the set time of which God had spoken to him. And Abraham called the name of his son that was born unto him, whom Sarah bare to him, Isaac. And Abraham circumcised his son Isaac being eight days old, as God had commanded him. And Abraham was an hundred years old, when his son Isaac was born unto him. . . .

And Sarah saw the son of Hagar the Egyptian, which she had born unto Abraham, mocking. Wherefore she said unto Abraham, Cast out this bondwoman and her son: for the son of this bondwoman shall not be heir with my son, even with Isaac. And the thing was very grievous in Abraham's sight because of his son.

And God said unto Abraham, Let it not be grievous in thy sight because of the lad, and because of thy bondwoman; in all that Sarah hath said unto thee, hearken unto her voice; for in Isaac shall thy seed be called. And also of the son of the bondwoman will I make a nation, because he is thy seed. And Abraham rose up early in the morning, and took bread, and a bottle of water, and gave it unto Hagar, putting it on her shoulder, and the child, and sent her away. . . .

And it came to pass after these things, that God did tempt Abraham, and said, unto him, Abraham: and he said, Behold here I am. And he said, Take now thy son, thine only son Isaac, whom thou lovest, and get thee into the land of Moriah; and offer him there for a burnt offering upon one of the mountains which I will tell thee of.

And Abraham rose up early in the morning, and saddled his ass, and took two of his young men with him, and Isaac his son, and clave the wood for the burnt offering, and rose up, and went unto the place of which God had told him. Then on the third day Abraham lifted up his eyes, and saw the place afar off. And Abraham said unto his young men Abide ye here with the ass; and I and the lad will go yonder and worship, and come again to you. And Abraham took the wood of the burnt offering, and laid it upon Isaac his son; and he took the fire in his hand, and a knife; and they went both of them together. And Isaac spake unto Abraham his father, and said, My father: and he said, Here am I, my son. And he said, Behold the fire and the wood: but where is the lamb for a burnt offering? And Abraham said, My son, God will provide himself a lamb for a burnt offering: so they went both of them together. And they came to the place which God had told him of; and Abraham built an altar there, and laid the wood in order, and bound Isaac his

[1] Genesis, Chapters 21-30; Exodus, Chapters 19-21. King James translation.

son, and laid him on the altar upon the wood. And Abraham stretched forth his hand and took the knife to slay his son. And the angel of the Lord called unto him out of heaven, and said, Abraham, Abraham: and he said, Here am I. And he said, Lay not thine hand upon the lad, neither do thou anything unto him: for now I know that thou fearest God, seeing thou hast not withheld thy son, thine only son from me. And Abraham lifted up his eyes, and looked, and behold behind him a ram caught in a thicket by his horns: and Abraham went and took the ram, and offered him up for a burnt offering in the stead of his son.

* * * * *

And Isaac was forty years old when he took Rebekah to wife, the daughter of Bethuel the Syrian of Padan-aram, the sister to Laban the Syrian. And Isaac intreated the Lord for his wife, because she was barren: and the Lord was intreated of him, and Rebekah his wife conceived. And the children struggled together within her; and she said, If it be so, why am I thus? And she went to enquire of the Lord. And the Lord said unto her, Two nations are in thy womb, and two manner of people shall be separated from thy bowels: and the one people shall be stronger than the other people; and the elder shall serve the younger.

And when her days to be delivered were fulfilled, behold there were twins in her womb. And the first came out red, all over like an hairy garment; and they called his name Esau. And after that came his brother out, and his hand took hold on Esau's heel; and his name was called Jacob: and Isaac was threescore years old when she bare them. And the boys grew: and Esau was a cunning hunter, a man of the field; and Jacob was a plain man, dwelling in tents. And Isaac loved Esau, because he did eat of his venison: but Rebekah loved Jacob.

And Jacob sod pottage: and Esau came from the field, and he was faint: And Esau said to Jacob, Feed me, I pray thee, with that same red pottage; for I am faint: therefore was his name called Edom. And Jacob said, Sell me this day thy birthright. And Esau said, Behold, I am at the point to die; and what profit shall this birthright do to me? And Jacob said, Swear to me this day; and he sware unto him: and he sold his birthright unto Jacob. Then Jacob gave Esau bread and pottage of lentiles; and he did eat and drink, and rose up, and went his way: thus Esau despised his birthright. . . .

And Isaac dwelt in Gerar: And the men of the place asked him of his wife; and he said, She is my sister; for he feared to say, She is my wife; lest said he, the men of the place should kill me for Rebekah; because she was fair to look upon. And it came to pass, when he had been there a long time, that Abimelech king of the Philistines looked out at a window, and saw, and, behold, Isaac was sporting with Rebekah his wife. And Abimelech called Isaac, and said, Behold, of a surety she is thy wife: and how saidst thou, She is my sister? And Isaac said unto him, Because I said, Lest I die for her. And Abimelech said, What is this thou hast done unto us? one of the people might lightly have lien with thy wife, and thou shouldest have brought guiltiness upon us. And Abimelech charged all his people, saying, He that toucheth this man or his wife shall surely be put to death. . . .

And it came to pass, that when Isaac was old, and his eyes were dim, so that he could not see, he called Esau his eldest son, and said unto him, My son: and he said unto him, Behold, here am I. And he said, Behold now, I am old, and I know not the day of my death: Now therefore take, I pray thee, thy weapons, thy quiver and thy bow, and go out to the field, and take me some venison; And make me savoury meat, such as I love, and bring it to me, that I may eat; that my soul may bless thee before I die. And Rebekah heard when Isaac spake to Esau his son. And Esau went to the field to hunt for venison, and to bring it.

And Rebekah spake unto Jacob her son, saying, Behold, I heard thy father speak unto Esau thy brother, saying, Bring me venison and make me savoury meat, that I may eat, and bless thee before the Lord before my death. Now therefore, my son, obey my voice according to that which I command thee. Go now to the flock, and fetch me from thence two good kids of the goats; and I will make them savoury meat for thy father, such as he loveth: And thou shalt bring it to thy father, that he may eat, and that he may bless thee before his death. And Jacob said to Rebekah his mother, Behold, Esau my brother is a hairy man, and I am a smooth man: My father peradventure will feel me, and I shall seem to him as a deceiver; and I shall bring a curse upon me, and not a blessing. And his mother said unto him, Upon me be thy curse, my son: only obey my voice, and go fetch me them. And he went, and fetched, and brought them to his mother: and his mother made savoury meat, such as his father loved. And Rebekah took goodly raiment of her eldest son Esau, which were with her in the house, and put them upon Jacob her younger son: And she put the skins of the kids of the goats upon his hands, and upon the smooth of his neck: And she gave the savoury meat and the bread, which she had prepared into the hand of her son Jacob.

And he came unto his father, and said, My father: and he said, Here am I: who art thou, my son? And Jacob said unto his father, I am Esau thy firstborn; I have done according as thou badest me; arise, I pray thee, sit and eat of my venison, that thy soul may bless me. And Isaac said unto his son, How is it thou hast found it so quickly, my son? And he said, Because the Lord thy God brought it to me. And Isaac said unto Jacob, Come near, I pray thee, that I may feel thee, my son, whether thou be my very son Esau or not. And Jacob went near unto Isaac his father; and he felt him, and said, The voice is Jacob's voice, but the hands are the hands of Esau. And he discerned him not, because his hands were hairy, as his brother Esau's hands; so he blessed him. And he said, Art thou my very son Esau? And he said, I am. And he said, Bring it near to me, and I will eat of my son's venison, that my soul may bless thee. And he brought it near to him, and he did eat: and he brought him wine, and he drank. And his father Isaac said unto him, Come near now, and kiss me, my son. And he came near, and kissed him: and he smelled the smell of his raiment, and blessed him, and said, See, the smell of my son is as the smell of a field which the Lord hath blessed: Therefore God give thee of the dew of heaven, and the fatness of the earth, and plenty of corn and wine: Let people serve thee, and nations bow down to thee; be lord over thy brethren, and let thy mother's sons bow down to thee: cursed be every one that curseth thee, and blessed be he that blesseth thee.

And it came to pass, as soon as Isaac had made an end of blessing Jacob, and Jacob was yet scarce gone out from the presence of Isaac his father, that Esau his brother came from his hunting. And he also had made savoury meat, and brought it unto his father, and said unto his father, Let my father arise, and eat of his son's venison, that thy soul may bless me. And Isaac his father said unto him, Who art thou? And he said, I am thy son, thy firstborn Esau. And Isaac trembled very exceedingly, and said, Who? where is he that hath taken venison, and brought it me, and I have eaten of all before thou camest, and have blessed him? yea, and he shall be blessed. And when Esau heard the words of his father, he cried with a great and exceeding bitter cry, and said unto his father, Bless me, even me also, O my father. And he said, Thy brother came with subtilty, and hath taken away thy blessing. . . . Behold, I have made him thy lord and all his brethren have I given to him for servants; and with corn and wine have I sustained him: and what shall I do now unto thee, my son? And Esau said unto his father, Hast thou but one blessing, my father? bless me, even me also, O my father. And Esau lifted up his voice and wept. And Isaac his father answered and said unto him, Behold, thy dwelling shall be the fatness of the earth, and of the dew of heaven from above; and by thy sword shalt thou live, and shalt serve thy brother; and it shall come to pass when thou shalt have the dominion, that thou shalt break his yoke from off thy neck. And Esau hated Jacob because of the blessing wherewith his father blessed him: and Esau said in his heart, The days of mourning for my father are at hand; then will I slay my brother Jacob.

* * * * *

[And it came to pass that Jacob abode with Laban, and served seven years for his daughter, Rachel,] and they seemed unto him but a few days for the love he had to her.

And Jacob said unto Laban, Give me my wife, for my days are fulfilled, that I may go in unto her. And Laban gathered together all the men of the place, and made a feast. And it came to pass in the evening, that he took Leah his daughter, and brought her to him; and he went in unto her. And Laban gave unto his daughter Leah Zilpah his maid for an handmaid. And it came to pass, that in the morning, behold, it was Leah: and he said to Laban, What is this thou hast done unto me? did not I serve with thee for Rachel? wherefore then hast thou beguiled me? And Laban said, It must not be so done in our country, to give the younger before the firstborn. Fulfill her week, and we will give thee this also for the service which thou shalt serve with me yet seven other years. And Jacob did so, and fulfilled her week: and he gave him Rachel his daughter to wife also. And Laban gave to Rachel his daughter Bilhah his handmaid to be her maid. And he went in also unto Rachel, and he loved also Rachel more than Leah, and served with him yet seven other years.

And when the Lord saw that Leah was hated, he opened her womb: but Rachel was barren. . . .

And when Rachel saw that she bare Jacob no children, Rachel envied her sister; and said unto Jacob, Give me children, or else I die. And Jacob's anger was kindled against Rachel: and he said, Am I in God's stead, who hath withheld from thee the fruit of the womb? And she said, Behold my maid Bilhah, go in unto her; and she shall bear upon my knees, that I may also have children by her. . . . When Leah saw that she had left bearing, she took Zilpah her maid, and gave her Jacob to wife. . . .

And God remembered Rachel, and God hearkened to her, and opened her womb. And she conceived, and bare a son; and said, God hath taken away my reproach: And she called his name Joseph; and said, The Lord shall add to me another son.

And it came to pass, when Rachel had born Joseph, that Jacob said unto Laban, Send me away, that I may go unto mine own place, and to my country. Give me my wives and my children, for whom I have served thee, and let me go: for thou knowest my service which I have done thee. And Laban said unto him, I pray thee, if I have found favour in thine eyes, tarry: for I have learned by experience that the Lord hath blessed me for thy sake. And he said, Appoint me thy wages, and I will give it. And he said unto him, Thou knowest how I have served thee, and how thy cattle was with me. For it was little which thou hadst before I came, and it is now increased unto a multitude; and the Lord hath blessed thee since my coming: and now when shall I provide for mine own house also? And he said, What shall I give thee? And Jacob said, Thou shalt not give me anything: if thou wilt do this thing for me, I will again feed and keep thy flock. I will pass through all thy flock today, removing from thence all the speckled and spotted cattle, and all the brown cattle among the sheep, and the spotted and speckled among the goats; and of such shall be my hire. So shall my righteousness answer for me in time to come, when it shall come for my hire before thy face: every one that is not speckled and spotted among the goats, and brown among the sheep, that shall be counted stolen with me. And Laban said, Behold, I would it might be according to thy word. And he removed that day the he goats that were ringstraked and spotted, and all the she goats that were speckled and spotted, and every one that had some white in it, and all the brown among the sheep, and gave them into the hand of his sons. And he set three days' journey betwixt himself and Jacob: and Jacob fed the rest of Laban's flocks.

And Jacob took him rods of green poplar, and of the hazel and chestnut tree; and pilled whitestrakes in them, and made the white appear which was in the rods. And he set the rods which he had pilled before the flocks in the gutters in the watering troughs when the flocks came to drink, that they should conceive when they came to drink. And the flocks conceived before the rods, and brought forth cattle ringstraked, speckled, and spotted. And Jacob did separate the lambs, and set the faces of the flocks toward the ringstraked, and all the brown in the flock of Laban; and he put his own flocks by themselves, and put them not unto Laban's cattle. And it came to pass, whensoever the stronger cattle did conceive, that Jacob laid the rods before the eyes of the cattle in the gutters, that they might conceive among the rods. But when the cattle were feeble, he put them not in: so the feebler were Laban's, and the stronger Jacob's. And the man increased exceedingly, and had much cattle, and maidservants, and menservants, and camels, and asses.

II

And it came to pass on the third day in the morning, that there were thunders and lightnings, and a thick cloud upon the mount, and the voice of the trumpet exceeding loud; so that all the people that was in the camp trembled. And Moses brought forth the people out of the camp to meet with God; and they stood at the nether part of the mount. And mount Sinai was altogether on a smoke, because the Lord descended upon it in fire: and the smoke thereof ascended as the smoke of a furnace, and the whole mount quaked greatly. And when the voice of the trumpet sounded long, and waxed louder and louder, Moses spake, and God answered him by a voice. And the Lord came down upon mount Sinai, on the top of the mount: and the Lord called Moses up to the top of the mount; and Moses went up and the Lord said unto Moses, Go down, charge the people, lest they break through unto the Lord to gaze, and many of them perish. And let the priests also, which come near to the Lord, sanctify themselves, lest the Lord break forth upon them. And Moses said unto the Lord, The people cannot come up to mount Sinai: for thou chargedst us, saying, Set bounds about the mount, and sanctify it. And the Lord said unto him, Away, get thee down, and thou shalt come up, thou, and Aaron with thee: but let not the priests and the people break through to come up unto the Lord, lest he break forth upon them. So Moses went down unto the people, and spake unto them.

And God spake all these words, saying. I am the Lord thy God, which have brought thee out of the land of Egypt, out of the house of bondage.

Thou shalt have no other gods before me.

Thou shalt not make unto thee any graven image, or any likeness of any thing that is in heaven above, or that is in the earth beneath, or that is in the water under the earth:

Thou shalt not bow down thyself to them, nor serve them: for I the Lord thy God am a jealous God, visiting the iniquity of the fathers upon the children unto the third and fourth generation of them that hate me:

And shewing mercy unto thousands of them that love me, and keep my commandments.

Thou shalt not take the name of the Lord thy God in vain; for the Lord will not hold him guiltless that taketh his name in vain.

Remember the sabbath day, to keep it holy.

Six days shalt thou labour, and do all thy work:

But the seventh day is the sabbath of the Lord thy God; in it thou shalt not do any work, thou, nor thy son, nor thy daughter, thy manservant, nor thy maidservant, nor thy cattle, nor thy stranger that is within thy gates:

For in six days the Lord made heaven and earth, the sea, and all that in them is, and rested the seventh day: wherefore the Lord blessed the sabbath day, and hallowed it.

Honor thy father and thy mother: that thy days may be long upon the land which the Lord thy God giveth thee.

Thou shalt not kill.

Thou shalt not commit adultery.

Thou shalt not steal.

Thou shalt not bear false witness against thy neighbor.

Thou shalt not covet thy neighbor's house, thou shalt not covet thy neighbor's wife, nor his manservant, nor his maidservant, nor his ox, nor his ass, nor anything that is thy neighbor's.

And all the people saw the thunderings, and the lightnings, and the noise of the trumpet, and the mountain smoking: and when the people saw it, they removed, and stood afar off. And they said unto Moses, Speak thou with us, and we will hear: but let not God speak with us, lest we die. And Moses said unto the people, Fear not: for God is come to prove you, and that his fear may be before your faces, that ye sin not. And the people stood afar off, and Moses drew near unto the thick darkness where God was.

And the Lord said unto Moses, Thus thou shalt say unto the children of Israel, Ye have seen that I have talked with you from heaven. Ye shall not make with me gods of silver, neither shall ye make unto you gods of gold.

An altar of earth thou shalt make unto me, and shalt sacrifice thereon thy burnt offerings, and thy peace offerings, thy sheep, and thine oxen: in all places where I record my name I will come unto thee, and I will bless thee. And if thou wilt make me an altar of stone, thou shalt not build it of hewn stone: for if thou lift up thy tool upon it, thou hast polluted it. Neither shalt thou go up by steps unto mine altar, that thy nakedness be not discovered thereon.

Now these are the judgments which thou shalt set before them.

If thou buy an Hebrew servant, six years he shall serve: and in the seventh he shall go out free for nothing. If he came in by himself, he shall go out by himself: if he were married, then his wife shall go out with him. If his master have given him a wife, and she have born him sons or daughters; the wife and her children shall be her master's, and he shall go out by himself. And if the servant shall plainly say, I love my master, my wife, and my children; I will not go out free; then his master shall bring him unto the judges; he shall also bring him to the door, or unto the door post; and his master shall bore his ear through with an aul; and he shall serve him forever. . . .

He that smiteth a man so that he die, shall be surely put to death. And if a man lie not in wait, but God deliver him into his hand; then I will appoint thee a place whither he shall flee. But if a man come presumptuously upon his neighbor, to slay him with guile; thou shalt take him from mine altar, that he may die.

And he that smiteth his father, or his mother, shall be surely put to death.

And he that stealeth a man, and selleth him, or if he be found in his hand, he shall surely be put to death.

And he that curseth his father, or his mother, shall surely be put to death.

And if men strive together, and one smite another with a stone, or with his fist, and he die not, but keepeth his bed: If he rise again, and walk abroad upon his staff, then shall he that smote him be quit: only he shall pay for the loss of his time, and shall cause him to be thoroughly healed.

And if a man smite his servant, or his maid, with a rod, and he die under his hand; he shall be surely punished. Notwithstanding, if he continue a day or two, he shall not be punished: for he is his money.

If men strive, and hurt a woman with child, so that her fruit depart from her, and yet no mischief follow: he shall be surely punished, according as the woman's husband will lay upon him; and he shall pay as the judges determine. And if any mischief follow, then thou shalt give life for life. Eye for eye, tooth for tooth, hand for hand, foot for foot. Burning for burning, wound for wound, stripe for stripe.

And if a man smite the eye of his servant, or the eye of his maid, that it perish; he shall let him go free for his eye's sake. And if he smite out his manservant's tooth or his maidservant's tooth; he shall let him go free for his tooth's sake.

If an ox gore a man or a woman, that they die: then the ox shall be surely stoned, and his flesh shall not be eaten; but the owner of the ox shall be quit. But if the ox were wont to push with his horn in time past, and it hath been testified to his owner, and he hath not kept him in, but that he hath killed a man or a woman; the ox shall be stoned, and his owner also shall be put to death. If there be laid on him a sum of money, then he shall give for the ransom of his life whatsoever is laid upon him. Whether he have gored a son, or have gored a daughter, according to this judgment shall it be done unto him. If the ox shall push a manservant or a maidservant; he shall give unto their master thirty shekels of silver, and the ox shall be stoned.

And if a man shall open a pit, or if a man shall dig a pit, and not cover it, and an ox or an ass fall therein; the owner of the pit shall make it good, and give money unto the owner of them; and the dead beast shall be his.

And if one man's ox hurt another's, that he die; then they shall sell the live ox, and divide the money of it; and the dead ox also they shall divide. Or if it be known that the ox hath used to push in time past, and his owner hath not kept him in; he shall surely pay ox for ox; and the dead shall be his own.

QUESTIONS FOR DISCUSSION

1. How do you respond to the stories about Abraham's willingness to offer Isaac as a sacrifice, Isaac's method of obtaining the blessing and the birthright, and Jacob's securement of payment from Laban? What do these stories have to do with morality?
2. Would it be fair to say of Abraham, Isaac, and Jacob that each was basically an egoist trying to obtain all he could for himself?
3. List the Ten Commandments. Could they be reduced to less than ten without loss of content? Are they broad enough to cover all aspects of life? How are the injunctions beginning with "Now these are the judgments which thou shalt set before them," related to those preceding them?
4. Are the doctrines presented in this section more helpful, or less, than the efforts of the philosophers we have considered, in answering moral questions?

READINGS FOR IMMEDIATE REFERENCE

The Old Testament. Genesis; Exodus, Chapters 1-24, 32-35; Deuteronomy, Chapters 1-12.

The Koran, translated by J. M. Rodwell. New York: E. P. Dutton, 1909, Suras 2, 3, 6, 11, 14-16, 19, 21, 22, 29, 37, 87.

The Pearl of Great Price. Salt Lake City: The Church of Jesus Christ of Latter Day Saints, 1902, Book of Moses; Book of Abraham.

REFERENCES FOR COMPREHENSIVE KNOWLEDGE

Albright, W. F. *From Stone Age to Christianity*. Baltimore: Johns Hopkins Press, 1940. A history of Judaism by a leading contemporary archeologist.

Freud, Sigmund. *Moses and Monotheism*. New York: Vintage Books, 1957. A psychoanalyst looks at the stories in the Old Testament.

Meek, T. J. *Hebrew Origins*. New York: Harper, 1936. A standard text.

Also see:

Adler, Joshua. *The Philosophy of Judaism*. New York: Philosophical Library, 1960.

Asch, Sholem. *Moses*. New York: G. P. Putnam, 1951. (fiction)

Pfeiffer, R. H. *Introduction to the Old Testament*, rev. ed. New York: Harper, 1948.

Robinson, T. H. and Oesterley, O. E. *A History of Israel*. New York: Oxford University Press, 1932.

II. THE NEW TESTAMENT

Jesus, like Socrates, and perhaps like Buddha and Lao-tse, wrote nothing himself; thus our knowledge of his life and beliefs comes from secondary sources. According to present calculations, he was born in 4 B.C. to Mary and her husband, Joseph, a carpenter and a descendant of Abraham. We know little about his youth, but at the age of thirty he was attracted by his cousin, John the Baptist, who taught that the judgment day was near and that the people should repent of their sins and be baptized. Jesus was baptized and, in turn, baptized John, then spent forty days in the wilderness fasting and conquering temptations. On returning to his home in Galilee, Jesus, too, preached repentance, and he also performed numerous miracles, attracting many followers and some disciples. He continued preaching and healing for approximately three years, becoming increasingly antagonized by—and anathema to—the sect of Pharisees, the legalistic form of Judaism, until he was finally brought to trial. Although he was not judged guilty by the Roman ruler, he was crucified, probably at the age of thirty-three.

Only two sustained speeches of Jesus, The Sermon on the Mount in Matthew and the Sermon in the Upper Room in John, are recorded in the Gospels. The following selection is the former, followed by Paul's classic statement concerning the meaning of love. As you read, keep two questions in mind: is it possible for a human being to live according to the principles here advocated; and, if it is, should people live the kind of life thus recommended? Is Jesus' ethic practical, and is it advisable?

The Sermon on the Mount[1]

And Jesus went about all Galilee, teaching in their synagogues, and preaching the gospel of the kingdom, and healing all manner of sickness and all manner of disease among the people. And his fame went throughout all Syria: and they brought unto him all sick people that were taken with divers diseases and torments, and those which were possessed with devils, and those

[1] Matthew, Chapters 4-7; Romans, Chapter 12. King James translation.

which were lunatick, and those that had the palsy; and he healed them. And there followed him great multitudes of people from Galilee, and from Decapolis, and from Jerusalem, and from Judaea, and from beyond Jordan.

And seeing the multitudes, he went up into a mountain: and when he was set, his disciples came unto him: And he opened his mouth, and taught them, saying, Blessed are the poor in spirit: for theirs is the kingdom of heaven. Blessed are they that mourn: for they shall be comforted. Blessed are the meek: for they shall inherit the earth. Blessed are they which do hunger and thirst after righteousness: for they shall be filled. Blessed are the merciful: for they shall obtain mercy. Blessed are the pure in heart: for they shall see God. Blessed are the peacemakers: for they shall be called the children of God. Blessed are they which are persecuted for righteousness' sake; for theirs is the kingdom of heaven. Blessed are ye, when men shall revile you, and persecute you, and shall say all manner of evil against you falsely, for my sake. Rejoice, and be exceedingly glad; for great is your reward in heaven: for so persecuted they the prophets which were before you.

Ye are the salt of the earth: but if the salt have lost his savour, wherewith shall it be salted? it is thenceforth good for nothing, but to be cast out, and to be trodden under foot of men. Ye are the light of the world. A city that is set on an hill cannot be hid. Neither do men light a candle, and put it under a bushel, but on a candlestick; and it giveth light unto all that are in the house. Let your light so shine before men, that they may see your good works, and glorify your Father which is in heaven.

Think not that I am come to destroy the law, or the prophets: I am not come to destroy, but to fulfil. For verily I say unto you, Till heaven and earth pass, one jot or one tittle shall in no wise pass from the law, till all be fulfilled. Whosoever therefore shall break one of these least commandments, and shall teach men so, he shall be called the least in the kingdom of heaven: but whosoever shall do and teach them, the same shall be called great in the kingdom of heaven. For I say unto you, That except your righteousness shall exceed the righteousness of the scribes and Pharisees, ye shall in no case enter into the kingdom of heaven.

Ye have heard that it was said by them of old time, Thou shalt not kill; and whosoever shall kill shall be in danger of the judgment: But I say unto you, that whosoever is angry with his brother without a cause shall be in danger of the judgment; and whosoever shall say to his brother, Raca, shall be in danger of the council: but whosoever shall say, Thou fool, shall be in danger of hell fire. Therefore if thou bring thy gift to the altar, and there rememberest that thy brother hath ought against thee; Leave there thy gift before the altar, and go thy way; first be reconciled to thy brother, and then come and offer thy gift. Agree with thine adversary quickly, whilst thou art in the way with him; lest at any time the adversary deliver thee to the judge, and the judge deliver thee to the officer, and thou be cast into prison. Verily I say unto thee, Thou shalt by no means come out thence, till thou hast paid the uttermost farthing.

Ye have heard that it was said by them of old, Thou shalt not commit adultery: But I say unto you, That whosoever looketh on a woman to lust after her hath committed adultery with her already in his heart. And if thy right eye offend thee, pluck it out, and cast it from thee: for it is profitable for thee that one of thy members should perish, and not that thy whole body should be cast into hell. And if thy right hand offend thee, cut it off, and cast it from thee: for it is profitable for thee that one of thy members should perish, and not that thy whole body should be cast into hell. It hath been said, Whosoever shall put away his wife, let him give her a writing of divorcement: But I say unto you, That whosoever shall put away his wife, saving for the cause of fornication, causeth her to commit adultery: and whosoever shall marry her that is divorced committeth adultery.

Again, ye have heard that it hath been said by them of old time, Thou shalt not forswear thyself, but shalt perform unto the Lord thine oaths: But I say unto you, Swear not at all; neither by heaven; for it is God's throne: Nor by the earth; for it is his footstool: neither by Jerusalem; for it is the city of the great King. Neither shalt thou swear by thy head, because thou canst not make one hair white or black. But let your communication be, Yea, yea; Nay, nay: for whatsoever is more than these cometh of evil.

Ye have heard that it hath been said, An eye for an eye, and a tooth for a tooth: But I say unto you, That ye resist not evil: but whosoever shall smite thee on thy right cheek, turn to him the other also. And if any man will sue thee at the law, and take away thy coat, let him have thy cloak also. And whosoever shall compel thee to go a mile, go with him twain. Give to him that asketh thee, and from him that would borrow of thee turn not thou away.

Ye have heard that it hath been said, Thou shalt love thy neighbor, and hate thine enemy. But I say unto you, Love your enemies, bless them that curse you, do good to them that hate you, and pray for them which despitefully use you, and persecute you; that ye may be the children of your Father which is in heaven: for he maketh his sun to rise on the evil and on the good, and sendeth rain on the just and on the unjust. For if ye love them which love you, what reward have ye? do not even the publicans the same? And if ye salute your brethren only, what do ye more than others? do not even the publicans so? Be ye therefore perfect, even as your Father which is in heaven is perfect.

Take heed that ye do not your alms before men, to be seen of them: otherwise ye have no reward of your Father which is in heaven. Therefore when thou doest thine alms, do not sound a trumpet before thee, as the hypocrites do in the synagogues and in the streets, that they may have glory of men. Verily I say unto you, They have their reward.

But when thou doest alms, let not thy left hand know what thy right hand doeth: that thine alms may be in secret: and thy Father which seeth in secret himself shall reward thee openly.

And when thou prayest, thou shalt not be as the hypocrites are: for they love to pray standing in the synagogues and in the corners of the streets, that they may be seen of men. Verily I say unto you, They have their reward. But thou, when thou prayest, enter into thy closet, and when thou hast shut thy door, pray to thy Father which is in secret; and thy Father which seeth in secret shall reward thee openly. But when ye pray, use not vain repetitions, as the heathen do: for they think, that they shall be heard for their much speaking. Be not ye therefore like unto them: for your Father knoweth what things ye have need of, before ye ask him. After this manner therefore pray ye: Our Father which art in heaven, Hallowed be thy name. Thy kingdom come. Thy will be done in earth, as it is in heaven. Give us this day our daily bread. And forgive us our debts, as we forgive our debtors. And lead us not into temptation, but deliver us from evil: For thine is the kingdom, and the power, and the glory, for ever. Amen. For if ye forgive men their trespasses, your heavenly Father will also forgive you: but if ye forgive not men their trespasses, neither will your Father forgive your trespasses.

Moreover, when ye fast, be not, as the hypocrites, of a sad countenance: for they disfigure their faces, that they may appear unto men to fast. Verily I say unto you, They have their reward. But thou, when thou fastest, anoint thine head, and wash thy face; that thou appear not unto men to fast, but unto thy Father which is in secret: and thy Father, which seeth in secret, shall reward thee openly.

Lay not up for yourselves treasures upon earth, where moth and rust doth corrupt, and where thieves break through and steal: But lay up for yourselves treasures in heaven, where neither moth nor rust doth corrupt, and where thieves do not break through nor steal: for where your treasure is, there will your heart be also. The light of the body is the eye: if therefore thine eye be single, thy whole body shall be full of light. But if thine eye be evil, thy whole body shall be full of darkness. If therefore the light that is in thee be darkness, how great is that darkness!

No man can serve two masters: for either he will hate the one, and love the other; or else he will hold to the one, and despise the other. Ye cannot serve God and mammon. Therefore I say unto you, Take no thought for your life, what ye shall eat, or what ye shall drink; nor yet for your body, what ye shall put on. Is not the life more than meat, and the body than raiment? Behold the fowls of the air: for they sow not, neither do they reap, nor gather into barns; yet your heavenly Father feedeth them. Are ye not much better than they? Which of you by taking thought can add one cubit unto his stature? And why take ye thought for raiment? Consider the lilies of the field, how they grow; they toil not, neither do they spin: And yet I say unto you, That even Solomon in all his glory was not arrayed like one of these. Wherefore, if God so clothe the grass of the field, which today is, and tomorrow is cast into the oven, shall he not much more clothe you, O ye of little faith? Therefore, take no thought, saying, What shall we eat? or, What shall we drink? or, Wherewithal shall we be clothed? (For after all these things do the Gentiles seek:) for your heavenly Father knoweth that ye have need of all these things. But seek ye first the kingdom of God, and his righteousness; and all these things shall be added unto you. Take therefore no thought for the morrow: for the morrow shall take thought for the things of itself. Sufficient unto the day is the evil thereof.

Judge not, that ye be not judged. For with what judgment ye judge, ye shall be judged: and with what measure ye mete, it shall be measured to you again. And why beholdest thou the mote that is in thy brother's eye, but considerest not the beam that is in thine own eye? Or how wilt thou say to thy brother, Let me pull out the mote out of thine eye; and, behold, a beam is in thine own eye? Thou hypocrite, first cast out the beam out of thine own eye; and then shalt thou see clearly to cast out the mote out of thy brother's eye.

Give not that which is holy unto the dogs, neither cast ye your pearls before swine, lest they trample them under their feet, and turn again and rend you.

Ask, and it shall be given you; seek, and ye shall find; knock, and it shall be opened unto you: for everyone that asketh receiveth; and he that seeketh findeth; and to him that knocketh it shall be opened. Or what man is there of you, whom if his son ask bread, will he give him a stone? Or if he ask a fish, will he give him a serpent? If ye then, being evil, know how to give good gifts unto your children, how much more shall your Father which is in heaven give good things to them that ask him? Therefore all things whatsoever ye would that men should do to you, do ye even so to them: for this is the law and the prophets.

Enter ye in at the strait gate: for wide is the gate, and broad is the way, that leadeth to destruction, and many there be which go in thereat: because strait is the gate, and narrow is the way, which leadeth unto life, and few there be that find it.

Beware of false prophets, which come to you in sheep's clothing, but inwardly they are ravening wolves. Ye shall know them by their fruits. Do men gather grapes of thorns, or figs of thistles? Even so every good tree bringeth forth good fruit; but a corrupt tree bringeth forth evil fruit. A good tree cannot bring forth evil fruit, neither can a corrupt tree bring forth good fruit. Every tree that bringeth not forth good fruit is hewn down, and cast into the fire. Wherefore by their fruits ye shall know them.

Not every one that saith unto me, Lord, Lord, shall enter into the kingdom of heaven; but he that doeth the will of my Father, which is in heaven. Many will say to me in that day, Lord, Lord, have we not prophesied in thy name? and in thy name have cast out devils? and in thy name done many wonderful works? And then will I profess unto them, I never knew you: depart from me, ye that work iniquity.

Therefore whosoever heareth these

sayings of mine, and doeth them, I will liken him unto a wise man, which built his house upon a rock: and the rain descended, and the floods came, and the winds blew, and beat upon that house; and it fell not: for it was founded upon a rock. And every one that heareth these sayings of mine, and doeth them not, shall be likened unto a foolish man, which built his house upon the sand: and the rain descended, and the floods came, and the winds blew, and beat upon that house; and it fell: and great was the fall of it. And it came to pass, when Jesus had ended these sayings, the people were astonished at his doctrine: for he taught them as one having authority, and not as the scribes.

* * * * *

Let love be without dissimulation. Abhor that which is evil; cleave to that which is good. Be kindly affectioned one to another with brotherly love; in honour preferring one another; not slothful in business; fervent in spirit; serving the Lord; rejoicing in hope; patient in tribulation; continuing instant in prayer; distributing to the necessity of saints; given to hospitality. Bless them that persecute you: bless, and curse not. Rejoice with them that do rejoice, and weep with them that weep. Be of the same mind one toward another. Mind not high things, but condescend to men of low estate. Be not wise in your own conceits. Recompense to no man evil for evil. Provide things honest in the sight of all men. If it be possible, as much as lieth in you, live peaceably with all men. Dearly beloved, avenge not yourselves, but rather give place unto wrath: for it is written, Vengeance is mine; I will repay, saith the Lord. Therefore, if thine enemy hunger, feed him; if he thirst, give him drink: for in so doing thou shalt heap coals of fire on his head. Be not overcome of evil, but overcome evil with good.

QUESTIONS FOR DISCUSSION

1. Can you summarize this sermon in terms of a few central ideas?
2. Do you think the advice Jesus gave about turning the other cheek, giving to borrowing neighbors, and not seeking after mammon is both practical and advisable in the modern world? If not, of what value is the sermon?
3. Do you agree with Voltaire when he said: "Christianity is such a worthy enterprise that I am surprised no one has tried it yet"?

READINGS FOR IMMEDIATE REFERENCE

The New Testament. Compare The Gospel According to Matthew, Chapters 3-11, 21-28 with The Gospel According to John, Chapters 1-3, 13-21.

The Koran, translated by J. M. Rodwell. New York: E. P. Dutton, 1909, Suras 2-6, 19, 23, 57, 61.

Gandhi, Mohandas. *Autobiography*. Boston: Beacon Press, 1957, Chapters 13-16.

REFERENCES FOR COMPREHENSIVE KNOWLEDGE

Dibelius, Martin. *Jesus.* Philadelphia: Westminister Press, 1949. A Protestant view.

Klausner, Joseph. *Jesus of Nazareth.* New York: Macmillan, 1925. A Jewish view.

Ricciotti, G. *The Life of Christ.* New York: A. L. Bruce, 1945. A Roman Catholic view.

Schweitzer, Albert. *The Quest of the Historical Jesus.* New York: Macmillan, 1910. An important book in the history of critical analyses. Examines what writers from different centuries have interpreted Jesus to be.

Also see:

Cadbury, H. J. *Jesus: What Manner of Man?* New York: Macmillan, 1947.

Edman, Irwin. *The Mind of Paul.* New York: Henry Holt, 1935.

Goodspeed, E. J. *The Life of Jesus.* New York: Harper, 1950.

Grant, Frederick C. *The Gospels: Their Origin and Growth.* New York: Harper, 1957.

Streeter, B. H. *The Four Gospels.* New York: Macmillan, 1925.

III. *GAUTAMA BUDDHA*

The life of Buddha is shrouded in mystery, myth and fact, all inextricably mixed. Modern scholars say he was born Siddartha Gautama, the son of a local chieftain in Northern India, probably in the early sixth century B.C., the supposed dates varying from 560 to 487. He grew to manhood amidst wealth and opportunity, was raised to be an orthodox Hindu, and at nineteen married a princess who bore him a son. Tradition says he was not satisfied with life, especially after viewing the Four Passing Sights: an old man, a diseased man, a dead man, and a calm monk. At twenty-six (or twenty-nine), he renounced his privileges, left his home and family and began to seek for the attitude of mind adopted by the monk, one which would allow him to live peacefully in a world filled with suffering. He tried reading the Vedas, performing ceremonies, contemplating, and observing rigid self-discipline and fasting—one account says he fasted until he could touch his stomach and feel his backbone—but nothing brought the desired peace of mind. After six years of search, enlightenment came while Buddha sat beneath the Bo tree: the cause of suffering is desire. Therefore, if suffering is an evil which should be eliminated, desire must be overcome, including the desire to overcome desire. He returned to his friends to tell them of his discovery, and from that time he was called The Enlightened One, The Buddha. He spent the remainder of his life, approximately fifty years, teaching others the path to enlightenment.

Your reading selection is taken from the first two sermons Buddha gave, and the Dhammapada, one of the earliest and most revered collections of his teachings. Do you find his teachings similar to any other theories we have considered? What reasons could he give for saying that we should overcome desire rather than satisfy it? Are they good reasons? Are the Four Noble Truths the most satisfactory means for achieving the end desired?

The Four Noble Truths[1]

On seeing their old teacher approach, the five bhikkhus agreed among themselves not to salute him, nor to address him as a master, but by his name only. "For," so they said, "he has broken his vow and has abandoned holiness. He is no bhikkhu but Gotama, and Gotama has become a man who lives in abundance and indulges in the pleasures of worldliness."

But when the Blessed One approached in a dignified manner, they involuntarily rose from their seats and greeted him in spite of their resolution. Still they called him by his name and addressed him as "friend Gotama."

When they had thus received the Blessed One, he said: "Do not call the Tathagata by his name nor address him as 'friend,' for he is the Buddha, the Holy One. The Buddha looks with a kind heart equally on all living beings, and they therefore call him 'Father.' To disrespect a father is wrong; to despise him, is wicked."

"The Tathagata," the Buddha continued, "does not seek salvation in austerities, but neither does he for that reason indulge in worldly pleasures, nor live in abundance. The Tathagata has found the middle path."

"There are two extremes O Bhikkhus, which the man who has given up the world ought not to follow—the habitual practice, on the one hand, of self-indulgence which is unworthy, vain and fit only for the worldly-minded—and the habitual practice, on the other hand, of self-mortification, which is painful, useless and unprofitable.

"Neither abstinence from fish or flesh, nor going naked, nor shaving the head, nor wearing matted hair, nor dressing in a rough garment, nor covering oneself with dirt, nor sacrificing to Agni, will cleanse a man who is not free from delusions.

"Reading the Vedas, making offerings to priests, or sacrifices to the gods, self-mortification by heat or cold, and many such penances performed for the sake of immortality, these do not cleanse the man who is not free from delusions.

"Anger, drunkenness, obstinacy, bigotry, deception, envy, self-praise, disparaging others, superciliousness and evil intentions constitute uncleanness; not verily the eating of flesh.

"A middle path, O Bhikkhus, avoiding the two extremes, has been discovered by the Tathagata—a path which opens the eyes, and bestows understanding, which leads to peace of mind, to the higher wisdom, to full enlightenment, to Nirvana!

"What is that middle path, O Bhik-

[1] From Buddha's "The Sermon at Benares," "A Sermon on Abuse," and the *Dhammapada,* Chapters 1, 3 and parable commentary, translated by Samuel Beal. LaSalle, Illinois: The Open Court Publishing Co., 1912. Reprinted by permission.

khus, avoiding these two extremes, discovered by the Tathagata—that path which opens the eyes, and bestows understanding, which leads to peace of mind, to the higher wisdom, to full enlightenment, to Nirvana?

"Let me teach you, O Bhikkhus, the middle path, which keeps aloof from both extremes. By suffering, the emaciated devotee produces confusion and sickly thoughts in his mind. Mortification is not conducive even to worldly knowledge; how much less to a triumph over the senses!

"He who fills his lamp with water will not dispel the darkness, and he who tries to light a fire with rotten wood will fail. And how can anyone be free from self by leading a wretched life, if he does not succeed in quenching the fires of lust, if he still hankers after either worldly or heavenly pleasures. But he in whom self has become extinct is free from lust; he will desire neither worldly nor heavenly pleasures, and the satisfaction of his natural wants will not defile him. However, let him be moderate, let him eat and drink according to the needs of the body.

"Sensuality is enervating; the self-indulgent man is a slave to his passions, and pleasure-seeking is degrading and vulgar.

"But to satisfy the necessities of life is not evil. To keep the body in good health is a duty, for otherwise we shall not be able to trim the lamp of wisdom, and keep our mind strong and clear. Water surrounds the lotus-flower, but does not wet its petals.

"This is the middle path, O Bhikkhus, that keeps aloof from both extremes." . . .

Then the Buddha said:

"He who recognizes the existence of suffering, its cause, its remedy, and its cessation has fathomed the four Noble Truths. He will walk the right path.

"Right views will be the torch to light his way. Right aspirations will be his guide. Right speech will be his dwelling place on the road. His gait will be straight, for it is right behavior. His refreshments will be the right way of earning his livelihood. Right efforts will be his steps: right thoughts his breath; and right contemplation will give him the peace that follows in his footprints.

"Now, this, O Bhikkhus, is the noble truth concerning suffering:

"Birth is attended with pain, decay is painful, disease is painful, death is painful. Union with the unpleasant is painful, painful is separation from the pleasant; and any craving that is unsatisfied, that too is painful. In brief, bodily conditions which spring from attachments are painful.

"Now this, O Bhikkhus, is the noble truth concerning the origin. Verily, it is that craving which causes the renewal of existence, accompanied by sensual delight, seeking satisfaction now here, now there, the craving for the gratification of the passions, the craving for a future life, and the craving for happiness in this life.

"Now this is the noble truth concerning the destruction of suffering: "Verily it is the destruction, in which no passion remains, of this very thirst: It is the laying aside of, the being free from, the dwelling no longer upon this thirst.

"Now this is the noble truth concerning the way which leads to the destruction of sorrow. Verily; it is this noble eightfold path; that is to say:

1. right views
2. right aspirations
3. right speech
4. right behavior
5. right livelihood
6. right effort
7. right thoughts
8. right contemplation

"This, then, is the noble truth concerning the destruction of sorrow. By the practice of loving kindness I have attained liberation of heart, and thus I am assured that I shall never return in renewed births. I have even now attained Nirvana."

And when the Blessed One had thus set the royal chariot wheel of truth rolling onward, a rapture thrilled through all the universes.

And when the doctrine was propounded, the venerable Kondanna, the oldest one among the five bhikkhus, discerned the truth with his mental eye, and he said: "Truly, O Buddha, our Lord, thou hast found the truth!" Then the other bhikkhus, too, joined him and exclaimed: "Truly, thou art the Buddha, thou hast found the truth."

* * * * *

And the Blessed One observed the ways of society and noticed how much misery came from malignity and foolish offenses done only to gratify vanity and self-seeking pride. And the Buddha said: "If a man foolishly does me wrong, I will return to him the protection of my ungrudging love; the more evil comes from him, the more good shall go from me; the fragrance of goodness always comes to me and the harmful air of evil goes to him."

A foolish man, learning that the Buddha observed the principle of great love which commends the return of good for evil, came and abused him. The Buddha was silent, pitying his folly.

When the man had finished his abuse, the Buddha asked him, saying: "Son, if a man declined to accept a present made to him, to whom would it belong?" And he answered: "In that case, it would belong to the man who offered it."

"My son," said the Buddha, "thou hast railed at me, but I decline to accept thy abuse, and request thee to keep it thyself. Will it not be a source of misery to thee? As the echo belongs to the sound, and the shadow to the substance, so misery will overtake the evil-doer without fail."

The abuser made no reply, and Buddha continued: "A wicked man who reproaches a virtuous one is like one who looks up and spits at heaven; the spittle soils not the heaven, but comes back and defiles his own person. The slanderer is like one who flings dust at another when the wind is contrary; the dust does but return on him who threw it. The virtuous man cannot be hurt and the misery that the other would inflict comes back on himself."

The abuser went away ashamed, but he came again and took refuge in the Buddha, the Dharma, and the Sangha.

* * * * *

And Buddha said: "All that we are is the result of what we have thought: it is founded on our thoughts, it is made up of our thoughts. If a man speaks or acts with an evil thought, pain follows him, as the wheel follows the foot of the ox that draws the carriage: If a man speaks or acts with a pure thought, happiness follows him, like a shadow that never leaves him.

"He abused me, he beat me, he defeated me, he robbed me"—in those who harbor such thoughts, hatred will never cease; in those who do not harbor such thoughts, hatred will cease. For hatred does not cease by hatred at any time: hatred ceases by love—that is an old rule.

He who lives looking for pleasures only, his senses uncontrolled, immoderate in his food, idle and weak, will certainly be overthrown by temptation, as the wind throws down a weak tree. He who lives without looking for pleasures, his senses well controlled, moderate in his food, faithful and strong, will certainly not be overthrown, any more than the wind throws down a rocky mountain. . . .

The thoughtless man, even if he can recite a large portion of the law, but is not a doer of it, has no share in the priesthood, but is like a cowherd counting the cows of others. The follower of the law, even if he can recite only a small portion of the law, but, having forsaken passion and hatred and foolishness, possesses true knowledge and serenity of mind, he, caring for nothing in this world or that to come, has indeed a share in the priesthood. . . .

As a fletcher makes straight his arrow, a wise man makes straight his trembling and unsteady thought, which is difficult to guard, difficult to hold back. It is good to tame the mind, which is difficult to hold in and flighty, rushing wherever it listeth; a tamed mind brings happiness. Let the wise man guard his thoughts, for they are difficult to perceive, very artful, and they rush wherever they list. . . .

Knowing that this body is fragile like a jar, and making his thought firm like a fortress, one should attack Mara, the tempter, with the weapon of knowledge, one should watch him when conquered, and should never rest. Before long, alas! this body will lie on the earth, despised, without understanding, like a useless log.

* * * * *

Kisa Gotami had an only son, and he died. In her grief she carried the dead child to all her neighbors, asking them for medicine, and the people said: "She has lost her senses. The boy is dead."

At length, Kisa Gotami met a man who replied to her request: "I cannot give thee medicine for thy child, but I know a physician who can."

And the girl said: "Pray tell me, sir; who is it?" And the man replied: "Go to Sakyamuni, the Buddha."

Kisa Gotami repaired to the Buddha

and cried: "Lord and Master, give me the medicine that will cure my boy."

The Buddha answered: "I want a handful of mustard-seed." And when the girl in her joy promised to procure it, the Buddha added: "The mustard-seed must be taken from a house where no one has lost a child, husband, parent, or friend."

Poor Kisa Gotami now went from house to house, and the people pitied her and said: "Here is mustard-seed; take it!" But when she asked, "Did a son or daughter, a father or mother, die in your family?" they answered her: "Alas! the living are few, but the dead are many. Do not remind us of our deepest grief." And there was no house but some beloved one had died in it.

Kisa Gotami became weary and hopeless, and sat down at the wayside, watching the lights of the city, as they flickered up and were extinguished again. At last the darkness of the night reigned everywhere. And she considered the fate of men, that their lives flicker up and are extinguished again. And she thought to herself: "How selfish am I in my grief! Death is common to all; yet in this valley of desolation there is a path that leads him to immortality who has surrendered all selfishness."

The Buddha said: "The life of mortals in this world is troubled and brief and combined with pain. For there is not any means by which those that have been born can avoid dying; after reaching old age there is death; of such a nature are living beings. As ripe fruits are early in danger of falling, so mortals when born are always in danger of death. As all earthen vessels made by the potter end in being broken, so is the life of mortals. Both young and adult, both those who are fools and those who are wise, all fall into the power of death; all are subject to death.

"Of those who, overcome by death, depart from life, a father cannot save his son, nor kinsmen their relations. Mark! while relatives are looking on and lamenting deeply, one by one mortals are carried off, like an ox that is led to the slaughter. So the world is afflicted with death and decay, therefore the wise do not grieve, knowing the terms of the world.

"Not from weeping nor from grieving will any one obtain peace of mind; on the contrary, his pain will be the greater and his body will suffer. He will make himself sick and pale, yet the dead are not saved by his lamentation. He who seeks peace should draw out the arrow of lamentation, and complaint, and grief. He who has drawn out the arrow and has become composed will obtain peace of mind; he who has overcome all sorrow will become free from sorrow, and be blessed."

* * * * *

And Punna, wishing to preach the path to enlightenment, sought the Buddha, and the Buddha said, "But, O Punna, the men of that country are violent, cruel and savage. When they become angry at you and do you harm, what will you think then?"

"I shall think them truly good and kind folk, for whilst they speak angry and insolent words, they refrain from striking or stoning me."

"They are very violent folk, Punna. What if they strike or stone you?"

"I shall think them kind and good not to smite me with their staff and sword."

"And what if they do so?"

"I shall think them kind and good indeed who free me from this vile body with so little pain."

"Well said, Punna, well said. With your gift of patience, you may indeed essay this task. Go, Punna, yourself saved, save others."

QUESTIONS FOR DISCUSSION

1. Does Buddha give the same meaning to the doctrine of the Middle Path as did Aristotle? If so, how do you account for the similar teachings? If not, which theory is superior?
2. Restate the Four Noble Truths giving reasons (either Buddha's or your own) to explain why they should be considered to be truths. Does the elimination of desire seem to you to be a worthy ideal?
3. What is the point of the story about Punna? Would any other theories we have discussed make the same point?

READINGS FOR IMMEDIATE REFERENCE

Buddha. *The Dhammapada,* translated by Max Muller. New York: Oxford University Press, 1912.

Arnold, Edwin. *The Light of Asia.* New York: Macmillan, 1892.

REFERENCES FOR COMPREHENSIVE KNOWLEDGE

Brewster, E. H. *Life of Gotama the Buddha.* London: Routledge and Kegan Paul, 1926. Discusses the sources for our knowledge as well as the life.

Burtt, E. A. *The Teachings of the Compassionate Buddha.* New York: New American Library, 1955. Selections from original sources with connecting commentary.

Pratt, James B. *The Pilgrimage of Buddhism.* New York: Macmillan, 1928. A standard history by a sympathetic western interpreter.

Also see:

Bell, Charles. *The Religion of Tibet.* New York: Oxford University Press, 1931.

Carus, Paul. *The Gospel of Buddha.* LaSalle: Open Court Publishing Co., 1917.

David, C. A. Rhys. *Buddhism.* New York: Henry Holt, 1912.

Keith, A. B. *Buddhist Philosophy in India and Ceylon.* Oxford: Clarendon Press, 1923.

Suzuki, D. T. *Zen Buddhism.* New York: Doubleday, 1956.

Thomas, E. J. *A History of Buddhist Thought,* 2nd ed. New York: Barnes and Noble, 1951.

IV. LAO-TSE

Lao-tse, meaning "The Old Philosopher," is a name given to Li Erh, founder of Taoism, a religion which dominated Chinese thought for nearly a thousand years. His life is so legendary that many authorities doubt his existence at all, but tradition says he was born in 604 B.C. and that he held the post of curator in the imperial archives at the court of Chow. After a long time he is said to have tired of society, doubted the wisdom of government, resigned his post, and retired to live in seclusion. His quiet was so disturbed by curious visitors, including Confucius who was then a young teacher, that he decided upon flight to the west. He obtained a two-wheel carriage drawn by two black oxen and went, pausing only long enough to compose the Tao Teh Ching for his friend, Yin Hsi, the gatekeeper. Nothing is known of the remainder of his life.

The Tao Teh Ching advises man to look at Nature to determine how to live. Accordingly, in understanding this moral theory, notice what he says about natural phenomena: water, vegetation, trees. Is his account of Nature's processes accurate and complete, and are the moral injunctions necessarily related to these descriptions? Do you find this form of Chinese thought similar to Buddhism—or to Christianity? Do all religions teach the same moral precepts?

Nature, Man, and the Tao[1]

2

When all began to recognize beauty as beauty, then ugliness came into existence:
When all began to recognize the good as good, then evil came into existence.
Existence and non-existence have a common origin;
Difficult and easy succeed one another;
Long and short oppose one another;
High and low exclude one another;
Theme and harmony blend with one another;
Before and after follow one another.
Because these things are so the wise man remains inert and so enjoys the

[1] From *The Great Sinderesis: The Tao Teh Ching,* by Lao-tse, translated by Orde Poynton. Adelaide: The Hassell Press, 1949. Reprinted by permission of the translator.

power to instruct without speaking.
Because objects have existence one does not repudiate them:
Because they have life one does not take possession of them:
Because they take action one does not depend upon them,
For when their activities are done they do not endure:
Yet even though they are ephemeral they should not on this account be repudiated.

7

Heaven and Earth are long enduring:
They are long enduring because they do not live to further their own ends.
Because this is so the Wise Man
Keeps himself in the background and so comes to the forefront;
Is regardless of his personal safety and so is preserved;
Takes no account of his own interests and thereby satisfies his own interests.

8

Supreme Virtue may be compared to water.
The essence of water is that it enriches everything, yet it is not aggressive:
It lies in places that are despised by all.
Thereby it has attained the Way.
In choosing a habitation esteem good soil:
In respect to affections esteem their depth:
In social relations esteem kindliness:
In conversation esteem truthfulness.
In regard to government esteem good order:
In the conduct of business esteem ability:
In carrying out changes esteem timeliness.

16

Attain to complete emptiness:
Hold fast to calm and sincerity.
All things are creations
That we can see retrogress;
For things that flourish
All return to their source.
Returning to the source may be styled "attaining calm,"
And this may be named "reverting to destiny."
Reverting to destiny may be styled "attaining permanence,"
And knowledge of the permanent may be named "enlightenment."
Ignorance of the permanent is a failing that will occasion disaster.
He who understands the permanent is forbearing;
He who is forbearing is just;
He who is just is supreme;
He who is supreme is of the Cosmos;
He who is of the Cosmos commands the Way;
He who commands the Way is immortal—
Though his body may decay he is not destroyed.

17

Pre-eminent rulers—the people are unaware of their existence:
Those of the second order—the people love and praise them:

Those of the third order—the people
fear them:
Those of the fourth order—the people
despise them.
Where confidence is lacking
How exceedingly will distrust flourish.
When his public duties are fulfilled and
his plans have succeeded
The people all say—"We did this ourselves."

19

When ingenuity is renounced and brilliance banished
The people will benefit a hundredfold:
When social virtue is renounced and
duty banished
The people will be obedient and affectionate:
When craftsmanship is renounced and
profit banished
Robbers and thieves will disappear.
These three facts reveal the defects of
culture.
Therefore you should order those who
depend upon you
To become simple and natural,
To be unselfish and have few wants.

25

There is something that is altogether
formless:
It existed before Heaven and Earth
were created.
It is silent and it is fathomless;
Self-established it does not alter;
It operates everywhere and is inexhaustible;
It is able to function as the Mother
of the World.
I do not know a name that would describe it—
The symbol that represents it is the
symbol of the Way.
If I must give a name to describe it,
I would call it "Supreme."
Supremacy implies decline,
Decline implies dissolution,
Dissolution implies rebirth.

Because the Way is Supreme
Heaven is Supreme,
Earth is Supreme,
A ruler of men is Supreme.
Within the boundaries of a kingdom
There are four things which are
Supreme,
And a ruler of men is one of them.

Man is subject to the law of the Earth;
The Earth is subject to the law of
Heaven;
Heaven is subject to the law of the
Way;
The Way is subject to its own law.

34

The Great Way flows to the left and to
the right:
Everything depends upon it and the
living are no exception.
Its merit is perfect and cannot be described:
It clothes and nourishes all things
yet does not act as their master.
It is for ever without desires:
It can be named with the insignificant.
All things return to it, yet it does not act
as their master.
It can be named as possessing greatness.
He who, to the end of his day, never

acts as though he himself were great
Can then perfect his greatness.

37

The Way is persistently inactive, yet it is ever active.
If barons and kings could grasp this principle,
Everything would be changed of itself.
If in that which is changed, desires should become operative,
We may control them through the Primordial Substance.
The nameless Primordial Substance will make them devoid of desires:
Devoid of desires they will be calmed
And all in the Cosmos will become secure.

44

Reputation or life—which is to be more esteemed?
Life or property—which is more precious?
Getting or losing—which is more harmful?
In truth, great distraint must beget great loss:
Much hoarding must occasion heavy plundering.

He who understands sufficiency will not be humiliated:
He who understands when to stop will not perish,
But will be able long to endure.

49

The Wise Man does not have a constant mind,
But he takes the mind of the people as his mind.
To the righteous we must be righteous,
And to the unrighteous also we must be righteous:
This is the Sinderesis of Righteousness.
To the truthful we must be truthful,
And to the untruthful also we must be truthful:
This is the Sinderesis of Truthfulness.
Wise Men shut themselves away because the world confuses their minds:
Wise Men are all children.

57

Through controls a kingdom may be governed:
Through the element of surprise weapons may be used to advantage:
But through inertia the world may be grasped.
How can we know that this is so?
By this—
When the empire is beset with restrictions and interdicts,
Then the people become stricken by poverty:
When the people have plenty of sharp weapons
Kingdoms and homesteads become the scene of disorder:
When men have a profusion of clever devices
Many unforeseen situations arise:
When numerous laws and orders are promulgated
Bandits and thieves flourish.
Therefore the Wise Man says—
"When I do nothing the people change of themselves:
When I delight in inertia the people correct themselves:
When I have nothing to do with af-

fairs the people make themselves rich:
When I desire nothing the people conform to nature."

67

The whole world says that this Way of mine is so wonderful that it is beyond description:
But it is just because it is so wonderful that it is beyond description.
Were it capable of description it would long since have become of no account.

I possess three treasures which I hold and guard:
The first is called "affection";
The second is called "moderation";
The third is called "Not venturing to be a leader in the world."

He who is affectionate is capable of courage:
He who is moderate is capable of liberality:
He who does not venture to lead the world is capable of discharging the highest offices.

Today we have courage without affection:
We have liberality without moderation:
We have leaders but no followers.
This is to perish.

He who assails through his love will conquer:
He who is assailed through love will be secure:
Heaven protects he who saves others through his love for them.

76

When a man is born he is soft and pliant,
But when he dies he is hard and rigid.
Living plants and trees are flexible and delicate,
But when they die they become withered and dry.
Even so he who is firm and strong is a disciple of death.
While he who is pliable and weak is a disciple of life.
Hence it is the feeble weapon which triumphs,
And it is the mighty tree that is cut down.
It is the powerful and the great that are brought low,
And it is the pliant and weak who are raised up.

77

The Way of the Cosmos is like the drawing of a long bow:
The head is bent down and the heel is bent up:
That which is excessive is reduced,
That which is insufficient is increased.
For the Way of the Cosmos is to take from that which has too much
And to add to that which has not enough.
The way of men is not like this,
For they take from those who have insufficient
That they may give more to those who have a superfluity.
Who can possess abundance and give it to the world?
Only he who possesses the Way.
Therefore the Wise Man acts but does not rely on his actions:

He achieves merit yet holds no official position:
He has no desire to appear to be wise.

81

Sincere conversation is not elegant;
Elegant conversation is not sincere.
An honest man does not discriminate;
He who discriminates is not honest.
A man who is discerning is not ostentatious;
He who is ostentatious is not discerning.
The Wise Man does not spare himself.
The more he helps others the more he has for himself:
The more he gives to others the more he has for himself.
The Way of the Cosmos brings profit without hurt:
The Way of the Wise Man brings achievement without conflict.

QUESTIONS FOR DISCUSSION

1. Write a short philosophical essay stating clearly Lao-tse's conclusions and the reasons he gives to support them.
2. How is Lao-tse's moral theory similar to Buddha's? To Jesus'? To any of the philosophical theories we have considered?
3. Do you agree that the abolition of laws, the practice of non-contention and the quest for humility are ways to improve mankind?

READINGS FOR IMMEDIATE REFERENCE

Lao-tse. *The Tao Teh Ching.*

Giles, H. A. *Chuang Tzu—Mystic, Moralist and Social Reformer*. Shanghai: Kelly and Walsh, 1926, Chapters 1-7.

REFERENCES FOR COMPREHENSIVE KNOWLEDGE

Legge, James. *The Texts of Taoism.* Oxford: Clarendon Press, 1891. Contains all the extant works plus commentary on their origins.

Waley, Arthur. *Three Ways of Thought in Ancient China.* London: Allen and Unwin, 1939. Buddhism, Confucianism, Taoism. A standard work.

Yutang, Lin. *The Wisdom of Lao-tse*. New York: Random House, 1948. Texts plus commentary by a leading interpreter of Chinese thought for the western world.

Also see:

Bonsall, B. S. *Confucianism and Taoism.* London: Epworth Press, 1934.

Chan, Wing-tsit. *Religious Trends in Modern China.* New York: Columbia University Press, 1953.

Latourette, K. S. *The Chinese, Their History and Culture,* third ed. New York: Macmillan, 1946.

Waley, Arthur. *The Way and Its Power*. London: Allen and Unwin, 1934.

V. CONFUCIUS

Born K'ung Fu Tze in 550 B.C., Confucius was the youngest son of a local government functionary. His father died when he was three years old, and he lived in poverty during all his youth. At ninteen he was married and a son was born to him the next year, and two daughters later on. He held such governmental positions as keeper of the stores and superintendent of the herds during his twenties, and at twenty-two he opened a school for those interested in the principles of right conduct and government. He continued his teaching and scholarship for the next twenty years, building a widely respected reputation, particularly through the activities of his many disciples. When Confucius was fifty-two, the Duke of Lu invited him to become the chief magistrate and a reformation swept the state. As a contemporary said: "He strengthened the ruler. Dishonesty and dissoluteness hid their heads. Loyalty and good faith became the characteristics of the men, and chastity and docility those of the women. He was the idol of the people." However, the ruler of a neighboring kingdom sent the Duke a present of "a troop of fine horses and a large company of beautiful women, trained in music and dancing." The Duke neglected Confucius' teachings, so he withdrew from government to spend the rest of his life as a wandering teacher. He died in 479 B.C.

Traditionally, this selection was a part of the Li Ki, the scripture of Confucianism although it probably was written by Tsetzu, Confucius' grandson and Mencius' teacher. Lin Yutang, one of the leading interpreters of Chinese culture for the western world, says the essence of Confucian ethics is "the moral effort to aspire to achieve the common place." Does this selection verify that conclusion?

The Moral Law and the Moral Man[1]

What is God given is what we call human nature. To fulfill the law of our human nature is what we call the moral law. The cultivation of the moral law is what we call culture.

The moral law is a law from whose operation we cannot for one instant in our existence escape. A law from which we may escape is not the moral law. Wherefore it is that the moral man (or the superior man) watches diligently over what his eyes cannot see and is in fear and awe of what his ears cannot hear.

There is nothing more evident than that which cannot be seen by the eyes and nothing more palpable than that which cannot be perceived by the senses. Wherefore the moral man watches diligently over his secret thoughts.

When the passions, such as joy, anger, grief, and pleasure have not awakened, that is our *central* self, or moral being. When these passions awaken and each and all attain due measure and degree, that is *harmony*, or the moral order.

Our central self or moral being is the great basis of existence, and *harmony* or moral order is the universal law in the world.

When our true central self and harmony are realized, the universe then becomes a cosmos and all things attain their full growth and development.

Confucius remarked: "The life of the moral man is an exemplification of the universal moral order (chung-yung, usually translated as "the Mean"). The life of the vulgar person, on the other hand, is a contradiction of the universal moral order.

"The moral man's life is an exemplification of the universal order, because he is a moral person who unceasingly cultivates his true self or moral being. The vulgar person's life is a contradiction of the universal order, because he is a vulgar person who in his heart has no regard for, or fear of, the moral law."

Confucius remarked: "To find the central clue to our moral being which unites us to the universal order, that indeed is the highest human attainment. For a long time, people have seldom been capable of it."

Confucius remarked: "I know now why the moral life is not practiced. The wise mistake moral law for something higher than what it really is; and the foolish do not know enough what moral law really is. I know now why the moral law is not understood. The noble natures want to live too high, high above their moral ordinary self; and ignoble natures do not live high enough, i.e., not up to their moral ordinary true self. There is no one who does not eat and drink. But few there are who really know flavor." . . .

[1] From *The Conduct of Life,* translated by Ku Hung Ming. London: John Murray Co., 1906, Sections 1-29. [I have made some slight changes in the order of the sections. C.M.]

The moral law is to be found everywhere, and yet it is a secret.

The simple intelligence of ordinary men and women of the people may understand something of the moral law; but in its utmost reaches there is something which even the wisest and holiest of men cannot understand. The ignoble natures of ordinary men and women of the people may be able to carry out the moral law; but in its utmost reaches even the wisest and holiest of men cannot live up to it.

Great as the Universe is, man is yet not always satisfied with it. For there is nothing so great but the mind of the moral men can conceive of something still greater which nothing in the world can hold. There is nothing so small but the mind of the moral man can conceive of something still smaller which nothing in the world can split.

The *Book of Songs* says: "The hawk soars to the heavens above and fishes dive to the depths below." That is to say, there is no place in the highest heavens above nor in the deepest waters below where the moral law is not to be found. The moral man finds the moral law beginning in the relation between man and woman; but ending in the vast reaches of the universe.

Confucius remarked: "The power of spiritual forces in the Universe—how active it is everywhere! Invisible to the eyes, and impalpable to the senses, it is inherent in all things, and nothing can escape its operation."

It is the fact that there are these forces which makes men in all countries fast and purify themselves and with solemnity of dress institute services of sacrifice and religious worship. Like the rush of mighty waters, the presence of unseen Powers is felt, sometimes above us, sometimes around us.

In the *Book of Songs* it is said:

> The presence of the Spirit:
> It cannot be surmised,
> How may it be ignored!

Such is the evidence of things invisible that it is impossible to doubt the spiritual nature of man.

Confucius said: "Truth does not depart from human nature. If what is regarded as truth departs from human nature, it may not be regarded as truth. The *Book of Songs* says: 'In hewing an axe handle, the pattern is not far off.' Thus, when we take an axe handle in our hand to hew another axe handle and glance from one to the other, some still think the pattern is far off. Wherefore the moral man in dealing with men appeals to the common human nature and changes the manner of their lives and nothing more.

"When a man carries out the principles of conscientiousness and reciprocity he is not far from the moral law. What you do not wish others should do unto you, do not do unto them.

"There are four things in the moral life of a man, not one of which I have been able to carry out in my life. To serve my father as I would expect my son to serve me: that I have not been able to do. To serve my sovereign as I would expect a minister under me to serve me: that I have not been able to do. To act towards my elder brothers as I would expect my younger brother to act towards me: that I have not been able to do. To be the first to behave towards friends as I would expect them to behave towards me: that I have not been able to do.

"In the discharge of the ordinary duties of life and in the exercise of care in ordinary conversation, whenever there is shortcoming, never fail to strive for improvement, and when there is much to be said, always say less than what is necessary; words having respect to actions and actions having respect to words. Is it not just this thorough genuineness and absence of pretense which characterizes the moral man?"

The moral man conforms himself to his life circumstances; he does not desire anything outside of his position. Finding himself in a position of wealth and honor, he lives as becomes one living in a position of wealth and honor. Finding himself in a position of poverty and humble circumstances, he lives as becomes one living in a position of poverty and humble circumstances. Finding himself in uncivilized countries, he lives as becomes one living in uncivilized countries. Finding himself in circumstances of danger and difficulty, he acts according to what is required of a man under such circumstances. In one word, the moral man can find himself in no situation in life in which he is not master of himself. . . .

Confucius remarked: "In the practice of archery we have something resembling the principle in a moral man's life. When the archer misses the center of the target, he turns round and seeks for the cause of his failure within himself." . . .

The moral life of man may be likened to traveling to a distant place: one must start from the nearest stage. It may also be likened to ascending a height: one must begin from the lowest step. The *Book of Songs* says:

"When wives and children and their sires are one,
'Tis like the harp and lute in unison.
When brothers live in concord and at peace
The strain of harmony shall never cease.
The lamp of happy union lights the home,
And bright days follow when the children come."

Confucius, commenting on the above, remarked: "In such a state of things what more satisfaction can parents have?"

* * * * *

Confucius remarked: "The Emperor Wu and his brother, Duke Chou, were indeed eminently pious men. Now, true filial piety consists in successfully carrying out the unfinished work of our forefathers and transmitting their achievements to posterity.

"In spring and autumn they repaired and put in order the ancestral temple, arranged the sacrificial vessels, exhibited the regalia and heirlooms of the family, and presented the appropriate offerings of the season.

"The principle in the order of precedence in the ceremonies of worship in the ancestral temple is, in the first place, to arrange the members of the family according to descent. Ranks are next considered, in order to give recognition to the principle of social distinction. Services rendered are next considered as a recognition of distinction in moral worth. In the general banquet those below take precedence of those above in pledging the company, in order to show that consideration is shown to the meanest. In conclusion, a separate feast is given to the elders, in order to recognize the principle of seniority according to age.

"To gather in the same places where our fathers before us have gathered; to perform the same ceremonies which they before us have performed; to play the same music which they before us have played; to pay respect to those whom they honored; to love those who were dear to them—in fact, to serve those now dead as if they were living, and now departed as if they were still with us: this is the highest achievement of true filial piety. . . .

Duke Ai (ruler of Lu, Confucius' native state) asked what constituted good government.

Confucius replied: "The principles of good government of the Emperors Wen and Wu are abundantly illustrated in the records preserved. When the men are there, good government will flourish, but when the men are gone, good government decays and becomes extinct. With the right men, the growth of good government is as rapid as the growth of vegetation is in the right soil. Indeed, good government is like a fast-growing plant. The conduct of government, therefore, depends upon the men. The right men are obtained by the ruler's personal character. To cultivate his personal character, the ruler must use the moral law. To cultivate the moral law, the ruler must use the moral sense (*jen,* or principles of true manhood).

"The moral sense is the characteristic attribute of man. To feel natural affection for those nearly related to us is the highest expression of the moral sense. The sense of justice (*yi* or propriety) is the recognition of what is right and proper. To honor those who are worthier than ourselves is the highest expression of the sense of justice. The relative degrees of natural affection we ought to feel for those who are nearly related to us and the relative grades of honor we ought to show to those worthier than ourselves: these give rise to the forms and distinctions in social life (*li,* or principles of social order). For unless social inequalities have a true and moral basis (or unless those being ruled feel their proper place with respect to their rulers), government of the people is an impossibility.

"Therefore it is necessary for a man of the governing class to set about regulating his personal conduct and character. In considering how to regulate his personal conduct and character, it is necessary for him to do his duties toward those nearly related to him. In considering how to do his duties toward those nearly related to him, it is necessary for him to understand the nature and organization of human society. In considering the nature and organization of human society it is necessary for him to understand the laws of God.

"The duties of universal obligation are five, and the moral qualities by which they are carried out are three. The duties are those between ruler and subject, between father and son, between husband and wife, between elder brother and younger, and those in the intercourse between friends. These are the five duties of universal obligation. Wisdom, compassion and courage—these are the three universally recognized moral qualities of man. It matters not in what way men come to the exercise of these moral qualities, the result is one and the same.

"Some men are born with the knowledge of these moral qualities; some acquire it as the result of education; some acquire it as the result of hard experience. But when the knowledge is acquired, it comes to one and the same thing. Some exercise these moral qualities naturally and easily; some because they find it advantageous to do so; some with effort and difficulty. But when the achievement is made it comes to one and the same thing."

Confucius went on to say: "Love of knowledge is akin to wisdom. Strenuous attention to conduct is akin to compassion. Sensitiveness to shame is akin to courage.

"When a man understands the nature and use of these three moral qualities, he will then understand how to put in order his personal conduct and character. When a man understands how to put in order his personal conduct and character, he will understand how to govern men. When a man understands how to govern men, he will then understand how to govern nations and empires.

"For every one called to the government of nations and empires there are nine cardinal directions to be attended to:

1. Cultivating his personal conduct.
2. Honoring worthy men.
3. Cherishing affection for, and doing his duty toward, his kindred.
4. Showing respect to the high ministers of state.
5. Identifying himself with the interests and welfare of the whole body of public officers.
6. Showing himself as a father to the common people.
7. Encouraging the introduction of all useful arts.
8. Showing tenderness to strangers from far countries.
9. Taking interest in the welfare of the princes of the Empire.

"When the ruler pays attention to the cultivation of his personal conduct, there will be respect for the moral law. When the ruler honors worthy men, he will not be deceived. When the ruler cherishes affection for his kindred, there will be no disaffection among the members of his family. When the ruler shows respect to the high ministers of state, he will not make mistakes. When the ruler identifies himself with the interests and welfare of the body of public officers, there will be a strong spirit of loyalty among the gentlemen of the country. When the ruler becomes a father to the common people, the mass of the people will exert themselves for the good of the state. When the ruler encourages the introduction of all useful arts, there will be sufficiency of wealth and revenue in the country. When the ruler shows kindness to the strangers from far countries, people from all quarters of the world will flock to the country. When the ruler takes interest in the condition and welfare of the princes of the Empire, he will inspire awe and respect for his authority throughout the whole world. . . .

"If the people in inferior positions do not have confidence in those above them, government of the people is an impossibility. There is only one way to gain confidence for one's authority: if a man is not trusted by his friends, he will not have confidence in those above him. There is only one way to be trusted by one's friends: if a man is not affectionate toward his parents, he will not be trusted by his friends. There is only one way to be affectionate toward one's parents: if a man, looking into his own heart, is not true to himself, he will not be affectionate toward his parents. There is only one way for a man to be true to himself. If he does not know what is good, a man cannot be true to himself.

"Being true to oneself is the law of God. Trying to be true to oneself is the law of man.

"He who is naturally true to himself is one who, without effort, hits upon what is right, and without thinking understands what he wants to know, whose life is easily and naturally in harmony with the moral law. Such a one is what we call a saint or a man of divine nature. He who learns to be his true self is one who finds out what is good and holds fast to it.

"In order to learn to be one's true self, it is necessary to obtain a wide and extensive knowledge of what has been said and done in the world; critically to inquire into it; carefully to ponder over it; clearly to sift it; and earnestly to carry it out.

"It matters not what you learn; but when you once learn a thing, you must never give it up until you have mastered it. It matters not what you inquire into, but when you inquire into a thing, you must never give it up until you have thoroughly understood it. It matters not what you try to think out, but when you once try to think out a thing you must never give it up until you have got what you want. It matters not what you try to sift out, but when you once try to sift out a thing, you must never give it up until you have sifted it out clearly and distinctly. It matters not what you try to carry out, but when you once try to carry out a thing you must never give it up until you have done it thoroughly and well. If another man succeed by one effort, you will use a hundred efforts. If another man succeed by ten efforts, you will use a thousand efforts.

"Let a man really proceed in this manner, and, though dull, he will surely become intelligent; though weak, he will surely become strong."

To arrive at understanding from being one's true self is called nature, and to arrive at being one's true self from understanding is called culture. He who is his true self has thereby understanding, and he who has understanding finds thereby his true self.

* * * * *

Truth means the fulfilment of our self; and moral law means following the law of our being. Truth is the beginning and end (the substance) of material existence. Without truth there is no material existence. It is for this reason that the moral man values truth.

Truth is not only the fulfilment of

our own being; it is that by which things outside of us have an existence. The fulfilment of our being is moral sense. The fulfilment of the nature of things outside of us is intellect. These, moral sense and intellect, are the powers or faculties of our being. They combine the inner or subjective and outer or objective use of the power of the mind. Therefore, with truth, everything done is right.

Thus absolute truth is indestructible. Being indestructible, it is eternal. Being eternal, it is self-existent. Being self-existent, it is infinite. Being infinite, it is vast and deep. Being vast and deep, it is transcendental and intelligent. It is because it is vast and deep that it contains all existence. It is because it is transcendental and intelligent that it embraces all existence. It is because it is infinite and eternal that it fulfils or perfects all existence. In vastness and depth it is like the Earth. In transcendental intelligence it is like Heaven. Infinite and eternal, it is the Infinite itself.

Such being the nature of absolute truth, it manifests itself without being seen; it produces effects without motion; it accomplishes its ends without action.

The principle in the course and operation of nature may be summed up in one word: because it obeys only its own immutable law, the way in which it produces the variety of things is unfathomable.

Nature is vast, deep, high, intelligent, infinite and eternal. The heaven appearing before us is only this bright, shining mass; but in its immeasurable extent, the sun, the moon, stars and constellations are suspended in it, and all things are embraced under it. The Earth, appearing before us, is but a handful of soil; but in all its breadth and depth, it sustains mighty mountains without feeling their weight; rivers and seas dash against it without causing it to leak. The mountain appearing before us is only a mass of rock; but in all the vastness of its size, grass and vegetation grow upon it, birds and beasts dwell on it, and treasures of precious minerals are found in it. The water appearing before us is but a ladleful of liquid; but in all its unfathomable depths, the largest crustaceans, dragons, fishes, and turtles are produced in them, and all useful products abound in them. . . .

Therefore every system of moral laws must be based upon the man's own consciousness, verified by the common experience of mankind, tested by due sanction of historical experience and found without error, applied to the operations and processes of nature in the physical universe and found to be without contradiction, laid before the gods without question or fear, and able to wait a hundred generations and have it confirmed without a doubt by a Sage of posterity. The fact that he is able to confront the spiritual powers of the universe without any fear shows that he understands the laws of God. The fact that he is prepared to wait a hundred generations for confirmation from the Sage of posterity without any misgiving shows that he understands the laws of man.

Wherefore it is that it is true of the really great moral man that every move he makes becomes an example for generations; every act he does becomes a model for generations and every word he utters becomes a guide for generations. Those who are far away look up to him, while those who are near do not decrease their respect for him. In the *Book of Songs* it is said:

"There they found no fault of him,
Here they never tire of him;
Thus from day to day and night to night
They will perpetuate his praise!"

There never was a moral man who did not answer this description and who yet could obtain timely recognition throughout the world.

QUESTIONS FOR DISCUSSION

1. What does Confucius mean by the statement: "The moral man finds the moral law beginning in the relation between man and woman; but ending in the vast reaches of the universe"?
2. Write a short essay describing how you would live if you were to follow the Confucian ethic.
3. Do you find any similarities between Confucius' teachings and other ethical theories, either religious or philosophical?

READINGS FOR IMMEDIATE REFERENCE

Confucius. *Analects,* translated by Arthur Waley. London: Allen and Unwin, 1938.

Mencius. *Book of History,* translated by James Legge. New York: Oxford University Press, 1895.

REFERENCES FOR COMPREHENSIVE KNOWLEDGE

Creel, H. G. *Confucius, The Man and the Myth.* New York: John Day Co., 1949.

———. *Chinese Thought from Confucius to Mao Tse-tung.* Chicago: University of Chicago Press, 1953. Together, a comprehensive survey of Confucius' thought and its influence.

Waley, Arthur. *Three Ways of Thought in Ancient China.* London: Allen and Unwin, 1939. Buddhism, Confucianism, Taoism. A standard work.

Also see:

Chan, Wing-tsit. *Religious Trends in Modern China.* New York: Columbia University Press, 1953.

Johnston, R. F. *Confucianism and Modern China.* New York: Appleton-Century, 1935.

Liu, Wu-chi. *A Short History of Confucian Philosophy.* Baltimore: Penguin Books, 1955.

Wilhelm, Richard. *Confucius and Confucianism.* New York: Harcourt, Brace, 1931.

BIBLIOGRAPHY FOR CHAPTER SIX

READINGS FOR IMMEDIATE REFERENCE

Butler, Joseph. *Five Sermons,* Stuart M. Brown, ed. New York: Liberal Arts Press, 1950.

Wheelwright, Philip. *A Critical Introduction to Ethics,* 3rd ed. New York: Odyssey Press, 1959, Chapters 8, 11.

Yutang, Lin. *The Importance of Living.* New York: John Day Co., 1937.

REFERENCES FOR COMPREHENSIVE KNOWLEDGE

Haydon, A. E. *Man's Search for the Good Life.* New York: Harper, 1937. A comparative study of the world's religions by one of America's leading interpreters of oriental thought.

Sneath, E. Hershey. *The Evolution of Ethics as Revealed in the Great Religions.* New Haven: Yale University Press, 1927. A statement of the different views of religious ethics by representative writers.

Also see:

D'Arcy, Martin C. *The Mind and Heart of Love,* rev. ed. London: Faber and Faber, 1954.

Garnett, A. Campbell. *Religion and the Moral Life.* New York: Ronald Press, 1955.

Harkness, Georgia. *The Recovery of Ideals.* New York: Scribners, 1937.

Sorley, W. R. *Moral Values and the Idea of God.* Cambridge: Cambridge University Press, 1919.

Chapter Seven

RELIGIOUS METAPHYSICS

I. THE OLD TESTAMENT

Unlike philosophical metaphysical theories which are complex and deal with many diverse problems, religious accounts of reality tend to localize their concern into one central question, "What can man know of God?" For if man can have this knowledge, all other metaphysical questions can be answered deductively. This selection, traditionally ascribed to Moses, presents one of the most influential answers to that question. As you read look for the particular points which are made—what was created on each day, whether the account given in Chapter One is compatible with the account given in Chapter Two, why man was made mortal and how, and also for the conception of God implied by these particulars. Does this account of the Creation seem to you to be reasonable? Or is that a proper question?

The Story of Creation[1]

CHAPTER I

In the beginning, God created the heaven and the earth. And the earth was without form, and void; and darkness was upon the face of the deep. And the Spirit of God moved upon the face of the waters. And God said, Let there be light: and there was light. And God saw the light, that it was good and God divided the light from the darkness. And God called the light Day, and the darkness he called Night. And the evening and the morning were the first day.

And God said, Let there be a firmament in the midst of the waters, and let it divide the waters from the waters. And

[1] Genesis, Chapters 1-3. King James translation.

God made the firmament, and divided the waters which were under the firmament from the waters which were above the firmament: and it was so. And God called the firmament Heaven. And the evening and the morning were the second day.

And God said, Let the waters under the heaven be gathered together unto one place, and let the dry land appear: and it was so. And God called the dry land Earth; and the gathering together of the waters called he Seas: and God saw that it was good. And God said, Let the earth bring forth grass, the herb yielding seed, and the fruit tree yielding fruit after his kind, whose seed is in itself, upon the earth: and it was so. And the earth brought forth grass, and herb yielding seed after his kind, and the tree yielding fruit, whose seed was in itself, after his kind: and God saw that it was good. And the evening and the morning were the third day.

And God said, Let there be lights in the firmament of the heaven to divide the day from the night; and let them be for signs, and for seasons, and for days, and years: and let them be for lights in the firmament of the heaven to give light upon the earth: and it was so. And God made two great lights; the greater light to rule the day, and the lesser light to rule the night: he made the stars also. And God set them in the firmament of the heaven to give light upon the earth. And to rule over the day and over the night, and to divide the light from the darkness: and God saw that it was good. And the evening and the morning were the fourth day.

And God said, Let the waters bring forth abundantly the moving creature that hath life, and fowl that may fly above the earth in the open firmament of heaven. And God created great whales, amd every living creature that moveth, which the waters brought forth abundantly, after their kind, and every winged fowl after his kind: and God saw that it was good. And God blessed them, saying, Be fruitful, and multiply, and fill the waters in the seas, and Let fowl multiply in the earth. And the evening and the morning were the fifth day.

And God said, Let the earth bring forth the living creature after his kind, cattle, and creeping thing, and beast of the earth after his kind: and it was so. And God made the beast of the earth after his kind, and cattle after their kind, and everything that creepeth upon the earth after his kind: and God saw that it was good.

And God said, Let us make man in our image, after our likeness: and let them have dominion over the fish of the sea, and over the fowl of the air, and over the cattle, and over all the earth, and over every creeping thing that creepeth upon the earth. So God created man in his own image, in the image of God created he him; male and female created he them. And God blessed them, and God said unto them, Be fruitful, and multiply, and replenish the earth, and subdue it: and have dominion over the fish of the sea, and over the fowl of the air, and over every living thing that moveth upon the earth.

And God said, Behold, I have given you every herb bearing seed, which is upon the face of all the earth, and every tree, in the which is the fruit of a tree yielding seed; to you it shall be for meat. And to every beast of the earth, and to every fowl of the air, and to every thing that creepeth upon the earth, wherein there is life, I have given every green herb for meat: and it was so. And God saw everything that he had made, and, behold, it was very good. And the evening and the morning were the sixth day.

CHAPTER II

Thus the heavens and the earth were finished, and all the host of them. And on the seventh day God ended his work which he had made; and he rested on the seventh day from all his work which he had made. And God blessed the seventh day, and sanctified it: because that in it he had rested from all his work which God created and made.

These are the generations of the heavens and of the earth when they were created, in the day that the Lord God made the earth and the heavens. And every plant of the field before it was in the earth, and every herb of the field before it grew: for the Lord God had not caused it to rain upon the earth, and there was not a man to till the ground. But there went up a mist from the earth, and watered the whole face of the ground. And the Lord God formed man of the dust of the ground, and breathed into his nostrils the breath of life; and man became a living soul.

And the Lord God planted a garden eastward in Eden; and there he put the man whom he had formed. And out of the ground made the Lord God to grow every tree that is pleasant to the sight, and good for food; the tree of life also in the midst of the garden, and the tree of knowledge of good and evil. And a river went out of Eden to water the garden; and from thence it was parted, and became into four heads. The name of the first is Pison: that is it which compasseth the whole land of Havilah, where there is gold; And the gold of that land is good: there is bdellium and the onyx stone. And the name of the second river is Gihon: the same is it that compasseth the whole land of Ethiopia. And the name of the third river is Hiddekel: that is it which goeth toward the east of Assyria. And the fourth river is Euphrates. And the Lord God took the man, and put him into the garden of Eden to dress it and to keep it. And the Lord God commanded the man, saying, Of every tree of the garden thou mayest freely eat: But of the tree of the knowledge of good and evil, thou shalt not eat of it: for in the day that thou eatest thereof thou shalt surely die.

And the Lord God said, It is not good that man should be alone; I will make him an help meet for him. And out of the ground the Lord God formed every beast of the field, and every fowl of the air; and brought them unto Adam to see what he would call them: and whatsoever Adam called every living creature, that was the name thereof. And Adam gave names to all cattle, and to the fowl of the air, and to every beast of the field; but for Adam there was not found an help meet for him. And the Lord God caused a deep sleep to fall upon Adam, and he slept: and he took one of his ribs, and closed up the flesh instead thereof; and the rib, which the

Lord God had taken from man, made he a woman, and brought her unto the man. And Adam said, This is now bone of my bones, and flesh of my flesh: she shall be called Woman, because she was taken out of Man. Therefore shall a man leave his father and his mother, and shall cleave unto his wife: and they shall be one flesh. And they were both naked, the man and his wife, and were not ashamed.

CHAPTER III

Now the serpent was more subtil than any beast of the field which the Lord God had made. And he said unto the woman, Yea, hath God said, Ye shall not eat of every tree of the garden? And the woman said unto the serpent, We may eat of the fruit of the trees of the garden: But of the fruit of the tree which is in the midst of the garden, God hath said, Ye shall not eat of it, neither shall ye touch it, lest ye die. And the serpent said unto the woman, Ye shall not surely die: for God doth know that in the day ye eat thereof, then your eyes shall be opened, and ye shall be as gods, knowing good and evil. And when the woman saw that the tree was good for food, and that it was pleasant to the eyes, and a tree to be desired to make one wise, she took of the fruit thereof, and did eat, and gave also unto her husband with her; and he did eat.

And the eyes of them both were opened, and they knew that they were naked; and they sewed fig leaves together, and made themselves aprons. And they heard the voice of the Lord God walking in the garden in the cool of the day: and Adam and his wife hid themselves from the presence of the Lord God amongst the trees of the garden. And the Lord God called unto Adam, and said unto him, Where art thou? And he said, I heard thy voice in the garden, and I was afraid, because I was naked; and I hid myself. And he said, Who told thee that thou wast naked? Hast thou eaten of the tree, whereof I commanded thee that thou shouldest not eat? And the man said, The woman whom thou gavest to be with me, she gave me of the tree, and I did eat. And the Lord God said unto the woman, What is this that thou hast done? And the woman said, the serpent beguiled me, and I did eat. And the Lord God said unto the serpent, Because thou hast done this, thou art cursed above all cattle, and above every beast of the field; upon thy belly shalt thou go, and dust shalt thou eat all the days of thy life: and I will put enmity between thee and the woman, and between thy seed and her seed; it shall bruise thy head, and thou shalt bruise his heel. Unto the woman he said, I will greatly multiply thy sorrow and thy conception; in sorrow thou shalt bring forth children; and thy desire shall be to thy husband, and he shall rule over thee. And unto Adam he said, Because thou hast hearkened unto the voice of thy wife, and hast eaten of the tree, of which I commanded thee, saying, Thou shalt not eat of it: cursed is the ground for thy sake; in sorrow shalt thou eat of it all the days of thy life; thorns also and thistles shall it bring forth to thee; and thou shalt eat the herb of the field; in the sweat of thy face shalt thou eat bread, till thou return unto the ground; for out of it wast thou taken; for dust thou art, and unto dust shalt thou return. And

Adam called his wife's name Eve; because she was the mother of all living. Unto Adam also and to his wife did the Lord God make coats of skins, and clothed them.

And the Lord God said, Behold, the man is become as one of us, to know good and evil: and now, lest he put forth his hand, and take also of the tree of life, and eat, and live for ever: therefore the Lord God sent him forth from the garden of Eden, to till the ground from whence he was taken. So he drove out the man; and he placed at the east of the garden of Eden Cherubims, and a flaming sword which turned every way, to keep the way of the tree of life.

QUESTIONS FOR DISCUSSION

1. List the events which took place on each day of the week of Creation. Does the order in which they occurred raise any problems?
2. Did Adam and Eve fall because they chose to or was this part of God's plan? What problems are raised if either view is adopted? What conception of God is implied by each alternative?
3. Are bearing children and obedience to Adam fitting punishments, in your opinion, to be given to Eve? And everlasting work to Adam? What would you consider to be a fitting punishment?
4. Should the Bible be read as being literally God's word? What problems are raised if you answer either affirmatively or negatively?

READINGS FOR IMMEDIATE REFERENCE

Noss, J. B. *Man's Religions,* rev. ed. New York: Macmillan, 1956. For other conceptions of creation see pp. 22 (primitive), 48-52 (Egyptian), 62-65 (Babylonian), 103-107 (Teutonic), 124-127 (Vedic), 131-134 (Brahman), 280-282 (Sikh), 400-401 (Shinto), and 441-452 (Zoroastrian).

REFERENCES FOR COMPREHENSIVE KNOWLEDGE

Breasted, James H. *The Dawn of Conscience.* New York: Scribners, 1933. Selections and commentary illustrating the growth of morality. A standard work.

Fraser, James G. *The Golden Bough.* New York: Macmillan, 1953. A thoroughly documented study which contends that religion grew out of magic, just as science grows out of religion.

Skinner, James. *A Critical and Exegetical Commentary on Genesis.* New York: Scribners, 1910. Demonstrates the application of Higher Criticism to the study of the Bible.

Also see:

Finegan, Jack. *Light from the Ancient Past.* Princeton: Princeton University Press, 1946.

Meek, T. J. *Hebrew Origins.* New York: Harper, 1936.

Moore, G. F. *The Birth and Growth of Religion.* New York: Scribners, 1926.

Murray, Gilbert. *The Five Stages of Greek Religion.* Oxford: Clarendon Press, 1925.

II. *THOMAS AQUINAS*

Thomas Aquinas was born in 1225, the seventh son of a noble family living in southern Italy. At the age of five he was sent to the Abbey at Monte Cassino where he remained for nine years. He then attended the University of Naples, where he became acquainted with the recently organized Dominican Order, which he joined in 1244, despite his family's vigorous objections. He studied in Paris with Albertus Magnus, the champion of Aristotle, whose works had recently been rediscovered to the western world, and in 1252 he began his own career as teacher and author. In 1259 he was appointed theological advisor to the papal court and in 1272 was commissioned to reorganize the curriculum in all Dominican schools. In 1274 he was appointed by Pope Gregory X to attend the General Council at Lyon as his personal delegate; however, Aquinas became ill shortly after leaving Naples and died before he reached France. His students said that his teaching was characterized by originality and vitality, and one of his contemporaries spoke of him as a man "large in physique and character with great composure and courtesy." Since the Encyclical, *Aeterni Patrias,* issued by Pope Leo XIII in 1879, the works of Aquinas have provided the basis for Roman Catholic religious education.

This selection, too, is concerned with our knowledge of God's existence: is it self-evident, or can it be demonstrated? Notice the distinctions Aquinas makes between "self-evident" and "demonstration." Are the objections he raises important ones, and are his answers satisfactory? In the five proofs, pay careful attention to the reasons he gives for saying causation (motion or contingent being) could not go on to infinity.

Proofs for God's Existence[1]

QUESTION II

Article I

WHETHER THE EXISTENCE OF GOD IS SELF-EVIDENT?

We proceed thus to the First Article: It seems that the existence of God is self-evident.

Objection 1. Now those things are said to be self-evident to us the knowledge of which is naturally in us, as we can see in regard to first principles. But as Damascene says, "the knowledge of God is naturally implanted in all." Therefore the existence of God is self-evident.

Objection 2. Further, those things are said to be self-evident, which are known as soon as the terms are known, which the Philosopher says is true of the first principles of demonstration. Thus, when the nature of a whole and of a part is known, it is at once known that every whole is greater than its part. But as soon as the meaning of the word "God" is understood, it is at once seen that God exists. For by this word is signified that thing than which nothing greater can be conceived. But that which exists actually and in the intellect is greater than that which exists only in the intellect. Therefore, since as soon as the word "God" is understood it exists in the intellect, it also follows that it exists actually. Therefore the proposition "God exists" is self-evident.

Objection 3. Further, the existence of truth is self-evident. For whoever denies the existence of truth grants that truth does not exist. And, if truth does not exist, then the proposition "Truth does not exist" is true. But if there is anything true, there must be truth. But God is truth itself: "I am the way, the truth, and the life." (John 14:6) Therefore "God exists" is self-evident.

On the contrary, No one can think the opposite of what is self-evident, as the Philosopher states concerning the first principles of demonstration. But the opposite of the proposition "God is" can be thought, for, "The fool said in his heart, There is no God." (Ps. 53:1) Therefore, that God exists is not self-evident.

I answer that, A thing can be self-evident in either of two ways. On the one hand, self-evident in itself, though not to us; on the other, self-evident in itself, and to us. A proposition is self-evident because the predicate is included in the notion of the subject, as "Man is an animal," for animal is contained in the essence of man. If therefore the essence of the predicate and subject be known at all, the proposition will be self-evident to all as is clear with regard to the first principles of demonstration, the terms of which are common

[1] From *Summa Theologica,* by Thomas Aquinas, translated by the English Dominican Fathers. New York: Benziger Brothers, Inc., 1920, First Part, Question 2, Articles 1-3. Reprinted by permission.

things that no one is ignorant of, such as being and non-being, whole and part, and the like. If, however, there are some to whom the essence of the predicate and subject is unknown, the proposition will be self-evident in itself, but not to those who do not know the meaning of the predicate and subject of the proposition. Therefore, it happens, as Boethius says, that "there are some concepts of the mind self-evident only to the learned, as that incorporeal substances are not in space." Therefore I say that this proposition, "God exists," of itself is self-evident, for the predicate is the same as the subject, because God is His own existence, as will be hereafter shown. Now because we do not know the essence of God, the proposition is not self-evident to us, but needs to be demonstrated by things that are more known to us, though less known in their nature—namely, by effects.

Reply Objection 1. To know that God exists in a general and confused way is implanted in us by nature, since God is man's Happiness. For man naturally desires happiness, and what is naturally desired by man must be naturally known to him. This, however, is not to know absolutely that God exists, just as to know that someone is approaching is not the same as to know that Peter is approaching, even though it is Peter who is approaching. For there are many who imagine that man's perfect good which is Happiness, consists in riches, and others in pleasures, and others in something else.

Reply Objection 2. Perhaps not everyone who hears this word "God" understands it to signify something than which nothing greater can be thought, seeing that some have believed God to be a body. Yet, granted that everyone understands the word "God" to mean this, nevertheless, it does not therefore follow that he understands that what the word signifies exists actually, but only that it exists in the intellect. Nor can it be argued that it actually exists, unless it be admitted that there actually exists something than which nothing greater can be thought. And this is what is not admitted by those who hold that God does not exist.

Reply Objection 3. The existence of truth in general is self-evident, but the existence of a First Truth is not self-evident to us.

Article II

WHETHER IT CAN BE DEMONSTRATED THAT GOD EXISTS?

We proceed thus to the second article. It seems that the existence of God cannot be demonstrated.

Objection 1. For it is an article of faith that God exists. But what is of faith cannot be demonstrated, because a demonstration produces scientific knowledge, whereas faith is of the unseen, as is clear from the Apostle (Heb. 11:1). Therefore it cannot be demonstrated that God exists. . . .

Objection 3. Further, if the existence of God were demonstrated, this could only be from His effects. But His effects are not proportioned to Him, since He is infinite and His effects are finite, and between the finite and infinite there is no proportion. Therefore, since a cause cannot be demonstrated by an effect not proportioned to it, it seems that the existence of God cannot be demonstrated.

On the contrary, the Apostle says: *The invisible things of Him are clearly seen, being understood by the things that are made* (*Rom.* 1:20). But this would not be unless the existence of God could be demonstrated through the things that are made; for the first thing we must know of anything is, whether it exists.

I answer that, Demonstration can be made in two ways: One is through the cause, and is called *propter quid,* and this is to argue from what is prior absolutely. The other is through the effect, and is called a demonstration *quid;* this is to argue from what is prior relatively only to us. When an effect is better known to us than its cause, from the effect we proceed to the knowledge of the cause. And from every effect the existence of its proper cause can be demonstrated, so long as its effects are better known to us; because, since every effect depends upon its cause, if the effect exists, the cause must pre-exist. Hence the existence of God, in so far as it is not self-evident to us, can be demonstrated from those of His effects which are known to us.

Reply Objection 1. The existence of God and other like truths about God, which can be known by natural reason, are not articles of faith, but are preambles to the articles, for faith presupposes natural knowledge, even as grace presupposes nature and perfection the perfectible. Nevertheless, there is nothing to prevent a man, who cannot grasp a proof, from accepting, as a matter of faith, something which in itself is capable of being scientifically known and demonstrated. . . .

Reply Objection 3. From effects not proportioned to the cause no perfect knowledge of that cause can be obtained. Yet from every effect the existence of the cause can be clearly demonstrated, and so we can demonstrate the existence of God from His effects; though from them we cannot know God perfectly as He is in His essence.

Article III

WHETHER GOD EXISTS?

We proceed thus to the Third Article:—It seems that God does not exist.

Objection 1. For if one of two contraries be infinite, the other would be altogether destroyed. But the name *God* means that He is infinite goodness. If, therefore, God existed, there would be no evil discoverable; but there is evil in the world. Therefore God does not exist.

Objection 2. Further, it is superfluous to suppose that what can be accounted for by a few principles has been produced by many. But it seems that everything we see in the world can be accounted for by other principles, supposing God did not exist. For all natural things can be reduced to one principle, which is nature; and all voluntary things can be reduced to one principle, which is human reason, or will, therefore there is no need to suppose God's existence.

On the contrary, It is said in the person of God: *I am Who am* (Exod. 3:14).

I answer that, The existence of God can be proved in five ways. The first and more manifest way is the argument from motion. It is certain, and evident to our senses, that in the world some things are in motion. Now whatever is moved is moved by another, for nothing can be moved except it is in potentiality to that towards which it is moved whereas a thing moves inasmuch as it is in act. For motion is nothing else than the reduction of something from potentiality to actuality. But nothing can be reduced from potentiality to actuality, except by something in a state of actuality. Thus that which is actually hot, as fire, makes wood, which is potentially hot, to be actually hot, and thereby moves and changes it. Now it is not possible that the same thing should be at once in actuality and potentiality in the same respect, but only in different respects. For what is actually hot cannot simultaneously be potentially hot; but it is simultaneously potentially cold. It is therefore impossible that in the same respect and in the same way a thing should be both mover and moved, i.e., that it should move itself. Therefore, whatever is moved must be moved by another. If that by which it is moved be itself moved, then this also must needs be moved by another, and that by another again. But this cannot go on to infinity, because then there would be no first mover, and, consequently, no other mover, seeing that subsequent movers move only inasmuch as they are moved by the first mover; as the staff moves only because it is moved by the hand. Therefore, it is necessary to arrive at a first mover, moved by no other; and this everyone understands to be God.

The second way is from the nature of efficient cause. In the world of sensible things we find there is an order of efficient causes. There is no case known (neither is it, indeed, possible) in which a thing is found to be the efficient cause of itself; for so it would be prior to itself, which is impossible. Now in efficient causes it is not possible to go on to infinity, because in all efficient causes following in order, the first is the cause of the intermediate cause, and the intermediate is the cause of the ultimate cause, whether the intermediate cause be several, or one only. Now to take away the cause is to take away the effect. Therefore, if there be no first cause among efficient causes, there will be no ultimate, nor any intermediate, cause. But if in efficient causes it is possible to go on to infinity, there will be no first efficient cause, neither will there be an ultimate effect, nor any intermediate efficient causes; all of which is plainly false. Therefore it is necessary to admit a first efficient cause, to which everyone gives the name God.

The third way is taken from possibility and necessity, and runs thus. We find in nature things that are possible to be and not to be, since they are found to be generated, and to be corrupted, and consequently, it is possible for them to be and not to be. But it is impossible for these always to exist, for that which can not-be at sometime is not. Therefore, if everything can not-be, then at one time there was nothing in existence. Now if this were true, even now there would be nothing in existence, because that which does not exist begins to exist only through something already existing. Therefore, if at one time nothing was in existence, it would have been impossible for anything to have begun to exist; and thus even now nothing would be in existence—which is absurd. Therefore, not all beings are merely possible, but there must exist something the existence of which is necessary. But every necessary thing either has its necessity caused by another, or not. Now it is impossible to go on to infinity in necessary things which have their necessity caused by another, as had been already proved in regard to efficient causes. Therefore we cannot but admit the existence of some being having of itself its own necessity, and not receiving it from another, but rather causing in others their necessity. This all men speak of as God.

The fourth way is taken from the gradation to be found in things. Among beings there are some more and some less good, true, noble, and the like. But *more* and *less* are predicated of different things according as they resemble in their different ways something which is the maximum, as a thing is said to be hotter according as it more nearly resembles that which is hottest; so that there is something which is truest, something best, something noblest, and, consequently, something which is most being, for those things that are greatest in truth are greatest in being, as it is written in *Metaph.* II (*Metaph.* Ia, 1 993b30). Now the maximum in any genus is the cause of all in that genus, as fire, which is the maximum of heat, is the cause of all hot things, as is said in the same book. (993b25). Therefore there must also be something which is to all beings the cause of their being, goodness, and every other perfection; and this we call God.

The fifth way is taken from the governance of the world. We see that things which lack knowledge, such as natural bodies, act for an end, and this is evident from their acting always, or nearly always in the same way, so as to obtain the best result. Hence it is plain that they achieve their end, not fortuitously, but designedly. Now whatever lacks knowledge cannot move towards an end, unless it be directed by some being endowed with knowledge and intelligence; as the arrow is directed by the archer. Therefore some intelligent being exists by whom all natural things are directed to their end; and this being we call God.

Reply Objection 1. As Augustine says: "Since God is the highest good, He would not allow any evil to exist in His works, unless His omnipotence and goodness were such as to bring good even out of evil." This is part of the infinite goodness of God, that He should allow evil to exist, and out of it produce good.

Reply Objection 2. Since nature works for a determinate end under the direction of a higher agent, whatever is done by nature must be traced back to God as to its first cause. So likewise whatever is done voluntarily must be traced back to some higher cause other than human reason and will, since these can change and fail; for all things that are changeable and capable of defect must be traced back to an immovable and self-necessary first principle, as has been shown.

QUESTIONS FOR DISCUSSION

1. Why is the existence of God not self-evident, and why should it be demonstrated?
2. According to Aquinas, why cannot causation (or motion, contingency or gradation) go on to infinity? Are his reasons persuasive?
3. Why does Aquinas reject the argument given in Article 1, Objection 2, the ontological argument, to prove God's existence? Read Anselm's work, listed below, for a statement of the argument, and the article by Norman Malcolm, "Anselm's Ontological Arguments," in the *Philosophical Review,* January, 1960; then decide whether Aquinas' reasons for rejecting the argument are sufficient.
4. How do you respond to the attempt to prove God's existence by logical argument? Is this a belief one should try to prove or one to be taken on faith?

READINGS FOR IMMEDIATE REFERENCE

Aquinas, Thomas. *Summa Theologica.* New York: Benziger Brothers, 1920. Part I, QQ. 1-26.

Anselm of Canterbury. *Proslogium.* LaSalle, Illinois: Open Court, 1903. Chapters 1-4 and Appendix.

Hume, David. *Dialogues Concerning Natural Religion.* New York: Hafner Publishing Co., 1954. Chapters 2, 5-9.

Pascal, Blaise. *Pensées.* New York: Dutton and Co., 1912. Sections 233-241.

REFERENCES FOR COMPREHENSIVE KNOWLEDGE

Aquinas, Thomas. *Summa Contra Gentiles,* translated by English Dominican Fathers. New York: Benziger Brothers, 1927-29.

Joyce, G. H. *Principles of Natural Theology,* 3rd ed. New York: Longmans, Green, 1951. A clear and comprehensive statement of Thomistic thought.

Pegis, Anton C. *The Wisdom of Catholicism.* New York: Random House, 1949. A collection of essays by both past and present authors.

Also see:

Copleston, F. C. *Aquinas.* London: Pelican Books, 1955.

D'Arcy, Martin. *Thomas Aquinas.* London: Clonmore, 1930.

Gilson, Etienne. *The Philosophy of St. Thomas Aquinas.* London: Heffer, 1924.

———. *God and Philosophy.* New York: Oxford University Press, 1941.

Jay, Eric. *The Existence of God, A Commentary on St. Thomas Aquinas' Five Ways.* New York: Allenson, 1946.

Maritain, Jacques. *An Essay in Christian Philosophy.* New York: Philosophical Library, 1955.

Martindale, G. C. *The Faith of the Roman Church.* London: Methuen, 1927.

III. REINHOLD NIEBUHR

Now we turn to the protestant tradition and specifically to one of the most influential Protestant theologians in the twentieth century: Reinhold Niebuhr. Born in Missouri in 1892, two years earlier than his equally famous brother, Richard, Niebuhr received his education at Elmhurst College and Yale Divinity School, and from 1913 to 1928 served as minister to the Bethel Evangelical Church in Detroit. During this time, Henry Ford, universally praised for both his generosity and efficiency, instituted the five-dollar day and the assembly line. But Niebuhr saw both acts as a facade for exploitation, as ruthless as they were scientific, and he joined with many of his congregation in helping to foster the labor movement. At the same time he became convinced that the confidence in reason and good will which marked liberal Christian thought was too naive to make Christianity effective. Accordingly, while he moved politically to the left, he also moved theologically to the right, returning to the same theological position which characterized original Protestantism. In 1928, he joined the faculty at Union Theological Seminary, where he continued to teach until his retirement in 1958. He has published many books, edited the periodical, *Christianity and Crisis,* and has exerted a profound influence on Protestant thought from the printed page, classroom, pulpit, and lecture platform.

This selection is taken from his 1939 Gifford Lectures, *The Nature and Destiny of Man,* in which he discusses the two ways by which man can know of God: the general propositions of personal-individual revelation and the specific social-historical revelations given in the Bible. He contends that neither Catholicism nor liberal Protestantism has understood the essence of Christian thought adequately, and that only such a knowledge of God, obtained in these ways, can enable man to make an accurate estimate of his own nature and destiny.

Personal and Historical Revelations[1]

The revelation of God to man is always a twofold one, a personal-individual revelation, and a revelation in the context of social-historical experience. Without the public and historical revelation the private experience of God would remain poorly defined and subject to caprice. Without the private revelation of God, the public and historical revelation would not gain credence. Because all men have, in some fashion, the experience of a reality beyond themselves, they are able to entertain the more precise revelations of the character and purpose of God as they come to them in the most significant experiences of prophetic history. . . . Private revelation is the testimony in the consciousness of every person that his life touches a reality beyond himself, a reality deeper and higher than the system of nature in which he stands.

St. Paul speaks of this experience of God when he declares that even without a further revelation men are "without excuse" if they do not glorify God as God but become vain in their imagination and make themselves God (Romans 1:20). The experience of God is not so much a separate experience, as an overtone implied in all experience. The soul which reaches the outermost rims of its own consciousness, must also come in contact with God, for He impinges upon that consciousness.

Schleiermacher describes this experience of God as the experience of "unqualified dependence." This is one of its aspects but not its totality. It is one of its aspects because there is, in all human consciousness, at least a dim recognition of the insufficient and dependent character of all finite life, a recognition which implies the consciousness of the reality upon which dependent existence depends. An equally important characteristic of the experience of God is the sense of being seen, commanded, judged and known from beyond ourselves. This experience is described by the Psalmist in the words: "O Lord, thou hast searched me, and known me. Thou knowest my downsitting and mine uprising, . . . and art acquainted with all my ways." (Ps. 139). . . . If any one should maintain that this sense of the impingement of God upon human life is a delusion by which man glorifies himself, one might call attention to the fact that in the book of Job exactly the same experience is described by one who is not grateful for it but protests against it. The constant demands and judgments of God seem to him to place life under an intolerable strain: "What is man, that thou shouldest magnify him? and that thou shouldest set thine heart upon him? and that thou shouldest visit him every morning, and try him every moment?" He feels that the divine demands

[1] The selection from Chapter 5, of *The Nature and Destiny of Man,* Volume I, by Reinhold Niebuhr (Copyright 1941 Charles Scribner's Sons) is reprinted with the permission of Charles Scribner's Sons.

are too exacting for human weakness: "let me alone; for my days are vanity," and he looks forward to the day when death will make the visitations of God impossible: "for now shall I sleep in the dust; and thou shalt seek me in the morning, but I shall not be" (Job 7:16-21). This impious protest against the ever-present accusing God is perhaps a more perfect validation of the reality of the experience than any pious words of gratitude for it.

The experience so described is in some sense identical or associated with what is usually called "conscience." The actual nature of conscience is, of course, variously defined in various philosophies. It may be regarded as the social obligations and judgments which all men must face, or it may be defined as the obligation and judgment under which the rational or intelligible self places the empirical, the sensible or the partial self. The significance of the Biblical interpretation of conscience lies precisely in this, that a universal human experience, the sense of being commanded, placed under obligation and judged is interpreted as a relation between God and man in which it is God who makes demands and judgments upon man. Such an interpretation of a common experience is not possible without the presuppositions of the Biblical faith. . . . But once accepted the assumption proves to be the only basis of a correct analysis of all the factors involved in the experience; for it is a fact that man is judged and yet there is no vantage point in his own life, sufficiently transcendent, from which the judgment can take place. . . .

Our approach to other human personalities offers an illuminating analogy of the necessity and character of "revelation" in our relation to God. We have various evidence that, when dealing with persons, we are confronting a reality of greater depth than the mere organism of animal life. We have evidence that we are dealing with a "Thou" of such freedom and uniqueness that a mere external observation of its behavior will not only leave the final essence of that person obscure but will actually falsify it. This person, this other "Thou," cannot be understood until he speaks to us; until his behavior is clarified by the "word" which comes out of the ultimate and transcendent unity of his spirit. Only such a word can give us the key by which we understand the complexities of his behavior.

In the same way, the God whom we meet as "The Other" at the final limit of our own consciousness, is not fully known to us except as specific revelations of His character augment this general experience of being confronted beyond ourselves.

In Biblical faith these specific revelations are apprehended in the context of a particular history of salvation in which specific historical events become special revelations of the character of God and of His purposes. Without the principle of interpretation furnished by this "special revelation" the general experience or the personal revelation involved in conscience becomes falsified, because it is explained merely as man facing the court of social approval or disapproval or as facing his own "best self." In that case, whatever the provisional verdict, the final verdict always is, "I know nothing against myself," and the conclusion drawn from this verdict must be and is, "I am thereby justified."

The fact that a culture which identifies God with some level of human consciousness, either rational or superrational, or with some order of nature, invariably falsifies the human situation and fails to appreciate either the total stature of freedom in man or the complexity of the problem of evil in him, is the most telling negative proof for the Biblical faith. Man does not know himself truly except as he knows himself confronted by God. Only in that confrontation does he become aware of his full stature and freedom, and of the evil in him. . . .

The general revelation of personal human experience, the sense of being confronted with a "wholly other" at the edge of human consciousness, contains three elements, two of which are not too sharply defined, while the third is not defined at all. The first is the sense of reverence for a majesty and of dependence upon an ultimate source of being. The second is the sense of moral obligation laid upon one from beyond oneself and of moral unworthiness before a judge. The third, most problematic of the elements in religious experience, is the longing for forgiveness. All three of these elements become more sharply defined as they gain the support of other forms of revelation. The first, the sense of dependence upon a reality greater and more ultimate than ourselves, gains the support of another form of "general" revelation, the content of which is expressed in the concept of the Creator and the creation. Faith concludes that the same "Thou" who confronts us in our personal experience is also the source and Creator of the whole world. The second element in personal religion, the experience of judgment, gains support from the prophetic-Biblical concept of judgment in history. The whole of history is seen as validation of the truth in the personal experience that God stands over against us as our judge. The third element, the longing for reconciliation after this judgment (and it must be regarded provisionally as a longing rather than an assurance), becomes the great issue of the Old Testament interpretation of life. The question is: is God merciful as well as just? And if He is merciful, how is His mercy related to His justice? This is the question which hovers over the whole of Biblical religion. Because Christian faith believes the final answer to this ultimate question to be given in Christ, it regards the revelation in Christ a final revelation, beyond which there can be no further essential revelation. For this reason it speaks of Christ as "the express image of his person." Here the whole depth and mystery of the divine are finally revealed.

In these three types of revelation God becomes specifically defined as (1) Creator, (2) Judge and (3) Redeemer. It is significant that each term represents a definition of divine transcendence in increasingly specific and sharply delineated terms; and yet in each the relation of God to the world is preserved. They must be studied in order.

To speak of God as Creator of the world, is to regard the world in its totality as a revelation of His majesty and self-sufficient power. . . . The fact that the world is not self-derived, self-explanatory and self-sufficing but points beyond itself, is used as evidence for the doctrine of Creation and to point to the glory of the Creator. In a sense, St. Paul makes use of the cosmological argument, but not in such a way as to be subject to the Kantian criticism. It is not assumed that the reality of God can be proved by the fact that the contingent and dependent character of all finite being implies that the whole of the sensible world "rests upon some intelligible being that is free from all empirical conditions and itself contains the ground of the possibility of all appearances." Rather, the creation is contemplated as pointing to a Creator, already known in man's moral experience. . . .

This doctrine is expressed in a "mythical" or supra-rational idea. Genetically, the idea of creation is related to primitive concepts in which God is pictured as fashioning the world as the potter moulds his clay. . . . The Bible retains this "primitive" concept because it preserves and protects the idea of the freedom of God and His transcendence. These are lost or imperilled by the more rational concept of "first cause" (which takes the place of God in naturalistic philosophies), and of the concept of a form—giving *nous,* which creates by forming the previously formless stuff or matter (which is the basic conception of divinity in idealistic philosophies).

The doctrine of creation preserves the transcendence and freedom of God without implying that the created world is evil because it is not God. On the contrary, Biblical religion consistently maintains the goodness of creation precisely on the ground that it is created by God. Moreover, this doctrine of creation escapes the error of the naturalists who, by regarding causality as the principle of meaning, can find no place for human freedom and are forced to reduce man to the level of nature. It also escapes the error of the rationalists who make *nous* into the ultimate principle of meaning, and are thereby tempted to divide man into an essentially good reason, which participates in or is identified with the divine, and an essentially evil physical life.

To reject the principle of natural causation as the final principle of interpreting the unity of the world is not to interpret the world merely from the standpoint of man's internal problem or to read psychic attributes of man into nature. The fact is, that the relation of things to each other in the chain of natural causation is not an adequate explanation of their specific givenness, for this irrational givenness must be regarded either as merely chance or caprice, or the order of the world must be related to a more ultimate realm of freedom. . . . [Thus,] the Biblical doctrine of creation derives both the formless stuff and the forming principle from a more ultimate divine source.

* * * * *

In the history of revelation, the counterpart of the sense of moral obligation experienced by every man is the covenant relation between God and His people. In this covenant we have the basic Biblical idea of the character of human history. It is not regarded as evil by reason of being involved in finiteness. Its ideal possibility is that a particular nation, Israel, should serve not its own purpose but the will of God, according to the covenant between God and His people. But the prophetic consciousness discerns that this ideal possibility is not fulfilled. Israel fails to fulfill its special mission not by reason of any inertia of nature, or any finiteness of mind, or any inability to comprehend the divine mission. On the contrary, the basis of the sin of Israel, according to the prophets, lies in the temptation of the nation to identify itself too completely with the divine will of which it is only an historical instrument. Israel makes this mistake particularly; but the prophets discern the same mistake in each of the great empires who become executors of divine judgment upon Israel.

The real evil in the human situation, according to the prophetic interpretation, lies in man's unwillingness to recognize and acknowledge the weakness, finiteness and dependence of his position, in his inclination to grasp after a power and security which transcend the possibilities of human existence, and in his effort to pretend a virtue and knowledge which are beyond the limits of mere creatures. The whole burden of the prophetic message is that there is only one God ("I am the first, and I am the last; and beside me there is no God." Is. 44:6) and that the sin of man consists in the vanity and pride by which he imagines himself, his nations, his cultures, his civilizations to be divine. Sin is thus the unwillingness of man to acknowledge his creatureliness and dependence upon God and his effort to make his own life independent and secure. . . .

The catastrophes of history by which God punishes this pride, it must be observed, are the natural and inevitable consequences of men's effort to transcend their mortal and insecure existence and to establish a security to which man has no right. One aspect of this human pride is man's refusal to acknowledge the dependent character of his life. Thus Egypt exists by the beneficences of nature in terms of the Nile's rhythmic seasons, but, according to Ezekiel, she imagines herself the author of this source of her wealth: "Behold, I am against thee, Pharaoh, king of Egypt, the great dragon that lieth in the midst of his rivers, which hath said, My river is mine own, and I have made it for myself" (Ezek. 29:3). One might write pages on the relevance of this prophetic judgment upon the self-sufficiency of modern man whose technical achievements obscure his dependence upon vast natural processes beyond his control and accentuate the perennial pride of man in his own power and security. . . .

Jesus' parable of the rich fool stands squarely in this whole Biblical interpretation of sin. The rich fool imagines himself secure for many years by reason of his filled granaries. He declares: "Soul, thou has much goods laid up for many years; take thine ease, eat, drink and be merry." But God said unto him, "Thou fool, this night thy soul shall be required of thee: then whose shall those things be, which thou hast provided?" (Luke 12:19-20). . . .

The serious view which the Bible takes of this sin of man's rebellion against God naturally leads to an interpretation of history in which judgment upon sin becomes the first category of interpretation. The most obvious meaning of history is that every nation, culture and civilization brings destruction upon itself by exceeding the bounds of creatureliness which God has set upon all human enterprises. All nations fall prey to the same temptation of pride and all finally face the same doom. . . .

But this interpretation leaves an important and ultimate problem unsolved. The further question is whether there is a resource in the heart of the Divine which can overcome the tragic character of history and which can cure as well as punish the sinful pride in which man inevitably involves himself. . . .

From the standpoint of Christian faith the life and death of Christ become the revelation of God's character with particular reference to the unsolved problem of the relation of His judgment to His mercy, of His wrath to His forgiveness. Christian faith sees in the Cross of Christ the assurance that judgment is not the final word of God to man; but it does not regard the mercy of God as a forgiveness which wipes out the distinctions of good and evil in history and make judgment meaningless. All the difficult Christian theological dogmas of Atonement and justification are efforts to explicate the ultimate mystery of divine wrath and mercy in its relation to man. The good news of the gospel is that God takes the sinfulness of man into Himself; and overcomes in His own heart what cannot be overcome in human life, since human life remains within the vicious circle of sinful self-glorification on every level of moral advance.

This is rightly regarded as the final revelation of the personality of God. Christian faith regards the revelation in Christ as final because this ultimate problem is solved by the assurance that God takes man's sin upon Himself and into Himself and that without this divine initiative and this divine sacrifice there could be no reconciliation and no easing of man's uneasy conscience. This revelation is final not only as a category of interpreting the total meaning of history but also as a solution for the problem of the uneasy conscience in each individual. . . .

The difficult conception of the "suffering servant" as the Messiah and messenger of God, suffering for the sins of the guilty though himself guiltless, and revealing thereby not simply the beauty of vicarious suffering in history but the very character of the divine, is thus rightly regarded by Christian faith as the ultimate revelation of God. . . .

[However,] it could not be claimed that this interpretation of the Christian revelation is consistently held in Christianity itself. There have always been interpretations of the revelation of Christ . . . regarded as under the influence of Platonism and Hellenism. For them, the problem of human existence is not primarily the problem of sin but the problem of finiteness. Their concern is to prove that God can speak to man and make Himself known, a proposition which Hebraic-Biblical faith has never doubted, since it rests upon the very presupposition of such a relationship between God and man. This type of Christianity does not give a Greek or Platonic answer to the problem of time and eternity but it is Greek in regarding this problem as primary. . . .

The modern liberal Protestant interpretation of Christianity is usually removed one further step from the Biblical faith. In this modern interpretation, even the time-eternity issue, which dominates Catholic thought, is not taken seriously; and the problem of sin is not understood at all. This version of Christian faith is obviously informed by, and is an accommodation to, the general presuppositions of modern culture. The optimism of this culture makes the central message of the gospel, dealing with sin, grace, forgiveness and justification, seem totally irrelevant. The naturalism of the culture also reduces the time and eternity problem to meaninglessness.

In consequence, the Christology of this type of Christianity is primarily interested in rejecting the rationally absurd orthodox doctrine of the two natures of Christ. Modern liberal Christianity does not understand that this rationally absurd doctrine contains the basic affirmation of the Christian faith. . . . Since the orthodox doctrine is rejected, the Christ of orthodox faith is transmuted into the "historic Jesus" who "incarnates values worthy of our highest devotion." . . .

Sometimes modern liberal versions of Christianity become uneasy about the special significance assigned to Jesus. They realize that they are perpetuating an estimate of his significance which is not compatible with their philosophical and theological presuppositions and which is no more than an attenuated form of the orthodox faith. In that case the effort is made to maintain some contact with the traditional faith by affirming simply that Jesus was a very, very, very good man, but that, of course, a better man might appear, at a future date. These moderns do not understand that they cannot transcend the relativities of history by the number of superlatives which they add to their moral estimate of Jesus and that they have not faced the problem of the nature of the criterion by which they judge Jesus to be good. They do not see that all historical judgments are based upon an explicit or implicit assumption about the character of history itself; and that there can be no judgment about the character of history which does not rest upon a further assumption about the relation of history to eternity. . . .

Thus, the essence of Biblical religion is not primarily the problem of how finite man can know God but how sinful man is to be reconciled to God, and how history is to overcome the tragic consequences of its "false eternals," its proud and premature efforts to escape finiteness.

QUESTIONS FOR DISCUSSION

1. What factors in both personal and social revelation provide the evidence for concluding that God is a Creator, Judge, and Saviour? In either case could Niebuhr's evidence be used to conclude that God has different characteristics?
2. Why does Niebuhr say "the problem of human existence is the problem of sin"? Do you agree?
3. In what ways does Niebuhr believe his views to be superior to Catholicism and liberal Protestantism?
4. Do you believe Niebuhr's method for gaining knowledge of God is superior to Aquinas'?

READINGS FOR IMMEDIATE REFERENCE

Niebuhr, Reinhold. *The Children of Light and the Children of Darkness.* New York: Scribners, 1945, Chapter 1.

———. *Moral Man and Immoral Society.* New York: Scribners, 1932, Chapters 3, 9, 10.

———. *The Nature and Destiny of Man.* New York: Scribners, 1941, Vol. I, Chapters 5-7; Vol. II, Chapters 1-4.

Fosdick, Harry Emerson. *As I See Religion.* New York: Harper, 1932, Chapter 1.

REFERENCES FOR COMPREHENSIVE KNOWLEDGE

Niebuhr, Reinhold. *Christian Realism and Political Problems.* New York: Scribners, 1953.

———. *Christianity and Power Politics.* New York: Scribners, 1940.

———. *Faith and History.* New York: Scribners, 1949.

———. *Pious and Secular America.* New York: Scribners, 1958.

———. *The Structure of Nations and Empires.* New York: Scribners, 1960.

Kegley, C. W. and Bretall, R. W. *Reinhold Niebuhr: His Religious, Social and Political Thought.* New York: Macmillan, 1956. The best of a small but growing number of comprehensive analyses.

Also see:

Barth, Karl. *The Doctrine of the Word of God.* London: T. and T. Clark, 1936.

Brunner, Emil. *Revelation and Reason.* Philadelphia: Westminster Press, 1946.

Davies, D. L. *Reinhold Niebuhr, Prophet from America.* New York: MacWhelan, 1948.

Harland, Gordon. *The Thought of Reinhold Niebuhr.* New York: Oxford University Press, 1960.

Niebuhr, H. Richard. *The Meaning of Revelation.* New York: Macmillan, 1942.

Tillich, Paul. *The Courage to Be.* New Haven: Yale University Press, 1952.

———. *Dynamics of Faith.* New York: Harper, 1956.

IV. JAN VAN RUYSBROEK

Little is known about the life of Jan van Ruysbroek beyond certain dates and events. In 1293, he was born near Brabant in the Low Countries; in 1317, he was ordained a priest; in 1351, he entered the Augustinian order, later becoming prior of the convent near Brussels; in 1381, he died. However, he is representative of a religious tradition which transcends ecclesiastical organizations, one which flourished in Christianity from the thirteenth to the sixteenth centuries and always has been an essential part of the eastern religions—mysticism. In common with St. John of the Cross, Meister Eckhart, and Jacob Boehme, van Ruysbroek maintains that neither rational argument nor knowledge of the Bible is sufficient to bring man to a knowledge of God; only the immediate intuitive experience of God's presence can give man that knowledge.

In this selection van Ruysbroek, in commenting on Matthew 25:6, gives some description—and feeling—of the progressive development of the soul towards union with God, together with an account of that mystical experience, insofar as it can be explained. What is your reaction to mysticism? Do you consider it a profound insight or a psychological aberration?

The Mystical Experience[1]

"See, the Bridegroom comes: go out and meet Him." St. Matthew the Evangelist writes these words for us, and Christ spoke them to His disciples, and to all men, as we may read in the parable of the virgins. This Bridegroom is Christ, and man's nature is the bride, whom God has made in the image and likeness of Himself. And in the beginning he had set her in the highest place, and in the fairest and richest and most splendid of dwellings, that was in paradise. And to her He had subjected all creatures, and He had adorned her with graces, and to her He had given a commandment: and had she showed obedience, she would have deserved to live steadfast and secure in everlasting

[1] From *The Spiritual Espousals*, by Jan van Ruysbroek, translated by Eric Colledge. New York: Harper and Brothers, 1953, pp. 43-4, 179-190. Reprinted by permission. Canadian permission by Faber and Faber.

wedlock with her Bridegroom and never to fall into any distress or sin.

Then there came a knave, the fiend from hell, cunningly in the guise of a serpent, and he was envious of this and he deceived the woman, and the two of them deceived the man, in whom humanity first existed. And by false counsel he seduced her, Nature, the bride of God. And she was driven out into a strange land, poor and wretched, and was made prisoner and oppressed and enslaved by her foes, as if she should never return to her native land or have pardon.

But when God thought it time, and when He had pity on this anguish of His subjects, then He sent His only-begotten Son on earth, into a splendid court and into a glorious temple, which was the body of the glorious maiden Mary. There He espoused this bride, our nature, and united her with His Person by the noble virgin's most pure blood. The priest who blessed the bride, that was the Holy Ghost. The angel Gabriel brought the command. The glorious maiden gave the consent.

Thus has Christ, our plighted Bridegroom, united our nature with Him, and has visited us in a strange land, and has taught us with heavenly laws and with the uttermost faith. And He has labored and striven as a champion against our foes, and He has broken open the prison and has won the battle, and by His death has dealt death to our death, and has ransomed us with His blood and has set us free with the waters of His baptism, and has enriched us with His sacraments and His gifts, so that we may go out clad in all virtues, as He says and meet Him in the court of glories, and enjoy Him without end and evermore.

Now Christ, the master teaching truth, says: "See the Bridegroom comes, go out and meet Him." In these words, Christ our true love teaches us four things. First, He gives us a command in that He says "See." Those who shut their eyes and neglect this command, they are all condemned. In the next words He shows us what we shall see, that is the coming of the Bridegroom. Then thirdly He teaches us and commands what we should do, in that He says "Go out." Fourthly, when He says "To meet Him," He makes plain to us the profit and use of all our labor and all our life, that is, a loving meeting with the Bridegroom.

Let us expound and make plain these words as they concern the supernatural life of the contemplation of God, which a few men can achieve in this manner or can savor, by way of their exalted and excellent form of living.

* * * * *

THE LIFE OF CONTEMPLATION OF GOD

This contemplation establishes us in a purity which is above all our understanding, for it is a peculiar adornment and a heavenly crown and in addition an everlasting reward for all virtue and all life. And no one can attain to this through knowledge or skill, nor with any exercise, but only he whom God will unite with Him in spirit, and will illumine with Himself, is able to contemplate God, and no one else.

The secret nature of the Divinity

is everlastingly active in contemplation and love, and is everlastingly in delectation in the uniting of the Persons in the unity of Their essence. In this uniting in the essential unity of God all inward spirits are one with God in a loving flowing-out, and they are one in themselves, that same oneness that the Divine essence itself is, as they have the manner of blessedness. And in this high unity of the Divine natures, the heavenly Father is a source and a beginning of all the works that are worked in heaven and in earth. And He says in the hidden depths of our spirit: "See the Bridegroom comes, go out to meet Him." . . .

But there are few who can attain to this Divine contemplation, because of men's own ineptitude and inability, and because the light by which men contemplate is a hidden light. And therefore no one shall utterly understand the depths of what we now expound by means of any instruction or of any narrow observation of his own. For all words and everything which a man of his natural powers is able to learn and understand, all this is far beneath the truth which I mean, and foreign to it. But the man who is united with God and illumined by this truth, he is able, through the truth, to understand it. And therefore I desire that every man who does not in the delectable unity of his spirit understand or feel this, that he remain unperturbed and leave matters as they are. For what I wish to say is true, and Christ the everlasting Truth has Himself said it in His teaching in many places. And therefore he who shall understand this must have died to himself and live to God, and he must turn his face to the eternal light in the depths of his spirit, where the secret truth reveals itself without mean.

I. "See."

The conditions for seeing.

For the heavenly Father wishes that we should see, because He is a Father of light. And therefore He speaks eternally, without men and without ceasing, in the secret places of our spirit, one single unfathomable word and nothing more. And in this word He enunciates Himself and all things. And this word is nothing else than "See"; and this is going-out and the birth of the Son of everlasting light, in Whom men recognize and see all blessedness.

A. The Necessary Ability

If the spirit is now with God to contemplate God without means in this Divine light, there are three things which are necessary to man. The first is that he must be well ordered in all virtues from without, and that within he must be unhindered, and that he be empty from all outward works, just as though he performed nothing. For if within he is preoccupied with any work of virtue, so he is distracted by images. As long as this lasts in him, he is unable to contemplate. Secondly, he must within depend on God with compelling intention and love, just as a kindled and glowing fire that never again can be put out. And when he feels himself to be thus, then he is able to contemplate. Thirdly, he must have lost himself in a lack of manner, and in a darkness in which all contemplative men fare in delectation, and can never again find themselves in any way natural to the creature.

B. The Illumining Word

In the depths of this darkness, in which the loving spirit has died to itself, begins the revelation of God and the eternal life. For in this darkness there shines and there is born an incomprehensible light, which is the Son of God, in Whom we contemplate eternal life. And in this light we see. And this Divine light is given in the simple being of the spirit, where the spirit receives the clarity which is God Himself. . . . And the spirit becomes immediately the very clarity which it receives.

Behold how this secret clarity in which man contemplates all that he has desired, in the manner of the emptiness of the spirit, this clarity is so great that the loving contemplative sees and feels in his depths where he rests nothing except an incomprehensible light. And according to the manner of this single nakedness which embraces all things, he finds himself and feels himself to be that very light by which he sees, and nothing else.

And in this you have the first point of how one sees in the Divine light. Blessed are the eyes that see thus, for they possess the eternal life.

II. "The Bridegroom comes."

The illumination, and its effect.

After we have thus come to see, we may joyfully contemplate the eternal coming of our Bridegroom, and this is the second matter, of which we will now speak.

When is then this coming of our Bridegroom which is eternal? That is the new birth and a new illumination without cease. For the depths from which the clarity shines forth, and which are the clarity itself, are living and fruitful. And therefore the revelation of the eternal light is ceaselessly renewed in the hidden places of the spirit. Behold, all works of the creature and all exercises of virtue may here pass away, for here God alone is His only work in the highest excellence of the spirit. And here there is nothing else than an eternal contemplation and beholding of the light, with the light and in the light. And the coming of the Bridegroom is so swift that He is always come and is always dwelling within us with all His riches; and ceaselessly and ever and again He is coming in His own Person with new clarity, just as if He never were come before. For to be come consists in an eternal now, without time which is constantly received in new joy and new delight.

Behold how the gladness and the joy which this Bridegroom brings in His coming are unfathomable and immeasurable, for so is He Himself. And therefore the eyes of the spirit, with which it contemplates and gazes upon its Bridegroom, are opened so wide that they never may be closed again. For this beholding and contemplating of the spirit remains eternally in the secret revelation of God, and the understanding of the spirit is opened so wide against the coming of the Bridegroom that the spirit itself becomes the wideness which it comprehends.

And so with God is God comprehended and seen, wherein lies all our blessedness. . . .

III. "Go Out": our life with God, remaining in Him and flowing out from Him, when we have attained to Him, our first image.

Now the Spirit of God says within the secret out-flowing of our spirit: "Go out in an eternal contemplation and delectation, according to the manner of God."

A. The Reasons making possible this co-existence

a. That which God by His Nature possesses is possessed by us through love. All the riches which are natural in God we possess through love in God, and God possesses them in us, through the immeasurable love which is the Holy Ghost. For in this love men savor everything for which they can yearn. And therefore through this love we die to ourselves and go forth in a loving flowing-out, in darkness, and lacking all manner. There the spirit is embraced in the Holy Trinity, eternally remaining in the superessential unity in rest and in delectation. And in this same unity, according to the manner of fruitfulness, the Father is in the Son and the Son in the Father, and all creatures are in Them both. And this is above any differentiation of Persons, for here, so far as reason is concerned, we understand the nature of Fatherhood and Sonhood in a living fruitfulness of the Divine natures.

b. Our flowing-out in God, our first image, is cause of our being. Out of this there springs and begins an everlasting going out and an everlasting work without beginning. For since the Almighty Father in the depths of His fruitfulness has perfectly comprehended Himself, the Son is the everlasting Word of the Father, proceeding forth as a Second Person in the Divinity. And through the everlasting birth, all creatures proceed forth everlastingly, before ever they have been created in time, So they have seen and acknowledged God in themselves, discreetly according to the *ratio vivens,* and with that difference which is His, not, however, a difference in every respect, for everything which is in God is God.

This everlasting going-out and this eternal life which we evermore have in God, and which we are without ourselves, this is a cause of our being created in time. . . . This everlasting being and life which we have and are in the eternal wisdom of God, that is like to God. For it remains eternally without differentiation in the Divine Being, and it flows out eternally, through the birth of the Son, with difference and with differentiation according to the *ratio vivens.* And through these two points our being and life are so like to God that they ceaselessly acknowledge and imagine Him in this likeness as He is in Being and in Person. For even though, as the reason is concerned, all is here discretion and difference, this likeness is still one with that same image of the Holy Trinity which is the wisdom of God, in which God contemplates Himself and all things in an eternal instant before which nothing came, after which nothing goes. With a single glance He contemplates Himself and all things; and this is the image and likeness of God, and our image and likeness, for in this God makes the image of Himself and of all things. In this image like to God, all creatures have an everlasting life, outside themselves, as it were in their everlasting examplar. And the Holy Trinity made us in this everlasting image and in this likeness.

B. How we attain to God, our First Image, and how in Contemplation and Delectation with Him we remain in Him and Flow out from Him.

And therefore God would have us go forth from ourselves in this Divine light, and supernaturally attain to this image, which is our own life, and possess it with Him, operatively and in delectation, in everlasting blessedness. . . .

And therefore men who are inward and contemplative must go out, according to the manner of contemplation, beyond reason and beyond discretion; and beyond their created nature, with an everlasting beholding in this inborn light, and so they shall become transformed, and one with this same light by which they see, and which they are. And so contemplative men attain to that everlasting image in which they are made, and they contemplate God and all things without any discretion in a single act of beholding in Divine clarity. And this is the most excellent and most profitable contemplation to which a man can attain in this life. For in this contemplation best of all does man remain free and master of himself, and he can increase in every meritorious form of living, each time that with love he turns inward, beyond all that men can understand. For he remains free and master of himself in inwardness and in virtue. And that beholding virtue and above all merit, for it is the crown and the prize for which we strive, and which in this manner we now have and possess, for the life of contemplation is the light of heaven. . . .

This going-out of the contemplative man is also loving. For through delectable love he passes beyond his created nature, and finds and savors the riches and the joy which are God Himself, and which cause the secret places of the spirit to be immediately transfused, when now he stands made like to the high excellence of God.

IV. "To Meet Him": the loving ascent, through the Holy Ghost, to the delectation of the Godhead

When the inward contemplative man has thus attained his everlasting image, and in this purity, by means of the Son, possesses the bosom of the Father, he is illumined with Divine Truth. And each hour he receives afresh the everlasting birth, and he goes out, according to the manner of the light in a Divine contemplation. And from this there springs the fourth point and the last, which is a loving meeting, in which above all else our highest blessedness consists.

You shall know that the heavenly Father, as He is a living depth, has gone operatively with all that lives in Him into His Son, as into the everlasting wisdom which is He; and this same wisdom, and all that lives in it, is operatively returned again into the Father, that is into the same depths, whence it proceeds. And from this meeting springs the third Person, between the Father and the Son, that is the Holy Ghost, the love of Them both, Who is one with both of Them in the same nature. And the Holy Ghost embraces and transfuses, operatively and in delectation, the Father and the Son and all that lives in Them, with so great riches and joy that concerning this all creatures must evermore be silent. For the incomprehensible miracle that lies in this love everlastingly exceeds the comprehension of all creatures. But in the spirit, above himself and one with the Spirit of God, man understands and savors this wonder without wonderment, and tastes and sees without measure as God does, the riches which are God, in the unity of the living depths where man possesses Him according to the manner of His uncreated being.

Then this most blessed meeting in us according to God's manner is ceaselessly renewed operatively. . . . Just as the Father ceaselessly contemplates all things anew in the birth of His Son, so all things are loved anew by the Father and by the Son in the flowing-out of the Holy Ghost. . . .

Now this operative meeting and this loving embrace are in their depths delectable and without manner. For God's impenetrable lack of manner is so dark and so without manner that in itself it comprehends all the Divine manners, and the work and the attributes of the Persons in the rich embrace of Their essential unity; and in the abyss of God's namelessness it makes a Divine delectation. And in this there is a delectable passing over and a flowing-away and a sinking-down into the essential nakedness, with all the Divine names and all manners and all living reason which has its image in the mirror of Divine truth: all these fall away into this simple nakedness, wanting manner and without reason. For in this unfathomable joy of simplicity, all things are embraced in a delectable blessedness, and the depths themselves remain uncomprehended, except it be in our essential unity with God. Before this all created personality must fail, and all that lives in God, for here there is nothing but an eternal resting in a delectable embrace of the flowing-out of love.

And this is in the being without manner which all inward spirits have chosen above all things. This is the dark silence in which all lovers are lost. But could we thus, as I have told, so prepare ourselves in virtues, we should then hasten to divest ourselves of this our mortal flesh, and we should launch ourselves on the waves of this blessedness, and no creature could ever call us back again.

That we in delectation may possess this essential unity, and that we may clearly contemplate Unity in Trinity, grant to us that Love which denies no prayer addressed to its Divinity.

Amen. Amen. Amen.

QUESTIONS FOR DISCUSSION

1. Is it possible to discuss the mystical experience philosophically, examining reasons and conclusions? Does van Ruysbroek? If so, are his reasons good ones? If not, why should one accept his account of the experience?
2. Is mysticism the essential element in all religious thought?
3. In your opinion, which of the ways we have discussed is the best way to know of God?

READINGS FOR IMMEDIATE REFERENCE

Dewey, John. *A Common Faith.* New Haven: Yale University Press, 1934, Chapter 2.

Eckhart, Meister. *Talks of Instruction,* Sections 1-8, 15-23.

Maugham, W. Somerset. *The Razor's Edge.* New York: Doubleday, Doran, 1944. (fiction)

St. John of the Cross. *The Dark Night of the Soul,* Book II, Chapters 11, 17.

REFERENCES FOR COMPREHENSIVE KNOWLEDGE

James, William. *The Varieties of Religious Experience.* New York: Longmans, Green, 1902. A thorough analysis with many examples by one of America's leading philosophers and psychologists.

Underhill, Evelyn. *Mysticism.* New York: E. P. Dutton, 1911. Still a standard work of explanation and defense.

Also see:

Inge, W. R. *Christian Mysticism.* New York: Noonday Press, 1956.

Jones, Rufus M. *The Inner Life.* New York: Macmillan, 1916.

———. *New Studies in Mystical Religion.* New York: Macmillan, 1927.

Stace, W. T. *Mysticism and Philosophy.* Philadelphia: Lippincott, 1960.

V. BHAGAVAD-GITA

Hinduism has many scriptures. The earliest, the Vedas, were composed from 1000 to 2000 B.C. and are largely hymns of praise for the various gods, eleven on each of three levels of reality. The Upanishads were started about the eighth century B.C. and are philosophical speculations about man and the cosmos. The epic period, from the fourth century B.C. to the fourth century A.D., saw the production of the Ramayana and the Mahabharata, which are stories about the lives of the people, together with a miscellany of history, mythology, politics, law, philosophy, and theology. Finally, the Vedantas were composed about the ninth century and represent a return to the speculative interest of the Upanishads. The Bhagavad-Gita originally was a section of Book Six of the Mahabharata, but because of its great subsequent influence it is accorded a separate position today. The author is unknown, as is the date of composition, but of universal concern are its problems: should one kill his fellow man in war; and the more general question, what is good? It is small wonder that many people have agreed with Mahatma Gandhi's estimate: "To me, the Gita represents all that is highest in the religious life of man."

The Gita first tells man the end which he should seek to achieve in life, then discusses the various means he can use to achieve this end. What is the end, and how many different methods are discussed? Which is the best?

Many Ways to Know God[1]

ARJUNA said:

O Krishna, seeing these my kinsmen, gather here desirous to fight, my limbs fail me, my mouth is parched; my body shivers, my hair stands on end, my Gandiva (bow) slips from by hand, my skin is burning. O Keshava (Krishna, the slayer of Keshi), I am not able to stand upright, my mind is in a whirl and I see adverse omens. O Krishna, neither do I see any good in slaying my own people in this strife. I desire neither

[1] From the *Bhagavad-Gita,* translated by Swami Paramananda. Boston: The Ramakrishna Vedanta Society, 1903, Chapters 1, 2, 4-6, 9, 12, 18. [The chapter heads and sentence numbers have been omitted. C.M.]

victory, nor kingdom, nor pleasures. Teachers, uncles, sons and grandsons, grandfathers, fathers-in-law, brothers-in-law, besides other kinsmen, for whose sake empire, enjoyment and pleasures are desired, they themselves stand here in battle, forsaking life and wealth. What avail, then, is kingdom, enjoyment, or even life, O Govinda (Krishna)? These warriors I do not wish to kill, even though I am killed by them, not even for the dominion over the three worlds, how much less for the sake of this earth, O slayer of Madhu. . . .

With my nature overpowered by pity and depression and mind confused about duty, I implore Thee (O Krishna) tell me with certainty what is good for me. I am Thy disciple, instruct me, who have taken refuge in Thee. For I see not what can remove this grief which withers my senses, even if I should obtain unrivalled and flourishing dominion over the earth and rulership over the gods.

SANJAYA said:

Gudakesha (Arjuna), the conqueror of his foes, having thus spoken to the Lord of the senses (Krishna), said: "I shall not fight, O Govinda!" and became silent. O descendant of King Bharata, Hrishikesha (Krishna), as if smilingly, spoke these words to him (Arjuna), who was thus grief-stricken in the midst of the two armies.

THE BLESSED LORD said:

Thou hast been mourning for those who should not be mourned for and yet thou speakest (apparent) words of wisdom; but the truly wise mourn not either for the dead or for the living. It is not that I have never existed before, nor thou, nor all these kings. Nor is it that all of us shall cease to exist hereafter. As in this body the embodied soul passes through childhood, youth and old age, in the same manner it goes from one body to another; therefore the wise are never deluded regarding it (the soul). O son of Kunti, the feelings of heat, cold, pleasure, pain, are produced from the contact of the senses with sense-objects; they are with beginning and end, transitory. Therefore, O Bharata, endure them (bravely). O mighty among men, he is fit to attain immortality who is serene and not afflicted by these sensations, but is the same in pleasure and pain. There is no existence for the unreal and the real can never be non-existent. The Seers of Truth know the nature and final ends of both. Know That to be indestructible by which all this is pervaded. No one is ever able to destroy that Immutable. These bodies are perishable; but the dwellers in these bodies are eternal, indestructible and impenetrable. Therefore fight, O descendant of Bharata!

He who considers this (Self) as a slayer or he who thinks that this (Self) is slain, neither of these knows the Truth. For It does not slay, nor is It slain. This (Self) is never born, nor does It die, nor after once having been, does It go into non-being. This (Self) is unborn, eternal, changeless, ancient. It is never destroyed even when the body is destroyed. O son of Pritha, how can he slay or cause the slaying of another who knows this (Self) to be indestructible, eternal, unborn and immutable? As man casts off worn-out garments and puts on others which are new, similarly the embodied soul, casting off worn-out bodies, enters into others which are new. Sword cannot pierce It (Self), fire cannot burn It, water cannot wet It, and air cannot dry It. It cannot be pierced, nor burned, nor wet, nor dried. It is eternal, all-pervading, unchangeable, immovable, everlasting. This (Self) is said to be unmanifested, unthinkable, unchangeable; therefore knowing this to be so, thou shouldst not grieve. But even if thou thinkest that this (Self) is subject to constant birth and death, even then, O mighty-armed, thou shouldst not grieve. For that which is born death is certain, and for the dead birth is certain. Therefore grieve not over that which is unavoidable.

* * * * *

Thus I have declared unto thee the wisdom of Self-realization. Listen now, O son of Pritha, regarding Yoga, by knowing which thou shalt be freed from the bonds of Karma (cause and effect). In this (Yoga) there is neither waste of effort nor possibility of evil results. Even a little practice of this (Yoga) delivers one from great fear. O son of Kuru, in this (Yoga), the well-resolved mind is single and one-pointed; but the purposes of the irresolute mind are many-branched and endless. O son of Pritha, those who delight in the flowery speech of the unwise and are satisfied with the mere letter of the Vedas (Scriptures) saying: "There is naught else"; and those who are full of desires for self-gratification, regarding heaven as their highest goal, and are engaged in many intricate Scriptural rites just to secure pleasure and power as the result of their deeds for their future incarnations; whose discrimination is stolen away by the love of power and pleasure and who are thus deeply attached therein, (for such people) it is impossible to obtain either firm conviction (in purpose) or God-consciousness.

The Vedas deal with the three *Gunas.* O Arjuna, be thou free from these three Gunas; free from the pairs of opposites (cold and heat, pleasure and pain); ever steadfast, be thou free from (thoughts of) acquiring or keeping and self-possessing. To the Brahmana, the knower of Truth, all the Vedas are of as little use as a small water-tank is during the time of a flood, when water is everywhere. To work alone thou hast the right, but never to the fruits thereof. Be thou neither actuated by the fruits of action, nor be thou attached to inaction. O Dhananjaya, abandoning attachment and regarding success and failure alike, be steadfast in Yoga and perform thy duties. Evenmindedness is called Yoga. O Dhananjaya, work (with desire for results) is far inferior to work with understanding. Therefore seek refuge in the Yoga of understanding. Wretched indeed are those who work for results.

ARJUNA said:

O Keshava, what are the signs of the man of steady wisdom, one who has attained God-consciousness? How does the man of steady wisdom speak? How does he sit? How does he walk?

The Blessed Lord said:

O Partha, when a man is satisfied in the Self by Self alone and has completely cast out all desires from the mind, then he is said to be of steady wisdom. He whose mind is not agitated in calamities and who has no longing for pleasure, free from attachment, fear and anger, he indeed is said to be a saint of steady wisdom. He who is free from all attachment and neither rejoices on receiving good nor is vexed on receiving evil, his wisdom is well-established. When he completely withdraws his senses from sense-objects as the tortoise withdraws its limbs, then his wisdom becomes well-established. The embodied, through the practice of abstinence (i.e. not giving food to the senses), can deaden the feelings of the senses, but longing still lingers in the heart; all longings drop off when he has seen the Supreme. O son of Kunti, dangerous are the senses, they even carry away forcibly the mind of a discriminative man who is striving for perfection. The man of steady wisdom, having subdued them all (senses), becomes fixed in Me, the Supreme. His wisdom is well-established whose senses are under control. Thinking of sense-objects, man becomes attached thereto. From attachment arises longing and from longing anger is born. From anger arises delusion; from delusion, loss of memory is caused. From loss of memory, the discriminative faculty is ruined and from the ruin of discrimination, he perishes.

But the self-subjugated attains peace and moves among objects with the senses under control, free from any longing or aversion. In peace there is an end to all misery and the peaceful mind soon becomes well-established in wisdom. There is no wisdom for the unsteady and there is no meditation for the unsteady and for the unmeditative there is no peace. How can there be any happiness for the peaceless? For the mind that yields to the uncontrolled and wandering senses, carries away his wisdom just as a boat on water is carried away by wind. Therefore, O mighty-armed, his wisdom is established whose senses are well-restrained from all objects of sense. That which is night to all beings, therein the self-subjugated remains awake; and in that where all beings are awake, that is night for the knower of Self: As the ocean remains calm and unaltered though the waters flow into it, similarly a self-controlled saint remains unmoved when desires enter into him; such a saint alone attains peace, but not he who craves the objects of desire.

That man attains peace who, abandoning all desires, moves about without attachment and longing, without the sense of "I" and "mine." O son of Pritha, this is the state of dwelling in Brahman (absolute Truth); having attained this, no one is ever deluded. Being established in this knowledge even at the end of life, one attains oneness with Brahman (The Supreme). . . .

O sinless one, in this world twofold is the path already described by me. The path of wisdom is for the meditative and the path of work is for the active. A man does not attain to freedom from action by non-performance of action, nor does he attain to perfection merely by giving up action. No one can ever rest even for an instant without performing action, for all are impelled by the Gunas (qualities), born of Prakriti (Nature), to act incessantly. He who, restraining the organs of action, sits holding thoughts of sense-objects in mind, that self-deluded one is called a hypocrite. But, O Arjuna, he who, controlling the senses by the mind, follows without attachment the path of action with his organs of action, he is esteemed.

* * * * *

Him the sages call wise whose undertakings are devoid of desire for results and of plans, whose actions are burned by the fire of wisdom. Having abandoned attachment for the fruits of action, ever content and dependent on none, though engaged in action, yet he does nothing. Being freed from longing, with self under control, and giving up all sense of possession (ownership), he is not tainted by sin merely by performing bodily action. Content with whatever comes without effort, undisturbed by the pairs of opposites (pleasure and pain, heat and cold), free from envy, even-minded in success and failure, though acting (he) is not bound. One whose attachment is gone, who is liberated, whose mind is well-established in wisdom, who works for sacrifice alone, his whole Karma melts away. Brahman (absolute Truth) is the offering, Brahman is the oblation, the sacrificial fire is (another form of) Brahman and by Brahman is the sacrifice performed. Thus, by performing actions with the consciousness of Brahman, he reaches Brahman alone.

Some Yogis offer sacrifices to the Devas, while others perform sacrifice in the fire of Brahman by offering self by the self alone. Some offer the sense of hearing and other senses as oblation in the fire of control; still others offer sound and other sense-objects as oblation in the fire of the senses. Others offer all the actions of the senses and the functions of the vital forces as oblation in the fire of self-control, lighted by wisdom. Some offer wealth as sacrifice; some, austerity and Yoga as sacrifice; still others, of rigid vow and self-control, offer study of the Scriptures and wisdom as sacrifice. Yet others offer as sacrifice the outgoing breath in the incoming and the incoming breath in the outgoing, stopping the courses of the outgoing and incoming breaths; thus they constantly practice Pranayama. Whereas others, regulating their food, offer the functions of the vital forces in the Prana itself as sacrifice. All the knowers of sacrifice, burning off their sins (impurities) by the performance of sacrifice and drinking the nectar of the remnant of sacrifice, go to the eternal Brahman (absolute Truth). O best of the Kurus (Arjuna), not even this world is for the non-performer of sacrifice, how much less is the other (world). All these various sacrifices are given in the Vedas (the revelation of Brahman or absolute Truth). Know them all to be born of action; knowing thus thou shalt be freed. O Parantapa (Arjuna), wisdom-sacrifice is far superior to the sacrifice performed with material objects. The entire realm of action, O Partha, ends in wisdom. . . .

Arjuna said:

O Krishna, renunciation of action thou praisest and then again Yoga (performance of action); tell me with certainty which of the two is better? . . .

The Blessed Lord said:

Renunciation (of action) and performance of action both lead to liberation. But of the two, performance of action is superior to renunciation of action. . . .

He who performs actions, surrendering them to Brahman and abandoning all attachment, is not polluted by sin, as a lotus-leaf by water. Karma Yogins, for self-purification alone, perform actions with body, with mind, with intellect, even with the senses, abandoning all attachment. The steady-minded, by giving up all (attachment for) the fruits of action, obtains peace, born of steadfastness. The unsteady (fickle), being attached to fruits through desire, is ever bound (by action).

* * * * *

He who has conquered himself by the Self, he is the friend of himself; but he whose self is unconquered, his self acts as his own enemy like an external foe. The Supreme Self of the self-subjugated and serene-minded, is ever undisturbed in heat and cold, pleasure and pain, as well as in honor and dishonor. He who is satisfied with wisdom and direct vision of Truth, who has conquered the senses and is ever undisturbed, to whom a lump of earth, a stone and gold are the same, that Yogi is said to be a Yukta (a saint of established wisdom). He is esteemed who looks with equal regard upon well-wishers, friends, enemies, neutrals, a mediator, the hateful, relatives, upon the righteous and the unrighteous.

A Yogi should constantly practice concentration of the heart, remaining in seclusion alone, subduing his body and mind and being free from longing and possession (sense of ownership). In a cleanly spot having established his seat firmly, neither too high nor too low, with a cloth, skin and Kusha grass, placed one on the other; being seated there, making the mind one-pointed and subduing the activities of mind and senses, let him practice Yoga for self-purification. Let him hold his body, head and neck erect and motionless, fixing the gaze on the tip of his nose, not looking around. Being serene-hearted and fearless, ever steadfast in the vow of Brahmacharya and controlling the mind, let him sit steadfastly absorbed in thoughts of Me, regarding Me as his supreme goal. Thus ever keeping himself steadfast, the Yogi of subdued mind attains eternal peace and freedom, which abide in Me. But, O Arjuna, (the practice of) Yoga is not for him who eats too much or who does not eat at all, nor for him who sleeps too much or keeps awake (in excess). He who is moderate in eating and recreation, moderate in his efforts in work, moderate in sleep and wakefulness (his practice of) Yoga becomes the destroyer of all misery.

When the mind, completely subdued, rests in Self alone, free from longing for all objects of desire, then he is said to be a Yukta (steadfast in Self-knowledge). As a lamp placed in a windless spot does not flicker, the same simile is used to define a Yogi of subdued mind, practicing union with the Self. . . .

He whose passions are quieted and mind perfectly tranquil, who has become one with Brahman, being freed from all impurities, to such a Yogi comes supreme bliss. Thus constantly holding the mind steadfast, the Yogi, whose sins are shaken off, easily attains the infinite bliss, born of contact with Brahman. He whose heart is steadfastly engaged in Yoga, looks everywhere with the eyes of equality, seeing the Self in all beings and all beings in the Self. He who sees Me in all and all in Me, from him I vanish not, nor does he vanish from Me.

* * * * *

[Now] I shall declare to thee, who art without evil thought, this great secret, wisdom together with realization, knowing which thou shalt be freed from evil. This is the king of sciences, king of secrets, the supreme purifier; it is realized by direct perception and is endowed with righteousness, easily performed and imperishable. O Parantapa (Arjuna), the men who have no faith in this Dharma (science of Self-knowledge), without attaining Me, return to the path of death and re-birth. By My unmanifested Form all this world is pervaded; all beings dwell in Me, but I do not dwell in them. Behold My Divine Yoga! Beings do not dwell in Me; (although) the Creator and Supporter of all beings, (yet) My Self dwells not in them. As the air, vast and always moving everywhere, exists in Akasha (space and ether), even so, know thou, all beings exist in Me. O son of Kunti, all beings, at the end of a cycle, go back to my Prakriti (Nature); again, at the beginning of a cycle, I send them forth. Ruling over My Prakriti, I send forth again and again this vast multitude of beings, who are helplessly impelled by Nature.

O conqueror of wealth (Arjuna), these acts (of creation and dissolution) do not bind Me, sitting as one unconcerned and unattached to these acts. O son of Kunti, with Me as the presiding Deity, Prakriti (Nature) sends forth the moving and the unmoving. For this reason the world wheels round and round. Fools, unaware of My Supreme state, as the great Lord of beings, disregard Me dwelling in human form. They are of vain hopes, of vain deeds, of vain knowledge, and senseless, possessed with the deluding nature of Rakshasas (unclean, passionate and godless creatures) and Asuras (creatures of darkness and of ignorance). But, O son of Kunti, the great-souled ones, possessing the Divine Nature, knowing Me as Immutable and as the Source of beings, worship Me with single-minded devotion. . . .

He who, with devotion offereth to Me a leaf, a flower, a fruit and water, that love-offering I accept, made by the pure-hearted. Whatever thou doest, whatever thou eatest, whatever thou offerest as oblation, whatever thou givest and the austerities thou performest, O son of Kunti, do that as an offering to Me. Thus thou shalt be freed from the bonds of action that bears good and evil fruit; and thy soul, being steadfastly engaged in this devotion of renunciation, liberated thou shalt come unto me.

Alike am I to all beings; hated or beloved there is none to Me. But those who worship Me with devotion, they are in Me and I am in them. Even if the most wicked worships Me with undivided devotion, he should be regarded as good, for he is rightly resolved. Very soon he becomes a righteous soul and attains to eternal peace. Know thou, O son of Kunti, that my devotee never perishes. O Partha, even those who are of inferior birth,—women, Vaishyas (merchant class) and Sudras (servant class),—even they, by taking refuge in Me, attain to the Supreme Goal.

What need is there, then, to speak of the holy Brahmanas and the royal Sages! Having come into this transitory and joyless world, do thou worship Me. Fill thy mind with Me, be thou My devotee, worship Me and bow down to Me; thus, steadfastly uniting thy heart with Me alone and regarding Me as thy Supreme Goal, thou shalt come unto Me.

* * * * *

But those who contemplate the Imperishable, the Undefinable, Unmanifested, Omnipresent, Unthinkable, Unchangeable, Immovable and Eternal, having subdued all the senses, even-minded everywhere, and engaged in doing good to all beings, verily they attain unto Me. Greater is their difficulty whose minds are set on the Unmanifested, for the goal of the Unmanifested is very arduous for the embodied to attain. But those who, surrendering all actions to Me and regarding Me as the Supreme Goal, worship Me with single-hearted devotion, for them whose hearts are thus fixed on Me, O son of Pritha, I become ere long the Saviour from the ocean of mortal Samsara (world of birth and death). Fix thy mind on Me alone and rest thine understanding in Me, thus thou shalt doubtlessly live in Me hereafter. O Dhananjaya, if thou art unable to fix thy mind steadfastly on Me, then, by faithful practice of devotion, do thou seek to reach Me. If thou art also unable to practice devotion, then be thou intent on working for Me. Even by performing actions for My sake, thou shalt attain perfection. If thou art not able to do even this, then, taking refuge in Me alone, and self-controlled, do thou surrender the fruits of all actions.

Knowledge is indeed better than blind practice; meditation excels knowledge; surrender of the fruits of action is more esteemed than meditation. Peace immediately follows surrender. He who hates no creature and is friendly and compassionate to all, who is free from attachment and egotism, equal-minded in pleasure and pain, and forgiving, who is ever content and meditative, self-subjugated and possessed with firm conviction, with mind and intellect dedicated to Me, he who is thus devoted to Me is dear to Me. He by whom the world is not afflicted and who is not afflicted by the world, who is free from elation, envy, fear and anxiety, he is dear to Me. He who is free from all external dependence, pure, efficient, unattached, undisturbed, and has given up all (selfish) undertakings, he who is thus devoted to Me is dear to Me. He who neither rejoices, nor hates, nor sorrows, nor desires and who has renounced good and evil, he who is thus full of devotion is dear to Me. He who is the same to friend and foe and also in honor and dishonor, the same in heat and cold, pleasure and pain, free from all attachment, he who is alike in praise and blame, is silent, content with everything, homeless, steadyminded, such a devoted soul is dear to Me.

Those who follow this immortal Dharma (teaching) as declared (by Me) and who are possessed with faith, regarding Me as the Supreme Goal, such devotees are exceedingly dear to Me.

* * * * *

Thus wisdom, most profound of all secrets, has been declared unto thee by Me; pondering over it fully, do as thou likest. Hear again My Supreme Word, most profound of all; for thou art My dearly beloved, therefore I shall speak for thy good.

Fill thy heart with Me, be thou devoted to Me, do thou worship Me and bow down to Me. Thus thou shalt attain unto Me. Truly I promise thee, for thou art dear to Me. Giving up all Dharmas (righteous and unrighteous actions), come unto Me alone for refuge. I shall free thee from all sins; grieve not. This should never be spoken by thee to one who is devoid of austerity or without devotion, nor to one who does not render service, nor to one who speaks ill of Me. He who, with supreme devotion to Me, will declare this deeply profound secret to My devotees, doubtless he shall come unto Me. There is none among men who does dearer service to Me than he, nor shall there be any other on earth dearer to Me than he. And he who shall study this Sacred Dialogue between us, by him I shall be worshipped with sacrifice of wisdom. Such is My conviction. And even that man who shall hear this, full of faith and without malice, he too, being freed from evil, shall attain to the sacred region of those of righteous deeds.

QUESTIONS FOR DISCUSSION

1. Describe four methods for attaining oneness with God as described in the Gita. What are the advantages and disadvanges of each, as you understand them?
2. Are any, or all, of these methods similar to any of our previously considered ways to know God, or does Hinduism present a unique method?
3. Does the Gita advocate the loss of self-identity or the identification of the self with the Brahman as the ultimate goal in life? Would one alternative have different implications for the moral life than the other? (See Schweitzer's comments on pp. 353-354.)

READINGS FOR IMMEDIATE REFERENCE

Bhagavad Gita. Chapters 1-12, 18.
Burtt, E. A. *Man Seeks the Divine*. New York: Harper, 1957, pp. 287-299.

REFERENCES FOR COMPREHENSIVE KNOWLEDGE

Bouquet, A. C. *Hinduism*. London: Hutchinson's University Library, 1949. Historical and philosophical, with original source material and commentary.
Gandhi, Mohandas. *Autobiography*. Boston: Beacon Press, 1957. How Hindu tolerance can be applied to problems in the modern world.
Menen, Aubrey. *The Ramayana*. New York: Scribners, 1954. The Hindu epic in a modern (and slightly irreverent) form.
Pratt, James B. *India and Its Faiths*. New York: Houghton Mifflin, 1915. Still one of the most sympathetic and comprehensive accounts.

Also see:
Dasgupta, S. *A History of Indian Philosophy*. Cambridge: Cambridge University Press, 1932.
Eliot, Charles. *Hinduism and Buddhism*. London: Routledge and Kegan Paul, 1921.
Hiriyana, M. *Essentials of Indian Philosophy*. London: Allen and Unwin, 1949.
Radhakrishnan, S. *The Hindu View of Life*. London: Allen and Unwin, 1927.

BIBLIOGRAPHY FOR CHAPTER SEVEN

READINGS FOR IMMEDIATE REFERENCE

Bertocci, Peter. *An Introduction to the Philosophy of Religion*. New York: Prentice-Hall, 1951, Chapters 11-18.
Burtt, E. A. *Types of Religious Philosophy*, rev. ed. New York: Harper, 1951, pp. 99-117, 217-225, 261-267.

REFERENCES FOR COMPREHENSIVE KNOWLEDGE

Hartshorne, Charles. *Philosophers Speak of God*. Chicago: University of Chicago Press, 1953. Original sources from both East and West, together with brief critical comments.
Tennant, F. R. *Philosophical Theology*. Cambridge: Cambridge University Press, 1928. A careful analysis of the knowing process in volume I provides the basis for a restatement of the teleological argument in volume II.

Also see:
Baillie, John. *Our Knowledge of God*. New York: Scribners, 1939.
Gilson, Etienne. *God and Philosophy*. New York: Oxford University Press, 1941.

Heschel, Abraham. *God in Search of Man.* Philadelphia: Jewish Publication Society of America, 1956.

Hocking, W. E. *The Meaning of God in Human Experience.* New Haven: Yale University Press, 1912.

Jones, Rufus. *Pathways to the Reality of God.* New York: Macmillan, 1931.

Taylor, A. E. *Does God Exist?* New York: Macmillan, 1947.

Chapter Eight

RELIGIOUS METHOD

1. JOHN CALVIN

John Calvin, one of the earliest successful reformers, was born in France in 1509, the second son of a local tax collector. As a youth, he showed great promise as a scholar, and when he went to the University of Paris (at the same time as Francis Xavier and François Rabelais) he intended to prepare himself for the priesthood. For two years he was known to his fellow students as "all Logic and Latin," but suddenly he left his studies to read for the law, which he did for another year. When he was twenty-one he experienced a sudden conversion to Protestantism and, fearing for his life, spent some time in hiding, other times in jail. Five years later, in 1536, he published the *Institutes,* one of the most influential treatises of the Reformation. A year later he was elected preacher of the Church of St. Pierre in Geneva, where he remained, except for a period of exile of three years, for the rest of his life. As the spiritual leader of the community he exercised increasing influence over the lives of the people until Geneva virtually became a theocracy. He was an excellent organizer and teacher, attracting young men from all over Europe to study with him. Physically he was of medium height, with a dark yet pallid complexion. He ate and slept sparingly, dressed simply, lived austerely, had a keen and retentive memory, and was a moving, but not flamboyant, speaker. He wrote many tracts and commentaries and was continuously engaged in revising the *Institutes,* even at the time of his death in 1564.

In this selection Calvin discusses the nature of man, and the resulting implications for the concepts of reason and freedom. Look for the reasons he gives to support his conclusions and, hence, what he conceives to be an acceptable method for reaching reliable conclusions.

Reason, Sin, and Predestination[1]

There is much reason in the old adage, which so strongly recommends to man the knowledge of himself. For if it be thought disgraceful to be ignorant of whatever relates to the conduct of human life, ignorance of ourselves is much more shameful, which causes us, in deliberating on subjects of importance, to grope our way in miserable obscurity, or even in total darkness. But we must be on our caution not to make preposterous use of this precept, as some philosophers have done, for the end they propose is that man may not remain ignorant of his own dignity and excellence, which may swell him with vain confidence, and inflate him with pride. The knowledge of ourselves which we need consists, first, in considering what was bestowed on us at our creation, and the favors we continually receive from the Divine benignity; secondly, we should contemplate our miserable condition since the fall of Adam, the sense of which tends to destroy all boasting and confidence, to overwhelm us with shame, and to fill us with real humility. . . .

Since it could not have been a trivial offense, but must have been a detestable crime, that was so severely punished by God, we must consider the nature of Adam's sin, which kindled the dreadful flame of Divine wrath against the whole human race. The vulgar opinion concerning the intemperance of gluttony is quite puerile; as though the sum and substance of all virtues consists in an abstinence from one particular kind of fruit, when they were diffused on every side all the delights which could possibly be desired. We must therefore look further, because the prohibition of the tree of knowledge of good and evil was a test of obedience, that Adam might prove his willing submission to the Divine government. And the name itself shows that the precept was given for no other purpose than that he might be contented with his condition, and not aim with criminal cupidity at any higher. For the promise which authorized him to expect eternal life, as long as he should eat of the tree of life, and, on the other hand, the dreadful denunciation of death, as soon as he should taste of the tree of knowledge of good and evil, were calculated for the probation and exercise of his faith. Hence it is easy to infer by what means Adam provoked the wrath of God against him. Augustine, indeed, properly observes, that pride was the first of all evils, because, if ambition had not elated man beyond what was lawful and right, he might have continued in his honorable situation. . . .

And it is also to be observed that

[1] From *A Compend of the Institutes of the Christian Religion,* by John Calvin, edited by Hugh Thompson Kerr, Jr., Board of Christian Education of the Presbyterian Church, 1939, Book II, Chapters 1, 2, and 4; Book III, Chapters 21, 23. Reprinted by permission.

when the first man rebelled against the government of God, he not only was ensnared by the allurements of Satan, but despised the truth, and turned aside to falsehood. And there certainly can be no reverence of God left, where his word is contemned; for we preserve a sense of his majesty and the purity of his worship, no longer than we implicitly attend to his voice. Infidelity, therefore, was the root of that defection. And from hence sprang ambition and ingratitude, since Adam, by coveting more than was granted, offered an indignity to the Divine goodness, which had so greatly enriched him. Thus, infidelity opened the gate to ambition and ambition produced obstinacy, so that they cast off the fear of God and precipitated themselves whithersoever they were led by their lawless desires. . . .

As the spiritual life of Adam consisted in a union to his Maker, so an alienation from him was the death of his soul. Nor is it surprising that he ruined his posterity by his defection, which has perverted the whole order of nature in heaven and earth. "The creatures groan," says Paul, "being made subject to vanity, not willingly." If the cause be inquired, it is undoubtedly that they sustain part of the punishment due to the demerits of man, for whose use they were created. And his guilt being the origin of that curse which extends to every part of the world, it is reasonable to conclude its propagation to all his offspring. Therefore, when the Divine image in him was obliterated, and he was punished with the loss of wisdom, strength, sanctity, truth and righteousness, with which he had been adorned, but which were succeeded by the dreadful pests of ignorance, importance, impurity, vanity and iniquity, he suffered not alone, but involved all his posterity with him, and plunged them into the same miseries. This is that hereditary corruption which the fathers called *original sin;* meaning by sin, the depravation of a nature previously good and pure.

* * * * *

Thus, it is certain that Adam was not only the progenitor, but as it were the root of mankind, and therefore that all the race was necessarily vitiated in his corruption. The Apostle explains this by the comparison between him and Christ: "As," says he, "by one man sin entered into the world, and death by sin, and so death passed upon all men, for that all have sinned," so, by the grace of Christ, righteousness and life have been restored to us. . . . And Christ himself, the heavenly Judge, declares, in the most unequivocal terms, that all are born in a state of depravity and corruption, when he teaches, that "whatsoever is born of the flesh is flesh," and that, therefore, the gate of life is closed against all who have not been regenerated. . . .

However, philosophers, indeed, with general consent, pretend that in the mind presides reason, which like a lamp illuminates with its counsels, and like a queen governs the will; for it is so irradiated with Divine light as to be able to give the best counsels, and endued with such vigor as to be qualified to govern in the most excellent manner. . . . They assert that the understanding is endued with reason, that most excellent guide to a good and a happy life, provided it only maintains itself in its own excellence, and exerts its innate power; but that the inferior affection of the soul, which is called sense, and by which it is seduced into error, is of such a nature that it may be tamed and gradually conquered by the rod of reason. They place the will in the middle station between reason and sense, as perfectly at liberty, whether it chooses to obey reason, or to submit to the violence of sense. . . . This, then, is the substance of the opinion of all the philosophers, that the reason of the human understanding is sufficient for its proper government; that the will, being subject to it, is indeed solicited by sense to evil objects, but, as it has a free choice, there can be no impediment to its following reason as its guide in all things. . . .

But I am here obliged to repeat that he who feels the most consternation, from a consciousness of his own calamity, poverty, nakedness, and ignominy, has made the greatest proficiency in the knowledge of himself. But man cannot assume to himself even the least particle beyond his just right, without ruining himself by vain confidence, and incurring the guilt of enormous sacrilege, by transferring to himself the honor which belongs to God. And whenever our minds are pestered with this cupidity, to desire to have something of our own, which may reside in ourselves rather than in God, we may know that this idea is suggested by the same counsellor, who excited in our first parents the desire of resembling "gods, knowing good and evil." . . .

Yet let us not forget that these are most excellent gifts of the Divine Spirit, which for the common benefit of mankind he dispenses to whomsoever he pleases. Now, if it has pleased the Lord that we should be assisted in physics, logic, mathematics, and other arts and sciences, let us make use of them; lest, if we neglect to use the blessings therein freely offered to us by God, we suffer the just punishment of our negligence. But, lest any one should suppose a man to be truly happy, when he is admitted to possess such powerful energies for the discovery of truth relating to the elements of this world, it must likewise be added, that all that faculty of understanding, and the understanding which is the consequence of it, is, in the sight of God, a fleeting and transitory thing, where there is not a solid foundation of truth.

* * * * *

We now proceed to show what human reason can discover, when it comes to the kingdom of God, and to that spiritual wisdom, which consists chiefly in three things: to know God; his paternal favor towards us, on which depends our salvation; and the method of regulating our lives according to the rule of the law. In the first two points, but especially in the second, the most sagacious of mankind are blinder than moles. I do not deny that some judicious and apposite observations concerning God may be found scattered in the writings of the philosophers; but they always betray a confused imagination. The Lord afforded them some slight sense of his Divinity, that they might not be able to plead ignorance as an excuse for impiety. But they saw the objects presented to their view in such a manner, that by the sight they were not even directed to the truth, much less did they arrive at it. . . . Besides, these few truths with which they, as it were, fortuitously besprinkle their books, with what numerous and monstrous falsehoods are they defiled! Lastly, they never had the smallest idea of that certainty of the Divine benevolence towards us, without which the human understanding must necessarily be full of immense confusion. Human reason, then, neither approaches, nor tends, nor directs its views toward this truth, to understand who is the true God, or in what character he will manifest himself to us. . . .

Thus, we experience how frequently we fall into error even when our intention is good. Our reason is overwhelmed with deceptions in so many forms, is obnoxious to so many errors, stumbles at so many impediments, and is embarrassed in so many difficulties, that it is very far from being a certain guide. . . . And the reason of our mind, whithersoever it turns, is unhappily given over to vanity. . . .

Let us hold this, then, as an undoubted truth, which no opposition can ever shake—that the mind of man is so completely alienated from the righteousness of God, that it conceives, desires, and undertakes everything that is impious, perverse, base, impure, and flagitious; that his heart is so thoroughly infected by the poison of sin, that it cannot produce anything but what is corrupt; and that if at any time men do anything apparently good, yet the mind always remains involved in hypocrisy and fallacious obliquity, and the heart enslaved by inward perverseness.

* * * * *

The covenant of life not being equally preached to all, and among those to whom it is preached not always finding the same reception, this diversity discovers the wonderful depth of the Divine judgment. Nor is it to be doubted that this variety also follows, subject to the decision of God's eternal election. If it be evidently the result of the Divine will, that salvation is freely offered to some, and others are prevented from attaining it,—this immediately gives rise to important and difficult questions, which are incapable of any other explication, than by the establishment of pious minds in what ought to be received concerning election and predestination. . . .

Predestination, by which God adopts some to the hope of life, and adjudges others to eternal death, no one, desirous of the credit of piety, dares absolutely to deny. We maintain, that both foreknowledge and predestination belong to God; that it is preposterous to represent one as dependent on the other. When we attribute foreknowledge to God, we mean that all things have ever been, and perpetually remain, before his eyes, so that to his knowledge nothing is future or past, but all things are present; and present in such a manner, that he does not merely conceive of them as ideas formed in his mind, as things remembered by us appear present to our minds, but really beholds and sees them as if actually placed before him. And this foreknowledge extends to the whole world, and to all the creatures. Predestination we call the eternal decree of God, by which he has determined to himself, what he would have to become of every individual of mankind. For they are not all created with a similar destiny; but eternal life is foreordained for some, and eternal damnation for others. Every man, therefore, being created for one or the other of these ends, we say, he is predestinated either to life or to death. This God has not only testified to in particular persons, but has given a specimen of it in the whole posterity of Abraham, which should evidently show the future condition of every nation to depend upon his decision. . . .

In conformity, therefore, to the clear doctrine of the Scripture, we assert, that by an eternal and immutable counsel, God has once and for all determined, both whom he would admit to salvation, and whom he would condemn to destruction. We affirm that this counsel, as far as concerns the elect, is founded on his gratuitous mercy, totally irrespective of human merit; but that to those whom he devoted to condemnation, the gate of life is closed by a just and irreprehensible, but incomprehensible, judgment. In the elect, we consider calling as an evidence of election, and justification as another token of its manifestation, till they arrive in glory, which constitutes its completion. As God seals his elect by vocation and justification, so by excluding the reprobate from the knowledge of his name and the sanctification of his Spirit, he affords an indication of the judgment that awaits them. . . .

When the human mind hears these things, its petulance breaks all restraint, and it discovers as serious and violent agitation as if alarmed by the sound of a martial trumpet. They object, were they not, by the decree of God, antecedently predestinated to that corruption which is now stated as the cause of condemnation? When they perish in their corruption, therefore, they only suffer the punishment of that misery into which, in consequence of his predestination, Adam fell, and precipitated his posterity with him. Is he not unjust, therefore, in treating his creatures with such cruel mockery?

I confess, indeed, that all the descendants of Adam fell by the Divine will into that miserable condition in which they are now involved; and this is what I asserted from the beginning, that we must always return at last to the sovereign determination of God's will, the cause of which is hidden in himself. But it follows not, therefore, that God is liable to this reproach. For we will answer them thus in the language of Paul: "O man, who art thou that repliest against God? Shall the thing formed say to him that formed it, Why hast thou made me thus? Hath not the potter power over the clay, of the same lump, to make one vessel unto honor and another unto dishonor?" For what appears to be the meaning of this, but that God possesses power, that cannot be resisted, of doing anything whatsoever according to his pleasure. . . .

Other people falsely and wickedly charge God with a violation of equal justice, because, in his predestination, he observes not the same uniform course of proceeding towards all. If he finds all guilty, they say, let him punish all alike; if innocent, let him withhold the rigor of justice from all. What is it they require? If all are guilty, then they shall

all suffer the same punishment. We confess the guilt to be common, but we say that some are relieved by Divine mercy. They say, Let it relieve all. But we reply, Justice requires that he should likewise show himself to be a just judge in the infliction of punishment. When they object to this, what is it but attempting to deprive God of the opportunity to manifest his mercy, or to grant it to him, at least, on the condition that he wholly abandon his justice. Wherefore there is the greatest propriety in these observations of Augustine: The whole mass of mankind having fallen into condemnation in the first man, the vessels that are formed from it to honor, are not vessels of personal righteousness, but of Divine mercy; and the formation of others to dishonor, is to be attributed, not to iniquity, but to the Divine decree, etc. While God rewards those whom he rejects with deserved punishment, and to those whom he calls, freely gives undeserved grace, he is liable to no accusation, but may be compared to a creditor, who has power to release one, and enforce his demands on another. For as Paul says, that "God hath concluded all under sin, that he might have mercy upon all," it must at the same time, be added, that he is debtor to none; for no man "hath first given to Him" to entitle him to demand a recompense.

* * * * *

Thus, man is so enslaved by sin, as to be of his own nature incapable of an effort, or even an inspiration, towards that which is good. Augustine somewhere compares the human will to a horse, obedient to the direction of his rider; and God and the devil he compares to riders. "If God rides it, he, like a sober and skillful rider, manages it in graceful manner, stimulates its tardiness; restrains its immoderate celerity; represses its wantonness and wildness; tames its perverseness, and conducts it into the right way. But if the devil has taken possession of it, he, like a foolish and wanton rider, forces it through pathless places, hurries it into ditches, drives it down over precipices, and excites it into pride, obstinancy and ferocity." . . .

Those whom the Lord does not favor with the government of his Spirit, he abandons, in righteous judgment, to the influence of Satan. Wherefore, the Apostle says, that "the God of this world hath blinded the minds of them which believe not," who are destined to destruction, "lest the light of the gospel should shine unto them." The blinding of the wicked, and all those enormities which attend it, are called the works of Satan, the cause of which must nevertheless be sought only in the human will, from which proceeds the root of evil, and in which rests the foundation of the kingdom of Satan, that is, sin. . . .

We are not afraid to allow, what Paul very strenuously asserts, that all, without exception, are depraved and addicted to wickedness, but with him we add, that the mercy of God does not permit all to remain in depravity. Therefore, since we all naturally labor under the same disease, they alone recover to whom the Lord has been pleased to apply his healing hand. The rest, whom he passes by in righteous judgment, putrefy in their corruption till they are entirely consumed.

QUESTIONS FOR DISCUSSION

1. What is the doctrine of original sin? Was God responsible for sin entering the world? How does Calvin answer this problem—or is it a problem?
2. Why does Calvin believe that philosophers' ideas about reason are mistaken?
3. How do you respond to the doctrine of predestination? What reasons are given to support it? What reasons could be given to deny it?
4. According to Calvin, how do we gain reliable knowledge? Do you think his answer is a typical Christian answer?

READINGS FOR IMMEDIATE REFERENCE

Calvin, John. *Institutes of the Christian Religion*. Philadelphia: Westminster Press, 1939, Book I, Chapters 15, 18; Book II, Chapters 1-5; Book III, Chapters 11, 21-23.

Channing, William Ellery. "The Moral Argument Against Calvinism," *The Works of William Ellery Channing*. Boston: American Unitarian Society, 1900.

Edwards, Jonathan. "God Glorified in Man's Dependence"; "The Insufficiency of Reason as a Substitute for Revelation"; "Sinners in the Hands of an Angry God" in *The Works of Jonathan Edwards*. Princeton, 1830.

REFERENCES FOR COMPREHENSIVE KNOWLEDGE

Augustine. *On Free Will*.

Luther, Martin. *On the Bondage of the Will*.

Paul: *Epistle to the Romans*. Classical statements of the doctrines of original sin, predestination, and grace.

Machen, J. G. *The Christian Doctrine of Man*. New York: Macmillan, 1937. A careful statement of the position, and a sympathetic defense.

McGiffert, A. C. *Protestant Thought Before Kant*. New York: Scribners, 1929. A thoughtful, scholarly, and highly readable historical account.

Also see:

Cole, S. G. *History of Fundamentalism*. New York: R. R. Smith, 1931.

Mackinnon, James. *The Origins of the Reformation*. New York: Dillenberger, 1939.

McGiffert, A. C. *Martin Luther: The Man and His Works*. New York: Century, 1912.

McNeill, J. T. *The History and Character of Calvinism*. New York: Oxford University Press, 1954.

Weber, Max. *The Protestant Ethic and the Spirit of Capitalism*. New York: Scribners, 1958.

II. THOMAS AQUINAS

For biographical material see Chapter Seven, p. 286.
Let us now turn to a representative from Roman Catholicism to consider his judgment concerning the competence of human reason. In this selection Aquinas discusses the relationship between reason and faith, giving reasons for believing that faith is both necessary and more important. Do you agree with the reasons he gives to support this conclusion?

Reason and Faith[1]

In what way it is possible to make known the divine truth. Now in those things which we hold about God there is truth in two ways. For certain things that are true about God wholly surpass the capability of human reason, for instance that God is three and one: while there are certain things to which even natural reason can attain, for instance, that God is, that God is one, and others like these, which even the philosophers proved demonstratively of God, being guided by the light of natural reason.

That certain divine truths wholly surpass the capability of human reason, is most clearly evident. For since the principle of all the knowledge which the reason acquires about a thing, is the understanding of that thing's essence, because according to the Philosopher's teaching the principle of a demonstration is what a thing is, it follows that our knowledge about a thing will be in proportion to our understanding of its essence. Wherefore, if the human intellect comprehends the essence of a particular thing, for instance a stone or a triangle, no truth about that thing will surpass the capability of human reason. But this does not happen to us in relation to God, because the human intellect is incapable by its natural power of attaining to the comprehension of His essence: since our intellect's knowledge, according to the mode of the present life, originates from the senses: so that things which are not objects of sense cannot be comprehended by the human intellect, except in so

[1] From *Summa Contra Gentiles,* by Thomas Aquinas, translated by the English Dominican Fathers. New York: Benziger Brothers, Inc., 1927-29, Book I, Chapters 3-4, 7-8. Reprinted by permission.

far as knowledge of them is gathered from sensibles. Now sensibles cannot lead our intellect to see in them what God is, because they are effects unequal to the power of their cause. And yet our intellect is led by sensibles to the divine knowledge so as to know about God that He is, and other such truths, which need to be ascribed to the first principle. Accordingly some divine truths are attainable by human reason, while others altogether surpass the power of human reason.

Again. The same is easy to see from the degrees of intellects. For if one of two men perceives a thing with his intellect with greater subtlety, the one whose intellect is of a higher degree understands many things which the other is altogether unable to grasp; as instanced in a yokel who is utterly incapable of grasping the subtleties of philosophy. Now the angelic intellect surpasses the human intellect more than the intellect of the cleverest philosopher surpasses that of the most uncultured. For an angel knows God through a more excellent effect than does man, for as much as the angel's essence, through which he is led to know God by natural knowledge, is more excellent than sensible things, even than the soul itself, by which the human intellect mounts to the knowledge of God. And the divine intellect surpasses the angelic intellect much more than the angelic surpasses the human. For the divine intellect by its capacity equals the divine essence, wherefore God perfectly understands of Himself what He is, and He knows all things that can be understood about Him: whereas the angel knows not what God is by his natural knowledge, because the angel's essence, by which he is led to the knowledge of God, is an effect unequal to the power of its cause. Consequently an angel is unable by his natural knowledge to grasp all that God understands about Himself: nor again is human reason capable of grasping all that an angel understands by his natural power. Accordingly just as a man would show himself to be a most insane fool if he declared the assertions of a philosopher to be false because he was unable to understand them, so, and much more, a man would be exceedingly foolish, were he to suspect of falsehood the things revealed by God through the ministry of His angels, because they cannot be the object of reason's investigations.

Furthermore. The same is made abundantly clear by the deficiency which every day we experience in our knowledge of things. For we are ignorant of many of the properties of sensible things, and in many cases we are unable to discover the nature of those properties which we perceive by our sense. Much less therefore is human reason capable of investigating all the truths about that most sublime essence. . . .

The remark of Aristotle likewise agrees with this conclusion. He says that "our intellect is related to the prime beings, which are most evident in their nature, as the eye of an owl is related to the sun."

Sacred Scripture also gives testimony to this truth. We read in Job:

"Peradventure thou wilt comprehend the steps of God, and wilt find out the Almighty perfectly?" (11:7) And again: "Behold, God is great, exceeding our knowledge." (*Job* 36:26) And St. Paul: "We know in part." (*I Corinthians* 13:9)

Therefore, we should not immediately reject as false, following the opinion of the Manicheans and many other unbelievers, everything that is said about God even though it cannot be investigated by reason.

That the truth about divine things which is attainable by reason is fittingly proposed to man as an object of belief. While then the truth of the intelligible things of God is twofold, one to which the inquiry of reason can attain, the other which surpasses the whole range of human reason, both are fittingly proposed by God to man as an object of belief. We must first show this with regard to that truth which is attainable by the inquiry of reason, lest it appear to some, that since it can be attained by reason, it was useless to make it an object of faith by supernatural inspiration.

Now three disadvantages would result if this truth were left solely to the inquiry of reason. One is that few men would have knowledge of God: because very many are hindered from gathering the fruit of diligent inquiry, which is the discovery of truth, for three reasons. Some indeed on account of an indisposition of temperament, by reason of which many are naturally indisposed to knowledge: so that no efforts of theirs would enable them to reach to the attainment of the highest degree of human knowledge, which consists in knowing God. Some are hindered by the needs of household affairs. For there must needs be among men some who devote themselves to the conduct of temporal affairs, who would be unable to devote so much time to the leisure of contemplative research as to reach the summit of human inquiry, namely the knowledge of God. And some are hindered by laziness. For in order to acquire the knowledge of God in those things which reason is able to investigate, it is necessary to have a previous knowledge of many things: since almost the entire consideration of philosophy is directed to the knowledge of God: for which reason metaphysics, which is about divine things, is the last of the parts of philosophy to be studied. Wherefore it is not possible to arrive at the inquiry about the aforesaid truth except after a most laborious study: and few are willing to take upon themselves this labor for the love of a knowledge, the natural desire for which has nevertheless been instilled into the mind of man by God.

The second disadvantage is that those who would arrive at the discovery of the aforesaid truth would scarcely succeed in doing so after a long time. First, because this truth is so profound, that it is only after long practice that the human intellect is enabled to grasp it by means of reason. Secondly, because many things are required beforehand, as stated above. Thirdly, because at the time of youth, the mind, when tossed about by the various movements of the passions, is not fit for the knowledge of so sublime a truth, whereas calm gives prudence and knowledge. Hence mankind would remain in the deepest darkness of ignorance, if the path of reason were the only available way to the knowledge of God: because the knowledge of God which especially makes men perfect and good, would be acquired only by a few, and by these only after a long time.

The third disadvantage is that much falsehood is mingled with the investigations of human reason, on account of the weakness of our intellect in forming its judgments, and by reason of the admixture of phantasms. Consequently many would remain in doubt about those things even which are most truly demonstrated, through ignoring the force of the demonstration: especially when they perceive that different things are taught by the various men who are called wise. Moreover among the many demonstrated truths, there is sometimes a mixture of falsehood that is not demonstrated, but assumed for some probable or sophistical reason which at times is mistaken for a demonstration. Therefore it was necessary that definite certainty and pure truth about divine things should be offered to man by way of faith.

Accordingly, the divine clemency has made this salutary commandment, that even some things which reason is able to investigate must be held by faith: so that all may share in the knowledge of God easily, and without doubt or error.

Hence, it is written: "Henceforward you walk not as also the Gentiles walk in the vanity of their mind, having their understanding darkened" (*Ephesians* 4:17-18). And again: "All thy children shall be taught of the Lord" (*Isaiah* 54:13). . . .

That those things which cannot be investigated by reason are fittingly proposed to man as an object of faith. It may appear to some that those things which cannot be investigated by reason ought not to be proposed to man as an object of faith: because divine wisdom provides for each thing according to the mode of its nature. We must therefore prove that it is necessary also for those things which surpass reason to be proposed by God to man as an object of faith.

For no man tends to do a thing by his desire and endeavor unless it be previously known to him. Wherefore since man is directed by divine providence to a higher good than human frailty can attain in the present life, as we shall show in the sequel, it was necessary for his mind to be bidden to something higher than those things to which our reason can reach in the present life, so that he might learn to aspire, and by his endeavors to tend to something surpassing the whole state of the present life. And this is especially competent to the Christian religion, which alone promises goods spiritual and eternal: for which reason it proposes many things surpassing the thought of man: whereas the old law which contained promises of temporal things, proposed few things that are above human inquiry. It was with this motive that the philosophers, in order to wean men from sensible pleasures to virtue, took care to show that there are other goods of greater account than those which appeal to the senses, the taste of which things affords much greater delight to those who devote themselves to active or contemplative virtues.

Again, it is necessary for this truth to be proposed to man as an object of faith in order that he may have truer knowledge of God. For then alone do we know God truly, when we believe that He is far above all that man can possibly think of God, because the divine essence surpasses man's natural knowledge, as stated above. Hence by the fact that certain things about God are proposed to man, which surpass his reason, he is strengthened in his opinion that God is far above what he is able to think.

There results also another advantage from this, namely, the checking of presumption which is the mother of error. For some there are who presume so far on their wits that they think themselves capable of measuring the whole nature of things by their intellect, in that they esteem all things true which they see, and false which they see not. Accordingly, in order that man's mind might be freed from this presumption, and seek the truth humbly, it was necessary that certain things far surpassing his intellect should be proposed to man by God. . . .

That the truth of reason is not in opposition to the truth of the Christian faith. Now though the aforesaid truth of the Christian faith surpasses the ability of human reason, nevertheless those things which are naturally instilled in human reason cannot be opposed to this truth. For it is clear that those things which are implanted in reason by nature, are most true, so much so that it is impossible to think them to be false. Nor is it lawful to deem false that which is held by faith, since it is so evidently confirmed by God. Seeing then that the false alone is opposed to the true, as evidently appears if we examine their definitions, it is impossible for the aforesaid truth of faith to be contrary to those principles which reason knows naturally.

Again. The same things which the disciple's mind receives from its teacher is contained in the knowledge of the teacher, unless he teach insincerely, which it were wicked to say of God. Now the knowledge of naturally known principles is instilled into us by God, since God Himself is the author of our nature. Therefore the divine Wisdom also contains these principles. Consequently whatever is contrary to these principles, is contrary to the divine Wisdom; wherefore it cannot be from God. Therefore those things which are received by faith from divine revelation cannot be contrary to our natural knowledge.

Moreover. Our intellect is stayed by contrary arguments, so that it cannot advance to the knowledge of truth. Wherefore if conflicting knowledges were instilled into us by God, our intellect would thereby be hindered from knowing the truth. And this cannot be ascribed to God.

Furthermore. Things that are natural are unchangeable so long as nature remains. Now contrary opinions cannot be together in the same subject. Therefore God does not instill into man any opinion or belief contrary to natural knowledge.

Hence the Apostle says "The word is nigh thee even in thy heart and in thy mouth. This is the word of faith which we preach." (*Romans* 10:8) Yet because it surpasses reason some look upon it as though it were contrary thereto; which is impossible.

This is confirmed also by the authority of Augustine who says . . . "That which truth shall make known can nowise be in opposition to the holy books whether of the Old or of the New Testament."

From this we may evidently conclude that whatever arguments are alleged against the teachings of faith, they do not rightly proceed from the first self-evident principles instilled by nature. Wherefore they lack the force of demonstration, and are either probable or sophistical arguments, and consequently it is possible to solve them.

In what relation human reason stands to the truth of faith. It would also seem well to observe that sensible things from which human reason derives the source of its knowledge, retain a certain trace of likeness to God, but so imperfect that it proves altogether inadequate to manifest the substance itself of God. For effects resemble their causes according to their own mode, since like action proceeds from like agent; and yet the effect does not always reach to a perfect likeness to the agent. Accordingly human reason is adapted to the knowledge of the truth of faith, which can be known in the highest degree only by those who see the divine substance, in so far as it is able to put together certain probable arguments in support thereof, which nevertheless are insufficient to enable us to understand the aforesaid truth as though it were demonstrated to us or understood by us in itself. And yet however weak these arguments may be, it is useful for the human mind to be practiced therein, so long as it does not pride itself on having comprehended or demonstrated; since although our view of the sublimest things is limited and weak, it is most pleasant to be able to catch but a glimpse of them.

QUESTIONS FOR DISCUSSION

1. Why should beliefs provable by reason still be accepted on faith? Does Aquinas give reasons to prove this conclusion? If so, what does this do to the conclusion's validity?
2. Do reason and faith always come to the same conclusion? Can you think of instances where they do? Where they do not?
3. Does faith or reason tell what the limits of reason are? If the former, then why should any reason be used at all? If the latter, why is faith needed? Can you say both are necessary without accepting these implications?
4. Is Aquinas' judgment about reason's competence the same as Calvin's?

READINGS FOR IMMEDIATE REFERENCE

Aquinas, Thomas. *Summa Contra Gentiles,* Book I, Chapters 3-11.
Dewey, John. *A Common Faith.* New Haven: Yale University Press, 1934, Chapter 1.
Maritain, Jacques. *The Range of Reason.* New York: Scribners, 1942, Chapters 1, 7, 16.

REFERENCES FOR COMPREHENSIVE KNOWLEDGE

Copleston, F. C. *Aquinas.* London: Penguin Books, 1955. Biographical, historical, and philosophical.
Gilson, Etienne. *The Christian Philosophy of St. Thomas Aquinas.* London: Sheed and Ward, 1957. A comprehensive and readable statement by one of the leading neo-Thomists.
Also see p. 292.

III. GEORGE FOX

Born in 1624 in Drayton, Leicestershire, the son of a weaver, Fox grew to manhood during the English civil war. He was apprenticed to a shoemaker, but in 1647 he felt the command of God to go forth alone and to preach. In doing so he denounced all kinds of social evils, and as a result spent more than six years in jails in different places and at different times. By 1651, he was organizing small groups of Quakers or, as they called themselves, members of the Religious Society of Friends, in all parts of England. He was a powerful and persuasive speaker and many were converted to his teachings, but frequently he was charged with blasphemy, creating a public disturbance, and failure to show respect for authority. He was therefore in and out of jail and many of his followers fled to America to live on the large preserve granted to William Penn, an early convert. Because in 1666 his vigorous health was broken by a particularly severe imprisonment, some of his activities had to be curtailed. Nevertheless, during the next decade he travelled to the West Indies and America, Holland and North Germany preaching and organizing, encouraging and helping. In 1680, he returned to England to spend his last years preparing his *Journal,* working chiefly in and around London, and helping to draft the Toleration Act. He died in 1691 at the age of sixty-five.

Fox's *Journal* is the record of his daily activities as recollected during his old age. How does he believe that reliable knowledge is achieved?

The Inner Light[1]

In my very young years I had a gravity and stayedness of mind and spirit not usual in children. . . .

When I came to eleven years of age I knew pureness and righteousness; for while a child I was taught how to walk to be kept pure. The Lord taught me to be faithful in all things, and to act faithfully two ways, viz. inwardly, to God, and outwardly, to man; and to keep to Yea and Nay in all things. . . .

As I grew up, my relations thought

[1] From *The Journal of George Fox.* Philadelphia: Friends' Book Store, 1875, pp. 55-76.

to have made me a priest, but others persuaded to the contrary. Whereupon I was put to a man who was a shoe maker by trade, and dealt in wool. . . . While I was with him he was blessed, but after I left him he broke and came to nothing.

I never wronged man or woman in all that time; for the Lord's power was with me and over me, to preserve me. While I was in that service I used in my dealings the word Verily, and it was a common saying among those that knew me, "If George says verily, there is no altering him." When boys and rude persons would laugh at me, I let them alone and went my way; but people had generally a love to me for my innocency and honesty.

Then, at the command of God, the ninth of the Seventh month, 1643, I left my relations, and broke off all familiarity or fellowship with young or old. . . . As I traveled through the country, professors took notice of me, and sought to be acquainted with me; but I was afraid of them, for I was sensible they did not possess what they professed.

During the time I was at Barnet a strong temptation to despair came upon me. I then saw how Christ was tempted, and mighty troubles I was in. Sometimes I kept myself retired to my chamber, and often walked solitary in the Chase to wait upon the Lord. I wondered why these things should come to me. I looked upon myself, and said, "Was I ever so before?" Then I thought, because I had forsaken my relations I had done amiss against them.

So I was brought to call to mind all my time that I had spent, and to consider whether I had wronged any; but temptations grew more and more, and I was tempted almost to despair; and when Satan could not effect his design upon me that way, he laid snares and baits to draw me to commit some sin, whereof he might take advantage to bring me to despair.

I was about twenty years of age when these exercises came upon me; and some years I continued in that condition, in great trouble; and fain I would have put it from me. I went to many a priest to look for comfort, but found no comfort from them.

From Barnet I went to London, where I took a lodging, and was under great misery and trouble there; for I looked upon the great professors of the city of London, and saw all was dark and under the chain of darkness. . . .

Being returned into Leicestershire, my relations would have had me married; but I told them I was but a lad, and must get wisdom. . . . Then I went to Coventry, where I took a chamber for a while at a professor's house, till people began to be acquainted with me, for there were many tender people in that town. After some time I went into my own country again, and continued about a year, in great sorrow and trouble, and walked many nights by myself. . . .

About the beginning of the year 1646, as I was going to Coventry, and approaching towards the gate, a consideration arose in me, how it was said that "All Christians are believers, both Protestants and Papists"; and the Lord opened to me that if all were believers, then they were all born of God, and passed from death to life; and that none were true believers but such; and, though others said they were believers, yet they were not. At another time, as I was walking in a field on a First-day morning, the Lord opened unto me that being bred at Oxford or Cambridge was not enough to fit and qualify men to be ministers of Christ; and I wondered at it, because it was the common belief of people. But I saw it clearly as the Lord opened it unto me, and I was satisfied, and admired the goodness of the Lord, who had opened this thing unto me that morning. So that which opened in me I saw struck at the priest's ministry.

But my relations were much troubled that I would not go with them to hear the priest; for I would go into the orchard or the fields, with my Bible, by myself. I asked them, "Did not the Apostle say to believers that they needed no man to teach them, but as the anointing teacheth them?" . . . So neither them, nor any of the dissenting people, could I join with; but was as a stranger to all, relying wholly upon the Lord Jesus Christ.

At another time it was opened in me that God, who made the world, did not dwell in temples made with hands. This at first seemed a strange word, because both priests and people used to call their temples, or churches, dreadful places, holy ground, and the temples of God. But the Lord showed me clearly that He did not dwell in these temples which men had commanded and set up, but in people's hearts. . . .

I had also great openings concerning the things written in the Revelations; and when I spoke of them the priests and professors would say that was a sealed book, and would have kept me out of it. But I told them Christ could open the seals, and that they were the nearest things to us, for the epistles were written to the saints that lived in former ages, but the Revelations were written of things to come.

I fasted much, walked abroad in solitary places many days, and often took my Bible, and sat in hollow trees and lonesome places till night came on; and frequently in the night walked mournfully about by myself; for I was a man of sorrow in the time of the first workings of the Lord in me.

During all this time I was never joined in profession of religion with any, but gave myself up to the Lord, having forsaken all evil company, taken leave of father and mother, and all other relations, and traveled up and down as a stranger in the earth, which way the Lord inclined my heart; taking a chamber to myself in the town where I came, and tarrying, sometimes more, sometimes less, in a place. For I durst not stay long in a place, being afraid both of professor and profane, lest, being a tender young man, I should be hurt by conversing much with either. For this reason I kept much as a stranger, seeking heavenly wisdom and getting knowledge from the Lord, and was brought off from outward things to rely on the Lord alone. . . .

Now, after I had received that opening from the Lord, that to be bred at Oxford or Cambridge was not sufficient to fit a man to be a minister of Christ, I regarded the priests less, and looked more after the dissenting people. Among them I saw there was some tenderness; and many of them came afterwards to be convinced, for they had some openings.

But as I had forsaken the priests, so I left the separate preachers also, and those esteemed the most experienced people; for I saw there was none among them all that could speak to my condition. When all my hopes in them and in all men were gone, so that I had nothing outwardly to help me, nor could I tell what to do, then, oh, then, I heard a voice which said, "There is one, even Christ Jesus, that can speak to thy condition"; and when I heard it, my heart did leap for joy.

Then the Lord let me see why there was none upon the earth that could speak to my condition, namely, that I might give Him all the glory. For all are concluded under sin, and shut up in unbelief, as I had been; that Jesus Christ might have the preeminence, who enlightens, and gives grace, and faith, and power. Thus when God doth work, who shall hinder it? and *this I knew experimentally*.

My desire after the Lord grew stronger, and zeal in the pure knowledge of God, and of Christ alone, without the help of any man, book, or writing. For though I read the Scriptures that spoke of Christ and of God, yet I knew Him not, but by revelation, as He who hath the key did open, and as the Father of Life drew me to His Son by His Spirit. Then the Lord gently led me along, and let me see His love, which was endless and eternal, surpassing all the knowledge that men have in the natural state, or can obtain from history or books and that love let me see myself, as I was without Him. . . .

One day, when I had been walking solitarily abroad, and was come home, I was taken up in the love of God, so that I could not but admire the greatness of His love; and while I was in that condition, it was opened unto me by the eternal light and power, and I therein clearly saw that all was done and to be done in and by Christ, and how He conquers and destroys this tempter the devil, and all his works, and is atop of him; and that all these troubles were good for me, and temptations for the trial of my faith, which Christ had given me.

The Lord opened me, that I saw all through these troubles and temptations. My living faith was raised, that I saw all was done by Christ the life, and my belief was in Him.

* * * * *

About this time there was a great meeting of the Baptists, at Broughton, in Leicestershire, with some that had separated from them, and people of other notions went thither, and I went also. Not many of the Baptists came, but many others were there. The Lord opened my mouth, and the everlasting truth was declared amongst them, and the power of the Lord was over them all. For in that day the Lord's power began to spring, and I had great openings in the Scriptures. Several were convinced in those parts and were turned from darkness to light, from the power of Satan unto God, and many were raised up to praise God. . . .

A report went abroad of me, that I was a young man that had a discerning spirit; whereupon many came to me, from far and near, professors, priests, and people. The Lord's power broke forth, and I had great openings and prophecies, and spoke unto them of the things of God, which they heard with attention and silence, and went away and spread the fame thereof. . . .

The Lord opened to me three things relating to those three great professions in the world,—law, physic, and divinity (so called). He showed me that the physicians were out of the wisdom of God, by which the creatures were made; and knew not the virtues of the creatures, because they were out of the Word of wisdom, by which they were made. He showed me that the priests were out of the true faith, of which Christ is the author; the mystery of which faith is held in a pure conscience. He showed me also that the lawyers were out of the equity, out of the true justice, and out of the law of God, which went over the first transgression, and over all sin, and answered the Spirit of God that was grieved and transgressed in man; and that these three ruled the world out of the wisdom, out of the faith, and out of the equity and law of God; one pretending the cure of the body, another the cure of the soul, and the third the protection of the property of the people. But I saw they were all out of the wisdom, out of the faith, out of the equity and perfect law of God.

And as the Lord opened these things unto me I felt that His power went forth over all, by which all might be reformed if they would receive and bow unto it. The priests might be reformed and brought into the true faith, which is the gift of God. The lawyers might be reformed and brought into the law of God, which answers that indwelling Spirit of God which is in every one transgressed and which yet, if heeded, brings one to love his neighbor as himself. This lets man see that if he wrongs his neighbor, he wrongs himself; and teaches him to do unto others as he would they should do unto him. The physicians might be reformed and brought into the wisdom of God, by which all things were made and created; that they might receive a right knowledge of the creatures, and understand their virtues, which the Word of wisdom, by which they were made and are upheld, hath given them.

Abundance was opened concerning these things; how all lay out of the wisdom of God, and out of the righteousness and holiness that man at the first was made in. But as all believe in the Light, and walk in the Light,—that Light with which Christ hath enlightened every man that cometh into the world,—and become children of the Light, and of the day of Christ, all things, visible and invisible, are seen, by the divine Light of Christ, the spiritual heavenly man, by whom all things were created. . . .

Now the Lord God opened to me by His invisible power that every man was enlightened by the divine Light of Christ, and I saw it shine through all; and that they that believed in it came out of condemnation to the Light of life, and became the children of it; but they that hated it; and did not believe in it, were condemned by it, though they made a profession of Christ. This I saw in the pure openings of the Light without the help of any man; neither did I then know where to find it in the Scriptures; though afterwards, searching the Scriptures, I found it. For I saw, in that Light and Spirit which was before the Scriptures were given forth, and which led the holy men of God to give them forth, that all, if they would know God or Christ, or the Scriptures aright, must come to that Spirit by which they that gave them forth were led and taught.

On a certain time, as I was walking in the fields, the Lord said unto me, "Thy name is written in the Lamb's book of life, which was before the foundation of the world": and as the Lord spoke it, I believed, and saw in it the new birth. Some time after the Lord commanded me to go abroad into the world, which was like a briery, thorny wilderness. When I came in the Lord's mighty power with the Word of life into the world, the world swelled, and made a noise like the great raging waves of the sea. Priests and professors, magistrates and people, were all like a sea when I came to proclaim the day of the Lord amongst them, and to preach repentance to them.

I was sent to turn people from darkness to the Light, that they might receive Christ Jesus; for to as many as should receive Him in His Light, I saw He would give power to become the sons of God; which power I had obtained by receiving Christ. I was to direct people to the Spirit that gave forth the Scriptures, by which they might be led into all truth, and up to Christ and God, as those had been who gave them forth.

Yet I had no slight esteem of the holy Scriptures. They were very precious to me; for I was in that Spirit by which they were given forth; and what the Lord opened in me I afterwards found was agreeable to them. . . .

When the Lord God and His Son Jesus Christ sent me forth into the world to preach His everlasting gospel and kingdom, I was glad that I was commanded to turn people to that inward Light, Spirit, and Grace, by which all might know their salvation and their way to God; even that Divine Spirit which would lead them into all truth, and which I infallibly knew would never deceive any.

But with and by this divine power and Spirit of God, and the Light of Jesus, I was to bring people off from all their own ways to Christ, the new and living way. And I was to bring them off from the world's teachers, made by men, to learn of Christ, who is the Way, the Truth, and the Life, of whom the Father said, "This is my beloved Son, hear ye Him"; and off from all the world's worships, to know the spirit of Truth in the inward parts, and to be led thereby; that in it they might worship the Father of spirits, who seeks such to worship Him. And I saw that they that worshipped not in the Spirit of Truth, knew not what they worshipped.

And I was to bring people off from all the world's religions, which are vain, that they might know the pure religion; might visit the fatherless, the widows, and the strangers, and keep themselves from the spots of the world. Then there would not be so many beggars, the sight of whom often grieved my heart, as it denoted so much hard-heartedness amongst them that professed the name of Christ.

I was to bring people off from Jewish ceremonies, and from heathenish fables, and from men's inventions and worldly doctrines . . . ; and from all their beggarly rudiments, with their schools and colleges for making ministers of Christ,—who are indeed ministers of their own making, but not of Christ's; and from all their images, and crosses, and sprinkling of infants, with all their holy-days (so-called), and all their vain traditions.

Moreover, when the Lord sent me forth into the world, He forbade me to put off my hat to any, high or low; and I was required to Thee and Thou all men and women, without any respect to rich or poor, great or small. . . .

About this time I was sorely exercised in going to their courts to cry for justice, in speaking and writing to judges and justices to do justly; in warning such as kept public houses for entertainment that they should not let people have more drink than would do them good; in testifying against wakes, feasts, May-games, sports, plays, and shows, which trained up people to vanity and looseness and led them from the fear of God. . . .

I was moved, also, to cry against all sorts of music, and against the mountebanks playing tricks on their stages; for they burthened the pure life, and stirred up people's minds to vanity. . . .

The earthly spirit of the priests wounded my life; and when I heard the bell toll to call people together to the steeple-house, it struck at my life; for it was just like a market-bell, to gather people together, that the priest might set forth his ware for sale. Oh, the vast sums of money that are gotten by the trade they make of selling the Scriptures, and by their preaching, from the highest bishop to the lowest priest! What one trade else in the world is comparable to it? Notwithstanding the Scriptures were given forth freely, and Christ commanded His ministers to preach freely, and the prophets and apostles denounced judgments against all covetous hirelings and diviners for money.

But in this free Spirit of the Lord Jesus was I sent forth to declare the Word of life and reconciliation freely, that all might come to Christ, who gives freely, and who renews up into the image of God, which man and woman were in before they fell, that they might sit down in heavenly places in Christ Jesus.

QUESTIONS FOR DISCUSSION

1. What is your initial response to Fox's saying continually that "the Lord opened unto me . . .," "The Lord made me to see . . .," etc.? How could you demonstrate that his claims were or were not true?
2. What is Fox's judgments about lawyers, doctors, and priests? How does he believe they should perform their services?
3. What positive teachings does he hold? What do modern Quakers believe about such topics as war, church organizations, and theology?

READINGS FOR IMMEDIATE REFERENCE

Fox, George. *Autobiography*. Philadelphia: Ferris and Leach, 1919.

Jones, Rufus. *Pathways to the Reality of God*. New York: Macmillan, 1931, Chapters 1, 2, 5, 8.

Trueblood, D. Elton. *The Logic of Belief*. New York: Harper, 1942, Chapters 7, 9-12.

REFERENCES FOR COMPREHENSIVE KNOWLEDGE

Jones, Rufus. *Studies in Mystical Religion*. New York: Macmillan, 1909.

———. *New Studies in Mystical Religion*. New York: Macmillan, 1927. Studies by the most famous modern spokesman for the Society of Friends.

Trueblood, D. Elton. *The Trustworthiness of Religious Experience*. London: Allen and Unwin, 1939.

———. *Philosophy of Religion*. New York: Harper, 1957. Statements of belief by a philosophically persuasive contemporary Quaker.

Also see:

Braithwaite, W. C. *The Beginnings of Quakerism,* rev. ed. Cambridge: Cambridge University Press, 1955.

Brayshaw, A. N. *The Quakers: Their Story and Message,* rev. ed. New York: Harper, 1953.

Grubb, Edward. *What is Quakerism?* rev. ed. London: Allen and Unwin, 1949.

IV. WILLIAM ELLERY CHANNING

Born in Newport, Rhode Island in 1780, Channing was raised as an orthodox Calvinist and attended Harvard, preparing himself for the ministry. Following graduation in 1798, he went to Virginia where he lived with the David Randolph family, acting as the tutor to their children. While there he came in contact with both deism and Pietism. When he returned to Boston in 1800 he went to preach in a Congregational church. Gradually he turned away from his Calvinist origins, the complete break coming in 1819 with the sermon he preached at the ordination of the Rev. Jared Sparks. From that time on he was known as "the apostle of Unitarianism." He traveled extensively in Europe and America and took a keen interest in all public questions, speaking and writing about such topics as slavery, the annexation of Texas, the British West Indies, and usury. Physically he was short and slight, with unusually large eyes and a powerful mellifluous voice. He was largely responsible for the spread of Unitarianism in America during the first half of the nineteenth century, was a close friend of Horace Mann, and the minister to Ralph Waldo Emerson. He died in 1842 at the age of sixty-two.

In the following sermon Channing argues that Christianity is a "rational" religion. Notice how he defines "rational" and the reasons he gives for claiming that Christianity has these characteristics. Would you agree with Channing's estimate of the origin and significance of the doctrines of original sin and the Trinity? Is Channing as confident of reason's abilities as he says he is?

Christianity Is a Rational Religion[1]

Christianity is a rational religion. Were it not so, I should be ashamed to profess it. I am aware that it is the fashion with some to decry reason, and to set up revelation as an opposite authority. This error, though countenanced by good men, ought to be earnestly withstood: for it virtually surrenders our religion into the hands of the unbeliever. It places our religion in hostility

[1] From "Christianity a Rational Religion," *The Works of William Ellery Channing*. Boston: American Unitarian Association, 1891, pp. 233-246.

to human nature, and gives to its adversaries the credit of vindicating the rights and noblest powers of the mind.

We must never forget that our rational nature is the greatest gift of God. It is a greater gift than any outward aid or benefaction, and no doctrine which degrades it can come from its Author. The development of it is the end of our being. Revelation is but a means, and is designed to concur with nature, providence, and God's spirit in carrying forward reason to its perfection. I glory in Christianity because it enlarges, invigorates and exalts my rational nature. I can conceive no sacrilege greater than to prostrate or renounce the highest faculty which we have derived from God.

In so doing we should offer violence to the divinity within us. Christianity wages no war with reason, but is one with it, and is given to be its helper and friend.

I wish, in the present discourse, to illustrate and confirm the views now given. My remarks will be arranged under two heads. I propose, first, to show that Christianity is founded on and supposes the authority of reason, and cannot therefore oppose it without subverting it. My object in this part of the discourse will be to expose the error of those who hope to serve revelation by disparaging reason. I shall then, in the second place, compare Christianity and the light of reason, to show their accordance. My aim, under this head, will be to vindicate the gospel from the reproaches of the unbeliever, and to strengthen the faith and attachment of its friends. . . .

I am to begin with showing that the Christian revelation is founded on the authority of reason, and here it may be proper to settle the meaning of the word "reason". . . . First, it belongs to reason to comprehend universal truths. This is among its most important offices. There are particular and there are universal truths. The last are the noblest; and the capacity of perceiving them is the distinction of intelligent beings. Let me give some illustrations. I see a stone falling to the ground. This is a particular truth: but I do not stop here. I believe that not only this particular stone falls towards the earth, but that every particle of matter tends towards all other matter. Here is a universal truth, a principle extending to the whole material creation and essential to its existence. . . . Again, I see with my eyes, I traverse with my hands, a limited space; but this is not all. I am sure that, beyond the limits which my limbs or senses reach, there is an unbounded space; that, go where I will, an infinity will spread around me. Here is another universal truth, and this belongs to reason. . . .

I now proceed to the second function of reason, which is indeed akin to the first. Reason is the power which tends and is perpetually striving to reduce our various thoughts to unity or consistency. Perhaps the most fundamental conviction of reason is, that all truths agree together,—that inconsistency is the mark of error. Its intensest, most earnest effort is to bring concord into the intellect, to reconcile what seem to be clashing views. On the observation of a new fact, reason strives to incorporate it with former knowledge. It can allow nothing to stand separate in the mind. It labors to bring together scattered truths, and to give them the strength and beauty of a vital order. Its end and delight is harmony. . . .

After these explanations, I proceed to the discussion of the two leading principles. First, I am to show that revelation is founded on the authority of reason. Let me state a few of the considerations which convince me of the truth of this position. The first is, that reason alone makes us capable of receiving a revelation. It must exist previously and operate, or we should be wholly unprepared for the communications of Christ. Consider to whom revelation is sent. Why is it given to men rather than to brutes? The answer is obvious. These lack reason; and lacking this, they have no capacity or preparation for revealed truth. And not only would revelation be lost on the brute; let it speak to the child before his rational faculties have been awakened, and it might as well speak to a stone. Reason is the preparation and ground of revelation.

The truth will be still more obvious if we consider not only to whom, but in what way, Christian revelation is communicated. How is it conveyed? In words. Did it make these words? No. They were in use ages before its birth. If the hearers of Jesus had not previously attached ideas to the terms which he employed, they could not have received his meaning. He might as well have spoken to them in a foreign tongue. Thus the ideas which enter into Christianity subsisted before. They were ideas of reason.

Revelation, we must remember, is not our earliest teacher. Man is not born with the single power of reading God's word; and sent immediately to that guide. His eyes open first on another volume,—that of the creation. Long before he can read the Bible he looks round on the earth and sky. He reads the countenances of his friends, and hears and understands their voices. He looks, too, by degrees, within himself, and acquires some ideas of his own soul. Thus his first school is that of nature and reason, and this is necessary to prepare him for a communication from Heaven. . . . Revelation, then, does not stand alone, nor is it addressed to a blank and passive mind. It was meant to be a joint worker with other teachers, with nature, Providence, conscience, our rational powers; and as these all are given us by God, they cannot differ from each other.

God must agree with himself. He has but one voice. It is man who speaks with jarring tongues. Nothing but harmony can come from the Creator; and, accordingly, a religion claiming to be from God can give no surer proof of falsehood than by contradicting those previous truths which God is teaching by our very nature. We have thus seen that reason prepares us for a divine communication, and that it furnishes the ideas of materials of which revelation consists. This is my first consideration.

I proceed to the second point. I affirm that revelation rests on the authority of reason, because to this faculty it submits the evidences of its truth. . . . I take the New Testament in hand, and on what ground do I receive its truth as divine? I see nothing on its pages but the same letters in which other books are written. No miraculous voice from heaven assures me that it is God's word, nor does any mysterious voice within my soul command me to believe the supernatural works of Christ. How, then, shall I settle the question? I must examine it by the same rational faculties by which other subjects are tried. I must ask what are its evidences, and I must lay them before reason, the only power by which evidence can be weighed. I have not a distinct faculty given me for judging a revelation. I have not two understandings, one for inquiring into God's word and another into his works. As with the same bodily eye I now look on the earth, now on the heavens, so with the same power of reason I examine now nature, now revelation. Reason must collect and weigh the various proofs of Christianity. . . . Reason must prescribe the tests or standards to which a professed communication from God should be referred; and among these none are more important than that moral law which belongs to the very essence and is the deepest conviction of the rational nature. Revelation, then, rests on reason, and in opposing it would act for its own destruction.

I have given two views. I have shown that revelation draws its ideas or materials from reason, and that it appeals to this power as the judge of its truth. I now assert, thirdly, that it rests on the authority of reason, because it needs this faculty to be its interpreter. How is the right of interpretation, the real meaning, of Scriptures to be ascertained? I answer, by reason. I know of no process by which the true sense of the New Testament is to pass from the page into my mind without the use of my rational faculties. . . . There is no miraculous simplicity in the Scriptures. In truth, no book can be written so simply as to need no exercise of reason. Almost every word has more than one meaning, and judgment is required to select the particular sense intended by the writer. . . . I open the New Testament and my eye lights on this passage: "If thy right hand offend thee, cut it off and cast it from thee." Is this language to be interpreted in its plainest and most obvious sense? Then I must mutilate my body. I look again, and I find Jesus using these words to the Jews: "Fill ye up the measure of your iniquities." Am I to interpret this according to the letter? Then Jesus commanded his hearers to steep themselves in crime. It is only by a deliberate use of reason that we can penetrate beneath the figurative hyperbolical, and often obscure style of the New Testament, to the real meaning.

Let me go to the Bible, dismissing my reason and taking the first impression which the words convey, and there is no absurdity, however gross, into which I shall not fall. I shall ascribe a limited body to God, and unbounded knowledge to man, for I read of God having limbs, and of man knowing all things. Nothing is plainer than that

I must compare passage with passage, and limit one by another, and especially limit all by those plain and universal principles of reason which are called common-sense, or I shall make revelation the patron of every folly and vice. So essential is reason to the interpretation of the Christian records. Revelation rests upon its authority. Can it then oppose it, or teach us to hold it in light esteem?

* * * * *

I have now completed my views of the first principle which I laid down in this discourse; namely, that the Christian revelation rests on the authority of reason. Of course, it cannot oppose reason without undermining and destroying itself. I maintain, however, that it does not oppose,—that it perfectly accords with reason. This is my second great position, and to this I ask your continued attention.

Earlier I said that universality and consistency are among the chief attributes of reason. Do we find these in Christianity? If so, its claim to the character of a rational religion will be established.

That a religion be rational nothing more is necessary than that its truths should agree with one another. Now I affirm that the Christian doctrines have this agreement. I go to the Gospel, and I first compare its various parts with one another. Among these I find perfect harmony; and what makes this more remarkable is, that Christianity is not taught systematically or like a science. Jesus threw out his precepts incidentally, or as they were required by the occasion, and yet, when they are brought together they form a harmonious whole. . . .

But this is not enough. A rational religion must agree not only with itself, but with all other truths. I take, then, Christianity into the creation; I place it by the side of nature. Do they agree? I say, Perfectly. I can discover nothing, in what claims to be God's word, at variance with His works. When I consult nature with the lights modern science affords, I see continually multiplying traces of the doctrine of One God. The more I extend my researches into nature, the more I see that it is a whole, the product of one wisdom, power and goodness. It bears witness to one Author. . . . Again, when I look round on the creation, I see nothing to lead me to suspect that its Author confines his love to a few. The sun sends no brighter beam into the palace of the proudest king than into the hut of the meanest peasant. The clouds select not one man's fields rather than his neighbor's but shed down their blessings on rich and poor, and still more, on the just and unjust. . . . Again, when I look through nature, nothing strikes me more than the union which subsists among all its works. The humblest plant has intimate connections with the air, the clouds, the sun. Harmony is the great law of nature, and how strikingly does Christianity coincide here with God's works, for what is the design of this religion but to bring the human race, the intelligent creation of God, into a harmony like that which knits together the outward universe? . . .

When I carry Christianity within and

compare it with the human soul, I again see that it is consistent with the great truths I discover there. When I look into the soul, I am at once struck with its immeasurable superiority to the body. . . . In Christianity, with what strength is the supremacy of the spiritual nature brought out. What contempt does Jesus cast on the body and its interests, when compared with the redemption of the soul. Another great truth dawns on me when I look within. I learn more and more that the great springs of happiness are in the mind, and that the efforts of men to secure peace by other processes are vain strivings; and Christianity is not only consistent with, but founded on, this great truth; teaching us that the kingdom of heaven is within us. . . .

Having shown that Christianity has the character of consistency, I proceed to the second mark of reason on a religion, that is, universality; and this I claim for Christianity. This, indeed is one of the most distinguishing features of our religion, and so obvious and striking as to need little illustration. When I examine the doctrines, precepts and spirit of Christianity, I discover nothing narrow, temporary, local. Its aim is to direct the mind to the Infinite Being, and to an infinite good. It is not made up, like other religions, of precise forms and details; but it inculcates immutable and all-comprehending principles of duty, leaving every man to apply them for himself to the endless variety of human conditions. . . . The more I examine Christianity, the more I am struck with its universality. I see in it a religion made for all regions and all times, for all classes and all stages of society. It is fitted, not to the Asiatic or the European, but to the essential principles of human nature,—to man under the tropical or polar skies, to all descriptions of intellect and condition. . . .

I do and must feel that the claim of Christianity to the honor of being a rational religion is fully established. As such I commend it to you. As such it will more and more prove itself in proportion as you study and practice it. You will never find cause to complain that by adopting it you have enslaved or degraded your highest powers. Here, then, I might stop, and might consider my work as done. But I am aware that objections have been made to the rational character of our religion which may still linger in the minds of some of my hearers. A brief notice of these may aid the purpose, and will form a proper conclusion, of this discourse.

* * * * *

It has been strenuously maintained that Christianity contains particular doctrines which are irrational, and which involve the whole religion to which they are essential in their own condemnation. To this class of objections I have a short reply. I insist that these offensive doctrines do not belong to Christianity, but are human additions. What doctrine is most frequently adduced to fix the charge of irrationality on the gospel? It is the Trinity. This is pronounced by the unbeliever a gross offense to reason. It teaches that there is one God, and yet that there are three divine persons. They love each other, converse with each other, and yet they are, according to the doctrine, not different beings, but one. Is this a rational doctrine? I answer, No. I can as easily believe that the whole human race are one man, as that three infinite persons, performing such different offices, are one God. But I maintain that because the Trinity is irrational, it does not follow that the same reproach belongs to Christianity; for this doctrine is no part of the Christian religion. I know there are passages which are continually quoted in its defense; but allow me to prove doctrines in the same way,—that is, by detaching texts from their connection and interpreting them without reference to the general current of Scripture, and I can prove anything and everything from the Bible. . . .

Christianity has often been reproached with teaching that God brings men into life totally depraved, and condemns immense multitudes to everlasting misery for sins to which their nature has irresistibly impelled them. This is said to be irrational. I certainly shall not attempt to vindicate this theological fiction. A more irrational doctrine could not, I think, be contrived; and it is something worse,—it is as immoral in its tendency as it is unreasonable. It is suited to alienate men from God and from one another. Were it really believed (which it cannot be), men would look up with dread and detestation to the Author of their being, and look round with horror on their fellow-creatures. It would dissolve society. All confidence, esteem, love, would die. What good man could consent to be a parent, if his offspring were to be born to this infinitely wretched inheritance? I say the doctrine is of immoral tendency; but I do not say that they who profess it are immoral. The truth is, that none do or can hold it in its full and proper import. . . .

I have now completed my vindication of the claim of the gospel to the character of a rational religion; and my aim has been, not to serve a party, but the cause of our common Christianity. At the present day, one of the most urgent duties of its friends is to rescue it from the reproach of waging war with reason. The character of our age demands this. There have been times when Christianity, though loaded with unreasonable doctrines, retained its hold on men's faith; for men had not learned to think. But that day is gone, and the spirit of freedom which has succeeded it is subjecting Christianity to a scrutiny more and more severe: and if this religion cannot vindicate itself to the reflecting, the calm, the wise, as a reasonable service, it cannot stand.

QUESTIONS FOR DISCUSSION

1. Is Channing's definition of "reason" satisfactory? Do you agree that Christianity is rational in that it is consistent, coherent, and comprehensive?
2. Are the doctrines of the Trinity and original sin human additions or essential elements in the Christian faith? What doctrines are essential? How can these questions be answered?

3. Given this sermon as indicative of Channing's views, how would he respond to the selection from Calvin, and why? How would Calvin respond to Channing's? In your view, which man makes the more accurate estimate of man's nature and reason's competence?
4. Does Channing rely only, or even basically, on reason for gaining knowledge? Can you find instances where he does not? Are they important?

READINGS FOR IMMEDIATE REFERENCE

Channing, William Ellery. "Unitarian Christianity"; "Unitarianism Most Favorable to Piety"; "Likeness to God"; "The Evidence of Revealed Religion" in *The Works of William Ellery Channing*. Boston: American Unitarian Association, 1891.

Niebuhr, Reinhold. *The Nature and Destiny of Man*. Scribners, 1941. Vol. I, Chapters 7-8.

Parker, Theodore. "The Transient and Permanent in Christianity," *The Critical and Miscellaneous Writings of Theodore Parker*. 1843.

REFERENCES FOR COMPREHENSIVE KNOWLEDGE

Channing, William Henry. *The Life of William E. Channing*. Boston: American Unitarian Association, 1880. A standard biography.

Edgell, David P. *William E. Channing: An Intellectual Portrait*. Boston: Beacon Press, 1955. An explanation and analysis of his leading ideas.

Robertson, John D. *A History of Freethought in the Nineteenth Century*. New York: G. P. Putnam, 1930. In both America and Europe.

Also see:

Brotherston, B. *A Philosophy for Liberalism*. Boston: Beacon Press, 1934.

Fosdick, Harry Emerson. *The Modern Use of the Bible*. New York: Macmillan, 1925.

Sellars, Roy Wood. *Religion Comes of Age*. New York: Macmillan, 1928.

Wright, Conrad. *The Beginnings of Unitarianism in America*. Boston: Beacon Press, 1955.

V. ALBERT SCHWEITZER

One of the outstanding men of the twentieth century, Albert Schweitzer has made significant contributions to the fields of philosophy, theology, music, and medicine, while he has been living and preaching the ideals of humanitarianism. Born in 1875, the eldest son of a minister, Schweitzer grew to manhood in the small Alsatian village of Gunsbach. He attended the Universities of Strasbourg and Paris, returning to the former in 1899 with doctorates in philosophy and theology to become a member of the philosophy faculty and an assistant minister at the Church of St. Nicholas. The next six years he taught, preached, and wrote books on Jesus, Paul, Bach, and Kant, in addition to his interests in building organs and performing as a concert organist. In 1905, at the age of thirty, he added the study of medicine to his interests, graduating with his third doctoral degree in 1912. The following year he married and went to French equatorial Africa to design, build, and maintain a hospital. Except for occasional trips to Europe and America, he has remained in Africa ever since. He has continued his scholarly activities while there, editing Bach's works and writing multi-volume works on Indian philosophy and the philosophy of civilization, along with nearly a dozen single-volume studies. He is a tall man with an astonishing capacity for work, and nearly all who have lived with him report him to be at once forceful and compassionate. He has received many awards and honors, among them the Nobel Peace Prize.

Schweitzer contends that the Eastern religions are logical but empty ethically and that Christianity is filled with logical paradoxes but is primarily ethical, both in its origins and meaning. Accordingly, the beliefs and practices of Christianity are independent of theology and organization. Do you agree?

Logical and Ethical Religions[1]

When examining the fundamental ideas of the higher religions, we notice three lines of distinction which are determinative for the character of each religion. The first is that between optimistic and pessimistic; the second that between monistic and dualistic; thirdly, there is the greater or lesser extent to which ethical motives are present.

A religion is optimistic if it represents the conviction that the forces at work in the natural world have their origin in a perfect primal force, which leads all things toward perfection through a natural development. The religious mind is said to hold a pessimistic view, if it cannot conceive the forces at work in the world of sense as the expression of divine goodness and perfection. It, therefore, does not rest its hopes on possibilities of development within this physical world, but looks beyond into the world of pure, spiritual being.

A religion is monistic if it considers God to be the sum-total of all the forces at work in the universe, and, therefore, believes that in the knowledge of the universe we can attain to perfect knowledge of God. Thus, in its very nature, monism is pantheistic. A religion is dualistic if it does not make any attempt to arrive at a full knowledge of the nature of God by examining the forces which are active in the natural world, but seeks to realize Him in accordance with the ideal conceptions of Him that we carry within us. Of necessity this leads to the idea that this God stands to a certain extent in contrast with the forces of Nature, however great may be the difficulties which this involves for human reasoning. The God whom we have within us as an ideal is an ethical Personality; on the one hand, the happenings due to the forces at work in the universe being no ethical character. Thus, the dualistic religion is theistic.

The distinctions we have so far touched upon concern more the philosophical conceptions on which a religion may be based. It is the ethical content, however, that determines its inner nature. The great question, therefore, which each religion must be asked is, how far it produces permanent and profound incentives to the inward perfecting of personality and to ethical activity.

* * * * *

Indian religion likes to represent itself as the religion of universal sympathy. It talks a good deal about the compassion which we should feel for all creatures. At the same time, however, it preaches the ideal of being absolutely without interest and of ceasing from all activity, and maintains that even the enthusiasm for doing good must be considered as a passion which in the end

[1] Reprinted with permission of The Macmillan Company from *Christianity and the Religions of the World,* by Albert Schweitzer, translated by Johanna Powers. First published in 1923 by Allen and Unwin, Chapter 1. Permission for Canada by George Allen and Unwin Ltd.

has to be overcome. From intellectual compassion the Brahmanist and the Buddhist do not advance to the compassion of deed. Why, indeed, should they render material assistance to a creature in distress? The only help which they can give, without being inconsistent, is to enable the individual to look behind the veil, and to tell him that he must die to life and world and thus rise to the passionless state. In the Indian mind intellectualism consumes the ethical element. . . .

Brahmanism and Buddhism make an impression because they represent a type of religion that is unified in itself, being the result of consistent reasoning on the world and on life. They present a logical, monistic-pessimistic view of world and life. But it is a poverty-stricken religion. Its God is mere empty spirituality. Its last word to man is absolute negation of life and of the world. Its ethical content is meagre. It is a mysticism which makes man lose his individual existence in a god that is dead. . . .

All the leading religious thinkers of China are at one in holding the conviction that the forces which are at work in the world are good. Therefore, in their opinion, true piety consists in understanding the meaning of the world and in acting in accordance with it. Being consistent monistic thinkers, they do not attain to the conception of a personal God; but whereas for the Indians God remains absolute, lifeless spirituality, he is to the Chinese the mere sum-total of the forces at work in the world. This Power, which they conceive as being above all things and in all things, they call "Heaven". . . .

What does it mean to think and live in harmony with Heaven? It means to become like the forces of nature, which work in unobtrusive, unselfish ways, not appearing to be busy outwardly, but solely in inward strength. That is why they accomplish such great things. . . .

Yet, we must say, Chinese piety is built on sand. It is based on the assumption that in the working of the forces of Nature we may read all that we believe and affirm in the religion of love, and that, therefore, meditation on the nature of the universe leads us to that religion. It is an illusion. Knowledge of the world does not lead so far. . . .

As speculations about the world, the religions of China and India are unassailable. All religious philosophy of Nature, somehow, follows similar tracks, either towards pessimism or towards optimism. Religion, however, has not only to explain the world. It has also to respond to the need I feel of giving my life a purpose. The question on which ultimately the decisive judgment must be based is, whether a religion is truly and vitally ethical or not. When it comes to this final test, the logical religions of the East fail. Logical thought about the nature of the universe cannot reach an ethic.

* * * * *

Compared with the logical religions of the East, the Gospel of Jesus is illogical. It presupposes a God who is an Ethical Personality, and who is, therefore, so to speak, outside the world. When trying to answer questions to the relation between this Ethical Personality and the forces at work in the world, Christianity cannot rise above the mist. It must hold fast the belief that God is the sum-total of the forces working in the world, that all that is, is in God. So far, therefore, Christianity, too is obliged to think on monistic and pantheistic lines. And yet it does not rest satisfied with conceiving God as the sum-total of the forces that are active in the world, for the God of monism and pantheism —the God of Nature philosophies—is impersonal and has no ethical character. For this reason, Christianity accepts all the difficulties of the dualistic view; it is ethical theism and apprehends God as a Will that is distinct from the world and compels us not to conform to the world.

Again and again, in the course of centuries, Christianity has sought to harmonize the philosophical and ethical conceptions of God, but it has never succeeded. It carries within itself, unresolved, the antinomy between monism and dualism, between logical and ethical religion.

Neither can Christianity definitely choose between pessimism and optimism. It is pessimistic, not only because, like Brahmanism and Buddhism, it realizes that imperfection, pain, and sorrow are essential features of the natural world, but for this additional and still more important reason, that in man it finds a will which does not answer to the will of the ethical God and which, therefore, is evil.

Again, Christianity is optimistic, because it does not abandon the world, does not, as do Brahmanism and Buddhism, withdraw from it in the negation of life and of the world, but assigns to man a place in this world and commands him to live in it and to work in it in the spirit of the ethical God. Further, Christianity gives him the assurance that thereby God's purpose for the world and for man is being fulfilled; it cannot, however, explain how. For what significance have the ethical character and the ethical activity of the religious individual in the infinite happenings of the Universe? What do they accomplish? We must admit that the only answer we have to this question is, that thereby the will of God is fulfilled.

All problems of religion, ultimately, go back to this one—the experience of God I have within myself differs from the knowledge concerning Him which I derive from the world. In the world He appears to me as the mysterious, marvellous creative Force; within me He reveals Himself as ethical Will. In the world He is impersonal Force, within me He reveals Himself as Personality. The God who is known through philosophy and the God whom I experience as ethical Will do not coincide. They are one; but how they are one I do not understand.

Which is the more vital knowledge of God? The knowledge derived from my experience of Him as ethical Will. The knowledge concerning God which is derived from nature is always imperfect and inadequate, because we perceive the things in the world from without only. I see the tree grow and I see it cover itself with leaves and blossoms; but I do not understand the forces which effect this; their generative power remains a mystery to me. In myself, on the other hand, I know things from within. The creative force which produces and sustains all that is, reveals itself in me in a way in which I do not get to know it elsewhere, namely as ethical Will, as something which desires to be creative within me. . . . My life is completely and unmistakably determined by the experience of God revealing Himself within me as ethical Will and desiring to take hold of my life. . . .

All profound religion is mystical. To be freed from the world by being in God: that is the longing we have within us, so long as we do not numb ourselves in thoughtlessness. A union with God, however, which is realized through the intellectual act of "knowing," as conceived in the Eastern religions, must always remain a dead spirituality. It does not effect a re-birth, in God, into living spirituality. Living spirituality, real redemption from the world, cannot come but from that union with God which is ethically determined. The religions of the East are logical mysticism, Christianity alone is ethical mysticism. . . .

Christianity must, clearly and definitely, put before men the necessity of a choice between logical religion and ethical religion, and it must insist on the fact that the ethical is the highest type of spirituality, and that it alone is living spirituality. Thus Christianity shows itself as the religion which, penetrating and transcending all knowledge, reaches forward to the ethical, living God, who cannot be found through contemplation of the world, but reveals Himself in man only. And it is thus that Christianity speaks with all the authority of its inherent truth.

* * * * *

The[1] ideal would be that Jesus should have preached religious truth in a form independent of any connection with any particular period and such that it could be taken over simply and easily by each succeeding generation of men. That, however, He did not do.

And so we must reconcile ourselves to the fact that Jesus' religion of love made its appearance as part of a system of thought that anticipated a speedy end of the world. We cannot make it our own through the concepts in which he proclaimed it but must rather translate it into those of our modern view of the world.

Hitherto we have been doing this ingenuously and covertly. In defiance of what the words of the text said, we managed to interpret the teachings of Jesus as if it were in agreement with our own view of the world. Now, however, it must be clear to us that we can only harmonize these two things by an act, for which we claim the right of necessity.

We are obliged, that is, to admit the evident fact that religious truth varies from age to age.

How is this to be understood? So far as its essential spiritual and ethical nature is concerned, Christianity's reli-

[1] From *Out of My Life and Thought* by Albert Schweitzer. Copyright 1933, 1949 by Holt, Rinehart and Winston, Inc. Reprinted by permission of Holt, Rinehart and Winston, Inc. Permission for Canada by George Allen and Unwin, Ltd.

gious truth remains the same through the centuries. The variations belong only to the outward form which it assumes in the ideas belonging to different world-views. Thus Jesus' religion of love which made its first appearance within the framework of late Jewish eschatological expectation, finds a place later on within the late Greek, the medieval, and the modern views of the world. Nevertheless, it remains through the centuries what it is essentially. Whether it is worked out in terms of one system of thought or another is of only relative importance. What is decisive is the amount of influence over mankind won by the spiritual and ethical truth which it has held from the very first.

We of today do not, like those who were able to hear the preaching of Jesus, expect to see a Kingdom of God realizing itself in supernatural events. Our conviction is that it can only come into existence by the power of the spirit of Jesus working in our hearts and in the world. The one important thing is that we shall be as thoroughly dominated by the idea of the Kingdom as Jesus requires His followers to be. . . .

Jesus never undertakes to expound the late Jewish dogmas of the Messiah and the Kingdom. His concern is, not how believers ought to picture things, but that love, without which no one can belong to God, and attain to membership of the Kingdom, shall be powerful within it. The subject of all His preaching is love, and more generally, the preparation of the heart for the Kingdom. The Messianic dogma remains in the background. If He did not happen to mention it now and then, one could forget that it is presupposed all through. That explains why it was possible to overlook for so long the fact that His religion of love was conditioned by Time. . . .

The true understanding of Jesus is the understanding of will acting on will. The true relation to Him is to be taken possession of by Him. Christian piety of any and every sort is valuable only so far as it means the surrender of our will to His.

Jesus does not require of men today that they be able to grasp either in speech or in thought Who He is. He did not think it necessary to give those who actually heard His sayings any insight into the secret of His personality, or to disclose to them the fact that He was that descendant of David who was one day to be revealed as the Messiah. The one thing He did require of them was that they should actively and passively prove themselves men who had been compelled by Him to rise from being as the world to being other than the world, and thereby partakers of His peace. . . .

Many people are shocked on learning that the historical Jesus must be accepted as "capable of error" because the supernatural Kingdom of God, the manifestation of which He announced as imminent, did not appear.

What can we do in face of what stands clearly recorded in the Gospels? Are we acting in the spirit of Jesus if we attempt with hazardous and sophisticated explanations to force the sayings into agreement with the dogmatic teaching of His absolute and universal incapability of error? He Himself never made any claim to such omniscience. Just as He pointed out to the young man who addressed Him as "Good Master" (Mark 10:17) that God alone is good, so He would also have set His face against those who would have liked to attribute to Him a divine infallibility. Knowledge of spiritual truth is not called upon to prove its genuineness by showing further knowledge about the events of world history and matters of ordinary life. Its province lies on a quite different level from the latter's, and is quite independent of it.

The historical Jesus moves us deeply by His subordination to God. In this He stands out as greater than the Christ personality of dogma which, in compliance with the claims of Greek metaphysics, is conceived as omniscient and incapable of error.

* * * * *

Anyone can rescue his human life, in spite of his professional life, who seizes every opportunity for being a man by means of personal action, however unpretending, for the good of fellow men who need the help of a fellow man. Such a man enlists in the service of the spiritual and good. No fate can prevent a man from giving to others this direct human service side by side with his lifework. If so much of such service remains unrealized, it is because the opportunities are missed.

That everyone shall exert himself in that state of life in which he is placed, to practice true humanity toward his fellow men, on that depends the future of mankind. Enormous values come to nothing every moment through the missing of opportunities, but the values which do get turned into will and deed mean wealth which must not be undervalued. Our humanity is by no means so materialistic as foolish talk is continually asserting it to be. Judging by what I have learned about men and women, I am convinced that there is far more in them of idealist will power than ever comes to the surface in the world. Just as the water of the streams we see is small in amount compared to that which flows underground, so the idealism which becomes visible is small in amount compared with what men and women bear locked in their hearts, unreleased or scarcely released. To unbind what is bound, to bring the underground waters to the surface: mankind is waiting and longing for such as can do that.

QUESTIONS FOR DISCUSSION

1. Three problems particularly crucial in the Christian faith are evil, freedom, and the doctrine of the Trinity. Why are these problems? Can they be answered, or do you agree with Schweitzer that Christianity is not a logical religion?
2. "Religious truth varies with every age." What does Schweitzer mean by this statement? Does he offer evidence to support it? Could he?
3. Schweitzer has been called "an agnostic Christian." Is this appropriate?
4. In this chapter you've read selections ranging from the most orthodox to the least orthodox of Christian writers. Do they agree in their

judgments concerning reason's competence to gain reliable knowledge? If they do, does this raise any problems?

READINGS FOR IMMEDIATE REFERENCE

Schweitzer, Albert. *Christianity and the Religions of the World.* New York: Macmillan, 1923.

———. *Out of My Life and Thought.* New York: Henry Holt, 1933, Chapters 5, 6, 9, 13, epilogue.

———. *The Quest of the Historical Jesus.* New York: Macmillan, 1910, Chapters 1, 18-20.

Sorley, W. R. *Moral Values and the Idea of God.* Cambridge: Cambridge University Press, 1919, Chapters 1, 15, 16, 20.

REFERENCES FOR COMPREHENSIVE KNOWLEDGE

Schweitzer, Albert. *Civilization and Ethics.* London: A. and C. Black, 1923.

———. *Decay and Restoration of Civilization.* London: A. and C. Black, 1923.

———. *Indian Thought and Its Development.* London: Hodden, 1936.

———. *J. S. Bach.* London: A. and C. Black, 1923.

———. *The Mysticism of Paul the Apostle.* London: A. and C. Black, 1933.

———. *Philosophy of Civilization.* New York: Macmillan, 1938.

Kraus, Oskar. *Albert Schweitzer: His Work and His Philosophy.* New York: Macmillan, 1944.

Seaver, George. *Albert Schweitzer: The Man and His Mind.* New York: Macmillan, 1947. These two books are the best of a growing number of commentaries, most of them more laudatory than analytical.

Also see:

Campion, C. T. *Albert Schweitzer: Philosopher, Theologian, Musician, Doctor.* London: A. and C. Black, 1928.

Hagedorn, Herman. *Prophet in the Wilderness.* New York: Macmillan, 1947.

Mozley, E. N. *The Theology of Albert Schweitzer.* London: A. and C. Black, 1951.

Seaver, George. *Albert Schweitzer: Christian Revolutionary.* New York: Harper, 1955.

BIBLIOGRAPHY FOR CHAPTER EIGHT

READINGS FOR IMMEDIATE REFERENCE

Bennett, Charles A. *The Dilemma of Religious Knowledge.* New Haven: Yale University Press, 1931.

Burtt, E. A. *Types of Religious Philosophy,* rev. ed. New York: Harper, 1951, Chapter 17.

REFERENCES FOR COMPREHENSIVE KNOWLEDGE

Macintosh, Douglas Clyde. *The Problem of Religious Knowledge.* New York: Harper, 1940. An able analysis by a sympathetic philosopher.

Santayana, George. *Reason in Religion.* New York: Scribners, 1905. Religion is more closely related to poetry than to metaphysics or science.

Trueblood, D. Elton. *The Logic of Belief.* New York: Harper, 1942. An analysis by a leading contemporary Quaker.

Also see:

Arberry, A. J. *Reason and Revelation.* New York: Macmillan, 1957.

Brunner, Emil. *Revelation and Reason.* Philadelphia: Westminster Press, 1946.

Cassirer, Ernst. *Language and Myth.* New York: Harper, 1946.

DeWolf, L. H. *The Religious Revolt Against Reason.* New York: Harper, 1949.

Hick, John. *Faith and Knowledge.* Ithaca: Cornell University Press, 1957.

Chapter Nine

THE RELIGIOUS WAY

Of the three attitudes toward life that we are considering, religion is the one which, historically, has appealed to most people. Many people lack the patience for or confidence in analytical reasoning necessary to be attracted by philosophy, and those who accept the scientific attitude are limited largely to the western world and the past two centuries. But religion, the grounding of one's beliefs in a reality beyond natural phenomena, always has been and continues to be the way many people give meaning to their lives.

However, "religion" is a term which includes many diverse, even contradictory, beliefs. Isaac said that his wife was his sister, but the Ten Commandments say one should not lie. Calvin says that all human reasoning is corrupted by sin, but Channing says that Christianity makes use of reason. Buddha tells us to follow the middle path, but Lao-tse advises us to accept all that happens with equanimity. Schweitzer says that Christianity is not the logical religion that Aquinas proclaims it to be. Advocates of the religious way of life, then, do not always have the same beliefs.

A similar situation in "The Philosophical Way" was mitigated when we separated, clarified, and analyzed more carefully the questions comprising those beliefs, and the same procedure might be helpful in this situation. Let us examine our authors, then, and try at once to be both sympathetic to the religious point of view and also philosophical in our analyses as we clarify the conclusions and examine the reasons given to support them.

I. RELIGIOUS MORALITY

All religions are vitally interested in man's moral life. The scriptures are filled with prescriptions; religious leaders make judgments and sound exhortations; and many people believe there is no morality without religion; indeed, no institution rivals a church for its influence on the moral life. But what kind of guidance has it provided? What ends have been said to be valuable? What means for achieving those ends have been suggested? What reasons have been given to support these conclusions? In what respect are these views vulnerable?

In Chapter Five we saw that there are many different kinds of consideration relevant to moral judgments, ranging from "What is a moral motive?" to "How can one justify a moral theory?" and "How can we make moral decisions?" One of the important principles we recognized then, the difference between descriptive and prescriptive judgments, between saying what values one does have as distinct from what values he should have, is especially helpful when moral ideas are presented in an historical perspective.

In Genesis, for instance, we learned that Abraham drove his son, Ishmael, and his son's mother, Hagar, into the desert when a new son, Isaac was born to Sarah, his wife. He was willing to sacrifice Isaac as a burnt offering, even having him carry the wood to the altar. Isaac later said that his wife was his sister, and his son, Jacob, took advantage of his brother, Esau, to obtain the birthright, just as Jacob used deceit to secure his father's blessing. Jacob married the wrong girl because of a custom his father-in-law had forgotten to mention for seven years, and when he asked for his pay he had to resort to a unique breeding process to counter his father-in-law's treachery. In other words, in this book there are examples of lying, deceit, egoism, treachery, lack of compassion, polygamy (if not adultery), materialism and partiality.

Perhaps this conclusion is somewhat shocking, for Abraham is known to most people today as Paul saw him, the supreme example of faith, and Jacob was the father of the Twelve Tribes; yet these events are a matter of historical record. If they are mistaken, only inductive evidence is pertinent. But this is not to say that they were right—or that we should act this way; only that they did. This is descriptive, not prescriptive, morality, and in a scripture organized historically, such as the Old Testament, this distinction is most important when evaluating moral standards.

But this is not the whole story. Interspersed in this account is a genuinely prescriptive theory. Why did Abraham drive Ishmael and Hagar into the desert? Because the Lord approved Sarah's judgment. Why was he willing to offer Isaac as a sacrifice? Because God commanded him to do so. Why did Jacob deceive his father? That God's purposes might be fulfilled. In each case, then, these men should have acted as they did because their actions were sanctioned by God.

In general, all religious moral theories are justified by this kind of appeal, a point to be discussed later, but for now it is sufficient if we remember that while descriptive and prescriptive accounts are not kept separate in an historical record, they should be distinguished when one is making choices regarding moral conduct.

Another characteristic of moral theory emphasized by such philosophers as Bentham, Dewey and Aristotle concerns the consequences of an action. These men held that an act was morally good if its consequences were worthwhile, and some religious theories also have placed the locus of moral worth in the results of an act. Thus, if one's actions conform to certain moral rules one is acting morally, regardless of intentions or thoughts. One important form this kind of theory has taken in religious thought is known as *legalism.* The Ten Commandments is an explicit statement of this basis for judging moral worth. If one does not kill or commit adultery, steal or bear false witness, and if he keeps the Sabbath day holy and honors his parents, then his actions are morally good.

Many of the world's religions use this method for prescribing moral conduct. Consider this passage from the Laws of Manu, a Hindu scripture.

> Death is the penalty if one steals more than ten measures of grain; where the amount is less, he must pay a fine eleven times the value of the grain, and in either case be made to return the property to that owner. But cutting off the hand is enjoined for stealing less than one hundred but more than fifty palas; where the amount is less, however, one should ordain a fine eleven times as great as the worth of the thing stolen.[1]

Or take this injunction from the Koran.

> O ye true believers, come not to prayer when ye are drunken, but wait till ye can understand what ye utter; nor when ye are polluted, unless ye be travelling on the road, until ye have washed you. If ye be sick, or on a journey, or have come from an unclean place, or have touched a woman, and ye find not water, then rub pure sand, and bathe your face and your hands in it; verily, God is Lenient, Merciful.[2]

The Li-Ki, a Confucian writing, gives this advice to young men:

> Sons, in serving their parents, on the first crowing of the cock, should all wash their hands and rinse their mouth, comb their hair, draw over it the covering of silk, fix this with the hair-in, bind the hair at the roots with the fillet, brush the dust from that which is left free, and then

[1] From the *Ordinances of Manu,* Book VIII, translated by A. C. Burrell. London: Kegan Paul, Trench, Trubner & Co., 1891.

[2] From the *Koran,* Sura IV, London: J. M. Dent & Sons; New York: E. P. Dutton & Co., 1909.

put on their caps, leaving the ends of the strings hanging down. They should then put on their squarely made black jackets, knee-covers, and girdles, fixing in the last their tablets. From the left and right of the girdle they should hang their articles for use:—on the left side, the duster and handkerchief, the knife and whetstone, the small spike, and the metal speculum for getting fire from the sun; on the right, the archer's thimble for the thumb and the armlet, the tube for writing instruments, the knife-case, the larger spike, and the borer for getting fire from wood. They should put on their leggings, and adjust their shoe strings.[1] . . .

Or take religious prescriptions concerning a common subject; the position of women, for example. From the Old Testament:

Thy desire shall be to thy husband, and he shall rule over thee.[2]

From the Laws of Manu (India):

No act is to be done according to her own will by a young girl, a young woman, or even by an old woman, though in their own houses. In her childhood, a girl should be under the will of her father; in her youth, of her husband; her husband being dead, of her sons; a woman should never enjoy her own will. She must never wish separation of herself from her husband, father or sons, for by separation from them a woman would make both families contemptible. She must always be cheerful and clever in household business, with the furniture well cleaned and with not a free hand in expenditures.[3]

From the Confucian scriptures:

Sons' wives should serve their parents-in-law as they served their own. Once they are dressed, they should go to their parents and parents-in-law. On getting to where they are, with bated breath and gentle voice, they should ask if their clothes are too warm or too cold, whether they are ill or pained, or uncomfortable in any part; and if they be so, they should proceed reverently to stroke and scratch the place. They should in the same way, going before or following after, help and support their parents in quitting or entering the home. In bringing in the basin for them to wash, the younger will carry the stand and the elder the water; they will beg to be allowed to pour out the water, and when the washing is concluded, they will hand the towel. They will ask whether they want anything, and then respectfully bring it. All this they will do with an appearance of pleasure to make their parents feel at ease.[4]

[1] From *Sacred Books of the East,* Vol. XXVII, translated by James Legge. Oxford: Clarendon Press, 1885, p. 114.

[2] From Genesis, 3:16.

[3] From the *Ordinances of Manu,* Book V, translated by A. C. Burrell. London: Kegan Paul, Trench, Trubner & Co., 1891.

[4] From *Sacred Books of the East,* Vol. XXVII, translated by James Legge. Oxford: Clarendon Press, 1885, p. 114.

This method for determining moral activity, then, is widely used in religious thought. What are its sources of appeal? In the first place, by emphasizing the results, legalism makes immoral activities easily identifiable and hence punishable. By specifying which actions should or should not be done, it makes morality a matter of conformity to stated and therefore known rules. It gives people a common source for their beliefs and therefore becomes a force for uniting a community. Legal codes, by reflecting the past experience of people, thus enables them to benefit from previous knowledge and to avoid earlier mistakes. Add to these advantages the belief that God sanctions such conduct and one can see that legalistic moral theories are justified by significant and meaningful reasons.

However, there also are certain important disadvantages to this approach. If you will notice, most legalistic theories emphasize a negative approach, telling men what they should not do, not what they should do. Eight of the Ten Commandments are negative commands. Moreover, no matter how many laws are given, there are never enough to cover every eventuality. The Laws of Manu do not say who should govern a woman when she has neither father, husband, nor son. The Ten Commandments as originally stated are supplemented considerably in the statements following. In addition, laws stated in one place sometimes are contradicted by other laws. Thus, the injunction "Thou shalt not kill" was given as one of the Ten Commandments, but later on killing was said to be justified under certain circumstances: when a son harms or curses his parents; when one man kills another; when a man's ox harms other people. Indeed, the Mosaic Law seems to sanction killing when it asserts a "life for a life."

Another important disadvantage of legalism is its ambiguity. Words in the law require interpretation. How does one act when he "honors" his father and mother? By not being identified with them? How does one keep the Sabbath day "holy"? By resting all day? And what does it mean to "rest"? In addition, by placing emphasis exclusively on actions, legalism does not seem to make extenuating circumstances or one's motives relevant to a moral judgment. Thus many religious legalisms sanction the law of retribution: the punishment should be identical to the criminal act. The Laws of Manu make the punishment more severe as the theft is greater, and the Mosaic Law makes the matter quite clear: "Life for life, eye for eye, tooth for tooth, hand for hand, foot for foot, burning for burning, wound for wound, stripe for stripe."

Finally, legalism appears to discourage individual moral growth.

By identifying morality with written rules, one is encouraged to learn the law rather than consider the rights and obligations relevant to each situation. By prescribing all conduct, legalism leaves no room for creative thought in searching out the requirements for moral behavior. Indeed, if one does not violate the laws, he does not even have to think about his own moral achievements, or lack of them. All that is required by legalism is that one learn what others have said constitutes moral behavior.

In spite of its advantages, this kind of approach to morality results in rules which are ambiguous, negative, contradictory, requiring continual interpretation and discouraging both creative thought and individual initiative. This is why there are few instances in religious literature in which a strict legalism has been held. A complete moral theory must consider more than just how a person acts; therefore philosophers such as Kant and Epictetus have emphasized the role of motives in judging moral worth; and so have spokesmen for the religious way of life.

Jesus says He came to "fulfill" (complete?) the law, and he does so by adding the element of intent. "Ye hath heard that it hath been said by them of olden times, thou shalt not kill, but I say unto you that whosoever is angry with his brother without a cause shall be in danger of the judgment." Not only should one not commit adultery but he should not desire to, for "whosoever looketh on a woman to lust after her hath committed adultery with her already in his heart." And when one keeps the Sabbath Day holy he should not act as the publicans do, "praying in the synagogues and on the corners of the streets, that they may be seen of men"; rather, he should have a pure heart, praying to the Father in secret.

Buddha, too, places emphasis on the person's motives. The good life does not result from reciting the laws or memorizing the scriptures, for these deal only with the outward manifestations of one's true self. The inner life is most important, for "all that we are is the result of what we have thought: it is founded on our thoughts, it is made up of our thoughts." Thus, if one can control his thinking, he will control his life, the Four Noble Truths and the eight-fold path providing the means to do so.

What kind of motive is morally good? The central idea emphasized by each of our authors is love. Jesus says we should love our enemies as well as our friends, do good to them who misuse us and have compassion on those who hate us. Buddha reminds us that one evil act elicits another, and that this chain of cause and effect can be broken only by one who repays evil with good. Lao-tse advises us to act like water which "benefits all things without competing with them," and like the growing grain which yields to the forces of wind and weather which seek to destroy it.

What are the characteristics of love, considered as a moral motive? Ordinarily, we consider love to be a feeling, an emotion, perhaps a desire. We identify it with the affective life of man. But love really has its foundation in the intellect. Paul recognized this when he said: "Rejoice with them that do rejoice, and weep with them that do weep. Be of the same mind one toward the other." Before we can rejoice with others, we must know they are rejoicing, and before we can weep, we must be aware of others' weeping. We cannot be of the same mind one toward the other until we know what is in the mind of others. In this sense, to love means to understand, to know of the experiences which please or displease others, to discern their interests and antipathies.

To forget that love requires intelligent understanding is to open the possibility for a serious misapplication of the principle, even at the time one thinks he is using it. In its most innocuous form, this is characterized by a vague and undiscriminating sentimentalism, an attitude in which one loves everybody without loving anybody. Because the object of one's love is abstract and general, a person can express love without loving a person, can feel compassion when there are no objects for his compassion. So love becomes a warm feeling without external objects or even manifestations.

However, thinking that love is only a feeling can have much more serious implications in a person's life. During the courting period, for instance, many young people identify love with the affective life, believing that if their emotional needs are satisfied, this is a sure sign of their being in love. All too frequently they fail to learn of their intended mates' interests and abilities, deficiencies and aspirations. As a result, when that factual side is forced upon them, as it is in marriage, the "love" foundation is unable to support the burden, and the consequences can be unhappiness, despair, bitterness, even divorce. If marriage is to be properly based on love, it must start with the understanding.

But knowledge is not enough; love does involve a feeling, but a special kind of feeling. To love means that one projects himself into the life of another; he feels joy as the other does, and he experiences sorrow with the same intensity and depth of feeling as the person loved. This love is not the same as the feeling of personal satisfaction experienced when one's emotional needs are satisfied. Nor is it the feeling of sympathy in which the experiences of life affect one the same way they affect others. Rather, love is the feeling of empathy, the imaginative projection of one's own consciousness into the life of another. It involves one in living the lives of others, but without having their bodies. It requires that we appreciate their accomplishments and share their disappointments as they experience them; that we enlarge our interests and our "self" to include the needs and interests of others outside our own body.

To love, in this sense, is an arduous task. We have the interests and problems which attach to our own body, and frequently they are more than enough to occupy our attention and energy. Moreover, even if we can project our lives beyond our own bodies, it is difficult to know what gives joy or sorrow to others. Even with the best of intentions we think in terms of analogies, thinking other's interests are similar to our own, but frequently this is not true. And even when we can love with understanding and empathy the experience is difficult to maintain because the affairs of the body and the world continually crowd in on our own lives.

To love fully, then, requires a sensitivity to understand the interests of others and to respond with empathy. It requires, also, a wisdom to know what those interests are and how to share them without encroaching on another's privacy. Finally, love requires strength to share the burdens and exalt in the joys of a life outside one's own body. Thus, when Jesus tells us we should love our neighbor, he is requiring that the best in human motivation should precede our actions, that we should endeavor to understand and appreciate his interests and experiences as he does. When Jesus tells us we should love God, he is asking for our total commitment, for he is asking us to think and feel with compassion toward the universe as God does. In this light, then, the admonition that we should love our enemy is a minor, although significant, achievement.

Thus, when one's motive is that of love toward all things, his attitude will be one of equanimity and composure. Lao-tse tells us that toward the "righteous we must be righteous, and to the unrighteous also we must be righteous. To the truthful we must be truthful, and to the untruthful also we must be truthful." Jesus tells us that we should correct our own attitudes before we try to remove the mote from our brother's eye. And Buddha sets a willingness to accept misfortune without anger as the prime condition for a peaceful existence. There is, then, considerable agreement among these leaders that motives are most important for judging moral worth and that a moral motive is exemplified by love. Such a teaching has been called a *self-perfectionist* moral theory. It is most succinctly summed up in St. Augustine's comment that a religious ethic requires only that we "love and then act."

Besides concern for moral consequences and motives, religious writers, like philosophers, have been concerned with the problem of justification. Why should one accept these prescriptions as constituting moral values? What reasons can be given to justify these conclusions?

Philosophers offered many different kinds of justification. Nietzsche appealed to the competitive aspects of nature, Bentham to man's desire for pleasure, Aristotle to the agreements among people. What kinds of justification have religious writers offered?

Buddha's theory is to be justified naturalistically. If your experience proves that life is suffering, then you can examine the validity of the second Noble Truth, that suffering is caused by desire. If you believe this, the third step, that desire should be overcome, could be experienced to be true, after which the fourth step, the eight fold path, would provide the means to do so. Buddha, then, asks each person to experience the truth for himself. Lao-tse says we should be noncompetitive because nature is noncompetitive, and Confucius finds the locus of moral worth in both nature and human nature. Among the eastern religions, then, the justification is an appeal to natural phenomena or human experience. This is why some people in the West believe the pantheism or agnosticism of these beliefs makes them philosophies rather than religions.

In the West, the justifications offered have been of two kinds. First, as suggested earlier, certain rules should be accepted as defining morality because they have been given by God. His wisdom is greater than ours, and therefore we should accept what He tells us. Another justification is suggested in Jesus' statement: ". . . and He will reward thee openly." We should do what is commanded because it is for our own good, either in this world or in immortality. Doing good now is the means for achieving a later reward. In this sense, love of God and love of man is the best way to achieve egoistically conceived benefits.

The first kind of justification, essentially, is the appeal to authority, one of the methods for establishing belief discussed by Peirce. In assessing its strength you could profitably return to that discussion on page 155, but for the present it is sufficient to point to one crucial problem raised by this method. *How* do you decide which authority to accept? The God of Abraham told him to drive one son into the desert and offer the remaining one as a sacrifice. The God of Moses proclaimed that the Ten Commandments define morality.

The God of Jesus sanctioned the law of love. To decide which God one should accept seems to require another standard by which the highest authority can be determined, and if this is so, the method of authority is a secondary method for obtaining knowledge. That, perhaps, is why the religious justification frequently lapses into the second form: you should do good because you expect to reap personal benefits. However, such a justification makes God and His commandments merely a means for achieving one's own ends, and far from placing God in the center of the moral life, He is of only secondary importance to one's own interests.

Regardless of which justification is used, moral values are said to originate from God. But how do we know that God exists? This is the step which takes us from ethics to metaphysics.

II. RELIGIOUS METAPHYSICS

Unlike philosophers who have written on metaphysical questions, religious writers have reduced the multiplicity of problems to one of central importance. Rather than discussing whether sense experience is reliable or how different things can be the same, religious writers see the natural world, with such problems, and man, with his finitude, as part of a larger reality, God's creation. The answer to all metaphysical questions, then, depends on answering just one: "How can we know about God?" If we can know of that which is the source for all other things, that which is most real, then all other problems can be answered deductively. What answers could be given to this question?

As we saw in our discussion of philosophical method, there are many ways by which knowledge can be obtained. Some men, like Hume, rely on sense experience; others, like Descartes, trust the results of logical argument; still others, like Bergson, accept only intuitive knowledge. Each of these finds his counterpart in religious thought.

In the Old Testament, for instance, sense experience of God was not viewed as unusual. Abraham received guidance verbally and Moses saw and talked with Him. In our own time, Joseph Smith, the founder of Mormonism, repeats these claims:

> When the light rested on me, I saw two personages, whose brightness and glory defy all description, standing above me in the air. One of them spake unto me, calling me by name, and said, pointing to the other—"This is My Beloved Son. Hear Him."[1]

Some people, then, claim sensory experience of God, but more than that, they also claim knowledge of his wishes and activities. The author of the book of Genesis, traditionally Moses, gives an account of the earth's origins as God created it, and does so in specific detail. Thus, on the first day, He created light and dark; on the second, Heaven; on the third, the earth, seas, grass, herbs and fruit trees; on the fourth, the sun, moon and stars; on the fifth, fish, fowl and whales; on the sixth, animals, cattle, reptiles (insects?) and man; and on the seventh, He rested.

Is this a reliable method to gain knowledge of God? We already have discussed this problem in Chapter Five so there is no need to reopen the issue beyond recalling that such knowledge must answer the arguments that it is partial, limited, changeable, inadequate, incomplete and biased. Moreover, when applied to the concept of God, there are certain implications which some people find objectionable. If God is known through sense experience and is known to speak, walk and act like other human beings, then one could argue that His majesty is diminished by making Him into a him. In addition, one of His traditional attributes, omnipotence, appears to be limited, for He has a body existing in space. Finally, the very specific accounts of His activities raise certain problems: What "light" was created on the first day when the sun, moon and stars were not created until the fourth? How could vegetable life exist without sunlight? What is meant by the word "day"? When was the original "water" created? etc.

All of these issues raise a central problem crucial to any such claimed knowledge of God: anthropomorphism, that of man making God in man's own image. Many religious people believe the method of sense experience tends to confuse man's conception of God with God's own nature and to think that because they visualize God in this way He must be this. Those who reject this method, then, are hesitant about claiming such specific knowledge. For instance, the Rig Veda, one of the earliest of the Hindu scriptures, portrays the creation in this way:

> Then was not non-existent nor existent:
> There was no realm of air, no sky beyond it.
> What covered it, and where?—and what gave shelter?—
> Was water there, unfathomed depth of water?—

[1] From *Pearl of Great Price* by Joseph Smith. Salt Lake City: Church of Jesus Christ of Latter-day Saints, 1902. Section 3, Chapter 2.

Death was not there, nor was there aught immortal:
No sign was there, the day's and night's divider.
That one thing breathless, breathed by its own nature:
Apart from it was nothing whatsoever.

Darkness there was: at first concealed in darkness,
This all was undiscriminated chaos.
All that existed then was void and formless:
By the great power of warmth was born that unit.

Thereafter rose desire in the beginning,
Desire, the primal seed and germ of spirit.
Sages who searched with their hearts' thought discovered
The existent's kinship in the non-existent.

Transversely was their severing line extended:
What was above it then, and what below it?—
There were begetters, there were mighty forces,
Free action here and energy up yonder.

Who verily knows and who can here declare it,
Whence it was born and whence comes this creation?—
The gods are later than this world's production.
Who knows, then, whence it first came into being?—

He, the first origin of this creation,
Whether he formed it all or did not form it,
Whose eye controls this world in highest heaven,
He verily knows it—or perhaps he knows it not![1]

A second, and more widely accepted method for knowing God is to "experience" His presence, to know, as Niebuhr says, He is there "at the limits of consciousness." This experience is analogous to knowing another person, for just as you are aware there is a depth of personality beyond your knowledge of him, so the religious experience shows there is "a reality deeper and higher than the system of nature in which man stands."

This method for knowing of God is based on experience, but of a special kind. It is similar to one's knowledge of his own feelings, his pains, aspirations and disappointments. They are experienced, indeed, they are among the most important of one's experiences, but only their manifestations can be known by others. No one else can feel your pain, nor can he understand your hopes; at best, he can know only your report of the experiences. In the same way, knowledge of

[1] From *The Hymns of Rig Veda,* translated by R. T. H. Griffith. Benares: E. J. Lazarus, 1896.

God can be experienced by a person although others have no way of sharing—or verifying—your experience.

However, there are degrees of privateness, and there are ways to train the mind so it can be more receptive to this kind of knowledge. Niebuhr believes that our knowledge of God comes from personal-private revelation, but that this must be supplemented by the social-historical revelation of God's nature as given in the Bible. Personally, one can experience God when he feels dependent, is being judged, and feels forgiveness, and these experiences duplicate His successive revelation as Creator, Judge, and Redeemer. In this way, one's experience of God is not merely personal, for there is a standard beyond himself to which he can compare his knowledge, as can others, and thus know that his private experience corresponds to a reality beyond his own conceptions.

For van Ruysbroek, and certain portions of the Bhagavad-Gita, man's intuitive knowledge can be increased by education and practice. Van Ruysbroek points to the scriptural statement, "See, the bridegroom comes, go out to meet him," as an indication of the successive steps one takes between the need to look spiritually for God to the "delectable passing over and flowing away and sinking down in the essential nakedness where all the Divine Names fall away into this simple nakedness, wanting manner and without reason." There is no standard beyond the experience itself to which it can be compared, but it is analogous to any wedding in which two people are united in blissful harmony, an experience with profound meaning but one which neither requires nor offers an explanation.

This method for knowing of God escapes the difficulties of sense experience yet maintains that God's presence is to be experienced. If one should doubt the reliability of this kind of experience, all he needs to do is make himself more receptive, through prayer and faith. As Plato said: "To those who have such knowledge, instruction is unnecessary; to those who do not, no instruction is possible." Yet it can reasonably be asked how one knows that this is knowledge of God and not knowledge of some private pain or hope. Just because one feels a presence how can he tell it is God's, the Devil's, or simply wish fulfillment? Niebuhr's answer to this problem already was suggested, but that answer is open to the objection that either the Bible does not reveal God to have these characteristics or that I do not experience Him as Niebuhr says I do. Another kind of test suggested is that one can prepare himself to receive this knowledge. In the Christian tradition, prayer and fasting are the traditional means for making oneself receptive, and certain mystics have given detailed instructions to follow. In the West, St. John of the Cross set out in great detail these steps and the pitfalls attendant to each level of achievement, and in the East, the practice of Yoga has been refined to an art. The Bhagavad-Gita tells us to find a quiet spot, seat ourselves comfortably, hold our body, neck, and head erect, fix our gaze on the tip of the nose and strive to make our mind "one pointed."

But the test of correct preparation, too, is subject to difficulties. Many who have experienced God did not prepare themselves to do so. Paul and St. Augustine provide good examples. Then there were others who did prepare themselves and who have not experienced Him, as all forgotten or unsuccessful novitiates testify. Proper training, then, is neither a necessary nor a sufficient condition to assure one's knowledge of God; it seems to be an accidental rather than an essential part of the experience.

The fact seems to be that this method is so private that it provides its own evidence, and no other reasons can be given to support the claim. This means that no one can challenge the experience, for, like pain, it is so personal that outside arguments simply are not relevant. But also, it means that one cannot defend his claim against reasoned analysis. To put the point in Plato's terminology again: "The power of dialectic alone can reveal this." The claim to know God by "experience," then, is neither challengeable nor provable.

However, others within the religious tradition have held a bolder rationalism, insisting that God's existence can be proven by logical argument. Aquinas offers five such proofs.

The first three, and one form of the fourth, have certain similarities. They all begin with evidence derived from sensory experience: objects move; some objects depend on others for existence; some objects are more perfect specimens of their species. In order to explain how these things came to be what they are, you must assume the existence of a prior motion or cause or contingent being. However, this method of explanation cannot continue indefinitely, for "if in efficient causes it is possible to go on to infinity, there will be no first efficient cause, neither will there be an ultimate effect, nor any intermediate efficient causes; all of which is plainly false." Or again, to quote the crucial passage: "If at one time nothing was in existence, it would have been impossible for anything to have begun to exist; and thus even now nothing would be in existence—which is absurd." Thus, an infinite chain of causes or motions is not possible; we must assume there is an Uncaused Cause, an Unmoved Mover, a Being which Necessarily exists. This Being is called "God." This is the *cosmological* proof.

The fourth argument begins somewhat differently. Sense experience demonstrates that some objects are more perfect than others; a Mongoloid is not as representative of man as the philosopher Aristotle. But if things can be judged according to their degree of perfection, there must be an ultimate perfection by which all things can be judged; and what is perfect is called God. But if God were merely the idea of perfection and did not exist, He would be lacking one of the attributes of perfection, namely existence. Therefore, in order for God to fully satisfy the definition of perfection, He must exist. In this form the argument is known as the *ontological* proof, although Aquinas specifically rejects this form, turning his own argument into a variant of the cosmological proof.

The fifth argument is still different. Objects without intelligence show adaptation to ends appropriate to them: birds fly south in the winter; vegetable life responds to the coldness of winter and the warmth of spring. Moreover, objects in the world show an interdependence which could not be merely fortuitous: grass grows so cows can have nourishment and give milk which, in turn, is drunk by humans who then have strength to water the grass so it will grow, etc. Since this inter-adaptability extends from the largest phenomena in the universe to the smallest particle, the universe must be the creation of an original Designer who directs all objects to their proper end. Thus the *teleological* argument.

Unlike the privateness of personal experience this method for gaining knowledge of God is susceptible to philosophical analysis, and many philosophers have examined it carefully. Both Hume and Kant have raised a number of objections which those who affirm the arguments' persuasiveness must meet to make them cogent.

Take the teleological argument first. (1) Just because we think there is design, it does not follow that there is, since we have no evidence to prove that the universe is similar to what we think it is. As Hume says: "What peculiar privilege has this little agitation of the brain we call *thought*, that we must thus make it the model of the whole universe?" (2) Even if there is design, it does not follow there was a Designer, for it might have been the result of natural processes. (3) Even if there was a Designer, it does not follow there was only one, for, as in the building of a house, many might have participated, many hands making the burden light. (4) Even if there was one Designer, it does not follow that he is all-wise, for, again from Hume: "Many worlds might have been botched and bungled throughout an eternity, ere this system was struck out." Finally, (5) even if He is all wise, it does not follow that He is all good, for, like

Descartes' evil genius, His main intent might be to fool men into thinking there is a designer.

The ontological argument is accepted by both Descartes and Spinoza and a reference to their forms of presenting it on pages 33 and 180 might be useful at this point. However, two crucial points should be raised: (1) Can one have an idea of perfection as such? We might have an idea of a perfect tree or perfect man, but can we conceive of perfection without applying it to some object? (2) If we can, then does it follow that existence is a necessary part of perfection? Is an idea with a physical counterpart more or less perfect than an idea without one?

Finally, the cosmological argument must deal with these objections: (1) The argument is superfluous, for all we need to control nature is knowledge of the immediately preceding causes, not the whole chain of causation. (2) Knowledge of a cause and effect relationship is possible only when the two are experienced in conjunction, but since the First Cause, by definition, is said to exist prior to all experience, this requirement cannot be met. (3) Even if it could, there is no reason to believe that God's causation of the universe is similar to our own idea of causation, for this commits the fallacy of faulty analogy. (4) It is as reasonable to assume that causation has continued for an infinite length of time as it is to assume that God exists infinitely. (5) At best, the argument would prove that God is all powerful but would have nothing to say about His goodness or knowledge. And (6) the argument really is circular, for to say that "unmoved mover" is what is meant by "God," is to assume a meaning not justified by any other kind of evidence or definition.

For some, these arguments have merely proven provocative, for discussion of the proofs continues to be significant and meaningful; but for other people, the criticisms have been sufficient to show that reasoning cannot bring one to a knowledge of God. In this situation some who advocate the religious way of life fall back on Pascal's wager for justification. This is not a way to prove God's existence; it is a belief that we will benefit by believing that He exists. Pascal, a seventeenth-century mathematician and mystic, said the evidence to prove God's existence is not persuasive, but neither is the evidence to prove His nonexistence. However, even in the absence of evidence we still must choose whether to believe. Only two choices are open to us: to believe He exists or not to believe. We cannot be agnostic, waiting until there is more evidence before making our choice, for this is to say that as of now we choose not to believe. And there are only two alternatives which could be true: either God does exist or He does not. If we now combine the two possible beliefs and the two possibilities concerning God's existence, we have four alternatives. First, we can believe God exists and it might turn out that He does, in which case one would have both peace of mind in this life and eternal reward in the next. Second, we might believe He exists and He does not, in which case the peace of mind and sense of security given by the belief would not be diminished, even though there were no immortality. Third, we might believe He does not exist, and He might not, in which case you will have gained nothing in this life by your nonbelief, although you will have lost nothing in the next life either. Finally, we might believe He does not exist, and He does, in which case you can expect eternal punishment in the next life with nothing gained by your skepticism now. Therefore, even in the absence of evidence, you still are justified in believing that God exists, for you have everything to gain and nothing to lose.

Whether the wager is a satisfactory substitute—or supplement—to the other methods for gaining knowledge of God is a matter for you to consider, but you should remember that the conception of God implied by this wager is a relevant consideration. But quite apart from your response, perhaps we should remind ourselves of the insight of the *Bhagavad Gita* that all methods for gaining knowledge of God are justified as long as they are pursued with sincerity and oneness of purpose. Sense experience, mysticism, experience "at the edge of consciousness," and logical argument are the ones examined here, but there are others such as worship, reading the scriptures, work and service which might also be effective. The important thing is that one be seeking sincerely, trying to "fill thy heart with Me, be thou devoted to Me, do thou worship Me and bow down to Me. Thus thou shalt attain unto Me."

Let us close our discussion by stating the basic philosophical problem which underlies any method for gaining knowledge of God. Do we know God as He is, or only what we understand Him to be? The difference is important, for the first alternative entitles us to talk about reality; the second, only about our idea of reality. In Chapter Five, we mentioned some of the difficulties attending the claim that we know reality as it is: our experience might be partial, incomplete and distorted; our descriptions might be inaccurate; we are assuming that linguistic expression is similar to the world. In the case of our knowledge of God, all these problems are raised, plus the problem as to how a finite mind can comprehend an Infinite Being. However, if we choose the other alternative, claiming only that these methods give us our understanding of God, then we run the risk of anthropomorphism, making God conform to our image of Him.

This problem can be avoided by saying that all such rational analyses are beside the point since they are only the philosopher's way of trying to explain an inexplicable experience. This alternative is accepted by many who advocate the religious way of life, and it does avoid the issue. But the implication also should be clear: the religious way of life basically is mystical, neither requiring a defense nor offering a justification. Whether this alternative is preferable or whether any of the methods for knowing of God can meet the objections raised is a matter still open to further discussion.

III. RELIGIOUS METHOD

So we come to the last, and in some ways the most crucial, problem of the religious way of life: how do we gain reliable knowledge? When faced with this problem, the philosophical way says that careful analytical human reasoning is the best method, and to think philosophically means to look for careful definitions, adequate evidence, and the resulting implications. Do writers in the religious tradition share this confidence in human reasoning? Do they believe that man's unaided mind can arrive at Truth? In short, is reason competent?

Your readings have not included representatives from the Eastern religions on the point, but what you have read should be enough to point the direction of their answer. Buddha's Four Noble Truths are justified naturalistically, from a person's own experience and thought, not from the acceptance of an authority. Confucian teachings emphasize that moral guidance is to be found by consulting the nature of man. Lao-tse asks man to study nature to discover the rules for correct behavior. The Bhagavad-Gita tells man to use whatever methods are appropriate to his own background. If we might add to this, the Buddhist scripture, the Surangama Sutra, provides an interesting argument to prove that the mind is not inside the head. In short, for the Eastern religions, there is no supernaturalism and hence man's own abilities are the only source for gaining reliable knowledge. To many observers, eastern religious thought thus is indistinguishable from its philosophy.

Because the answer of the Eastern religions seemed relatively obvious, the reading selections dealt only with the Christian answer to the problem. In them, there were two representatives from the orthodox side of Christian thought, one Protestant and one Catholic, one representative from a theologically more moderate position, the

Society of Friends, and two from the liberal side, one Unitarian and the other an "agnostic Christian." What have they—and hence Christianity—said about the competence of human reasoning? Let us briefly recall their answers.

Calvin insists that "our reason is overwhelmed with deceptions in so many forms, is obnoxious to so many errors, stumbles at so many impediments, and is embarrassed in so many difficulties, that it is very far from being a certain guide." The reason for Calvin's despair is easy to discover, for he holds that Adam fell because of the sin of pride, a sin transmitted to his posterity, which makes men, when they use their reason, "conceive, desire, and undertake everything that is impious, perverse, base, impure and flagitious." Man's heart is "so thoroughly infected by the poison of sin, that it cannot produce anything but what is corrupt." Accordingly, if man is to achieve reliable knowledge, he must rely on a source greater than himself: God. This is God's world; hence man must allow His spirit to guide him in his search for truth.

Aquinas has a greater confidence in human reasoning, for he believes that unaided reasoning can prove not only the existence of God but His attributes and unity, and the existence, freedom, and immortality of the soul as well. Indeed, reason can even prove that reason cannot prove everything. First, all reasoning originates with sense experience, but we know our senses inform us of only a part of the object being viewed; hence we know there is more which could be known than is known. Second, experience demonstrates there are degrees of intellect, ranging from the yokel to the philosopher. Since everything we know exhibits this gradation, this is a reason for believing that degrees of intellect extend beyond this life also. Third, philosophers are the first to admit how little they know, but to know this, they must know there is more to be known than they now know. Fourth, if reasoning were the only way to know of God, most men would be excluded from this knowledge, for many of them cannot follow a philosophical argument; others, who can, do not have the time; and still others are lacking in inclination. Finally, there are some who are led to the wrong conclusions by contrary arguments. Since reason is thus limited, is fallible, not universally applicable and erroneous, it is better "that even things which reason is able to investigate must be held by faith; so that all may share in the knowledge of God easily, and without doubt or error." Reason is competent but only when guided by faith.

Fox teaches that the Spirit should guide man in all he does, whether it be in reading the scriptures, converting unbelievers, reforming the professions, or calling everyone by the familiar form, "thee" or "thou." What the spirit dictates might seem silly, perhaps illegal, to men guided by worldly wisdom, and the true believer must be willing to accept the consequences of their judgment. However, man's judgments are transitory and fleeting while God's wisdom is eternal, so what greater good can a man achieve than to "declare the Word of life and reconciliation freely that all might come to Christ"?

Channing says that Christianity is a rational religion in that it presupposes the use of reason to understand the Christian message, it is consistent both within itself and with the world of experience, and it is of universal application. Indeed, reason can tell that the doctrines of original sin and the Trinity are merely human additions to essential Christian principles. However, Channing conceives of reason, not as the originating source for knowledge, but as the propagating means, for he asks, "In what way is Christian revelation communicated?" and he insists that reason "proves the truth of revelation." Hence, while reason both understands and communicates religious ideas, all such ideas have their origin in revelation.

Finally, Schweitzer contends that Christianity is not a logical religion for it is both optimistic and pessimistic, monotheistic and polytheistic. It has not resolved the problem of evil: how God can be all powerful, as He is if He is the Creator of the universe, and all good, as the traditional view insists, and yet permit evil in the world, as there must be if Jesus is to redeem man. Nor has Christianity adequately dealt with the problem of freedom: how man can make choices, as he must if he is to be rewarded or punished, when he lives in a world created and governed by God.

But such problems really are beside the point. Christianity, in its origins, did not pretend to be a logical religion, nor is one who experiences the Christian message attracted by its logical cogency. To be a Christian is to "allow ourselves to be gripped by the Ethical God who reveals himself in us, and to yield our will to His." Theology, then, is a man-made addition to the Christian message, each age interpreting Christ in terms of its own presuppositions.

Do these spokesmen for different forms of Christian thought agree in their estimates of reason's competence? The answer of the most liberal author, Schweitzer, is remarkably similar to that of the most orthodox, Calvin. Both believe that reliable knowledge is obtained only when God enters man's soul to guide his thoughts. They do differ when reporting the content of that experience: Calvin emphasizes its redemptive features, Schweitzer, its compassion, but they agree that reason is inferior and hence must be subordinated to revelation. This conclusion also is accepted by Aquinas, Fox and Channing, in spite of their other differences.

Nor should this conclusion be surprising; it simply is an implication of the Christian view of life. The natural world, and everything in it, including man's reason, is only part of a larger reality, one created and governed by God. Accordingly, at best, man's reason can grasp a part of the whole; at worst, he grasps that inadequately. Reliable knowledge comes only when God reveals the larger view of reality to man, only as man can supplement his finitude with God's infinite wisdom.

Moreover, this conclusion helps to explain why we reached certain other conclusions. It explains why self-perfection as an ethical goal is difficult for human beings to achieve, being bound up in nature as they are, seeking but always failing to follow the admonition: "Be ye therefore perfect, even as your Father which is in heaven is perfect." It explains why moral rules are justified by an appeal to God's authority, since there is no more important source for knowledge in the universe. It explains why all metaphysical questions could be answered as deductions from the answer to one, for if we know of God, His attributes tell us of His creation. Reality, then, is more than nature; man is more than reason: only knowledge of the supernatural life, given by a supernatural being, can make the natural life understandable and meaningful.

This seems to be the ultimate ground on which the religious way of life rests its case: God reveals reliable knowledge to those who are part of His creation. But a philosopher seeing this conclusion would want to examine it more carefully, and he might want to argue something like this. Remember, there is a difference between the source and the content of knowledge, and while I am willing to admit your knowledge might have originated from a supernatural source, I would claim you understand only *your* own ideas of it. Your knowledge is *your* knowledge, and you have no way to get outside your own understanding to determine whether what you say are God's ideas really are His ideas.

This means, then, that your own claims are in a most precarious position. If you insist that your ideas are the same as God's ideas, you are putting your own understanding on a par with God's, thereby making yourself subject to the most grievous of all sins: pride. But worse still, you are saying God thinks as you do, and hence you are making Him in your image. If, on the other hand, you admit God's knowledge might be different from your understanding of it, you must abandon all claims to the certain belief that your knowledge is identical to God's, admitting even that it might possibly be mistaken. So, the religious position results either in pride, dogmatism, and anthropomorphism or uncertainty, tentativeness, and even the admission of error.

What would the advocate of a religious way of life say to this kind of criticism? He might want to examine the argument carefully, looking again at the reasons and conclusions given, to discover if and where errors in the analysis have occurred. But to approach it this way is to adopt the philosophical method of careful, analytical reasoning. More likely he would point out that the whole argument presupposes reason's competence, for the philosopher has assumed that his finite knowledge can explain adequately God's infinite wisdom, but that reason is unable to do so is the very foundation on which religious thought rests. Ultimately, the religious man probably would abandon the argument because he knows that the living experience of God's presence was sufficient ground to establish all beliefs, and he views with compassion, as did William Blake, in his "The Scoffers," those who have not yet received the blessedness which comes from such knowledge.

> Mock on, mock on; Voltaire, Rousseau.
> Mock on, mock on; 'tis all in vain;
> You throw but dust against the wind
> And the wind blows it back again.
>
> And every stone becomes a gem
> Reflected in the beams divine;
> Blown back, they blind the mocking eye,
> But still in Israel's paths they shine.
>
> The atoms of Democritus
> And Newton's particles of light
> Are sands upon the Red sea shore,
> Where Israel's tents do shine so bright.

IV. RELIGION AS A WAY OF LIFE

A final paragraph will complete our discussion. What kind of person would one be if his attitude toward life were dominately religious? In the first place, he probably would be concerned with his own purpose in life and with the deeper problems of human existence. Secondly, he would understand these problems in a broader perspective than their natural characteristics and would tend to see temporal problems in terms of infinity, daily activities in terms of eternal purposes. Third, he would have considerable concern for his relationships with other people, he would take the notion of compassion seriously, and he would place obedience to God's commandments above social approval or personal advantage. Finally, if he were confronted by those who are philosophically inclined, those who insist on analyzing, examining and arguing, he probably would be irritated at first, but soon would view them with compassion because he would know that they were doing the best they could, being limited as they were by their finite and fallible methods of human reasoning.

QUESTIONS FOR DISCUSSION

1. Do you believe that religious moral theories are superior or inferior to the philosophical theories we considered? Which kind of theory has had the most influence on people? On you?
2. Analyze Pascal's wager. What presuppositions does it make regarding the nature of God?
3. Consider the validity of this argument: Religion is either a branch of philosophy or else it is incomprehensible, for regardless of the origins of the claims of knowledge, either they must be expressed in language and in terms of reasons and conclusions, which makes them subject to philosophical investigation, or else they are not expressed in language with reasons and conclusions, in which case they cannot be understood.

READINGS FOR IMMEDIATE REFERENCE

Freud, Sigmund. *The Future of an Illusion*. New York: Anchor Books, 1951.

Gibran, Kahlil. *The Prophet*. New York: Harper, 1933.

REFERENCES FOR COMPREHENSIVE KNOWLEDGE

Burtt, E. A. *Types of Religious Philosophy*, rev. ed. New York: Harper, 1951. A standard text on the history and nature of Christian thought.

Noss, J. B. *Man's Religions*, rev. ed. New York: Macmillan, 1956. An historical account and philosophical analysis of the world's leading religions. A standard text.

Also see:

Burtt, E. A. *Man Seeks the Divine*. New York: Harper, 1957.

Huxley, Aldous. *The Perennial Philosophy*. New York: Harper, 1945.

Russell, Bertrand. *Why I am Not a Christian*. New York: Simon and Schuster, 1957.

Smith, Huston. *Man's Religions*. New York: Harper, 1958.

White, Andrew D. *A History of the Warfare Between Science and Theology*. New York: Appleton, 1896.

SCIENCE

Chapter Ten

SCIENTIFIC METHOD

1. MORRIS R. COHEN AND ERNEST NAGEL

Morris Cohen, born in Russia in 1880, was brought to the United States when he was twelve years old. He grew to manhood in New York City's East Side where his father was a tailor. He attended City College and received his doctorate from Harvard University in 1906 where he studied with Royce, James, Santayana, and Perry. He returned to the City College of New York to teach mathematics and philosophy until his retirement in 1938. He achieved considerable fame as a teacher, and his erudition, dialectical skill, and philosophical interest in subjects outside technical philosophy made him widely respected, both in America and abroad. His contributions to the philosophy of law are particularly noteworthy. He died in 1947.

Ernest Nagel was born in Czechoslovakia in 1901. He came to America as a youth and attended City College, from which he graduated in 1923, having studied with Cohen. He received his doctorate from Columbia in 1930 and joined the faculty the following year. There he has remained—teaching, writing, lecturing, and editing *The Journal of Philosophy* and *The Journal of Symbolic Logic*. His main interests have been in the philosophy of science. In 1954 he was elected president of the American Philosophical Association.

This selection consists of an example of scientific reasoning from the Greeks, and an account of the principles which characterize scientific method. Note them carefully, making certain you understand why each element is mentioned by the authors, for in the second and third selections you will be asked to look for similarities; and in the fourth you will be asked to evaluate how satisfactorily certain experiments meet the standards for competent scientific inquiry.

Logic and Scientific Method[1]

In the second book of his fascinating *History*, Herodotus recounts the sights that met him on his travels to Egypt. The river Nile aroused his attention:

Now the Nile, when it overflows, floods not only the Delta, but also the tracts of country on both sides of the stream which are thought to belong to Libya and Arabia, in some places reaching to the extent of two days' journey from its banks, in some even exceeding that distance, but in others falling short of it.

Concerning the nature of the river, I was not able to gain any information either from the priests or from others. I was particularly anxious to learn from them why the Nile, at the commencement of the summer solstice, begins to rise, and continues to increase for a hundred days—and why, as soon as that number is past, it forthwith retires and contracts its stream, continuing low during the whole of the winter until the summer solstice comes around again. On none of these points could I obtain any explanation from the inhabitants, though I made every inquiry, wishing to know what was commonly reported—they could neither tell me what special virtue the Nile has which makes it so opposite in its nature to all other streams, nor why, unlike every other river, it gives forth no breezes from its surface.

Some of the Greeks, however, wishing to get a reputation for cleverness, have offered explanations of the phenomena of the river, for which they have accounted in three different ways. Two of these I do not think it worth-while to speak of, further than simply to mention what they are. One pretends that the Etesian winds [the northwest winds blowing from the Mediterranean] cause the rise of the river by preventing the Nile-water from running off into the sea. But in the first place it has often happened, when the Etesian winds did not blow, that the Nile has risen according to its usual wont; and further, if the Etesian winds produced the effect, the other rivers which flow in a direction opposite to those winds ought to present the same phenomena as the Nile, and the more so as they are all smaller streams, and have a weaker current. But these rivers, of which there are many both in Syria and in Libya, are entirely unlike the Nile in this respect.

The second opinion is even more unscientific than the one just mentioned, and also, if I may so say, more marvellous. It is that the Nile acts so strangely because it flows from the ocean, and that the ocean flows all round the earth.

The third explanation, which is very much more plausible than either of the others, is positively the furthest from the truth; for there is really nothing in what it says, any more than in the other theories. It is, that the inundation of the Nile is caused by the melting of snows. Now, as the Nile flows out of Libya [Central Africa], through Ethiopia, into Egypt, how is it possible that it can be formed of melted snow, running, as it does, from the hottest regions of the world into cooler countries? Many are the proofs whereby anyone capable of reasoning on the subject may be convinced that it is most unlikely this should be the case. The first and strongest argument is furnished by the winds, which always blow hot from these regions. The second is,

[1] From *An Introduction to Logic and Scientific Method* by Morris R. Cohen and Ernest Nagel, copyright, 1934, by Harcourt, Brace and World. Inc., Chapters 11, 20. Reprinted by permission.

that rain and frost are unknown there. Now, whenever snow falls, it must of necessity rain within five days; so that, if there were snow, there must be rain also in those parts. Thirdly, it is certain that the natives of the country are black with the heat, that the kites and the swallows remain there the whole year, and that the cranes, when they fly from the rigors of a Scythian winter, flock thither to pass the cold season. If then, in the country whence the Nile has its source, or in that through which it flows, there fell ever so little snow, it is absolutely impossible that any of these circumstances could take place. . . .

This excerpt from Herodotus illustrates clearly the Greek zest for scientific knowledge and speculation. But it also illustrates the great difference between the habit of simple acceptance of apparently stray, disconnected information, and the attitude that searches for some order in facts which are only superficially isolated. The observable inundation of the Nile was to many a brute fact, unconnected with other familiar but isolated facts. For Herodotus, however, the behavior of the Nile was not simply a brute fact. It presented a *problem* that could be resolved only by finding some general *connection* between the periodic inundation of the Nile and *other* facts.

It is an utterly superficial view, therefore, that the truth is to be found by "studying the facts." It is superficial because no inquiry can even get under way until and unless *some difficulty is felt* in a practical or theoretical situation. It is the difficulty, or problem, which guides our search for some *order among the facts,* in terms of which the difficulty is to be removed. We could not possibly discover the *reasons* for the inundation of the Nile unless we first recognized in the inundation a *problem* demanding solution.

If some problem is the occasion for inquiry, the *solution* of the problem is the goal and function of the inquiry. What constitutes a satisfactory solution of a problem, and in particular of the problem: Why does the Nile overflow its banks? The sort of answer for which Herodotus was looking was the discovery of a connection between the fact of the Nile's behavior and *other* facts; in virtue of that connection, apparently isolated facts would be seen to be *ordered* facts. And in general, scientific investigations must begin with some problem, and aim at an order connecting what at first sight may seem unrelated facts. But the ability to perceive in some brute experience the occasion for a problem, and especially a problem *whose solution has a bearing on the solution of other problems,* is not a common talent among men. For no rule can be given by means of which men can learn to ask significant questions. It is a mark of scientific genius to be sensitive to difficulties where less gifted people pass by untroubled with doubt.

* * * * *

The method of science does not seek to impose the desires and hopes of men upon the flux of things in a capricious manner. It may indeed be employed to satisfy the desires of men. But its successful use depends upon seeking, in a deliberate manner, and irrespective of what men's desires are, to recognize, as well as to take advantage of, the structure which the flux possesses.

1. Consequently, scientific method aims to discover what the facts truly are, and the use of the method must be guided by the discovered facts. But, as we have repeatedly pointed out, what the facts are cannot be discovered without reflection. Knowledge of the facts cannot be equated to the brute immediacy of our sensations. When our skin comes into contact with objects having high temperatures or with liquid air, the immediate experiences may be similar. We cannot, however, conclude without error that the temperatures of the substances touched are the same. Sensory experience sets the *problem* for knowledge, and just because such experience is immediate and final it must become informed by reflective analysis before knowledge can be said to take place.

2. Every inquiry arises from some felt problem, so that no inquiry can even get under way unless some selection or sifting of the subject matter has taken place. Such selection requires, we have been urging all along, some hypothesis, preconception, prejudice, which guides the research as well as delimits the subject matter of inquiry. Every inquiry is specific in the sense that it has a definite problem to solve, and such solution terminates the inquiry. It is idle to collect "facts" unless there is a problem upon which they are supposed to bear.

3. The ability to formulate problems whose solution may also help solve other problems is a rare gift, requiring extraordinary genius. The problems which meet us in daily life can be solved, if they can be solved at all, by the application of scientific method. But such problems do not, as a rule, raise far-reaching issues. The most striking applications of scientific method are to be found in the various natural and social sciences.

4. The "facts" for which every inquiry reaches out are propositions for whose truth there is considerable evidence. Consequently what the "facts" are must be determined by inquiry, and cannot be determined antecedently to inquiry. Moreover, what we believe to be the facts clearly depends upon the stage of our inquiry. There is therefore no sharp line dividing facts from guesses or hypotheses. During any inquiry the status of a proposition may change from that of hypothesis to that of fact, or from that of fact to that of hypothesis. Every so-called fact, therefore, *may* be challenged for the evidence upon which it is asserted to be a fact, even though no such challenge is actually made.

Hypotheses and Scientific Method. The method of science would be impossible if the hypotheses which are suggested as solutions could not be elaborated to reveal what they imply. The full meaning of a hypothesis is to be discovered in its implications.

1. Hypotheses are suggested to an inquirer by something in the subject matter under investigation, and by his previous knowledge of other subject matters. No rules can be offered for obtaining fruitful hypotheses, any more than rules can be given for discovering significant problems.

2. Hypotheses are required at every stage of an inquiry. It must not be forgotten that what are called general prin-

ciples or laws (which may have been confirmed in a previous inquiry) can be applied to a present, still unterminated inquiry only with some risk. For they may not in fact be applicable. The general laws of any science function as hypotheses, which guide the inquiry in all its phases.

3. Hypotheses can be regarded as suggestions of possible connections between actual facts or imagined ones. The question of the truth of hypotheses need not, therefore, always be raised. The necessary feature of a hypothesis, from this point of view, is that it should be statable in a determinate form, so that its implications can be discovered by logical means.

4. The number of hypotheses which may occur to an inquirer is without limit, and is a function of the character of his imagination. There is a need, therefore, for a technique to choose between the alternative suggestions, and to make sure that the alternatives are in fact, and not only in appearance, *different* theories. Perhaps the most important and best explored part of such a technique is the technique of formal inference. For this reason, the structure of formal logic has been examined at some length. The object of that examination has been to give the reader an adequate sense of what formal validity means, as well as to provide him with a synoptic view of the power and range of formal logic.

5. It is convenient to have on hand—in storage, so to speak—different hypotheses whose consequences have been carefully explored. It is the task of mathematics to provide and explore alternative hypotheses. Mathematics receives hints concerning what hypotheses to study from the natural sciences; and the natural sciences are indebted to mathematics for suggestions concerning the type of order which their subject matter embodies.

6. The deductive elaboration of hypotheses is not the sole task of scientific method. Since there is a plurality of possible hypotheses, it is the task of inquiry to determine which of the possible explanations or solutions of the problem is in best agreement with the facts. Formal considerations are therefore never sufficient to establish the material truth of any theory.

7. No hypothesis which states a general proposition can be demonstrated as absolutely true. We have seen that all inquiry which deals with matters of fact employs probable inference. The task of such investigations is to select that hypothesis which is the most probable on the factual evidence; and it is the task of further inquiry to find other factual evidence which will increase or decrease the probability of such a theory.

Evidence and Scientific Method. Scientific method pursues the road of systematic doubt. It does not doubt *all* things, for this is clearly impossible. But it does question whatever lacks adequate evidence in its support.

1. Science is not satisfied with psychological certitude, for the mere intensity with which a belief is held is no guarantee of its truth. Science demands and looks for logically adequate grounds for the propositions it advances.

2. No single proposition dealing with matters of fact is beyond every signifi-

cant doubt. No proposition is so well supported by evidence that other evidence may not increase or decrease its probability. However, while no single proposition is indubitable, the body of knowledge which supports it, and of which it is itself a part, is better grounded than any alternative body of knowledge.

3. Science is thus always ready to abandon a theory when the facts so demand. But the facts must really demand it. It is not unusual for a theory to be modified so that it may be retained in substance even though "facts" contradicted an earlier formulation of it. Scientific procedure is therefore a mixture of a willingness to change, and an obstinacy in holding on to, theories apparently incompatible with facts.

4. The verification of theories is only approximate. Verification simply shows that, within the margin of experimental error, the experiment is *compatible* with the verified hypothesis.

System in The Ideal of Science. The ideal of science is to achieve a systematic interconnection of facts. Isolated propositions do not constitute a science. Such propositions serve merely as an opportunity to find the logical connection between them and other propositions.

1. "Common sense" is content with a miscellaneous collection of information. As a consequence, the propositions it asserts are frequently vague, the range of their application is unknown, and their mutual compatibility is generally very questionable. The advantages of discovering a system among facts is therefore obvious. A condition for achieving a system is the introduction of accuracy in the assertions made. The limit within which propositions are true is then clearly defined. Moreover, inconsistencies between propositions asserted become eliminated gradually because propositions which are part of a system must support and correct one another. The extent and accuracy of our information is thus increased. In fact, scientific method differs from other methods in the accuracy and number of facts it studies.

2. When, as frequently happens, a science abandons one theory for another, it is a mistake to suppose that science has become "bankrupt" and that it is incapable of discovering the structure of the subject matter it studies. Such changes indicate rather that the science is progressively realizing its ideal. For such changes arise from correcting previous observations or reasoning, and such correction means that we are in possession of more reliable facts.

3. The ideal of system requires that the propositions asserted to be true should be connected without the introduction of further propositions for which the evidence is small or nonexistent. In a system the number of unconnected propositions and the number of propositions for which there is no evidence are at a minimum. Consequently, in a system the requirements of simplicity, as expressed in the principle of Occam's razor, are satisfied in a high degree. For that principle declares that entities should not be multiplied beyond necessity. This may be interpreted as a demand that whatever is capable of proof

should be proved. But the ideal of system requires just that.

4. The evidence for propositions which are elements in a system accumulates more rapidly than that for isolated propositions. The evidence for a proposition may come from its own verifying instances, or from the verifying instances of *other* propositions which are connected with the first in a system. It is this systematic character of scientific theories which gives such high probabilities to the various individual propositions of a science.

The Self-Corrective Nature of Scientific Method. Science does not desire to obtain conviction for its propositions in *any* manner and at *any* price. Propositions must be supported by logically acceptable evidence, which must be weighed carefully and tested by the well-known canons of necessary and probable inference. It follows that the *method* of science is more stable, and more important to men of science, than any particular result achieved by its means.

1. In virtue of its method, the enterprise of science is a self-corrective process. It appeals to no special revelation or authority whose deliverances are indubitable and final. It claims no infallibility, but relies upon the methods of developing and testing hypotheses for assured conclusions. The canons of inquiry are themselves discovered in the process of reflection, and may themselves become modified in the course of study. The method makes possible the noting and correction of errors by continued application of itself.

2. General propositions can be established only by the method of repeated sampling. Consequently, the propositions which a science puts forward for study are either confirmed in all possible experiments or modified in accordance with the evidence. It is this self-corrective nature of the method which allows us to challenge any proposition, but which also assures us that the theories which science accepts are more probable than any alternative theories. By not claiming more certainty than the evidence warrants, scientific method succeeds in obtaining more logical certainty than any other method yet devised.

3. In the process of gathering and weighing evidence, there is a continuous appeal from facts to theories or principles, and from principles to facts. For there is nothing intrinsically indubitable, there are no absolutely first principles, in the sense of principles which are self-evident or which must be known prior to everything else.

4. The method of science is thus essentially circular. We obtain evidence for principles by appealing to empirical material, to what is alleged to be "fact"; and we select, analyze, and interpret empirical material on the basis of principles. In virtue of such give and take between facts and principles, everything that is dubitable falls under careful scrutiny at one time or another.

* * * * *

On the whole it may be said that the safety of science depends on there being men who care more for the justice of their methods than for any results obtained by their use. For this reason it is unfortunate when scientific research in the social field is largely in the hands of those not in a favorable position to oppose established or popular opinion.

We may put it the other way by saying that the physical sciences can be more liberal because we are sure that foolish opinions will be readily eliminated by the shock of facts. In the social field, however, no one can tell what harm may come of foolish ideas before the foolishness is finally, if ever, demonstrated. None of the precautions of scientific method can prevent human life from being an adventure, and no scientific investigator knows whether he will reach his goal. But scientific method does enable large numbers to walk with surer step. By analyzing the possibilities of any step or plan, it becomes possible to anticipate the future and adjust ourselves to it in advance. Scientific method thus minimizes the shock of novelty and the uncertainty of life. It enables us to frame policies of action and of moral judgment fit for a wider outlook than those of immediate physical stimulus or organic response.

Scientific method is the only effective way of strengthening the love of truth. It develops the intellectual courage to face difficulties and to overcome illusions that are pleasant temporarily but destructive ultimately. It settles differences without any external force by appealing to our common rational nature. The way of science, even if it is up a steep mountain, is open to all. Hence, while sectarian and partisan faiths are based on personal choice or temperament and divide men, scientific procedure unites men in something nobly devoid of all pettiness. Because it requires detachment, disinterestedness, it is the finest flower and test of a liberal civilization.

QUESTIONS FOR DISCUSSION

1. Can you give a scientific explanation for the reason why Herodotus was mistaken in rejecting the third alternative? If you were to follow the authors' account of the scientific method, how would you go about explaining the phenomenon of the Nile's rise?
2. Look again at the selections from Dewey (p. 104) and Peirce (p. 151). Do you notice many similarities between them and this selection? Is scientific method the same as philosophical method? The same as the religious advocates' method?
3. Why do the authors say scientific method "is the finest flower and test of a liberal civilization"? Do you agree? Is it the best method for obtaining reliable knowledge?

READINGS FOR IMMEDIATE REFERENCE

Cohen, Morris and Nagel, Ernest. *An Introduction to Logic and Scientific Method.* New York: Harcourt, Brace, 1934, Chapters 13, 14, 17, 20.

Beardsley, Monroe C. *Practical Logic*. New York: Prentice-Hall, 1950, Chapters 12-15.

Conant, James B. *Science and Common Sense*. New Haven: Yale University Press, 1951, Chapter 3.

REFERENCES FOR COMPREHENSIVE KNOWLEDGE

Bacon, Francis. *Novum Organum,* Parts I and II. Scientific method as understood by one of its sixteenth-century founders.

Mill, John Stuart. *A System of Logic*. London, 1867. Books III and IV concentrate on the problem of induction.

Also see:

Black, Max. *Critical Thinking,* rev. ed. New York: Prentice-Hall, 1952.

Campbell, Norman. *What is Science?* New York: Dover, 1952.

Larrabee, H. A. *Reliable Knowledge*. Boston: Houghton Mifflin, 1945.

Poincaré, Henri. *Science and Hypothesis*. London: Walter Scott, 1905.

II. P. W. BRIDGMAN

Bridgman was born in Cambridge, Massachusetts, in 1882, and was educated there, receiving his Ph.D. from Harvard in 1908. He joined the Harvard faculty the same year, becoming Hollis Professor of Mathematics and Natural Philosophy in 1926 and Higgins University Professor in 1950. His main interest was in the thermodynamic behavior of materials at high pressure, and he was awarded the Nobel Prize in Physics in 1946 for his investigations. In addition, he wrote extensively on the philosophy and implications of science; his most popular book was *The Logic of Modern Physics,* from which the following selection is taken. He died in 1961.

In this article, Bridgman discusses four concepts: the nature of empirical knowledge; what constitutes an "explanation"; the function of models in scientific investigation; and the purpose and reliability of mathematics. As you read, look for the information which he conveys on these topics, but also determine whether he believes that the scientific method involves the same procedures that Cohen and Nagel describe.

Mathematics, Explanations, and Scientific Method[1]

Although many aspects of the processes by which we obtain knowledge of the external physical world are much beyond the scope of our present inquiry, one matter must be mentioned in detail because it tacitly underlies all our discussion, the fact, namely, that all results of measurement are only approximate. That such is true is evident after the most superficial examination of any measuring process; any statement about numerical relations between measured quantities must always be subject to the qualification that the relation is valid only within limits. Furthermore, all experience seems to be of this character; we never have perfectly clean-cut knowledge of anything, but all our experience is surrounded by a twilight zone, a penumbra of uncertainty, into which we have not yet penetrated. This penumbra is as truly an unexplored

[1] Reprinted with permission of the publisher from *The Logic of Modern Physics* by P. W. Bridgman. Copyright 1927 by The Macmillan Company, Chapter II.

region as any other region beyond experiment, such as the region of high velocities, for example, and we must hold no preconceived notions as to what will be found within the region. The penumbra is to be penetrated by improving the accuracy of measurement. Within what was at one time penumbra has been found the displacement of angular position of the stars near the edge of the solar disc, and within the penumbra as yet unpenetrated we look for such effects as the equivalence of mass and energy. Many of the great discoveries of the future will probably be made within the penumbra: we have already mentioned that increased knowledge of phenomena of a cosmic scale is to be obtained by increasing the accuracy of measurement of the very small.

It is a general consequence of the approximate character of all measurement that no empirical science can ever make exact statements. This was fairly obvious in the case of mechanics, but it required a Gauss[1] to convince us that the geometry in which we are interested as physicists is an empirical subject, and that one cannot say that actual space is Euclidean, but only that actual space approaches to ideal Euclidean space within a certain degree of approximation. I believe that we are compelled to go still further, and recognize that arithmetic, so far as it purports to deal with actual physical objects, is also affected with the same penumbra of uncertainty as all other empirical science. A typical statement of empirical arithmetic is that 2 objects plus 2 objects makes 4 objects. This statement acquires physical meaning only in terms of certain physical operations, and these operations must be performed in time. Now the penumbra gets into this situation through the concept of object. If the statement of arithmetic is to be an exact statement in the mathematical sense the "object" must be a definite clean-cut thing, which preserves its identity in time with no penumbra. But this sort of thing is never experienced, and as far as we know does not correspond exactly to anything in experience. If our objects are tumblers of water, we discover when our observation reaches a certain stage of refinement that the amount of water is continually changing by evaporation and condensation, and we are bothered by the question whether the object is still the same after it has waxed and waned. Coming to solids, we eventually discover that even solids evaporate, or condense gases on them, and we see that an object with identity is an abstraction corresponding exactly to nothing in nature. Of course the penumbra of uncertainty which surrounds our arithmetical statements because of this property of physical objects is so exceedingly tenuous that practically we are not aware of its existence, and expect never to find undiscovered phenomena within the penumbra. But in principle we must recognize its presence, and must further recognize that *all* empirical science must be of this character. . . .

Perhaps the climax of our task of interpreting and correlating nature is reached when we are able to find an explanation of phenomena; with the

[1] C. F. Gauss, *Gesammelte Werke,* especially vols. IV and VIII.

finding of the explanation we are inclined to feel that our understanding of the situation is complete. We now have to ask what is the nature of the explanation which we set as the goal of our efforts. The answer is not easy to give, and there may be difference of opinion about it. We shall get the best answer to this, as to so many other questions, by adopting the operational point of view, and examining what we do in giving an explanation. I believe that examination will show that the essence of an explanation consists in reducing a situation to elements with which we are so familiar that we accept them as a matter of course, so that our curiosity rests.[1] "Reducing a situation to elements" means, from the operational point of view, discovering familiar correlations between the phenomena of which the situation is composed. . . .

In this view of explanation there is no implication that the "element" is either a smaller or a larger scale thing than the phenomenon being explained; thus we may explain the properties of a gas in terms of its constituent molecules, or perhaps some day we shall become so familiar with the idea of a non-Euclidean space that we shall *explain* (instead of describe) the gravitational attraction of a stone by the earth in terms of a space-time curvature imposed by all the rest of the matter in the universe.

If this is accepted as the true nature of explanation, we see that an explanation is not an absolute sort of thing, but what is satisfactory for one man will not be for another. The savage is satisfied by explaining the thunderstorm as the capricious act of an angry god. The physicist demands more and requires that the familiar elements to which we reduce a situation be such that we can intuitively predict their behavior. Thus even if the physicist believed in the existence of the angry god, he would not be satisfied with this explanation of the thunderstorm because he is not so well acquainted with angry gods as to be able to predict when anger is followed by a storm. He would have to know why the god had become angry and why making a thunderstorm eased his ire. But even with this additional qualification, scientific explanation is obviously still a relative affair—relative to the elements or axioms to which we make reduction and which we accept as ultimate. These elements depend to a certain extent on the purpose in view, and also on the range of our previous physical experience. If we are explaining the action of a machine, we are satisfied to reduce the action to the push and pull of the various members of the machine, it being accepted as an ultimate that these members transmit pushes or pulls. But the physicist who has extended his experimental knowledge further, may want to explain how the members transmit pushes or pulls in terms of the action on each other of the electrons in their orbits in the atoms. The character of our explanatory structure will depend on the character of our experimental knowledge, and will change as this changes.

Formally, there is no limit to the process of explanation, because we can

[1] The ultimate elements of explanation are analogous to the axioms of formal mathematics.

always ask what is the explanation of the elements in terms of which we have given the last explanation. But the point of view of operations shows that this is mere formalism which ends only in meaningless jargon, for we soon arrive at the limit of our experimental knowledge, and beyond this the operations involved in the concepts of our explanations become impossible and the concepts become meaningless.

As we extend experimental knowledge and push our explanations further and further, we see that the explanatory sequence may be terminated in several possible ways. In the first place, we may never push our experiments beyond a stage into which the elements with which we are already familiar do not enter. In this case explanation is very simple: it involves nothing essentially new, but merely the disentanglement of complexities. The kinetic theory of gases, in explaining the thermal properties of a gas in terms of ordinary mechanical properties of the molecules, suggests such a situation. Or, secondly, our experiments may bring us into contact with situations novel to us, in which we can recognize no familiar elements, or at least must recognize that there is something in addition to the familiar elements. Such a situation constitutes an explanatory crisis and explanation has to stop by definition. Or thirdly, we may try to force our explanations into a predetermined mold, by formally erecting or inventing beyond the range of present experiment ultimates more or less like elements already familiar to us, and seek to explain all present experience in terms of these chosen ultimates.

Leaving for the present the third possibility, which is within our control to accept or reject, and is a formal matter, it is merely a question of experimental fact which of the first two possibilities corresponds to the actual state of affairs. The most perfunctory examination of the present state of physics shows that we are now facing the second of these possibilities, and that in the new experimental facts of relativity, and in all quantum phenomena, we are confronted with an explanatory crisis. It has often been emphasized that Einstein's theory of gravitation does not seek at all to give an explanation of gravitational phenomena, but merely describes and correlates these phenomena in comparatively simple mathematical language. No more attempt is made to reduce the gravitational attraction between the earth and the sun to simple terms than was made by Newton. In the realm of quantum phenomena it is of course the merest commonplace that our old ideas of mechanics and electrodynamics have failed, so that it is a matter of the greatest concern to find how many, or indeed whether any, elements of the old situations can be carried over into the new.

An examination of many of the so-called "explanations" of quantum theory constitutes at once a justification of the definition of explanation given above, and of the statement that in quantum phenomena we are at an explanatory crisis. For the endeavor of all these quantum explanations is to find in every new or more complicated situation the same elements which have already been met in simpler situations, and which are therefore relatively more familiar. For example, many quantum phenomena are made to involve the emission of energy when an electron jumps from one orbit to another. But always the elements to which reduction is made are themselves quantum phenomena, and these are still so new and unfamiliar that we feel an instinctive need for explanation in other terms. We seek to understand why the electron emits energy when it jumps.

The explanatory crisis which now confronts us in relativity and quantum phenomena is but a repetition of what has occurred many times in the past. A similiar crisis confronted Prometheus when he discovered fire, and the first man who observed a straw sticking to a piece of rubbed amber, or a suspended lodestone seeking the north star. Every kitten is confronted with such a crisis at the end of nine days. Whenever experience takes us into new and unfamiliar realms, we are to be at least prepared for a new crisis.

Now what are we to do in such a crisis? It seems to me that the only sensible course is to do exactly what the kitten does, namely, to wait until we have amassed so much experience of the new kind that it is perfectly familiar to us, and then to resume the process of explanation with elements from our new experience included in our list of axioms. Not only will observation show that this is what is now actually being done with respect to quantum and gravitational phenomena, but it is in harmony with the entire spirit of our outlook on nature. All our knowledge is in terms of experience; we should not expect or desire to erect an explanatory structure different in character from that of experience. Our experience is finite; on the confines of the experimentally attainable it becomes hazy, and the concepts in terms of which we describe it fuse together and lose independent meaning. Furthermore, at every extension of our experimental range we must be prepared to find, and as a matter of fact we have often found, that we encounter phenomena of an entirely novel character for which previous experience has given us no preparation. The explanatory structure proposed above has all these properties; it is finite, being terminated by the edge of experiment, the final stages of our explanations are hazy in that it becomes more and more difficult to distinguish elements of familiar experience, and every now and then we must admit new elements into our explanations.

* * * * *

When one thinks of an atom as a thing with any geometrical properties at all, I believe he will find that what he essentially does is to imagine a model, multiplying all the hypothetical dimensions by a factor large enough to bring it to a magnitude of ordinary experience. This large scale model is given properties corresponding to those of the physical thing. For example, the model of the atom which was accepted in the fall of 1925 contains electrons rotating in orbits, and every now and then an electron jumps from one orbit to another, and simultaneously energy is radiated from the atom. Such a model is satisfactory if it offers the counterpart of all the phenomena of the original atom. Now I believe the only meaning that any one can find in his statement that the space of the atom is Euclidean is that he believes that he can construct in Euclidean space a model with all the observed properties of the atom. This possibility may or may not be sufficient to give real physical significance to the statement that the space of the atom is Euclidean. The situation here is very much the same as it was with respect to mechanisms. The model may have many more properties than correspond to measurable properties of the atom, and in particular, the operations by which the space of the model is tested for its Euclidean character may (and as a matter of fact I believe *do*) not have any counterpart in operations which can be carried out on the atom. Further, we cannot attach any *real* significance to the statement that the space of the atom is Euclidean unless we can show that no model constructed in non-Euclidean space can reproduce the measurable properties of the atom.

In spite of all this, I believe that the model is a useful and indeed unescapable tool of thought, in that it enables us to think about the unfamiliar in terms of the familiar. There are, however, dangers in its use: it is the function of criticism to disclose these dangers, so that the tool may be used with confidence.

Closely related to the mental model are mental constructs, of which physics is full. There are many sorts of constructs: those in which we are interested are made by us to enable us to deal with physical situations which we cannot directly experience through our senses, but with which we have contact indirectly and by inference. Such constructs usually involve the element of invention to a greater or less degree. A construct containing very little of invention is that of the inside of an opaque solid body. We can never experience directly through our senses the inside of such a solid body, because the instant we directly experience it, it ceases by definition to be the inside. We have here a construct, but so natural a one as to be practically unavoidable. An example of a construct involving a greater amount of invention is the stress in an elastic body. A stress is by definition a property of the interior points of a body which is connected mathematically in a simple way with the forces acting across the free surface of the body. A stress is then, by its very nature, forever beyond the reach of direct experience, and it is therefore a construct. The entire structure of a stress corresponds to nothing in direct experience; it is related to force, but is itself a six-fold magnitude, whereas a force is only three-fold. . . .

But we have every reason to be satisfied with our construct of stress. In the first place, from the formal point of view, it is a good construct because there is a unique correspondence between it and the physical data in terms of which it is defined; and in the second place we have a right to ascribe physical reality to it because it is uniquely connected with other physical phenomena, *independent of those which entered its definition.* This last requirement, in fact, from the operational point of view, amounts to nothing more than a definition of what we mean by the reality of things not given directly by experience. Since now in addition to satisfying the formal requirements, experience shows that a stress is most useful in correlating phenomena, we are justified in giving to this construct of stress a prominent place among our concepts. . . .

Another indispensable and most interesting construct is that of the atom. This is evidently a construct, because no one ever directly experienced an atom, and its existence is entirely inferential. The atom was invented to explain constant combining weights in chemistry. For a long time there was no other experimental evidence of its existence, and it remained a pure invention, without physical reality, useful in discussing a certain group of phenomena. It is one of the most fascinating things in physics to trace the accumulation of independent new physical information all pointing to the atom, until now we are as convinced of its physical reality as of our hands and feet.

A construct which had to be abandoned because it did not turn out to have physical reality, and which furthermore was not sufficiently useful in the light of newly discovered phenomena, was that of a caloric fluid. . . .

The moral of all this is that constructs are most useful and even unavoidable things, but that they may have great dangers, and that a careful critique may be necessary to avoid reading into them implications for which there is no warrant in experience, and which may most profoundly affect our physical outlook and course of action.

Practically all the formulations of theoretical physics are made in mathematical terms; in fact to obtain such formulations is generally felt to be the goal of theoretical physics. It is then evidently pertinent to consider what the nature of the mathematics is to which we assign so prominent a rôle.

We have in the first place to understand why it is possible to express physical relations in mathematical language at all. I am not sure that there is much meaning in this question. It is the merest truism, evident at once to unsophisticated observation, that mathematics is a human invention. Furthermore, the mathematics in which the physicist is interested was developed for the explicit purpose of describing the behavior of the external world, so that it is certainly no accident that there is a correspondence between mathematics and nature. The correspondence is not by any means perfect, however, but there is always in mathematics a precise quality to which none of our information about nature ever attains. The theorems of Euclid's geometry illustrate this in a preeminent degree. The statement that there is just one straight line between two points and that this is the shortest possible path between the points is entirely different in character from any information ever given by physical measurement, for all our measurements are subject to error. It is possible, nevertheless, to give a certain real physical meaning to the ideally precise statements of geometry, because it is a result of everyday experience that as we refine the accuracy of our physical measurements the quantitative statements of geometry are verified within an ever-decreasing margin of error. From this arises that view of the nature of mathematics which apparently is most commonly held; namely that if we could eliminate the imperfections of our measurements, the relations of mathematics would be exactly verified. Abstract mathematical principles are supposed to be active in nature, controlling natural phenomena, as Pythagoras long ago tried to express with his harmony of the spheres and the mystic relations of numbers.

This idealized view of the connection of mathematics with nature could be maintained only during that historical period when the accuracy of physical measurement was low, and must now be abandoned. For it is no longer true that the precise relations of Euclid's geometry may be indefinitely approximated to by increasing the refinements of the measuring process, but there are essential physical limitations to the very concepts of length, etc., which enter the geometrical formulations, set by the discrete structure of matter and of radiation. . . .

Mathematics appears to fail to correspond exactly to the physical situation in at least two respects. In the first place, there is the matter of errors of measurement in the range of ordinary experience. Now mathematics can deal with this situation, although somewhat clumsily, and only approximately, by specifically supplementing its equations by statements about the limit of error, or replacing equations by inequalities—in short, the sort of thing done in every discussion of the propagation of error of measurement. In the second place, and much more important, mathematics does not recognize that as the physical range increases, the fundamental concepts become hazy, and eventually cease entirely to have physical meaning, and therefore must be replaced by other concepts which are operationally quite different. For instance, the equations of motion make no distinction between the motion of a star into our galaxy from external space, and the motion of an electron about the nucleus, although physically the meaning in terms of operations of the quantities in the equations is entirely different in the two cases. The structure of our mathematics is such that we are almost forced, whether we want to or not, to talk about the inside of an electron, although physically we cannot assign any meaning to such statements. As at present constructed, mathematics reminds one of the loquacious and not always coherent orator, who was said to be able to set his mouth going and go off and leave it. What we would like is some development of mathematics by which the equations could be made to cease to have meaning outside the range of numerical magnitude in which the physical concepts themselves have meaning. In other words, the problem is to make our equations correspond more closely to the physical experience back of them; it evidently needs some sort of new invention to accomplish this.

QUESTIONS FOR DISCUSSION

1. What is Bridgman's judgment about the nature and reliability of mathematics? Does he offer good reasons to support his view?
2. Do you understand an "explanation" to be what Bridgman says it is? What other meanings could be given to "explanation"?
3. Taking these two selections together, can you formulate a statement of the nature of scientific method?

READINGS FOR IMMEDIATE REFERENCE

Bridgman, P. W. *The Logic of Modern Physics*. New York: Macmillan, 1927, Chapters 1, 2, 4.

Planck, Max. *Scientific Autobiography*. London: Williams and Norgate, 1956, pp. 121-150.

Poincaré, Henri. *Science and Hypothesis*. London: Walter Scott, 1905, Chapter 9.

REFERENCES FOR COMPREHENSIVE KNOWLEDGE

Bridgman, P. W. *The Nature of Some of our Physical Concepts*. New York: Philosophical Library, 1952.

———.*Reflections of a Physicist*. New York: Philosophical Library, 1950.

———. *The Way Things Are*. Cambridge: Harvard University Press, 1959.

Whitehead, A. N. *Science and the Modern World*. New York: Macmillan, 1925. The origins, nature, and implications of the physical sciences as seen by one of this century's leading mathematicians and philosophers.

Also see:

Duhem, Pierre. *The Aim and Structure of Physical Theory*. Princeton: Princeton University Press, 1953.

Einstein, Albert. *Evolution of Physics*. New York: Simon and Schuster, 1938.

Heisenberg, Werner. *Philosophic Problems of Nuclear Science*. New York: Pantheon, 1952.

Robbins, H. and Courant, R. *What is Mathematics?* New York: Oxford University Press, 1941.

III. MAX WEBER

Weber was born in Erfurt, Germany, in 1864. His original interest was in the practice of law, but gradually it shifted to legal history, then history in general, economics, and finally sociology. He was elected to the faculty of the University of Berlin in 1893, and also taught at Freiburg, Heidelberg, and Munich. His main intellectual interest was in challenging the Marxian concept of economic determinism, and his most famous work, *The Protestant Ethic and the Spirit of Capitalism,* was written to demonstrate the importance of religious and ethical ideas in shaping historical events. This work led him to consider the still larger problem of whether there are identifiable causes for social phenomena. To find an answer he studied the religions of the world and travelled extensively. His conclusions were printed in a series of posthumously published volumes. Despite continual poor health he had a keen interest in social and political affairs and played a key role in establishing the Weimar republic following World War I. He died in 1920 at the age of fifty-six.

In this selection Weber considers some of the factors which make the study of human beings and their institutions different from the study of the physical sciences, and he questions the possibility of making a scientific study of society. Since this volume was written in 1910, you should ask yourself whether any (or all) of the problems he mentions have been eliminated, or mitigated, by the techniques of social scientists today.

Methodology in the Social Sciences[1]

There is no absolutely "objective" scientific analysis of culture—or put perhaps more narrowly but certainly not essentially differently for our purposes —of "social phenomena" independent of special and "one-sided" viewpoints according to which—expressly or tacitly, consciously or unconsciously—they are selected, analyzed and organized for expository purposes. The reasons for this

[1] From *On the Methodology of the Social Sciences* by Max Weber, translated by Edward Shils and Henry Finch. Glencoe, Ill.: The Free Press, 1949, pp. 72-84. Reprinted by permission.

lie in the character of the cognitive goal of all research in social science which seeks to transcend the purely *formal* treatment of the legal or conventional norms regulating social life.

The type of social science in which we are interested is an *empirical science* of concrete *reality*. Our aim is the understanding of the characteristic uniqueness of the reality in which we move. We wish to understand on the one hand the relationships and the cultural significance of individual events in their contemporary manifestations and on the other the causes of their being historically *so* and not *otherwise*. Now, as soon as we attempt to reflect about the way in which life confronts us in immediate concrete situations, it presents an infinite multiplicity of successively and coexistently emerging and disappearing events, both "within" and "outside" ourselves. The absolute infinitude of this multiplicity is seen to remain undiminished even when our attention is focused on a single "object," for instance, a concrete act of exchange, as soon as we seriously attempt an exhaustive description of *all* the individual components of this "individual phenomena," to say nothing of explaining it causally. All the analysis of infinite reality which the finite human mind can conduct rests on the tacit assumption that only a finite portion of this reality constitutes the object of scientific investigation, and that only it is "important" in the sense of being "worthy of being known." But what are the criteria by which this segment is selected?

It has often been thought that the decisive criterion in the cultural sciences, too, was in the last analysis, the "regular" recurrence of certain causal relationships. The "laws" which we are able to perceive in the infinitely manifold stream of events must—according to this conception—contain the scientifically "essential" aspect of reality. As soon as we have shown some causal relationship to be a "law," i.e., if we have shown it to be universally valid by means of comprehensive historical induction or have made it immediately and tangibly plausible according to our subjective experience, a great number of similar cases order themselves under the formula thus attained. Those elements in each individual event which are left unaccounted for by the selection of their elements subsumable under the "law" are considered as scientifically unintegrated residues which will be taken care of in the further perfection of the system of "laws." Alternatively they will be viewed as "accidental" and therefore scientifically unimportant *because* they do not fit into the structure of the "law"; in other words, they are not typical of the event and hence can only be the objects of "idle curiosity." Accordingly, even among the followers of the Historical School we continually find the attitude which declares that the ideal which all the sciences, including the cultural sciences, serve and towards which they should strive even in the remote future is a system of propositions from which reality can be "deduced." As is well known, a leading natural scientist believed that he could designate the "factually unattainable" ideal goal of such a treatment of cultural reality as a sort of *"astronomical"* knowledge.

Let us not, for our part, spare ourselves the trouble of examining these matters more closely—however often they have already been discussed. The first thing that impresses one is that the "astronomical" knowledge which was referred to is not a system of laws at all. On the contrary, the laws which it presupposes have been taken from other disciplines like mechanics. But it too concerns itself with the question of the *individual* consequence which the working of these laws in an unique *configuration* produces, since it is these individual configurations which are *significant* for us. Every individual constellation which it "explains" or predicts is causally explicable only as the consequence of another equally individual constellation which has preceded it. As far back as we may go into the grey mist of the far-off past, the reality to which the laws apply always remains equally *individual*, equally *undeducible* from laws. A cosmic "primeval state" which had no individual character or less individual character than the cosmic reality of the present would naturally be a meaningless notion. . . .

The social-scientific interest has its point of departure, of course, in the *real,* i.e., concrete, individually-structured configuration of our cultural life in its universal relationships which are themselves no less individually-structured, and in its development out of other social cultural conditions, which themselves are obviously likewise individually structured. It is clear here that the situation which we illustrated by reference to astronomy as a limiting case (which is regularly drawn on by logicians for the same purpose) appears in a more accentuated form. Whereas in astronomy, the heavenly bodies are of interest to us only in their *quantitative* and exact aspects, the *qualitative* aspect of phenomena concerns us in the social sciences. To this should be added that in the social sciences we are concerned with psychological and intellectual (*geistig*) phenomena the emphatic understanding of which is naturally a problem of a specifically different type from those which the schemes of the exact natural sciences in general can or seem to solve.

Despite that, this distinction in itself is not a distinction in principle, as it seems at first glance. Aside from pure mechanics, even the exact natural sciences do not proceed without qualitative categories. Furthermore, in our own field we encounter the idea (which is obviously distorted) that at least the phenomena characteristic of a money-economy—which are basic to our culture—are quantifiable and on that account subject to formulation as "laws." Finally it depends on the breadth or narrowness of one's definition of "law" as to whether one will also include regularities which because they are not quantifiable are not subject to numerical analysis. Especially insofar as the influence of psychological and intellectual (*geistige*) factors is concerned, it does not in any case exclude the establishment of *rules* governing rational conduct. Above all, the point of view still persists which claims that the task of psychology is to play a role comparable to mathematics for the *Geisteswissenschaften* in the sense that it analyzes the complicated phenomena of social life into their psychic conditions and effects, reduces them to their most elementary possible psychic factors and then analyzes their functional interdependences. Thereby, a sort of "chemistry" if not "mechanics" of the psychic foundations of social life would be created. Whether such investigations can produce valuable and—what is something else—useful results for the cultural sciences, we cannot decide here. But this would be irrelevant to the question as to whether the aim of social-economic knowledge in our sense, i.e., knowledge of *reality* with respect to its cultural *significance* and its causal relationships can be attained through the quest for recurrent sequences.

Let us assume that we have succeeded by means of psychology or otherwise in analyzing all the observed and imaginable relationships of social phenomena into some ultimate elementary "factors," that we have made an exhaustive analysis and classification of them and then formulated rigorously exact laws covering their behavior. What would be the significance of these results for our knowledge of the *historically* given culture or any individual phase thereof, such as capitalism, in its development and cultural significance? As an analytical tool, it would be as useful as a textbook of organic chemical combinations would be for our knowledge of the biogenetic aspect of the animal and plant world. In each case, certainly an important and useful preliminary step would have been taken. In neither case can concrete reality be deduced from "laws" and "factors."

This is not because some higher mysterious powers reside in living phenomena (such as "dominants," "entelechies," or whatever they might be called). This, however, is a problem in its own right. The real reason is that the analysis of reality is concerned with the *configuration* into which those (hypothetical!) "factors" are arranged to form a cultural phenomenon which is historically significant to us. Furthermore, if we wish to "explain" this individual configuration "causally" we must invoke other equally individual configurations on the basis of which we will explain it with the aid of those (hypothetical!) "laws."

The determination of those (hypothetical) "laws" and "factors" would in any case only be the first of the many operations which would lead us to the desired type of knowledge. The analysis of the historically given individual configuration of those "factors" and their *significant* concrete interaction, conditioned by their historical context and especially the *rendering intelligible* of the basis and type of this significance would be the next task to be achieved. This task must be achieved, it is true, by the utilization of the preliminary analysis but it is nonetheless an entirely new and *distinct* task. The tracing as far into the past as possible of the individual features of these historically evolved configurations which are *contemporaneously* significant, and their historical explanation by antecedent and equally individual configurations would be the third task. Finally the prediction of possible future constellations would be a conceivable fourth task.

For all these purposes, clear concepts and the knowledge of those (hypothetical) "laws" are obviously of great value as heuristic means—but only as such. Indeed they are quite indispensable for this purpose. But even in this function their limitations become evident at a decisive point. In stating this, we arrive at the decisive feature of the method of the cultural sciences. We have designated as "cultural sciences" those disciplines which analyze the phenomena of life in terms of their cultural significance. The *significance* of a configuration of cultural phenomena and the basis of this significance cannot however be derived and rendered intelligible by a system of analytical laws (*Gesetzesbegriffen*), however perfect it may be, since the significance of cultural events presupposes a *value-orientation* towards these events. The concept of culture is a *value-concept.* Empirical reality becomes "culture" to us because and insofar as we relate it to value ideas. It includes those segments and only those segments of reality which have become significant to us because of this value-relevance. Only a small portion of existing concrete reality is colored by our value-conditioned interest and it alone is significant to us.

It is significant because it reveals relationships which are important to us due to their connection with our values. Only because and to the extent that this is the case is it worthwhile for us to know it in its individual features. We cannot discover, however, what is meaningful to us by means of a "presuppositionless" investigation of empirical data. Rather perception of its meaningfulness to us is the presupposition of its becoming an *object* of investigation. Meaningfulness naturally does not coincide with laws as such, and the more general the law the less the coincidence. For the specific meaning which a phenomenon has for us is naturally *not* to be found in those relationships which it shares with many other phenomena. . . .

The *goal* of our investigation is not reached through the exposition of those laws and concepts, precise as it may be. The question as to what should be the object of universal conceptualization cannot be decided "presuppositionlessly" but only with reference to the *significance* which certain segments of that infinite multiplicity which we call "commerce" have for culture. We seek knowledge of an historical phenomenon, meaning by historical: significant in its individuality (*Eigenart*). And the decisive element in this is that only through the presupposition that a finite part alone of the infinite variety of phenomena is significant, does the knowledge of an individual phenomenon became logically meaningful. Even with the widest imaginable knowledge of "laws," we are helpless in the face of the question: how is the *causal explanation* of an *individual* fact possible—since a *description* of even the smallest slice of reality can never be exhaustive? The number and type of causes which have influenced any given event are always infinite and there is nothing in the things themselves to set some of them apart as alone meriting attention. A chaos of "existential judgments" about countless individual events would be the only result of a serious attempt to analyze reality "without presuppositions." And even this result is only seemingly possible, since every single perception discloses on closer examination an infinite number of constituent perceptions which can never be exhaustively expressed in a judgment.

Order is brought into this chaos only on the condition that in every case only a *part* of concrete reality is interesting and *significant* to us, because only it is related to the *cultural values* with which we approach reality. Only certain sides of the infinitely complex concrete phenomenon, namely those to which we attribute a general *cultural significance*—are therefore worthwhile knowing. They alone are objects of causal explanation. And even this causal explanation evinces the same character; an *exhaustive* causal investigation of any concrete phenomena in its full reality is not only practically impossible—it is simply nonsense.

* * * * *

What is the consequence of all this?

Naturally, it does not imply that the knowledge of *universal* propositions, the construction of abstract concepts, the knowledge of regularities and the attempt to formulate "laws" have no scientific justification in the cultural sciences. Quite the contrary, if the causal knowledge of the historians consists of the imputation of concrete effects to concrete causes, a *valid* imputation of any individual effect without the application of *"nomological" knowledge*—i.e., the knowledge of recurrent causal sequences—would in general be impossible. Whether a single individual component of a relationship is, in a concrete case, to be assigned causal responsibility for an effect, the causal explanation of which is at issue, can in doubtful cases be determined only by estimating the effects which we *generally* expect from it and from the other components of the same complex which are relevant to the explanation. In other words, the *"adequate"* effects of the causal elements involved must be considered in arriving at any such conclusion.

The extent to which the historian (in the widest sense of the word) can perform this imputation in a reasonably certain manner with his imagination sharpened by personal experience and trained in analytic methods and the extent to which he must have recourse to the aid of special disciplines which make it possible, varies with the individual case. Everywhere, however, and hence also in the sphere of complicated economic processes, the more certain and the more comprehensive our general knowledge the greater is the *certainty* of imputation. This proposition is not in the least affected by the fact that even in the case of all so-called "economic laws" without exception, we are concerned here not with "laws" in the narrower exact natural science sense, but with *adequate* causal relationships expressed in rules and with the application of the category of "objective possibility." The establishment of such regularities is not the *end* but rather the *means* of knowledge. It is entirely a question of expediency, to be settled separately for each individual case, whether a regularly recurrent causal relationship of everyday experience should be formulated into a "law."

Laws are important and valuable in the exact natural sciences, in the measure that those sciences are *universally valid.* For the knowledge of historical phenomena in their concreteness, the most general laws, because they are most devoid of content are also the least valuable. The more comprehensive the validity,—or scope—of a term, the more it leads us away from the richness of reality since in order to include the common elements of the largest possible number of phenomena, it must necessarily be as abstract as possible and hence *devoid* of content. In the cultural sciences, the knowledge of the universal or general is never valuable in itself.

The conclusion which follows from the above is that an "objective" analysis of cultural events, which proceeds according to the thesis that the ideal of science is the reduction of empirical reality to "laws," is meaningless. It is not meaningless, as is often maintained, because cultural or psychic events for instance are "objectively" less governed by laws. It is meaningless for a number of other reasons. Firstly, because the knowledge of social laws is not knowledge of social reality but is rather one of the various aids used by our minds for attaining this end; secondly, because knowledge of *cultural* events is inconceivable except on a basis of the significance which the concrete constellations of reality have for us in certain *individual* concrete situations. In *which* sense and in *which* situations this is the case is not revealed to us by any law; it is decided according to the *value-ideas* in the light of which we view "culture" in each individual case. "Culture" is a finite segment of the meaningless infinity of the world process, a segment on which *human beings* confer meaning and significance.

This is true even for the human being who views a *particular* culture as a mortal enemy and who seeks to "return to nature." He can attain this point of view only after viewing the culture in which he lives from the standpoint of his values, and finding it "too soft." This is the purely logical-formal fact which is involved when we speak of the logically necessary rootedness of all historical entities (*historische Individuen*) in "evaluative ideas." The transcendental presupposition of every *cultural science* lies not in our finding a certain culture or any "culture" in general to be *valuable* but rather in the fact that we are *cultural beings,* endowed with the capacity and the will to take a deliberate attitude towards the world and to lend it *significance.* Whatever this significance may be, it will lead us to judge certain phenomena of human existence in its light and to respond to them as being (positively or negatively) meaningful. Whatever may be the content of this attitude—these phenomena have cultural significance for us and on this significance alone rests its scientific interest. . . .

All knowledge of cultural reality, as may be seen, is always knowledge from *particular points of view.* When we require from the historian and social research worker as an elementary presupposition that they distinguish the important from the trivial and that he should have the necessary "point of view" for this distinction, we mean that they must understand how to relate the events of the real world consciously or unconsciously to universal "cultural values" and to select out those relationships which are significant for us. If the notion that those standpoints can be derived from the "facts themselves" continually recurs, it is due to the naive self-deception of the specialist who is unaware that it is due to the evaluative ideas with which he unconsciously approaches his subject matter, that he has selected from an absolute infinity a tiny portion with the study of which he *concerns* himself.

In connection with this selection of individual special "aspects" of the event which always and everywhere occurs, consciously or unconsciously, there also occurs that element of cultural-scientific work which is referred to by the often-heard assertion that the "personal" element of a scientific work is what is really valuable in it, and that personality must be expressed in every work if its existence is to be justified. To be sure, without the investigator's evaluative ideas, there would be no principle of selection of subject-matter and no meaningful knowledge of the concrete reality. Just as without the investigator's conviction regarding the significance of particular cultural facts, every attempt to analyze concrete reality is absolutely meaningless, so the direction of his personal belief, the refraction of values in the prism of his mind, gives direction to his work. And the values to which the scientific genius relates the object of his inquiry may determine, i.e., decide the "conception" of a whole epoch, not only concerning what is regarded as "valuable" but also concerning what is significant or insignificant, "important" or "unimportant" in the phenomena.

Accordingly, cultural science in our sense involves "subjective" presuppositions insofar as it concerns itself only with those components of reality which have some relationship, however indirect, to events to which we attach cultural *significance*. Nonetheless, it is entirely *causal* knowledge exactly in the same sense as the knowledge of significant concrete natural events which have a qualitative character. . . .

However, there emerges from this the meaninglessness of the idea which prevails occasionally even among historians, namely, that the goal of the cultural sciences, however far it may be from realization, is to construct a closed system of concepts, in which reality is synthesized in some sort of *permanently* and *universally* valid classification and from which it can again be deduced. The stream of immeasurable events flows unendingly towards eternity. The cultural problems which move men from themselves ever anew and in different colors, and the boundaries of that area in the infinite stream of concrete events which acquires meaning and significance for us, i.e., which becomes an "historical individual," are constantly subject to change. The intellectual contexts from which it is viewed and scientifically analyzed shift. The points of departure of the cultural sciences remain changeable throughout the limitless future as long as a Chinese ossification of intellectual life does not render mankind incapable of setting new questions to the externally inexhaustible flow of life. A systematic science of culture, even only in the sense of a definitive, objectively valid, systematic fixation of the problems which it should treat, would be senseless in itself. Such an attempt could only produce a collection of numerous, specifically particularized, heterogeneous and disparate viewpoints in the light of which reality becomes "culture" through being significant in its unique character.

QUESTIONS FOR DISCUSSION

1. Does Weber's point about the importance of individual selectivity in the social sciences apply equally to the other sciences? How would they deal with this problem, or is it a problem?
2. Can science establish universally true conclusions? Why?
3. Having read accounts of scientific method as given by philosophers, a physical scientist, and a social scientist, can you now formulate the procedures characteristic of scientific method and its potential difficulties? If so, apply it to the solution of the following problem: During the summer I noticed that the peas at the ends of the rows in my garden were not growing as well as those in the middle, and I wondered what was the cause. Can you, as scientist, tell me how to go about finding the answer?

READINGS FOR IMMEDIATE REFERENCE

Weber, Max. *On the Methodology of the Social Sciences.* Glencoe: Free Press, 1949.

Kaufman, Felix. *Methodology in the Social Sciences.* New York: Humanities Press, 1958.

REFERENCES FOR COMPREHENSIVE KNOWLEDGE

Durkheim, Emile. *The Rules of Sociological Method,* 8th ed. Glencoe: Free Press, 1950. A classic statement of the procedures and problems.

Also see:

Gardiner, Patrick. *The Nature of Historical Explanation.* New York: Oxford University Press, 1952.

Kris, Ernst. "Validation of Psychoanalytic Propositions," *Freedom and Experience,* eds. S. Hook and M. Konvitz. Ithaca: Cornell University Press, 1947.

Mandelbaum, Maurice. *The Problem of Historical Knowledge.* New York: Liveright, 1938.

Skinner, B. F. *Science and Human Behavior.* New York: Macmillan, 1953.

IV. SOME REPRESENTATIVE EXPERIMENTS

You have read what philosophers, physicists, and sociologists have said about scientific method, its nature and potential difficulties. This is your opportunity to examine some experiments yourself to see how satisfactorily they were done. Each of these experiments has been an important milestone in the history of science, so read them carefully and evaluate them thoughtfully.

---

1. WILLIAM HARVEY

Born in 1578, Harvey was the leading physician in England during the first half of the seventeenth century, having had James I, Charles I, and Francis Bacon among his patients. His theory of the circulation of the blood was vigorously opposed when first presented in lecture form in 1616, but by his death in 1657 it was generally accepted.

The Motion of the Heart[1] *(1628)*

In the first place, then, when the chest of a living animal is laid open and the capsule that immediately surrounds the heart is slipped up or removed, the organ is seen now to move, now to be at rest; there is a time when it moves, and a time when it is motionless.

These things are more obvious in the colder animals, such as toads, frogs, serpents, small fishes, crabs, shrimps, snails, and shell-fish. They also become more distinct in warm-blooded animals, such as the dog and hog, if they be attentively noted when the heart begins to flag, to move more slowly, and, as it were, to die: the movements then become slower and rarer, the pauses longer, by which it is made much more easy to perceive and unravel what the motions really are, and how they are performed. In the pause, as in death, the heart is soft, flaccid, exhausted, lying, as it were, at rest.

In the motion, the interval in which this is accomplished, three principal circumstances are to be noted.

1. That the heart is erected, and rises upwards to a point, so that at this time it strikes against the breast and the pulse is felt externally.

[1] From *On the Motion of the Heart and Blood in Animals.* Cambridge, 1847, Chapter 2.

2. That it is everywhere contracted, but more especially towards the sides so that it looks narrower, relatively longer, more drawn together. The heart of an eel taken out of the body of the animal and placed upon the table or the hand, shows these particulars; but the same things are manifest in the hearts of all small fishes and of those colder animals where the organ is more conical or elongated.

3. The heart being grasped in the hand, is felt to become harder during its action. Now this hardness proceeds from tension, precisely as when the forearm is grasped, its tendons are perceived to become tense and resilient when the fingers are moved.

4. It may further be observed in fishes, and the colder-blooded animals, such as frogs, serpents, etc., that the heart, when it moves, becomes of a paler color, when quiescent of a deeper blood-red color.

From these particulars it appears evident to me that the motion of the heart consists in a certain universal tension—both contraction in the line of its fibres, and constriction in every sense. It becomes erect, hard, and of diminished size during its action; the motion is plainly of the same nature as that of the muscles when they contract in the line of their sinews and fibres; for the muscles, when in action, acquire vigor and tenseness, and from soft become hard, prominent, and thickened: and in the same manner the heart.

We are therefore authorized to conclude that the heart, at the moment of its action, is at once constricted on all sides, rendered thicker in its parietes and smaller in its ventricles, and so made apt to project or expel its charge of blood. This, indeed, is made sufficiently manifest by the preceding fourth observation in which we have seen that the heart, by squeezing out the blood that it contains, becomes paler, and then when it sinks into repose and the ventricle is filled anew with blood, that the deeper crimson color returns. But no one need remain in doubt of the fact, for if the ventricle be pierced the blood will be seen to be forcibly projected outwards upon each motion or pulsation when the heart is tense.

These things, therefore, happen together or at the same instant: the tension of the heart, the pulse of its apex, which is felt externally by its striking against the chest, the thickening of its parietes, and the forcible expulsion of the blood it contains by the constriction of its ventricles.

Hence the very opposite of the opinions commonly received appears to be true; inasmuch as it is generally believed that when the heart strikes the breast and the pulse is felt without, the heart is dilated in its ventricles and is filled with blood; but the contrary of this is the fact, and the heart, when it contracts (and the impulse of the apex is conveyed through the chest wall) is emptied. Whence the motion which is generally regarded as the diastole of the heart, is in truth its systole. And in like manner the intrinsic motion of the heart is not the diastole but the systole; neither is it in the diastole that the heart grows firm and tense, but in the systole, for then only, when tense, is it moved and made vigorous.

2. JOSEPH PRIESTLEY

Priestley was born in 1733, one of six children. As a young man he aspired to a business career, but his aunt, who raised him after he was orphaned, saw to it that he was prepared for the ministry. At one parish he also taught school, and this experience was the origin of his scientific interests. He performed many experiments with gases and electricity, and was elected to the Royal Academy at the age of thirty-three. However, his political views were liberal, and as a result his home and papers were burned by a mob in 1791. He fled to America where he lived until his death in 1804.

The Discovery of Oxygen[1] *(1775)*

On the 8th of this month I procured a mouse, and put it into a glass vessel, containing two ounce-measures of the air from mercurius calcinatus. Had it been common air, a full-grown mouse, as this was, would have lived in it about a quarter of an hour. In this air, however, my mouse lived a full half hour; and though it was taken out seemingly dead, it appeared to have been only exceedingly chilled; for upon being held to the fire, it presently revived, and appeared not to have received harm from the experiment.

By this I was confirmed in my conclusion, that the air extracted from mercurius calcinatus, etc., was, *at least, as good* as common air, but I did not certainly conclude that it was any *better;* because, though one mouse would live only a quarter of an hour in a given quantity of air, I knew it was not impossible but that another mouse might have lived in it half an hour; so little accuracy is there in this method of ascertaining the goodness of air: and indeed I have never had recourse to it for my own satisfaction, since the discovery of that most ready, accurate, and elegant test that nitrous air furnishes. But in this case I had a view to publishing the most generally satisfactory account of my experiments that the nature of the thing would admit of.

This experiment with the mouse, when I had reflected upon it some time, gave me so much suspicion that the air into which I had put it was better than common air, that I was induced, the day after, to apply the test of nitrous air to a small part of that very quantity of air which the mouse had breathed so long; so that, had it been common air, I was satisfied it must have been very nearly, if not altogether, as noxious as possible, so as not to be affected by nitrous air; when, to my surprise again, I found that though it had been breathed

[1] Reprinted by permission of the publishers from Leonard K. Nash, *Plants and Atmosphere*—Harvard Case Histories in Experimental Science. Cambridge, Mass.: Harvard University Press, Copyright, 1950, 1952, by The President and Fellows of Harvard College, pp. 44-45.

so long, it was still better than common air. For after mixing it with nitrous air, in the usual proportion of two to one, it was diminished in the proportion of 4½ to 3½; that is, the nitrous air had made it two ninths less than before, and this in a very short space of time; whereas I had never found that, in the longest time, any common air was reduced more than one fifth of its bulk by any proportion of nitrous air, nor more than one fourth by any phlogistic process whatever. Thinking of this extraordinary fact upon my pillow, the next morning I put another measure of nitrous air to the same mixture, and, to my utter astonishment, found that it was farther diminished to almost one half of its original quantity. I then put a third measure to it; but this did not diminish it any farther; but, however, left it one measure less than it was after the mouse was taken from it. . . .

As common air takes about half of its bulk of nitrous air, before it begins to receive any addition to its dimensions from more nitrous air, and this air took more than four half-measures before it ceased to be diminished by more nitrous air, and even five half-measures made no addition to its original dimensions, I conclude that it was between four and five times as good as common air. It will be seen that I have since procured air better than this, even between five and six times as good as the best common air I have ever met with.

3. URBAIN JEAN JOSEPH LEVERRIER

Born in 1811, Leverrier had many interests. He was a productive researcher and popular instructor in chemistry until 1837 when a teaching position in astronomy opened at the University of Paris and he became an astronomer, being "docile to circumstances." He was elected to the French Academy largely because of his investigations concerning Uranus. In 1854 he became director of the Paris Observatory and devoted the remainder of his life to revising astronomical charts to make them conform to the knowledge then known. He completed this task only three weeks before his death in 1877.

The Motions of Uranus[1] *(1846)*

The theory of Uranus at the present time absorbs the attention of astronomers. It has been the subject of many hypotheses, more or less plausible, which, however, aside from geometric considerations cannot have any real value. Several societies have even proposed the theory as a subject for competi-

[1] Reprinted by permission of the publishers from Harlow Shapley and Helen E. Howarth, *A Source Book in Astronomy*. Cambridge, Mass.: Harvard University Press, 1929, pp. 250-254.

tion. I believe, therefore, that because of the importance of the question, I should rapidly recount its history. One can better judge the goal of my work, the course I have travelled, and the results at which I have arrived.

In 1820, there were available regular meridian observations extending over a period of forty years. The planet had, moreover, been observed nineteen times between 1690 and 1771 by Flamsteed, Bradley, Mayer, and Lemonnier. These astronomers had seen it as a star of the sixth magnitude. On the other hand, the analytical expressions for the perturbations which Jupiter and Saturn produce on Uranus are to be found developed in the first volume of the Mecanique Celeste. Using all these data, one should have expected to be able to construct exact tables for the planet. This is what Bouvard, Member of the Academy of Science, undertook. But he encountered unforeseen difficulties. . . .

It was found impossible to represent at the same time the nineteen older observations and the numerous modern ones. In this embarrassing situation the learned member of the academy throws doubt upon the accuracy of the older observations; he discards them completely and takes into account only the modern observations. But one should note that though the observations of Flamsteed, Bradley, Mayer, and Lemonnier are not as exact as those of the astronomers of our epoch, one may not with any plausibility be allowed to consider them infested with such enormous errors as those of which the present tables accuse them. The author of these tables actually suggests, however, that this is his opinion, although he adds, after reviewing the difficulties which he had encountered: "the future shall have the burden of demonstrating whether the difficulty of reconciling the two systems is really connected with the inaccuracy of observations, or whether it depends on some strange and unperceived force which may be exerted on the planet."

The twenty-five years which have elapsed since that epoch have shown us that the present tables, which do not represent the older positions, are in no better agreement with the positions observed in 1845. May this disagreement be attributed to lack of precision in the theory? Or rather has not the theory been applied to the observations with sufficient exactitude in the work which has served as a basis for the present table? Or finally, might it be that Uranus is subjected to other influences besides those which result from the action of the Sun, of Jupiter, and of Saturn? And, in this case, might one succeed, by a careful study of the disturbed motion of the planet, in determining the cause of these unforeseen irregularities? And could one come to the point of fixing the spot in the sky where the investigations of observing astronomers ought to discover the strange body, the source of all the difficulties?

LETTER FROM J. S. ENCKE, SEPT. 1846.

No mail went to Hamburg yesterday and, therefore, I could not announce to you the discovery of the Leverrier planet. Accordingly, I can today give you more information. In the Comptes Rendus for August 31, 1846, M. Leverrier has given the following elements, deduced from the deviations of Uranus from its orbit, computed on the basis of the known masses:

Semi-major axis 36.154
Period of
revolution . . . 217.387 years (sidereal)
Eccentricity 0.10761
Perihelion . . . . 284° 45′
Mean longitude on
Jan. 1, 1847 . . . . 318° 47′
Mass 1/9300

And from this it follows:

Heliocentric True Longitude,
Jan. 1, 1847 . . . . 326° 32′
Distance from the Sun 33.06

In a letter which arrived on Sept. 23, M. Leverrier especially urged Dr. Galle to search for the planet. Probably he was guided by the supposition mentioned in his article that the planet could be identified through showing a disk. The same evening Galle compared with the sky the excellent maps which Dr. Bremiker has plotted, and almost immediately noticed, very near the position which Leverrier predicts, a star of the eighth magnitude which was missing on the chart. It was immediately measured three different times by Galle with reference to a star in Bessel's catalogue (each measure consisting of five observations), and was once measured by me. The results of these comparisons are as follows:

Sidereal Time	R.A. diff. + 1m	Dec. diff. + 1
22h 52m	25 s. 84	1′ 35″.9
23 47	25 . 30	37 .9
0 52	25 . 34	35 .9
1 8	25 . 26	37 .3

Although on the whole there is shown here a progression, nevertheless, the discrepancies in this first series were so noticeable that it cannot be depended upon. Therefore, we waited until the next evening. At that time, to be sure, the weather interfered, cloudiness interrupting the observations. Nevertheless, motion exactly in the direction of the Leverrier elements was decisive, for we found, using the same star. [See below]

Similarly, on the 25th of September, when Galle compared the star five times and I, ten times, the motion was confirmed. . . .

The star seemed to be only a trifle fainter than Piazzi XXI, 344, and, therefore, fully as bright as the eighth magnitude. Yesterday the atmospheric conditions were favorable. We recognized a disk, the diameter of which, using bright cross wires and a magnification of 320, we found to be 2″.9; Galle found 2″.7. When we subsequently used a bright field, I measured the planet greater than 3″.2 and Galle considerably smaller than 2″.2; but by this time the air had become much more unfavorable so that the first measurements are more to be

Sept. 24	20h	7m	+ 1m 21s.56	+ 1′16″.4	Galle (5 Obser.)
	21	11	21 .30	14 .8	Galle (5 Obser.)
	22	20	21 .08	14 .4	Encke (4 Obser.)

trusted. I believe that the diameter is probably 2″.5, or perhaps somewhat greater, but not as large as 3″.0. In this respect, also, the prediction of Leverrier, who assumed 3″.3, is fully confirmed.

It would be superfluous to add anything more. This is the most brilliant of all planetary discoveries, because purely theoretical researches have enabled Leverrier to predict the existence and the position of a new planet. Permit me to add that the prompt discovery was possible only because of the excellent Academy Star Charts by Bremiker; the disk can be recognized only when one knows that it exists.

4. CLAUDE BERNARD

One of the most distinguished of all physiologists, Bernard was born in 1813 and aspired to be a playwright until he was nearly thirty years old. A chance appointment as a laboratory assistant allowed him to develop his creativity in other ways; his work was so thorough and voluminous that a special professorship at The Sorbonne was created for him in 1854. He was elected to the French Academy in 1869 and was the first scientist accorded a public funeral in Notre Dame. He died in 1878.

The Origins of Diabetes[1] *(1865)*

First example—one day, rabbits from the market were brought into my laboratory. They were put on the table where they urinated, and I happened to observe that their urine was clear and acid. This fact struck me, because rabbits, which are herbivora, generally have turbid and alkaline urine; while on the other hand carnivora, as we know, have clear and acid urine. This observation of acidity in the rabbits' urine gave me an idea that these animals must be in the nutritional condition of carnivora. I assumed they had probably not eaten for a long time, and that they had been transformed by fasting, into veritable carnivorous animals, living on their own blood. Nothing was easier than to verify this preconceived idea or hypothesis by experiment. I gave the rabbits grass to eat; and a few hours later, their urine became turbid and alkaline. I then subjected them to fasting and after twenty-four hours or thirty-six hours at most, their urine again became clear and strongly acid; then after eating grass, their urine became alkaline again, etc. I repeated this very simple experiment a great many times, and always with the same result. I then repeated it

[1] Reprinted by permission of Abelard-Schuman, Ltd., New York, from *An Introduction to the Study of Experimental Medicine* by Claude Bernard, 1949, pp. 152-153.

on a horse, an herbivorous animal which also has turbid and alkaline urine. I found that fasting, as in rabbits, produced prompt acidity of the urine, with such an increase in urea, that it spontaneously crystallizes at times in the cooled urine. As a result of my experiments, I thus reached the general proposition which then was still unknown, to wit, that all fasting animals feed on meat, so that herbivora then have urine like that of carnivora.

We are here dealing with a very simple, particular fact which allows us easily to follow the evolution of experimental reasoning. When we see a phenomenon which we are not in the habit of seeing, we must always ask ourselves what it is connected with, or putting it differently, what is its proximate cause; the answer or the idea, which presents itself to the mind, must then be submitted to experiment. When I saw the rabbits' acid urine, I instinctively asked myself what could be its cause. The experimental idea consisted in the connection, which my mind spontaneously made, between acidity of the rabbits' urine, and the state of fasting which I considered equivalent to a true flesh-eater's diet. The inductive reasoning which I implicitly went through was the following syllogism: the urine of carnivora is acid; now the rabbits before me have acid urine, therefore they are carnivora, i.e., fasting. This remained to be established by experiment.

But to prove that my fasting rabbits were really carnivorous, a counterproof was required. A carnivorous rabbit had to be experimentally produced by feeding it with meat, so as to see if its urine would then be clear, as it was during fasting. So I had rabbits fed on cold boiled beef (which they eat very nicely when they are given nothing else). My expectation was again verified, and as long as the animal diet was continued, the rabbits kept their clear and acid urine.

To complete my experiment, I made an autopsy on my animals, to see if meat was digested in the same way in rabbits as in carnivora. I found, in fact, all the phenomena of an excellent digestion in their intestinal reactions, and I noted that all the chyliferous vessels were gorged with very abundant white, milky chyle, just as is carnivora. But apropos of these autopsies which confirmed my ideas on meat digestion in rabbits, lo and behold a fact presented itself which I had not remotely thought of, but which became, as we shall see, my starting point in a new piece of work.

5. CHARLES DARWIN

Born in 1809, Darwin studied for both the ministry and medical professions before joining the crew of the *Beagle* in 1831 as naturalist for a five-year cruise around the world. During this time he gathered data and started to develop the theory which he finally published in the *Origin of Species* in 1859. In spite of the many controversies this book caused, Darwin continued his studies calmly and systematically, "with a love of science, unbounded patience in long reflecting over any subject, industry in observing and collecting facts and a fair share of invention as well as common sense," as he described himself. He died in 1882.

The Theory of Evolution[1] (*1871*)

It is notorious that man is constructed on the same general type or model as other mammals. All the bones in his skeleton can be compared with corresponding bones in a monkey, bat, or seal. So it is with his muscles, nerves, blood-vessels and internal viscera. The brain, the most important of all the organs, follows the same law, as shown by Huxley and other anatomists. Bischoff, who is a hostile witness, admits that every chief fissure and fold in the brain of man has its analogy in that of the orang; but he adds that at no period of development do their brains perfectly agree; nor could perfect agreement be expected, for otherwise their mental powers would have been the same. . . .

It may, however, be worth while to specify a few points, not directly or obviously connected with structure, by which this correspondence or relationship is well shown.

Man is liable to receive from the lower animals, and to communicate to them, certain diseases, as hydrophobia, variola, the glanders, syphilis, cholera, herpes, etc.; and this fact proves the close similarity of their tissues and blood, both in minute structure and composition, far more plainly than does their comparison under the best microscope, or by the aid of the best chemical analysis. Monkeys are liable to many of the same non-contagious diseases as we are; thus Rengger, who carefully observed for a long time the *Cebus Azarae* in its native land, found it liable to catarrh, with the usual symptoms, and which, when often recurrent, led to consumption. These monkeys suffered also from apoplexy, inflammation of the bowels, and cataract in the eye. The younger ones when shedding their milk-teeth often died from fever. Medicines produced the same effect on them as on us. Many kinds of monkeys have a strong taste for tea, coffee, and spirituous liquors; they will also, as I have myself seen, smoke tobacco with pleasure. Brehm asserts that the natives of north-eastern Africa catch the wild baboons by exposing vessels with strong beer, by which they are made drunk. He has seen some of these animals, which he kept in confinement, in this state; and he gives a laughable account of their behavior and strange grimaces. On the following morning they were very cross and dismal; they held their aching heads with both hands, and wore a most pitiable expression: when beer or wine was offered them, they turned away with disgust, but relished the juice of

[1] From *The Descent of Man,* London, 1871, Chapter 1.

lemons. An American monkey, an Ateles, after getting drunk on brandy, would never touch it again, and thus was wiser than many men. These trifling facts prove how similar the nerves of taste must be in monkeys and man, and how similarly their whole nervous system is affected.

Man is infested with internal parasites, sometimes causing fatal effects; and is plagued by external parasites, all of which belong to the same genera or families as those infesting other mammals, and in the case of scabies to the same species. Man is subject, like other mammals, birds, and even insects, to that mysterious law, which causes certain normal processes, such as gestation, as well as the maturation and duration of various diseases, to follow lunar periods. His wounds are repaired by the same process of healing; and the stumps left after the amputation of his limbs, especially during an early embryonic period, occasionally possess some power of regeneration, as in the lowest animals.

The whole process of that most important function, the reproduction of the species, is strikingly the same in all mammals, from the first act of courtship by the male, to the birth and nurturing of the young. Monkeys are born in almost as helpless a condition as our own infants; and in certain genera the young differ fully as much in appearance from the adults as do our children from their full-grown parents. It has been urged by some writers, as an important distinction, that with man the young arrive at maturity at a much later age than with any other animal: but if we look to the races of mankind which inhabit tropical countries the difference is not great, for the orang is believed not to be adult till the age of from ten to fifteen years. Man differs from woman in size, bodily strength, hairiness, etc., as well as in mind, in the same manner as do the two sexes of many mammals. So that the correspondence in general structure, in the minute structure of the tissues, in chemical composition and in constitution, between man and the higher animals, especially the anthropomorphous apes, is extremely close.

Man is developed from an ovule, about the 125th of an inch in diameter which differs in no respect from the ovules of other animals. The embryo itself at a very early period can hardly be distinguished from that of other members of the vertebrate kingdom. At this period the arteries run in arch-like branches, as if to carry the blood to branchiae which are not present in the higher vertebrate, tho the slits on the sides of the neck still remain, marking their former position. At a somewhat later period, when the extremities are developed, "the feet of lizards and mammals," as the illustrious Von Baer remarks, "the wings and feet of birds, no less than the hands and feet of man, all arise from the same fundamental form." It is, says Prof. Huxley, "quite in the later stages of development that the young human being presents marked differences from the young ape, while the latter departs as much from the dog in its developments, as the man does. Startling as this last assertion may appear to be, it is demonstrably true."

After the foregoing statements made by such high authorities, it would be superfluous on my part to give a number of borrowed details, showing that the embryo of man closely resembles that of other mammals. It may, however, be added, that the human embryo likewise resembles certain low forms when adult in various points of structure. For instance, the heart at first exists as a simple pulsating vessel; the excreta are voided through a cloacal passage; and the os coccyx projects like a true tail, "extending considerably beyond the rudimentary legs." In the embryos of all air-breathing vertebrates, certain glands, called the corpora Wolffiana, correspond with and act like the kidneys of mature fishes. Even at a later embryonic period, some striking resemblances between man and the lower animals may be observed. Bischoff says that the convolutions of the brain in a human foetus at the end of the seventh month reach about the same state of development as in a baboon when adult. The great toe, as Prof. Owen remarks, "which forms the fulcrum when standing or walking is perhaps the most characteristic peculiarity in the human structure;" but in an embryo, about an inch in length, Prof. Wyman found "that the great toe was shorter than the others; and, instead of being parallel to them, projected at an angle from the side of the foot, thus corresponding with the permanent condition of this part in the quadrumana."

6. SIGMUND FREUD

Freud was born in 1856; his interest in Darwin suggested a scientific career. He completed a medical degree in 1881, and had already established himself as an authority on diseases of the nervous system when his interest in hypnosis turned his career toward psychological phenomena. In 1900 he published his *Interpretation of Dreams,* and in 1902 was appointed Professor of Neuro-pathology at the University of Vienna. He retained this post until 1938 when, after watching his books burned by the Nazis, he went to live in England. He died there a year later.

An Interpretation of Dreams[1] (*1920*)

A young woman who had already been married for a number of years dreamt as follows: She was at the theatre with her husband and one side of the stalls was quite empty. Her husband told her that Elise L. and her fiancé also wanted to come, but could only get bad seats, three for a florin

[1] From *A General Introduction to Psychoanalysis* by Sigmund Freud. By Permission of Liveright, Publishers, New York. Copyright © R 1948, S. Hoch, pp. 110-111. Canadian permission by George Allen and Unwin, Ltd.

and a half, and of course they could not take those. She replied that in her opinion they did not lose much by that.

The first thing stated by the dreamer is that the occasion giving rise to the dream is alluded to in the manifest content: her husband had really told her that Elise L., an acquaintance of about her own age, had become engaged, and the dream is the reaction to this piece of news. We know already that in many dreams it is easy to point to some such occasion occurring on the day before, and that this is often traced by the dreamer without any difficulty. This dreamer supplies us with further information of the same sort about other elements in the manifest dream. To what did she trace the detail of one side of the stalls being empty? It was an allusion to a real occurrence of the week before, when she had meant to go to a certain play and had therefore booked seats *early*, so early that she had to pay extra for the tickets. On entering the theatre it was evident that her anxiety had been quite superfluous, for one side of the stalls was almost empty. It would have been time enough if she had bought the tickets on the actual day of the performance and her husband did not fail to tease her about having been in *too great a hurry*. Next, what about the one florin and a half? (1 fl. 50) This was traced to quite another context which had nothing to do with the former, but it again refers to some news received on the previous day. Her sister-in-law had had a present of 150 florins from her husband and had rushed off *in a hurry*, like a silly goose, to a jeweler's shop and spent it all on a piece of jewelry. What about the number three? She knew nothing about that unless this idea could be counted an association, that the engaged girl, Elise L., was only three months younger than she herself who had been married ten years. And the absurdity of taking three tickets for two people? She had nothing to say to this and refused to give any more associations or information whatever.

Nevertheless, her few associations have provided us with so much material that it is possible to discover the latent dream-thoughts. We are struck by the fact that in her statements references to time are noticeable at several points, which form a common basis for the different parts of this material. She had got the theatre tickets *too soon*, taken them in *too great a hurry*, so that she had to pay extra for them; in the same way her sister-in-law had *hurried* off to the jeweler's with her money to buy an ornament with it, as though she might *miss something*. If the strongly emphasized points: "too early," "too great a hurry," are connected with the occasion for the dream (namely, the news that her friend, only three months younger than herself, had now found a good husband after all) and with the criticism expressed in her asperity about her sister-in-law, that it was *folly* to be so precipitate, there occurs to us almost spontaneously the following construction of the latent dream-thoughts, for which the manifest dream is a highly distorted substitute:

"It was really *foolish* of me to be in such a hurry to marry! Elise's example shows me that I too could have found a husband later on." (The over-haste is represented by her own conduct in buying the tickets and that of her sister-in-law in buying the jewelry. Going to the theatre is substituted for getting married.) This would be the main thought; perhaps we may go on, though with less certainty: "And I might have had one a hundred times better for the money!" (150 florins is 100 times more than one florin and a half.) If we may substitute the dowry for the money, it would mean that the husband is bought with the dowry: both the jewelry and the bad seats would stand for the husband. It would be still more desirable if we could see some connection between the element "three tickets" and a husband; but our knowledge does not as yet extend to this. We have only found out that the dream expresses *deprecation* of her own husband and regret at having *married so early*.

QUESTIONS FOR DISCUSSION

1. There are several crucial questions to ask of any scientific experiment: (1) have all the relevant factors been controlled; (2) does prediction correspond to experimentation; (3) could the same data be explained with a different hypothesis? When you apply these questions to the preceding experiments, what can you say about the reliability of the conclusions?
2. What are the advantages of the scientific way for obtaining reliable knowledge? What are its disadvantages? Do you think it is a better way than the methods used by philosophy or religion?

READINGS FOR IMMEDIATE REFERENCE

Bernard, Claude. *Introduction to Experimental Medicine*. New York: Schuman, 1949, Chapter 3.

Darwin, Charles. *The Descent of Man*. London, 1871, Chapters 1-3, 7, 21.

———. *The Origin of Species*. London, 1859, Chapter 15.

Freud, Sigmund. *A General Introduction to Psychoanalysis*. New York: Liveright, 1948, Part II.

Harvey, William. *The Motion of the Heart and Blood in Animals*. Cambridge, 1847, Chapters 2-5, 9-17.

REFERENCES FOR COMPREHENSIVE KNOWLEDGE

Barnett, S. A. *A Century of Darwin*. Cambridge: Harvard University Press, 1958.

Chauvois, Louis. *William Harvey*. New York: Philosophical Library, 1957.

Conant, James B. *Overthrow of the Phlogiston Theory*. Cambridge: Harvard University Press, 1950.

Jones, Ernest. *The Life and Works of Sigmund Freud*. New York: Basic Books, 1953-57.

Olmstead, James. *Claude Bernard and the Experimental Method in Medicine*. New York: Schuman, 1952.

BIBLIOGRAPHY FOR CHAPTER TEN

READINGS FOR IMMEDIATE REFERENCE

Churchman, C. W. *Methods of Inquiry*. St. Louis: St. Louis Educational Publishers, 1950, Part I.

Copi, Irving M. *Introduction to Logic,* rev. ed. New York: Macmillan, 1961, Chapter 13.

Northrup, F. C. S. *Logic of the Sciences and the Humanities*. New York: Macmillan, 1947, Chapters 1-4, 8, 13, 14, 21.

REFERENCES FOR COMPREHENSIVE KNOWLEDGE

Harvard Case Histories in Experimental Science. (8 vols.) Cambridge: Harvard University Press, 1950-54. A series of original documents, together with analyses, of many crucial experiments in the history of science.

Also see:

Beveridge, W. B. *The Art of Scientific Investigation,* rev. ed. New York: Norton, 1957.

Braithwaite, R. B. *Scientific Explanation*. Cambridge: Cambridge University Press, 1953.

Ritchie, A. D. *Studies in the History and Methods of the Sciences*. New York: Oxford University Press, 1912.

Simpson, George. "Biology and the Nature of Science," *Science*. Vol. 139, (Jan. 11, 1963), 81-88.

Chapter Eleven

SCIENTIFIC METAPHYSICS

I. *AUGUSTE COMTE*

Comte, the "father of sociology," was born in 1798, the son of a French tax collector. He graduated from the Ecole Polytechnique, receiving a thorough grounding in the sciences, but he also read widely in philosophy, being particularly attracted to Hume. While in his early twenties, he became interested in the communal living plans of Saint-Simon and devoted nearly a decade to organizing and fostering these projects. In time, he returned to the Polytechnique as an instructor in mathematics. During his spare hours he wrote *The Positive Philosophy,* the first volume appearing in 1830; the sixth, which contained a preface which so angered his superiors that he lost his teaching position, in 1842. Thereafter, his life was a continual series of disasters: lawsuits, poverty, illness, an unfortunate marriage and divorce, and frequent, always unsuccessful, attempts to obtain a professorship. Toward the end of his life, his early interest in religion was reasserted in the religion of humanity, a form of belief in which philosophers and scientists replaced the saints, and satisfying the needs of men was substituted for the worship of God. He died in 1857, having been supported by public subscription for the last nine years of his life.

Comte believed man's thinking has gone through three stages, the theological, metaphysical and positive. Notice the characteristics of each stage and the factors which gave rise to its being changed. Also, Comte contends that the scientific stage is the highest. Are the reasons he gives to establish this claim satisfactory? Insofar as Comte speaks for the positivistic science, what is the scientific attitude toward metaphysical problems?

From Theology to Science[1]

In order to understand the true value and character of the Positive Philosophy, we must take a brief general view of the progressive course of the human mind, regarded as a whole; for no conception can be understood otherwise than through its history.

From the study of the development of human intelligence, in all directions, and through all times, the discovery arises of a great fundamental law, to which it is necessarily subject. The law is this: that each of our leading conceptions, each branch of our knowledge, passes successively through three different theoretical conditions: the Theological, or fictitious; the Metaphysical, or abstract; and the Scientific, or positive. In other words, the human mind, by its nature, employs in its progress three methods of philosophizing, the character of which is essentially different, and even radically opposed: viz., the theological method, the metaphysical, and the positive. Hence arise three philosophies, or general systems of conceptions on the aggregate of phenomena, each of which excludes the others. The first is the necessary point of departure of the human understanding; and the third is its fixed and definite state. The second is merely a state of transition. . . .

There is no science which, having attained the positive stage, does not bear marks of having passed through the others. Some time since it was (whatever it might be) composed, as we can now perceive, of metaphysical abstractions; and, further back in the course of time, it took its form from theological conceptions. We shall have only too much occasion to see, as we proceed, that our most advanced sciences still bear very evident marks of the two earlier periods through which they have passed.

The progress of the individual mind is not only an illustration, but an indirect evidence of that of the general mind. The point of departure of the individual and of the race being the same, the phases of the mind of a man correspond to the epochs of the mind of the race. Now, each of us is aware, if he looks back upon his own history, that he was a theologian in his childhood, a metaphysician in his youth, and a natural philosopher in his manhood. All men who are up to their age can verify this for themselves.

Besides the observation of facts, we have theoretical reasons in support of this law.

The most important of these reasons arises from the necessity that always exists for some theory to which to refer our facts, combined with the clear impossibility that, at the outset of human knowledge, men could have formed theories out of the observation of facts.

[1] From *The Positive Philosophy,* by Auguste Comte, translated by Harriet Martineau. London: George Bell and Sons, 1896, Introduction, Chapter 1; Book VI, Chapters 6-8, 10-11, 13. [I have made some slight changes in the order of the chapters. C.M.]

All good intellects have repeated, since Bacon's time, that there can be no real knowledge but that which is based on observed facts. This is incontestable, in our present advanced stage; but, if we look back to the primitive stage of human knowledge, we shall see that it must have been otherwise then. If it is true that every theory must be based upon observed facts, it is equally true that facts cannot be observed without the guidance of some theory. Without such guidance, our facts would be desultory and fruitless; we could not retain them: for the most part we could not even perceive them.

Thus, between the necessity of observing facts in order to form a theory, and having a theory in order to observe facts, the human mind would have been entangled in a vicious circle, but for the natural opening afforded by Theological conceptions. This is the fundamental reason for the theological character of the primitive philosophy. This necessity is confirmed by the perfect suitability of the theological philosophy to the earliest researches of the human mind. It is remarkable that the most inaccessible questions,—those of the nature of beings, and the origin and purpose of phenomena,—should be the first to occur in a primitive state, while those which are really within our reach are regarded as almost unworthy of serious study. The reason is evident enough: —that experience alone can teach us the measure of our powers; and if men had not begun by an exaggerated estimate of what they can do, they would never have done all that they are capable of. Our organization requires this.

* * * * *

We may now proceed to a direct examination of the successive periods, estimating the rational character of each, on the one hand; and, on the other, exhibiting its filiation to the preceding, and its tendency to prepare for the following; so as to realize by degrees the positive concatenation whose principle has been already established. . . .

The theological period of humanity could begin no otherwise than by a complete and usually very durable state of pure Fetishism, which allowed free exercise to that tendency of our nature by which Man conceives of all external bodies as animated by a life analogous to his own, with differences of mere intensity. This primitive character of human speculation is established by the biological theory of Man in the *a priori* way; and in the opposite way, by all the precise information that we can obtain of the earliest social period; and again, the study of individual development confirms the analysis of the collective. . . .

In a purely philosophical view,—that is, in regard to its function of directing human speculation,—this earliest form of religious belief manifests in the smallest possible degree the theological quality of attacking the original torpor of the human faculties by furnishing some aliment to our conceptions, and some bond between them. Having done this, fetishism obstructs all advance in genuine knowledge. It is in this form, above all others, that the religious spirit is most directly opposed to the scientific, with regard to the simplest phenomena; and all idea of natural laws is out of the question when every object is a divinity with a will of its own. At this period of intellectual infancy, imaginary facts wholly overwhelm real ones; or rather, there is no phenomenon which can be distinctly seen in its genuine aspect. The mind is in a state of vague pre-occupation with regard to the external world, which, universal and natural as it is, is not the less a kind of permanent hallucination, proceeding from such a preponderance of the affective over the intellectual life, that the most absurd beliefs impair all direct observation of natural phenomena.

* * * * *

The intervention of the scientific spirit has only recently been direct and explicit; but not the less has it been concerned in all the successive modifications of the religious spirit. If man had been no more capable than monkeys and carnivorous animals of comparing, abstracting, and generalizing, he would have remained for ever in the rude fetishism which their imperfect organization forbids their surmounting. Man however can perceive likeness between phenomena, and observe their succession: and when these characteristic faculties had once found aliment and guidance under the first theological instigation, they gathered strength perpetually, and by their exercise reduced, more and more rapidly, the influence of the religious philosophy by which they had been cherished. The first general result of the rise of this spirit of observation and induction seems to me to have been the passage from fetishism to polytheism, beginning, as all such changes do, with the highest order of minds, and reaching the multitude at last. . . . The difference between the divinities of the two systems is the essential one that the gods, properly so called, have, from their indeterminate residence, a more general and abstract character. Each undertakes a special order of phenomena, but in a great number of bodies at the same time; so that each rules a department of some extent; whereas the fetish is inseparable from the one object in which it resides. When certain phenomena appeared alike in various substances, the corresponding fetishes must have formed a group, and at length coalesced into one principal one, which thus became a god; that is, an ideal and usually invisible agent, whose residence is no longer rigorously fixed. Thus, when the oaks of a forest, in their likeness to each other, suggested certain general phenomena, the abstract being in whom so many fetishes coalesced was no fetish, but the god of the forest. Thus, the intellectual transition from fetishism to polytheism is neither more nor less than the ascendancy of specific over individual ideas, in the second stage of human childhood, social as well as personal. . . .

When all bodies were no longer supposed to be divine in their nature, the secondary details of phenomena were set free for observation, without theological intermixture; and the religious conception related to beings distinct from the body, and residing elsewhere. The general conception of destiny or fate, introduced by polytheism, was also a substantial primitive ground for the principle of the invariableness of natural laws. While phenomena must then have appeared more irregular than we can conceive, polytheism exceeded its aim by presenting such a crowd of heterogeneous and unruly divinities as could not be reconciled with so much of regularity in the external world as must be admitted; and hence the creation of a particular god of immutability, whose supremacy must be acknowledged by all the rest, amidst their proper independence. Thus was the notion of Fate the necessary corrective of polytheism, from which it is naturally inseparable;—to say nothing of the aid it afforded in the final transition to monotheism. Thus polytheism disclosed an access to the ulterior principle of the invariableness of natural laws by subordinating the innumerable wills of its deities to some steady rules, however obscure those rules might be: and it sanctioned this nascent regularity, in certain respects, in relation to the moral world, which was, in that instance as in every other within the range of theology, the starting-point of all explanations of the physical world.

The Theological system arrived at the highest perfection of which it is capable when it substituted the providential action of a single Being, for the varied operations of the numerous divinities which had been before imagined. In the same way, in the last state of the Metaphysical system, men substituted one great entity (Nature) as the cause of all phenomena, instead of the multitude of entities at first supposed. In the same way again, the ultimate perfection of the Positive system would be to represent all phenomena as particular aspects of a single general fact; such as Gravitation, for instance.

* * * * *

The original and indispensable office of the theological philosophy is to lead the human mind out from the vicious circle in which it was confined by the two necessities of observing first, in order to form conceptions, and of forming theories first, in order to observe. The theological philosophy afforded an issue by likening all phenomena whatever to human acts; directly in the first instance, by supposing all bodies to have a life more or less like our own, and indirectly afterwards, by means of the more durable and suggestive hypothesis which adds to the visible system of things an invisible world, peopled by superhuman agents, who occasion phenomena by their actions on matter, otherwise inert. The second state is especially suitable to the human mind which begins to feel its difficulties and its needs; for every new phenomenon is accounted for by the supposition of a fresh volition in the ideal agent concerned, or, at most, by the easy creation of a new agent. However futile these speculations may now appear, we must remember that, in all times and everywhere, they have awakened human thought by offering to it the only material which it could at first accept. . . .

The moral and social grounds of this philosophy were as necessary as the intellectual. Its moral influence was to inspire Man with confidence enough for action, by animating him with a sense of a position of supremacy. There is something astonishing in the contrast between the actual powers of Man in an infant state and the indefinite control which he aspires to exercise over external nature; just as there is in his expectation of understanding matters which are inaccessible to reason. The practical and the speculative expectation alike belong to the theological philosophy. Supposing all phenomena to be regulated by superhuman will, Man may hope to modify the universe by his desires; not by his personal resources, but by the access which he believes himself to have to the imaginary beings whose power is unlimited; whereas, if he was aware from the beginning that the universe is subject to invariable laws, the certainty that he could no more influence than understand them would so discourage him that he would remain forever in his original apathy, intellectual and moral. We find ourselves able to dispense with supernatural aid in our difficulties and sufferings, in proportion as we obtain a gradual control over nature by a knowledge of her laws; but the early races of men were in an opposite condition. They could obtain confidence, and therefore courage, only from above, and through the illusion of an illimitable power residing there, which could, on any occasion, afford them irresistible aid.

* * * * *

Fixing our attention now upon the spiritual element which continues to be the most characteristic, even in this case, —we have seen how the metaphysical spirit must naturally obtain social sway at this period. After the Greek division of philosophy into natural and moral, the metaphysical spirit assumed two forms, which, in harmony with the distinction, became gradually antagonistic. The first, of which Plato must be considered the chief organ, most resembled the theological philosophy, which it at first tended rather to modify than to destroy. The second, whose type was Aristotle, approached much nearer to the positive philosophy, and tended to disengage the human understanding from all theological guardianship. The one was critical only on the side of polytheism, and superintended the organization of monotheism, under which it was itself absorbed by the theological spirit, and transmuted into religious philosophy; whereas, the other, occupied at first with the study of the external world, could not but be altogether critical, from its anti-theological tendency, in combination with its total lack of power to produce any organization whatever. It was under the direction of this last that the great revolutionary movement went on. Discarded by Platonism, while the best minds were engaged in the organization of the Catholic system, the Aristotelian spirit, which had been perpetually extending its inorganic domain, began to assume the ascendancy in philosophy, by gradually comprehending the moral, and even the social world under its sway, as soon as the need of a rational philosophy began to prevail. It was thus that, after the twelfth century, when the monotheistic system was in its glory, the growing triumph of scholasticism was actually working the destruction of the theological philosophy and authority. . . .

Scholasticism had realized the social

triumph of the metaphysical spirit, by disguising its organic impotence through its incorporation with the Catholic constitution, the political properties of which rendered an ample equivalent for the intellectual assistance which it provisionally received from the metaphysical philosophy. When this philosophy extended from the inorganic world to Man, implanting its entities in his moral and social nature, monotheistic faith began to be irretrievably perverted by admitting the alliance of reason. No longer resting on a natural universal obedience to a direct and permanent revelation, the faith subjected itself to the protection of demonstrations, which must necessarily admit of permanent controversy, and even of refutation; such as those which, in strange incoherence, were already named Natural Theology. This historical title is a good exponent of the temporary fusion of reason and faith, which could end in nothing but the absorption of faith by reason: it represents the contradictory dualism established between the old notion of God and the new entity of Nature, which were the respective centers of the theological and metaphysical philosophies. The antagonism of the two conceptions was reconciled for the moment by the intervention of the positive instinct, which offered the hypothesis of a God creating invariable laws, which he bound himself never to alter, and confided to Nature for special and continuous application;—a fiction which is in close analogy with that of politicians about constitution royalty. This supposition bears a characteristic metaphysical impress; and it made Nature the main object of contemplation and interest, reserving only a barren veneration for the majestic inertia of the supreme divinity, and therefore placing him at a remote distance from thought, which would naturally seek him less and less. Popular good sense never accepted this doctrine, which neutralized all theological ideas of arbitrary will and permanent action; and it is therefore no wonder that popular instinct urged the charge of atheism against so many learned assertors of Natural theology. At the present time, the case is so inverted, that that which was denounced by public reason as impiety is now considered to be religion *par excellence;* and it is laboriously cultivated by demonstrations which I have shown to be one of the chief causes of the mental destruction of monotheism. We thus see how the scholastic compromise brought about only a thoroughly contradictory situation, which could have no stability, though it was provisionally necessary to scientific progress.

Thus, the metaphysical philosophy takes possession of the speculative field after the theological has relinquished it, and before the positive is ready for it: so that in each particular case, the dispute about the supremacy of any of the three philosophies is reduced to the mere question of opportuneness, judged by a rational examination of the development of the human mind. The method of modification consists in substituting gradually the entity for a deity when religious conceptions become so generalized as to diminish perpetually the number of supernatural agents, as well as their active intervention, and at length arrive, professedly if not really, at rigorous unity. When supernatural action loses its original speciality, it consigns the immediate direction of the phenomenon to a mysterious entity, at first emanating from itself, but to which daily custom trains the human mind to refer more and more exclusively the production of each event. This strange process has favored the withdrawal of supernatural causes, and the exclusive consideration of phenomena; that is, the decline of the theological and the rise of the positive spirit. Beyond this, the general character of this philosophy is that of the theological, of which it is only a modification, though the chief. It has an inferior intellectual consistency, and a much less intense social power; so that it is much better adapted for a critical function than for any real organization: and it is those very qualities which disable it for resistance to the growth of the positive spirit. On the one hand, the increasing subtlety of metaphysical speculations is forever reducing their characteristic entities to mere abstract denominations of the corresponding phenomena, so as to render their own impotence ridiculous when they attempt explanations: a thing which would not have been possible, in an equal degree, with purely theological forms. On the other hand, its deficiency of organizing power, in consequence of its radical inconsistency, must prevent its maintaining any such political struggle as theology maintained against the spread of positive social philosophy. However, it obtains a respite by its own equivocal and mobile nature, which enables it to escape from rational discussion even more than the theological philosophy itself, while the positive spirit is as yet too imperfectly generalized to be able to attack the only substantial ground of their common authority, the universality which they can boast, but which it has not. However, this may be, we must admit the aptitude of metaphysics to sustain, provisionally, our speculative activity on all subjects till it can receive more substantial nourishment; at the same time carrying us over from the theological regime further and further in the direction of the positive.

* * * * *

Let us consider what is the proper development of the Positive Philosophy. As we have seen, the first characteristic is that it regards all phenomena as subjected to invariable natural laws. Our business is, seeing how vain is any research into what are called *Causes* whether first or final, to pursue an accurate discovery of these Laws, with a view to reducing them to the smallest possible number. By speculating upon causes, we could solve no difficulty about origin and purpose. Our real business is to analyze accurately the circumstances of phenomena, and to connect them by the natural relations of succession and resemblance. The best illustration of this is in the case of Gravitation. We say that the general phenomena of the universe are *explained* by it, because it connects under one head the whole immense variety of astronomical facts; exhibiting the constant tendency of atoms towards each other in direct proportion to their masses, and in inverse proportion to the squares of their distances; whilst the general fact itself is a mere extension of one which is perfectly familiar to us, and which we therefore say that we know: the weight of bodies on the surface of the earth. As to what weight and attraction are, we have nothing to do with that, for it is not a matter of knowledge at all. Theologians and metaphysicians may imagine and refine about such questions; but positive philosophy rejects them. When any attempt has been made to explain them, it has ended only in saying that attraction is universal weight, and that weight is terrestrial attraction: that is, that the two orders are identical; which is the point from which the question set out.

The true idea of the nature of research being thus attained, the next step was to determine the respective offices of observation and reasoning, so as to avoid the danger of empiricism on the one hand, and mysticism on the other. We have accordingly sanctioned, in the one relation, the now popular maxim of Bacon, that observed facts are the only basis of sound speculation; so that we agree to what I wrote a quarter of a century ago,—that no proposition that is not finally reducible to the enunciation of a fact, particular or general, can offer any real and intelligible meaning. On the other hand, we have repudiated the practice of reducing science to an accumulation of desultory facts, asserting that science, as distinguished from learning, is essentially composed, not of facts, but of laws, so that no separate fact can be incorporated with science till it has been connected with some other, at least by the aid of some justifiable hypothesis. . . .

Such is the nature of the positive method. The next inquiry is of its destination,—in regard to the individual, the race, speculative life and practical life. The theoretical office in regard to the individual consists in satisfying the double need of extending and connecting his real knowledge. The connection between our conceptions offered by the old philosophies, hindered their extension by providing beforehand an explanation to suit all imaginable cases; and the consequence would have been a total obstruction of knowledge, but for the secondary questions, pertaining to common affairs, which disclosed the operation of laws, without which Man could not have guided his conduct from hour to hour. From this accessory, special, and desultory positivity, genuine investigation proceeded at length, and manifested its aptitude, first to connect our conceptions, and by that very connection to extend them; and then, using every extension to perfect the anterior connection. Though the introduction of new facts may appear to disturb the positive arrangement, all experience proves—and the experience is now long enough to be relied on—that the positive method solves all such difficulties by its faithful subordination of conceptions to realities. Meeting these two needs as it meets those of order and progress in social affairs, its function may be simply described as constituting the general harmony of our intellectual system, so as to express the natural preeminence of statical over dynamical needs—those of existence over those of motion, in the case of the race as well as an individual. . . . It is this way that great philosophical minds become the intellectual guides of Humanity, undergoing first the mental revolution which they make easier and more speedy to the others by its manifestation in themselves. If this oneness of interest was evident amidst the extravagances of former philosophies, it must be complete and irresistible in the positive state—all minds speculating on a common basis, open to their examination, but untouched by their authority, and proceeding by a homogeneous course from the same starting-point to identical investigations,—their inequality affecting only the date of their success. The inverse action is clear;—that such an inevitable and unanimous concurrence must confirm the reality of the new conceptions, no less than their opportuneness. In another view, no partial intelligence can so separate itself from the general mass as not to be essentially carried on with it—even if it be—as an extreme case—that of a wise physician compelled to live among madmen, whose vehement convictions inevitably act upon his own. The most profound thinker will therefore never forget that all men must be regarded as coadjutors in discovering truth, as well as in applying it.

Social phenomena is the one branch of science which has not hitherto entered into the domain of Positive Philosophy. Theological and metaphysical methods, exploded in other departments, are as yet exclusively applied, both in the way of inquiry and discussion, in all treatment of social subjects, though the best minds are heartily weary of eternal disputes about divine right and the sovereignty of the people. This is the gap which has to be filled, to constitute, solid and entire, the Positive Philosophy.

QUESTIONS FOR DISCUSSION

1. Do you think the evidence, both personal and historical, supports Comte's description of the three-stage development of thought? Does he offer evidence? Could he? Should he?
2. Do you agree that "no proposition that is not finally reducible to the enunciation of a fact, particular or general, can offer any real and intelligible meaning"? Have you run across this belief in your previous readings? Can you think of a proposition which would deny it?
3. Do Comte's ideas presuppose a metaphysical theory? Can you have a scientific theory which is not based on a metaphysical theory?

READINGS FOR IMMEDIATE REFERENCE

Comte, Auguste. *The Positive Philosophy*. London: Bell, 1896, Books I, VI.

Poincaré, Henri. *The Foundations of Science*. New York: Science Press, 1921, pp. 321-355.

Tennant, F. R. *Philosophical Theology*. Cambridge: Cambridge University Press, 1956, Vol. I, Chapter 13.

REFERENCES FOR COMPREHENSIVE KNOWLEDGE

Comte, Auguste. *A General View of Positivism*. London: Bell, 1899.

Marvin, Francis. *Comte, the Founder of Sociology*. London: Chapman and Hall, 1936. Biographical and sympathetically analytic.

Also see:

Caird, Edward. *The Social Philosophy and Religion of Comte*. Glasgow, 1893.

Hayek, F. A. *The Counter-revolution in Science*. New York: Macmillan, 1938.

Mill, John Stuart. *Comte and Positivism*. London, 1875.

II. KARL PEARSON

Born in London in 1857, Pearson attended University College in London and Cambridge University, being admitted to the practice of law in 1881. That same year he began teaching mathematics part time at University College and, upon being appointed to a professorship in applied mathematics some five years later, he left the legal profession never to return. During the 1890's his interests shifted to biology, especially to the application of mathematics to biological research. In 1912 he was appointed Galton Professor of Eugenics. In addition he lectured on astronomy, supervised mechanical drawing classes, acted as counselor and confidant to many, and continued his own studies on the uses of statistics in biology. He retired in 1933 and died in 1937 at the age of eighty.

This selection from Pearson's very influential *Grammar of Science* contains both a critical and a constructive side. In the former he also evidences the positivistic belief that all which is meaningful in the study of metaphysics can be understood by the methods of science, the remainder being the product of imagination; in the latter, he gives an account of reality as known by the scientist. After having read several metaphysical theories, both philosophical and religious, do you find yourself in agreement with his criticisms? And after having thought about the problems of metaphysics do you find yourself in agreement with his solutions?

Positivism and Our Knowledge of the External World[1]

The reader may perhaps feel that I am laying stress upon *method* at the expense of material content. Now this is the peculiarity of scientific method, that when once it has become a habit of mind, that mind converts *all* facts whatsoever into science. The field of science is unlimited; its material is endless, every group of natural phenomena, every phase of social life, every stage of past or present development is material for science. *The unity of all science consists alone in its method, not in its material.* The man who classifies

[1] From the book *The Grammar of Science* by Karl Pearson. Everyman's Library. Reprinted by permission of E. P. Dutton and Co., Inc., New York and J. M. Dent and Sons, Ltd., London, 1920, Chapters 1, 2.

facts of any kind whatever, who sees their mutual relation and describes their sequences, is applying the scientific method and is a man of science. The facts may belong to the past history of mankind, to the social statistics of our great cities, to the atmosphere of the most distant stars, to the digestive organs of a worm, or to the life of a scarcely visible bacillus. The material of science is coextensive with the whole physical universe, not only that universe as it now exists, but with its past history and the past history of all life therein. When every fact, every present or past phenomenon of that universe, every phase of present or past life there, has been examined, classified, and co-ordinated with the rest, then the mission of science will be completed. What is this but saying that the task of science can never end till man ceases to be, till history is no longer made, and development itself ceases? . . .

Now I want to draw the reader's attention to two results which flow from the above considerations, namely: that the material of science is coextensive with the whole of life, physical and mental, of the universe, and furthermore that the limits of our perception of the universe are only apparent, not real. It is no exaggeration to say that the universe was not the same for our great-grandfathers as it is for us, and that in all probability it will be utterly different for our great-grandchildren. The universe is a variable quantity, which depends upon the keenness and structure of our organs of sense, and upon the fineness of our powers and instruments of observation. Let us briefly consider the first remark, which defines the unlimited scope of science. To say that there are certain fields—for example, *metaphysics*—from which science is excluded, wherein its methods have no application, is merely to say that the rules of methodological observation and the laws of logical thought do not apply to the facts, if any, which lie within such fields. These fields, if indeed any such exist, must lie outside any intelligible definition which can be given of the word Knowledge. If there are facts, and sequences to be observed among those facts, then we have all the requisites of scientific classification and knowledge. If there are no facts, or no sequences to be observed among them, then the possibility of *all* knowledge disappears.

The greatest assumption of everyday life—the inference which the metaphysicians tell us is wholly beyond science—namely, that other beings have consciousness as well as ourselves, seems to have just as much or as little *scientific* validity as the statement that an earth-grown apple would fall to the ground if carried to the planet of another star. Both are beyond the range of experimental demonstration, but to assume uniformity in the characteristics of brain "matter" under certain conditions seems as scientific as to assume uniformity in the characteristics of stellar "matter." Both are only working hypotheses and valuable insofar as they simplify our description of the universe.

Yet the distinction between science and metaphysics is often insisted upon, and not unadvisedly, by the devotees of both. If we take any group of physical or biological facts—say, for example, electrical phenomena or the development of the ovum—we shall find that though physicists or biologists may differ to some extent in their measurements or in their hypotheses, yet in the fundamental principles and sequences the professors of each individual science are in practical agreement among themselves. A similar if not yet so complete agreement is rapidly springing up in both mental and social sciences, where the facts are more difficult to classify and the bias of individual opinion is much stronger. . . .

The case is quite different with metaphysics and those other supposed branches of human knowledge which claim exemption from scientific control. Either they are based on an accurate classification of facts, or they are not. But if their classification of facts were accurate, the application of the scientific method ought to lead their professors to a practically identical system. Now one of the idiosyncrasies of metaphysicians lies in this: that each metaphysician has his own system, which to a large extent excludes that of his predecessors and colleagues. Hence we must conclude that metaphysics are built either on air or on quicksand—either they start from no foundation in facts at all, or the superstructure has been raised before a basis has been found in the accurate classification of facts. I want to lay special stress on this point. There is no short cut to truth, no way to gain a knowledge of the universe except through the gateway of scientific method. The hard and stony path of classifying facts and reasoning upon them is the only way to ascertain truth. It is the reason and not the imagination which must ultimately be appealed to. The poet may give us in sublime language an account of the origin and purport of the universe, but in the end it will not satisfy our aesthetic judgment, our idea of harmony and beauty, like the few facts which the scientist may venture to tell us in the same field. . . . The poet is a valued member of the community, for he is known to be a poet; his value will increase as he grows to recognize the deeper insight into nature with which modern science provides him. The metaphysician is a poet, too, often a very great one, but unfortunately he is not known to be a poet, because he strives to clothe his poetry in the language of reason, and hence it follows that he is liable to be a dangerous member of the community. . . . The touchstone of science is the universal validity of its results for all normally constituted and duly instructed minds. Because the glitter of the great metaphysical systems becomes dross when tried by this touchstone, we are compelled to classify them as interesting works of the imagination, and not as solid contributions to human knowledge.

It must not be supposed that science for a moment denies the existence of some of the problems which have hitherto been classed as philosophical or metaphysical. On the contrary, it recognizes that a great variety of physical and biological phenomena lead directly to these problems. But it asserts that the methods hitherto applied to these problems have been futile, because they have been unscientific. The classifications of facts hitherto made by the system-mongers have been hopelessly inadequate or hopelessly prejudiced. Until the scientific study of psychology, both by observation and experiment, has advanced immensely beyond its present limits—and this may take generations of work—science can only answer to the great majority of "metaphysical" problems, "I am ignorant." Meanwhile it is idle to be impatient or to indulge in system-making. The cautious and laborious classification of facts must have proceeded much further than at present before the time will be ripe for drawing conclusions.

* * * * *

Scientific ignorance may either arise from an insufficient classification of facts, or be due to the unreality of the facts with which science has been called upon to deal. . . . This is the actual state of the case with those mental and spiritual phenomena which are said to lie outside the proper scope of science, or which appear to be disregarded by scientific men.

No better example can be taken than the range of phenomena which are entitled Spiritualism. Here science is asked to analyze a series of facts which are to a great extent unreal, which arise from the vain imaginings of untrained minds and from atavistic tendencies to superstition. So far as the facts are of this character, no account can be given of them, because, like the witch's supernatural capacity, their unreality will be found at bottom to make them self-contradictory. Combined, however, with the unreal series of facts are probably others, connected with hypnotic and other conditions, which are real and only incomprehensible because there is as yet scarcely any intelligent classification or true application of scientific method. The former class of facts will, like astrology, never be reduced to law, but will one day be recognized as absurd; the other, like alchemy, may grow step by step into an important branch of science.

* * * * *

We must strive to define a little more closely in what the material of science consists. We have seen that the legitimate field of science embraces all the mental and physical facts of the universe. But what are these facts in themselves, and what is for us the criterion of their reality?

Let us start our investigation with some "external object," and as apparent simplicity will be satisfied by taking a familiar requisite of the author's calling, namely, a blackboard, let us take it. We find an outer rectangular frame of brownish-yellow color, which on closer inspection we presume to be wood, surrounding an inner fairly smooth surface painted black. We can measure a certain height, thickness, and breadth, we notice a certain degree of hardness, weight, resistance to breaking, and, if we examine further, a certain temperature, for the board feels to us cold or warm. Now although the blackboard at first sight appears a very simple object, we see that it at once leads us up to a very complex group of properties. In common talk, we attribute all these properties to the blackboard, but when we begin to think over the matter carefully we shall find that the real link between them is by no means so simple as it seems to be. To begin with, I receive certain impressions of size and shape and color by means of my organs of sight, and these enable me to pronounce with very considerable certainty that the object is a blackboard made of wood and coated with paint, even before I have touched or measured it. I *infer* that I shall find it hard and heavy, that I could if I pleased saw it up, and that I should find it to possess various other properties which I have learned to *associate* with wood and paint. These inferences and associations are something which I add to the sight-impressions, and which I myself contribute from my past experience and put into the object—blackboard. . . . The sense-impressions which determine the reality of the external object may be very few indeed, the object may be largely constructed by inferences and association, but *some* sense-impressions there must be if I am to term the object real, and not the product merely of my imagination. . . .

A sense-impression, if sufficiently strong, leaves in our brain some more or less permanent trace of itself, which is rendered manifest in the form of association whenever an immediate sense-impression of a like kind recurs. The stored effects of past sense-impressions form to a great extent what we are accustomed to speak of as an "external object." Of this account, such an object must be recognized as largely constructed by ourselves; we add to a greater or less number of immediate sense-impressions an associated group of stored sense-impressions. . . .

Just how close then can we actually get to this supposed world outside ourselves? Just as near as but no nearer than the brain terminals of the sensory nerves. We are like the clerk in the central telephone exchange who cannot get nearer to his customers than his end of the telephone wires. We are indeed worse off than the clerk, for to carry out the analogy properly we must suppose him never to have been outside the telephone exchange, never to have seen a customer, or any one like a customer—in short, never, except through the telephone wire, to have come in contact with the outside universe. Of that "real" universe outside himself he would be able to form no direct impression; the real universe for him would be the aggregate of his constructs from the messages which were caused by the telephone wires in his office. About those messages and the ideas raised in his mind he might reason and draw his inferences: and his conclusions would be correct—for what? For the world of telephonic messages, for the types of messages which go through the telephone. . . .

Very much in the position of such a telephone clerk is the conscious *ego* of each one of us seated at the brain terminals of the sensory nerves. Not a step nearer than those terminals can the *ego* get to the "outer world," and what in and for themselves are the subscribers to its nerve exchange it has no means of ascertaining. Messages in the form of sense-impressions come flowing in from that "outside world," and these we analyze, classify, store up, and reason about. But of the nature of "things-in-themselves," of what may exist at the other end of our system of telephone wire, we know nothing at all.

But the reader, perhaps, remarks, "I not only see an object, but I can *touch* it. I can trace the nerve from the tip of my finger to the brain. I am not like the telephone clerk, I can follow my network of wires to their terminals and find what is at the other end of them." Can you, reader? Think for a moment whether your *ego* has for one moment got away from his brain-exchange. The sense-impression that you call touch was just as much as sight felt only at the brain end of a sensory nerve. What has told you also of the nerve from the tip of your finger to your brain? Why, sense-impressions also, messages conveyed along optic or tactile sensory nerves. In truth all you have been doing is to employ one subscriber to your telephone exchange to tell you about the wire that goes to a second, but you are just as far as ever from tracing out for yourself the telephone wires to the individual subscriber and ascertaining what his nature is in and for himself. . . .

Reality of the external world lies for science and for us in combinations of form and color and touch—sense-impressions as widely divergent from the thing "at the other end of the nerve" as the sound of the telephone from the subscriber at the other end of the wire. We are cribbed and confined in this world of sense-impressions like the exchange clerk in his world of sounds, and not a step beyond can we get. As his world is conditioned and limited by his particular network of wire, so ours is conditioned by our nervous system, by our organs of sense. Their peculiarities determine what is the nature of the outside world which we construct. It is the similarity in the organs of sense and in the perceptive faculty of all normal human beings which makes the outside world the same, or *practically* the same, for them all. To return to the analogy, it is as if two telephone exchanges had very nearly identical groups of subscribers. In this case a wire between the two exchanges would soon convince the imprisoned clerks that they had something in common and peculiar to themselves. . . .

If at different times we meet with two groups of sense-impressions which differ very little from each other, we term them the same object or individual, and in practical life the test of identity is sameness in sense-impressions. The individuality of an object consists for us in the sameness of the great majority of our sense-impressions at two instants of time. In the case of growth, or rapid change in a group of sense-impressions, these instants must be taken closer and closer together as the rapidity increases. An impress of this sameness is then formed in the mind of the observer, and this constitutes in the case of the "external world" the recognition of individuality, in the case of the "internal world," the feeling of the continuity of the *ego*.

These considerations are more important than they may appear to the reader at first sight. Are we forced to assume a shadowy "thing in itself" behind a group of sense-impressions in order to account for the permanency of objects, their existence as individuals? We have seen by the examples cited that the "thing in itself" would have to be supposed as transient as the sense-impressions, the permanency of which it is introduced to explain. We are not, however, thrown back on any metaphysical inquiry to define for practical and scientific purposes the sameness of objects. Looking out of my window I see in a *certain* corner of my garden an ash-tree, with boughs of a *certain* form and shape, the sun is playing upon it and a *certain* light and shade is visible, the wind is turning over the leaves of the western branches. All this forms a complex group of sense-impressions. I close my eyes, and on opening them I have again a complex group of sense-impressions, but slightly differing from the last, for the sun has left some leaves and fallen on others, and the wind is still; but there is a sameness in the great majority of the sense-impressions of the two groups, and accordingly I term them one and the same individual tree—the ash-tree in my garden. If any one tells me that the sameness is due to some "thing-in-itself" which introduces the permanency into the group of sense-impressions, I can as little accept or deny his assertion as he forsooth can demonstrate anything about this shadowy thing-in-itself. . . . Such unknowables do not assist us in grasping why groups of sense-impressions remain more or less permanently linked together. Our experience is that they are so linked, and their association is at the present, and may ever remain, as mysterious as is now the process by which the impresses of past sense-impressions are involuntarily linked together in the brain.

We are now, I think, in a position to clearly grasp what we mean by the facts of science; we see that its field is ultimately based upon sensations. The familiar side of sensations, sense-impressions, excite the mind to the formations of constructs and conceptions, and these again, by association and generalization, furnish us with the whole range of material to which the scientific method applies. Shall we say that there are limits to the scientific method—that our power of knowledge is imprisoned within the narrow bounds of sense-impression? The question is an absurd one until it has been demonstrated that a definition can be found for knowledge, which shall include what does not lie in the plane of men's thought. Our only experience of thought is associated with the brain of man; no inference can possibly be legitimate which carries thought any further than nervous systems akin to his. But human thought has its ultimate source in sense-impressions, beyond which it cannot reach. We can therefore only show that our knowledge is of necessity limited by demonstrating that there are problems within the sphere of man's thought, the only sphere where thought can be legitimately said to exist, which can never be solved. Such a demonstration I, for one, have never met with, and I believe that it can never be given. . . . The very word "knowledge" only applies to the product of the scientific method. Other methods, here or elsewhere, may lead to fantasy, as that of the poet, or of the metaphysician, to superstition, but never to knowledge. There is no easy or short road to knowledge, for it can be gained, if at all, only by the long and patient toiling of many groups of workers, perhaps through several centuries.

QUESTIONS FOR DISCUSSION

1. List Pearson's objections to metaphysical theory. Do they seem to you to be cogent? Does he violate any of them in his own constructive theory?
2. Do you find his analysis of the "same" experiences satisfactory? Has he made any assumptions? If so, are they metaphysical in nature?
3. Comte's and Pearson's judgments about metaphysical thought are widely held among scientists. This view has been characterized (by a philosopher, incidentally) as being like "a blind man in a dark room looking for a black cat which isn't there." Do you agree with this estimate, or do Spinoza, Plato, Royce, Aquinas *et al.* have a more justified position?

READINGS FOR IMMEDIATE REFERENCE

Pearson, Karl. *The Grammar of Science*. London: Dent, 1920, Chapters 1-3, 7, 12.

Mach, Ernst. *The Science of Mechanics*. LaSalle, Ill.: Open Court Publ. Co., 1902, pp. 481-494.

Pap, Arthur. *Elements of Analytic Philosophy*. New York: Macmillan, 1949, pp. 402-408.

REFERENCES FOR COMPREHENSIVE KNOWLEDGE

Duhem, Pierre. *The Aim and Structure of Physical Theory*. Princeton: Princeton University Press, 1953. The purpose of scientific thought is to classify, not explain.

Poincaré, Henri. *The Foundations of Science*. New York: Science Press, 1921. Detailed studies of the particular sciences plus a defense of scientific thought as being nominalistic.

Also see:

Mach, Ernst, *Popular Scientific Lectures*. LaSalle, Ill.: Open Court Publ. Co., 1953.

Margenau, Henry. *The Nature of Physical Reality*. New York: McGraw-Hill, 1950.

Meyerson, Emile. *Identity and Reality*. London: Allen and Unwin, 1930.

Schlick, Moritz. *Philosophy of Nature*. New York: Philosophical Library, 1949.

III. PHILIPP FRANK

Born in 1884, Frank was educated in Austria, graduating from the University of Vienna. He taught at various European universities including his alma mater where he was a member of the Vienna circle, a group of philosophers and scientists, including Moritz Schlick, who met weekly to discuss problems of mutual interest. These meetings eventuated in a magazine, *Erkenntnis,* a series of world-wide conferences on the relationships between philosophy and science and the foundations of the important contemporary body of thought known as logical positivism. Frank went to the University of Prague as professor of theoretical physics in 1932, but he left in 1938 when Czechoslovakia was taken by the Nazis. He taught at Cambridge for a year, but eventually settled in the United States, where he has continued to write and teach to the present time.

In this recently published book Frank examines the historical and theoretical relationships between science and philosophy, then comes to an analysis of why theories of high generality are accepted or rejected by scientists; which is the substance of this selection. He considers several alternatives, rejecting most and concluding that the concept of purpose is of fundamental importance. Do you agree? If so, does it follow that a description of reality is part of a theory of value; that metaphysics is a branch of axiology?

Scientific Theories and Purposiveness[1]

It is generally understood among scientists that from the purely scientific angle, a system of propositions is an acceptable theory if, and only if, the system is logically correct, and its conclusions are in agreement with observable facts. Since, certainly, not all conclusions can be checked by experiment, we should rather say that (the theory is acceptable *if* no conclusion is in disagreement) with experiment, provided the number of tests is sufficiently great. It makes no difference for "science in the modern sense" which type of concepts and which type of relations between concepts occur in the proposi-

[1] From Philipp Frank, *Philosophy of Science: The Link Between Science and Philosophy.* © 1957, Prentice-Hall, Inc., Englewood Cliffs, N.J., pp. 349-359. Reprinted by permission.

tion of the theory, provided no conclusion drawn from the theory is in disagreement with observations. Of course, we must always consider that the propositions of the theory consist not only of the relations between the basic concepts (or the basic symbols), but also of the "operational definitions" which connect those statements about basic symbols with statements about observable facts. According to these criteria, a theory is confirmed if it is in agreement with observable conclusions which have been tested by actual observations. But if a theory has been "confirmed" in the sense which we have described above, it cannot be concluded that it is "valid," but only that it *may* be valid. According to what criteria have scientists made a choice between several theories which may be valid?

In general, scientists would say that among several theories that are set up to account for a certain domain of observed facts, one will stand out as the best and will be accepted generally. If we follow Reichenbach's advice, we would say that we should accept the "most probable" theory. This means, according to the statistical theory of probability, that the theory should be accepted which shows "more" agreement with observed facts than the other theories. However, this agreement cannot be the only criterion of acceptance. If this were so, the best theory would be the mere description of facts; but this would be no theory at all. . . .

Most contemporary scientists would claim that among all theories that can account for the same observed facts the "simplest" theories are chosen, but the question arises of how to define the degree of simplicity. . . . During the long dispute between the wave theory and the corpuscular theory of light, one of the reasons for preferring the corpuscular was an argument of "simplicity." This theory led mathematically to the differential equations for the motion of a particle which are formulated by Newton's laws of motion. These laws lead to ordinary differential equations of the second order. The wave theory, however, led to the wave equation, which was a partial differential equation of the second order that had to be solved under restriction by boundary conditions. This was in the beginning of the nineteenth century a mathematical problem much less simple than the solution of ordinary differential equations. Hence, mathematical simplicity could be invoked in favor of the corpuscular theory. This difference in simplicity became, of course, less and less obvious the more the theory of partial differential equations developed. Hence, it is clear that how we judge the mathematical simplicity of a theory depends on the state of science at a certain period.

There is, of course, the question *why* "simple theories" should be preferred. Some scientists say that they prefer them because "simple" formulae allow easier and quicker computation of the result; they are "economical" because they save time and effort. Other authors, however, say that simple theories are more "elegant," more "beautiful"; they prefer simple theories for aesthetic reasons. . . .

If we investigate which theories have actually been preferred because of their simplicity, we find that the decisive reason for acceptance has been neither economic nor aesthetic, but rather what has often been called "dynamic." This means that the theory was preferred that proved to make science more dynamic, i.e., more fit to expand into unknown territory. This can be made clear by using an example that we have invoked frequently in this book: the struggle between the Copernican and the Ptolemaic systems. In the period between Copernicus and Newton a great many reasons had been invoked on behalf of one or the other system. Eventually, however, Newton advanced his theory of motion, which accounted excellently for all motions of celestial bodies (e.g., comets), while Copernicus as well as Ptolemy had accounted for only the motions in our planetary system. Even in this restricted domain, they neglected the "perturbations" that are due to the interaction between the planets. However, Newton's laws originated in generalizations of the Copernican theory, and we can hardly imagine how they could have been formulated if he had started with the Ptolemaic system. In this respect and in many others, the Copernican theory was the more "dynamic" one. . . .

If we look at the reasons why theories have been actually accepted, however, we soon notice that agreement with facts and simplicity are not the only qualities which a scientific theory is expected to possess. When we remember, for example, Francis Bacon's attitude toward the Copernican theory, we note that he prefers the geocentric (Ptolemaic) theory because it is more in agreement with common sense. . . . [But,] science has never been completely restricted to technological use. Therefore, criteria which are different from the "scientific" ones in the narrower sense have always intervened. If we again invoke an old example, the Copernican theory, we can easily see that a great many scientists and philosophers who have admitted that this system is "mathematically simple" and "in agreement with the facts" have rejected it for reasons of a completely different kind.

It is easily seen from well-known examples that fitness to support desirable conduct on the part of citizens or, briefly, to support moral behavior, has served through the ages as a reason for the acceptance of a theory. In antiquity, the physics of Aristotle and Plato seemed to be fitter, in this respect, than the physics of Epicurus. According to the first, the celestial bodies were made of a nobler material than our earth, while according to the "materialistic" doctrine of Epicurus, all these bodies consisted of the same elements. This latter doctrine, however, made it more difficult to teach the existence of a difference between material and spiritual beings. Since a great many educators and statesmen have been convinced that the belief in this difference is important for the education of good citizens, the Epicurean doctrine was rejected by powerful groups. . . .

Scientists and scientifically minded people in general have often been inclined to say that these "non-scientific" influences upon the acceptance of scientific theories are something which should not happen; but since they do happen, it is necessary to understand their status within a logical analysis of science. We have learned by a great many examples that the general principles of science are not unambiguously determined by the observed facts. If we add requirements of simplicity and agreement with common sense, the determination becomes narrower, but it does not become unique. We can still require their fitness to support desirable moral and political doctrines. All these requirements together enter into the determination of a scientific theory. The firm conviction of most scientists that a theory should be accepted "on scientific grounds" only, forms a philosophy which they absorbed as young scientists in the period when they started to acquire knowledge about the world: this philosophy claims that a "true" theory gives us a "picture of the physical reality," and that this theory can be found on the basis of observed facts. If a theory built up exclusively because of its agreement with observed facts told the "truth" about the world, it would be foolish to assume seriously that the acceptance of a scientific theory should be influenced by reasons of simplicity and agreement with common sense, let alone moral, religious, or political grounds. However, we have learned that "agreement with observed facts" never singles out one individual theory. There is never only one theory that is in complete agreement with all observed facts, but several theories that are in partial agreement. We have to select the final theory by a compromise. The final theory has to be in fair agreement with observed facts and must also be fairly simple. If we consider this point, it is obvious that such a "final" theory cannot be "The Truth."

However, this metaphysical concept of a true theory as a "replica of physical reality" is not prevalent in the scientific philosophy of today. A theory is now rather regarded as an instrument that serves some definite purpose. It must be helpful in predicting future observable facts on the basis of facts that have been observed in the past and in the present. The theory should also be helpful in the contribution of devices which can save us time and labor. The scientific theory is, in a way, a tool that produces other tools according to a practical scheme. Scientific theories are also accepted, however, because they give us a simple and beautiful world picture and support a philosophy which, in turn, supports a desirable way of life.

The question of which theory should be accepted can only be answered if we know whether predictions of facts, construction of devices, beauty, simplicity, or fitness to support moral and political aims should be preferred. We can understand this situation if we compare it with the question about the choice of an airplane. If we speak of an individual airplane, it makes no sense to ask whether it is "true" in the sense of being "perfect." We can only ask whether it is "good" or "perfect" for a certain purpose. If we set "speed" as our purpose, the perfect airplane will be different from the one which is perfect for the purpose of "endurance." The criterion of perfection will be different again if we choose "safety" or "fun" or "convenience for reading or sleeping" as our purpose. It is impossible to construct an airplane which fulfills all these purposes in a maximal way; we must achieve some compromise. In order to determine the kind of compromise which "should" be achieved, we must decide which is more important: speed or safety, fun or endurance? The answer to this question can certainly not be derived from physical or engineering science. From the view of "science proper," the purpose is arbitrary; science can only teach us how to construct a plane if we are given in advance the speed and the degree of safety that should be achieved. However, the desirable relation between speed and safety is dependent upon moral, political, and even religious opinions. . . .

We may ask why a certain scientific theory, e.g., the Copernican theory of planetary motion or Einstein's theory of relativity, has been accepted as true or perfect. According to the previous considerations, this question can only be answered if we first answer the question: What purpose is the theory to serve? Is it only the purely technical purpose of predicting observable facts? Or is it the purpose of obtaining a simple and elegant theory which will allow us to derive a great many facts from simple principles? We have to prefer the theory that fits our purpose. For some groups, the main purpose of scientific theories may be to serve as a support in teaching a desirable way of life, or in discouraging an undesirable one. These groups would accept theories which may give a rough picture of observed facts, provided we can get from them a picture of the world in which man plays the role that they regard as desirable.

If we wish to speak in a brief and rather perfunctory way, we may distinguish between two main purposes of a theory: use for the construction of devices (technological purposes), and use for direct guidance of human conduct. The actual acceptance of theories has always been a compromise between the technological and the sociological value of the theory. Human conduct has been directly influenced by the latter because specific religious and political views were encouraged, while technological influence upon human conduct has been rather indirect—technological changes bring about social changes which manifest themselves in changes in human conduct. Everybody knows of the "industrial revolution" in nineteenth-century England and the accompanying changes in human behavior. Probably the rise of atomic technology in our twentieth century will produce analogous changes in human life. . . .

This double role of scientific theories becomes even more obvious in biology. If we investigate the attitude of biologists toward very general questions, we may take as an example the question of whether or not living organisms have developed from inanimate matter. Here we find the conflict between the technological and the sociological purpose of theories in full bloom. Some prominent biologists say that "spontaneous generation" is highly probable, while others claim that according to their computations this probability is almost zero. One group believes that the biological theories should uphold human dignity because otherwise moral behavior could not be founded upon science. This dignity would be impaired if man is descended not only from apes, but even from earth and stone. Another group, however, believes that the assumption of spontaneous generation would uphold the belief in the unity of nature as a whole, and, on this basis, support a moral human behavior.

From all these considerations, we see that the validity of a scientific theory cannot be judged unless we ascribe a certain purpose to that theory. The achievement of that purpose depends upon the degree to which the different criteria for the acceptance of a theory are satisfied, agreement with observed facts, simplicity and elegance, agreement with common sense, fitness to support desirable human conduct, etc. Hence, the validity of a theory cannot be judged by "scientific" criteria in the narrower sense: agreement with observations and logical consistency. After application of all these criteria, there remains often a choice among several theories.

QUESTIONS FOR DISCUSSION

1. List the possible reasons which could be given for accepting a theory discussed by Frank, and the reasons he gives for rejecting the ones he does.
2. Do you agree with Frank that "agreement with the facts" is an inadequate reason for accepting a scientific theory?
3. Do you think that Frank's view is an advance, a regression or irrelevant to the views of Comte and Pearson?

READINGS FOR IMMEDIATE REFERENCE

Frank, Philipp. *Between Physics and Philosophy*. Cambridge: Harvard University Press, 1941, Essays 4, 5, 10.

———. *Philosophy of Science*. New York: Prentice-Hall, 1957, Chapters 1, 2, 12-15.

Dewey, John. *Logic: The Theory of Inquiry*. New York: Henry Holt, 1938, Chapters 22, 24.

REFERENCES FOR COMPREHENSIVE KNOWLEDGE

Frank, Philipp. *Einstein, His Life and Times*. New York: Knopf, 1947.

———. *Modern Science and Its Philosophy*. Cambridge: Harvard University Press, 1949.

———. *The Validation of Scientific Theories*. Boston: Beacon Press, 1957.

Also see:

Bridgman, Percy W. *The Logic of Modern Physics*. New York: Macmillan, 1927.

Peirce, Charles S. *Collected Papers,* Vol. VI, Book I. Cambridge: Harvard University Press, 1935.

IV. JOHN DALTON

Born in 1766, the son of a poor Quaker weaver, Dalton had little formal education, although he was teaching in a village school when he was no more than twelve years old. He farmed for some time but spent most of his life in Manchester teaching as a private tutor and in New College (later to become part of Oxford). Besides his teaching he was actively interested in scientific research. During more than half a century he recorded more than 200,000 meteorological observations, and his interest in optics led to the discovery of color blindness. In 1828 he was elected one of eight foreign associates of the French Academy, and in 1830 he was awarded an annual stipend by the British government. His life was very simple—broken each Thursday afternoon by a game of bowls, annual excursions to the Lake country, and an occasional visit to London, "a surprising place and well worth one's while to see once, but the most disagreeable place on earth for one of a contemplative turn to reside in constantly." He died in 1844, aged seventy-seven.

Not all scientists are positivistic toward metaphysics. The ancient theory of atomism has been revived and found to be fruitful in modern physical thought. In this selection you will read one of the earliest statements of this theory given in modern times. Look for the evidence Dalton gives to support his conclusion.

Modern Atomism[1]

"It seems probable to me that God in the beginning formed matter in *solid, massy, hard, impenetrable, movable* particles, of such *sizes* and *figures,* and with such other *properties,* and in such proportion to space as most conduced to the end for which he formed them; and that these primitive particles being solids, are incomparably harder than any porous bodies compounded of them; even so very hard as never to wear or break in pieces; no ordinary power being able to divide what God Himself made *One,* in the first creation. While the particles continue entire they may compose bodies of one and the same nature and texture in all ages; but should they wear away or break in pieces, the nature of things depending on them would be changed. Water and earth, composed of old worn particles and fragments

[1] From Henry Roscoe, *John Dalton and the Rise of Modern Chemistry.* New York: Cassell and Co., 1901, pp. 131-145. And from John Dalton, *A New System of Chemical Philosophy*. Manchester, 1810, Part I.

of particles, would not be of the same nature and texture now, with water and earth composed of *entire* particles in the beginning. And therefore that nature may be lasting, the changes of corporeal things are to be placed only in the various *separations* and new *associations,* and motions of these permanent particles; compound bodies being apt to break, not in the midst of solid particles, but where those particles are laid together, and only touch in a few points. . . .

God is able to create particles of matter of several *sizes* and *figures,* and in several proportions to the space they occupy, and perhaps of different *densities* and forces . . . At least I see nothing of contradiction in all this."

SIR ISAAC NEWTON.

As the ensuing lectures on the subject of *chemical elements* and their combinations will perhaps be thought by many to possess a good deal of novelty, as well as importance, it may be proper to give a brief historical sketch of the train of thought and experience which led me to the conclusions about to be detailed.

Having been long accustomed to make meteorological observations, and to speculate upon the nature and constitution of the atmosphere, it often struck me with wonder how a *compound* atmosphere, or a mixture of two or more elastic fluids, should constitute apparently a homogeneous mass, or one in all mechanical relations agreeing with a simple atmosphere.

Newton has demonstrated clearly, in the 23rd Prop. of Book 2 of the *Principia,* that an elastic fluid is constituted of small particles or atoms of matter, which repel each other by a force increasing in proportion as their distance diminishes. But modern discoveries having ascertained that the atmosphere contains three or more elastic fluids, of different specific gravities, it did not appear to me how this proposition of Newton would apply to a case of which he, of course, could have no idea.

The same difficulty occurred to Dr. Priestley, who discovered this compound nature of the atmosphere. He could not conceive why the oxygen gas, being specifically heaviest, should not form a distinct *stratum* of air at the bottom of the atmosphere, and the azotic gas one at the top of the atmosphere. Some chemists upon the Continent, I believe the French, found a solution of this difficulty (as they apprehended). It was *chemical affinity*. One species of gas was held in solution by the other; and this compound in its turn dissolved water; hence *evaporation, rain,* etc. This opinion of air dissolving water had long before been the prevailing one, and naturally paved the way for the reception of that which followed, of one kind of air dissolving another. It was objected that there were no decisive *marks* of chemical union, when one kind of air was mixed with another. The answer was, that the affinity was of a very *slight* kind, not of that energetic cast that is observable in most other cases.

I may add, by-the-bye, that this is now, or has been till lately, I believe, the prevailing doctrine in most of the chemical schools in Europe.

In order to reconcile or rather adapt this chemical theory of the atmosphere to the Newtonian doctrine of repulsive atoms or particles, I set to work to combine my atoms upon paper. I took an atom of water, another of oxygen, and another of azote, brought them together, and threw around them an atmosphere of heat. . . . I repeated the operation, but soon found that the watery particles were exhausted (for they make but a small part of the atmosphere). I next combined my atoms of oxygen and azote, one to one; but I found in time my oxygen failed; I then threw all the remaining particles of azote into the mixture, and began to consider how the general equilibrium was to be obtained.

My triple compounds of *water, oxygen,* and *azote* were wonderfully inclined, by their superior gravity, to descend and take the lowest place; the double compounds of *oxygen* and *azote* affected to take a middle station; and the azote was inclined to swim at the top. I remedied this defect by lengthening the wings of my heavy particles, that is, by throwing more heat around them, by means of which I could make them float in any part of the vessel; but this change unfortunately made the whole mixture of the same specific gravity as azotic gas—this circumstance could not for a moment be tolerated. In short, I was obliged to abandon the hypothesis of the chemical constitution of the atmosphere altogether, as irreconcilable to the phenomena. . . .

There was but one alternative left, namely, to surround every individual particle of *water,* of *oxygen,* and of *azote,* with heat, and to make them respectively centers of repulsion, the same in a *mixed* state as in a *simple* state. This hypothesis was equally pressed with difficulties; for, still my oxygen would take the lowest place, my azote the next, and my steam would swim upon the top.

In 1801 I hit upon an hypothesis which completely obviated these difficulties.

According to this, we were to suppose that the atoms of one kind did *not* repel the atoms of another kind, but only those of their own kind. This hypothesis most effectually provided for the diffusion of any one gas through another, whatever might be their specific gravities, and perfectly reconciled any mixture of gases to the Newtonian theorem. Every atom of both or all the gases in the mixture was the center of repulsion to the proximate particles of its own kind, disregarding those of the other kind. All the gases united their efforts in counteracting the pressure of the atmosphere, or any other pressure that might be opposed to them.

This hypothesis, however beautiful might be its application, had some improbable features.

We were to suppose as many distinct *kinds* of repulsive powers, as of gases; and, moreover, to suppose that *heat* was not the repulsive power in any one case; positions certainly not very probable. Besides, I found from a train of experiments which have been published in the *Manchester Memoirs,* that the diffusion of gases through each other was a *slow* process, and appeared to be a work of considerable effort.

Upon reconsidering this subject, it occurred to me that I had never contemplated the effect of *difference of size* in the particles of elastic fluids. By *size* I mean the hard particle at the center and the atmosphere of heat taken together. If, for instance, there be not exactly the same *number* of atoms of oxygen in a given volume of air as of azote in the same volume, then the *sizes* of the particles of oxygen must be different from those of azote. And if the *sizes* be different, then on the supposition that the repulsive power is heat, no equilibrium can be established by particles of unequal size pressing against each other. . . .

This idea occurred to me in 1805. I soon found that the *sizes* of the particles of elastic fluids *must* be different. For a measure of azotic gas and one of oxygen, if chemically united, would make nearly *two* measures of nitrous gas, and those *two* could not have *more* atoms of nitrous gas than the *one* measure had of azote or oxygen. . . . Hence the suggestion that all gases of different kinds have a difference in the *size* of their atoms; and thus we arrive at the reason for that diffusion of every gas through every other gas, without calling in any other repulsive power than the well-known one of heat.

This then is the present view which I have of the constitution of a mixture of elastic fluids.

The different *sizes* of the particles of elastic fluids under like circumstances of temperature and pressure being once established, it became an object to determine the relative *sizes* and *weights,* together with the relative *number* of atoms in a given volume. This led the way to the combinations of gases, and to the *number* of atoms entering into such combinations, the particulars of which will be detailed more at large in the sequel. Other bodies besides elastic fluids, namely liquids and solids, were subject to investigation, in consequence of their combining with elastic fluids. Thus a train of investigation was laid for determining the *number* and *weight* of all chemical elementary principles which enter into any sort of combination one with another. . . .

We endeavored to show that matter, though divisible in an *extreme degree,* is nevertheless not *infinitely* divisible. That there must be some point beyond which we cannot go in the division of matter. The existence of these ultimate particles of matter can scarcely be doubted, though they are probably much too small ever to be exhibited by microscopic improvements.

I have chosen the word *atom* to signify these ultimate particles, in preference to *particle, molecule,* or any other diminutive term, because I conceive it is much more expressive; it includes in itself the notion of *indivisible,* which the other terms do not. It may perhaps be said that I extend the application of it too far, when I speak of *compound atoms;* for instance, I call an ultimate particle of *carbonic acid* a *compound atom.* Now, though this atom may be divided, yet it ceases to be carbonic acid, being resolved by such division into charcoal and oxygen. Hence I conceive there is no inconsistency in speaking of compound atoms, and that my meaning cannot be misunderstood.

It has been imagined by some philosophers that all matter, however unlike, is probably the same thing; and that the great variety of its appearances arises from certain powers communicated to it, and from the variety of combinations and arrangements of which it is susceptible. From the notes I borrowed from Newton in the last lecture, this does not appear to have been his idea. Neither is it mine. I should apprehend there are a considerable number of what may be properly called *elementary* principles, which never can be metamorphosed, one into another, by any power we can control. We ought, however, to avail ourselves of every means to reduce the number of bodies or principles of this appearance as much as possible; and after all we may not know what elements are absolutely indecomposable, and what are refractory, because we do not apply the proper means for their reduction.

* * * * *

Whether the ultimate particles of a body, such as water, are all alike, that is, of the same figure, weight, etc. is a question of some importance. From what is known, we have no reason to apprehend a diversity in these respects: if it does exist in water, it must equally exist in the elements constituting water, namely, hydrogen and oxygen. Now it is scarcely possible to conceive how the aggregates of dissimilar particles should be so uniformly the same. If some of the particles of water were heavier than others, if a parcel of the liquid on any occasion were constituted principally of these heavier particles, it must be supposed to affect the specific gravity of the mass, a circumstance not known. Similar observations may be made on other substances. Therefore we may conclude that *the ultimate particles of all homogeneous bodies are perfectly alike in weight, figure, etc.* In other words, every particle of water is like every other particle of water; every particle of hydrogen is like every other particle of hydrogen. . . .

When any body exists in the elastic state, its ultimate particles are separated from each other to a much greater distance than in any other state; each particle occupies the center of a comparatively large sphere, and supports its dignity by keeping all the rest, which by their gravity, or otherwise are disposed to encroach upon it, at a respectful distance. When we attempt to conceive the *number* of particles in an atmosphere, it is somewhat like attempting to conceive the number of stars in the universe; we are confounded with the thought. But if we limit the subject, by taking a given volume of any gas, we seem persuaded that, let the divisions be ever so minute, the number of particles must be finite; just as in a given space of the universe, the number of stars and planets cannot be infinite.

Chemical analysis and synthesis go no farther than to the separation of particles one from another, and to their reunion. No new creation or destruction of matter is within the reach of chemical agency. We might as well attempt to introduce a new planet into the solar system, or to annihilate one already in existence, as to create or destroy a particle of hydrogen. All the changes we can produce, consist in separating particles that are in a state of cohesion or combination, and joining those that were previously at a distance.

In all chemical investigations, it has justly been considered an important object to ascertain the relative *weights* of the simples which constitute a compound. But unfortunately the enquiry has terminated here; whereas from the relative weights in the mass, the relative weights of the ultimate particles or atoms of the bodies might have been inferred, from which their number and weight in various other compounds would appear, in order to assist and to guide future investigations, and to correct their results. Now it is one great object of this work, to show the importance and advantage of ascertaining *the relative weights of the ultimate particles, both of simple and compound bodies, the number of simple elementary particles which constitute one compound particle, and the number of less compound particles which enter into the formation of one more compound particle.*

* * * * *

The greatest difficulty attending the mechanical hypothesis, arises from different gases observing different laws. Why does water not admit its bulk of every kind of gas alike? This question I have duly considered, and though I am not yet able to satisfy myself completely, I am nearly persuaded that the circumstance depends upon the weight and number of the ultimate particles of the several gases: Those whose particles are lightest and single being least absorbable, and the others more according as they increase in weight and complexity. (Subsequent experience renders this conjecture less probable.) An enquiry into the relative weights of the ultimate particles of bodies is a subject, as far as I know, entirely new: I have lately been prosecuting this enquiry with remarkable success. The principle cannot be entered upon in this paper; but I shall just subjoin the results, as far as they appear to be ascertained by my experiments.

TABLE OF THE RELATIVE WEIGHTS OF THE ULTIMATE PARTICLES OF GASEOUS AND OTHER BODIES

Hydrogen	1
Azote	4·2
Carbon	4·3
Ammonia	5·2
Oxygen	5·5
Water	6·5
Phosphorus	7·2
Phosphuretted hydrogen	8·2
Nitrous gas [nitric oxide]	9·7
Ether	9·6
Gaseous oxide of carbon	9·8
Nitrous oxide	13·9
Sulphur	14·4
Nitric acid	15·2
Sulphuretted hydrogen	15·4
Carbonic acid	15·3
Alcohol	15·1
Sulphureous acid	19·9
Sulphuric acid	25·4
Carburetted hydrogen from stag. water	6·3
Olefiant gas	5·3

QUESTIONS FOR DISCUSSION

1. What was the problem raised by his account of water, oxygen and azote (nitrogen), and how did the atomic theory resolve it?
2. Does Dalton believe that atoms differ qualitatively or quantitatively —or both?
3. Compare Dalton's theory to the selection from Lucretius on pp. 169-177, giving special attention to the reasons given to support the conclusion. Are they the same? If so, how do you account for this? If not, which has the better reasons?

READINGS FOR IMMEDIATE REFERENCE

Hobbes, Thomas. *Elements of Philosophy*. Chapters 8-15, 26.

Nash, Leonard K. "The Atomic Molecular Theory," *Harvard Case Studies in Experimental Science*. Cambridge: Harvard University Press, 1954.

REFERENCES FOR COMPREHENSIVE KNOWLEDGE

Dalton, John. *New System of Chemical Philosophy*. Manchester, 1810.

Roscoe, H. E. and Harden, A. *A New View of the Origin of Dalton's Atomic Theory*. London: Methuen, 1912. The theory came from his empirical studies, not his speculations.

Also see:

Freund, Ira. *The Study of Chemical Composition*. Cambridge: Cambridge University Press, 1904.

Heisenberg, Werner. *Philosophic Problems of Nuclear Science*. New York: Pantheon, 1952.

Henry, W. C. *Life of Dalton*. London, 1854.

Neville-Polley, L. J. *John Dalton*. New York: Oxford University Press, 1920.

V. J. W. N. SULLIVAN

Born in England in 1886, Sullivan was interested as a boy in music and mathematics, in which he was largely self-taught. After his graduation from University College he wrote technical articles for industrial firms, served in World War I and became the science editor for *The Athenaeum* in 1921. He published many books, including biographies of such diverse men as Newton, Beethoven and Galileo. He once described himself as "an extreme form of introvert" having little interest in such things as "politics, business, social gathering and royal processions," but following his death in 1937, the *Times* of London spoke of him as "one of the most accomplished men of our generation," one who was particularly adept at stating contemporary scientific theories in nontechnical language.

In this selection Sullivan contends that the traditional Newtonian presuppositions of science no longer are justified, and hence a new set of beliefs is necessary. Notice particularly his description of Newtonian physics and his reasons for saying they are limited. Is the alternative he suggests similar to any theory you have read in earlier chapters? How is his belief in freedom justified?

The Limitations of Science[1]

We have seen that the scientific account of our universe appears clearest and most convincing when it deals with inanimate matter. Here we feel that the account is relatively satisfactory because it does, on the whole, meet the kind of interest we take in these phenomena. The age, position, size, velocity, chemical constitution of a star is, for instance, the kind of information we want about a star. And to be told that matter consists of little electrified particles arranged with respect to one another in certain ways makes us feel that our curiosity about matter has very largely been met.

But when we come to the sciences dealing with life, the state of affairs is less satisfactory. Many of the questions that seem to us quite fundamental have not been met. What, for instance, makes us regard a living organism as a whole, and not merely as the sum of its parts?

[1] From *The Limitations of Science* by J. W. N. Sullivan. Copyright 1933 by The Viking Press, Inc. Reprinted by permission of The Viking Press, Inc., Chapter 6.

What does this vague notion of "wholeness" or "individuality" really amount to? Even if every bodily activity of the animal was explained in terms of physical and chemical changes, we should still feel that our question was unanswered unless what appears as the *purposive order* of those changes was also accounted for. But "purpose" is not yet a scientific notion. It is not employed in the physical and chemical sciences, and the majority of biologists or, at least, of physiologists, are reluctant to introduce any ideas which have not been found necessary in these sciences. This is doubtless an excellent procedure so far as certain limited classes of problems are concerned, but it also seems to lead to the consequence that the most obvious and fundamental problems of biology are not even approached. The case has been put forcibly, but fairly, by Professor Whitehead. Speaking of the application of the notions of physics and chemistry to life he says:

> The brilliant success of this method is admitted. But you cannot limit a problem by reason of a method of attack. The problem is to understand the operations of an animal body. There is clear evidence that certain operations of certain animal bodies depend upon the foresight of an end and the purpose to attain it. It is no solution of the problem to ignore this evidence because other operations have been explained in terms of physical and chemical laws. The existence of a problem is not even acknowledged. It is vehemently denied. Many a scientist has patiently designed experiments for the *purpose* of substantiating his belief that animal operations are motivated by no purposes. He has perhaps spent his spare time in writing articles to prove that human beings are as other animals so that "purpose" is a category irrelevant for the explanation of their bodily activities, his own activities included. Scientists animated by the purpose of proving that they are purposeless constitute an interesting subject for study.

* * * * *

Psychology, contrasted with the physical sciences, seems even more inadequate. The psychological theory that sticks most closely to the terms of mechanics is Behaviorism, and we have seen that that theory is hopelessly inadequate.[1] Psycho-analysis, it is true, introduces primary concepts which are not mechanical, but these concepts are far too vague and indefinite to be called scientific. Such a concept as Freud's libido, for example, is called upon to explain so much that it explains nothing. So far as a scientific explanation is concerned, no more is gained by saying that the most amazingly diverse manifestations all come about through the libido than by saying that they all come about through the Will of God. The explanation admittedly explains everything—and therefore explains nothing.

We conclude, therefore, that it is only in the sciences dealing with inanimate matter that a reasonably adequate set of primary concepts has yet been isolated. We say "reasonably adequate" because in relativity and quantum theory, even these concepts are undergoing extensive revision. Nevertheless, they have been a tremendous success over three centuries, and it is doubtless owing to this success that scientific men have

[1] It gives a too simple account of the mind, failing adequately to account for memory, imagination, and the ability to understand the same idea given in different words, among other difficulties.—C.M.

been led to adopt them in fields where they would not, perhaps, naturally suggest themselves. What are these concepts, and how were they isolated? The answer to this question will enable us to realize the nature and limitations of the scientific method, and also show us how baseless is the hope that these concepts will ever suffice to cover the whole of experience.

Scientific method, as we see from the work of its founders, Copernicus, Kepler, Galileo, began by quite consciously and deliberately selecting and abstracting from the total elements of our experience. From the total wealth of impressions received from nature these men fastened upon some only as being suitable for scientific formulation. These were those elements that possess *quantitative* aspects. Between these elements mathematical relations exist, and these men were convinced that mathematics is the key to the universe. . . . Galileo had no doubt that mathematics is the one true key to natural phenomena. It was this persuasion that gave these men their criterion for selection amongst the total elements of their experience. They confined their attention to those elements amongst which mathematical relations exist. Bodies, for instance, have for their measurable aspects size, shape, weight, motion. Such other characteristics as they possess were regarded as belonging to a lower order of reality. The real world is the world of mathematical characteristics. In fact, our minds are so constructed, Kepler said, that they can know nothing perfectly except quantities.

With Galileo this separation of the mathematical from the other qualities became a perfectly clear and definite doctrine. Kepler had supposed that the non-mathematical qualities actually did belong to bodies, but that they were somehow less real. Galileo went further than this, and stated that the non-mathematical properties are all entirely subjective. They have no existence at all apart from our senses. Thus colors, sounds, odors, and so on exist, as such, wholly in our minds. They are, in reality, motions of some kind or another in the external world, and these motions, impinging on our senses, give rise to these sensations of color, sound, and so on. It is mind that peoples the world with the songs of birds, the colors of the sunset, etc. In the absence of mind the universe would be a collection of masses of various sizes, shapes, and weights, drifting without color, sound, or odor, through space and time. . . .

With this reduction of the real world to colorless, soundless, odorless bodies in motion, the notions of space and time underwent a profound change. To the medieval philosophers the temporal process was the transformation of potentiality into actuality. The purpose of everything was to reach a higher state of being, culminating in union with God. The whole of the past, up to the present moment, was the ground already won, as it were. As the process continues, the ground won increases; the future is being drawn into the present. This process goes on until the final culmination is reached, when time stands still. We see how different is this notion of time from the mathematical time introduced by Galileo. Time, as it appears in science, may be likened to an ever-moving mathematical point. The present moment, which has no finite duration, is merely a boundary point between a vanished past and a non-existent future. Time, conceived in this way, can be represented very simply mathematically as a straight line, successive points on the line representing successive instants of time. . . .

With this change in the notion of time comes a corresponding change in the notion of cause. When all things were regarded as moving towards union with God, then union with God was regarded as the final cause of all change. The cause of a process was to be found in the end towards which it tended. The reason why things happened was to be found in the purpose the happening served. With the new notion of time the future, being non-existent, had no influence on present happenings. The cause of anything happening now was to be found in its immediate past. Further, all that really happens are motions—motions of the constituent particles of the bodies forming the real world. And these motions are themselves the products of preceding motions. . . .

We see that the scientific outlook, as presented by Galileo, constitutes a really amazing revolution in thought. The vivid world of the medievalist, a world shot through with beauty and instinct with purpose, a world having an intimate relation to his own destiny and an intelligible reason for existing in the light of that destiny, is dismissed as an illusion. It has no objective existence. The real world, as revealed by science, is a world of material particles moving, in accordance with mathematical laws, through space and time.

* * * * *

[The] first indication that these concepts were not all-sufficient came when men tried to fashion a mechanical theory of light. This endeavor led to the creation of the ether, the most unsatisfactory and wasteful product of human ingenuity that science has to show. For generations this monster was elaborated. Miracles of mathematical ingenuity were performed in the attempt to account for the properties of light in terms of the Newtonian concepts. The difficulties became ever more heartbreaking until, after the publication of Maxwell's demonstration that light is an electromagnetic phenomenon, they seemed to become insuperable. . . . The construction of ethers became a decaying industry, and largely because there was so little demand for the product. For it had dawned on men of science that there was, after all, nothing sacrosanct about the Newtonian entities. It might be that his list of ultimates, mass, force, and so on, was not exhaustive. Instead of reducing electricity to these terms, it might be better to add it to the list. This was done. After a certain amount of hesitation, and a few last desperate efforts to make electricity mechanical, electricity was added to the list of irreducible elements.

This may seem to have been a simple and obvious step to take, but it was, in reality, of profound significance. For the Newtonian concepts were all of a kind that one seemed to understand intimately. Thus the mass of a body was the quantity of matter in it. Inertia was that familiar property of matter which makes it offer resistance to a push. Force was a notion derived from our experience of muscular effort. Of course, all these concepts, in order to be of use to science, had to be given quantitative expression. They entered our calculations as mathematical symbols. In the case of electricity its nature is precisely what we did not know. Attempts to represent it in familiar terms—as a condition of strain in the ether, or what not—had been given up. All that we knew about electricity was the way it affected our measuring instruments. The precise description of this behavior gave us the mathematical specification of electricity and this, in truth, was all we knew about it. . . .

With the realization [that we know nothing about an object but its mathematical structure] it is no long step to Eddington's position that a knowledge of mathematical structure is the only knowledge that the science of physics can give us. Of all the philosophical speculations which have been hung on to the new physics, this seems to be the most illuminating and the best-founded. It seems to be true that "exact" science is a knowledge of what Eddington calls "pointer-reading"—the readings on an instrument of some kind. We assume, of course, that these readings refer to various qualities of the external world, but all we actually know about these qualities, for the purposes of exact science, is the way they affect our measuring instruments.

* * * * *

The fact that science is confined to a knowledge of structure is obviously of great humanistic importance. For it means that the problem of the nature of reality is not prejudged. We are no longer required to believe that our response to beauty, or the mystic's sense of communion with God, have no objective counterpart. It is perfectly possible that they are what they have so often been taken to be, clues to the nature of reality. . . .

The outlook just described may fairly be said to be a result of the new scientific self-consciousness. It is more than a mere speculation. But some of the other views that have been put forth by our scientific philosophers seem a good deal less secure. We have, for instance, Sir James Jeans' view that the universe is a thought in the mind of a Supreme Mathematician. His reason for thinking this seems to be that "*all* the pictures which science now draws of nature, and which alone seem capable of according with observational fact, are mathematical pictures." Moreover, these mathematical pictures are not pictures of anything we can imagine. On the wave theory, for example, an electron is a system of waves in a three-dimensional space. This sounds intelligible. We can identify this space with the physical space of our perceptions, and imagine the waves as being waves in some kind of ether. But we find that two electrons require a six-dimensional space, three electrons nine dimensions, and so on. It is evident that the space being talked of can have nothing to do with the space of perception. Also, we find that the waves being talked of are extremely elusive. . . . From this, and similar instances, Sir James Jeans concludes that the universe is more like a thought than it is like anything else. . . .

[But taking a next step,] that the universe is a thought in a mathematical mind, seems a very long one. Sir James Jeans appears to have been led to this conclusion by the difficulty of imagining anything material behaving in accordance with the equations that modern physicists have found. He says:

> The concepts which now prove to be fundamental to our understanding of nature—a space which is finite; a space which is empty, so that one point differs from another solely in the properties of the space itself; four-dimensional, seven and more dimensional spaces; a space which forever expands; a sequence of events which follows the laws of probability instead of the laws of causation—or, alternatively, a sequence of events which can only be fully and consistently described by going outside space and time, all these concepts seem to my mind to be structures of pure thought, incapable of realization in any sense which would be described as material.

The state of affairs described by Jeans certainly makes it likely that whatever it is that behaves in this extraordinary way is not something that we can represent to ourselves in terms of familiar concepts. The "atom" of Victorian science could be pictured as a tiny grain of sand. The "electron" of modern physics certainly cannot be pictured as an even tinier grain of sand. But surely this is not surprising? Why should not the intimate workings of nature outrun our capacity for pictorial representation? Lord Kelvin said that he could understand nothing of which he could not make a mechanical model, and for that reason he never accepted Maxwell's electromagnetic theory of light. That seems to us now a strange criterion. Why should a man suppose that nature must be the kind of thing that a nineteenth-century engineer can reproduce in his workshop? . . .

Nevertheless, although they adopt very different routes, both Eddington and Jeans arrive at very much the same conclusion, namely, that the ultimate nature of the universe is mental. We have seen that Jeans has been led to this conclusion by the impossibility of conceiving anything save pure thought to which the modern mathematical description of the universe could apply. Eddington reaches his conclusion by reflecting that the only direct knowledge we possess is knowledge of mental states. All other knowledge, such as our knowledge of the material universe, is inferred knowledge—often the product of a long and complicated chain of inference. He holds the well-known theory that all our knowledge of the external world comes to us in the form of physical stimuli which travel along the nerves to the brain. Having arrived at the brain these stimuli are somehow transformed into, or give rise to, mental states, which are apparently of an entirely different nature from the physical stimuli. But, he argues, the only link in this chain of whose *nature* we know anything is the last link—the mental state. Are we to suppose that this link is something absolutely different in kind from the other links?

Consider vision, for example. The

process starts with the vibrating atoms of an external object. These vibrating atoms give rise to what the older physics called waves in the ether, but which the newer physics cannot yet satisfactorily describe. This physical process, whatever it may be, reaches the eye, and causes another physical process there. This, in turn, leads presumably to molecular movements in the brain. There then occurs the whole dissimilar phenomenon we call seeing a glowing red patch. This phenomenon appears so unlike those that preceded it that an absolute breach of continuity seems to have occurred. But why should we suppose this? We have seen that the only knowledge we have of the vibrating atoms, ether waves, and so on, is knowledge of their *structure*. This tells us nothing about their nature. May it not be, then, that their nature is the same as that of the red patch, namely, mental? This is, in essence, what Professor Eddington asserts. . . .

Jeans, as we have seen, goes even further, and would make the universe even more fully mental, being, indeed, a thought in the mind of God.

The humanistic importance of this outlook, in the minds of its authors, seems to be that it leaves us more free to attach the traditional significance to our aesthetic, religious or, compendiously, mystic experiences. It does not actively reinforce any particular religious interpretation of the universe, but it cuts the ground from under those arguments which were held to prove that any such interpretation is necessarily illusory. This it does by showing that science deals with but a partial aspect of reality, and that there is no faintest reason for supposing that everything science ignores is less real than what it accepts. The question as to why science can afford to ignore these other elements has also been answered by Eddington. Why is it that science forms a closed system? Why is it that the elements of reality it ignores never come in to disturb it? The reason is that all the terms of physics are defined in terms of one another. The abstractions with which physics begins are all it ever has to do with. By starting with "point-events," for instance, we can, mathematically, grind out one expression after another until we come to the mathematical specification of "matter." From this specification we can continue until we arrive back at our starting point.

We are doing what the dictionary compiler did when he defined a violin as a small violoncello, and a violoncello as a large violin. But what we have left out of this description is the process by which the mind of the scientist makes contact with one of the entities, namely, matter, which appears in this mathematical chain. It is in virtue of his recognition of this entity that the cycle of definitions has a meaning for him, and gives him genuine information. Similarly, to one who has seen either a violin or a violoncello, the dictionary definition gives information. But as long as the abstractions of physics form a closed cycle it is obviously immune from all disturbance from factors it has neglected.

It is not quite clear that this immunity will endure. The above analysis applies only to "field" physics which, as we have mentioned, covers a very large part of physics. But it does not cover the whole of physics, and the hope that it could be made to do so grows steadily less. In atomic and sub-atomic phenomena we seem to be faced by a state of affairs that lies right outside the cyclic scheme. The most disconcerting characteristic of this region is that strict causality, a cardinal assumption in science, does not seem to apply. In the motions of individual atoms and electrons there seems to be an element of free-will. Determinism has broken down, and the principle of indeterminacy has taken its place. There is great difference of opinion at present as to whether this is a genuine discovery, or as to whether it is a merely temporary technical device. Einstein, Max Planck, and others, think that strict causality will ultimately be restored in physics, while such men as Eddington and Schrödinger think that determinism must be definitely abandoned.

If the principle of indeterminacy comes to be definitely established, it will obviously have important philosophic consequences. It will make it easier to believe that our intuition of free-will is not an illusion. Moreover, instead of regarding the course of nature as the mere unrolling of a vast machine where every product is predetermined, we shall be freer to attribute to nature a genuine creative advance. And the distinction between the natural and the supernatural, as Eddington has pointed out, would be appreciably diminished. Indeed, if this principle be definitely admitted it will lead to the greatest revolution in scientific thought, and in the philosophy based on it, that has yet occurred.

[Thus] the new self-consciousness of science has resulted in the recognition that its claims were greatly exaggerated. By making "matter and motion" the sole reality, it dismissed other aspects of our experience, those that seemed to us to have the greatest significance and which, finally, made life worth living, as illusory. Science, in spite of all its practical benefits, had seemed to many thoughtful men, perhaps to the majority, to have darkened life. That the new attitude of science, as explained by such men as Eddington and Jeans, has obtained such widespread attention is not, therefore, surprising. It was the metaphysical doctrines that accompanied science that were found so depressing.

QUESTIONS FOR DISCUSSION

1. What were the primary concepts Galileo and Newton used for explaining reality? What evidence, and what reasons, suggest they no longer are satisfactory?
2. What are Eddington's and Jeans' views of Reality? Compare the arguments they use to arrive at this conclusion with those employed by Royce on p. 133.
3. What reasons can be given to support the conclusion that science sees the world as mechanistic and deterministic? What reasons can be given to deny this conclusion? What implications, for both science and life, follow from Sullivan's assertion that "our intuition of free-

will is not an illusion"? Write a short essay which embodies your answers.

READINGS FOR IMMEDIATE REFERENCE

Sullivan, J. W. N. *The Limitations of Science.* New York: Viking Press, 1933, Chapters 5-7.

Meyerson, Emile. *Identity and Reality.* London: Allen and Unwin, 1930.

Peirce, Charles S. "Chance: The Doctrine of Necessity Examined," *Collected Papers.* Cambridge: Harvard University Press, 1935, Vol. VI, Book I, Chapter 2.

REFERENCES FOR COMPREHENSIVE KNOWLEDGE

Sullivan, J. W. N. *Aspects of Science.* New York: Knopf, 1925.

———. *Beethoven: His Spiritual Development.* New York: Knopf, 1927.

———. *Galileo.* New York: Dutton, 1928.

———. *Sir Isaac Newton.* New York: Macmillan, 1938.

Burtt, E. A. *The Metaphysical Foundations of Modern Science.* New York: Harcourt, Brace, 1949. A thorough and incisive analysis of Newtonian principles. A standard work.

Also see:

Eddington, Arthur S. *The Expanding Universe.* Cambridge: Cambridge University Press, 1933.

———. *The Nature of the Physical World.* Cambridge: Cambridge University Press, 1928.

More, Louis T. *The Limitations of Science.* New York: Henry Holt and Co., 1915.

Jeans, James. *The Growth of Physical Science.* Cambridge: Cambridge University Press, 1951.

———. *The Mysterious Universe.* New York: Macmillan, 1932.

———. *Physics and Philosophy.* Cambridge: Cambridge University Press, 1933.

BIBLIOGRAPHY FOR CHAPTER ELEVEN

READINGS FOR IMMEDIATE REFERENCE

Burtt, E. A. *The Metaphysical Foundations of Modern Science.* New York: Harcourt, Brace, 1949, Chapters 1-3, 7, 8.

Whitehead, A. N. *Science and the Modern World.* New York: Macmillan, 1925, Chapters 1-4, 9.

REFERENCES FOR COMPREHENSIVE KNOWLEDGE

Campbell, Norman. *What is Science?* New York: Dover, 1952.

———. *The Foundations of Science.* New York: Dover, 1957. Together, a lucid statement of the philosophical bases of science.

Sarton, George. *A History of Science.* Cambridge: Harvard University Press, 1952. Combines a reporting of experimentation with an analysis of theoretical foundations.

Also see:

Butterfield, Herbert. *The Origins of Modern Science,* rev. ed. New York: Macmillan, 1957.

Dampier, W. C. *A History of Science*. Cambridge: Cambridge University Press, 1942.

Toulmin, Stephen. *The Philosophy of Science*. London: Hutchinson's University Library, 1953.

Wiener, Philip. *Readings in Philosophy of Science*. New York: Scribners, 1953.

Chapter Twelve

SCIENTIFIC MORALITY

1. RUTH F. BENEDICT

Ruth Fulton Benedict was born in New York in 1887. Her father died when she was only two, and after his death her mother supported the family by teaching. She graduated from Vassar in 1909 and continued on there as a member of the faculty, teaching English and publishing poetry for nearly two decades. In 1919 she attended a summer session at Columbia University where, among others, she studied with Franz Boas, the dean of American anthropologists. She became so interested in her studies that she gave up her other career to complete a doctoral degree in anthropology. She stayed on at Columbia to teach, and during the last few years of her life was chairman of the department. Besides teaching, she studied numerous cultures, particularly Indian tribes in the Southwestern part of the United States. She was especially interested in their religious beliefs, mythology and folklore. She wrote extensively about her experiences and observations among primitive peoples, as well as on topics of a more general nature. She died in 1948.

In this selection from her widely read *Patterns of Culture,* Mrs. Benedict describes the society of the Dobuans in the southwest Pacific. In addition to the intrinsic interest the selection has, ask yourself how this material is relevant to the problems of morality. Are any of the distinctions you made earlier helpful in assessing its contribution?

Life Among the Dobuans[1]

The Dobuans amply deserve the character they are given by their neighbors. They are lawless and treacherous. Every man's hand is against every other man. They lack the smoothly working organization of the Trobriands, headed by honored high chiefs and maintaining peaceful and continual reciprocal exchanges of goods and privileges. Dobu has no chiefs. It certainly has no political organization. In a strict sense it has no legality. And this is not because the Dobuan lives in a state of anarchy, Rousseau's "natural man" as yet unhampered by the social contract, but because the social forms which obtain in Dobu put a premium upon ill will and treachery and make of them the recognized virtues of their society.

Nothing could be further from the truth, however, than to see in Dobu a state of anarchy. Dobuan social organization is arranged in concentric circles, within each of which specified traditional forms of hostility are allowed. No man takes the law into his own hands except to carry out these culturally allowed hostilities within the appropriate specified group. The largest functioning Dobuan grouping is a named locality of some four to twenty villages. It is the war unit and is on terms of permanent international hostility with every other similar locality. Before the days of white control no man ventured into an alien locality except to kill and to raid. One service, however, the localities exact of each other. In cases of death and serious illness, when it is necessary to find out by divination the person who is responsible, a diviner is brought from an enemy locality. Diviners within the locality are thus not called upon to face the dangers attendant upon divining a culprit, and a practitioner is called in to whom distance gives a certain immunity.

Danger indeed is at its height within the locality itself. Those who share the same shore, those who go through the same daily routine together, are the ones who do one another supernatural and actual harm. They play havoc with one's harvest, they bring confusion upon one's economic exchanges, they cause disease and death. Everyone possesses magic for these purposes and uses it upon all occasions. People with whom one associates daily are the witches and sorcerers who threaten one's affairs. . . .

Marriage, of course, must be with someone outside the susu [mother's family]. It remains within the locality, and therefore it allies two villages between which enmity runs high. Marriage brings with it no amelioration of hostility. From its beginning the institutions that surround it make for conflict and hard feeling between the two groups. . . .

From marriage until death the couple live in alternate years in the village of the husband and the village of the wife. Each alternate year one spouse has the

[1] From *Patterns of Culture* by Ruth F. Benedict. New York: Houghton Mifflin Co., copyright, 1934, Chapter 5. Reprinted by permission.

backing of his own group and commands the situation. The alternate year the same spouse is a tolerated alien who must efface himself before the owners of his spouse's village. . . . [By all the traditional means at its command] Dobuan society demands that during the year in the spouse's village the spouse who is on alien territory play a role of humiliation. All the owners of the village may call him by his name. He may never use the name of any one of them. There are several reasons why personal names are not used in Dobu as in our own civilization, for when personal names are used it signifies that important liberties may be taken by the namer. It denotes prestige in relation to the person named. Whenever the village makes or receives gifts in betrothal, in the exchange of marriage gifts which is renewed year after year, or at death, the spouse who is married in and resident there for the year must absent himself. He is a perpetual outsider.

These are, however, the least of the indignities of his position. There is tension of a more important sort. The village in which the couple are living at the moment is seldom satisfied with the behavior of the spouse who has married in. Because of the marital exchanges between the two villages, which continue with much the same formalities from the wedding till the death of one of the spouses, the marriage is an important investment of the susu. The men of the mother's line have an economic right to play an active role in it. It is easy for the spouse who is on home ground to turn to his susu, especially to the mother's brother, for support in the marital quarrels that recur constantly in Dobu. The mother's brother is usually only too willing to lecture the outsider publicly or send him or her packing from the village with obscene abuse.

Tension of an even more intimate kind is also present. Faithfulness is not expected between husband and wife, and no Dobuan will admit that a man and woman are ever together even for the shortest interval except for sexual purposes. The outsider spouse of the year is quick to suspect unfaithfulness. Usually he has grounds. In the suspicion-ridden atmosphere of Dobu the safest liaison is with a village "brother" or a village "sister." During the year when one is in one's own village circumstances are propitious and supernatural dangers at a minimum. Public opinion strongly disapproves of marriage between such classificatory "brothers" and "sisters." It would disrupt the village to have obligatory marital exchanges between two parts of the settlement. But adultery within this group is a favorite pastime. It is celebrated constantly in mythology, and its occurrence in every village is known to everyone from early childhood. It is a matter of profoundest concern to the outraged spouse. He (it is as likely to be she) bribes the children for information, his own or any in the village. If it is the husband, he breaks his wife's cooking-pots. If it is the wife, she maltreats her husband's dog. He quarrels with her violently, and no quarrel can go unheard in the close-set, leaf-thatched houses of Dobu. He throws himself out of the village in a fury. As a last resort of impotent rage he attempts suicide by one of several traditional methods, no one of which is surely fatal. He is usually saved and by this means he enlists his wife's susu; in fear of what his relatives might do if the outraged spouse succeeded in his attempts at suicide, they are moved to a more conciliatory behavior. They may even refuse to take any further steps in the matter, and the partners to the marriage may remain sullenly and angrily together. The next year the wife can retaliate similarly in her own village.

* * * * *

The fierce exclusiveness of ownership in Dobu is nowhere more violently expressed than in the beliefs about hereditary proprietorship of yams. The line of yams descends within the susu as surely as the blood in the veins of its members. The seed yams are not pooled even in the gardens of the married pair. Each of them cultivates his own garden, planted with seed yams of his hereditary line, and they are made to grow by magical incantations owned individually and secretly in his susu line. The universal dogma of their society is that only yams of one's own blood line will grow in one's garden, brought to fruition by the magical incantations that have descended with the seed. . . .

Food is never sufficient in Dobu, and everyone goes hungry for the last few months before planting if he is to have the requisite yams for seed. The greatest Dobuan delinquency is the eating of one's seed yams. The loss is never made up. It would be impossible for the husband or wife to make it good, for yams not of the matrilineal line would not grow in one's garden. Even one's own susu does not make up so flagrant a bankruptcy as a loss of seed. One who would fall so low as to eat his yams for planting is a bad bet backed not even by his own clan. He is for life the Dobuan beachcomber. . . .

The violence of Dobuan regard for ownership and the degree to which it involves the victimizing of others and their reciprocating suspicion and ill will are grossly reflected in their religion. . . . In Dobu there is no propitiation of supernatural beings, no gifts or sacrifices to cement cooperation between gods and petitioners. The supernatural beings that are known in Dobu are a few secret magical names, the knowledge of which, like the discovery of the name "Rumpelstiltchen" in the folktale, gives the power of command. . . .

Every activity has its relevant incantations, and one of the most striking of all Dobuan beliefs is that no result in any field of existence is possible without magic. . . . Yams cannot grow without their incantations, sex desire does not arise without love-magic, exchanges of valuables in economic transactions are magically brought about, no trees are protected from theft unless malevolent charms have been placed upon them, no wind blows unless it is magically called, no disease or death occurs without the machinations of sorcery or witchcraft.

The magical incantations, therefore, are of incomparable importance. The violence with which success is coveted is faithfully reflected in the fierce competition for magical formulae. These are never owned in common. There are no secret societies whose prerogative they are. There are no groups of brothers to all of whom they descend. Even co-operation within the susu never extends so far as to give its members joint benefit in the powers of an incantation. The susu merely channels the strict individual inheritance of magic. . . .

The magical incantations of Dobu must be word-perfect to be effective, and there are often specific leaves or woods that must be used with them with symbolic actions. They are most of them examples of sympathetic magic and depend upon the technique of mentioning bush-growing water plants to the new-leafed yam that it may imitate their luxuriance, or describing the hornbill's rending of a tree stump to ensure the ravages of gangosa. The incantations are remarkable for their malevolence and for the degree to which they embody the Dobuan belief that any man's gain is another's loss. . . .

[During the planting season] no magical watch is set upon the yams, no magical thieving is undertaken. But when they are somewhat grown it is necessary to root them solidly in one's own place. For yams are conceived as persons and are believed to wander nightly from garden to garden. The vines remain behind but the tubers are gone. Toward the middle of the morning they normally return. For this reason yams are not dug early in the morning when garden work is usually done; it would be in vain. Their return must be compliantly awaited. Also when the yams are growing they resent too early curtailment of their freedom; therefore the husbanding incantations are not begun until the plants have reached a certain stage of growth. These incantations lure the roaming yams to remain in one's own garden at the expense of the garden in which they are planted. Gardening in Dobu is as competitive as the struggle for an inheritance. A man has no notion that another gardener can plant more yams than he can or make more yams grow from his seed tubers. Whatever harvest his neighbor has in excess of his own is thought to have been magically thieved from his own or someone else's garden. Therefore physical guard is mounted by the man over his own garden from this time until harvesting, he uses whatever charms he knows to attract his neighbor's yams, and he opposes the charms of his neighbor's by countercharms. . . .

Disease charms have a malevolence all their own. Every man and woman in the Tewara village owns from one to five. Each is a specific charm for a particular disease, and the person who owns the incantation owns also the incantation for removing the same affliction. Some persons have a monopoly of certain diseases and hence are sole owners of the power to cause it and the power to cure it. Whoever has elephantiasis or scrofula in the locality, therefore, knows at whose door to lay it. The charms make the owner powerful and are greatly coveted.

The incantations give their possessors an opportunity for the most explicit expression of malignity the culture allows. Ordinarily such expression is tabu. The Dobuan does not risk making a public challenge when he wishes to injure a person. He is obsequious and redoubles the shows of friendship. He believes that sorcery is made strong by intimacy and he waits the opportunity for treachery. But in placing his disease-charm upon his enemy and in teaching his charm to his sister's son he has full license for malevolence. It is an occasion out of reach of his enemy's eye or ear, and he lays aside his pretenses. He breathes the spell into the excreta of the victim or into a creeper which he lays across the path of his enemy, hiding nearby to see that the victim actually brushes against it. In communicating the spell the sorcerer imitates in anticipation the agony of the final stages of the disease he is inflicting. He writhes upon the ground, he shrieks in convulsion. Only so, after faithful reproduction of its effects, will the charm do its destined work. The diviner is satisfied. When the victim has brushed against the creeper he takes the bit of vine home with him and lets it wither in his hut. When he is ready for his enemy's death he burns it in his fire.

* * * * *

So far we have avoided mention of Dobuan economic exchanges. The passion for endless reciprocal commercial transactions that grips so much of Melanesia is present also in Dobu. The passionately desired and passionately resented success which lies closest to the heart of every Dobuan is sought primarily in two fields, the field of material possessions and the field of sex. Sorcery is another field, but in these connections it is an instrument rather than an end, a means for attaining and defending success in the primary activities.

Material success in a community ridden with treachery and suspicion like Dobu must necessarily offer many contrasts to the economic goals that are recognized in our civilization. Accumulation of goods is ruled out at the beginning. Even one successful harvest spied out by others and never admitted by the gardener is occasion enough for the practice of fatal sorcery. Ostentatious display is likewise debarred. The ideal commercial technique would be a system of counters that pass through each man's hands but may not remain with him as a permanent possession. It is precisely the system that obtains in Dobu. The high point of life in these islands is in international exchange which includes a dozen islands that lie in a roughly drawn circle approximately one hundred and fifty miles in diameter. These islands constitute the Kula ring which Dr. Malinowski has described also for the Trobriands, the partners of Dobu to the north. . . .

The Kula ring is a circle of islands around which one kind of valuable travels in one direction and another in the other in semi-annual exchange. The men of each island make long voyages across the open seas, carrying shell necklaces in clockwise direction and armshells counter-clockwise. Each man has his partner in the exchanging island to each direction and bargains for advantage by every means in his control. Eventually the valuables make full circle, and new ones of course may be added. The armshells and the necklaces are all named with personal names, and certain ones possess a traditional excessive value in proportion to their fame. . . .

The most prolific source of bad feeling is the sharp practice known as wabuwabu. To wabuwabu is to get many spondylus shell necklaces from different places to the south on the security of one armshell left at home in the north; or vice versa, many armshells from the north on a security that cannot meet them, promising the one valuable which one possesses to many different persons in return for their gifts that are being solicited. It is sharp practice, but it is not entirely confidence tricksterıng. . . .

Suppose I, Kisian of Tewara, go to the Trobriands and secure an armshell named Monitor Lizard. I then go to Sanaroa and in four different villages secure four different shell necklaces, promising each man who gives me a shell necklace Monitor Lizard in later return. I, Kisian, do not have to be very specific in my promise. Later when four men appear in my home at Tewara each expecting Monitor Lizard, only one will get it. The other three are not defrauded permanently, however. They are furious, it is true, and their exchange is blocked for the year. Next year, when I, Kisian, go again to the Trobriands I shall represent that I have four necklaces at home waiting for those who give me four armshells. I obtain more armshells than I obtained previously and pay my debts a year late.

To wabuwabu successfully is a great achievement, one of the most envied in Dobu. The great mythical hero of the Kula was an expert in it. Like all Dobuan practices it stresses one's own gains at the expense of another's loss. It allows one to reap personal advantage in a situation in which others are victimized. The Kula is not the only undertaking in which a man may risk wabuwabu. The term covers also the victimizing of others in the marital exchanges. The series of payments that are set up between two villages during betrothal involve considerable property. A man who dares to run the risk may enter into an engagement in order to reap the economic profits. When the balance of the exchanges is heavily on his side, he breaks off the betrothal. There is no redress. A person who gets away with it proves thereby that his magic is stronger than the magic of the village he has outraged, which will, of course, attempt his life. He is an enviable person.

* * * * *

The attitudes that we have discussed, those involved in marriage, magic, gardening, and economic exchange, are all expressed in the strongest terms in behavior at the time of death. Dobu, in Dr. Fortune's words, "cowers under a death as under a whipping," and looks about immediately for a victim. True to Dobuan dogma, the victim is the person nearest to the dead; that is, the spouse. They believe that the person with whom one shares the bed is the person to charge with one's fatal illness. The husband has used his disease-causing incantations, and the wife has used witchcraft. For though women also may know the disease-charms, men attribute to them a special technique of villainy, one that strangely resembles the European tradition of witches on their broomsticks. Dobuan witches leave their bodies sleeping beside their husbands and fly through the air to cause accident—a man's fall from a tree or a canoe's drifting from its moorings are due to flying witches—or to abstract the soul from an enemy, who will thereupon weaken and die. Men are in terror of these machinations of their women.

* * * * *

Life in Dobu fosters extreme forms of animosity and malignancy which most societies have minimized by their institutions. Dobuan institutions, on the other hand, exalt them to the highest degree. The Dobuan lives out without repression man's worst nightmares of the ill will of the universe, and according to his view of life virtue consists in selecting a victim upon whom he can vent the malignancy he attributes alike to human society and to the powers of nature. All existence appears to him as a cutthroat struggle in which deadly antagonists are pitted against one another in a contest for each one of the goods of life. Suspicion and cruelty are his trusted weapons in the strife and he gives no mercy, as he asks none.

QUESTIONS FOR DISCUSSION

1. What evidence does Mrs. Benedict give for saying that the Dobuans are lawless but do not live in an anarchy?
2. Does your author believe the Dobuans should live this way? Or that we should? Does she give reasons to support these conclusions? Could she? Should she?
3. In Chapter Five we saw that there are many facets to an ethical theory. Which of those distinctions could be applied in order to understand Mrs. Benedict's contributions to the subject?

READINGS FOR IMMEDIATE REFERENCE

Benedict, Ruth. *Patterns of Culture*. New York: Houghton Mifflin, 1934, Chapters 4-8.

Malinowski, Bronislaw. *Argonauts of the Western Pacific*. New York: Dutton, 1950, Chapters 1-3.

REFERENCES FOR COMPREHENSIVE KNOWLEDGE

Benedict, Ruth. *The Chrysanthemum and the Sword*. New York: Houghton Mifflin, 1946.

———. *Science and Politics*. New York: Viking Press, 1943.

———. *Zuñi Mythology*. New York: Columbia University Press, 1935.

Fortune, R. F. *Sorcerers of Dobu*. London: Routledge, 1932. The full study from which most of Mrs. Benedict's report was taken.

Also see:

Boas, Franz. *Anthropology and Modern Life*. New York: Norton, 1928.

———. *Race, Language and Culture*. New York: Macmillan, 1940.

Kroeber, A. L. *The Nature of Culture*. Chicago: University of Chicago Press, 1952.

Malinowski, Bronislaw. *Magic, Science and Religion*. Boston: Beacon Press, 1948.

Mead, Margaret. *New Lives for Old*. New York: Morrow, 1953.

Montague, Ashley. *On Being Human*. New York: Schuman, 1950.

II. WILLIAM GRAHAM SUMNER

Born in Paterson, New Jersey, in 1840, the son of an uneducated railroad repairman who had come from England four years earlier, Sumner grew to manhood in Hartford, Connecticut, and graduated from Yale in 1863. He studied on the continent for three years and tutored at his alma mater for three more before he was ordained a priest and assigned a parish in the Protestant Episcopal church. In 1872 he accepted a position on the faculty at Yale where students reported him to be a stimulating, querulous, and iconoclastic teacher, although, as a person, he was unusually sensitive and compassionate. He had a working knowledge of a dozen languages, mostly acquired after he was forty-five, served on the Connecticut State Board of Education for twenty-eight years and was well-known as a dynamic and forthright public lecturer. He retired in 1909 and died within a year.

In this selection, from one of the most influential books in the social sciences, Sumner describes, historically and psychologically, the origins of morality; speaks of what today are such familiar ideas as folkways and mores, in-groups and out-groups; discusses the causes of change and the role of the dissenter; and says there is no standard outside the mores by which the mores can be judged as good or bad. When you have finished reading, ask yourself whether his conclusions are justified by his analysis, and whether it is possible to have a scientific morality—or any morality—as we have been studying it in previous chapters.

Folkways and Ethical Relativism[1]

If we put together all that we have learned from anthropology and ethnography about primitive man and primitive society, we perceive that the first task of life is to live. Men begin with acts, not with thoughts. Every moment brings necessities which must be satisfied at once. Need was the first experience, and it was followed at once by a blundering effort to satisfy it. It is

[1] From *Folkways* by William Graham Sumner. Boston: Ginn and Co., Copyright 1906, Chapters 1, 2, and 5. [The paragraph numbers have been omitted. C.M.]

generally taken for granted that men inherited some guiding instincts from their beast ancestry, and it may be true, although it has never been proved. If there were such inheritances, they controlled and aided the first efforts to satisfy needs. Analogy makes it easy to assume that the ways of beasts had produced channels of habit and predisposition along which dexterities and other psychophysical activities would run easily. Experiments with newborn animals show that in the absence of any experience of the relation of means to ends, efforts to satisfy needs are clumsy and blundering. The method is that of trial and failure, which produces repeated pain, loss, and disappointments. Nevertheless, it is a method of rude experiment and selection. The earliest efforts of men were of this kind. Need was the impelling force. Pleasure and pain, on the one side and the other, were the rude constraints which defined the line on which efforts must proceed. The ability to distinguish between pleasure and pain is the only psychical power which is to be assumed. Thus ways of doing things were selected which were expedient. They answered the purpose better than other ways, or with less toil and pain. Along the course on which efforts were compelled to go, habit, routine, and skill were developed. The struggle to maintain existence was carried on, not individually, but in groups. Each profited by the other's experience; hence there was concurrence towards that which proved to be most expedient. All at last adopted the same way for the same purpose; hence the ways turned into customs and became mass phenomena. Instincts were developed in connection with them. In this way folkways arise. The young learn them by tradition, imitation, and authority. The folkways, at a time, provide for all the needs of life then and there. They are uniform, universal in the group, imperative and invariable. As time goes on, the folkways become more and more arbitrary, positive, and imperative. If asked why they act in a certain way in certain cases, primitive people always answer that it is because they and their ancestors always have done so. A sanction also arises from ghost fear. The ghosts of ancestors would be angry if the living should change the ancient folkways. . . .

It is of the first importance to notice that, from the first acts by which men try to satisfy needs, each act stands by itself, and looks no further than the immediate satisfaction. From recurrent needs arise habits for the individual and customs for the group, but these results are consequences which were never conscious, and never foreseen or intended. They are not noticed until they have long existed, and it is still longer before they are appreciated. Another long time must pass, and a higher stage of mental development must be reached, before they can be used as a basis from which to deduce rules for meeting, in the future, problems whose pressure can be foreseen. The folkways, therefore, are not creations of human purpose and wit. They are like products of natural forces which men unconsciously set in operation. . . . From this it results that all the life of human beings, in all ages and stages of culture, is primarily controlled by a vast mass of folkways handed down from the earliest existence of the race, having the nature of the ways of other animals, only the topmost layers of which are subject to change and control, and have been somewhat modified by human philosophy, ethics, and religion, or by other acts of intelligent reflection. . . .

The folkways, being ways of satisfying needs, have succeeded more or less well, and therefore have produced more or less pleasure or pain. Their quality always consisted in their adaptation to the purpose. If they were imperfectly adapted and unsuccessful, they produced pain, which drove men on to learn better. The folkways are, therefore, (1) subject to a strain of improvement towards better adaptation of means to ends, as long as the adaptation is so imperfect that pain is produced. They are also (2) subject to a strain of consistency with each other, because they all answer their several purposes with less friction and antagonism when they cooperate and support each other. The forms of industry, the forms of the family, the notions of property, the constructions of rights, and the types of religion show the strain of consistency with each other through the whole history of civilization. The two great cultural divisions of the human race are the oriental and the occidental. Each is consistent throughout; each has its own philosophy and spirit; they are separated from top to bottom by different mores, different standpoints, different ways, and different notions of what societal arrangements are advantageous. In their contrast they keep before our minds the possible range of divergence in the solution of the great problems of human life, and in the views of earthly existence by which life policy may be controlled. If two planets were joined in one, their inhabitants could not differ more widely as to what things are best worth seeking, or what ways are most expedient for well-living. . . .

It is evident that the "ways" of the older and more experienced members of a society deserve great authority in any primitive group. We find that this rational authority leads to customs of deference and to etiquette in favor of the old. The old in turn cling stubbornly to tradition and to the example of their own predecessors. Thus tradition and custom become intertwined and are a strong coercion which directs the society upon a fixed line, and strangles liberty. Children see their parents always yield to the same custom and obey the same persons. They see that the elders are allowed to do all the talking, and that if an outsider enters, he is saluted by those who are at home according to rank and in fixed order. All this becomes rule for children, and helps to give to all primitive customs their stereotyped formality.

The conception of "primitive society" which we ought to form is that of small groups scattered over a territory. The size of the groups is determined by the conditions of the struggle for existence. The internal organization of each group corresponds to its size. A group of groups may have some relation to each other which draws them together and differentiates them from others. Thus a differentiation arises between ourselves, the we-group, or in-group, and everybody else, or the others-group, out-groups. The insiders in a we-group are in a relation of peace, order, law, government, and industry, to each other. Their relation to all outsiders, or others-groups, is one of war and plunder, except so far as agreements have modified it.

The relation of comradeship and peace in the we-group and that of hostility and war towards the others-group are correlative to each other. The exigencies of war with outsiders are what make peace inside, lest internal discord should weaken the we-group for war. These exigencies also make government and law in the in-group, in order to prevent quarrels and enforce discipline. Thus war and peace have reacted on each other and developed each other, one within the group, the other in the intergroup relation. The closer the neighbors, and the stronger they are, the intenser is the warfare, and then the intenser is the internal organization and discipline of each. Sentiments are produced to correspond. Loyalty to the group, sacrifice for it, hatred and contempt for outsiders, brotherhood within, warlikeness without,—all grow together, common products of the same situation. These relations and sentiments constitute a social philosophy. It is sanctified by connection with religion. Men of an others-group are outsiders with whose ancestors the ancestors of the we-group waged war. The ghosts of the latter will see with pleasure their descendants keep up the fight, and will help them. Virtue consists in killing, plundering and enslaving outsiders.

Ethnocentrism is the technical name for this view of things in which one's own group is the center of everything, and all others are scaled and rated with reference to it. Folkways correspond to it to cover both the inner and the outer relation. Each group nourishes its own pride and vanity, boasts itself superior, exalts its own divinities, and looks with contempt on outsiders. Each group thinks its own folkways the only right ones, and if it observes that other groups have other folkways, these excite its scorn.

* * * * *

The folkways are the "right" way to satisfy all interests, because they are traditional, and exist in fact. They extend over the whole of life. There is a right way to catch game, to win a wife, to make one's self appear, to cure disease, to honor guests, to treat comrades or strangers, to behave when a child is born, on the warpath, in council, and so on in all cases which can arise. The ways are defined on the negative side, that is, by taboos. The "right" way is the way which the ancestors used and which has been handed down. The tradition is its own warrant. It is not held subject to verification by experience. The notion of right is in the folkways. It is not outside of them, of independent origin, and brought to them to test them. In the folkways, whatever is, is right. This is because they are traditional, and therefore contain in themselves the authority of the ancestral ghosts. When we come to the folkways we are at the end of our analysis. The notion of right and ought is the same in regard to all the folkways, but the degree of it varies with the importance of the interest at stake. The obligation of conformable and cooperative action is far greater under ghost fear and war than in other matters, and the social sanctions are severer, because group interests are supposed to be at stake. . . . The morality of a group at a time is the sum of the taboos and prescriptions in the folkways by which right conduct is defined. Therefore morals can never be intuitive. They are historical, institutional and empirical.

World philosophy, life policy, right, rights, and morality are all products of the folkways. They are reflections on, and generalizations from, the experience of pleasure and pain which is won in efforts to carry on the struggle for existence under actual life conditions. The generalizations are very crude and vague in their germinal forms. They are all embodied in folklore, and all our philosophy and science have been developed out of them. . . .

When the elements of truth and right are developed into doctrines of welfare, the folkways are raised to another plane. They then become capable of producing inferences, developing into new forms, and extending their constructive influence over men and society. Then we call them the mores. The mores are the folkways, including the philosophical and ethical generalizations as to societal welfare which are suggested by them, and inherent in them, as they grow.

The mores necessarily consist, in a large part, of taboos, which indicate the things which must not be done. These taboos always contain a greater element of philosophy than the positive rules, because the taboos contain reference to a reason, as, for instance, that the act would displease the ghosts. . . . The taboos carry on the accumulated wisdom of generations, which has almost always been purchased by pain, loss, disease, and death. Other taboos contain inhibitions of what will be injurious to the group. The laws about the sexes, about property, about war, and about ghosts, have this character. They always include some social philosophy. They are both mystic and utilitarian, or compounded of the two. . . .

The range of societal activity may be greatly enlarged, interests may be extended and multiplied, the materials by which needs can be supplied may become far more numerous, the processes of societal cooperation may become more complicated, and contract or artifice may take the place of custom for many interests; but, if the case is one which touches the ways or interests of the masses, folkways will develop on and around it by the same process as that which has been described as taking place from the beginning of civilization. The ways of carrying on war have changed with all new inventions of weapons or armor, and have grown into folkways of commanding range and importance. The factory system of handicrafts has produced a body of folkways in which artisans live, and which distinguish factory towns from commercial cities or agricultural villages. The use of cotton instead of linen has greatly affected modern folkways. The applications of power and machinery have changed the standards of comfort of all classes. The folkways, however, have kept their character and authority through all the changes of form which they have undergone.

* * * * *

It is most important to notice that, for the people of a time and place, their own mores are always good, or rather that for them there can be no question of the goodness or badness of their mores. The reason is because the standards of good and right are in the mores themselves. If the life conditions change, the traditional folkways may produce pain and loss, or fail to produce the same good as formerly. Then the loss of comfort and ease brings doubt into the judgment of welfare, and thus disturbs the unconscious philosophy of the mores. Then a later time will pass judgment on the mores. Another society may also pass judgment on the mores. In our literary and historical study of the mores we want to get from them their educational value, which consists in the stimulus or warning as to what is, in its effects, societally good or bad. This may lead us to reject or neglect a phenomenon like infanticide, slavery, or witchcraft, as an old "abuse" and "evil," or to pass by the crusades as a folly which cannot recur. Such a course would be a great error. Everything in the mores of a time and place must be regarded as justified with regard to that time and place. "Good" mores are those which are adapted to the situation. [On the other hand,] "bad" mores are those which are not so adapted. The mores are not so stereotyped and changeless as might appear, because they are forever moving towards more complete adaptation to conditions and interests, and also towards more complete adjustment to each other. People in mass have never made or kept up a custom in order to hurt their own interests. They have made innumerable errors as to what their interests were and how to satisfy them, but they have always aimed to serve their interests as well as they could. This gives the standpoint for the student of the mores. All things in them come before him on the same plane. They all bring instruction and warning. They all have the same relation to power and welfare. The mistakes in them are component parts of them. We do not study them in order to approve some of them and condemn others. They are all equally worthy of attention from the fact that they existed and were used. The chief object of study in them is their adjustment to interests, their relation to welfare, and their coordination in a harmonious system of life policy. For the men of the time there are no "bad" mores. What is traditional and current is the standard of what ought to be. The masses never raise any questions about such things. If a few raise doubts and questions, this proves that the folkways have already begun to lose firmness and the regulative element in the mores has begun to lose authority. This indicates that the folkways are on their way to a new adjustment.

* * * * *

[However,] dissent is always unpopular in the group. Groups form standards of orthodoxy as to the "principles" which each member must profess and the ritual which each must practice. Dissent seems to imply a claim of superiority. It evokes hatred and persecution. Dissenters are rebels, traitors, and heretics. We see this in all kinds of subgroups. Noble and patrician classes, merchants, artisans, religious and philosophical sects punish by social penalties dissent from, or disobedience to, their code of group conduct. The modern trades union, in its treatment of a "scab," only presents another example. The group also, by a majority, adopts a programme of policy and then demands of each member that he shall work and make sacrifices for what has been resolved upon for the group interest. He who refuses is a renegade or apostate with respect to the group doctrines and interests. He who adopts the mores of another group is a still more heinous criminal. The medieval definition of a heretic was one who varied in life and conversation, dress, speech, or manner from the ordinary members of the Christian community. The first meaning of "Catholic" in the fourth century was a summary of the features which were common to all Christians in social and ecclesiastical behavior; those were Catholic who conformed to the mores which were characteristic of Christians. If a heretic was better than the Catholics, they hated him more. That never excused him before the church authorities. They wanted loyalty to the ecclesiastical corporation. Persecution of a dissenter is always popular in the group which he has abandoned. Toleration of dissent is no sentiment of the masses.

* * * * *

For every one the mores give the notion of what ought to be. This includes the notion of what ought to be done, for all should cooperate to bring to pass, in the order of life, what ought to be. All notions of propriety, decency, chastity, politeness, order, duty, right, rights, discipline, respect, reverence, cooperation and fellowship, especially all things in regard to which good and ill depend entirely on the point at which the line is drawn, are in the mores. The mores can make things seem right and good to one group or one age which to another seem antagonistic to every instinct of human nature. The thirteenth century bred in every heart such a sentiment in regard to heretics that inquisitors had no more misgivings in their proceedings than men would have now if they should attempt to exterminate rattlesnakes. The sixteenth century gave to all such notions about witches that witch persecutors thought they were waging war on enemies of God and man. Of course the inquisitors and witch persecutors constantly developed the notions of heretics and witches. They exaggerated the notions and then gave them back again to the mores, in their expanded form, to inflame the hearts of men with terror and hate and to become, in the next stage, so much more fantastic and ferocious motives. Such is the reaction between the mores and the acts of the living generation. The world philosophy of the age is never anything but the reflection on the mental horizon, which is formed out of the mores, of the ruling ideas—which are in the mores themselves. It is from a failure to recognize the to and fro in this reaction that the current notion arises that mores are produced by doctrines. The "morals" of an age are never anything but the consonance between what is done and what the mores of the age require. The whole revolves on itself, in the relation of the specific to the general, within the horizon formed by the mores. Every attempt to win an outside standpoint from which to reduce the whole to an absolute philosophy of truth and right, based on an unalterable principle, is a delusion.

QUESTIONS FOR DISCUSSION

1. How does Sumner define (1) folkways, (2) mores, (3) ethnocentrism, and (4) morality?
2. Is his theory another form of hedonism or is the pleasure-pain principles he mentions only an incidental part of his thought? Also, what is the logical status of "adjustment"; essential or accidental?
3. What conclusion(s) would you say this selection provides, and with what evidence?
4. Is this a descriptive or prescriptive theory? If the former, is it a generalization of the material presented in Mrs. Benedict's selection? If the latter, how does it prove that each society ought to have the standards it does?

READINGS FOR IMMEDIATE REFERENCE

Sumner, William Graham. *Folkways.* Boston: Ginn, 1906, Chapters 1-3, 15.

Stace, W. T. *The Concept of Morals.* New York: Macmillan, 1937, Chapters 1, 2.

White, Leslie. *The Science of Culture.* New York: Farrar, Straus, 1949, Chapters 1, 2, 4, 6, 7, 14.

REFERENCES FOR COMPREHENSIVE KNOWLEDGE

Asch, Solomon E. *Social Psychology.* New York: Prentice-Hall, 1952. A vigorous criticism of ethical relativism, especially in Chapter 13.

Westermarck, Edward. *The Origin and Development of Moral Ideas.* New York: Macmillan, 1906. Historically one of the first, and philosophically one of the most important, statements of ethical relativism.

Also see:

Herkovits, M. J. *Man and His Works.* New York: Knopf, 1948.

Kluckhohn, Clyde. *Society and Culture,* rev. ed., New York: Knopf, 1953.

Linton, Ralph. *The Study of Man.* New York: Appleton-Century, 1936.

Westermarck, Edward. *Ethical Relativity.* New York: Harcourt, Brace, 1932.

Wissler, Clark. *Man and Culture.* New York: Crowell, 1923.

III. THOMAS HENRY HUXLEY

Huxley was born in England in 1825. Although his father was a teacher, he received little formal schooling, having attended only "two years of pandemonium" by the time he was fifteen. However, among other books, he had read Hamilton's *Logic,* and at seventeen was greatly attracted to Carlyle's writings. Soon after, he entered upon medical studies, graduating in 1845 and, like Darwin earlier, joined the crew of a scientific exploration ship to study animals and plants. He returned to England in 1850 to collate and publish his findings, and was elected to the Royal Society and offered several positions in university science faculties because of them. When the *Origin of Species* was published in 1859, Huxley found it to be the intellectual framework within which his own studies could be understood, and he spent much of his remaining life defending and providing additional evidence, largely anatomical, to support the theory. In addition, he served on no less than ten Royal Commissions, was secretary and then President of the Royal Society for fifteen years, was a member of the London and National School boards, was a widely respected public lecturer much in demand and continued to be a teacher and researcher of high repute. After 1870, he became increasingly involved in controversy with religious leaders, contending that "since the second century what had assumed to itself the title of Orthodox Christianity was a varying compound of some of the best and some of the worst elements of Paganism and Judaism." His always poor health broke completely in 1885, although he did not die until 1895. His famous grandsons, Aldous and Julian, continue the iconoclastic tradition of their grandfather today.

Can the theory of evolution provide the basis for a prescriptive ethical theory? Huxley believes it can, and this selection demonstrates how. What ends are advocated by the theory, and what are the best means for achieving those ends? Are either the ends or the means necessarily related to the theory of evolution?

Evolution and Ethics[1]

My present enterprise has a certain analogy to that of the daring adventure of Jack and the Bean-stalk. I beg you to accompany me in an attempt to reach a world which, to many, is probably strange, by the help of a bean. It is, as you know, a simple, inert-looking thing. Yet, if planted under proper conditions, of which sufficient warmth is one of the most important, it manifests active powers of a very remarkable kind. A small green seedling emerges, rises to the surface of the soil, rapidly increases in size and, at the same time, undergoes a series of metamorphoses which do not excite our wonder as much as those which meet us in legendary history, merely because they are to be seen every day and all day long.

By insensible steps, the plant builds itself up into a large and various fabric of root, stem, leaves, flowers, and fruit, every one molded within and without in accordance with an extremely complex but, at the same time, minutely defined pattern. In each of these complicated structures, as in their smallest constituents, there is an immanent energy which, in harmony with that resident in all the others, incessantly works towards the maintenance of the whole and the efficient performance of the part which it has to play in the economy of nature. But no sooner has the edifice, reared with such exact elaboration, attained completeness, than it begins to crumble. By degrees, the plant withers and disappears from view, leaving behind more or fewer apparently inert and simple bodies, just like the bean from which it sprang; and, like it, endowed with the potentiality of giving rise to a similar cycle of manifestations. . . .

The value of a strong intellectual grasp of the nature of this process lies in the circumstance that what is true of the bean is true of living things in general. From very low forms up to the highest—in the animal no less than in the vegetable kingdom—the process of life presents the same appearance of cyclical evolution. Nay, we have but to cast our eyes over the rest of the world and cyclical change presents itself on all sides. It meets us in the water that flows to the sea and returns to the springs; in the heavenly bodies that wax and wane, go and return to their places; in the inexorable sequence of the ages of man's life; in that successive rise, apogee, and fall of dynasties and of states which is the most prominent topic of civil history. . . .

But there is another aspect of the cosmic process, so perfect as a mechanism, so beautiful as a work of art. Where the cosmopoietic energy works through sentient beings, there arises, among its other manifestations, that which we call pain or suffering. This baleful product of evolution increases in quantity and in intensity, with advancing grades of animal organization, until it attains its highest level in man. Fur-

[1] From *Evolution and Ethics and Other Essays* by Thomas Henry Huxley. New York: D. Appleton and Co., Copyright, 1898, Essay 2.

ther, the consummation is not reached in man, the mere animal; nor in man, the whole or half savage; but only in man, the member of an organized polity. And it is a necessary consequence of his attempt to live in this way; that is, under those conditions which are essential to the full development of his noblest powers.

Man, the animal, in fact, has worked his way to the headship of the sentient world, and has become the superb animal which he is, in virtue of his success in the struggle for existence. The conditions having been of a certain order, man's organization has adjusted itself to them better than that of his competitors in the cosmic strife. In the case of mankind, the self-assertion, the unscrupulous seizing upon all that can be grasped, the tenacious holding of all that can be kept, which constitute the essence of the struggle for existence, have answered. For his successful progress, throughout the savage state, man has been largely indebted to those qualities which he shares with the ape and the tiger; his exceptional physical organization; his cunning, his sociability, his curiosity, and his imitativeness; his ruthless and ferocious destructiveness when his anger is roused by opposition.

But, in proportion as men have passed from anarchy to social organization, and in proportion as civilization has grown in worth, these deeply ingrained serviceable qualities have become defects. After the manner of successful persons, civilized man would gladly kick down the ladder by which he has climbed. He would be only too pleased to see "the ape and tiger die." But they decline to suit his convenience; and the unwelcome intrusion of these boon companions of his hot youth into the ranged existence of civil life adds pains and griefs, innumerable and immeasurably great, to those which the cosmic process necessarily brings on the mere animal. In fact, civilized man brands all these ape and tiger promptings with the name of sins; he punishes many of the acts which flow from them as crimes; and, in extreme cases, he does his best to put an end to the survival of the fittest of former days by axe and rope.

* * * * *

[We want to know] whether there is, or is not, a sanction for morality in the ways of the cosmos. . . .

Two thousand five hundred years ago, the value of civilization was as apparent as it is now; then, as now, it was obvious that only in the garden of an orderly polity can the finest fruits humanity is capable of bearing be produced. But it had also become evident that the blessings of culture were not unmixed. The garden was apt to turn into a hothouse. The stimulation of the senses, the pampering of the emotions, endlessly multiplied the sources of pleasure. The constant widening of the intellectual field indefinitely extended the range of that especially human faculty of looking before and after, which adds to the fleeting present those old and new worlds of the past and the future, wherein men dwell the more the higher their culture. But that very sharpening of the sense and that subtle refinement of emotion, which brought such a wealth of pleasures, were fatally attended by a proportional enlargement of the capacity for suffering; and the divine faculty of imagination, while it created new heavens and new earths, provided them with the corresponding hells of futile regret for the past and morbid anxiety for the future. Finally, the inevitable penalty of over-stimulation, exhaustion, opened the gates of civilization to its great enemy, ennui; the stale and flat weariness when man delights not, nor woman either; when all things are vanity and vexation; and life seems not worth living except to escape the bore of dying.

Even purely intellectual progress brings about its revenges. Problems settled in a rough and ready way by rude men, absorbed in action, demand renewed attention and show themselves to be still unread riddles when men have time to think. The beneficient demon, doubt, whose name is Legion and who dwells amongst the tombs of old faiths, enters into mankind and thenceforth refuses to be cast out. Sacred customs, venerable dooms of ancestral wisdom, hallowed by tradition and professing to hold good for all time, are put to the question. Cultured reflection asks for their credentials; judges them by its own standards; finally, gathers those of which it approves into ethical systems, in which the reasoning is rarely much more than a decent pretext for the adoption of foregone conclusions.

One of the oldest and most important elements in such systems is the conception of justice. Society is impossible unless those who are associated agree to observe certain rules of conduct towards one another; its stability depends on the steadiness with which they abide by that agreement; and, so far as they waver, that mutual trust which is the bond of society is weakened or destroyed. . . . This observance of a common understanding, with the consequent distribution of punishments and rewards according to accepted rules, received the name of justice, while the contrary was called injustice. Early ethics did not take much note of the animus of the violator of the rules. But civilization could not advance far, without the establishment of a capital distinction between the case of involuntary and that of wilful misdeed; between a merely wrong action and a guilty one. And, with increasing refinement of moral appreciation, the problem of desert, which arises out of this distinction, acquired more and more theoretical and practical importance. If life must be given for life, yet it was recognized that the unintentional slayer did not altogether deserve death; and, by a sort of compromise between the public and the private conception of justice, a sanctuary was provided in which he might take refuge from the avenger of blood. . . .

Now when the ancient sage, whether Indian or Greek, who had attained to this conception of goodness, looked the world, and especially human life, in the face, he found it as hard as we do to bring the course of evolution into harmony with even the elementary requirements of the ethical ideal of the just and the good.

If there is one thing plainer than another, it is that neither the pleasures nor the pains of life, in the merely animal world, are distributed according to desert; for it is admittedly impossible for the lower orders of sentient beings to deserve either the one or the other. If there is a generalization from the facts of human life which has the assent of thoughtful men in every age and country, it is that the violator of ethical rules constantly escapes the punishment which he deserves; that the wicked flourishes like a green bay tree, while the righteous begs his bread; that the sins of the fathers are visited upon the children; that, in the realm of nature, ignorance is punished just as severely as wilful wrong; and that thousands upon thousands of innocent beings suffer for the crime, or the unintentional trespass of one. . . .

In the great Semitic trial of this issue, Job takes refuge in silence and submission; the Indian and the Greek, less wise perhaps, attempt to reconcile the irreconcilable and plead for the defendant. To this end, the Greeks invented Theodicies; while the Indians devised what, in its ultimate form, must rather be termed a Cosmodicy. For, though Buddhism recognizes gods many and lords many, they are products of the cosmic process; and transitory, however long enduring, manifestations of its eternal activity. In the doctrine of transmigration, whatever its origin, Brahminical and Buddhist speculation found, ready to hand, the means of constructing a plausible vindication of the ways of the cosmos to man. If this world is full of pain and sorrow; if grief and evil fall, like the rain, upon both the just and the unjust; it is because, like the rain, they are links in the endless chain of natural causation by which past, present, and future are indissolubly connected; and there is no more injustice in the one case than in the other. Every sentient being is reaping as it has sown; if not in this life, then in one or other of the infinite series of antecedent existences of which it is the latest term. The present distribution of good and evil is, therefore, the algebraical sum of accumulated positive and negative deserts; or, rather, it depends on the floating balance of the account. For it was not thought necessary that a complete settlement should ever take place. Arrears might stand over as a sort of "hanging gale"; a period of celestial happiness just earned might be succeeded by ages of torment in a hideous nether world, the balance still overdue for some remote ancestral error.

* * * * *

Let us now set our faces westwards, towards Asia Minor and Greece and Italy, to view the rise and progress of another philosophy, apparently independent, but no less pervaded by the conception of evolution.

The sages of Miletus were pronounced evolutionists; and, however dark may be some of the sayings of Heraclitus of Ephesus, who was probably a contemporary of Gautama, no better expressions of the essence of the modern doctrine of evolution can be found than are presented by some of his pithy aphorisms and striking metaphors. . . .

But when the focus of Greek intellectual activity shifted to Athens, the leading minds concentrated their attention upon ethical problems. Forsaking the study of the macrocosm for that of the microcosm, they lost the key to the thought of the great Ephesian, which, I imagine, is more intelligible to us than it was to Socrates, or to Plato. Socrates, more especially, set the fashion of a kind of inverse agnosticism, by teaching that the problems of physics lie beyond the reach of the human intellect; that the attempt to solve them is essentially vain; that the one worthy object of investigation is the problem of ethical life; and his example was followed by the Cynics and the later Stoics. Even the comprehensive knowledge and the penetrating intellect of Aristotle failed to suggest to him that in holding the eternity of the world, within its present range of mutation, he was making a retrogressive step. The scientific heritage of Heraclitus passed into the hands neither of Plato nor of Aristotle, but into those of Democritus. But the world was not yet ready to receive the great conceptions of the philosopher of Abdera. It was reserved for the Stoics to return to the track marked out by the earlier philosophers; and, professing themselves disciples of Heraclitus, to develop the idea of evolution systematically. In doing this, they not only omitted some characteristic features of their master's teaching, but they made additions altogether foreign to it. One of the most influential of these importations was the transcendental theism which had come into vogue. . . .

The consequences of this step were momentous. For if the cosmos is the effect of an immanent, omnipotent, and infinitely beneficent cause, the existence in it of real evil, still less of necessarily inherent evil, is plainly inadmissible. Yet the universal experience of mankind testified then, as now, that, whether we look within us or without us, evil stares us in the face on all sides; that if anything is real, pain and sorrow and wrong are realities.

It would be a new thing in history if *a priori* philosophers were daunted by the factious opposition of experience; and the Stoics were the last men to allow themselves to be beaten by mere facts. "Give me a doctrine and I will find the reasons for it," said Chrysippus. So they perfected, if they did not invent, that ingenious and plausible form of pleading, the Theodicy; for the purpose of showing firstly, that there is no such thing as evil; secondly, that if there is, it is the necessary correlate of good; and, moreover, that it is either due to our own fault, or inflicted for our benefit. Theodicies have been very popular in their time, and I believe that a numerous, though somewhat dwarfed, progeny of them still survives. So far as I know, they are all variations of the theme set forth in those famous six lines of the "Essay on Man," in which Pope sums up Bolingbroke's reminiscences of stoical and other speculations of this kind—

All nature is but art, unknown to thee;
All chance, direction which thou canst not see;
All discord, harmony not understood;
All partial evil, universal good;
And spite of pride, in erring reason's spite,
One truth is clear: whatever is is right.

* * * * *

Modern thought is making a fresh start from the base whence Indian and

Greek philosophy set out; and, the human mind being very much what it was six-and-twenty centuries ago, there is no ground for wonder if it presents indications of a tendency to move along the old lines to the same results. . . .

The propounders of what are called the "ethics of evolution," when the "evolution of ethics" would usually better express the object of their speculations, adduce a number of more or less interesting facts and more or less sound arguments, in favor of the origin of the moral sentiments, in the same way as other natural phenomena, by a process of evolution. I have little doubt, for my own part, that they are on the right track; but as the immoral sentiments have no less been evolved, there is, so far, as much natural sanction for the one as the other. The thief and the murderer follow nature just as much as the philanthropist. Cosmic evolution may teach us how the good and the evil tendencies of man may have come about; but, in itself, it is incompetent to furnish any better reason why what we call good is preferable to what we call evil than we had before. . . .

There is another fallacy which appears to me to pervade the so-called "ethics of evolution." It is the notion that because, on the whole, animals and plants have advanced in perfection of organization by means of the struggle for existence and the consequent "survival of the fittest"; therefore men in society, men as ethical beings, must look to the same process to help them towards perfection. I suspect that this fallacy has arisen out of the unfortunate ambiguity of the phrase "survival of the fittest." "Fittest" has a connotation of "best"; and about "best" there hangs a moral flavor. In cosmic nature, however, what is "fittest" depends upon the conditions. . . .

Men in society are undoubtedly subject to the cosmic process. As among other animals, multiplication goes on without cessation, and involves severe competition for the means of support. The struggle for existence tends to eliminate those less fitted to adapt themselves to the circumstances of their existence. The strongest, the most self-assertive, tend to tread down the weaker. But the influence of the cosmic process on the evolution of society is the greater the more rudimentary its civilization. Social progress means a checking of the cosmic process at every step and the substitution for it of another, which may be called the ethical process; the end of which is not the survival of those who may happen to be the fittest, in respect of the whole of the conditions which obtain, but of those who are ethically the best.

As I have already urged, the practice of that which is ethically best—what we call goodness or virtue—involves a course of conduct which, in all respects, is opposed to that which leads to success in the cosmic struggle for existence. In place of ruthless self-assertion it demands self-restraint; in place of thrusting aside, or treading down, all competitors, it requires that the individual shall not merely respect, but shall help his fellows; its influence is directed, not so much to the survival of the fittest, as to the fitting of as many as possible to survive. It repudiates the gladiatorial theory of existence. It demands that each man who enters into the enjoyment of the advantages of a polity shall be mindful of his debt to those who have laboriously constructed it; and shall take heed that no act of his weakens the fabric in which he has been permitted to live. Laws and moral precepts are directed to the end of curbing the cosmic process and reminding the individual of his duty to the community, to the protection and influence of which he owes, if not existence itself, at least the life of something better than a brutal savage.

It is from neglect of these plain considerations that the fanatical individualism of our time attempts to apply the analogy of cosmic nature to society. Once more we have a misapplication of the stoical injunction to follow nature; the duties of the individual to the state are forgotten, and his tendencies to self-assertion are dignified by the name of rights. . . .

Let us understand, once for all, that the ethical progress of society depends, not on imitating the cosmic process, still less in running away from it, but in combating it. It may seem an audacious proposal thus to pit the microcosm against the macrocosm and to set man to subdue nature to his higher ends; but I venture to think that the great intellectual difference between the ancient times with which we have been occupied and our day, lies in the solid foundation we have acquired for the hope that such an enterprise may meet with a certain measure of success.

The history of civilization details the steps by which men have succeeded in building up an artificial world within the cosmos. Fragile reed as he may be, man, as Pascal says, is a thinking reed: there lies within him a fund of energy, operating intelligently and so far akin to that which pervades the universe, that it is competent to influence and modify the cosmic process. In virtue of his intelligence, the dwarf bends the Titan to his will. In every family, in every polity that has been established, the cosmic process in man has been restrained and otherwise modified by law and custom; in surrounding nature, it has been similarly influenced by the art of the shepherd, the agriculturist, the artisan. As civilization has advanced, so has the extent of this interference increased; until the organized and highly developed sciences and arts of the present day have endowed man with a command over the course of non-human nature greater than that once attributed to the magicians. The most impressive, I might say startling, of these changes have been brought about in the course of the last two centuries; while a right comprehension of the process of life and of the means of influencing its manifestations is only just dawning upon us. We do not yet see our way beyond generalities; and we are befogged by the obtrusion of false analogies and crude anticipations. But Astronomy, Physics, Chemistry, have all had to pass through similar phases, before they reached the stage at which their influence became an important factor in human affairs. Physiology, Psychology, Ethics, Political Science must submit to the same ordeal. Yet it seems to me irrational to doubt that, at no distant period, they will work as great a revolution in the sphere of practice.

The theory of evolution encourages no millennial anticipations. If, for millions of years, our globe has taken the upward road, yet, some time, the summit will be reached and the downward route will be commenced. The most daring imagination will hardly venture upon the suggestion that the power and the intelligence of man can ever arrest the procession of the great year.

Moreover, the cosmic nature born with us and, to a large extent, necessary for our maintenance, is the outcome of millions of years of severe training, and it would be folly to imagine that a few centuries will suffice to subdue its masterfulness to purely ethical ends. Ethical nature may count upon having to reckon with a tenacious and powerful enemy as long as the world lasts. But, on the other hand, I see no limit to the extent to which intelligence and will, guided by sound principles of investigation, and organized in common effort, may modify the conditions of existence, for a period longer than that now covered by history. And much may be done to change the nature of man himself. The intelligence which has converted the brother of the wolf into the faithful guardian of the flock ought to be able to do something towards curbing the instincts of savagery in civilized man.

But if we may permit ourselves a larger hope of abatement of the essential evil of the world than was possible to those who, in the infancy of exact knowledge, faced the problem of existence more than a score of centuries ago, I deem it an essential condition of the realization of that hope that we should cast aside the notion that the escape from pain and sorrow is the proper object of life.

We have long since emerged from the heroic childhood of our race, when good and evil could be met with the same "frolic welcome"; the attempts to escape from evil, whether Indian or Greek, have ended in flight from the battlefield; it remains to us to throw aside the youthful over-confidence and the no less youthful discouragement of nonage. We are grown men, and must play the man

> . . . strong in will
> To strive, to seek, to find, and not to yield,

cherishing the good that falls in our way, and bearing the evil, in and around us, with stout hearts set on diminishing it. So far, we all may strive in one faith towards one hope:

> It may be that the gulfs will wash us down,
> It may be we shall touch the Happy Isles,
>
> . . . . but something ere the end,
> Some work of noble note may yet be done.

QUESTIONS FOR DISCUSSION

1. How does Huxley apply the theory of evolution to the problems of ethical theory? How is it similar to Nietzsche's approach? How is it different? Which has the weight of the evidence on his side?
2. Why is Huxley critical of the "fanatical individualism of our time"? Should he be?

3. What steps took Huxley from a description of the theory of evolution to the prescription of cooperation? Reconstruct his argument as carefully as you can.

READINGS FOR IMMEDIATE REFERENCE

Huxley, Thomas. *Evolution and Ethics*. New York: Appleton, 1898, Essays 1-3.

Darwin, Charles. *Descent of Man*. London, 1871, Chapters 4, 27.

REFERENCES FOR COMPREHENSIVE KNOWLEDGE

Spencer, Herbert. *The Data of Ethics*. London, 1879. An elaborate statement of the relationship between the theory of evolution and moral theory.

Also see:

Allee, Werden. *Cooperation Among the Animals: with Human Implications*. New York: Schuman, 1951.

Hobhouse, L. T. *Development and Purpose*. New York: Macmillan, 1927.

Keith, Arthur. *Evolution and Ethics*. New York: Putnam, 1947.

Mead, Margaret. *Cooperation and Competition Among Primitive Peoples*. New York: McGraw-Hill, 1937.

Simpson, George G. *The Meaning of Evolution: its significance for man*. New Haven: Yale University Press, 1950.

IV. ERICH FROMM

Born in 1900 in Frankfurt, Germany, Fromm studied in his home city, Munich and Berlin before receiving his doctoral degree from the University of Heidelberg at the age of twenty-two. In 1923, he began studying at the Berlin Institute for Psychoanalysis, spending the next decade in Berlin and Frankfurt teaching, researching and writing from an interdisciplinary orientation. He left Germany in 1933 and in 1941 published his influential *Escape from Freedom,* a psychoanalytic account of the rise of Naziism. He has taught at numerous universities, among them Columbia, Yale, Bennington and the New School for Social Research; has been a member of various psychiatric institutes, including the Washington School of Psychiatry and the William Alanson White Institute of Psychiatry; and has been much in demand as a public lecturer. At present, he divides his time between Mexico City where he is a professor at the National University of Mexico and teaching positions around New York City, all the time continuing to publish books and articles reflecting his deepening psychoanalytic insight and interest in the problems of human life and history.

In the book from which this selection has been taken, *The Sane Society,* Fromm contends that a society's sanity (and hence goodness) can be determined by how well it satisfies man's basic needs. What are those needs? How can they best be satisfied? Does Fromm offer reasons to support each kind of consideration?

Sanity, Love, and Reason[1]

Man, in respect to his body and his physiological functions, belongs to the animal kingdom. The functioning of the animal is determined by instincts, by specific action patterns which are in turn determined by inherited neurological structures. The higher an animal is in the scale of development, the more flexibility of action pattern and the less completeness of structural adjustment do we find at birth. In the higher primates we even find considerable intel-

[1] From *The Sane Society* by Erich Fromm. Copyright © 1955 by Erich Fromm, Chapters 3, 4. Reprinted by permission of Holt, Rinehart and Winston, Inc.

ligence; that is, use of thought for the accomplishment of desired goals, thus enabling the animal to go far beyond the instinctively prescribed action pattern. But great as the development within the animal kingdom is, certain basic elements of existence remain the same.

The animal "is lived" through biological laws of nature; it is part of nature and never transcends it. It has no conscience of a moral nature, and no awareness of itself and of its existence; it has no reason, if by reason we mean the ability to penetrate the surface grasped by the senses and to understand the essence behind that surface; therefore the animal has no concept of the truth, even though it may have an idea of what is useful.

Animal existence is one of harmony between the animal and nature; not, of course, in the sense that the natural conditions do not often threaten the animal and force it to a bitter fight for survival, but in the sense that the animal is equipped by nature to cope with the very conditions it is to meet, just as the seed of a plant is equipped by nature to make use of the conditions of soil, climate, et cetera, to which it has become adapted in the evolutionary process.

At a certain point of animal evolution, there occurred a unique break, comparable to the first emergence of matter, to the first emergence of life, and to the first emergence of animal existence. This new event happens when in the evolutionary process, action ceases to be essentially determined by instinct; when the adaption of nature loses its coercive character; when action is no longer fixed by hereditarily given mechanisms. When the animal transcends nature, when it transcends the purely passive role of the creature, when it becomes, biologically speaking, the most helpless animal, *man is born.* At this point, the animal has emancipated itself from nature by erect posture, the brain has grown far beyond what it was in the highest animal. This birth of man may have lasted for hundreds of thousands of years, but what matters is that a new species arose, transcending nature, that *life became aware of itself.*

Self-awareness, reason and imagination disrupt the "harmony" which characterizes animal existence. Their emergence has made man into an anomaly, into the freak of the universe. He is part of nature, subject to her physical laws and unable to change them, yet he transcends the rest of nature. He is set apart while being a part; he is homeless, yet chained to the home he shares with all creatures. Cast into this world at an accidental place and time, he is forced out of it, again accidentally. Being aware of himself, he realizes his powerlessness and the limitations of his existence. He visualizes his own end: death. Never is he free from the dichotomy of his existence: he cannot rid himself of his mind, even if he should want to; he cannot rid himself of his body as long as he is alive—and his body makes him want to be alive.

Reason, man's blessing, is also his curse; it forces him to cope everlastingly with the task of solving an insoluble dichotomy. Human existence is different in this respect from that of all other organisms; it is in a state of constant and unavoidable disequilibrium. Man's life cannot "be lived" by repeating the pattern of his species; *he* must live. Man is the only animal that can be *bored,* that can feel evicted from paradise. Man is the only animal who finds his own existence a problem which he has to solve and from which he cannot escape. He cannot go back to the prehuman state of harmony with nature; he must proceed to develop his reason until he becomes the master of nature, and of himself.

But man's birth ontogenetically as well as phylogenetically is essentially a negative event. He lacks the instinctive adaptation to nature, he lacks physical strength, he is the most helpless of all animals at birth, and in need of protection for a much longer period of time than any of them. While he has lost the unity with nature, he has not been given the means to lead a new existence outside of nature. His reason is most rudimentary, he has no knowledge of nature's processes, nor tools to replace the lost instincts; he lives divided into small groups, with no knowledge of himself or of others; indeed, the biblical Paradise myth expresses the situation with perfect clarity. Man, who lives in the Garden of Eden, in complete harmony with nature but without awareness of himself, begins his history by the first act of freedom, disobedience to a command. Concomitantly, he becomes aware of himself, of his separateness, of his helplessness; he is expelled from Paradise, and two angels with fiery swords prevent his return.

Man's evolution is based on the fact that he has lost his original home, nature—and that he can never return to it, can never become an animal again. There is only one way he can take: to emerge fully from his natural home, to find a new home—one which he creates, by making the world a human one and by becoming truly human himself.

When man is born, the human race as well as the individual, he is thrown out of a situation which was definite, as definite as the instincts, into a situation which is indefinite, uncertain and open. There is certainty only about the past, and about the future as far as it is death—which actually is return to the past, the inorganic state of matter.

The problem of man's existence, then, is unique in the whole of nature; he has fallen out of nature, as it were, and is still in it; he is partly divine, partly animal; partly infinite, partly finite. *The necessity to find ever-new solutions for the contradictions in his existence, to find ever-higher forms of unity with nature, his fellowmen and himself, is the source of all psychic forces which motivate man, of all his passions, effects and anxieties.*

The animal is content if its physiological needs—its hunger, its thirst and its sexual needs—are satisfied. Inasmuch as man is also animal, these needs are likewise imperative and must be satisfied. *But inasmuch as man is human, the satisfaction of these instinctual needs is not sufficient to make him happy; they are not even sufficient to make him sane. The archimedic point of the specifically human dynamism lies in this uniqueness of the human situation; the understanding of man's psyche must be based on the analysis of man's needs stemming from the conditions of his existence.*

The problem, then, which the human race as well as each individual has to solve is that of being born. . . . Slowly, the growing person learns to love, to develop reason, to look at the world objectively. He begins to develop his powers; to acquire a sense of identity, to overcome the seduction of his senses for the sake of an integrated life. Birth then, in the conventional meaning of the word, is only the beginning of birth in the broader sense. The whole life of the individual is nothing but the process of giving birth to himself; indeed, we should be fully born, when we die—although it is the tragic fate of most individuals to die before they are born. . . .

Man's life is determined by the inescapable alternative between regression and progression, between return to animal existence and arrival at human existence. Any attempt to return is painful, it inevitably leads to suffering and mental sickness, to death either physiologically or mentally (insanity). Every step forward is frightening and painful too, until a certain point has been reached where fear and doubt have only minor proportions. Aside from the physiologically nourished cravings (hunger, thirst, sex), all essential human cravings are determined by this polarity. Man has to solve a problem, he can never rest in the given situation of a passive adaptation to nature. Even the most complete satisfaction of all his instinctive needs does not solve his *human* problem; his most intensive passions and needs are not those rooted in his body, but those rooted in the very peculiarity of his existence. . . .

Man is torn away from the primary union with nature, which characterizes animal existence. Having at the same time reason and imagination, he is aware of his aloneness and separateness; of his powerlessness and ignorance; of the accidentalness of his birth and of his death. He could not face this state of being for a second if he could not find new ties with his fellow man which replace the old ones, regulated by instincts. Even if all his physiological needs were satisfied, he would experience his state of aloneness and individuation as a prison from which he had to break out in order to retain his sanity. In fact, the insane person is the one who has completely failed to establish any kind of union, and is imprisoned, even if he is not behind barred windows. The necessity to unite with other living beings, to be related to them, is an imperative need on the fulfillment of which man's sanity depends. This need is behind all phenomena which constitute the whole gamut of intimate human relations, of all passions which are called love in the broadest sense of the word.

There are several ways in which this union can be sought and achieved. Man can attempt to become one with the world by *submission* to a person, to a group, to an institution, to God. In this way he transcends the separateness of his individual existence by becoming part of somebody or something bigger than himself, and experiences his identity in connection with the power to which he has submitted. Another possibility of overcoming separateness lies in the opposite direction: man can try to unite himself with the world by having *power* over it, by making others a part of himself, and thus transcending his individual existence by domination. The common element in both submission and domination is the symbiotic nature of relatedness. Both persons involved have lost their integrity and freedom; they live on each other and from each other, satisfying their craving for closeness, yet suffering from the lack of inner strength and self-reliance which would require freedom and independence, and furthermore constantly threatened by the conscious or unconscious hostility which is bound to arise from the symbiotic relationship. The realization of the submissive (masochistic) or the domineering (sadistic) passion never leads to satisfaction. . . .

There is only one passion which satisfies man's need to unite himself with the world, and to acquire at the same time a sense of integrity and individuality, and this is *love*. *Love is union with somebody, or something, outside oneself, under the condition of retaining the separateness and integrity of one's own self*. It is an experience of sharing, of communion, which permits the full unfolding of one's own inner activity. The experience of love does away with the necessity of illusions. There is no need to inflate the image of the other person, or of myself, since the reality of active sharing and loving permits me to transcend my individualized existence, and at the same time to experience myself as the bearer of the active powers which constitute the act of loving. What matters is the particular quality of loving, not the object. Love is in the experience of human solidarity with our fellow creatures, it is in the erotic love of man and woman, in the love of the mother for the child, and also in the love of oneself, as a human being; it is in the mystical experience of union. In the act of loving, I am one with All, and yet I am myself, a unique, separate, limited, mortal human being. Indeed out of the very polarity between separateness and union, love is born and reborn.

Love is one aspect of what I have called the productive orientation: the active and creative relatedness of man to his fellow man, to himself and to nature. In the realm of *thought*, this productive orientation is expressed in the proper grasp of the world by reason. In the realm of *action*, the productive orientation is expressed in productive work, the prototype of which is art and craftsmanship. In the realm of *feeling*, the productive orientation is expressed in love, which is the experience of union with another person, with all men, and with nature, under the condition of retaining one's sense of integrity and independence. In the experience of love the paradox happens that two people become one, and remain two at the same time. Love in this sense is never restricted to one person. If I can love only one person, and nobody else, if my love for one person makes me more alienated and distant from my fellow man, I may be attached to this person in any number of ways, yet I do not love. If I say, "I love you," I say, "I love in you all of humanity, all that is alive; I love in you also myself." Self-love, in this sense, is the opposite of selfishness. The latter is actually a greedy concern with oneself which springs from and compensates for the lack of genuine love for oneself. Love, paradoxically, makes me more independent because it makes me stronger and happier—yet it makes me one with the loved person to the extent that individuality seems to be extinguished for the moment. In loving I experience "I am you," you—the loved person, you—the stranger, you—everything alive. In the experience of love lies the only answer to being human, lies sanity.

Productive love always implies a syndrome of attitudes; that of *care, responsibility, respect* and *knowledge.* If I love, I *care*—that is, I am actively concerned with the other person's growth and happiness; I am not a spectator. I am *responsible,* that is, I respond to his needs, to those he can express and more so to those he cannot or does not express. I *respect* him, that is (according to the original meaning of *re-spicere*) I look at him as he is, objectively and not distorted by my wishes and fears. I *know* him, I have penetrated through his surface to the core of his being and related myself to him from my core, from the center, as against the periphery, of my being.

Productive love when directed toward equals may be called *brotherly love.* In *motherly love* (Hebrew: *rachamim,* from *rechem*=womb) the relationship between the two persons involved is one of inequality; the child is helpless and dependent on the mother. In order to grow, it must become more and more independent, until he does not need mother any more. Thus the mother-child relationship is paradoxical and, in a sense, tragic. It requires the most intense love on the mother's side, and yet this very love must help the child to grow away from the mother, and to become fully independent. It is easy for any mother to love her child before this process of separation has begun—but it is the task in which most fail, to love the child and at the same time to let it go—and to *want* to let it go.

* * * * *

The fact that man has reason and imagination leads not only to the ability to experience love but also to orient himself in the world intellectually. This need can be compared with the process of physical orientation which develops in the first years of life, and which is completed when the child can walk by himself, touch and handle things, knowing what they are. But when the ability to walk and to speak has been acquired, only the first step in the direction of orientation has been taken. Man finds himself surrounded by many puzzling phenomena and, having reason, he has to make sense of them, has to put them in some context which he can understand and which permits him to deal with them in his thoughts. The further his reason develops, the more adequate becomes his system of orientation, that is, the more it approximates reality. But even if man's frame of orientation is utterly illusory, it satisfies his need for some picture which is meaningful to him. Whether he believes in the power of a totem animal, in the rain god, or in the superiority and destiny of his race, his need for some frame of orientation is satisfied. Quite obviously, the picture of the world which he has depends on the development of his reason and of his knowledge. Although biologically the brain capacity of the human race has remained the same for thousands of generations, it takes a long evolutionary process to arrive at *objectivity,* that is, to acquire the faculty to see the world, nature, other persons and oneself as they are, and not distorted by desires and fears. The more man develops this objectivity, the more he matures, the better can he create a human world in which he is at home. Reason is man's faculty for *grasping* the world by thought, in contradiction to intelligence, which is man's ability to *manipulate* the world with the help of thought. Reason is man's instrument for arriving at truth, intelligence is man's instrument for manipulating the world more successfully; the former is essentially human, the latter belongs to the animal part of man.

Reason is a faculty which must be practiced, in order to develop, and it is indivisible. By this I mean that the faculty for objectivity refers to the knowledge of nature as well as to the knowledge of man, of society and of oneself. It one lives in illusions about one sector of life, one's capacity for reason is restricted or damaged, and thus the use of reason is inhibited with regard to all other sectors. Reason in this respect is like love. Just as love is an orientation which refers to all objects and is incompatible with the restriction to one object, so is reason a human faculty which must embrace the whole of the world with which man is confronted.

The need for a frame of orientation exists on two levels; the first and the more fundamental need is to have some frame of orientation, regardless of whether it is true or false. Unless man has such a subjectively satisfactory frame of orientation, he cannot live sanely. On the second level, the need is to be in touch with reality by reason, to grasp the world objectively. But the necessity to develop his reason is not as immediate as that to develop some frame of orientation, since what is at stake for man in the latter case is his happiness and serenity, and not his sanity.

* * * * *

Summing up, it can be said that the concept of mental health follows from the very conditions of human existence, and it is the same for man in all ages and all cultures. Mental health is characterized by the ability to love and to create, by the emergence from incestuous ties to clan and soil, by a sense of identity based on one's experience of self as the subject and agent of one's powers, by the grasp of reality inside and outside of ourselves, that is, by the development of objectivity and reason.

QUESTIONS FOR DISCUSSION

1. What are the differences between animal and human life, submissiveness and love, reason and intelligence, sanity and insanity, as Fromm sees them? Would you disagree with any of his characterizations?
2. (1) What are the ends a sane society should seek to achieve, and (2) why should they be achieved? (3)What are the best means to do so, and (4) why are these the most effective? Which of these questions does Fromm answer, and how?
3. Do you find any important similarities between Fromm's thought and other ethical theories we have considered? Is his thought inferior or superior to the others'?

READINGS FOR IMMEDIATE REFERENCE

Fromm, Erich. *The Art of Loving*. New York: Harper, 1956.
———. *Man for Himself*. New York: Rinehart, 1947, Chapters 3, 4.
———. *The Sane Society*. New York: Henry Holt, 1955, Chapters 1-5.
Birnbach, Martin. *Neo-Freudian Social Philosophy*. Palo Alto: Stanford University Press, 1961. Chapter 8.
Jung, Carl. *Modern Man in Search of a Soul*. London: Kegan Paul, 1934.

REFERENCES FOR COMPREHENSIVE KNOWLEDGE

Fromm, Erich. *Escape from Freedom*. New York: Rinehart, 1941.
———. *The Forgotten Language*. New York: Henry Holt, 1951.
———. *Marx's Concept of Man*. New York: Ungar, 1961.
———. *Sigmund Freud's Mission*. New York: Harper, 1959.
Horney, Karen. *Neurosis and Human Growth*. New York: Norton, 1937. In western civilization, neurotic behavior is caused by a conflict between the desire for affection and the desire for power.

Also see:
Adler, Alfred. *Understanding Human Nature*. New York: Greenberg, 1946.
Alexander, Franz. *Our Age of Unreason*. Philadelphia: Lippincott, 1951.
Freud, Sigmund. *Civilization and Its Discontents*. London: Hogarth Press, 1955.
Jung, Carl. *Psychology and Religion*. New York: Oxford University Press, 1938.
Kardiner, Abram. *The Psychological Frontiers of Society*. New York: Columbia University Press, 1946.

V. HENRY MARGENAU AND BERTRAND RUSSELL

Margenau was born in 1901 in Bielefeld, Germany, living in that country until 1923 when he emigrated to America. He graduated from Midland College in 1924 and received his Ph.D. from Yale in 1929, a year before he became a naturalized citizen. He has taught at numerous universities (Nebraska, Yale, Munich, Berlin, California, Carleton) and has served as consultant for many firms and governmental agencies (Rand Corporation, General Electric, Lockheed, Atomic Energy Commission, Argonne National Laboratories,), but he has centered his operations at Yale University where he has been a member of the Philosophy Department since 1931.

A brief biographical sketch of Russell will be found on page 36.

We conclude this chapter with short selections from two contemporary philosophers who have made important contributions to science: the first to physics, the second to mathematics. Margenau contends that while science cannot provide a prescriptive ethical theory, only the application of scientific method to the problems of morality can provide reasonable and reliable answers to those problems. Russell believes that "a scientific society must be viewed with apprehension." Which man is correct—or is neither, or both? Can science answer prescriptive moral problems—including the judgment as to what its own purposes should be?

Scientific Method and the Moral Life[1]

The last section has dealt with attempts at augmenting physical reality and with their prospects, but attention was confined to problems of factual apperception and knowledge. All these attempts share with the philosophy developed in this book the quality of being insufficient for the representation of human experience in at least two major fields, the areas of feeling and of value judgments. It is of course not for the philosopher to say that these defects are necessary and are traceable to *fundamental* limitations of scientific method; nor is the scientist free to deny it. The proper attitude on the part of the phi-

[1] By permission, from *The Nature of Physical Reality,* by Henry Margenau. Copyright, 1950. McGraw-Hill Book Company, Inc., Chapter 21.

losopher is open-mindedness, while it is clearly the job of the scientist to recognize the insufficiencies and then to attempt their removal. He may not be successful; science may have essential limitations which are not at present within sight. But the gain for humanity that might attach to success is great enough to justify a straining after the smallest chance.

Let us not fall prey to an absurd and fraudulent argument which the enemies of science have concocted: that if science regulated the emotions, judgments, and actions of mankind, human beings would become regimented automata, and life would not be worth living. For there is a great difference between understanding phenomena well enough to control them when control is indicated, and not understanding them. Knowledge of the laws of motion of material bodies does not lessen one's pleasure in playing dice or in any activity where, for enjoyment or for any other purpose, one intentionally discards scientific treatment and invites the pleasant chicanery of chance; but such knowledge does help in the construction of houses and automobiles. To say that we are destined to become robots if society's functioning were known as accurately as the behavior of gases is an error because *knowing* and *regulating* are different things. Science may not create values, yet it alone provides the means for their realization.

Indifference of physical reality with respect to the affective qualities of experience is generally recognized and needs no emphasis here. A person dear to me is a valid construct in the same sense as, and therefore no more real than, the umbrella in my closet. Obviously, this kind of statement leaves out a wealth of aspects more cherished in life than the facts of reality. But here again it is not certain that the processes of scientific understanding, and with them the idea of reality, cannot be enlarged sufficiently to express that added richness of experience. . . .

As to values, however, the story is somewhat different. In my view, which is not the only one consistent with the epistemological theory presented in this book and therefore cannot be argued without an appeal to extrascientific convictions, natural science contains no *normative* principles dealing with ultimate goals; physical reality is the quintessence of cognitive experience and not of values. Its significance is in terms of stable *relations* between phases of experience, and since it draws its power from relations, reality cannot create an *unconditional* "thou shalt." To know physical reality is to know where to look when something is wanted or needed to be seen; it is to be able to cure when a cure is desired, to kill when killing is intended. But natural science will never tell whether it is good or bad to look, to cure, or to kill. It simply lacks the premise of an "ought."

Now some oughts are very easily smuggled into science. One may say that psychology, anthropology, and sociology can determine what is good for the human species, then regard this as a scientific finding and base upon it a scientific code of ethics. The multiple reference to science in this and similar proposals is unwittingly designed to camouflage the fact that the statement is in fact a recommendation of hedonism, albeit in a modern and altruistic form. But never can it relieve us from the necessity of an ultimate nonscientific commitment, in this instance from a dedication of ourselves to the maxim that *it is good to seek the goal of hedonism*. Methodologically, the acceptance of this "doctrine" or any of its competitors in the field of ethics is the counterpart of an acceptance of the principles and postulates of science. In consequence of their lying at different parts but in the same basic stratum of experience, moral postulates are not reducible to scientific ones, nor the reverse. I should regard the failure to recognize this as an impediment to the progress of both science and philosophy, as comparable to the error on the part of a metaphysician of the old school who takes science to be the description of some sort of preformed being.

Because of this irreducibility, however, there arises the possibility of erecting ethics and science as parallel structures, of utilizing the *formal* principles of science in an endeavor to make the appeal of ethics more firm and more universal. This chance looms here as a vague but promising conjecture, which we can only allude to in this book. Yet it should perhaps be said that the considerations set forth in it were largely prompted by the hope that clarity with respect to scientific method, once attained, might later lead to a decision on the applicability of that method to problems in the normative disciplines; in this sense, the present volume merely covers the preliminaries for a larger and most pressing task.

Should this conjecture be true, then a subject like ethics must be developed in three interlocking stages. It must form a postulational discipline in which (a) a basic code is adopted, (b) that basic code is developed through its formal consequences and applied to action, (c) these actions or their social consequences are tested against some standard of validity. The outcome of such tests decides the ethical correctness of the moral code.

The first reaction to this graceless and seemingly artificial proposal must be one of thorough skepticism, based on the argument that there is no objective standard of ethical validity; that only the adopted code itself can confer ethical validity and that therefore the whole procedure of validation, stage (c), is a trivial, rubber-stamping referral of the results of a given set of ethical postulates to the postulates which generated these results. And this would seem unscientific, nay futile.

But let it be said with emphasis that verification in science is not a simple matter either, is in many instances an equally circular undertaking. To the nonscientist, verification is likely to mean a look-and-see procedure, and artless comparison of what is *predicted* with what *is*. The analysis of the preceding chapters has shown how far this is from being true, how naive it is to suppose that a bare datum of immediate experience invariably carries theoretical significance. On the contrary, it is the formal structure of science that confers relevance on observations; theory determines to a large extent in what manner it will expose itself to test. Historically, therefore, the technique of verification, which is rarely present before a theory is born, developed along with scientific theory and attained refinement in the same measure as the theory did. Is it not unreasonable, then, to doubt the possibility of verifying ethical theory before trying to set up such a theory in postulational form?

In a crude way the opportunity for verifying ethical postulates is always present: it is to see whether the society practicing the code derived from the postulates survives. This corresponds to the naive scientific look-and-see thesis. On the scientific side, refinement of that thesis came about as theories advanced, and there seems to be little hope for ethics except in this same procedure of starting the postulational formalism with wholehearted acquiescence and developing methods of verification as it goes forward.

But an even greater difficulty, though a less fundamental one, lies in the accomplishment of task (a), the acceptance of a basic code. There is the important problem of getting it adopted, and this problem has its taproot in a strange practical attitude with regard to the ethical postulates. Concerning them we often display an irrational insistence on *a priori* evidence; we demand that they come to us accredited with absolute certainty or with divine sanction, forgetting altogether that *scientific* postulates are initially tentative and are confirmed with use. The postulates of arithmetic are not *certain* nor are they *true,* for there are many instances in our simplest experience which violate them thoroughly. One cloud in the sky plus another cloud do not always make two clouds. But successful science, valid in a large though not unlimited domain, has nevertheless proceeded from the axioms of arithmetic. Fuller realization of these facts may perchance make the problems of the normative sciences more tractable.

The Outlook for a Scientific Society[1]

Science in the course of a few centuries of its history has undergone an internal development which appears to be not yet completed. One may sum up this development as the passage from contemplation to manipulation. The love of knowledge to which the growth of science is due is itself the product of a twofold impulse. We may seek knowledge of an object because we love the object or because we wish to have power over it. The former impulse leads to the kind of knowledge that is contemplative, the latter to the kind that

[1] Reprinted from *The Scientific Outlook* by Bertrand Russell. By permission of W. W. Norton and Company, Inc. Copyright 1931 and 1959 by Bertrand Russell, Chapter 17. Canadian rights by George Allen and Unwin, Ltd.

is practical. In the development of science the power impulse has increasingly prevailed over the love impulse. The power impulse is embodied in industrialism and in governmental technique. It is embodied also in the philosophies known as pragmatism and instrumentalism. Each of these philosophies holds, broadly speaking, that our beliefs about any object are true in so far as they enable us to manipulate it with advantage to ourselves. This is what may be called a governmental view of truth. Of truth so conceived science offers us a great deal; indeed there seems no limit to its possible triumphs. To the man who wishes to change his environment science offers astonishingly powerful tools, and if knowledge consists in the power to produce intended changes, then science gives knowledge in abundance.

But the desire for knowledge has another form, belonging to an entirely different set of emotions. The mystic, the lover, and the poet are also seekers after knowledge—not perhaps very successful seekers, but none the less worthy of respect on that account. In all forms of love we wish to have knowledge of what is loved, not for purposes of power, but for the ecstasy of contemplation. "In knowledge of God standeth our eternal life," but not because knowledge of God gives us power over Him. Wherever there is ecstasy or joy or delight derived from an object there is the desire to know that object—to know it not in the manipulative fashion that consists of turning it into something else, but to know it in the fashion of the beatific vision, because in itself, and for itself, it sheds happiness upon the lover. In sex love as in other forms of love the impulse to this kind of knowledge exists, unless the love is purely physical or practical. This may indeed be made the touchstone of any love that is valuable. Love which has value contains an impulse towards that kind of knowledge out of which the mystic union springs.

Science in its beginnings was due to men who were in love with the world. They perceived the beauty of the stars and the sea, of the winds and the mountains. Because they loved them their thoughts dwelt upon them, and they wished to understand them more intimately than a mere outward contemplation made possible. "The world," said Heraclitus, "is an ever-living fire, with measures kindling and measures going out." Heraclitus and the other Ionian philosophers, from whom came the first impulse to scientific knowledge, felt the strange beauty of the world almost like a madness in the blood. They were men of Titanic passionate intellect, and from the intensity of their intellectual passion the whole movement of the modern world has sprung. But step by step, as science has developed, the impulse of love which gave it birth has been increasingly thwarted, while the impulse of power, which was at first a mere campfollower, has gradually usurped command in virtue of its unforeseen success. The lover of nature has been baffled, the tyrant over nature has been rewarded. As physics has developed, it has deprived us step by step of what we thought we knew concerning the intimate nature of the physical world. Color and sound, light and shade, form and texture, belong no longer to that external nature that the Ionians sought as the bride of their devotion. All these things have been transferred from the beloved to the lover, and the beloved has become a skeleton of rattling bones, cold and dreadful, but perhaps a mere phantasm. The poor physicists, appalled at the desert that their formulae have revealed, call upon God to give them comfort, but God must share the ghostliness of His creation, and the answer that the physicists think they hear to their cry is only the frightened beating of their own hearts. Disappointed as the lover of nature, the man of science is becoming its tyrant. What matters it, says the practical man, whether the outer world exists or is a dream, provided I can make it behave as I wish? Thus science has more and more substituted power-knowledge for love-knowledge, and as this substitution becomes completed science tends more and more to become sadistic. The scientific society of the future as we have been imagining it is one in which the power impulse has completely overwhelmed the impulse of love, and this is the psychological source of the cruelties which it is in danger of exhibiting.

Science, which began as the pursuit of truth, is becoming incompatible with veracity, since complete veracity tends more and more to complete scientific scepticism. When science is considered contemplatively, not practically, we find that what we believe we believe owing to animal faith, and it is only our disbeliefs that are due to science. When, on the other hand, science is considered as a technique for the transformation of ourselves and our environment, it is found to give us a power quite independent of its metaphysical validity. But we can only wield this power by ceasing to ask ourselves metaphysical questions as to the nature of reality. Yet these questions are the evidence of a lover's attitude towards the world. Thus it is only in so far as we renounce the world as its lovers that we can conquer it as its technicians. But this division in the soul is fatal to what is best in man. As soon as the failure of science considered as metaphysics is realized, the power conferred by science as a technique is only obtainable by something analogous to the worship of Satan, that is to say, by the renunciation of love.

This is the fundamental reason why the prospect of a scientific society must be viewed with apprehension. The scientific society in its pure form, which is what we have been trying to depict, is incompatible with the pursuit of truth, with love, with art, with spontaneous delight, with every ideal that man has hitherto cherished, with the sole exception of ascetic renunciation. It is not knowledge that is the source of these dangers. Knowledge is good and ignorance is evil: to this principle the lover of the world can admit no exception. Nor is it power in and for itself that is the source of danger. What is dangerous is power wielded for the sake of power, not power wielded for the sake of genuine good. The leaders of the modern world are drunk with power; the fact that they can do something that no one previously thought it possible to do is to them a sufficient reason for doing it. Power is not one of the ends of life, but merely a means to other ends, and until men remember the ends that power should subserve, science will not do what it might to minister to the good life. But what then are the ends of life, the reader will say. I do not think that one man has a right to legislate for another on this matter. For each individual the ends of life are those things which he deeply desires, and which if they existed would give him peace. Or, if it be thought that peace is too much to ask this side of the grave, let us say that the ends of life should give delight or joy or ecstasy. In the conscious desires of the man who seeks power for its own sake there is something dusty: when he has it he wants only more power, and does not find rest in contemplation of what he has. The lover, the poet and the mystic find a fuller satisfaction than the seeker after power can ever know, since they can rest in the object of their love, whereas the seeker after power must be perpetually engaged in some fresh manipulation if he is not to suffer from a sense of emptiness. I think therefore that the satisfactions of the lover, using that word in its broadest sense, exceed the satisfactions of the tyrant, and deserve a higher place among the ends of life. When I come to die I shall not feel that I have lived in vain. I have seen the earth turn red at evening, the dew sparkling in the morning, the snow shining under a frosty sun; I have smelt rain after drought, and have heard the stormy Atlantic beat upon the granite shores of Cornwall. Science may bestow these and other joys upon more people than could otherwise enjoy them. If so, its power will be wisely used. But when it takes out of life the moments to which life owes its value, science will not deserve admiration, however cleverly and however elaborately it may lead men along the road to despair. The sphere of values lies outside science, except in so far as science consists in the pursuit of knowledge. Science as the pursuit of power must not obtrude upon the sphere of values, and scientific technique, if it is to enrich human life, must not outweigh the ends which it should serve. . . .

Our world has a heritage of culture and beauty, but unfortunately we have been handing on this heritage only to the less active and important members of each generation. The government of the world, by which I do not mean its ministerial posts but its key-positions of power, has been allowed to fall into the hands of men ignorant of the past, without tenderness towards what is traditional, without understanding of what they are destroying. There is no essential reason why this should be the case. To prevent it is an educational problem, and not a very difficult one. Men in the past were often parochial in space, but the dominant men of our age are parochial in time. They feel for the past a contempt that it does not deserve, and for the present a respect that it deserves still less. The copybook maxims of a former age have become outworn, but a new set of copybook maxims is required. First among these I should put: "It is better to do a little good than much harm." To give content to this maxim it would of course be necessary to instil some sense of what is good. Few men in the present day, for example, can be induced to believe that there is no inherent excellence in rapid locomotion. To climb from Hell to Heaven is good, though it be a slow and laborious process; to fall from Heaven to Hell is bad, even though it be done with the speed of Milton's Satan. Nor can it be said that a mere increase in the production of material commodities is in itself a thing of great value. To prevent extreme poverty is important, but to add to the possessions of those who already have too much is a worthless waste of effort. To prevent crime may be necessary, but to invent new crimes in order that the police may show skill in preventing them is less admirable. The new powers that science has given to man can only be wielded safely by those who, whether through the study of history or through their own experience of life, have acquired some reverence for human feelings and some tenderness towards the emotions that give color to the daily existence of men and women. . . . A world without delight and without affection is a world destitute of value. These things the scientific manipulator must remember, and if he does his manipulation may be wholly beneficial. All that is needed is that men should not be so intoxicated by new power as to forget the truths that were familiar to every previous generation. Not all wisdom is new, nor is all folly out of date.

Man has been disciplined hitherto by his subjection to nature. Having emancipated himself from this subjection, he is showing something of the defects of slave-turned-master. A new moral outlook is called for in which submission to the powers of nature is replaced by respect for what is best in man. It is where this respect is lacking that scientific technique is dangerous. So long as it is present, science, having delivered man from bondage to nature, can proceed to deliver him from bondage to the slavish part of himself. The dangers exist, but they are not inevitable, and hope for the future is at least as rational as fear.

QUESTIONS FOR DISCUSSION

1. Do Margenau's comments regarding the implicit hedonism in the social scientists' ethical judgments seem to you to be correct when applied to the other selections in this chapter?
2. Do you think Margenau's method for formulating ethical principles would be useful and justified?
3. Why does Russell express skepticism regarding a scientific society? Do you share his pessimism? Does he have a solution? Do you?

READINGS FOR IMMEDIATE REFERENCE

Margenau, Henry. "Ethical Science," *Scientific Monthly*, November, 1949, pp. 290-296.

Russell, Bertrand. *The Impact of Science on Society*. New York: Columbia University Press, 1951, Chapters 1, 2, 6, 7.

———. *The Scientific Outlook.* New York: Norton, 1931, Chapters 3-5, 13, 17.

———. *Unpopular Essays.* London: Allen and Unwin, 1950, Chapters 3, 9, 10.

Oppenheimer, J. Robert. *Foundations for World Order.* Denver: University of Denver Press, 1949. Chapter 2.

REFERENCES FOR COMPREHENSIVE KNOWLEDGE

Margenau, Henry. *The Foundations of Physics.* New York: J. Wiley and Sons, 1936.

Russell, Bertrand. *The Analysis of Matter.* London: Kegan Paul, 1927.

———. *An Analysis of Mind.* London: Allen and Unwin, 1921.

———. *Human Knowledge: Its Scope and Limits.* London: Allen and Unwin, 1948.

———. *Icarus or the Future of Science.* London: Kegan Paul, 1924.

———. *An Inquiry into Meaning and Truth.* London: Allen and Unwin, 1940.

———. *Our Knowledge of the External World.* London: Allen and Unwin, 1914.

———. *Political Ideals.* New York: Century, 1917.

———. *Power: A New Social Analysis.* New York: Norton, 1938.

———. *The Problems of Philosophy.* London: William and Norgate, 1912.

———. *Religion and Science.* London: Butterworth-Nelson, 1935.

———. *Why I am Not a Christian.* London: Watts, 1927.

———. *Why Men Fight.* New York: Century, 1916.

Schilpp, Paul A. *The Philosophy of Bertrand Russell,* rev. ed. New York: Tudor, 1952. Discussion of different phases of Russell's thought by various authorities, together with Russell's answers.

BIBLIOGRAPHY FOR CHAPTER TWELVE

READINGS FOR IMMEDIATE REFERENCE

Brandt, Richard. *Ethical Theory.* New York: Prentice-Hall, 1959, Chapter 3.

Hall, Everett. *Modern Science and Human Values.* Princeton: Van Nostrand, 1956, Chapters 8-10.

REFERENCES FOR COMPREHENSIVE KNOWLEDGE

Breasted, James H. *The Dawn of Conscience.* New York: Scribners, 1934.

Hobhouse, L. T. *Morals in Evolution,* 5th ed. New York: Henry Holt, 1931.

Kohler, Wolfgang. *The Place of Values in a World of Fact.* New York: Liveright, 1938.

Windle, B. C. *Science and Morals.* London: Burns and Oates, 1919.

Chapter Thirteen

THE SCIENTIFIC WAY

Of the three attitudes we are considering, the one accepted today most widely in the western world, at least superficially, is science. Philosophy's adherents always have been few, for to view life philosophically requires rigorous thinking about speculative problems, a combination too demanding for many people. Those who view life religiously, although still large in number, have been decreasing steadily during the past two centuries. However, science has made the world in which we live. It has made possible an increasingly high degree of material comfort. It has revolutionized such diverse fields as medicine, mining, and agriculture. Scientific evidence has become important in such sacrosanct areas as law and education. In this century, science even dominates philosophy, as seen in the dominant schools of pragmatism and positivism, while evolution and higher criticism of the Bible have had a significant effect on religious thought.

Probably the main reason for science's successes has been its ability to control nature, to use the earth's resources for fulfilling man's desires. This control in turn has resulted from the belief that the world can be viewed as it really is, apart from the private beliefs of an observer. How has science achieved this impartiality? What method leads to reliable knowledge? These are the problems to which we now turn.

I. SCIENTIFIC METHOD

Some scientists doubt that there is a scientific method, believing, rather, that each area of investigation has its own unique techniques. However, if we analyze the procedures used in a variety of scientific experiments, there are certain general procedures which are present in all scientific investigations, although each need not be present in every experiment. This is the scientific eight-fold path.

(1) First, there is a problem which has troubled the investigator enough to warrant investigation. Why did Priestley's mouse live

longer than expected; why was Uranus' motion unpredictable; why do dreams recur? These problems might arise from the experimenter's own experience, as is usually the case, but they also can originate from the desire to duplicate another's experiments, or the suspicion that his conclusions are mistaken.

(2) Possible solutions to the problem or hypotheses are then proposed. Knowledge of these also comes from different sources: one's own experience, as did Bernard's; knowledge of the literature, as did Leverrier's; knowledge of analogous problems, as did Priestley's; or one's own imaginative resources, as did Freud's. Then, assuming that a given hypothesis is correct, (3) predictions are made. These might be either logical deductions, usually hypothetical statements, as were Bernard's, or mathematical calculations predicting a quantitative result, as were Leverrier's.

(4) The next step is the most important part of the method: experimentation. In this step, the scientist tries to discern the relevant cause, separating, if you will, what is essential from what is accidental to an understanding of the phenomenon experienced. Then, (5) if successful, he might want to explain why this particular factor caused this particular phenomenon, and thus we have a theory; for example, Darwin explaining why there are so many similarities among animals, Bernard explaining why malnutrition causes acid urine, and Harvey explaining why the heart is a brighter red when it is full.

(6) Out of the data thus collected, relevance and order must be established, and thus the use of classification or naming: oxygen, diabetes, Neptune, libido. (7) The information might have some utility, as it did in Harvey's, Priestley's, Bernard's, Darwin's, and Freud's cases, although for the scientist, as distinct from the technician, this is irrelevant. And finally, (8), there are further problems requiring investigation, as both Bernard and Darwin suggest.

In general, these are the procedures followed in all scientific investigations. However, in a discussion of scientific method certain aspects are more significant than others, so let us concentrate our attention on two of them: the function of theory in scientific method and the nature of experimentation.

Some people believe that science deals only with "facts," with observing sensory phenomena, but both the preceding account of scientific method and our authors' comments suggest that this view is inadequate. Scientific method makes use of theory in at least two distinct ways.

In the first place, an hypothesis is a theory. Leverrier proposed alternative ideas to explain the irregularities of Uranus' motion. Priestley supposed his good air would support a mouse longer than ordinary air. There was an idea, then, to be tested by experimentation; indeed, the idea or theory helped to determine what the experimentation would be.

The ability to formulate a theory which gives a possible explanation is what sets the scientist off from an ordinary observer. As Cohen and Nagel observe, when Herodotus wondered what causes the Nile to flood, not merely that it did, and proposed three alternative explanations, he was thinking as a scientist. The fact that none of his alternatives could account for additional observations (how could the cause be melting snow when all the people in the area have dark skins?) also points out that "the full meaning of a hypothesis is to be discovered in its implications."

Bridgman and Weber also point to the need for theory to guide inquiry, the former observing that the idea of a reality composed of atoms has been fruitful in explaining further observations, while the belief in a caloric fluid was abandoned because it could not do so; and Weber says: "Order is brought into this chaos only on the condition that in every case only a part of concrete reality is interesting and significant to us." Scientists, then, do not merely observe facts; "some hypothesis, preconception, prejudice guides their research."

The second place in which theory is important in scientific method occurs after experimentation, for many scientists want to explain why they observed what they did. In some cases, this explanation involves only a repetition of the evidence, as is suggested by Harvey, but more frequently a theory is a generalized explanation based on the particularized bits of evidence. Animals have many similarities; therefore, Darwin suggested, they must have had a common origin. The recurrence of an identical dream can be explained, Freud said, by the presence of an unconscious in which all distasteful experiences are recorded and retained. Bernard theorized that a starving rabbit really lives on its own flesh, and that is why his urine had the characteristics of a meat eating animal.

How do these theories originate, and how can one tell whether they are correct? Perhaps this is one area in which the genuinely creative scientist can be distinguished most easily, for the ability to relate data requires much more than the ability to observe phenomena. However, a theory is a guess, and can be disputed by other theories. Perhaps animals did not have a common origin, but were all made from the same basic pattern by an all powerful Creator. Perhaps there is no unconscious mind, the similarities of dreams being caused by the similarities of sleeping habits. Theories, then, originate in the mind of the observer, being limited not only by the observations he makes but by the mental horizons of his own time. Thus, the savage explains thunder as the act of a capricious god while the contemporary physicist explains it in other terms. Both utilize ideas with which they are familiar, and so new theories sound reasonable, but when either the categories of explanation change or they no longer are sufficient to explain experienced phenomena, a new kind of theory will be given. As Bridgman said: "We must wait until we have amassed so much experience of a new kind that it is perfectly familiar to us, and then we will resume the process of explanation."

Scientific method, then, is not merely the accumulating of data, not notebook keeping; it involves choosing the relevant data and explaining why it is relevant, both kinds of activity being theoretical in origin and nature.

A second crucial area of scientific method is experimentation. All of our authors agree that scientific problem solving involves the use of experimental methods, and that controlled investigation seeks out the essential causes of the phenomena observed. It is for this reason that scientific method is intimately concerned with the concept of causation.

Traditionally, four methods for distinguishing the essential from the accidental causes have been used. John Stuart Mill, a nineteenth-century philosopher, named and explained them in this way:

1. *The method of agreement.* "If two or more instances of a phenomenon under investigation have only one circumstance in common, the circumstance in which alone all the instances agree is the cause (or effect) of the given phenomenon."[1] Thus, to take an instance: I am faced with a problem, brown spots in my lawn, and I wonder what is causing them. The one factor which my hypothesis suggests as a cause I shall keep constant while I change all the others; then I shall observe whether the spots will still be there. My hypothesis is that I, the gardener, am causing these spots. In order to test my hypothesis, I shall continue to cut the lawn but I shall see to it that the lawn will be treated with different amounts of water, sunshine, children and dogs, cosmic rays, and songs from the neighbor's canary; then I shall observe the lawn to see if the spots are still there.

[1] *A System of Logic,* Vol. I, p. 451.

In logical terms the method can be stated thus:

If *a* and *b* and *c* and *d* and *e* and. . . , then *x*.
If *a* and not *b* and not *c* and not *d* and not *e* and not . . . , then *x*.

The letter *a* stands for cutting the lawn, *b* for regular watering, *c* the scuffling of children, *d*, *e* . . . for other possible causes, and *x* for the phenomenon being investigated, the presence of brown spots in my lawn. Do I see the brown spots after cutting the lawn and after I have changed the other factors?

2. *The method of difference.* "If an instance in which the phenomenon under investigation occurs, and an instance in which it does not occur, have every circumstance in common save one, that one occurring in the former; the circumstance in which alone the two instances differ, is the effect, or the cause, or an indispensable part of the cause, of the phenomenon."[1] In logical terms:

If *a* and *b* and *c* and *d* and *e* and . . . , then *x*
If *not a* and *b* and *c* and *d* and *e* and . . . , then *not x*

So, to return to my lawn, I reverse the method of agreement and keep all the factors constant except one and then see whether the brown spots also disappear. I give it the same amounts of water, dogs, children, gophers, etc., but I modify one factor: I do not cut the lawn. Do the brown spots disappear?

3. *The method of concomitant variation.* "Whatever phenomenon varies in any manner whenever another phenomenon varies in some particular manner, is either a cause or an effect of that phenomenon, or is connected with it through some fact of causation.[2] In logical terms:

If *a* and *b* and *c* and *d* and *e* and . . . , then *x*
If ½ *a* and *b* and *c* and *d* and *e* and . . . , then ½ *x*
If ¾ *a* and *b* and *c* and *d* and *e* and . . . , then ¾ *x*
.
.
.

I look for proportional relationships. I keep everything constant again, only I cut the lawn every third time and observe whether the brown spots are one third as numerous.

4. *The method of residues.* "Subtract from any phenomenon such part as is known by previous inductions to be the effect of certain

[1] *Ibid.*, p. 452.
[2] *Ibid.*, p. 464.

antecedents, and the residue of the phenomenon is the effect of the remaining antecedents."[1] Again, in logical terms:

If *a* and *b* and *c* and *d* and *e* and . . . , then *x*
But if *b*, then *not x*
if *c*, then *not x*
if *d*, then *not x*
.
.
.
Therefore, if *a*, then *x*

So, what have I learned from previous experience concerning the possible causes? That gophers cause holes, not brown spots. That children trample the grass, but do not make this kind of spot. That too much water makes a lawn brown, but not in spots. But I experienced at our previous home that when I cut the lawn there were brown spots in it. What conclusion should I draw? Goodbye lawnmower!

Is the conclusion justified? Have I determined the essential cause? Certainly these methods are helpful, for if the spots are present every time I cut the lawn, other factors being different; if they are absent every time I do not cut it, other factors being the same; and if there are only a third as many when I cut the lawn every third week; then the evidence suggests that my cutting the lawn is the cause of the spots. If I could use all four methods several times each, my conclusion would be that much more reliable.

However, am I certain this conclusion is correct? No, for while I was concerned with the conditions relevant to one hypothesis, other factors might have affected the brown spots without my being aware of them. What about the habits of the lawn moth? Or the crab grass? Or my wife's method of hanging clothes on the clothes line? These might have been relevant factors, which I did not consider; so when I thought I was controlling the possible causes I was not doing so at all. In other words, that part of the logical expression of each method stated as ". . ." conceals a difficulty in experimentation, for there is always the possibility that a factor not considered by the experimentation is the essential cause and that the inductive methods have isolated an accidental one. Any scientific conclusion, then, is only probably true, not certainly so.

Additional evidence also supports this conclusion. In order to know the cause of such a phenomenon as brown spots in a lawn a very large number of possible causes must be considered, but when

[1] *Ibid.*, p. 460.

living things are investigated "they present an infinite multiplicity of successively and co-existing emerging and disappearing events," as Weber says. This is the reason why many biologists believe the techniques so successful in the physical sciences are not applicable for the biological sciences. But beyond that, there is a question whether inductive experimentation can deal with all kinds of phenomena. Consider the nature of life itself. What about the nature of mind and the mental processes? Can the scientific method satisfactorily explain how a person can understand the same concept given in different words, how one retains knowledge, the phenomenon of (apparently) choosing to give attention to one thing rather than another, and the experience of educability, the ability to learn and adjust rather than merely react to situations?

The answer to these questions is that perhaps we cannot apply inductive experimentation to these aspects of life now, but we can do so more satisfactorily in the future. That might be true, but there are even more fundamental problems scientific method must consider. When living things know they are being subjected to scientific experimentation, do they act differently than when they are not, and, more importantly, does the experimenter have a technique to control this possibly significant factor? How reliable are TV rating polls, for instance, when they are based on the viewing habits of people who know their viewing habits are being recorded? Beyond that, knowledge of the results of an experiment itself becomes a factor in assessing the reliability of the experiment's conclusion. Thus, experimenters many years ago discovered a positive correlation between color preference and intelligence. But before going further, suppose you ask yourself whether you prefer a brilliant red to a pastel blue. Have you your answer? Now, I will report that they discovered that the more intelligent people preferred pastel colors. Does your knowing this now make any difference as to your own preference? If so, then your knowledge becomes a factor which the previous testing, which demonstrated this conclusion, did not take into account.

Scientific conclusions, then, must be re-evaluated continually, and in assessing their reliability several questions always should be kept in mind: (1) have all the possible factors been considered? (2) has the announced cause been the essential, not the accidental, one? (3) have the characteristics of living things been adequately controlled? (4) has the knowledge of being part of an experiment been a relevant factor which has been controlled? and (5) how does knowledge of the results affect the reliability of the experiment?

These are among the reasons for deciding that any conclusion arrived at by the scientific method should be considered to be tentative and probably true, but saying this should not obscure another facet of the scientific method: application of these principles makes conclusions continually more reliable, for the method is self-correcting. This is so for several reasons. Any conclusion can be re-examined by someone else; thus possible errors will be eliminated by re-investigation, as was the situation with Leverrier. As new techniques and instruments are developed, the crude experiments of an earlier age are refined and the conclusions made more reliable. Who today would test the goodness of air by placing a mouse in it, as did Priestley? Finally, there is a continual interaction between theory and fact, for hypotheses help to discern which facts are relevant and the facts observed help to determine which of competing hypotheses will be more reliable for making accurate predictions. Thus, as past experimentation is re-examined and present experience and thought are combined, errors are eliminated and conclusions made more reliable.

Perhaps this point should be emphasized, for sometimes one concludes that changing scientific conclusions gives a reason for doubting their reliability. Thus, in 1900, geologists estimated the earth to be 100,000,000 years old; in 1930, 2,000,000,000 years; in 1950, 4,000,000,000 years; and today, 4,500,000,000. So, the argument goes, if scientists change their minds on these (and all other) matters, we really should not take their conclusions too seriously, for what they believe today they will doubt tomorrow.

Not only does this argument miss the point of the method's self-correcting features just mentioned, but it ignores the basic candor which characterizes the scientist's search for truth. Many people would rather ignore a previously held opinion now shown to be false, or explain it away, than admit their error, but scientific method rests on free inquiry and public verification which makes the scientist willing to admit his mistakes and correct his conclusions. While scientific conclusions do change continuously, then, it does not follow that they are merely changing for the sake of change, for their reliability improves as new knowledge is obtained.

Obtaining new knowledge is of the essence, for scientific method is self-perpetuating. Any conclusion can be re-examined either by new techniques or by skeptical minds, and investigation of a problem invariably leads to an awareness of new uninvestigated problems. But beyond these reasons, conclusions regarding living things must change continually to keep pace with their growth, and evidence relating to human behavior constantly must be re-examined to account for their changes and increased knowledge. It is not likely, then, that we will ever run out of scientific problems, or that we will have enough money or men to investigate all the problems which might be investigated.

In conclusion, how can scientific method be characterized? It has many similarities with the philosopher's method, for both believe that reliable knowledge is achieved only by the use of careful analytical human reasoning. Both make use of *inductive logic*. The methods of agreement, difference, concomitant variation and residues are techniques for distinguishing between essential and accidental causes. We are reminded of certain inductive errors, the fallacy of hasty generalization, drawing a conclusion without adequate evidence, the fallacy of *post hoc, ergo propter hoc,* confusing a temporal sequence with real causation; the fallacy of forced hypothesis, believing that one factor is the only possible cause, and the fallacy of false analogy, assuming one phenomenon necessarily is similar to another. Add to these the general point that induction provides evidence as the reason given to support a conclusion, a technique used in both philosophy and science, and the similarities are obvious.

Deductive logic also plays a part in both disciplines. Hypothetical arguments serve the same function in philosophy as prediction does in science, both pointing the way to anticipated conclusions. False disjunctions should be avoided in science as well as in philosophy, for from the fact that one hypothesis is not the cause it does not follow that a stated alternative must be. And contradictions, so valuable in philosophy for pointing to a lack of clarity, are important in science for pointing to the disparity between hypothesis and observation.

However, science and philosophy have different views regarding the importance of *semantics*. Much of our discussion of philosophical method centered around ways for making definitions: genus and differentia, stipulation, denotation and use were four of the techniques mentioned. But here the subject has hardly been mentioned because scientific method makes definition either a preliminary in helping to formulate the problem to be investigated, or else a means for classifying information to make clear its relationships to other data. In both cases, the stipulative method for making definitions is used, defining words carefully and precisely so that they refer only to the field of inquiry being investigated.

Except for minimizing the role of semantics and emphasizing the central role of experimentation for providing reasons to support conclusions, the scientific method has much in common with the philosophical method. However, these techniques are applied in different areas, perhaps ultimately to different kinds of problems. If we return to Plato's doctrine of the divided line, science investigates the realm of the visible, while philosophy turns to that of the intelligible. Problems the scientist takes to be important are known by sense experience and are changing continually; so the only way reliable knowledge can be achieved is by a constant narrowing of interest and refining of problem. The problems and outlook of the scientist, then, tend to make him increasingly specialized. The problems that philosophers take to be important originate with knowledge from the visible realm but go beyond it to those of a more general nature: how does this information help us to understand any more clearly what is Good? Or True? Or Beautiful? Knowing this about experience tells us what about reality? Thus, the philosopher's problems become increasingly difficult to answer as the scientist accumulates more knowledge.

Insofar as method is concerned, then, science and philosophy use many of the same techniques and the same general principles for gaining reliable knowledge, but they differ mainly in the kind of problem that they take to be significant. If there were no scientific knowledge, philosophers would have no problems, but if science did not merge into the more general and theoretical areas of thought, it would have no direction. Each, in its own way, demonstrates the way human reasoning can deal with the problems of human beings.

II. SCIENTIFIC METAPHYSICS

Today, the dominant attitude of science toward metaphysics is positivistic and skeptical. At best, scientists view metaphysical inquiry as did Comte, a stage in the development of man's thought, one which grew out of—and improved upon—theological speculations but one which has been superseded as more reliable methods for gaining knowledge have been developed. Frequently, however, metaphysical theories are not spoken of so kindly, being judged, in Pearson's words, "as built either on air or on quicksand—either they start from no foundation in facts at all, or the superstructure has been raised before a basis has been found in the accurate classification of facts." People who make such theories, he adds, are like poets, but "more liable to be dangerous members of the community because they strive to clothe their poetry in the language of reason." Accordingly, to title a section "scientific metaphysics" is to radically confuse concepts, if not to record a contradiction in terms.

For the positivistic scientist there are good reasons for adopting this conclusion. Science gathers facts while metaphysics is merely speculative. The former's conclusions are empirically verifiable while the latter's are without verification. Scientists usually agree with each other, but every metaphysician may have his own unique theory. If there are differences, scientists have a commonly accepted method for mitigating, if not removing them; but metaphysicians cannot even agree on a procedure for resolving their differences, much less resolve them. The scientific way is precise, empirical, verifiable, and leads to commonly accepted conclusions; the metaphysician's is vague, speculative, personal and leads, usually, to disagreements—with no way to resolve them.

Why, then, should a discussion of scientific metaphysics be continued? In the first place, a positivistic attitude does not deny the importance, even the relevance, of metaphysical questions. Again, as Pearson says: "It must not be supposed that science for a moment denies the existence of some of the problems which have hitherto been classed as philosophical or metaphysical." The real objection, he says, is methodological, for "the methods hitherto applied to these problems have been futile because they have been unscientific." So scientific metaphysics is not impossible, in principle. Moreover, there have been other scientists not so positivistic who have developed theories about the nature of reality, some of which have had considerable influence on science itself. Finally, scientific method makes certain assumptions concerning the nature of reality, and also has important implications for our understanding of nature. Since science is not totally distinct from metaphysics, let us consider two facets of that relationship, turning first to a metaphysical question important in its own right but particularly central to scientific thought, the problem of freedom and determinism, and then to a brief consideration of some theories suggested by non-positivistic scientists.

Let us put the problem of determinism in its most frightening form:

> He rubbed his hands. For of course, they didn't content themselves with merely hatching out embryos: any cow could do that.
>
> "We also predestine and condition. We decant our babies as socialized human beings, as Alphas or Epsilons, as future sewage workers or future . . ." He was going to say "future World controllers," but correcting himself said "future Directors of Hatcheries," instead.
>
> The D.H.C. acknowledged the compliment with a smile.
>
> They were passing Metre 320 on Rack 11. A young Beta-Minus mechanic was busy with screw-driver and spanner on the blood-surrogate

pump of a passing bottle. The hum of the electric motor deepened by fractions of a tone as he turned the nuts. Down, down . . . a final twist, a glance at the revolution counter, and he was done. He moved two paces down the line and began the same process on the next pump.

"Reducing the number of revolutions per minute," Mr. Foster explained. "The surrogate goes round slower; therefore passes through the lung at longer intervals; therefore gives the embryo less oxygen. Nothing like oxygen-shortage for keeping an embryo below par." Again he rubbed his hands.

"But why do you want to keep the embryo below par?" asked an ingenuous student.

"Ass!" said the Director, breaking a long silence. "Hasn't it occurred to you that an Epsilon embryo must have an Epsilon environment as well as an Epsilon heredity?"

It evidently hadn't occurred to him. He was covered with confusion.

"The lower the caste," said Mr. Foster, "the shorter the oxygen." The first organ affected is the brain. After that the skeleton. At seventy percent of normal oxygen you get dwarfs. At less than seventy eyeless monsters. . . .

Their wandering through the crimson twilight had brought them to the neighborhood of Metre 170 on Rack 9. From this point onward Rack 9 was enclosed and the bottle performed the remainder of the journey in a kind of tunnel, interrupted here and there by openings two or three metres wide.

"Heat conditioning," said Mr. Foster.

Hot tunnels alternated with cool tunnels. Coolness was wedded to discomfort in the form of hard X-rays. By the time they were decanted the embryos had a horror of cold. They were predestined to emigrate to the tropics, to be miner and acetate silk spinner and steel workers. Later on their minds would be made to endorse the judgment of their bodies. "We condition them to thrive on heat," concluded Mr. Foster. "Our colleagues upstairs will teach them to love it."

"And that," put in the Director sententiously, "that is the secret of happiness and virtue—liking what you've *got* to do.

* * * * *

Mr. Foster was left in the Decanting room. The D.H.C. and his students stepped into the nearest lift and were carried up to the fifth floor.

INFANT NURSERIES. NEO-PAVLOVIAN CONDITIONING ROOMS announced the board.

The Director opened a door. They were in a large bare room, very bright and sunny; for the whole of the southern wall was a single window. Half a dozen nurses, trousered and jacketed in the regulation white viscose-linen uniform, their hair aseptically hidden under white caps, were engaged in setting out bowls of roses in a long row across the floor. Big bowls, packed tight with blossom. . . .

The nurses stiffened to attention as the D.H.C. came in.

"Set out the books," he said curtly.

In silence the nurses obeyed his command. Between the rose bowls the books were duly set out—a row of nursery quartos opened invitingly each at some gaily-colored image of beast or fish or bird.

"Now bring in the children."

They hurried out of the room and returned in a minute or two, each pushing a kind of tall dumb-waiter ladder, on all its four wire-netted shelves with eight-month-old babies, all exactly alike (a Bokanovsky Group, it was evident) and all (since their caste was Delta) dressed in khaki.

"Put them down on the floor."

The infants were unloaded.

"Now turn them so that they can see the flowers and books.". . .

The swiftest crawlers were already at their goal. Small hands reached out uncertainly, touched, grasped, unpetaling the transfigured roses, crumpling the illuminated pages of the books. The Director waited until all were happily busy. Then, "Watch carefully," he said. And lifting his hand, he gave the signal. The Head Nurse, who was standing by a switchboard at the other end of the room, pressed down a little lever.

There was a violent explosion, shriller and ever shriller, a siren shrieked. Alarm bells maddeningly sounded.

The children started, screamed; their faces were distorted with terror.

"And now," the Director shouted (for the noise was deafening), "now we proceed to rub in the lesson with a mild electric shock."

He waved his hand again, and the Head Nurse pressed a second lever. The screaming of babies suddenly changed its tone. There was something desperate, almost insane, about the sharp spasmodic yelps to which they now gave utterance. Their little bodies twitched and stiffened; their limbs moved jerkily as if to the tug of unseen wires.

"We can electrify that whole strip of floor," bawled the Director in explanation. "But that's enough," he signalled to the nurse.

The explosions ceased, the bells stopped ringing, the shriek of the siren died down from tone to tone into silence. The stiffly twitching bodies relaxed, and what had become the sob and yelp of infant maniacs broadened out once more into a normal howl of ordinary terror.

"Offer them the flowers and the books again."

The nurses obeyed; but at the approach of the roses, at the mere sight of those gaily-colored images of pussy and cock-a-doodle-doo and baa-baa black sheep, the infants shrank away in horror; the volume of their howling suddenly increased.

"Observe," said the Director triumphantly, "observe."

Books and loud noises, flowers and electric shocks—always in the infant mind these couples were uncompromisingly linked; and after two hundred repetitions of the same or a similar lesson would be wedded indissolubly. What man has joined, nature is powerless to put asunder![1]

Huxley then goes on to describe life in this *Brave New World* where each person, by heredity and environment, is determined to do the job he does—and to enjoy it. He contrasts this with the life of the savage, a throwback from the year 632 A.F. (After Ford) to the Christian tradition, one who mortifies his body, abhors promis-

[1] From *Brave New World* by Aldous Huxley. Copyright 1932 by Aldous Huxley. Reprinted by permission of Harper and Brothers, New York, and Chatto and Windus Ltd., London, pp. 14-17, 20-23.

cuous sexual relations, and is lost in a world devoted to efficiency and planning.

This book can be viewed from many points of view, for it contrasts hedonism with Christianity, the new world with the old, efficiency with tradition, but for our purpose its most important contribution is the recognition that if reality is mechanical and deterministic, those who understand its laws can control human life as well as nature. If determinism is true, human engineering is possible.

Why has science encouraged the belief in determinism? Partly because it grows out of a view of life commonly held by many people, and partly because of its own history.

The belief that reality is similar to a machine in which input equals output, that knowledge of all the causes gives an accurate understanding of the effect, was held long before the advent of modern science and has been expressed by many different writers. Among the earliest philosophers, Empedocles, for instance, suggested this view in the fifth century B.C., when he said that the elements composing reality "never cease changing place continually, now being all united by love into one, now being borne apart by the hatred engendered of strife, until they are brought together in the unity of all, and become subject to it." Anaxagoras said that love and strife are aspects of mind, thereby suggesting the Stoic's teaching, and the ancient Atomists—Democritus, Epicurus and Lucretius—contended that reality was deterministic, being no more than atoms bumping into each other. In more modern times Spinoza argued that there was no freedom, for there was no possible way things could be made to be other than what they are.

The acceptance of determinism also finds expression in religious thought. Calvin and his followers held to an uncompromising predestinarianism; indeed, Calvin himself held that there is double predestination, man being determined both to hear God's word and to respond to it. But one of the most eloquent statements of this position is Saint Paul's: "For none of us liveth unto himself, and no man dieth to himself. For whether we live, we live unto the Lord; and whether we die, we die unto the Lord. Whether we live, therefore, or die, we are the Lord's."[1] This world is God's creation; therefore whatever happens does so because He created it to be that way.

In both the philosophical and religious expressions of determinism, the conclusion is drawn because life is viewed as being governed by

[1] Romans, 14: 7-8.

forces over which man has no control. But beneath these expressions there is a basic impression which arises out of the common experience of men. Night follows day, the seasons come and go, thunder follows lightning, the moon passes through its phases, death always follows life. These things occur with regularity and can be verified by all. But they could not happen unless there was regularity in nature itself, unless there was a causal order behind our experience. Determinism, then, originates psychologically from man's experience of regularity.

However, there is a more particular reason why science has lent support to mechanical determinism. During the Middle Ages, science was part of theology, as was philosophy; hence it was viewed as purposive, each thing striving to develop its own natural end. With the challenges arising from astronomy, mathematics, and chemistry during the sixteenth century, the renewed emphasis on empiricism first stated fully by Francis Bacon in his *Novum Organum*, and the studies on perspective by the artists of the Renaissance, this view gradually lost its persuasiveness. By 1687, Newton could describe the principles of science, and his hopes for it, in this way:

> I wish I could derive all phenomena of nature by some kind of reasoning from mechanical principles; for I have many reasons to suspect that they all depend upon certain forces by which the particles of bodies are either mutually attracted and cohere in regular figures or are repelled and recede from each other.[1]

Thus, he hoped to fit all material events into a framework of relatively simple, and mathematically expressible, rules.

This was Newton's purpose, and it was the purpose of scientific thought for the next two centuries. The hope was that all knowledge could be reduced to a few basic propositions, for this would demonstrate that reality was governed by certain inexorable laws. Moreover, if one could know of these laws, he could control nature; in Bacon's phrase, science seeks for "that knowledge whose dignity is maintained by works of utility and power." And once one seeks knowledge of nature's determinate laws so that he can gain power over them, it is not a long step to Huxley's description in *Brave New World*.

Mechanistic determinism, then, arises from the common sense experience of regularity and the desire for simplicity; it is given

[1] *Mathematical Principles of Natural Philosophy*, translated by Andrew Mott. Berkeley: University of California Press, 1934. Preface.

expression in man's religious beliefs and philosophies and has provided the foundation for scientific endeavor for two centuries. If such a doctrine is so pervasive why is there any problem about it? Because it conflicts with two other equally basic kinds of experience. The first is the experience of choice. We think we are free to choose and can demonstrate that choice either by reading on or by closing this book and hence reading no further. If the determinist reminds us that we do not know all the causes which motivate our actions and that we mistakenly think we have just chosen, one has to admit he might be correct. But still, the experience of choosing itself is a fundamental datum of life, and regardless of its antecedents, the experience cannot be denied.

The second kind of evidence is the belief regarding responsibility. It is a widely, if not universally, held dictum that a person should neither be punished nor rewarded for actions he did not do. The reason for this belief is that the actions were not his, and hence he was not responsible. If what I do is caused by the laws of the universe, I should not, although I might, be punished, for *I* did not act. Thus, morality requires that one be free, and freedom is not possible if he lives in a deterministic world in which he is caused to act by forces over which he has no control.

How can these equally pervasive yet incompatible experiences be reconciled? That is the problem of determinism and freedom. Huxley's description suggests that freedom is an illusion and that a deterministic science can remake the world and life in it. Sullivan argues that science no longer rests on deterministic principles for all the evidence cannot be explained in this way. Some religious writers make a distinction between God's foreknowledge and His predestination, or say that an all-powerful God can relinquish some of his power to man. Some philosophers have said that an indeterminate world in which there is choice is more damaging to moral behavior than a determinate world, and others have argued that the whole problem is a pseudo-problem, one which can be cleared up by making certain distinctions. Whether these alternatives are satisfactory or not is a matter needing considerably more discussion, but insofar as science assumes the world processes are governed by deterministic laws, the *Brave New World* stands as the extreme description of what science can do.

There is no need to discuss in detail the metaphysical theories expressed by non-positivistic scientists. There are not many, they are not worked out carefully or completely and, for the most part, they are restatements of theories previously expressed by philosophers.

John Dalton made explicit the atomic theory suggested by the scientists Newton and Boyle, and earlier by the philosopher Hobbes. Still earlier, the theory was worked out carefully by Lucretius and stated by Epicurus and Democritus. Dalton contended that reality is composed of elementary particles called atoms which combine to make objects be what they are. He was led to this conclusion as the result of his study of gases, for he found that this theory helped to explain his observations more satisfactorily than did competing theories. His theory has proven to be fruitful for continuing scientific thought and Dalton now frequently is called the father of the atomic theory. Dalton did come to the theory from an empirical basis, but we should not forget that the theory was more than two millennia old when he stated it.

Sullivan contends that the history of science demonstrates its own limitations. Newton's mechanical determinism no longer is sufficient to support the findings in the physical sciences, Darwin's theory is useful but not complete for the biological sciences, and the social sciences are hardly developed enough to be considered as sciences. These limitations arise because the philosophy underlying science is not adequate. He suggests that a more satisfactory metaphysic is that suggested by Eddington and Jeans: all reality is the reality of an idea. Thus, he believes, only an idealist metaphysical theory, such as suggested by Royce, is sufficient.

Finally, Frank examines the reasons that scientists give for accepting theories of high generality and finds that they are not accepted merely because they tell us about reality, agree with the facts or can eventuate in accurate predictions. They are accepted because they enable us to achieve certain ends, and if those ends are achieved, the theory is good. Scientific thought, then, is a means to an end, just as Peirce and Dewey said, and now the question is, What end? But that is the problem to be examined in the next section.

However, science could give a complete and detailed account of reality, a satisfactory metaphysical theory, without having recourse to philosophical resources. Such an account could occur under two conditions: first, if all the sciences could be reduced to one, if physiology, biology and astronomy could be considered as aspects of physics, for instance; or second, if a theory of universal generality could be developed, one which could explain all scientific phenomena just as the theory of evolution can do in biology and the theory of relativity can do in physics. At present, however, these alternatives remain as unrealized possibilities.

Let us conclude this part of our inquiry by noting that metaphysical theories in their basic nature involve more than an appeal to sense experience and hence tend to go beyond the scientist's legitimate concern. To be sure, data from scientific experimentation have certain implications for metaphysical thought, and science itself rests on certain assumptions about what is real, but the dominant attitude is positivistic. Most scientists would be willing to turn all metaphysical questions over to philosophers, but probably would wonder, privately if not publicly, whether the philosophers were doing anything significant.

III. SCIENTIFIC MORALITY

Each of the three attitudes toward life which we are examining has one problem which is particularly difficult to handle. In religion, it was the problem of method: how can reason be used definitively to support conclusions when it is judged to be incomplete, even incompetent? In philosophy, it could be seen most clearly in the area of metaphysics: how can you choose one theory rather than another when each is persuasive, yet the two are incompatible? In science, the problem centers on the subject of morality: can scientific method tell one what he ought to do?

There are both obvious and subtle reasons why the combination of scientific method and moral issues raises a difficult problem. There is, of course, the threat of annihilation posed by thermonuclear war, the result of scientific achievement outstripping moral knowledge. There are the problems created by science giving the material comforts of life but no notion of the ends for which they exist. And there is always the threat of the *Brave New World,* the possibility that control over nature will become control over man.

But the issues are deeper than these, for we must look at the purposes of science as well as its consequences. Why do we desire scientifically verified knowledge? Why do we learn about natural phenomena, and what ends should we achieve by controlling them? Most important, can scientific method itself answer these questions? To put the problem in the form faced by the scientists: Can you, by using scientific method, determine what you *ought* to investigate, or what you ought to do with the information you derive? Can scientists answer moral questions, including the one concerning what their own purposes ought to be?

One of the views regarding moral questions held by scientists is known as *ethical relativism.* It has its origins in the study of different cultures, such as the descriptions given by Mrs. Benedict. She points out that the Dobuans have developed a society based on mutual distrust. No husband trusts his wife, nor does she trust him: marital fidelity is not expected. In trading, each man tries to deceive the other with false promises. In farming, only magic can counter a neighbor's treachery. In short, for the Dobuan, "suspicion and cruelty are his trusted weapons in strife and he gives no mercy, as he asks none."

Such descriptions give rise to the belief expressed by Sumner that "the standard of good and right are in the mores themselves." He suggests these standards originate from the satisfaction of primitive needs, are equated with pleasure and pain and since they are preserved by tradition and authority, reform is slow and reformers unpopular. He also explains the origin of ethnocentrism, enriches the vocabulary with (stipulative) definitions of folkways, mores, in-groups, out-groups, etc., but most important, he concludes not only that each society has its own standards, but that there is no standard by which the mores themselves can be evaluated. One can never get outside his own mores to judge their value for "the world philosophy of an age is never anything but the reflection on the mental horizon, which is formed out of the mores, or the ruling ideas—which are in the mores themselves. Every attempt to win an outside standpoint from which to reduce the whole to an absolute philosophy of truth and right, based on an unalterable principle, is a delusion."

To refer to one of our previous distinctions, page 218, Sumner is using a descriptive theory to justify a prescriptive theory: people do have different values; therefore each society should have the values it does. To put the conclusion first: people ought to value what they do because each society has its own values.

Ethical relativism might be saying less than this, insisting only that people do have different standards of values, but in this case judgments about a society's values, either that they are or are not valuable or that they can or cannot be judged, are not permissible. If one holds this view then he must be as careful as Mrs. Benedict to say only what values there are.

In the prescriptive form in which ethical relativism is often stated, certain problems are raised which need to be considered. Perhaps the best place to start is with the reason given to justify the conclusion. In Chapter Five we noted that a descriptive statement is justified by empirical evidence, and a prescriptive statement by appeal to a more inclusive theory than the particular ethical judgment, be it religious, metaphysical, historical, etc. Thus, the statement "People do like social security" could be verified by a public opinion poll but the statement "People ought to like social security" requires a different kind of justification, one like "because they live longer," or "because it makes more people happy."

If this general rule is justified, then the ethical relativist's reasons are of the wrong kind. He is saying that values ought to be relative to a culture because empirical evidence shows they are different in each culture. But from the fact that they are different, it does not follow that they should be different. To justify this conclusion, appeal must be made to a more inclusive theory, not to a recording of data.

Let us put the difficulty in another way. Reduce the argument to its logical constituents. The conclusion is that each society ought to have the standards it does have, and the reason is that each society has its own standards. Thus:

Each society has its own standards
∴ Each society ought to have the standards it has.

But notice, the major premise is unstated. To complete the argument, this premise would have to read: "If each society has its own standards, then each society ought to have the standards it does," and now the argument would be a valid hypothetical argument, as discussed on pp. 209-212.

$$a \supset b$$
$$a$$
$$\therefore b$$

But a valid argument can be silly, as we saw in Chapter Five; so whether the argument is true depends on the kind of evidence used to support the unstated major premise. Unfortunately, those who accept ethical relativism seldom attempt to provide evidence, even though their argument is neither valid nor true without it.

What kind of evidence could be given? Two different appeals might be made. The relativist might say that each society will have its own standards anyhow, so the statement, "If each society has its own standards, then it ought to have the standards it does," simply points to a condition which could not be otherwise. But this answer is not satisfactory, for now the "ought" in the consequent becomes empty, the statement pointing either to another form of descriptive determinism, "Each society will have the standards it does," or to a triviality: "If each society has its own standards, then it will have the standards it does." This alternative, then, makes moral questions either futile, for people couldn't have values different from what they have, or else innocuous, for then people value what they value.

The other kind of evidence is contained in the assertion that any standard one might use to judge a society's mores is itself only another society's mores, so all one is doing is evaluating one society by another's standards.

But surely this reason is mistaken, for, as we have seen, all sorts of moral standards have been proposed which are not the *de facto* mores of the group in which the theorist lived. Indeed, the reverse seems to have been the case, for Jesus said men should love each other precisely because in his society they did not, Kant advocated the categorical imperative because people did not take the notion of duty seriously enough, and Bentham advanced the moral calculus as a means to help people achieve the pleasure they did not know how to obtain.

However, suppose the relativist replies: "But that's not what I meant. I am not appealing to how people do act, but rather to the goals they believe they ought to achieve, and in this sense, Jesus and Kant and Bentham were simply expressing the ideals unique to their own age." Now the question becomes an empirical one, and evidence could be given whether the people of the first century did believe they ought to love their enemy any more than those in the nineteenth century did, or whether those latter day hedonists were any more hedonistic than those in the Roman Empire, and here, probably, the evidence would not be conclusive. So, justifying the implicit premise by saying there could be no other standards than a society's mores seems to rest either on a dogmatic assertion or on evidence which is mistaken or incomplete.

Or look at this whole problem in a different way. Inductive evidence requires that we admit possible exceptions. This is so because in experimentation we never can be certain that we have considered all possible explanations. Therefore, if the premise "If each society has its own standards, then each society should have the standards it does" is justified by inductive evidence, those making the assertion must admit it might be mistaken. But when an ethical relativist admits this, he no longer is a prescriptive relativist, for now he says: "If each society has its own standards, then perhaps it should have the standards it does." To say otherwise is to conclude more than the evidence justifies.

Prescriptive ethical relativism can be shown to be inadequate because it gives the wrong kind of reason and because it cannot provide evidence to support its implicit major premise. However, the difficulties can be stated even more simply. (1) To say, prescriptively, that whatever is, is what ought to be, is also to say that things should not be different from what they are. So, logically, a relativist should say that when a society's standards do change, they should not. To do so puts him not only on the side of conservatism but in the position of advocating inertia. And this is a conclusion few, if any, relativists would accept. (2) But, suppose he replies with yet another form of relativism, a relative relativism, that what is right at one time is not right at another, even within the same society. If this is what relativism stands for, then words like "good" and "right" lose their significance, for their different meanings might be contradictory. In this case, then, ethical relativism has become ethical nihilism; the insistence is that there are no moral standards and hence moral words should not be used, nor should moral judgments be made. The relativist, however, might reply that words still retain their meaning within that context and that there are no contradictions since contexts change. If this is his answer, though, it is sufficient to point out that when the same word is used twice, we are back to a variant of that ancient problem from which philosophy started: how can the same word have different meanings; the problem of the One and the Many. And the confrontation of such a metaphysical problem as this might be enough to stop even the most ardent ethical relativist.

Ethical relativism, then, is a complex and difficult doctrine. Perhaps the easiest way to know whether it is justified is to ask what it means, for it might be used to justify different conclusions. When you find this doctrine expounded, then, and it can be encountered frequently in the writings of social scientists, ask yourself which of the following conclusions is being drawn. (1) This is a descriptive statement, telling us some interesting, even exciting, information about other cultures. (2) It is trivial, saying only that people value what they value. (3) It is a causative explanation, telling us of the conditions which give rise to people having the values they do; it is one to be judged, like all other scientific investigations, by how adequately the essential causes have been separated from the accidental ones. (4) It is a plea for tolerance—that we can learn from other societies. (5) It is a prescriptive statement of ethical relativity and hence is a doctrine to be examined carefully, keeping the previously discussed distinction in mind.

However, not all scientists accept Sumner's view. Some, like Huxley and Fromm, propose as an alternative to ethical relativism the belief that there are certain universal needs which ought to be satisfied. They contend that these needs can be verified empirically, and hence moral theory is based on scientific evidence, and that the satisfaction of needs is what ought to be achieved, and hence the theory is prescriptive. In light of the preceding discussion, the two potential difficulties with this procedure are easy to state. First, of course, there is the matter of the empirical evidence. How was it obtained? Were the methods of experimental inquiry used? Were the essential factors separated from the accidental? Was there any circularity in defining the problem then adducing the evidence? Like any claimed scientific evidence, then, the conclusion must be examined for its empirical validity.

Secondly, the distinction between descriptive and prescriptive judgments enters again, reminding us that merely because people do have needs, it does not necessarily follow that their needs should be satisfied. Again, this is the wrong kind of reason to justify a prescriptive statement and the implicit major premise probably is without evidence. This is not to say that needs should not be satisfied; indeed, many of them probably should. But the reason they should is not that people have them. A description is different from a prescription, and just as you would be suspicious of a doctor who did not know the difference, so, too, you should be suspicious of a scientist who speaks as though he does not understand the difference.

The same kind of theory frequently is presented in hypothetical form: "If you want your needs satisfied then. . . ." In this case, the theory becomes understandable in terms of the distinction between means and ends. If the end, the satisfaction of needs, is accepted, then science can tell the best means to achieve those satisfactions. Huxley, for instance, sees survival as constituting man's fundamental need and asks how this can best be achieved. An observation of nature suggests what Nietzsche saw: competition is the law of nature. But Huxley says that the nature of man is to go beyond his animal origin, to repress his "ape and tiger" promptings, and to learn to act from cooperation, mutual respect, and compassion. This kind of activity involves combating the natural processes, "curbing the cosmic process and reminding the individual of his duty to the community to which he owes the life of something better than a brutal savage."

Fromm, a vigorous critic of ethical relativism, presents a theory which is similar to Huxley's, although it is psychologically oriented rather than biologically. Men have certain biological needs which can be satisfied by instinctive behavior, but they have other needs which only the development of reason can satisfy. The tension between instinct and reason, man's animal origins and his human potential, creates the main problem in life. Some individuals want to escape from freedom, deny their humanness, by allowing themselves to be controlled by a government, church, or business organization because they believe that if their physiological needs are satisfied, if they are happy, then the purpose of life has been achieved. Others, however, try to achieve sanity. To do so, one must develop both reason and love. One becomes rational when he understands the world—and himself—as it is, apart from all delusions and desires, and one loves when he can feel "union with somebody, or something, outside one's self, under the conditions of retaining the separateness and integrity of one's own self." Thus, if one wants to be insane, he should deny his humanness; if he wants to be sane, he should learn to love and reason.

Why should one want to be sane? Fromm does not appeal to empirical evidence; indeed, one of his major themes is that people in the twentieth century, especially those in highly industrialized societies, do not want to be sane. They value the security and happiness of animal existence above the freedom of human life. Rather, he suggests, as did Aristotle, that men should be sane because such an existence is appropriate to *human* behavior.

There is still another alternative for developing a scientific morality. Even if we admit science can only describe values or discover the best means to achieve a stated end, there still is the possibility that in the future scientific method can answer prescriptive questions. This is the point urged by Margenau. He believes scientific method involves adopting a basic code of behavior, elaborating its consequences, applying it to actions, and evaluating the results. He recognizes that his proposal is circular, for to evaluate a code, another code must be assumed, but he points out that science involves the same circularity yet has made many notable achievements. If moral theorists, he says, would give up their search for absolute and certain principles, a search abandoned long ago in science, and seek, rather, for tenative and relative goods, "the problems of the normative sciences may perchance be more tractable." Whether such a procedure would be successful requires the test of experience.

Perhaps we can best bring this discussion to a close by considering, with Russell, the moral problem which faces the scientist: "Why should I want to gain the knowledge I am seeking?" He might say that he simply desires to understand nature, to gain a knowledge of its elements and functioning. If this is his response, then he is saying that knowledge is an end in itself, a *summum bonum,* and, accordingly, he will view nature contemplatively. But he might also say that he studies nature to learn how to control it. Now the question becomes: "Control for what purpose?" He might say that he wishes to gain control because power is an end in itself, thus exhibiting a Nietzschean ethic. Or he might say that he desires power as a means to some other end: happiness; fulfilling God's commandments; destroying evil men elsewhere in the world. But if these are his reasons, then his knowledge is a means to achieve an end, but the end has not been derived by scientific method; he is working for goals set by others. At the very least, in order for a scientist to discover even his own goals he is led outside the realm of science altogether.

The difficulty here is in distinguishing between the attitude encouraged by scientific method and the applications of scientific research. If knowledge were an end in itself, the scientist would be like the philosopher, seeking to learn of nature and its processes. But when science is valued for what it can do, its purposes are determined by people and procedures outside of science, and the scientist's endeavors are directed to achieving ends others deem valuable.

Thus, the methods of science do not seem appropriate to answering the problems of moral theory, and the application of scientific knowledge can be used as the means for others, whether they be military leaders, dictators or businessmen, to achieve their purposes. Science, then, has no notion of its own goals, and, apparently, has no method for discovering them. It can become (and is?) a tool in the hands of unscrupulous men and nations to achieve the goods they value. As scientists learn increasingly how to gain power over things—and people—the question of the purposes for which that power is gained becomes ever more important. And as the consequences of technology become increasingly apparent, their implications become increasingly frightening. But most frightening of all is the recognition that science cannot provide answers to the moral problems created by its own technology; a scientist cannot determine even what his own, much less others', purposes should be. And so we are left with a powerful tool for controlling nature and no way of knowing why, when or whether that control should be used.

IV. SCIENCE AS A WAY OF LIFE

Of the three attitudes we are considering, science seems to have both the greatest potentialities and greatest limitations at the present time. It utilizes the method of repetitive verification, and hence increases the possibility for agreement among people. It minimizes personal preference, and thus enables us to see the world as it is. It has remade, and continues to remake, the physical world in which we live. Yet, it is more concerned with reliable techniques for gaining knowledge than with their implications. It ignores metaphysical questions. It confuses moral issues. It cannot even provide guidance for its own activities.

It might be that, given enough time, science's interest and competence in metaphysical and moral questions will increase, and it might also be that because of science's ability to control nature, we might achieve such a pleasant life that these questions no longer will be asked. But if it is a question of time, then one must decide whether the potentialities of science hold greater promise than the insights of philosophy and religion, especially when the former also has brought us to the very real possibility of total annihilation.

QUESTIONS FOR DISCUSSION

1. What advantages and disadvantages does the scientist's method for obtaining knowledge have when compared to the philosopher's method? To the religious man's method? Are the three incompatible?
2. Write a short philosophical essay on the problem of freedom and determinism. Define your terms, state the issue/s, explain the relevant reasons and justify your final conclusion.
3. Can you find examples of ethical relativism in other textbooks or the conversation of friends? If so, make use of the distinctions discussed on pp. 533-536 to determine what is being said.

READINGS FOR IMMEDIATE REFERENCE

Conant, James B. *On Understanding Science*. New Haven: Yale University Press, 1947, Essays 1, 4.

REFERENCES FOR COMPREHENSIVE KNOWLEDGE

Conant, James B. *Science and Common Sense*. New Haven: Yale University Press, 1951. A survey of knowledge in various fields together with an appraisal of their implications for a democratic society.

Lundberg, George A. *Can Science Save Us?* New York: Longmans, Green, 1947. The answer is no, and the book is provocative.

Also see:

Lynd, Robert S. *Knowledge for What?* Princeton: Princeton University Press, 1939.

Mumford, Lewis. *Technics and Civilization*. New York: Harcourt, Brace, 1934.

Reichenbach, Hans. *The Rise of Scientific Philosophy*. Berkeley: University of California Press, 1951.

Chapter Fourteen

TOWARDS A PHILOSOPHY OF LIFE

So now we come to the last stages of our inquiry. The preceding pages have attempted to introduce you to philosophy by both analysis and comparison. Our point of departure has been that philosophy is an activity, an outlook, a way of looking at life, developed, cultivated, and expressed in the writings of philosophers. As such, it has certain problems it must consider, moral, metaphysical, and methodological being among the more important, and it can be compared in its ability to answer these problems to competing ways of viewing life, religion and science. In a still larger view, this book has attempted to introduce you to philosophy in its original meaning, "the love of wisdom," by considering the realm of ideas, regardless of origin.

In this introduction, three purposes should have been fulfilled, and now is the time for you to determine what successes it has had for you. It has tried to provide information. What can you recall about the lives, and, which is more important, the thought of Plato? Aristotle? Descartes? Hume? Kant? Dewey? Russell? Aquinas? Fromm? In addition, many of the selections were included to provide stimulation for your own thinking. Have they done so? Finally, the preceding chapters have attempted to clarify certain problems by examining their nature, discussing alternative ways for answering them and noting what implications follow from each answer. The material in the reading selections has concentrated on the three main issues, morality, metaphysics and methodology; in Chapters Five, Nine and Thirteen certain other problems have been considered: The One and the Many; ethical relativism; our knowledge of God; the reliability of sense experience; etc. If you took the suggestion offered in the Note to the Reader, now is the time to take out your original statement of beliefs to see how, if at all, your own thinking has changed as a result of your reading, thought and discussion.

In the few remaining pages I want to direct your attention to two additional problems which grow out of the concern for clarification. The first concerns the developing of a philosophy of life; the second, the role of philosophy, in its narrower meaning, in that endeavor. By considering the answers to these two problems you should be able to appreciate more fully the importance and values of philosophy.

Each of us has some kind of philosophy of life, usually a compend of beliefs stemming from our parents, educational background, and experience. For the most part, these beliefs have been accepted without a serious analysis of their consistency or validity, presuppositions or implications, but, probably they are satisfactory to direct our lives. They never can be dismissed entirely, perhaps they cannot even be questioned seriously, but one of the underlying purposes of this book has been to ask you to raise some questions about your own philosophy of life; if you will, it has asked you to step outside yourself to examine your own ideas from the viewpoint of thoughtful writers from the East and the West, the present and the past. When compared to the alternatives thus seen to be available, have your past experiences and background given you a satisfactory philosophy of life? Do you still feel comfortable with what you have believed now that you know what else you *might* have believed? These are the underlying problems this book has attempted to raise.

It is not easy for any of us to answer these questions negatively, for the force of habit and the years of living in accordance with these beliefs are not shed easily. But if your reading and thinking has made the questions meaningful to you, if you have been jarred enough to ask yourself whether your past beliefs provide a sufficient basis for guiding your present and future life, then the following suggestions might be helpful.

In general, there are two ways you might proceed to formulate a philosophy of life. The first has been implied by the extensive bibliographies following each author and discussion. As you have read the selections in this book, certain writers may have seemed particularly incisive and cogent, and because you wanted to know more about their ideas you have read other books listed in the bibliographies. If you have, you can continue to take advantage of this method to develop your own way of life, for, in effect, you will be letting someone who has thought more deeply and extensively about life's problems than you be the guide to your thinking. In this sense, the *Readings for Immediate Reference* and the *References for Comprehensive Knowledge* will be the vehicles for leading you beyond this introductory stage of philosophical thought into the ongoing activity of making life meaningful.

However, letting others help you find your beliefs is not the same as having them do it for you. Read what they have to say, follow their analyses and arguments, but always re-think your mentors' thoughts in your own way. Do the reasons given support the conclusions drawn? Is the evidence sufficient? Are the definitions clear? What implications follow? Perhaps your initial impression will turn out to have been mistaken, or perhaps it will have been re-inforced, but regardless of the outcome, you will be continuing to learn and think about the ideas from which a philosophy of life can be formulated.

The second way has been suggested by the organization of the book. To have a way of life, answers must be found to certain crucial questions. To do this you must know what questions are pertinent, what answers might be given, and what reasons, whether they be the result of gathering evidence, formulating implications, or analyzing relationships, can be given to support each answer. If you can become aware of all the problems relevant to a philosophy of life and can make intelligent choices from among the alternative answers, then gradually you will develop your own philosophy of life.

These chapters have provided you with a start in that direction. Are the reasons given for denying the reliability of sense experience sufficient to cause you to search for a different basis for gaining knowledge? Was the argument against ethical relativism persuasive? Are any of the methods for knowing of God's existence satisfactory? Is moral behavior to be identified with the categorical imperative or the moral calculus—or neither? Once you can formulate your own answers to these and the other questions discussed in the preceding chapters you are on your way to understanding your own philosophy of life.

However, there are many other problems which need to be examined also. The whole realm of aesthetics, the nature of beauty, has not been touched. What is an aesthetic response? Should an artist seek to express his feelings or convey a message? Is there meaning in music? What makes a work of art good? Is aesthetic appreciation necessary for a way of life? The relationships between the individual and political life have barely been touched. Is political theory a part of ethics or history—or neither? Why is western style democracy better than communist democracy, or is it? Are freedom and organizational life incompatible? And there are other problems. The existentialists, for instance, ask whether life itself has a meaning. Those writing in the philosophy of history ask whether there is a pattern to history. And so forth. There are many questions a complete way of life must answer, then, and yours can develop as you become aware of them and examine carefully and thoughtfully how they might be answered.

Perhaps this sounds too challenging. After all, you might say, if I have a way of life which has served me well this far, one which has provided a satisfactory basis for my thinking to date, why should I continue to read and think, trying to find a new one? Especially why should I continue to search when I run the risk of failing to find any answers at all? The objection is both a fair and an important one. What reasons can be found to answer it?

Perhaps the most important reason is that continual search is sanctioned by all three of the ways of life we have considered. In science, the last step in scientific method is the recognition that further problems need investigation. The merely probable knowledge resulting from inductive experimentation plus the continual change in life itself makes any conclusion subject to error or inadequacy, and hence the need for more investigation. In religion, natural finite man is seeking to learn of God's supernatural infinite nature, so there always will be more which should be known than is now known. And if you have come this far in this book and have not been made aware of the existence of problems needing more investigation, this is not the time to try to be persuasive about the philosopher's continual search for knowledge. No way of life sanctions intellectual stagnation.

However, in the continuing quest for a way of life each of these three ways of thinking has its own unique advantages and disadvantages. Scientific method leads to conclusions which are publicly verifiable and empirical but it cannot be applied to moral issues and, for the most part, is willing to ignore all metaphysical problems for the present. This means that science is not a way of life as much as it is a method for obtaining knowledge about the world known by sense experience. Hence, the inquiry encouraged by science is directed toward empirical studies, but, as we have seen, they are only a part of a total way of life.

Religion is concerned with moral and metaphysical questions and it provides answers to these questions; thus it avoids the deficiencies of a scientific way. But religion can never justify its own claims. It insists that human reasoning is fallible and mistaken because it is only a part of the total creation. Yet it also claims that a given theology, one stated—and argued for—by human reason, is not mistaken but is identical to God's thoughts. Thus, while religion can provide a way of life, once it gives reasons to support its conclusions it is being untrue to its own premises.

The chief disadvantages of the philosophical search for a way of life are that it is difficult, continually demanding the best in human reasoning, and that it is complex, evidencing many alternative, even contradictory, beliefs. However, like religion, it is concerned with problems regarding the significance of human existence and provides answers to them; and like science, it places its emphasis on human reasoning, seeking to find agreements by careful analytical thought. Potentially, then, philosophical inquiry, unlike science, can provide a complete way of life for each individual, and, unlike religion, can provide a rational method for mitigating differences among individuals. Thus, there are certain advantages which accrue to a philosophical way of life which are not enjoyed by religion and science.

There are other advantages, too. One is philosophy's humanizing tendencies. Once one becomes aware of the realm of ideas he cannot help being impressed not only with its diversity but the fact that there are reasons which can be given to support every conclusion. This awareness should make one more appreciative of diversity, and hence more receptive to learning; more tolerant and less dogmatic; more willing to listen to others and less certain that he now has the final truth. Developing a tolerant attitude will make one genuinely educable, but more importantly, it is an attitude needed in the world today, for increased means of travel and communication are bringing people with diverse beliefs closer to each other every day, and we need to know why others think as they do in order to live with them in peace.

On a more personal level, the continual study of philosophy has certain practical benefits. Perhaps you have discovered while reading and discussing the material in this book that your own thinking has become sharper, that you can more readily separate reasons and conclusions, and that you are more aware of the need to look for evidence and foresee implications. These are side effects of philosophical inquiry, but they are important, for regardless of one's position in life, be he businessman, engineer, teacher or homemaker, clear thinking and the ability to discern relevance are invaluable assets. Moreover, the ability to think clearly leads to an increased ability to speak clearly and effectively, and where are such abilities not assets? Learning how to think philosophically has the added benefit of enabling one to penetrate to the heart of a problem, any problem, because he learns how to look at its logical constituents.

But the philosophical attitude has advantages outside one's professional life, too. Consider the matter of leisure time. Many people believe they have no leisure time, having far more things to do than there is time to do them. No doubt they are busy, but busy doing what? During the past decade I have conducted a little survey trying to find out how people spend their hours. I have distinguished between the things they *must* do and those they *might* do in their leisure time. Here is the way an average week is used by a student, a young mother, and a young father:

For the student

45 hours doing schoolwork (15 hours in class, 30 hours studying)
20 hours working at a part-time job
5 hours traveling to and from work and school
49 hours sleeping (seven hours of sleep every night)
10 hours eating (average of 1/2 hour every meal)
7 hours socializing (average of one hour a day)
136

For a young mother

70 hours working (average of 10 hours a day, seven days a week)
10 hours eating (average of 1/2 hour every meal)
49 hours sleeping (seven hours of sleep every night. Might be somewhat interrupted)
4 hours shopping
7 hours travel (transporting children to ballet lessons and to little league games)
5 hours socializing
145

For the young father

48 hours working (eight hours a day, six days a week)
6 hours traveling (average one hour each day to and from work)
7 hours with children (one hour a day)
6 hours working in the yard
10 hours eating (1/2 hour for every meal)
56 hours sleeping (average of eight hours a night)
5 hours socializing
138

These are average figures collected over the years, and you are invited to compare your own week with theirs. You might sleep more and work less, travel more and eat less, but always remember these are figures regarding the things which must be done as distinct from those which might be done.

Satisfy yourself on how you spend your own time, then consider that there is a total of 168 hours in every week. If you will note the totals in the preceding examples you will find that the average student still has thirty-two hours, nearly five hours a day, remaining every week *after* he has studied, worked, slept, traveled, and dated. The father has thirty hours; even a busy young mother has twenty-three hours, or more than three hours every day after everything else has been done! Thus, if you have thirty hours every week for doing what you would like to do, then you have over fifteen hundred hours every year, and, in a productive life of fifty years, more than seventy-five thousand hours!

Where does the time go? That is the question you should ask yourself continually. Beyond your professional life, what will your life amount to? Will it be a productive, useful, growing and significant existence, or will you vegetate day after day, failing to take advantage of the opportunities afforded by an all too short human existence? If you have caught the spirit of philosophical inquiry and have felt the urge to learn and think about the problems of human existence, you will find that at least some of those 75,000 hours will be as productive and meaningful, perhaps more so, than anything else you do.

The continued study of philosophy, then, can help in the quest for world understanding, make for increased tolerance, clarify one's thinking, make one more humane and help to make one's leisure hours productive. But in the final analysis, philosophy is not to be valued so much as a means to some other ends, valuable though they are, as it is to be valued as an end in itself. To be philosophical is to be reasonable, to express the qualities of a civilized man. To be philosophical is to be willing to learn; it is to be dissatisfied with one's present state of achievement; it is to ask oneself what is the meaning of life? It is to be a *human* being.

If you will let philosophy's method for dealing with life problems, its concern for the fundamental issues of human existence and some of its rich diversity of answers become part of your own attitude toward life, you will discover not only that you will gain new insights and thoughts you never considered before, but you will find that your own life will become more meaningful and significant, richer and deeper. Let yourself continue to grow intellectually, and you will continue to appreciate the profound wisdom which always has guided philosophical inquiry:

> No greater good can happen to a man than to discuss human excellence every day, as you have heard me examining myself and others, for, my friends, the unexamined life is not worth living.

READINGS FOR IMMEDIATE REFERENCE

James, William. "Philosophy and Its Critics," *Some Problems of Philosophy*. New York: Longmans, Green, 1911.

Whitehead, A. N. *Science and the Modern World*. New York: Macmillan, 1925, Chapters 9, 11, 12, 13.

REFERENCES FOR COMPREHENSIVE KNOWLEDGE

Dampier, W. C. *A History of Science and Its Relations with Philosophy and Religion*. New York: Macmillan, 1944. A concise yet comprehensive and thoughtful survey. A standard work.

Publications of the Conference on Science, Philosophy and Religion in their Relation to the Democratic Way of Life. New York: Norgate Press, 1941.

Also see:

Dingle, Herbert. *Through Science to Philosophy*. London: Allen and Unwin, 1938.

Raven, C. E. *Science, Religion and the Future*. Cambridge: Cambridge University Press, 1943.

Whitehead, A. N. *Essays in Science and Philosophy*. Cambridge: Harvard University Press, 1947.

GLOSSARY

The following list of definitions is intended as an aid for understanding some of the more technical words used in this book. The definitions are intended to be helpful rather than technically complete, and the list is not exhaustive. For definitions of other unknown words see:

Dictionary of Philosophy, edited by Dagobert D. Runes. New York: Philosophical Library, 1955.

Dictionary of Philosophy and Psychology, edited by James Baldwin. New York: Peter Smith, 1910.

Webster's New International Dictionary. New York: G. and C. Merriam, 1935.

absolutism. (1) Metaphysical. The theory that reality is one interconnected unity which is unconditioned, unqualified, and without relationships. Contrast with atomism. (Royce, Sullivan, Bhagavad-Gita) (2) Epistomological. The doctrine that objective truths exist and can be known. Contrast with skepticism. (Plato) (3) Ethical. The view that values exist independently of being valued by human beings. Opposed to relativism. (Kant, Jesus, Fromm. Criticized by Ayer, Sumner.)

agnosticism. Literally, "without knowledge." (1) Theological. The doctrine that man has not attained knowledge of God. Opposed to theism. (Comte, Epicurus. Opposed by the religious metaphysicians, pp. 281-319). (2) Less frequently, epistemological. The doctrine that man does not attain knowledge of any particular subject. Related to skepticism. Opposed to the claim that one has knowledge. (Hume)

a posteriori. Literally, "from the latter." A term applied to any proposition whose truth is derived from, and dependent upon, experience. "This paper is white." Opposed to *a priori.* (Peirce, Hume. See pp. 231-235.

a priori. Literally, "from the former." A term applied to any proposition whose truth depends solely on its meaning, independent of experience. "If A is larger than B, then B is smaller than A." Opposed to *a posteriori.* (Descartes, Spinoza. See pp. 216-217.)

atomism. Literally, "the uncuttable." A type of philosophy which asserts that reality is composed of separate, discrete, irreducible particles. Contrast with absolutism. (Epicurus, Lucretius, Dalton. Contrast with Royce, Spinoza. Discussed, p. 228.)

axiology. Literally, "theory of value." The branch of philosophy which deals with the nature, types, criteria, and status of value in every form whether it be ethical, aesthetic, economic, political, or religious. (Perry)

cosmology. Literally, "theory of the universe." (1) Metaphysical. In its larger sense, cosmology is synonymous with metaphysics and ontology. In a narrower sense, cosmology is contrasted with both: cosmology dealing with the origin and structure of the universe, ontology with the nature of being as such, and metaphysics including these two concepts. (2) Theological. The cosmological proof demonstrates God's existence by showing the necessity for a first cause. (Aquinas. Discussed, pp. 374-376.)

determinism. Literally, "to limit." The view that every event is totally conditioned by antecedent causes or, in a wider view, that the entire universe is governed by causal law. Closely related to fatalism, predestinarianism. Opposed to freedom, indeterminism. (Spinoza, Calvin, Epictetus. Criticized by Sullivan. Discussed, pp. 525-530.)

dualism. Literally, "two." (1) General. In any field of knowledge, all subject matter can be reduced to two irreducible principles, e.g., natural and supernatural, good and evil. Opposed to monism. (2) Metaphysical. The view that the universe is composed of two kinds of reality, e.g., matter and ideas, objects and forms. (Descartes, Plato, Aristotle) (3) Epistemological. The view that the object of knowledge is not identical with the object known. Related to phenomenalism. (Descartes, Plato, Pearson. Contrast with Peirce.)

empiricism. Literally, "in experiment." The type of philosophy which holds that all knowledge originates from, and is reducible to, experience. Accepts *a posteriori* knowledge; opposed to *a priori* knowledge. Contrasted with rationalism. (Hume, Ayer, Schlick, Russell. Criticized by Santayana, Royce, Bergson.)

epistemology. Literally, "theory of knowledge." The branch of philosophy which investigates the possibility, origins, methods, nature, reliability, and limitations of knowledge.

essence. Literally, "formed as if." (1) Logical. Those properties an object must have, as distinct from those it might have, in order to belong to a given class. Opposed to accidental, incidental. (Discussed, pp. 208-209.) (2) Metaphysical. A term used to characterize that which is permanent and unchanging. Closely related to *being* (literally, "that which is") and *substance* (literally, "to stand under"). Opposed to transitory, variable. (Plato, Aristotle, Lucretius, Aquinas. Criticized by Peirce, Schlick.)

ethics. Originally, "custom." That branch of philosophy, a part of axiology, which deals with the nature of the good and how it can be achieved. Includes several distinctions: (1) descriptive *vs.* prescriptive, the factual account of what goods people do consider to be valued (Benedict) *vs.* the account of the goals which people ought to consider as valuable (Fromm); (2) ethical judgments based on the motives of the actor (Kant) *vs.* judgments based on the consequences of the act (Moses); (3) extrinsic *vs.* intrinsic goods, those valued as a means to another end (Spinoza) *vs.* those valued for themselves (Aristotle); (4) a single highest good, a *summum bonum* (Aristotle) *vs.* a multiplicity of goods (Dewey). (Discussed, pp. 218-225, 361-370, 532-539.)

freedom. (1) As indeterminism, the free will is independent of all causation, including instinct, motives, and previous experience. Opposed to determinism. (2) As self-determinism, the free will is independent of external restraint, but acts in accordance with the ideals of the agent. Not incompatible with determinism. (Spinoza, Epictetus, Calvin. Criticized by Sullivan. Discussed, pp. 525-530.)

hedonism. Literally, "pleasure." (1) Psychological. All motivation is explained by reference to the desire to seek pleasure or to avoid pain. (2) Ethical. The goal of moral behavior, the only intrinsic good, is to achieve pleasure. (Bentham, Aristotle, Sumner. Criticized by Kant.)

idealism. (1) Metaphysical. More accurately, ideaism, the doctrine that reality is essentially composed of minds or ideas. Opposed to materialism. (Royce, Sullivan) (2) Epistemological. The doctrine that the mental life alone is knowable. Opposed to realism. (Royce, Buddha, Pearson. Discussed, pp. 228-230.) (3) Ethical. The doctrine that one should seek to realize universal values. Opposed to practicalism. (Kant, Jesus, Fromm)

intuitionism. Literally, "to look at." (1) Methodology. That type of knowledge which is direct, non-discursive, and immediate. Related to mysticism. Opposed to mediated knowledge. (Fox, Van Ruysbroek, Bhagavad-Gita) (2) Epistemological. The view that only intuitively known truths provide a satisfactory basis for knowledge. Opposed to empiricism. Contrast with rationalism. (Bergson, Santayana, Schweitzer) (3) Ethical. The view that the basic propositions of ethics are ultimate and underivative. (Russell)

logic. Originally, "belonging to reason." The branch of philosophy which deals with the problems and nature of clear thinking. Includes (1) *semantics,* literally, "significant meanings," that part which deals with the meanings of words and their relationships to objects; (2) *deduction,* literally "a leading down," that part which deals with valid forms of inference and determines whether conclusions necessarily are implied by premises; (3) *induction,* literally "to lead in," that part which deals with evidence and determines whether and when observations of particular instances can be used to justify acceptance of a general conclusion. (Discussed, pp. 203-216, 518-520.)

materialism. Literally, "stuff, matter." (1) Metaphysical. The view that everything in the universe, including life and ideas, can be reduced to, and explained in terms of, material particles. (Lucretius, Dalton. Discussed, pp. 227-228.) (2) Ethical. The belief that bodily satisfactions are either the only or the highest good. (Bentham, Epicurus. Criticized by Jesus, Kant.)

mechanism. Literally, "machine." Agrees with determinism that every event is totally conditioned by antecedent causes, but also rejects all ideas of design, purpose, and goal. Opposed to vitalism, teleology, freedom. (Spinoza. Criticized by Sullivan.)

metaphysics. Literally, "beyond the study of nature." The branch of philosophy which deals with the study of the nature of reality. (1) Traditionally, divided into *cosmology,* a study of the causes and processes of nature, and *ontology,* the nature of reality. (2) Today, is also divided into *speculative metaphysics,* theories about reality, and *reflective metaphysics,* an inquiry into the presuppositions of knowledge itself. (See pp. 225-236, 370-378, 524-532.)

methodology. Literally, "the theory of method." The branch of philosophy which deals with the problem of how we obtain reliable knowledge. Includes empiricism, intuitionism, rationalism, scientific method, and others as alternative answers. (Socrates. See pp. 203-218, 378-382, 515-524.)

monism. Literally, "oneness." The view that all reality is of the same kind, whether it be mental or material. Opposed to Dualism. (Royce, Lucretius, Spinoza, Van Ruysbroek. Criticized by Plato, Santayana.)

naturalism. (1) Metaphysical. The view that the universe and all things in it are self-existent, self-explanatory, self-directing, and self-operating. Opposed to supernaturalism. (Hume, Comte, Lucretius. Criticized by Niebuhr, Aquinas.) (2) Ethical. The view that all moral goals are determined entirely by the needs and characteristics of human beings. (Dewey, Huxley, Fromm. Criticized by Moses, Jesus.)

nominalism. Originally, "of names." The view, chiefly in Medieval philosophy, that universals do not exist, and that the mind can frame no concepts corresponding to general terms. Opposed to realism. (Hume. Opposed to Plato, Aquinas.)

ontology. Literally, "the study of being." (1) Metaphysical. In its larger sense, ontology is synonymous with metaphysics and cosmology. In a narrower sense, ontology deals with the nature of being rather than its causes, as does cosmology, and thus is a part of metaphysics. (2) Theological. The ontological proof demonstrates God's existence by asserting that the idea of a perfect being would not be perfect if it lacked existence. (Descartes, Spinoza. Discussed, pp. 375-376.)

phenomenalism. Literally, "to appear." The view that we cannot know things as they are, but only as they appear to us. Contrast with realism. (Pearson. Contrast with Peirce.)

positivism. The type of philosophy which insists that all knowledge propositions must be either verifiable, at least in principle, or logically deducible from such propositions. Contrast with speculation, *a priori, intuition, metaphysics.* (Ayer, Hume, Comte, Schlick. Criticized by Santayana.)

pragmatism. Literally, "a thing done." The philosophy, largely developed in America, which sees mind as an instrument for solving problems and looks to the "successful working" of ideas to determine their truth. Opposed to formalism and speculative metaphysics. (Peirce, Dewey, Frank)

rationalism. Literally, "of reason." (1) Methodological. The view that reasoning, usually beginning with *a priori* premises, can arrive deductively at reliable knowledge. Contrast with empiricism, intuitionism. (Descartes, Spinoza. Criticized by Peirce, Pearson.) (2) Metaphysical. The belief that ultimate reality can be known by human reasoning alone. (Philosophy, science. Contrast with religion.)

realism. Literally, "a thing." (1) Greek and medieval metaphysics. The view that universals and classes exist independent of particulars. Opposed to nominalism. (Plato, Aquinas) (2) Contemporary metaphysics. The view that objects exist independent of our knowledge of them. Opposed to idealism. (Peirce. Criticized by Royce.) (3) Epistemological. The view that sense experience gives us a true account of objects as they are. Contrast with phenomenalism. (Hume, Peirce, Comte. Criticized by Descartes, Royce. Contrast with Pearson.)

relativism. (1) Epistemological. The view that knowledge varies with the person, time, and place and that knowledge of things as they are is impossible. Opposed to realism. (Descartes. Criticized by Peirce.) (2) Ethical. The view that moral values depend on the attitude taken by some individual or group. Opposed to absolutism. (Dewey, Sumner, Benedict. Contrast to Jesus, Buddha, Lao-tse, Kant. Discussed, pp. 532-536.)

teleology. Literally, "the study of ends." (1) Metaphysical. The doctrine that events are to be explained by reference to final goals and purposes rather than merely antecedent causes. Opposed to mechanism. (Aristotle, Bergson) (2) Epistemological. The doctrine that mind is governed by purposes and interests as well as evidence in its search for truth. (Peirce, Dewey, Frank. Contrast with Comte, Schlick.) (3) Theological. The teleological proof demonstrates God's existence by asserting that the relationships among things evidence design which, in turn, suggests a designer. (Aquinas, Aristotle, Channing. Contrast with Spinoza. Discussed, pp. 375-376.)

theology. Literally, "the study of God." (1) Philosophical. The branch of philosophy which deals with the study of God and His relationship to the natural world. In the Christian sense, is opposed to naturalism. (Chapter seven. See pp. 370-378.) (2) Religious. The theoretical expression of any set of religious beliefs. (See pp. 241-383.)

vitalism. Originally, "to live." The doctrine that life is not totally explainable in terms of physical and chemical constituents, but requires an "élan vital" to complete the explanation. Opposed to mechanism. (Bergson)

INDEX OF AUTHORS AND TITLES

* Italicized numbers refer to pages where this author's ideas are discussed, although he is not mentioned by name.